Communications in Computer and Information Science 609

Commenced Publication in 2007
Founding and Former Series Editors:
Alfredo Cuzzocrea, Dominik Ślęzak, and Xiaokang Yang

Editorial Board

Simone Diniz Junqueira Barbosa
  *Pontifical Catholic University of Rio de Janeiro (PUC-Rio),
  Rio de Janeiro, Brazil*
Phoebe Chen
  La Trobe University, Melbourne, Australia
Xiaoyong Du
  Renmin University of China, Beijing, China
Joaquim Filipe
  Polytechnic Institute of Setúbal, Setúbal, Portugal
Orhun Kara
  TÜBİTAK BİLGEM and Middle East Technical University, Ankara, Turkey
Igor Kotenko
  *St. Petersburg Institute for Informatics and Automation of the Russian
  Academy of Sciences, St. Petersburg, Russia*
Ting Liu
  Harbin Institute of Technology (HIT), Harbin, China
Krishna M. Sivalingam
  Indian Institute of Technology Madras, Chennai, India
Takashi Washio
  Osaka University, Osaka, Japan

More information about this series at http://www.springer.com/series/7899

Paul M. Clarke · Rory V. O'Connor
Terry Rout · Alec Dorling (Eds.)

Software Process Improvement and Capability Determination

16th International Conference, SPICE 2016
Dublin, Ireland, June 9–10, 2016
Proceedings

Editors
Paul M. Clarke
Lero Irish Software Research Centre
Dublin City University
Dublin
Ireland

Rory V. O'Connor
Dublin City University
Dublin
Ireland

Terry Rout
Software Quality Institue
Griffith University
Brisbane, QLD
Australia

Alec Dorling
Impronova AB
Drabergsvagen, Lindome
Sweden

ISSN 1865-0929　　　　　　ISSN 1865-0937 (electronic)
Communications in Computer and Information Science
ISBN 978-3-319-38979-0　　　ISBN 978-3-319-38980-6 (eBook)
DOI 10.1007/978-3-319-38980-6

Library of Congress Control Number: 2016939056

© Springer International Publishing Switzerland 2016
This work is subject to copyright. All rights are reserved by the Publisher, whether the whole or part of the material is concerned, specifically the rights of translation, reprinting, reuse of illustrations, recitation, broadcasting, reproduction on microfilms or in any other physical way, and transmission or information storage and retrieval, electronic adaptation, computer software, or by similar or dissimilar methodology now known or hereafter developed.
The use of general descriptive names, registered names, trademarks, service marks, etc. in this publication does not imply, even in the absence of a specific statement, that such names are exempt from the relevant protective laws and regulations and therefore free for general use.
The publisher, the authors and the editors are safe to assume that the advice and information in this book are believed to be true and accurate at the date of publication. Neither the publisher nor the authors or the editors give a warranty, express or implied, with respect to the material contained herein or for any errors or omissions that may have been made.

Printed on acid-free paper

This Springer imprint is published by Springer Nature
The registered company is Springer International Publishing AG Switzerland

Preface

On behalf of the SPICE 2016 Conference Organizing Committee we are proud to present the proceedings of the 16th International Conference on Software Process Improvement and Capability dEtermination (SPICE 2016), held in Dublin, Ireland, during June 9–10, 2016.

The SPICE Project was formed in 1993 to support the development of an international standard for software process assessment. The work of the project eventually led to the finalization of ISO/IEC 15504 – Process Assessment, and its complete publication represented a climax for the work of the project. The standardization effort continues, with the publication of the first documents in the new ISO/IEC 330xx family of standards on process assessment.

As part of its charter to provide ongoing publicity and transition support for the emerging standard, the project organized a number of SPICE workshops and seminars, with invited speakers drawn from project participants. These have now evolved to a sustaining set of international conferences with broad participation from academia and industry with a common interest in model-based process improvement. This was the 16th in the series of conferences organized by the SPICE User Group to increase knowledge and understanding of the International Standard and of the technique of process assessment.

The conference program featured invited keynote talks, research papers, and industry experience reports on the most relevant topics related to software process assessment and improvement; a significant focus this year were detailed studies of aspects of process implementation, assessment, and improvement, and the expansion in the range and variety of relevant process models. Members of the Program Committee selected the papers for presentation following a peer-review process.

SPICE conferences have a long history of attracting attendees from industry and academia. This confirms that the conference covers topics that are up to date, important, and interesting. SPICE 2016 offered a unique forum for industry and academic professionals to discuss their needs and ideas in the area of process assessment and improvement and in related aspects of quality management.

On behalf of the SPICE 2016 Conference Organizing Committee, we would like to thank all participants. Firstly all the authors, whose quality work is the essence of the conference, and the members of the Program Committee, who helped us with their expertise and diligence in reviewing all of the submissions. As we all know, organizing a conference requires the effort of many individuals. We wish to thank also all the members of our Organizing Committee, whose work and commitment were invaluable.

June 2016

Paul M. Clarke
Rory V. O'Connor
Terry Rout
Alec Dorling

Organization

General Chair

Alec Dorling	Impronova AB, Sweden

Program Chair

Terry Rout	Griffith University, Australia

Local Organizing Chair

Paul M. Clarke	Lero, Dublin City University, Ireland

Proceedings Chair

Rory V. O'Connor	Lero, Dublin City University, Ireland

Program Committee

Béatrix Barafort	Luxembourg Institute of Science and Technology, Luxembourg
Luigi Buglione	Engineering Ingegneria Informatica SpA, Italy
Aileen Cater-Steel	University of Southern Queensland, Australia
Gerhard Chroust	Jonannes Kepler University of Linz, Austria
François Coallier	Ecole de technologie Superieure, Canada
Tony Coletta	Qual. IT. Consulting, Italy
Onur Demirors	Middle East Technical University, Turkey
Fabrizio Fabbrini	Italian National Research Council, Italy
Dennis Goldenson	Software Engineering Institute, USA
Christiane Gresse von Wangenheim	Federal University of Santa Catarina, Brazil
Victora Hailey	VHG Corporation, Canada
Linda Ibrahim	Enterprise SPICE, USA
Jørn Johansen	Whitebox, Denmark
Ravindra Joshi	Morphius Consulting, India
Ho-Won Jung	Korea University, South Korea
Giuseppe Lami	National Research Council, Italy
Marion Lepmets	Dundalk Institute of Technology, Ireland
Catriona Mackie	BT, UK
Antonia Mas Pichaco	Universidad de les Illes Balears, Spain
Fergal McCaffery	Dundalk Institute of Technology, Ireland

Tom McBride	University of Technology Sydney, Australia
Antanas Mitasiunas	Vilnius University, Lithuania
Takeshige Miyoshi	Miyoshi Art of Software Process Inc., Japan
Risto Nevalainen	FiSMA Association, Finland
Mark Paulk	The University of Texas at Dallas, USA
Saulius Ragaisos	Vilnius University, Lithuania
Alain Renault	Luxembourg Institute of Science and Technology, Luxembourg
Patricia Rodriguez-Dapena	SoftWcare SL, Spain
Clenio Salviano	CenPRA, Brazil
Jean-Martin Simon	CGI Business Consulting, France
Fritz Stallinger	Software Competence Center, Austria
Timo Varkoi	Spinet Oy, Finland
Bharathi Vijayakumar	Wipro Technologies, India
Murat Yilmaz	Çankaya University, Turkey

Local Organizing Committee

Paul M. Clarke	Lero, Dublin City University, Ireland
Rory V. O'Connor	Lero, Dublin City University, Ireland

Acknowledgments

The conference organizers wish to acknowledge the assistance and support of the SPICE User Group, SPICE 2016 Program Committee, and reviewers in contributing to a successful conference.

Contents

SPI in Regulated and Safety Critical Domains

Deriving Safety Case Fragments for Assessing MBASafe's Compliance
with EN 50128.. 3
   Barbara Gallina, Elena Gómez-Martínez, and Clara Benac Earle

Safety Critical Software Development – Extending Quality Management
System Practices to Achieve Compliance with Regulatory Requirements 17
   Andrzej Beniamin Bujok, Silvana Togneri MacMahon,
   Fergal McCaffery, Dick Whelan, Bernard Mulcahy,
   and William J. Rickard

The Use of Maturity/Capability Frameworks for Healthcare Process
Assessment and Improvement...................................... 31
   Mehmet Söylemez and Ayca Tarhan

Software Process Improvement Roadmaps – Using Design Patterns to Aid
SME's Developing Medical Device Software in the Implementation of IEC
62304 43
   Peter Rust, Derek Flood, and Fergal McCaffery

Gamification and Education Issues in SPI

Coverage of ISO/IEC 12207 Software Lifecycle Process
by a Simulation-Based Serious Game 59
   Alejandro Calderón and Mercedes Ruiz

A Gamification Approach to Improve the Software Development Process
by Exploring the Personality of Software Practitioners................ 71
   Mert Yilmaz, Murat Yilmaz, Rory V. O'Connor, and Paul Clarke

A Simulation and Gamification Approach for IT Service Management
Improvement 84
   Elena Orta and Mercedes Ruiz

Towards a Manifesto for Software Process Education, Training
and Professionalism... 98
   Jørn Johansen, Ricardo Colomo-Palacios, and Rory V. O'Connor

SPI in Agile and Small Settings

A Maturity Model for Integrating Agile Processes and User Centred Design ... 109
  Dina Salah, Richard Paige, and Paul Cairns

Analysis of Tools for Assessing the Implementation and Use of Agile
Methodologies in SMEs... 123
  *Mirna Muñoz, Jezreel Mejia, Brisia Corona, Jose A. Calvo-Manzano,
  Tomas San Feliu, and Juan Miramontes*

Evaluation of Agility Assessment Tools: A Multiple Case Study........... 135
  Onat Ege Adalı, Özden Özcan-Top, and Onur Demirörs

Exploring Processes in Small Software Companies: A Systematic Review ... 150
  Nirnaya Tripathi, Elina Annanperä, Markku Oivo, and Kari Liukkunen

SPI and Assessment

Developing Process Definition for Financial and Physical Resource
Management Process in Government Domain........................ 169
  Ebru Gökalp and Onur Demirörs

A Nominal Group Interview Technique to Support Lightweight Process
Assessments: Description and Experience Report 181
  Eduardo Miranda

The Issue of Reliability in Software Mediated Process Assessments........ 195
  *Anup Shrestha, Aileen Cater-Steel, Mark Toleman, Terry Rout,
  and Suren Behari*

Towards a Process Capability Assessment Model for Government Domain... 210
  Ebru Gökalp and Onur Demirörs

SPI and Project Management Concerns

Measuring Global Distance: A Survey of Distance Factors
and Interventions.. 227
  John Noll and Sarah Beecham

MAMD: Towards a Data Improvement Model Based on ISO 8000-6X
and ISO/IEC 33000... 241
  Ana G. Carretero, Ismael Caballero, and Mario Piattini

How to Integrate Risk Management in IT Settings Within Management
Systems? Comparison and Integration Perspectives from ISO Standards..... 254
  Béatrix Barafort, Antoni-Lluís Mesquida, and Antònia Mas

A Learning Tool for the ISO/IEC 29110 Standard: Understanding the
Project Management of Basic Profile 270
  Mary-Luz Sánchez-Gordón, Rory V. O'Connor,
  Ricardo Colomo-Palacios, and Sandra Sanchez-Gordon

Empirical Research Case Studies of SPI

The Role of Process in Early Software Defect Prediction: Methods,
Attributes and Metrics 287
  Rana Ozakinci and Ayca Tarhan

An Empirical Study on Software Testing Practices in Automotive 301
  Giuseppe Lami, Isabella Biscoglio, and Fabio Falcini

Empirically Derived Recommendations for Personalised Text-Based
Technical Support 316
  Solomon Gizaw, Jim Buckley, and Sarah Beecham

SPI Sustainment Model Validation: Two Exploratory Case Studies 334
  Nazrina Khurshid and Paul L. Bannerman

Knowledge and Human Communications Issues in SPI

An Investigation of Software Development Process Terminology 351
  Paul Clarke, Antoni-Lluís Mesquida, Damjan Ekert, J.J. Ekstrom,
  Tatjana Gornostaja, Milos Jovanovic, Jørn Johansen, Antonia Mas,
  Richard Messnarz, Blanca Nájera Villar, Alexander O'Connor,
  Rory V. O'Connor, Michael Reiner, Gabriele Sauberer,
  Klaus-Dirk Schmitz, and Murat Yilmaz

Representing Software Process in Description Logics: An Ontology
Approach for Software Process Reasoning and Verification 362
  Edward Kabaale, Lian Wen, Zhe Wang, and Terry Rout

A Behavior Tree-Based Model for Supporting the Analysis of Knowledge
Transferred in Software R&D Teams 377
  Alvaro Fernández Del Carpio

The Need for Obtaining Real Sponsor Satisfaction that Leads to Steady
Generation of SPI Effects 391
  Takeshige Miyoshi

Short Papers

Investigating the Suitability of Using Agile for Medical Embedded
Software Development 409
  Surafel Demissie, Frank Keenan, and Fergal McCaffery

Agile – Is it Suitable for Medical Device Software Development?......... 417
    Fergal McCaffery, Kitija Trektere, and Ozden Ozcan-Top

Using Enterprise SPICE in Very Small Entities...................... 423
    Linda Ibrahim, Ernest Wallmüller, and Wolfgang Daschner

Smart Requirements: How Smart Can They Get? 431
    Danilo Assmann

Current Challenges and Proposed Software Improvement Process for VSEs
in Developing Countries 437
    Tatsuya Nonoyama, Lian Wen, and Terry Rout

Erratum to: Software Process Improvement and Capability Determination ... E1
    Paul M. Clarke, Rory V. O'Connor, Terry Rout, and Alec Dorling

Author Index 445

SPI in Regulated and Safety Critical Domains

Deriving Safety Case Fragments for Assessing MBASafe's Compliance with EN 50128

Barbara Gallina[1(✉)], Elena Gómez-Martínez[2], and Clara Benac Earle[3]

[1] Mälardalen University, Västerås, Sweden
barbara.gallina@mdh.se
[2] University of East London, London, UK
e.gomez@uel.ac.uk
[3] Universidad Politécnica de Madrid, Madrid, Spain
cbenac@fi.upm.es

Abstract. According to EN 50129, manufacturers of rail vehicles shall justify via a safety case that their vehicles are adequately safe for their intended applications. MBASafe is a recently proposed and potentially innovative design and verification process. In the presence of compelling arguments concerning its adequacy as process evidence, MBASafe could support the safety claims within the required safety cases. In this paper, we contribute to partially justify the adequacy of MBASafe to act as process evidence. To do that, we first manually check if MBASafe includes EN 50128-compliant process elements, then we model MBASafe in compliance with Software Process Engineering Meta-model 2.0, then, we derive process-based arguments from the MBASafe process model by using MDSafeCer, the recently introduced Model Driven Safety Certification method. By doing so, we provide a twofold contribution: we further validate MDSafeCer in the rail domain and we strengthen MBASafe.

Keywords: EN 5012x · Model-driven safety certification · Process assessment

1 Introduction

According to the CENELEC standard series, manufacturers of rail vehicles shall justify via a safety case that their vehicles are adequately safe for their intended applications. More specifically, the CENELEC EN 50129-compliant safety case should include arguments aimed at explaining why the included evidence (e.g., safety and quality management) is adequate to support the safety claims. Arguments should specifically refer to the appropriate Safety Integrity Level (SIL) since the stringency from one level to another changes. Recently proposed and potentially innovative engineering methods could act as process-related evidence. However, to ease their acceptance within the rail industrial settings, the adequacy of these methods need to be justified. MBASafe [1] is a recently proposed

---

The original version of this chapter was revised. An erratum to this chapter can be found at 10.1007/978-3-319-38980-6_34

and potentially innovative model-driven process for the design and verification of software architectures. MBASafe has been validated in research settings in cooperation with industry [1]. The adoption of MBASafe in the rail domain, however, is not straightforward due to the current absence of compelling arguments concerning its adequacy, i.e., arguments aimed at explaining that the selection of process elements that composes MBASafe, aimed at guiding the design of rail vehicles-related subsystems, is compliant with the CENELEC requirements. MDSafer is a method aimed at speeding up the creation of process-based arguments, derived from process models, given in standardized process languages e.g., SPEM (Software Process Engineering Meta-model) 2.0 [2]. The usage and potential effectiveness of MDSafer has been illustrated in the automotive [3] and rail domain [4]. However, no in-depth illustration has been attempted so far. In this paper, we use MDSafeCer to derive part of the needed justification concerning the adequacy of MBASafe as safety and quality management evidence. By doing so we provide a twofold contribution: we further extend and validate MDSafeCer and we strengthen MBASafe by deriving safety case fragments aimed at showing its adequacy to design software sub-systems in compliance with EN 50128. More specifically, we consider the design of a door control management subsystem (within a specific train control monitoring system) in a suburban train. This subsystem is expected to have doors with a button that enables passengers to open them upon request. The malfunctioning of this system may endanger the system safety. The assumed Safety Integrity Level (SIL) is SIL 2. Given this system, we focus our attention on justifying adequacy with respect to SIL 2. Given the pattern-based nature of our justification, it can be flexibly changed to argue about a different level, where necessary.

The rest of the paper is organized as follows. In Sect. 2, we present essential background. In Sect. 3, we collect elements of EN 50128-compliance and we model in SPEM2.0 the compliant portion of MBASafe. In Sect. 4, we derive safety case fragments for arguing that MBASafe partially meets EN 50128. In Sect. 5, we discuss related work. Finally, concluding remarks and future work can be found in Sect. 6.

2 Background

In this section we present the essential background on which we base our work.

2.1 Safety Cases and Safety Cases Representation

A safety case is defined as "a structured argument, supported by a body of evidence, that provides a compelling, comprehensible and valid case that a system is safe for a given application in a given environment" [5]. Such argument typically includes process and product-based sub-arguments. To document safety cases, several approaches exist. GSN [6] is one of them and it is here selected because of its active community and its current level of maturity. GSN is a graphical notation, which permits users to structure their argumentation into flat or hierarchically nested graphs (constituted of a set of nodes and a set of edges), called goal structures. To make the paper self-contained, in Fig. 1, we recall a subset of the GSN concrete syntax used in Sect. 4. As Fig. 1 shows, all the nodes are characterized by an identifier (ID) and a statement, which is supposed to be written in natural language.

We recall that a *Goal* represents a claim about the system; a *Strategy* represents a method that is used to decompose a goal into sub goals; a *Solution* represents the evidence that a particular goal has been achieved; a *Context* represents the domain or scope in which a goal, evidence or strategy is given; *Supported by* represents an inferential (inference between goals) or evidential (link between a goal and the evidence used to substantiate it) relationship. Finally, *In context of* represents a contextual relationship. To create argumentation patterns, i.e., reusable goal structures, specific pattern constructs are at disposal, as shown in Fig. 1. Within patterns, in addition to the constructs presented in Fig. 1, curly brackets are also used to denote variables. SACM (Structured Assurance Case Metamodel) [7] is an OMG standard aimed at unify and standardize the graphical notations (including GSN) broadly used for documenting safety cases. At the time being SACM only addresses a subset of GSN modeling elements. Pattern constructs, for instance, are not addressed yet.

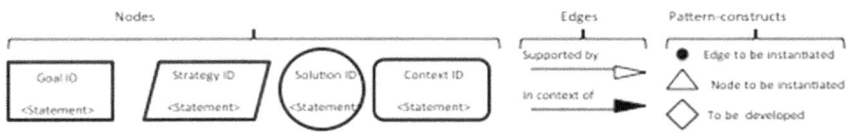

Fig. 1. Subset of GSN concrete syntax.

2.2 The CENELEC EN 5012x

The CENELEC EN 5012x is a family of standards that contains requirements and recommendations concerning processes to be followed for the development and assurance of safety-critical systems. This family of standards is used for the certification of railway systems and signaling control-command equipment. As it was documented within the deliverable D6.1 of the MODSafe project [8], Light Rail, Metros, Trams are still characterized by a diversified landscape of safety requirements, safety models, roles and responsibilities, safety approval, acceptance and certification schemes. However, convergence towards the CENELEC standard series is evident. In this section, we briefly present the portions of EN 50126, EN 50129 and EN 50128 that are necessary to understand Sect. 4.

EN 50126 - [9] defines a fourteen-phase process to manage Reliability, Availability, Maintainability and Safety at system level. The Risk Analysis Phase is the third phase. The objective of this phase is multi-fold: (1) identification of the hazards associated with the system; (2) estimation of the risk associated with the hazards; (3) development of a process for risk management. One of the outcome of the Risk Analysis phase is the assignment of a SIL to any safety relevant function or system or sub-system or component. A SIL specifies a target level of risk reduction and is typically defined in components that operate in a safety-critical system. There are four discrete integrity levels associated with SIL with SIL 4 the most dependable and SIL 1 the least. The SIL allocation is made taking into account the rate of dangerous failures and tolerable hazard rate of the function, system, sub-system or component. The SIL of a system to be developed is determined on system level. The software "inherits" the SIL as any other part of the system through decomposition. Then, EN 50128 defines what must be done to develop SW functions with that SIL.

EN 50129 - [10] defines the conditions that shall be satisfied in order that a safety-related electronic railway system/sub-system/equipment can be accepted as adequately safe for its intended application. These conditions are constituted of three types of evidence: Evidence of quality management, Evidence of safety management, and Evidence of functional and technical safety. The documentary evidence that these conditions have been satisfied shall be included in a structured safety justification document, known as the safety case. The safety case shall be structured in six parts. In this sub subsection we limit our attention to the following parts: Part 2 Quality Management Report, this shall contain the evidence of quality management, e.g., evidence of adequate organizational structures as well as evidence of adequate personnel competence and training; Part 3 Safety Management Report, this shall contain the evidence of safety management, e.g., evidence that the safety management process consists of a number of phases and activities, which are linked to form the safety life-cycle in compliance with EN 50126 and with EN 50128 at software sub-system level. The software architecture design phase should for instance be aligned with the system architecture design. Part 6 Conclusion, this shall summarize the evidence presented in the previous parts of the safety case, and argue that the relevant system/sub-system/equipment is adequately safe, subject to compliance with the specified application conditions.

It should be noted that the depth of the evidence presented and the extent of the supporting documentation should be appropriate to the SIL of the system/sub-system/equipment under scrutiny.

EN 50128 - [11] focuses on processes for the development, deployment and maintenance of safety-related software for railway control and protection applications. EN 50128 does not mandate the use of a particular software development lifecycle. It only provides normative tables and recommendations concerning specific process elements, e.g., roles, work products, techniques, tools, tasks. Illustrative software route maps are indicated, however, a process engineer is responsible for the selection and composition of adequate process elements aimed at achieving the required software integrity level. To make the paper self-contained, we recall those process elements related to the Software Architecture & Design Phase that are in relation with MBASafe.

Tasks and related work products - The design task should receive in input the Software Requirements Specification and should deliver in output the Software Architecture Specification, the Software Design Specification, the Software Interface Specifications, the Software Integration Test Specification, the Software/Hardware Integration Test Specification, and the Software Architecture and Design Verification Report. The verification task should receive in input all necessary system, hardware and software documentation and should deliver in output a Software Verification Plan a set of Software Verification Report(s), and a Software Quality Assurance Verification Report. The validation task should receive in input all necessary system, hardware and software documentation and should deliver in output a Software Validation Plan, a Software Validation Report and a Software Validation Verification Report.

Guideline - We limit our attention to Annex A. According to Table A.4, formal methods are recommended (R) for SIL 1 and SIL 2 and highly recommended (HR) for SIL 3 and SIL 4. More generally, modeling is HR for SIL1-4. According to Table A.5, formal proofs are R for SIL 1 and SIL 2 and HR for SIL 3 and SIL 4. According to Table A.17, petri nets are R for SIL 1 and SIL 2 and HR for SIL 3 and SIL 4. Finally, according to Table A.22, Object Oriented Detailed Design is R for SIL 1 and SIL 2 and HR for SIL 3 and SIL 4.

Roles - We limit our attention to Annex B. According to Table B.2, a designer shall: transform specified software requirements into acceptable solutions; own the architecture and downstream solutions; define or select the design methods and supporting tools; apply appropriate design principles and standards; develop component specifications where appropriate; maintain traceability to and from the specified software requirements; develop and maintain the design documentation; ensure design documents are under change and configuration control. With respect to expected competencies, a designer shall be competent in: engineering appropriate to the application area, the safety design principles, design analysis &design test methodologies, and understanding the problem domain. Moreover, a designer shall understand: the constraints imposed by the hardware platform, the operating system and the interfacing systems and the relevant parts of EN 50128. Finally, (s)he shall be able to work within design constraints in a given environment.

According to Table B.5, a verifier shall be: competent requirements engineering and experienced in the applications domain and in the safety attributes of the applications domain. Moreover, a verifier shall understand: the overall role of the system and the environment of application; analytical techniques and outcomes; the applicable regulations; and the requirements of EN 50128.

Finally, according to Table B.7, a validator shall be competent in: the domain where validation is carried out as well as various validation approaches/methodologies and be able to identify the most suitable method or combination of methods in a given context. Moreover, he/she shall be: experienced in safety attributes of applications domain; capable of deriving the types of validation evidence required from given specifications bearing in mind the intended application as well as of combining different sources and types of evidence and synthesize an overall view about fitness for purpose or constraints and limitations of the application. A validator shall also have analytical thinking ability and good observation skills as well as overall software understanding and perspective including understanding the application environment. Finally, he/she shall understand the requirements of EN 50128. It should be also mentioned that the verifier and validator can be the same person in case of SIL1 and SIL2.

2.3 SPEM 2.0

SPEM 2.0 [2] is the OMG's standard for systems and software process modelling. SPEM 2.0 supports the definition of reusable process content, i.e., work definition elements (e.g., tasks, etc.) as well as elements representing: who is responsible for the work (roles), how the work should be performed (guidance), what should be expected as in/output (work-products) and which tool should be used to perform the work. In Table 1, we recall a subset of SPEM 2.0 modelling elements, which can be interrelated to model static process structures.

Table 1. Subset of SPEM 2.0 modelling elements

Task	Role	WorkProduct	Tool	Guidance

2.4 Model-Driven Engineering Principles and Derived Methods

Model-driven Engineering (MDE) principles consist of the exploitation of models to capture characteristics at different abstraction levels of the development life-cycle. For automation purposes, vertical as well as horizontal model transformations are used to refine models (model-to-model transformations). A model transformation transforms a source model (compliant with one meta-model) into a target model compliant with the same or a different meta-model. A standard transformation can be defined as a set of rules to map source to the target. Each rule describes how to transform source instances to the identical target.

MBASafe - Gómez-Martínez et al. [1] propose a Model-Based methodology for Assessing (MBA) performance and safety requirements of critical systems at early stages of the design phase. Since this paper is only focused on safety certification, we simplify this methodology taking into account this perspective. We call the simplified methodology MBASafe. The methodology is constituted of four chained tasks, which can be iterated and are: (1) the *design* task (focus on the functional specification) is carried out by the designer and focuses on modeling the software system architecture by means of UML diagrams, being these diagrams the outcome of this step. (2) The non-functional *safety specification* task is carried out by the safety engineer and consists of specifying safety requirements using Safety Contract Fragments (SCF) [12]. SFCs are in turn mapped into OCL constraints and included within the UML diagrams. (3) The *transformation* task is aimed at obtaining a formal architectural specification. This activity is carried out by a Petri net expert (Verifier) who translates the UML diagrams augmented with OCL constraints into Generalized Stochastic Petri nets (GSPN) [13]. This transformation is divided into two steps. During the first step the UML diagrams are automatically translated using the ArgoSPE plugin [14]. During the second step, OCL constraints are manually transformed following the rules described in [1], which are based on the guidelines given in [15]. The results of the two steps are then merged using the algebra tool of GreatSPN [16]. (4) The *verification & validation* task is aimed at verifying via GreatSPN tool that the safety requirements are satisfied. In the case that the design does not meet the safety requirements, systematized recommendations to improve the design are formulated and a new iteration is carried out.

MDSafeCer - MDSafeCer (Model-driven Safety Certification) [3] is a method that adopts MDE principles to enable the semi-automatic generation of composable process-based argument-fragments within safety cases. Via MDSafeCer, process models compliant with a process modeling language meta-model (e.g., SPEM 2.0) are transformed into argumentation models compliant with SACM and presented via for instance GSN-goal structures. MDSafeCer generates process arguments based on a possible argumentation pattern, which is constituted of a top level claim stating that "the adopted p process is in compliance with the required {S} of standard- level {intLev}", where p, S, L are variables indicating respectively a specific process, a set of standards, a specific integrity level. This claim can be decomposed by showing that all the process activities have been executed and that in turn for each activity all the tasks have been executed and so on until an atomic process-related work-definition unit is reached.

3 Collecting and Modeling Elements of Compliance

To partly act as safety and quality management evidence, needed for process assessment, MBASafe must be the result of the selection and composition of process elements that can be considered compliant with respect to the CENELEC series. MBASafe is a methodology to be used at design phase. Thus, first, it should be aligned with the Software Architecture & Design Phase. As recalled in Sect. 2, according to the CENELEC EN 50128, this phase should be carried out by appropriate roles, according to specific guidelines, be constituted of specific tasks, consume and produce specific work products. Since, as recalled in Sect. 2, MBASafe contains some of the required elements, its compliance can be partially argued about. More specifically, the following list highlights the process elements that meet the EN 50128 requirements: all the tasks that compose MBASafe can be considered aligned with he Software Architecture & Design Phase. However, not all the required tasks are included in MBASafe.

This means that a company should be aware about what else should be performed. The task Transformation is not included in EN 50128 as a standalone task. It is implicitly expected to be executed (manually or automatically) in the case of usage of formal methods within the verification task. Also the current sets of MBASafe in/out work products can be aligned. However, the EN 50128 expected number of in/out work products is greater. MBASafe guidelines can be aligned. As seen in the background formal methods and more specifically petri nets are among the techniques suggested to perform verification. With respect to roles, MBASafe does not pose enough emphasis. Nothing about qualifications is defined. Finally, the current tools (e.g., translator, model checker, etc.) that are proposed to perform the tasks do not offer satisfying evidence concerning their quality. Thus, MBASafe as it is cannot be adopted in real settings.

To enable its usage in real settings, the presentation of MBASafe should be enhanced and its alignment clearly made explicit. More specifically, all input/output work products should be specified and aligned with EN 50128. Concerning roles, vagueness in terms of their responsibility and degree of independence should be eliminated. Concerning tools, rational and adequate justifications in terms of their quality should be provided. In alternative, other tools should be suggested. In Table 2, we illustrate the SPEM 2.0 models representing the augmented MBASafe tasks.

By construction, these augmented MBASafe tasks contain process elements that are in compliance with EN 50128. To explain this compliance, in Sect. 4 we derive process-based arguments and we document them in GSN. Besides the enhancement of the presentation, to satisfy all the EN 50128, MBASafe should, however, be further developed or combined with another methodology offering

Table 2. MBASafe tasks given in SPEM 2.0

Task-1	Task-2
<<mandatory input>> Safety requirements; <<performs, primary>> Designer; <<Used Tool>> Argo UML; A4, A22; Design; <<mandatory output>> UML diagrams defining: Software Design Specification, the Software Interface Specifications	<<mandatory input>> Safety requirements; <<performs, primary>> Designer; <<Used Tool>> Argo UML; A4, A22; Safety specification; <<mandatory output>> UML diagrams + OCL contracts defining: Software Design Specification, the Software Interface Specifications
Task-3	**Task-4**
<<mandatory input>> UML diagrams + OCL contracts; <<performs, primary>> Verifier; <<Used Tools>> Argo SPE + GreatSPN; A4, A5, A17; Transformation; <<mandatory output>> Petri net	<<mandatory input>> Petri net; <<performs, primary>> Verifier&Validator; <<Used Tool>> GreatSPN; A4, A5, A17; V&V; <<mandatory output>> V&V report

complementary support. Thus, given the awareness developed thanks to the performed gap analysis, we also indicate the undeveloped goals.

4 Arguing About EN 50128 Compliance via MDSafeCer

The aim of this section is to derive a process-based argument for arguing about MBASafe compliance with EN 50128. More specifically, our derived argument given in GSN argues that MBASafe is partially compliant with the EN 50128 requirements related to the design phase for a SIL2 subsystem. To derive such argument, we proceed compositionally and from the process models given in Table 2, by using MDSafeCer, we first derive sub-arguments that argue about compliance at task level. The derived sub-arguments are depicted in Table 3. Such arguments could be further developed to indicate the missing evidence (e.g., the missing work products).

To argue at phase level, the rules that were initially proposed by Gallina [3] need to be further developed. More specifically, we present additional rules that are needed to generate a pattern instance based on our pattern on *Process compliance*, represented in Fig. 2 and in Fig. 3, whose structure partially borrows

Table 3. Task-based arguments

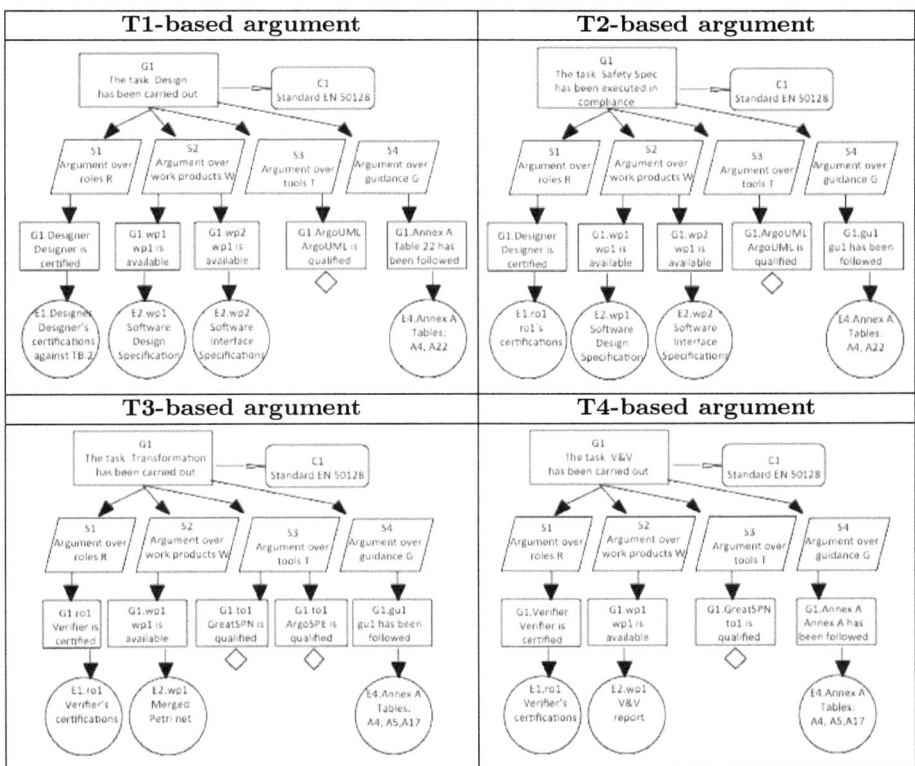

from the *Goal decomposition* pattern and incorporates the divide and conquer principle. For sake of clarity, it should be stated here that the semantic mapping was previously given and explained [3].

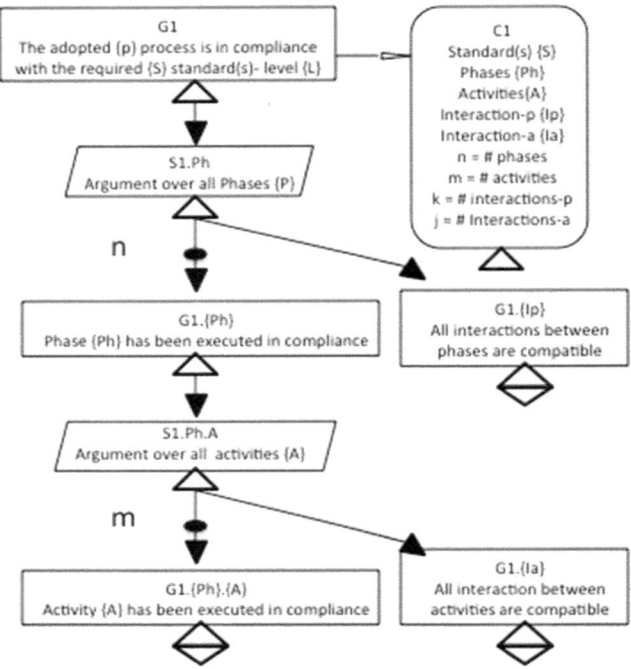

Fig. 2. Goal structure representing the *Process compliance* argumentation pattern.

For space reasons, Fig. 2 represents a pattern that considers only a 3-layer work-breaking-down structure. A process is divided into phases, which in turn are divided into activities. A richer hierarchy could be considered by breaking activities down further into tasks and finally tasks into steps. The 3-layer granularity is however sufficient for this paper since MBASafe can be considered a 2-layer hierarchy, i.e., a phase constituted of four activities. The four activities are named tasks in accordance with SPEM 2.0 models.

The additional needed rules are:

1. Create the top-level goal ID:G1 and statement: "The adopted p process is in compliance with the required {S} standard- level {intLev}". Create the context to be associated to G1. Context ID:C1 and statement: "Standard {S}", where S and L are variables. Create an inContextOf link to relate G1 and C1.

Develop the goal G1 further by creating one strategy.

(a) S1: "Argument over phases P".

2. Further develop strategy S1 by creating:

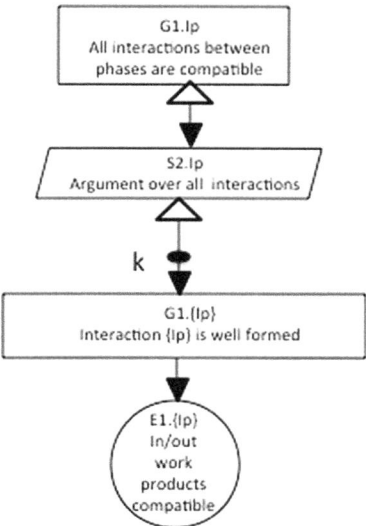

Fig. 3. Goal structure, continuation of the pattern in Fig. 2.

(a) for every phase ph in P, a goal G1.ph "Phase ph has been executed in compliance". Then, develop this goal further by creating an equivalent structure related to the lower level work decomposition.

(b) a goal G1.ip "All interactions {Ip} between Phases are compatible" and develop this goal further by creating one strategy: S2.Ip: "Argument over all interactions {Ip}". Further develop strategy S2.Ip by creating for every existing relation (representing an interaction between two phases) a goal G1.Ip "Interaction Ip is well formed" and develop this goal further by creating the corresponding solution E1.Ip "Ip In/out work products compatible" and the supportedBy link necessary to link S1.Ip with E1.Ip.

By aligning MBASafe-hierarchy with the pattern hierarchy and by manually following the above listed rules, we can easily derive the argument at the phase level, depicted in Fig. 4 and in Fig. 5 (note that for space reasons Fig. 5 does not present all the developed goals related to all the relations among tasks).

This argument can be easily composed with the sub-arguments, which were illustrated in Table 3. The compositional nature could be presented in a more advanced way by using modularized goal structures. Similarly, contracts could be used to clearly state the assumptions and guarantees that may exist between two sub goal-structures. In the context of distributed and heterogeneous management, where the responsibility for the provision of the different justifications might also be distributed and then integrated, contract-based goal structuring could be a winning solution.

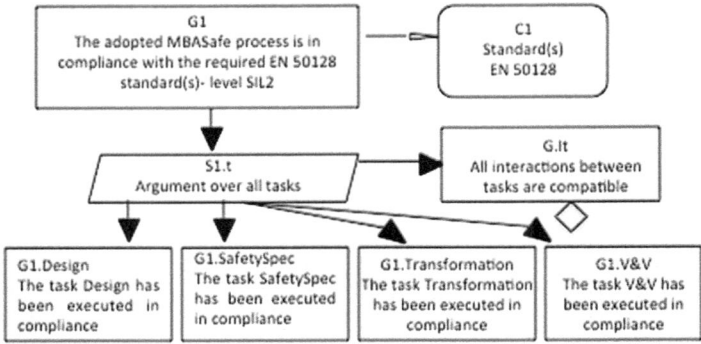

Fig. 4. Goal structure representing the argumentation pattern instance.

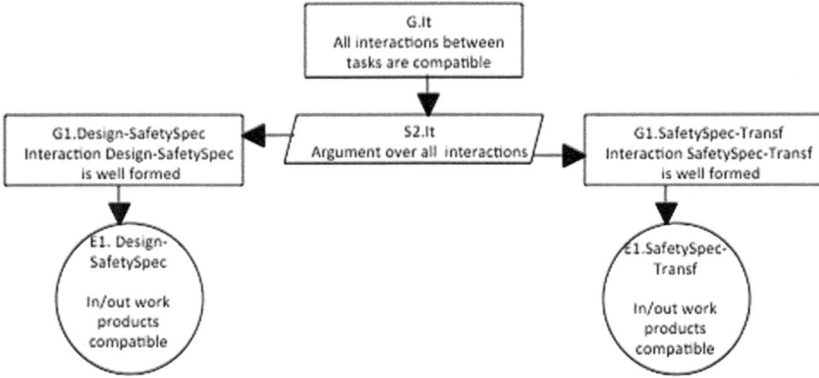

Fig. 5. Goal structure, continuation of the argumentation pattern instance.

5 Related Work

The current certification framework is traversing a crisis phase due to the growing complexity associated to the safety justifications that are required by the standards [17]. A balance between process and product-based justification is still not clear. Despite its necessity, process-based justification is proportionally less investigated. Bender et al. [18] in their work on the certification nature, conclude that for the time being process adherence (including personal qualifications), classified as indirect evidence, must be provided. They however do not propose any process-related argument. More recently, Nair et al. [19] recognize the relevance of process-based argumentation and similarly to what proposed by Gallina [3] argue about the core process elements. Nair et al. call the process-based argument as secondary confidence argument. In its effort aimed at strengthening via process-based evidence an existing method that targets provision of product-based evidence, our work represents a novelty and an effort to contribute to the achievement of the right balance. The possibility, in a long term, of deriving semi-automatically process-based arguments related to MBASafe will free time to be dedicated to the provision of product-based arguments.

6 Conclusion and Future Work

Since newly proposed and potentially innovative engineering methods suffer of low acceptance in rail industrial settings due to the requirements of the certification process, methods aimed at speeding up the provision of process-based arguments can be beneficial. In this paper, we have used MDSafeCer to show that MBASafe can be partly used as quality and safety management evidence within a safety case. More specifically, we have focused on specific portions of the CENELEC standard series related to software process compliance and we have argued by using GSN about compliance with EN 50128-related design.

In the future, to achieve a full compelling process argument, we will further develop MBASafe according to the findings. Ideally, all undeveloped goals should be replaced by well-founded and explained goals. Moreover, with respect to tool-support, in the context of SafeCer [20], a prototype implementation of MDSafeCer was integrated within Workflow Engine for Analysis, Certification and Testing (WEFACT), which is a tool that offers a flexible infrastructure for defining and executing processes as well as integrating other tools for rendering purposes. This implementation is expected to evolve in the framework of the recently funded ECSEL project AMASS. The initial goal of its evolution is to provide evidence with respect to the effectiveness of the approach in terms of time reduction (manual vs. semi-automatic work). Once the evidence is achieved, the intention is to provide an industry-friendly tool support. As future work, we also aim at focusing on evidence related to the system/subsystem behavior, i.e., technical evidence. To do that, we plan to derive product-based arguments by building on top of work presented by Sljivo et al. [21].

Acknowledgments. This work has been partially supported by the ARTEMIS project nSafeCer [20] and by the Swedish Foundation for Strategic Research via the SYNOPSIS project [22] and the Gen&ReuseSafetyCases project [23].

References

1. Gómez-Martínez, E., Rodríguez, R.J., Etxeberria Elorza, L., Illarramendi Rezabal, M., Benac Earle, C.: Model-based verification of safety contracts. In: Canal, C., Idani, A. (eds.) SEFM 2014 Workshops. LNCS, vol. 8938, pp. 101–115. Springer, Heidelberg (2015)
2. Object Management Group: Software & Systems Process Engineering Meta-Model (SPEM), v2.0. Full Specification formal/08-04-01 (2008)
3. Gallina, B.: A model-driven safety certification method for process compliance. In: 2nd International Workshop on Assurance Cases for Software-intensive Systems (ASSURE), pp. 204–209, November 2014

4. Gallina, B., Provenzano, L.: Deriving reusable process-based arguments from process models in the context of railway safety standards. AUJ **36**(4), 237–241 (2015)
5. Interim Defence Standard 00–56 Part 1 - Issue 5, in, UK MOD (2014)
6. GSN: Community Standard Version 1 (2011)
7. SACM. http://www.omg.org/spec/sacm/1.0
8. MODSafe Modular Urban Transport Safety and Security Analysis: Survey of current safety lifecycle approaches, DEL D6.1 TRIT WP6 100531 V1.0. Technical report (2010)
9. BS EN50126: Railway applications: The specification and demonstration of Reliability. Availability, Maintainability and Safety (RAMS) (1999)
10. BS EN50129: Railway applications Communication, signalling and processing systems Safety related electronic systems for signalling (2003)
11. BS EN50128: Railway applications - Communication, signalling and processing systems Software for railway control and protection systems (2011)
12. Söderberg, A., Johansson, R.: Safety contract based design of software components. In: IEEE International Symposium on Software Reliability Engineering Workshops (ISSREW), pp. 365–370 (2013)
13. Ajmone Marsan, M., Balbo, G., Conte, G., Donatelli, S., Franceschinis, G.: Modelling with Generalized Stochastic Petri Nets. Wiley Series in Parallel Computing. Wiley, New York (1995)
14. Gómez-Martínez, E., Merseguer, J.: ArgoSPE: model-based software performance engineering. In: Donatelli, S., Thiagarajan, P.S. (eds.) ICATPN 2006. LNCS, vol. 4024, pp. 401–410. Springer, Heidelberg (2006)
15. Liu, T.S., Chiou, S.B.: The application of Petri nets to failure analysis. Reliab. Eng. Syst. Safe. **57**(2), 129–142 (1997)
16. Baarir, S., Beccuti, M., Cerotti, D., De Pierro, M., Donatelli, S., Franceschinis, G.: The GreatSPN tool: recent enhancements. SIGMETRICS Perform. Eval. Rev. **36**(4), 4–9 (2009)
17. Gallina, B.: How to increase efficiency with the certification of process compliance. In: The 3rd Scandinavian Conference on SYSTEM & SOFTWARE SAFETY, Stockholm, 24–25 March (2015)
18. Bender, M., Maibaum, T., Lawford, M., Wassyng, A.: Positioning verification in the context of software/system certification. In: 11th International Workshop on Automated Verification of Critical Systems (AVOCS), Newcastle upon Tyne (UK), 12–15 Sept (2013)
19. Nair, S., Walkinshaw, N., Kelly, T., de la Vara, J.L.: An evidential reasoning approach for assessing confidence in safety evidence. In: IEEE 26th International Symposium on Software Reliability Engineering (ISSRE), pp. 541–552, November 2015
20. ARTEMIS-JU-269265: SafeCer-Safety Certification of Software-Intensive Systems with Reusable Components. http://www.safecer.eu/
21. Sljivo, I., Gallina, B., Carlson, J., Hansson, H.: Generation of safety case argument-fragments from safety contracts. In: Bondavalli, A., Di Giandomenico, F. (eds.) SAFECOMP 2014. LNCS, vol. 8666, pp. 170–185. Springer, Heidelberg (2014)
22. SYNOPSIS-SSF-RIT10-0070: SYNOPSIS project-safety Analysis for Predictable Software Intensive Systems. Swedish Foundation for Strategic Research
23. Gen&ReuseSafetyCases-SSF. http://www.es.mdh.se/projects/393-genreusesafetycases

Safety Critical Software Development – Extending Quality Management System Practices to Achieve Compliance with Regulatory Requirements

Andrzej Beniamin Bujok[1(✉)], Silvana Togneri MacMahon[1], Fergal McCaffery[1], Dick Whelan[2], Bernard Mulcahy[2], and William J. Rickard[3]

[1] Regulated Software Research Centre, Dundalk Institute of Technology,
Dublin Road, Dundalk, Ireland
{andrzej.bujok,silvana.macmahon,fergal.mccaffery}@dkit.ie
[2] Almir Business Limited, 2 Mungret Street, Limerick, Ireland
{dw,bm}@almir.biz
[3] Dabl Ltd., Carraig Court, Georges Avenue, Blackrock, Co., Dublin, Ireland
wjrickard@dabl.eu

Abstract. Software is increasingly being used to provide functionality in safety critical domains. The complexity involved in the development of software for these domains can bring challenges concerned with safety and security. International standards are published, providing information on practices which must be implemented in order to satisfy the regulations. This paper details an investigation of the relevant standards that companies need to implement in order to satisfy the regulatory requirements. A literature review was conducted which examines the relevant Quality management system, Risk Management and Software development standards across the safety critical domains. To examine the challenges in implementing these standards, interviews were conducted with a medical device software development company having a Quality management system in place and beginning to implement the relevant Software development standards. In addition, an interview was conducted with a consultancy company who have experience in the implementation and maintenance of Quality management systems in small and medium enterprises. Future work will focus on the integration of practices which need to be implemented by companies developing safety critical software.

Keywords: Quality management system · Risk management · Software development · Standards · Safety critical software development · Regulatory requirements · Integrated use of standards · Small and medium enterprises

1 Introduction

Software is increasingly being used to provide functionality in safety critical domains such as Medical device; Automotive; or Aviation, Space and Defence. For instance, a premium class car now contains 100 microprocessors and runs on 100 m lines of software code. To a software engineer this makes a car like a computer [1].

Safety-critical systems are defined as: *"systems whose failure could result in loss of life, significant property damage, or damage to the environment."* [2] As the use of software, whether embedded or standalone, grows in safety critical domains, functionality also increases thus improving quality of services being provided and the products being produced. For example, software is increasingly being used in medical devices for diagnostic [3] or treatment purposes [4–6].

However, the increased use of software brings new challenges concerned with safety and security issues. For example attackers have tried to infect medical devices with malware in order to steal confidential data [7]. Another example of a security issue is an instance when a team of computer security researchers was able to gain wireless access to a combination heart defibrillator and pacemaker and were able to reprogram it to shut down and to deliver jolts of electricity that would potentially be fatal if the device had been implanted within a patient. In this case, the researchers were hacking into a device in a laboratory [8]. These examples show the possibility that the confidential data about patient's health could be stolen and misused to cause some damage. As a result a considerable amount of attention is dedicated to these issues, not only on the country government and legal level but also there is a great need to solve them on international level [9, 10].

To have regulatory oversight of the safety critical domains government bodies issue regulatory requirements. In European countries they can be based on the regulatory framework provided by European Union (EU) Council [11], and in United States (US) by Federal Government [12]. In terms of medical devices and the healthcare domain, the EU Council directives [13] and US Code of regulations were issued [14]. If product or service complies with regulatory requirements, a certificate is issued, which entitles the organization to sell products on the market [15].

The paper examines how the use of Quality management system standards can be combined with the use of Software development and Risk management standards in order to implement practices which will allow developers to comply with the relevant regulations. This also ensures that issues concerning the safety and security of the software are avoided. The remainder of this paper is structured as follows. Section 2 presents a literature review of the relevant Quality management system (QMS) standards, Risk Management (RM) and Software development (SD) standards for a number of safety critical domains. This section presents an outline of the relevant standards that were examined for each of the safety critical domains and provides a brief description of the regulatory environments for the Medical; Automotive; and Aviation and Aerospace domains. Section 3 presents two mappings of these standards. One mapping focuses on an examination of QMS standards while the other focuses on SD standards related to safety critical domains. The purpose of the mapping is to identify a core set of requirements which are common across the standards and to identify those requirements which are specific to a certain domain. Section 4 presents the results of the interviews which were conducted to investigate the challenges experienced by companies attempting to integrate and implement the standards. Section 5 describes the research conducted to date and outlines next steps for the future work. Section 6 presents the conclusions of this paper.

2 Quality Management System, Software Development and Risk Management Standards in Safety Critical Domains

Non-government organizations for standardization produce standards which contribute to achieving compliance with the regulatory requirements for safety critical software development [16, 17] such as:

- ISO 9001:2015 – *Quality management systems Requirements* [18]
- ISO/IEC 15288:2015 *Systems and software engineering – System lifecycle processes* [19] and *ISO/IEC 12207:2008 – Systems and software engineering – Software lifecycle processes* [20]
- ISO 31000:2009 *Risk management – Principles and guidelines* [21] and *IEC 61508:2010 Functional safety of electrical/electronic/programmable electronic safety-related systems - General requirements*

Many standards are harmonized with respect to US regulations – *"Recognized Consensus Standards"* [22], and European directives [23]. Harmonized standards are: *"European Standards, adopted by CEN, CENELEC or ETSI, following a mandate or order issued by the European Commission. Compliance with harmonized standards, for which the reference numbers have been published in the Official Journal of the EU and which have been transposed into national standards, provides a presumption of conformity to the corresponding essential requirements of the EU Directives."* [24]

The need for implementation of several standards within one domain has resulted in organisations attempting to integrate the requirements of several standards. As a result, ISO organization published guidance on the Integrated use of management system standards [25]. Due to need to integrate an increasing number of standards this

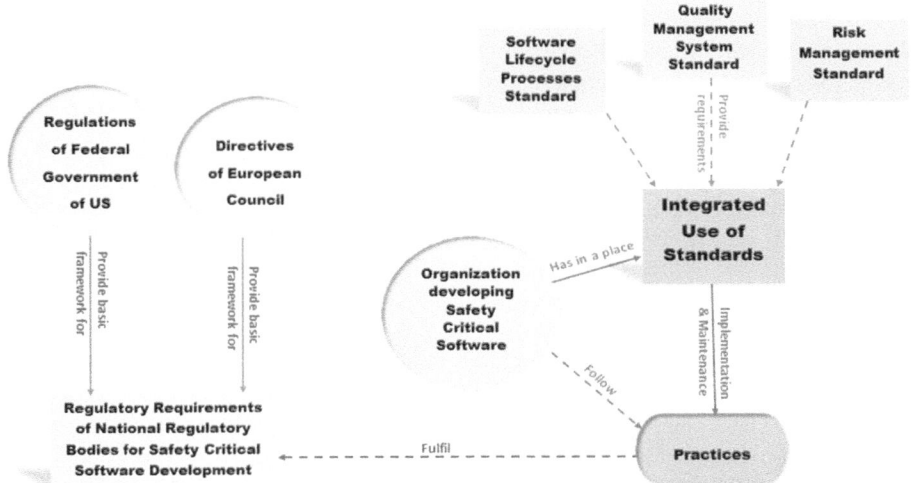

Fig. 1. Integrated requirements of Quality management system, Software development and Risk management standards implemented as required practices in safety critical domains.

publication is currently being revised. Figure 1 shows how Quality management system; Software development; and Risk management standards; represented by the fields at the top right side of diagram, are integrated and consequently implemented as practices. Organizations developing safety critical software need to have Quality management system standard in place and subsequently follow the practices from other standards. Such integrated use of standards provides practices that fulfil the regulatory requirements. In the following subsections there is an explanation of the standards that were examined for each of the listed above safety critical domains. During the initial phases of the research to date, the main focus is on the Medical device domain. This domain will be used as an exemplar of the research approach taken, which can then be applied to the other safety critical domains.

2.1 Standards in the Medical Device Domain

Significant research on Medical device domain has been conducted by other researchers from Regulated Software Research Centre at Dundalk Institute of Technology in Dundalk within last few years. Various fields related to medical device software development were investigated, such as Software process improvement and Roadmaps [26], Integration agile with a Medical device software development [27], Development of process assessment model for assessing medical IT networks against *IEC 80001-1* [28], Investigation of traceability within a medical device organization [29, 30], and others. This paper extends the research being conducted within the centre and through an examination of what standards organizations having *ISO 13485:2012 Medical devices – Quality management systems – Requirements for regulatory purposes* [31] or more generic QMS already in place, need to implement to fulfil the regulatory requirements for the development of software in safety critical domains. This section of the paper examines the standards which are relevant to the medical device domain.

For Medical device developers the *ISO 13485:2012* is seen as the first step in obtaining certification and CE mark for their product. However, QMS is not strictly related to Software development issues, therefore, the *IEC 62304:2006 Medical device software – Software life-cycle processes* [32] standard is also required. The QMS standard addresses the quality management issues but does not address the software lifecycle issues that are addressed by *IEC 62304*. *IEC 62304* is harmonized by the EU and the US and is used as a benchmark for Medical device software development to comply with regulatory requirements. *IEC 62304* standard requires that *ISO 13485:2012*; and *ISO 14971:2012 Medical devices — Application of risk management to medical devices* [33]; are also in place. And additionally there is a Technical report *IEC/TR 80002-1:2009 Medical device software Part 1: Guidance on the application of ISO 14971 to medical device software* [34]. Figure 2 shows the relevant standards, the requirements of which need to be in place to form the Integrated use of standards. Organizations developing medical device software, which are represented in the figure by the circle on the left side, need to have integrated use of standards in place and follow the implemented practices. Through the integrated use of these standards, the regulatory requirements represented by fields placed on the left side of the diagram can be fulfilled.

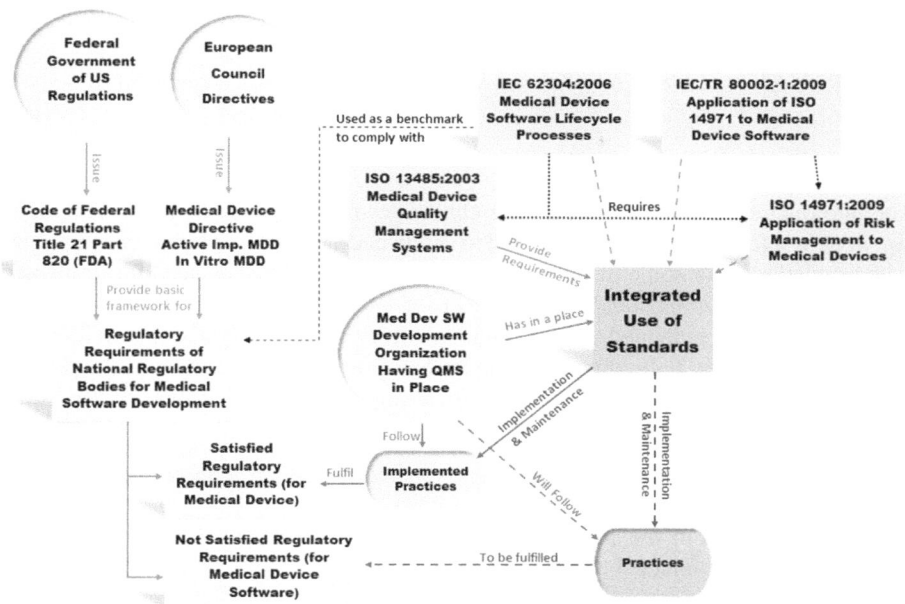

Fig. 2. Integrated requirements of ISO 13485, IEC 62304 and ISO 14971 implemented as required practices for Medical device software domain.

2.2 Standards in the Automotive Domain

The Automotive domain can be illustrated by diagram similar to the general one in Fig. 1, but there are specific standards for automotive domain, that are considered for integration in the general diagram.

- For QMS: *ISO/TS 16949:2009 Quality management systems — Particular requirements for the application of ISO 9001:2008 for automotive production and relevant service part organizations* [35]
- for SD: *ISO 15497:2000 Road vehicles – Development guidelines for vehicle based software* [36] and *ISO 26262-6:2011 Road vehicles — Functional safety Part 6: Product development at the software level* [37] together with *ISO 26262-8:2011 Road vehicles — Functional safety Part 8: Supporting processes* [38]
- for RM: *ISO 26262-9:2011 Road vehicles — Functional safety Part 9: Automotive Safety Integrity Level (ASIL)-oriented and safety-oriented analyses* [39].

2.3 Standards in the Aviation and Aerospace Domain

Similarly for the Aviation, Space and Defence domain there are specific standards:

- for QMS: *EN 9100: 2009 Quality Management Systems — Requirements for Aviation, Space and Defence Organizations* [40] and *EN 9115: 2013 Quality Management Systems — Requirements for Aviation, Space and Defence Organizations — Deliverable Software* [41]

- for SD: *RTCA DO-178C:2011 Software Consideration in Airborne Systems and Equipment Certification* [42]
- for RM: *EN 16601-80:2014 Space project management Risk management* [43]

2.4 Challenges of Software Development for Safety Critical Domains

The introduction of this paper identifies challenges faced by organizations developing software in safety critical domain related to safety and security issues and in compliance with regulations. For some of the safety critical domains there is a need for implementation of more than one standard. The need for knowledge of different standards and practices to be implemented, and of standards integration, gives another challenge to software developers. Following the completion of the literature review of the relevant standards related to each of the safety critical domains, two additional phases of the research process were completed as follows:

- A comparison of the QMS standards and related SD standards across the safety critical domains was performed
- An investigation of the challenges experienced by companies implementing these standards was conducted

The comparison of the standards was conducted to identify a core set of requirements which are common across the standards and to identify those requirements which are specific to a certain domain. Following the literature review and the mapping of the standards, the focus of the research was then to gain an understanding of the challenges that are experienced by companies when trying to integrate and implement these standards. The following section of this paper discusses the approach to and the results of the mapping of the standards. The results of the investigation of the challenges in implementing the standards are presented in Sect. 4.

3 Mapping of QMS and SD Standards Related to Different Domains

This section provides a description of the mappings of the standards that have been completed as part of this research. One mapping focuses on an examination of QMS standards while the other focuses on SD standards related to different safety critical domains. The future work will include also the mapping of RM standards. The purpose of the mapping was to examine areas which are common among the standards and also to investigate the differences among them. Initially the focus of the research was on Medical device domain and medical device software development, but was then expanded to examine the use of QMS, RM and aligned SD standards in other safety critical domains, like Automotive; and Aviation, Space & Defence.

It has been observed that the set of standards, which is necessary for medical device software development, as QMS, SD and RM, is common for other safety critical domains and that each domain has corresponding standards related to this domain. Accordingly, there is specific QMS for Medical device, specific QMS for Automotive, and specific

QMS for Aviation, Space and Defence domains. As a next step of the research on standards integration we need to define, what is common for these standards and develop common core.

Consequently the research subject has been expanded to:

- What are the required practices of integrated use of standards for safety critical software development domain to comply with regulatory requirements
- How can the implementation of integrated use of standards become more feasible for software developers in terms of small and medium enterprises

For the indicated domains – Medical device; Automotive; Aviation, Space and Defence; the cross industry cross reference mapping of sections and subsections for QMS standards has been conducted as a first step of standards mapping. As an outcome the cross reference table has been created presenting differences and what is common for researched industries. The sample of the table for QMS standards is introduced on Table 1. There are six different QMS standards represented in the table: *General ISO 9001 QMS*, which is foundation QMS and is used as a base for development of domain specific QMS standards, *Medical Device 13485 QMS, Aviation, Space and Defence EN 9100 AND EN 9115 QMS* and *Automotive ISO 16040 QMS*.

There are two vertical segments of the table. The left segment – *"Integrated Table of Sections and Subsections for QMS Standards"* has one column for Section Titles (titles). In the right segment – *"Numbers Accorded to Section Titles of QMS Standards"* there are six columns and each column represents one QMS standard. The column of titles has been populated with section titles from Medical device QMS standard first, followed by section titles from QMS standards of other domains. If, in some of the QMS standards, the new title of main section or sub/sub-sub section appeared, a new line was added to the table in order to include the new title. If the examined QMS standard

Table 1. The sample of mapping conducted of QMS standards for different safety critical domains.

Integrated Table of Sections and Subsections for QMS Standards	Numbers Accorded to Section Titles of QMS Standards					
Section Titles	Medical Device ISO 13485:2003	Aviation, Space and Defence BS/EN 9110:2009	Aviation, Space and Defence BS/EN 9115:2013	Automotive ISO/TS 16949:2009	General ISO 9001:2008	General ISO 9001:2015
Context of the organization	.	.	.	.	.	4
Understanding the organization and its context						4.1
Understanding the needs and expectations of interested parties						4.2
Determining the scope of the quality management system	.	.	.	.	.	4.3
Quality management system (and its processes)	4	4	4	4	4	4.4
General requirements	4.1	4.1	4.1	4.1	4.1	-
General requirements —Supplemental	-	-	-	4.1.1	-	-
Documentation requirements	4.2	4.2	4.2	4.2	4.2	-
General	.	4.2.1	4.2.1	4.2.1	.	.
Quality manual	.	4.2.2	4.2.2	4.2.2	.	.
Control of documents	.	4.2.3	4.2.3	4.2.3	.	.
Engineering specifications	.	.	.	4.2.3.1	.	.
Control of records	.	4.2.4	4.2.4	4.2.4	.	.
Records retention	.	.	.	4.2.4.1	.	.
Management responsibility/Leadership	5	5	5	5	5	5
Management commitment/Leadership and commitment	5.1	5.1	5.1	5.1	5.1	5.1
Process efficiency	.	.	.	5.1.1	.	.
General						5.1.1
Customer focus	5.2	5.2	5.2	5.2	5.2	5.1.2
Policy	.	.	.	.	.	5.2
Quality policy	5.3	5.3	5.3	5.3	5.3	5.2.1
Communicating the quality policy						5.2.2
Organizational roles, responsibilities and authorities	.	.	.	.	.	5.3
Planning	5.4	5.4	5.4	5.4	5.4	6

contains inserted title then in the related line the number of title is inserted to the column representing this QMS standard, if not, the dash mark is inserted.

This mapping is an initial stage of developing common core for QMS standards and common core for SD standards. This approach corresponds to the fact that also ISO have seen that organizations have had challenges in implementing multiple standards. To this end they published Annex SL within *ISO/IEC Directives, Part 1* publication [44]. This Annex SL provides framework for the future Management systems that will make them more generic, more easily applicable and more consistent and therefore their integration should be easier. This common framework consists of high level structure, identical core text and common terms and core definitions. There is number of standards including ISO 9001:2015 that already employed Annex SL [45]. ISO also addressed the challenges of multiple risk standards. They introduced *ISO 31000 Risk management – principles and guidelines* [21] that provides common framework that can be applied to any type of risk and is not specific to any industry or sector [21]. This attempt of ISO to harmonize Management systems and to harmonize Risk management processes by introducing common framework can be seen as a model for development of common framework for safety critical software standards. The presented mapping of QMS and SD standards is s first step of developing common core for these standards.

For all considered domains it was noticed that for the QMS standards the structure of main sections and first subsections is exactly the same, except of ISO 9001:2015. The differences were found in the second and higher subsections. The unified structure of QMS standards for different safety critical domains provides a good foundation for their integration. The presence of a common set of requirements in these standards allows for the identification of core set of QMS requirements which can then be extended to allow the additional requirements of a specific safety critical domain to be implemented.

Using the same approach the cross industry cross reference mapping of sections and subsection for SD standards has been conducted and subsequently the cross reference

Table 2. The sample of mapping conducted of SD standards for different safety critical domains.

Integrated Table of Sections and Subsections for SD Standards	Numbers Accorded to Section Titles of SD Standards				
Section Titles	Medical Device		Automotive		Aviation, Space & Defence
	IEC 62304:2006	IEC/TR 80002-3:2014	ISO 26262-6:2011	ISO 26262-8:2011	ISO/TR 15497:2000	DO-178C/ED-12C:2011
Software development PROCESS (Software lifecycle)	5	4.1	-	-	3	5.0
Medical device software life cycle processes	-	4	-	-	-	-
Software development planning (Project planning)	5.1	4.1.1	-	-	3.1	4.0
Initiation of product development at the software level (Interfaces within distributed developments)	-	-	5	5	-	-
Objectives/ Software Planning Process Objectives	-	-	5.1	5.1	-	4.1
Software Planning Process Activities	-	-	-	-	-	4.2
General/ Software Plans	-	-	5.2	5.2	-	4.3
Software Lifecycle Environment Planning	-	-	-	-	-	4.4
Software Development Environment	-	-	-	-	-	4.4.1
Language and Compiler Consideration	-	-	-	-	-	4.4.2
Software Test Environment	-	-	-	-	-	4.4.3
Software Development Standards	-	-	-	-	-	4.5
Review of the Software Planning Process	-	-	-	-	-	4.6
Inputs to this clause	-	-	5.3	5.3	-	-
Requirements and recommendations	-	-	5.4	5.4	-	-
Work products	-	-	5.5	5.5	-	-
Software requirements analysis (requirements specification)	5.2	4.1.2	-	-	3.3	5.1
Specification of software safety requirements	-	-	6	6	-	-
Objectives/ Software Requirements Process Objectives	-	-	6.1	6.1	-	5.1.1
Software Requirements Process Activities	-	-	-	-	-	5.1.2

table was created. The sample of the table is presented on Table 2. The structure of the table for SD standards is similar to the table for QMS standards. There are six columns representing different domains and SD standards related to these domains, and there is column for integrated section titles. The sample of the table shows that there are sections with significant differences. It has been realized that for SD there are more differences in section structure then for QMS. Therefore the development of common core appears more challenging comparing to QMS standards.

4 The Challenges of Compliance with Regulatory Requirements Related to Safety Critical Domains

The introduction of this paper identified challenges faced by organizations developing software in safety critical domains related to safety and security issues and to regulatory requirements. The research conducted on standards and their implementation shows the complexity of existing standards and how they relate to software development and to each other. The next phase of the research, presented in this section, examined the challenges faced by organizations developing software for a safety critical domain.

4.1 Medical Device Software Development & Compliance with Regulatory Requirements

Using Medical device software as an example of safety critical software domains that faces challenges related to compliance with regulatory requirements, an interview was conducted with an organization developing medical device software. The purpose of the interview was to examine their experience with standards implementation and main challenges that they face.

Previously, for the purpose of their activity they implemented QMS and they were *ISO 9001:2008 Quality management system* [46] compliant. The regulatory amendment issued in 2010 changed the classification of software meaning that software used for treatment and diagnosis as per the established definition of Medical device, could now be classified as a medical device in its own right [47]. This amendment changed their situation significantly. The amendment meant that they now needed to obtain the CE mark for their software as a proof of compliance with regulatory requirements. For this reason, the Quality assurance (QA) department was created and a QA specialist was employed within the organization. They had ISO 9001:2008 in place but, because of the classification of their software as a Medical device, they then implemented the ISO 13485:2012 standard as a first step in obtaining CE mark. In order to implement ISO 13485:2012, the company initially conducted a gap analysis between the requirements of ISO 9001:2008 and those additional requirements, which would need to be implemented in order to comply with ISO 13485:2012. In this way an integration of two systems, ISO 9001 and ISO 13485 was achieved and presently there are not two separate QMS in place and no duplicated requirements implemented.

The company is now beginning to implement the requirements of IEC 62304:2006. They identify the implementation of this standard as challenging. They see standard as being open to interpretation, and not specific in terms of which software development life-cycle should be used in order to comply with regulatory requirements. They find the requirements of this standard to be unclear and are not certain if their understanding is correct. In their opinion, with the many different software development lifecycles which are available for use there is continuous discussion within the company as to which of these lifecycles is appropriate for use for medical device software development. The company stated that even the opinions from specialist consultants on which of the lifecycles are suited for use were contradictory.

The company would like to follow the agile software lifecycle but because of the perceived lack of clarity regarding its suitability in terms of compliance with regulatory requirements, they follow the Waterfall lifecycle. From their point of view the regulations and directions are ambiguous and there are no guidelines provided on what is necessary. They find that the requirements of the standard are expressed at a high level and implementation can be challenging. They advised that a check-list which details an approach to the implementation of the requirements would be most helpful. They consider the implementation of the IEC 62304:2006 as a very robust approach, the implementation of which would be very challenging for small and medium enterprises (SME). Given constrains on SMEs the company feel that there is an issue with identifying the minimum requirements of standard that has to be implemented in order to comply with regulations.

Another issue for the company is concerned with safety classification. In their opinion, in the EU the regulations pertaining to the classification of devices is open for interpretation and not specific enough. The company noted that in the US on the FDA website there is a "Product Code Classification Database" where you can look at other products registered and compare, as a code classification guide. They stated that a similar site would be helpful which provides examples of the safety classification of devices under EU regulations. An incorrect safety classification of a device can have serious consequences for the company.

The interview confirmed that in the medical device domain there is presently no unified framework for safety critical software development that incorporates all of the best practices for safety critical software development. The selection of appropriate standards and necessary requirements, integration and implementation of these standard requirements causes significant challenges for SMEs.

4.2 Issues with Compliance with Regulatory Requirements Seen by Consultancy Company

Another interview was conducted with a Consultancy Company. This company provides assistance with the implementation and maintenance of QMS standards in SMEs. They have insight into the challenges concerned with QMS standard implementation that the SMEs face, and also they have experience with their approach to address these challenges. The purpose of the interview was to see their experience with QMS standard implementation and how they perceive the challenges with QMS implementation that the SMEs face. Building on their experience of implementing QMS in SMEs the consultancy company is now focussing on: how these systems can be expanded to include the required best practices in order to comply with the requirements for the development of software in safety critical domains. The other purpose of interview, based on their broad insight into the field of different international standards, was to investigate the challenges that the organization having QMS standard in place and developing software in safety critical domain have to face with implementing requirements of Software standards.

The Managing Director of the company said that from their experience the quality management systems are: *"well practised, they are well written and tangible"*. But in their opinion the software standards assume unlimited resources for implementation and maintenance of all standard procedures, but this is not the case of SMEs. From their experience there are number of small enterprises with limited human and financial resources, with experts in software development but without knowledge of regulatory requirements and about standard implementation. The other issue is concerned with the need for implementation of several standards which is the case of safety critical software development. They say that implementation of all standard requirements produces lots of overlying separate processes in place. The interview confirmed again that SME face the challenges related to the lack of resources which are necessary for standard implementation and maintenance. They have also insufficient knowledge about regulations and standards.

5 Future Works

To date the literature review and interviews with companies were conducted to identify the challenges that SMEs developing software in safety critical domains have to face. A cross industry mapping of section titles has been completed for QMS standards and for SD standards. A detailed mapping of standard requirements will be conducted as the next phase of the research process. Three different standard categories will be investigated. One mapping will be conducted for QMS standards, another mapping for Software development standards and another one for Risk management standards related to safety critical domains. For each of the standard categories, the outcome of the mapping will define the common requirements across the investigated domains and identify the requirements which are specific to each domain. Based on the defined common requirements for each standard category, a common core will be developed, one for QMS, one for SD and one for RM. These common cores will be a foundation for development of the Integrated use of standards. In the next stage the mapping of common cores will be conducted to investigate overlaying requirements and procedures. Based on this mapping the core of Integrated use of standards will be developed. This core of Integrated use will provide practices that include all investigated domains and all related standard categories. The further work will focus on standard requirements which are specific for different domains. The goal of this research is to develop the integrated use of management system standards as a unified framework for safety critical software development that incorporates all of best practices.

6 Conclusion

This paper has presented the results of a literature review which has examined how the integrated use of QMS and SD standards can address the challenges concerned with safety critical software development. To extend the results of the literature review and investigate the challenges in integrating and implementing the requirements of various standards, interviews were conducted with companies assisting in the implementation of QMS standards and with a company developing software in the medical device domain. These interviews combined with the results of the literature review revealed that organisations, particularly SME, struggle to integrate and implement the practices outlined in standards which are necessary for compliance with the regulations for software development in safety critical domains.

The research conducted to date has focused on an initial investigation of the challenges experienced by SMEs in the integration of QMS, RM and SD standards. The next phase of the research will focus on identifying requirements which are common within standard categories across safety critical domains and identifying which requirements are domain specific. This will form the basis for the development of a framework which can be used by SME already having a QMS in place to implement the requirements for software development in safety critical domains. The mapping of standards conducted to date will be expanded to examine the requirements of the standards. The mapping approach will cover all of investigated safety critical domains and related standard categories. The framework which will be developed as part of this research will assist organisations in addressing the challenges of complying with the regulatory requirements for software development across safety critical domains.

Acknowledgments. This research is supported by the Science Foundation Ireland Principal Investigator Programme, grant number 08/IN.1/I2030 (the funding of this project was awarded by Science Foundation Ireland under a co-funding initiative by the Irish Government and European Regional Development Fund),and by Lero - the Irish Software Research Centre (http://www.lero.ie) grant 10/CE/I1855 & 13/RC/20194.

References

1. Gapper, J.: Software is steering auto industry - FT.com. Financ. Times (2016)
2. Knight, J.: Safety critical systems: challenges and directions. In: International Conference on Software Engineering (2002)
3. Monti, M.M., Vanhaudenhuyse, A., Coleman, M.R., Boly, M., Pickard, J.D., Tshibanda, L., Owen, A.M., Laureys, S.: Willful modulation of brain activity in disorders of consciousness. N. Engl. J. Med. **362**, 579–589 (2010)
4. McHugh, M., McCaffery, F., MacMahon, S.T.: Improving safety in medical devices from concept to retirement. In: Furht, B., Agarwal, A. (eds.) Handbook of Medical and Healthcare Technologies, pp. 452–480. Springer, New York (2013)
5. Next Generation PDT, Next Generation PDT - New Generation Cancer Treatment Therapy. http://www.nextgenerationpdt.com/?loc=gbl. Accessed: 15 Feb 2016
6. National Cancer Institute, Radiation Therapy for Cancer. http://www.cancer.gov/about-cancer/treatment/types/radiation-therapy/radiation-fact-sheet#q1. Accessed: 15 Feb 2016

7. TrapX Labs, Anatomy of an Attack Medjack (Medical Device Hijack) (2015)
8. Fu, K.: ARCHIMEDES Ann Arbor Research Center for Medical Device Security. http://www.secure-medicine.org/. Accessed: 15 Feb 2016
9. European Council, MD Directives
10. U.S. FDA, Inspection, Compliance, Enforcement, and Criminal Investigations
11. McHugh, M., McCaffery, F., Casey, V.: How amendments to the medical device directive affects the development of medical device software (2011)
12. McHugh, M., McCaffery, F., Casey, V.: US FDA releases final rule on Medical Device Data Systems - what does this mean for device manufacturers? (2011)
13. European Commission, Council Directive 93/42/EEC, vol. L 269, September 2000
14. U.S. FDA, Code of Federal Regulations Title 21
15. U.S. FDA, FDA Agents - FDA Registration and U.S. Agent Representation
16. ISO, ISO - International Organization for Standardization. http://www.iso.org/iso/home.htm. Accessed: 15 Feb 2016
17. IEC, Welcome to the IEC - International Electrotechnical Commission: http://www.iec.ch/index.htm. Accessed: 15 Feb 2016
18. ISO, ISO 9001: 2015 Quality management systems Requirements … making excellence a habit (2015)
19. ISO/IEC, ISO/IEC 15288:2015 Systems and software engineering — Life cycle processes (2015)
20. ISO/IEC, ISO/IEC 12207:2008 Systems and software engineering — Software life cycle processes (2008)
21. ISO, ISO 31000:2009 Risk management – principles and guidelines (2009)
22. U.S. FDA, Recognized Consensus Standards
23. European Commission, Harmonised Standards - European Commission
24. NSAI, Standards Supporting EU Directives. http://www.nsai.ie/Our-Services/Standardization/Standards-Supporting-EU-Directives.aspx. Accessed: 17 Feb 2016
25. ISO, ISO publishes book + CD on integrated use of management system standards (2008-07-15) - ISO (2008). http://www.iso.org/iso/news.htm?refid=Ref1144. Accessed: 15 Jan 2016
26. Flood, D., McCaffery, F., Casey, V., Regan, G.: A Methodology for Software Process Improvement Roadmaps for Regulated Domains - Example with IEC 62366
27. McHugh, M., McCaffery, F., Casey, V., Pikkarainen, M.: Integrating agile practices with a medical device software development lifecycle. In: EuroSPI 2012, pp. 1–8 (2012)
28. MacMahon, S.T., McCaffery, F., Eagles, S., Keenan, F., Lepmets, M., Renault, A.: Development of a Process Assessment Model for assessing Medical IT Networks against IEC 80001-1
29. Regan, G., McCaffery, F., McDaid, K., Flood, D.: Investigation of traceability within a medical device organization. In: Woronowicz, T., Rout, T., O'Connor, R.V., Dorling, A. (eds.) SPICE 2013. CCIS, vol. 349, pp. 211–222. Springer, Heidelberg (2013)
30. McCaffery, F., Casey, V.: Med-Trace. In: O'Connor, R.V., Rout, T., McCaffery, F., Dorling, A. (eds.) SPICE 2011. CCIS, vol. 155, pp. 208–211. Springer, Heidelberg (2011)
31. ISO, EN ISO 13485:2012 Medical devices — Quality management systems — Requirements for regulatory purposes, July 2012
32. IEC, IEC 62304:2006 Medical device software—Software life cycle processes (2006)
33. ISO, EN ISO 14971:2012 Medical devices — Application of risk management to medical devices (ISO 14971:2007, Corrected version 2007-10-01) (2012)
34. IEC, IEC/TR 80002-1:2009 Medical device software Part: Guidance on the application of ISO 14971 to medical device software (2009)

35. ISO, ISO/TS 16949: 2009 Quality management systems — Particular requirements for the application of ISO 9001: 2008 for automotive production and relevant service part organizations (2009)
36. ISO, ISO/TR 15497:2000 Road Vehicles — Development guidelines for vehicle based software (2000)
37. ISO, ISO 26262-6:2011 Road vehicles — Functional safety Part 6: Product development at the software level (2011)
38. ISO, ISO 26262-8:2011 Road vehicles — Functional safety Part 8: Supporting processes (2011)
39. ISO, ISO 26262-9:2011 Road vehicles — Functional safety Part 9: Automotive Safety Integrity Level (ASIL)-oriented and safety-oriented analyses (2011)
40. EN, EN 9100: 2009 Quality Management Systems – Requirements for Aviation, Space and Defense Organizations (2009)
41. EN, EN 9115: 2013 Quality Management Systems — Requirements for Aviation, Space and Defense Organizations — Deliverable Software (2013)
42. RTCA, RTCA DO-178C:2011 Software Consideration in Airborne Systems and Equipment Certification (2011)
43. EN, BS EN 16601-80:2014 Space project management. Risk management (2014)
44. ISO, ISO/IEC Directives, Part 1 Consolidated ISO Supplement — Procedures specific to ISO (2014)
45. The 9000 Store, What is the New Annex SL Platform? http://the9000store.com/iso-9001-2015-annex-sl.aspx. Accessed: 25 Feb 2016
46. ISO, EN ISO 9001: 2008 Quality management systems Requirements (2008)
47. European Commission, DIRECTIVE 2007/47/EC, November 2000 (2007)

The Use of Maturity/Capability Frameworks for Healthcare Process Assessment and Improvement

Mehmet Söylemez[1(✉)] and Ayca Tarhan[2]

[1] TÜBİTAK - BİLGEM/Software Technologies Research Institute, 06100 Ankara, Turkey
mehmet.soylemez@tubitak.gov.tr
[2] Hacettepe University Computer Engineering Department Beytepe Yerleskesi, 06800 Ankara, Turkey
atarhan@hacettepe.edu.tr

Abstract. Process assessment enables to identify strengths and weaknesses of selected processes in a specific domain typically by referencing process maturity/capability frameworks. Assessment findings are usually transformed into action-items for process improvement. In healthcare domain where hospitals offer high-risk services to patients every day in a complex, dynamic, and multidisciplinary environment, establishing process thinking and effective process management is increasingly demanded but not an easy task to accomplish. In this study, we investigate the maturity/capability frameworks that are proposed or used for assessing and improving the healthcare processes. We searched the studies reported between the years 2000 and 2015 in scientific digital libraries and identified 29 studies out of 958 initially retrieved in a systematic way. This study provides an analysis of six studies out of 29 with respect to a number of research questions regarding context, scope, time coverage, and results as well as research method and contribution.

Keywords: Healthcare · Healthcare process · Process maturity · Process capability · Process assessment · Process improvement · Maturity model · Capability framework · Systematic mapping

1 Introduction

Healthcare is one of the most challenging business domains where hospitals provide high-risk services to patients every day. Service quality has direct impact on related costs and reputation of hospitals [1]. Establishing process thinking and achieving effective process management is vital to continually improve service quality in such a complex, knowledge-intensive, dynamic, and multidisciplinary environment [2].

Process assessment is the foundation step for process improvement activities. It investigates strong, weak, and/or missing points in definition and application of a set of selected processes in a specific business domain [3, 4]. Process assessment provides an understanding about current process situation and enables the rating of process quality by considering the degree of conformance to process quality frameworks or process reference models. Findings from a process assessment are usually transformed into action items to improve business processes [5, 6].

The application of process assessment and improvement methods in a hospital setting is not new. There are studies that make use of excellence models [7, 8] as well as Lean management principles and six-sigma [9–12]. Also, there are studies that propose or use maturity models per specialty [13–15]. Despite the existence of these sporadic studies, the number of articles that provide methodological support in general [16–18] and as specific to healthcare [19, 20] is scarce. Maturity/capability frameworks [5, 6, 21] have been successfully used in some domains such as system/software engineering and information technology for the purpose of process assessment and improvement in the last two decades. A business process maturity model, for example, is an instrument to assess and continually improve organizational processes [22]. Despite the abundance of the maturity models proposed in diverse domains [23], an overview of process assessment or improvement studies that refer to maturity/capability frameworks in healthcare settings is lacking. Such an overview could provide the state-of-the-art of existing applications as well as the methods used, and might be useful to highlight research directions for future implementations.

Based on the need stated above, in this study, we focus on the usage of process maturity/capability frameworks that have been taken as the base for healthcare process assessment or improvement. We have aimed at a systematic mapping [24] of the related studies as reported in the scientific digital libraries of (in alphabetical order); ACM, Emerald, IEEE Explore, Pubmed, ScienceDirect, Scopus, SpringerLink, Web of Science, and Wiley. We initially retrieved 958 studies, from which we identified 29 studies that refer to process maturity/capability frameworks for the assessment or improvement of healthcare processes, information systems (IS), or information technology (IT). We then selected six studies (out of 29) that focus solely on healthcare process assessment or improvement. Consequently, in this study, we provide a profile of these studies by analyzing them for the attributes of reference model, assessment model, research method and contribution, context and scope, time coverage, results, and benefits and challenges.

The remaining of this paper is organized as follows. Section 2 gives a summary of the few studies that overview maturity/capability frameworks, from the healthcare point of view. Section 3 explains research design and research questions to analyze the selected studies. Section 4 summarizes research results in response to the research questions. Section 5 closes the paper with conclusions and items for future work.

2 Related Studies

Wendler [23] provides an analysis of 237 articles published between 1999 and 2010. The study reveals that the maturity model research is dominated by the studies in the software engineering field and that most studies deal with the development of maturity models, where evaluations and validations are scarce. This is an initial systematic summary of maturity model research, and helps researchers to gain an understanding of the research gaps from a broad perspective. However, the study is not intended as specific to healthcare domain, and reports only six studies in this field.

Van Looy [25] provides a comprehensive overview of 69 maturity models. The study provides extensive reviews and comparisons of existing business process maturity models, including their structural characteristics and points of focus, such as assessment and improvement. However, this study is neither a systematic mapping nor intended as specific to healthcare domain, and reports only one study as related to this field.

Tarhan et al. [22] report a systematic review of the literature to obtain an overall understanding of the existence, characteristics, and use of generic maturity models in the BPM discipline. They follow a bottom-up approach to elicit empirical studies that refer to the models in order to show the degree of interest drawn by academia. As a result of the review, the authors conclude that current state of research on BPM maturity is in its early phases, and academic literature lacks methodical applications of many mainstream BPM maturity models that have been proposed. This review is for generic maturity models and not specific to healthcare domain, and the authors claim the need for and the lack of a unified and integrated model, around which domain-specific extensions and bodies of improvement practice can be devised.

Blondiau et al. [14] provide a comprehensive evaluation to identify major challenges and risks when it comes to the implementation and design of maturity models in healthcare organizations. The findings in the study are based on three projects conducted from 2008 to 2012 relating to distinct areas of health informatics and health information management. The first project provides a maturity model for measuring the information technology capability of a hospital. The second project provides a maturity model that can be used for measuring the effectiveness and reliability of a hospital's supply-chain management process. The third project provides a maturity model that focuses on intra- and inter-organizational aspects associated with optimizing cooperative processes in hospitals.

Rohner [26] provides a case study in which how process orientation can be applied in a medium-size hospital in Germany. The study reveals that due to abundance of concepts and theories in clinical process management, a comprehensive and target-oriented approach within the entire hospital is sparse. As a result of the case study, an additional net profit of several million euros a year is reported.

Gemmel et al. [27] adapt an existing tool proposed for business process orientation by McCormack and Johnson [28] to the specific context of healthcare. Their measurement tool consists of 35 questions measuring seven dimensions. Three dimensions (process view, process jobs, process management and measurement) are related to the components of business process orientation. The authors emphasize various benefits of measuring process orientation in the healthcare context.

Gillies and Howard [29] combine a process improvement approach derived from the Capability Maturity Model [21] with a model of competency derived from a previous work for becoming a skilled professional in healthcare. The authors provide a case study application on managing change from paper-based to electronic health records in primary care.

To the best of our knowledge, this study is the first attempt to systematically investigate the use of maturity/capability frameworks for healthcare process assessment and improvement. We see a constant need and also an increasing interest in healthcare community to use such frameworks, and hope that our efforts provide insights in directing new adaptations or implementations.

3 Research Design

The research purpose of this study is to identify and analyze the studies that propose or use process maturity/capability frameworks for healthcare process assessment or improvement as reported in the digital libraries of the scientific literature. Table 1 shows research questions that we identified to answer by an analysis of the included studies. We used systematic mapping (SM) as the empirical research method to search, identify and select the included studies. A systematic mapping is a method to identify, review, classify, and structure studies related to a specific research interest in a specific field [24].

Table 1. Research questions (RQs) of the study

RQ#	Research Question (*with an explanation of example answers*)
RQ-1	Which process maturity/capability framework(s) were proposed or used as the base for healthcare process assessment or improvement?
RQ-2	Which assessment method/model was proposed or used to assess healthcare processes?
RQ-3	What was the type of research method used in the study? (*As described in* [24]: *solution proposal, validation research, evaluation research, experience paper, comparison paper*)
RQ-4	What was the main contribution of the study to the field? (*A new process maturity/capability framework, a new assessment model/method, a new tool, etc.*)
RQ-5	What was the context of the study? (*Multiple hospitals, a single hospital, multiple departments, a single department, a clinical pathway, a healthcare process, etc.*)
RQ-6	What was the scope of the study? (*Identity of processes assessed*)
RQ-7	What was the time coverage of healthcare process assessment or improvement? (*Instant versus longitudinal*)
RQ-8	What maturity/capability level(s) were reported as a result of healthcare process assessment or improvement?
RQ-9	What were the reported benefits of carrying out healthcare process assessment or improvement?
RQ-10	What were the challenges of carrying out healthcare process assessment or improvement based on the usage of process maturity/capability framework?

In order to elicit the studies to answer the research questions, we ran four searches for the studies reported between the years 2000 and 2015 in the following digital libraries of the scientific literature (in alphabetical order): ACM, Emerald, Pubmed, ScienceDirect, Scopus, SpringerLink, Web of Science, and Wiley. Table 2 shows the searches ran in the digital libraries, and the number of studies initially retrieved and selected. The phrases searched in the title, abstract, and keywords of the studies are listed following Table 2.

Table 2. Number of studies initially retrieved and selected

Digital Lib.	Search-1		Search-2		Search-3		Search-4	
	Initially retrieved	Initially selected	Initially retrieved	Initially selected	Initially retrieved	Initially selected	Initially retrieved	Initially selected
ACM	135	2	35	0	85	1	4	0
Emerald	11	2	0	0	4	0	7	1
Pubmed	40	10	6	0	37	10	0	0
ScienceDirect	10	1	4	0	51	6	0	0
Scopus	192	11	6	1	58	10	4	2
SpringerLink	63	9	3	2	25	5	3	2
Web of Science	21	6	7	0	26	10	1	1
Wiley	45	1	37	0	0	0	38	0
TOTAL	**517**	**43**	**98**	**3**	**286**	**43**	**57**	**6**
TOTAL Initially Retrieved			958					
TOTAL Initially Selected			95					

Search-1:
    ((health OR healthcare) AND
    ("business process" OR "process management" OR
        "process improvement" OR "quality management") AND
    (maturity OR capability) AND
    (assessment OR appraisal OR evaluation))

Search-2:
    (("clinical pathway" OR "clinical guideline" OR "care pathway") AND
    (maturity OR capability) AND
    (assessment OR appraisal OR evaluation))

Search-3:
    ((health OR healthcare) AND
    ("maturity model" OR "maturity framework" OR "maturity grid" OR
        "capability model" OR "capability framework"))

Search-4:
    (("clinical pathway" OR "clinical guideline" OR "care pathway") AND
    ("maturity model" OR "maturity framework" OR "maturity grid" OR
        "capability model" OR "capability framework"))

The phrases to be searched were identified by running several searches with different texts and checking the scopes of the studies returned. For example in Search-1, we first searched the studies without the second sub-phrase (i.e., "business process" OR "process management" OR "process improvement" OR "quality management"), and noticed that the result set was too large and also frequently irrelevant to our scope since the evaluation or assessment of maturity or capability have different meanings in healthcare studies. Therefore, we added the second sub-phrase to Search-1. The searches 1 and 2 were aimed at retrieving potential studies on process assessment/ appraisal/evaluation, while the searches 3 and 4 were aimed at retrieving potential studies that propose or use maturity/capability frameworks for process assessment or improvement.

The searches were performed by one of the authors, and 958 studies were retrieved. Out of these studies, we initially selected 95 studies. After reviewing these studies in detail, we selected 29 studies that report process, IS, or IT assessments or improvements based on process maturity/capability frameworks. Then within these 29 studies, we selected six studies that focus solely on process assessments or improvements in various healthcare contexts. While selecting the studies, we excluded the ones; (i) that used generic business quality/excellence models such as EFQM or process management methods such as Lean or Six-sigma, (ii) that were not presented in English, (iii) that could not be accessed in full-text, (iv) that were retrieved as duplicates from different searches, and (v) books and gray literature. The studies initially and finally selected were reviewed by both of the authors and the inclusion/exclusion criteria was identified (and revised as necessary) iteratively in discussions held after the reviews.

4 Research Results

The distribution of the 29 studies as included in our SM study by years is shown in Fig. 1. The figure indicates that there is an increased attention on the subject in the last few years. Also, the distribution of the studies (17 out of 29 studies) that include process maturity/capability assessment or improvement, by subject category is shown in Fig. 2. Finally, Table 3 shows an analysis of six studies (out of 17) that focus solely on process assessment or improvement in different healthcare settings.

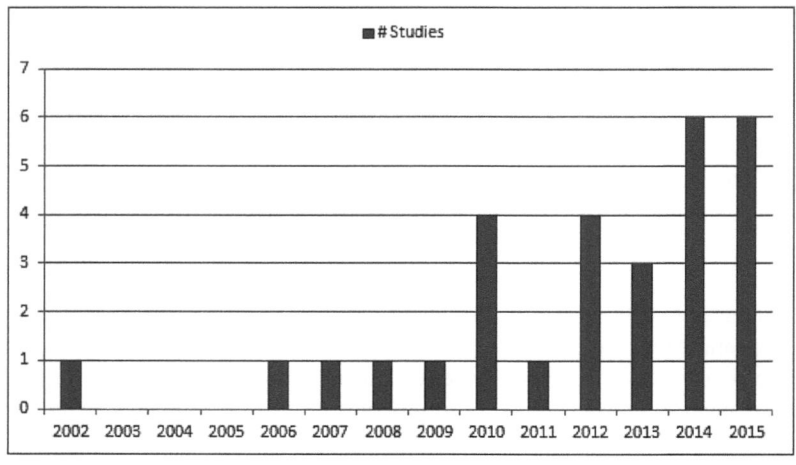

Fig. 1. Distribution of the studies included in our SM study by years (29 studies)

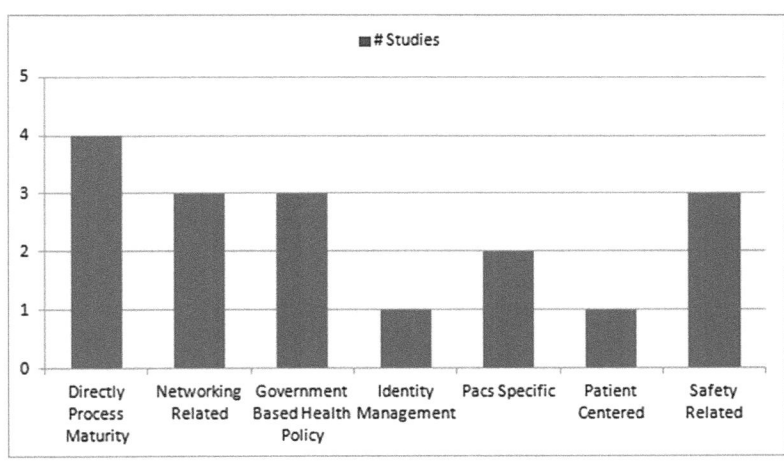

Fig. 2. Distribution of the studies that include process maturity/capability assessment or improvement by subject category (17 out of 29 studies)

Table 3. An analysis of six selected studies with respect to research questions

RQ#	S1 [31]	S2 [32]	S3 [15]	S4 [13]	S5 [33]	S6 [34]
RQ-1	Structured Process Improvement for Construction Environments - Facilities Management (SPICE-FM)	An empirically grounded maturity model	OMG's Business Process Maturity Model [6]	Hospital Cooperation Maturity Model (HCMM)	Act on Oncology (standardized operational process assessment tool) based on the structure of CMMI [21]	A maturity model to assess and advance networkability of health care providing organizations
RQ-2	Structure Process Improvement for Construction Environments - Facilities Management (SPICE-FM)	Not reported	A process assessment method adapted from SCAMPI [4] and ISO/IEC 15504 [3]	Hospital Cooperation Maturity Model (HCMM)	Act on Oncology (standardized operational process assessment tool) based on the structure of CMMI [21]	A maturity model to assess and advance networkability of health care providing organizations
RQ-3	Evaluation Research	Solution Proposal	Evaluation Research	Solution Proposal, Evaluation Research	Solution Proposal, Evaluation Research	Solution Proposal, Evaluation Research
RQ-4	SPICE-FM application within NHS facilities directorate	A new process maturity/capability framework for process management in hospitals	Assessing the healthcare processes of a hospital department in accordance to a well-known Business Process Maturity Model (BPMM)	A new process maturity/capability framework for assessing the quality of cooperation between and within hospitals	Standardized operational process assessment tool	A maturity model to assess and advance networkability of health care providing organizations
RQ-5	A facilities directorate of a major NHS trust within the northwest of England	Acute somatic hospitals in Switzerland	A single department (the ophthalmology department) of a hospital operating in the Netherlands	Five Swiss and German hospitals	Prostate Cancer Centers	Five public Swiss hospitals
RQ-6	NHS facilities management process	Process management process	Ophthalmology specific healthcare processes	Cooperation process between and within hospitals	Multidisciplinary care in Prostate	Networkability of health care

(Continued)

Table 3. (*Continued*)

RQ#	S1 [31]	S2 [32]	S3 [15]	S4 [13]	S5 [33]	S6 [34]
					Cancer Centers	providing organizations
RQ-7	Not reported	Not reported	Instant	Instant	Instant	Instant
RQ-8	SPICE FM maturity levels ranging from 1 to 5. Only key findings of key processed are evaluated and reported.	Not reported	Not reported	HCMM uses a four-staged approach, ranging from "Initial/Ad-hoc", "Committed", "Established/Focused", to "Optimized". 12 reference points with 3 dimensions were assessed for staged approach. The average levels are shown below. In strategy dimension: 0.9 In organization dimension: 0.92 In information dimension: 0.92	30 key process areas were assessed by using CMMI [21] maturity levels. According to this assessment: All key process areas of maturity level 1 have %100 fulfilment. 7 of the 16 key process areas of maturity level 2 have over %75 fulfilment. All key process areas of maturity level 3 have over %50 fulfilment. 1 of the 2 key process areas of maturity level 4 have over %50 fulfilment. 1 of the 2 key process areas of maturity level 5 have over %50 fulfilment.	Six components of the maturity model were assessed by a five-point CMMI-like set of maturity levels. According to this assessment, the average scores of hospitals' maturity levels are shown below: Hospital 1: 2.66 Hospital 2: 0.74 Hospital 3: 1.33 Hospital 4: 2.61 Hospital 5: 0.90
RQ-9	Continuous process improvement. FM processes capability assessment.	Identification of improvement potentials. The model introduced in this article apprehends this fact and offers a model with an adequate level of complexity, which addresses the specific problems that hospitals are currently facing. The empirically derived model reveals why existing, generic capability maturity models for process management are not applicable in the hospitals context.	Using a generic business process maturity model (BPMM) to assess the maturity of a department in a healthcare institution.	HCMM focuses on intra-organizational as well as inter-organizational aspects relevant to optimizing cooperative structures and processes in hospitals. HCMM conceptualizes an evolutionary improvement path for cooperation within and between hospitals. HCMM is intended to primarily support decision-making of hospital managers.	Act On Oncology provides a feasible tool to evaluate quality and efficiency of operational processes in prostate cancer centers. This tool was developed for implementing multidisciplinary care and improving process quality and efficiency.	Contributes to the knowledge base and addresses the problem space by identifying relevant components and detailed factors that determine maturity of networkability for health care providers. This enables development of a methodological framework to assess current state and give directions on advancing networkability maturity based on accepted models for maturity assessment.
RQ-10	The SPICE-FM model does not specifically deal with formulating and evaluating facilities management strategies of NHS trust	Comparatively high complexity on the one hand and their strong focus on topics like an adequate IT integration and process automation on the other hand make it inadequate for solving the problems felt in the hospital sector.	Mapping of the healthcare-specific processes to the BPMM's process areas was the most challenging yet critical step of the assessment.	Not reported	The selection of process areas was continuously challenged and revised if necessary.	Not reported

We have a number of inferences based on the answers to the research questions. From the answers to RQ-1 and RQ-2, we identify only one study (S3) that indicates a distinction between the models of process improvement and process assessment. This finding is consistent with the one observed for the generic business process maturity models proposed [30], and should be considered for the design of future studies.

From the answers to RQ-3, we infer that validation studies in addition to solution proposals and evaluation research are needed in the domain.

The answers to RQ-4, RQ-5, and RQ-6 show that there are maturity/capability frameworks proposed as specific to the needs (e.g. per specialty or management aspect like in S2, S4, S5, and S6) as well as the adaption of existing maturity/capability frameworks for the assessment or improvement of healthcare processes (like in S1 and S3).

Also, the answers to RQ-5 indicate that only two studies are related to processes within a single hospital department and specific diagnosis processes. Department- or diagnosis-specific processes are identified as clinical or care pathways, which specify care processes for a particular diagnosis. Clinical or care pathways consist of collaborative efforts of many healthcare professionals, and are developed to continuously improve the quality of patient care. We propose that further studies related to department- or diagnosis-specific processes are needed in the domain, since these processes directly affect human health and require high maturity due to being complex and having dedicated domain information. Consequently, we infer that the proposal and use of maturity/capability frameworks for the pathways would have different properties from those for managerial hospital processes such as supply-chain management.

The answers to RQ-7 indicate that the majority of the studies reported instant implementations rather than longitudinal work, which is another issue that should be considered in future studies.

From the answers to RQ-8, RQ-9, and RQ-10 we observe that specializing process areas and measurement dimensions for the intended purposes of use (like in S4, S5, and S6) might increase the ease of use of the frameworks in the domain. On the other hand, adaption of existing frameworks to specific contexts (like in S1 and S3) has significant challenges such as domain knowledge, assessment experience, and tailoring insight per specialty, on the side of the implementers.

A general observation from the analysis of the studies is the unavailability of methods or guidelines for adapting generic maturity models to the healthcare domain. This is partly due to the lack of a single generic maturity model that has been commonly accepted in academia and widely applied in practice [22]. On the other part, however, our perception is that some healthcare processes are so human-oriented and knowledge based that carrying out an effective process-based approach is not a simple action.

5 Conclusion

Process assessment and improvement is a necessity in many business environments and despite the significant challenges, healthcare domain is not an exception. In this study we investigated the existence and use of maturity/capability frameworks for healthcare process assessment or improvement. Within the 29 studies that we identified in a systematic way, we selected and analyzed six studies that focus solely on process assessment or improvement in various healthcare settings.

The analysis results show that application of generic maturity/capability frameworks to specific healthcare settings has difficulties. On the other hand, if new frameworks are developed (or adapted from generic ones) for specific contexts in healthcare, process assessment and improvement might bring significant benefits. The existence of widely-known maturity/capability frameworks constitutes an evidence, and the frameworks themselves might provide guidance when developing new models or adapting generic ones.

The analysis results also show that only two studies are related to processes within a single hospital department and specific diagnosis processes. The maturity of these processes is critical since they have a direct impact on human health. Therefore, there is a need for proposing and using maturity/capability frameworks for these processes. It might be insightful to first identify barriers and opportunities in defining/adapting these frameworks for specialty-based processes.

This study has limitations due to its search strings and selection criteria. As a future work, we plan to extend the search and review processes by snowballing of the included and related studies, and aim to make a comparison among the proposed process maturity/capability frameworks regarding their design and implementations.

References

1. Quaglini, S.: Information and communication technology for process management in healthcare: a contribution to change the culture of blame. J. Softw. Maint. Evol. Res. Pract. **22**, 435–448 (2010)
2. Kirchmer, M., Laengle, S., Masias, V.: Transparency-driven business process management in healthcare settings. IEEE Technol. Soc. Mag. **32**, 14–16 (2013). doi:10.1109/MTS.2013.2286427
3. ISO/IEC: ISO/IEC 15504-2: Information Technology-Process Assessment. Part 2: Performing an assessment (2003)
4. Team, S.: Standard CMMI Appraisal Method for Process Improvement (SCAMPI) A, Ver.1.3 (2011). doi:CMU/SEI-2011-HB-001
5. ISO/IEC: ISO/IEC 15504-4: Information Technology-Process Assessment. Part–4: Guidance on use for process improvement and process capability determination (2004)
6. OMG: Business Process Maturity Model (BPMM), Ver.1, Object Management Group (2008)
7. Langmann, G., Maier, R., Theisl, A., et al.: Erfolgreiche umsetzung des efqm-management-modells an der universitätsaugenklinik graz. Der Ophthalmol **108**, 351–363 (2011). doi:10.1007/s00347-010-2297-2
8. Holland, K., Fennell, S.: Clinical governance is "ACE" – using the EFQM excellence model to support baseline assessment. Int. J. Health Care Qual. Assur. **13**, 170–177 (2000)
9. Kim, C.S., Spahlinger, D.A., Kin, J.M., Billi, J.E.: Lean health care: what can hospitals learn from a world-class automaker? J. Hosp. Med. **1**, 191–199 (2006). doi:10.1002/jhm.68
10. Smith, C., Wood, S., Beauvais, B.: Thinking lean: implementing DMAIC methods to improve efficiency within a cystic fibrosis clinic. J. Healthc. Qual. **33**, 37–46 (2011). doi:10.1111/j.1945-1474.2010.00130.x

11. Hina-Syeda, H., Kimbrough, C., Murdoch, W., Markova, T.: Improving immunization rates using lean six sigma processes: alliance of independent academic medical centers national initiative III project. Ochsner J. **13**, 310–318 (2013)
12. Steinfeld, B., Scott, J., Vilander, G., et al.: The role of lean process improvement in implementation of evidence-based practices in behavioral health care. J. Behav. Health Serv. Res. **42**, 504–518 (2015). doi:10.1007/s11414-013-9386-3
13. Mettler, T., Blondiau, A.: HCMM - A maturity model for measuring and assessing the quality of cooperation between and within hospitals. In: Proceedings of the IEEE Symposium on Computer-Based Medical System (2012). doi:10.1109/CBMS.2012. 6266397
14. Blondiau, A., Mettler, T., Winter, R.: Designing and implementing maturity models in hospitals: an experience report from 5 years of research. Health Inf. J. (2015). doi:10.1177/1460458215590249
15. Tarhan, A., Turetken, O., van den Biggelaar, F.J.H.M.: Assessing Healthcare Process Maturity: Challenges Of Using A Business Process Maturity Model. Process. approach patient-centered care Deliv. Work. (ProCare 2015)
16. Bendell, T.: Structuring business process improvement methodologies. Total Qual. Manag. Bus. Excell. **16**, 969–978 (2005). doi:10.1080/14783360500163110
17. Damij, N., Damij, T., Grad, J., Jelenc, F.: A methodology for business process improvement and IS development. Inf. Softw. Technol. **50**, 1127–1141 (2008). doi:10.1016/j.infsof.2007.11.004
18. Vanwersch, R.J.B., Shahzad, K., Vanderfeesten, I., et al.: A critical evaluation and framework of business process improvement methods. Bus. Inf. Syst. Eng. **58**, 1–11 (2015). doi:10.1007/s12599-015-0417-x
19. Harris, J.K., Beatty, K.E., Barbero, C., et al.: Methods in public health services and systems research: a systematic review. Am. J. Prev. Med. **42**, S42–S57 (2012). doi:10.1016/j.amepre.2012.01.028
20. Bastian, N.D., Munoz, D., Ventura, M.: A mixed-methods research framework for healthcare process improvement. J. Pediatr. Nurs. **31**, e39–e51 (2015). doi:10.1016/j.pedn.2015.09.003
21. CMU/SEI: Capability Maturity Model Integration for Development v1.3, CMU/SEI-2010-TR-033 (2010)
22. Tarhan, A., Turetken, O., Reijers, H.A.: Business process maturity models: a systematic literature review. Inf. Softw. Technol. (2016). doi:10.1016/j.infsof.2016.01.010
23. Wendler, R.: The maturity of maturity model research: a systematic mapping study. Inf. Softw. Technol. **54**, 1317–1339 (2012). doi:10.1016/j.infsof.2012.07.007
24. Petersen, K., Feldt, R., Mujtaba, S., Mattsson, M.: Systematic mapping studies in software engineering. In: Proceedings of 12th International Conference on Evaluation and Assessment Software Engineering, EASE 2008, pp. 68–77 (2008). doi:10.1142/S0218194007003112
25. Van Looy, A.: Business Process Maturity-A Comparative Study on a Sample of Business Process Maturity Models. Springer, Heidelberg (2014)
26. Rohner, P.: Achieving impact with clinical process management in hospitals: an inspiring case. Bus. Process. Manag. J. **18**, 600–624 (2012). doi:10.1108/14637151211253756
27. Gemmel, P., Vandaele, D., Tambeur, W.: Hospital Process Orientation (HPO): the development of a measurement tool. Total Qual. Manag. Bus. Excell. **19**, 1207–1217 (2008). doi:10.1080/14783360802351488
28. McCormack, K., Johnson, W.: Business Process Orientation: Gaining the E-business Competitive Advantage. CRC Press, St Lucie Press, Delray Beach, FL (2001)

29. Gillies, A., Howard, J.: Managing change in process and people: combining a maturity model with a competency-based approach. Total Qual. Manag. Bus. Excell. **14**, 779–787 (2003)
30. Tarhan, A., Turetken, O., Ilisulu, F.: Business process maturity assessment: state of the art and key characteristics. In: 2015 41st Conference on Software Engineering and Advanced Applications, pp. 430–437 (2015). doi:10.1109/SEAA.2015.50
31. Amaratunga, D., Haigh, R., Sarshar, M., Baldry, D.: Assessment of facilities management process capability: a NHS facilities case study. Int. J. Health Care Qual. Assur. Inc. Leadersh. Health Serv. **15**, 277–288 (2002). doi:10.1108/09526860210442047
32. Cleven, A.K., Winter, R., Wortmann, F., et al.: Process management in hospitals: an empirically grounded maturity model. Bus. Res. **7**, 191–216 (2014). doi:10.1007/s40685-014-0012-x
33. Voigt, W., Hoellthaler, J., Magnani, T., et al.: "Act on oncology" as a new comprehensive approach to assess prostate cancer centres - method description and results of a pilot study. PLoS ONE **9**, 1–7 (2014). doi:10.1371/journal.pone.0106743
34. Fitterer, R., Rohner, P.: Towards assessing the networkability of health care providers: a maturity model approach. Inf. Syst. E-bus Manag. **8**, 309–333 (2010). doi:10.1007/s10257-009-0121-9

Software Process Improvement Roadmaps – Using Design Patterns to Aid SME's Developing Medical Device Software in the Implementation of IEC 62304

Peter Rust[✉], Derek Flood, and Fergal McCaffery

Regulated Software Research Centre and Lero,
Dundalk Institute of Technology, Dundalk, Ireland
{peter.rust,derek.flood,fergal.mccaffery}@dkit.ie

Abstract. One stated objective of the European Union is to encourage SME's expand their area of operation into other domains. The medical device domain is one such domain identified by the EU. Medical device software development must be carried out in a manner that compliance with certain medical device standards and regulations can be demonstrated. *IEC 62304, Medical device software - software life cycle processes*, is a standard that defines the processes that are required to be executed in order to develop safe software. SME software development organizations wishing to expand their operations into the medical device software development domain face serious challenges in demonstrating compliance with IEC 62304. The standard describes the set of processes, activities, and tasks that are required to be carried out, but importantly do not describe how they should be carried out. This paper describes the development of a roadmap that will aid software development SME's, entering the medical device software development domain, by the use of design patterns to generate "How-to" artefacts, overcome the challenge of demonstrating compliance.

Keywords: SME's · Medical device software · Medical device standards · Regulatory compliance · Software roadmap · Software process improvement · Software process improvement roadmaps · IEC 62304 · Design patterns

1 Introduction

In Europe, the medtech industry generates over €100 billion annually and employs approximately 575,000 people. As many as 95 % of these companies are small to medium enterprises (SME) [1]. SME software development organizations wishing to enter the medical device software development arena must be able to demonstrate that the processes, utilised in the development of the software, are compliant with IEC 62304 [2]. IEC 62304 is the Medical Device Software – software life cycle processes standard and it is harmonised in the European Union (EU) and the United States of America (USA). The path to regulatory compliance for software development organizations that are able to demonstrate compliance with IEC 62304 is shorter and they will be able to market their product both in the EU and USA. However, implementing

IEC 62304 within a medical device software development organization is not straightforward or easy. Höss et al. [3] describe a pilot project that they undertook to acquire skills in implementing IEC 62304 in a hospital-based environment (in-house manufacture). They concluded that the pilot project carried out at their facility clearly demonstrated that the interpretation and implementation of IEC 62304 is not feasible without appropriately qualified staff. They recognized that it could be carried out by a small team with limited resources although the initial effort is significant and a learning curve must be overcome.

Standalone software can now be classified as an active medical device [4]. IEC 62304 defines the life cycle requirements for medical device software. These requirements vary according to the safety classification assigned to the software system as defined by requirement 4.3. The software safety class is assigned according to the possible effects on the patient, operator, or other people resulting from a hazard to which the software system can contribute. The software safety classes are based on severity as follows:

Class A: no injury or damage to health is possible

Class B: non-serious injury is possible

Class C: death or serious injury is possible.

The life cycle requirements establish a common framework for medical device software life cycle processes, but critically the standard does not state how the processes should be implemented. SME's in the general software development sphere will have their own processes in place; however these may not be robust enough to satisfy the requirements of IEC 62304. The processes in place will require improvement and new processes will inevitably be required to be implemented.

The Capability Maturity Model® Integration (CMMI®) [5] and ISO/IEC 15504-5:2012 (SPICE) [6] are two software process improvement models that are directed at the general software development domain. These models are not robust enough to allow organizations achieve medical device regulatory compliance [7]. The development of MDevSPICE® (formerly known as Medi SPICE) has filled this void [7]. An MDevSPICE® assessment will identify the gaps that appear in an organization's processes, but critically, not how to fill these gaps.

During the initial research period, various methods were considered as a means for bringing the IEC 62304 standard to SME's developing medical device software. These included decision trees, flowcharts, roadmaps and design patterns. After a review of the literature and due consideration of the various methods, a roadmap was chosen as the most appropriate method. A roadmap was subsequently developed for the implementation of IEC 62304. During the process of developing the "how-to" artefacts that form a crucial part of the roadmap, it was noted that design patterns may have a role in developing these artefacts. This paper explores that avenue.

The remainder of this paper is structured in the following manner: Sect. 2 describes roadmaps and the roadmapping process. Section 3 introduces the concept of design patterns, outlining their history, the process of creating them and describing their structure. Section 4 presents a discussion while Sect. 5 presents the conclusions and future work.

2 Roadmaps and the Roadmapping Process

2.1 Development of the Roadmap

The definition of a roadmap for standards implementation has gone through a number of versions before the following was decided upon: "*A series of Activities, comprised of Tasks that will guide an organisation, through the use of specific "How-to's" towards compliance with regulatory standards*". To generate the roadmap for IEC 62304 the roadmap development method described by Flood et al. [8] has been applied. This method, described below, has been revised in light of the latest definition of a roadmap.

1. Identify requirements of the standard and rephrase them as Tasks;
2. Group the Tasks into logical Activities;
3. Order the Activities into a sequence by which they can be introduced into an organization in a rational manner;
4. Validate the generated roadmap;
5. Identify the "How-To's" that can meet the identified Tasks;
6. Validate the "How-To's" in a host organization.

Flood et al. [8, 9] have already applied the roadmapping process to ISO 14971 and IEC 62366 and these roadmaps have been validated with industry experts. A roadmap has also been developed for traceability in the medical device domain and now with the development of an IEC 62304 roadmap, the suite is nearing completion.

2.2 Process Used to Develop the Roadmap

In step 1 as described above the standard was decomposed into its elementary requirements and a total of 172 elementary requirements were identified. The requirements were then transformed into Tasks by the application of an action verb.

Taking as an example of the transformation process, IEC 62304, requirement 5.1.1 states that "*the manufacturer shall establish a software development plan (or plans) for conducting the activities of the software development process appropriate to the scope, magnitude, and software safety classifications of the software system to be developed.*" This was transformed into a Task defined as "*establish a software development plan. The plan is for the software system to be developed (for conducting the eight activities of the software development process), defining fully the software lifecycle model to be utilised.*"

In step 2 when the transformation of all the requirements was complete, the Tasks were analysed for particular keywords that would aid their grouping into logical Activities. The above Task was assigned the keyword "Planning". A total of seven Tasks were initially grouped according to this keyword and an Activity created titled "Software Development Planning". The generation of the final roadmap is described in Rust et al. [10]. Following the roadmap generation process, a total of five Tasks were allocated to the Software Development Planning Activity. The final allocation of Tasks to Activities is detailed in Table 1.

Table 1. Final number of tasks per activity

Ref	Activity	Final No of Tasks
1	QMS	1
2	RMS	1
3	Software Safety Classification	3
4	Software Development Planning Process	5
5	Software Configuration Management Process	4
6	Software Risk Management Process	9
7	Software Requirements Analysis Process	4
8	Software Architectural Design Process	10
9	Software Detailed Design Process	4
10	Software Unit Implementation and Verification Process	5
11	Software Integration and Integration Testing Process	6
12	Software System Testing Process	3
13	Software Release Process	6
14	Software Problem Resolution Process	8
15	Change Request Process	7
16	Software Maintenance Process	6

2.3 Structure of the Roadmap

The metaphor for the roadmap is detailed in Fig. 1 below. The metaphor presented below was designed to highlight the stage at which each of the Activities may be applied during the development of a medical device software project. It can be seen that a number of the processes may be ongoing for the duration of the software development process.

Each of the phases in the software development lifecycle is depicted to overlap as a number of Tasks may be performed in parallel. Taking an example of the Software Unit Implementation and Verification Process and the Software Detailed Design Process, it is feasible that during the second Task of the Software Detailed Design Process – *"Document a design with enough detail to allow correct implementation of each software unit"*, the organization may commence the first Task of the Software Unit Implementation – *"Implement each software unit"*.

Each task will be associated with an artefact in the "How-to" repository and will also be context dependent (Safety Classification). The artefacts will be constructed using design patterns as a building mechanism.

3 Design Patterns

3.1 What is a Design Pattern?

Christopher Alexander is an architect that introduced the concept of design patterns for the design of towns, communities, buildings and homes [11]. He compiled a catalogue of some 253 patterns to describe various elements and combinations of elements for

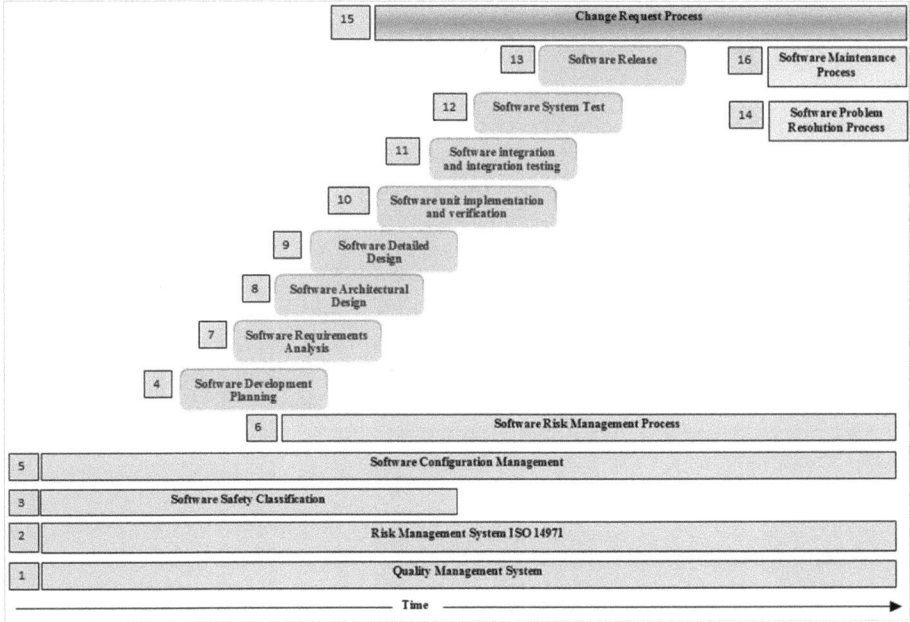

Fig. 1. Metaphor for the Roadmap

repeatable architectural design. Alexander stated, "Each pattern describes a problem which occurs over and over again in our environment, and then describes the core of the solution to that problem, in such a way that you can use this solution a million times over, without ever doing it the same way twice" [12].

While Alexander was talking about patterns for the design and construction of towns, houses and buildings, the concept can be applied to the design and "construction" of the "How-to" artefacts for standards implementation. Indeed, design patterns have been proposed for the following other domains:

- Object orientated software design [12].
- Business Process Modelling [13].
- Real time and embedded systems [14].
- Security risk orientated patterns [15].
- Architectural design patterns (computer) [16].
- Workflow patterns [17].
- Nurse practitioner practice patterns [18].
- Behaviour design patterns [19].
- Patterns for effective use cases [20].
- Pro HTML5 and CSS3 design patterns [21].

3.2 History of Design Patterns

Christopher Alexander describes in his *"book of two halves"*, A Pattern Language [11] and A Timeless Way of Building [22], how first the gate must be constructed and on passing through the gate the practice of building can be undertaken. Building the gate comprises the identification of the design patterns that constitute the language. Once that is complete the patterns are used to design and build concrete structures that are unique to the user of the language. The patterns are based on real life experience and can be reused time and time again without replication of a particular solution.

OOPSLA – Object-Oriented Programming, Systems, Languages, and Applications held its first conference in 1986 [23] and about 50 papers were presented. Among the presenters were Ralph Johnson, Ward Cunningham and Kent Beck. In 1987 Ward Cunningham and Kent Beck were working as consultants on a Smalltalk project that was having difficulty in completing [24]. Both had an interest in Alexander's design patterns. Alexander believed that the occupiers of a building should be involved in its design. Cunningham and Beck decided to allow the users of the software to complete the design. Cunningham developed a five pattern "language" that helped these novice designers take advantage of Smalltalk's strengths and avoid its weaknesses. The experiment was successful in that the project was completed.

Erich Gamma while conducting doctoral research became intrigued by Alexander's work and the reusability feature of design patterns. In August of 1993 [25], Kent Beck and Grady Booch sponsored a hillside retreat for a group of people who were also interested in pattern languages and wanted to build on Gamma's work. Present were Ward Cunningham, Ralph Johnson, Ken Auer, Hal Hilderbrand, Grady Booch, Kent Beck and Jim Coplien. The Hillside Group was established. In 1994 [24] they sponsored a conference on the Pattern Language of Programs (PloP-94) which was held at Allerton Park in Monticello, Illinois, a property of the University of Illinois at Urbana Champaign. The conference chair was Ralph Johnson and in the program chair, Ward Cunningham. The PloP conferences are held annually to this day. The use of design patterns in software engineering has greatly increased over the years. The book Design Patterns: Elements of Reusable Object-Oriented Software has sold over 500,000 copies since it was first published.

3.3 Process Used to Develop Design Patterns

A literature review conducted by the authors has unearthed various methods of developing Pattern Languages. This section describes a number of the more prominent methods and provides a justification of the methods selected to develop the Language.

Alexander et al. [11] describes the format adopted in writing their patterns as:

- First, there is a picture, which shows an archetypal example of the problem.
- Second, after the picture, each pattern has an introductory paragraph which sets the context for the pattern, by explaining how it helps to complete certain larger patterns.

- The essence of the problem is then described in one or two sentences.
- The body of the problem, which is the longest section, describes the empirical background of the pattern, the evidence for its validity and the range of ways it can be manifested in the building.
- The solution follows in the form of an instruction – so that you know exactly what you need to do, to build the pattern.
- The solution in the form of a labelled diagram follows indicating its main components.
- Lastly, the links to other patterns in the language are listed.

Gamma et al. [12] start by describing the four essential elements of a pattern:

1. **Name:** The pattern name is a handle we can use to describe a design problem, its solutions, and consequences in a word or two.
2. **Problem:** The problem describes when to apply the pattern.
3. **Solution:** The solution describes the elements that make up the design, their relationships, responsibilities, and collaborations.
4. **Consequences:** The consequences are the results and trade-offs of applying the pattern.

Each pattern is then described using a consistent format:

- **Pattern Name and Classification** - The pattern's name conveys the essence of the pattern. The pattern's classification falls under two headings purpose and scope.
- **Intent** - What does the design pattern do? What is its rationale and intent? What particular design issue or problem does it address?
- **Also Known As** - Other well-known names for the pattern, if any.
- **Motivation** - A scenario that illustrates a design problem and how the class and object structures in the pattern solve the problem.
- **Applicability** - What are the situations in which the design pattern can be applied?
- **Structure** - A graphical representation of the classes in the pattern using a notation based on the Object Modelling Technique (OMT).
- **Participants** - The classes and/or objects participating in the design pattern and their responsibilities.
- **Collaborations** - How the participants collaborate to carry out their responsibilities.
- **Consequences** - How does the pattern support its objectives? What are the trade-offs and results of using the pattern?
- **Implementation** - What pitfalls, hints, or techniques should you be aware of when implementing the pattern? Are there language-specific issues?
- **Sample Code** - Code fragments that illustrate how you might implement the pattern in C++ or Smalltalk.
- **Known Uses** - Examples of the pattern found in real systems.
- **Related Patterns** - What design patterns are closely related to this one?

Wellhausen and Fießer [26] offer their advice in writing patterns using the door lock as an example. Although they do not reference Alexander or Gamma, the pattern produced is very similar to that of the patterns proposed by Alexander and Gamma, starting first with the name and then with a picture or diagram followed by the context, problem, forces, solution and consequences. The sequence in which the design pattern should be addressed is detailed in Fig. 2 below.

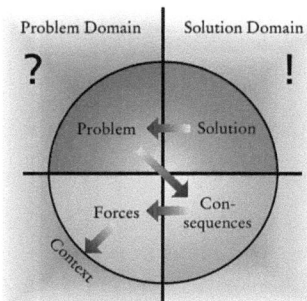

Fig. 2. Essential pattern sections and their writing order

Cunningham [27] provides the following tips for writing a pattern language:

- Pick a whole area.
- Make a list of all the things that you have learned about the area.
- Cast each item on your list as a solution.
- Write each item as a pattern. Include four paragraphs in total, the first two separated from the last two by the word "therefore".
- Organise them into sections, writing a short introduction to the section and listing each pattern in the section.
- Write an introduction to the language that hints at the forces that you will be addressing.

Arising out of a workshop at PLoP-95, Meszaros and Doble [28] collaborated on writing a pattern language for pattern writing. These patterns were reviewed at Plop-96 and were published in 1997.

There are recurring themes running throughout all of these contributions. With this in mind and that the patterns to be created are for standards implementation, the following format is being adopted:

- Name
- Software Safety Classification
- Context
- Problem
- Motivation (Forces)
- Solution
- Consequences
- Related Patterns
- ISO/IEC Reference
- Catalogue (Section)
- Alias

3.4 Structure of the Design Patterns

To demonstrate the process of writing a pattern language, using the tips for writing pattern languages proposed by Cunningham [27], and referencing the pattern development process described by Wellhausen and Fießer [26], the following steps were undertaken:

1. The area chosen is standards implementation in the medical device software development domain.
2. The standard to be implemented is IEC 62304 [6].
3. The requirements of IEC 62304 have been listed and cast as solutions.
4. The solution to the problem is to establish a software development plan.
5. The problem for which a pattern is to be written is "The software developer wants to demonstrate compliance with requirement 5.1.1 - Establish a Software Development Plan - for software classified as Class A."

Solution: The solution will describe the main essential elements that are required. The solution is not particular or specific because a pattern is like a template that can be applied in many different situations. In this instance, the solution is the actual software development plan for medical device software with a safety classification of Class A. In previous research, a software development plan template was designed to take account of all safety classifications A, B and C. This content of this template has been stripped down to include only those elements that are essential for compliance with IEC 62304 under a Class A safety classification. The design pattern solution for medical device software with a safety classification of Class B will only contain the additional elements that are required to achieve compliance for this safety classification. Similarly, the solution for medical device software with a safety classification of Class C will only contain those remaining elements that are required to complete a full software development plan for Class C software.

Problem: The problem describes when to apply the pattern. It explains the problem and its context. The problem for the software development team is that compliance with IEC 62304 must be demonstrated. A physical software development plan must be produced. IEC 62304 lists certain elements that must be addressed or referenced by the plan. For SME's with little or no experience in the medical device domain this can be a daunting task. The design pattern will not only define the problem but critically will provide a template for the solution.

Consequences: The consequences will describe the benefits and possible liabilities of using the pattern. Consider first the benefits of using the pattern, a plan for the medical device software development is established. The plan is safety classification dependent. Only those requirements that are necessary are considered. The software development team has identified only those activities of the software development process that are required for the particular safety classification and by means of the roadmap will be able to address these in a timely manner.

Secondly the liabilities must be considered. Planning is an iterative process. Failure to keep the plan up-dated may have detrimental consequences. The software development plan will include or reference certain other plans that are required by other activities and processes. As the software development proceeds, these plans will evolve and quite possibly change. Keeping the software development plan updated and circulated to all members of the team will ensure that every member of the team knows what artefacts are current. Failure may lead to members of the team using outdated artefacts.

Motivation (Forces): The reasons why the solution is required. The motivation will mirror the consequences. A software development plan is a necessary artefact to demonstrate compliance with IEC 62304. The software development plan requires that certain identified tasks be undertaken. The resources required to undertake the development must be identified and put in place. Failure to plan and failure to resource the development adequately will result in failure to achieve regulatory compliance.

Context: What is the situation when the pattern can be applied? List the elements that have already been completed. Referencing the roadmap, it can be established which elements that will be already underway at the point in time that the software development plan is required to be in place. The quality management, risk management and software configuration management processes will have commenced. The software system will have been assigned a safety classification of A, B or C. The level of planning required will vary depending on the safety classification assigned. In this instance a safety classification of Class A has been assigned, so only the design pattern for Class A software development plan need be considered.

Name: The pattern name is used to describe the problem, its solution and consequences in a short sentence. Naming a pattern in this way allows the user to easily find the correct pattern. The context can be established and work can start on the solution. The name chosen in this instance is - Establish Software Development Plan for a safety classification of Class A.

Catalogue: The catalogue will be used to group patterns in a meaningful way, so that the user can quickly see other patterns that may be useful. In this case the design pattern will be filed under the Planning entry in the catalogue.

Related Patterns: 5.2. Update the software development plan. 5.4. Identify supporting items. 5.5. Plan configuration items management control. X.X Documentation Plan.

IEC References: IEC 62304 requirement 5.1.1 The manufacturer shall establish a software development plan (or plans) for conducting the activities of the software development process appropriate to the scope, magnitude, and software safety classifications of the software system to be developed. The software development life cycle model shall either be fully defined or be referenced in the plan (or plans).

Alias: There are no known aliases at this time.

Artefact: The template for the software development plan for medical device software with a safety classification of Class A, which is compliant with IEC 62304, comprises twenty pages. Only those elements that are required by specific requirements are included. The elements are gathered in sections as detailed Rust et al. [29]. The contents page is reproduced hereunder (Fig. 3).

The Final Pattern: The final pattern comprises all the eleven sections described above, and detailed in Fig. 4 below.

```
Contents
1   Introduction ............................................................................................ 9
    1.1   Project Overview ............................................................................ 9
    1.2   Project Deliverables ....................................................................... 9
    1.3   Evolution of the Software Development Plan ........................... 10
    1.4   Reference Materials ..................................................................... 11
2   Project Organization ......................................................................... 12
    2.1   Process Model .............................................................................. 12
    2.2   Software Verification Planning .................................................. 14
    2.3   Risk Management [Software Risk Management IEC 62304] ... 15
    2.4   Monitoring and Controlling Mechanisms ................................. 16
3   Technical Process ............................................................................... 17
    3.1   Software Documentation ............................................................ 17
    3.2   Project Support Functions .......................................................... 19
4   Appendices .......................................................................................... 20
```

Fig. 3. Contents page from software development plan template Class A

Element	Structure
Name	Establish a Software Development Plan
Software Safety Classification	Class A
Context	The software system has been assigned a safety classification of A, B or C. The level of planning required varies depending on the safety classification. In this instance the safety classification is Class A.
Problem	The Manufacturer and hence the software developer wants to demonstrate compliance with requirement Clause 5.1.1 for software classified as Class A.
Motivation/Forces	A software development plan is a necessary artefact to demonstrate compliance with IEC 62304. The software development plan requires that certain identified tasks be undertaken. The resources required to undertake the development must be identified and put in place.
Solution	Establish a software development plan that complies with IEC 62304 for the designated safety classification assigned to the software system. In this instance the safety classification is Class A.
Consequences - Benefits & Liabilities	Benefits: A plan for the software development is established. The software developer has identified the activities of the software development process and will be able to address these in a timely manner. Liabilities: Planning is an iterative process. Failure to update the plan could have detrimental consequences.
Artefact - (The How To) Template	Software Development Plan Template Ref 5.1 Class A
Links to Related Patterns	5.2. Update the software development plan. 5.4. Identify supporting items. 5.5. Plan configuration items management control. X.X Documentation Plan
IEC Reference	5.1.1 The manufacturer shall establish a software development plan (or plans) for conducting the activities of the software development process appropriate to the scope, magnitude, and software safety classifications of the software system to be developed. The software development life cycle model shall either be fully defined or be referenced in the plan (or plans).
Alias	None known

Fig. 4. The final pattern

4 Discussion

IEC 62304 defines the processes required for the development of safe software for the medical device domain but does not tell the organization "how to" implement the processes. The generated roadmap, together with the "how-to" artefacts, when completed will fill this gap. The "how-to" artefacts will be developed using design patterns as described above. Each step on the roadmap will reference an appropriate design pattern that will contain the basic information that will guide the software development team in the implementation of the process. The software development team need only choose those processes which they require, which in turn will only reference the design patterns that are relevant to the software safety class of the medical device software. The software development team will be familiar with the concept of design patterns and will therefore be better positioned to understand and use the design patterns presented to them. The combination of the roadmap and the design patterns will guide the software development team in the production of the artefacts that will aid them in demonstrating compliance with the regulatory requirements.

5 Conclusions and Future Work

One of the stated objectives of the EU is to encourage software development SME's to enter other domains. Medical device software development is one such domain. However, the medical device software development domain is strictly regulated. The regulatory standards provide a description of all the necessary processes that must be planned for, executed and that the results of the execution are recorded and documented. The documents will be audited and compliance with the regulations and standards will be determined by the results of the audit. How to plan, execute and document their processes is the challenge for SME's entering the medical device software domain. The design patterns that identify the "how-to" element of the processes combined with the roadmap, will guide the SME's along the path to regulatory compliance in a timely and planned manner.

The roadmap is currently being validated by industry experts. The next stage of this work is to create more design patterns to help build additional "How-to" artefacts and have them trialled in SME medical device software development organizations that are new to the medical device domain.

Acknowledgement. This research is supported by the Science Foundation Ireland Principal Investigator Programme, grant number 08/IN.1/I2030 and by Lero - the Irish Software Research Centre (http://www.lero.ie) grant 10/CE/I1855 & 13/RC/20194.

References

1. About the Medtech sector | IMDA. http://www.imda.ie/Sectors/IMDA/IMDA.nsf/vPages/ Medtech_sector~about-the-medtech-sector!OpenDocument. Accessed 23 Feb 2016

2. IEC: IEC 62304:2006 - Medical device software – Software life cycle processes. ISO, Geneva, Switzerland (2006)
3. Höss, A., Lampe, C., Panse, R., Ackermann, B., Naumann, J., Jäkel, O.: First experiences with the implementation of the European standard EN 62304 on medical device software for the quality assurance of a radiotherapy unit. Radiat. Oncol. **9**, 10 (2014)
4. McHugh, M., McCaffery, F., Casey, V.: Standalone software as an active medical device. In: O'Connor, R.V., Rout, T., McCaffery, F., Dorling, A. (eds.) SPICE 2011. CCIS, vol. 155, pp. 97–107. Springer, Heidelberg (2011)
5. CMMI Product Team (2010), Capability Maturity Model® Integration for Development Version 1.2. Software Engineering Institute, Pittsburgh, PA (2010)
6. ISO/IEC: ISO/IEC 15504-5, Information technology - Process Assessment - Part 5: An Exemplar Process Assessment Model. ISO, Geneva, Switzerland (2012)
7. McCaffery, F., Dorling, A.: Medi SPICE development. Softw. Process Maint. Evol. Improv. Pract. J. **22**(4), 255–268 (2010)
8. Flood, D., McCaffery, F., Casey, V., McKeever, R., Rust, P.: A roadmap to ISO 14971 implementation. J. Softw. Process Evol. **27**(5), 319–336 (2015)
9. Flood, D., McCaffery, F., Casey, V., Regan, G.: A methodology for software process improvement roadmaps for regulated domains – example with IEC 62366. In: McCaffery, F., O'Connor, R.V., Messnarz, R. (eds.) EuroSPI 2013. CCIS, vol. 364, pp. 25–35. Springer, Heidelberg (2013)
10. Rust, P., Flood, D., McCaffery, F.: Software process improvement & roadmapping – a roadmap for implementing IEC 62304 in organizations developing and maintaining medical device software. In: Rout, T., O'Connor, R.V., Dorling, A. (eds.) SPICE 2015. CCIS, vol. 526, pp. 19–30. Springer, Heidelberg (2015)
11. Alexander, C., Ishikawa, S., Silverstein, M.: A Pattern Language: Towns, Buildings, Construction. OUP USA (1977)
12. Gamma, E., Helm, R., Johnson, R., Vlissides, J.: Design Patterns: Elements of Reusable Object-Oriented Software. Pearson Education, Upper Saddle River (1994)
13. Atwood, D.: BPM process patterns: repeatable design for BPM process models. BP Trends, May 2006
14. Douglass, B.P.: Doing Hard Time: Developing Real-time Systems with UML, Objects, Frameworks, and Patterns. Addison-Wesley Professional, Boston (1999)
15. Ahmed, N., Matulevičius, R.: Securing business processes using security risk-oriented patterns. Comput. Stand. Interfaces **36**(4), 723–733 (2014)
16. Schmidt, D.C., Stal, M., Rohnert, H., Buschmann, F.: Pattern-Oriented Software Architecture. Patterns for Concurrent and Networked Objects. Wiley, New York (2013)
17. van Der Aalst, W.: Workflow patterns. Distrib. Parallel Databases **14**, 5–51 (2003)
18. Fain, J., Melkus, G.: Nurse practitioner practice patterns based on standards of medical care for patients with diabetes. Diabetes Care **17**, 879–881 (1994)
19. Taylor, G., Wray, R.: Behavior design patterns: engineering human behavior models. Ann Arbor (2004)
20. Adolph, S., Cockburn, A., Bramble, P.: Patterns for effective use cases (2002)
21. Bowers, M., Synodinos, D., Sumner, V., Zack, A.: Pro HTML5 and CSS3 Design Patterns (2011)
22. Alexander, C.: The Timeless Way of Building - Christopher Alexander. OUP USA (1979)
23. OOPSLA. http://www.oopsla.org/oopsla-history/. Accessed 25 Feb 2016
24. History of Patterns. http://www.c2.com/cgi/wiki?HistoryOfPatterns. Accessed 04 Feb 2016
25. The Hillside Group - Wikipedia, the free encyclopedia. https://en.wikipedia.org/wiki/The_Hillside_Group. Accessed 26 Feb 2016

26. Wellhausen, T., Fießer, A.: How to write a pattern. In: European Conference on Pattern (2011)
27. Cunningham, W.: Tips For Writing Pattern Languages (1994). http://www.c2.com/cgi/wiki?TipsForWritingPatternLanguages. Accessed 02 Feb 2016
28. Meszaros, G., Doble, J.: A pattern language for pattern writing. Pattern Lang. Progr. Des. **3**, 529–574 (1998)
29. Rust, P., Flood, D., McCaffery, F.: Creation of an IEC 62304 compliant Software Development Plan. In: EuroasiaSPI (2015)

Gamification and Education Issues in SPI

Coverage of ISO/IEC 12207 Software Lifecycle Process by a Simulation-Based Serious Game

Alejandro Calderón[✉] and Mercedes Ruiz

Department of Computer Science and Engineering, University of Cádiz,
Avenida de La Universidad de Cádiz, 10, 11519 Puerto Real (Cádiz), Spain
{alejandro.calderon,mercedes.ruiz}@uca.es

Abstract. Software process is a very important area of knowledge that supports software development. However, we can observe a lack of methods and tools that allow teaching software process in a highly practical way and attached to the software development learning. In this paper, we analyze the software lifecycle process groups of the ISO/IEC 12207 and the current application of serious games and gamification techniques within the software process education scope. Moreover, we propose a simulation-based serious game for software project management teaching that can be used, at the same time, to educate learners in software process. The paper also maps the stages of the game lifecycle to the software lifecycle processes of the ISO/IEC 12207. Ten experts from the educational field have evaluated the idea of using the proposed serious game for software process education concluding that it helps learners acquire practical knowledge not only in the project management area but in the software process scope.

Keywords: ISO/IEC 12207 · Software process education · Serious games · Gamification

1 Introduction

Software engineering is a relevant field that provides a set of methods, tools and procedures for the development of quality software, within the constraints of cost and time. To succeed in this goal, the software industry relies on processes to structure the activities and tasks to develop and facilitate the collaborative work of all the stakeholders. However, according to the CHAOS reports from the Standish Group, there is a low percentage of successful Information Technology (IT) projects [1].

One of the main factors leading to this problem directly points to the people involved in the software development process and their training [2]. In many occasions, when training future software developers, maximum priority is given to theory, sidelining the importance of practical applications in real-life scenarios when it comes to software process education. There is a clear necessity within the software engineering scope that demands a best software process education, more attached to the practice and more realistic, where learners can learn within real-life scenarios [3].

On the other hand, ISO/IEC 12207 training in an industrial environment is traditionally performed by an expert in form of a seminar in a classroom environment [4].

This approach causes that practitioners do not learn properly and thoroughly the substantial details of the entire standard [4]. Consequently, practitioners are often demotivated and unsatisfied with their industrial and corporate training and they do not acquire the required skills to manage the life cycle of software. Hence, practitioners need more practical experience in software process to be enough experts to produce more quality software [5].

These necessities move trainers towards the development and use of methods and techniques to teach in a highly practical way, to promote active and interactive learning, and therefore increase the motivation and engagement of learners in software process education. Moreover, these necessities lead educational organizations and industry to design new training strategies for training software process practitioners as skilled and qualified professionals.

Serious games are powerful tools that allow participants to experiment, learn from their own mistakes and acquire experience in a free-risk environment. As training tools, serious games increase learners' conceptual knowledge, learners' confidence, improve retention, and increase task completion [6]. They also allow injecting fun in the training process with the goal to engage and motivate learners, therefore they improve learning outcomes to a high extent [7].

The main contributions of this paper are: (i) analyzing the use of serious games and gamification for software process education, (ii) providing a mapping between the different stages of a proposed serious game and the software life cycle processes of ISO/IEC 12207 [8], and (iii) evaluating the idea of using the proposed simulation-based serious game to educate and train learners and professionals in the field of software processes.

The structure of the paper is as follows: Sect. 2 shows the background of this study. Section 3 describes the serious game developed and evaluates the coverage of the life cycle processes of ISO/IEC 12207 of our serious game. Finally, Sect. 4 summarizes the paper and presents our conclusions and future work.

2 Background

2.1 ISO/IEC 12207

ISO/IEC 12207 is an international software engineering standard that establishes a common framework for software life cycle processes [8]. It contains processes, activities, and tasks that are to be applied during the acquisition of a software product or service and during the supply, development, operation, maintenance and disposal of software products. Hence, the standard provides a set of processes that cover the software life cycle from conception to the end of product.

As Fig. 1 shows, there are two main sub-divisions of processes: *system context processes* that deal with a standalone software system, service or product and *software specific processes* that are used in implementing a software product or service as an element of a system. The ISO/IEC 12207 standard comprises 43 processes and groups the activities that may be performed during the life cycle of a software system, service

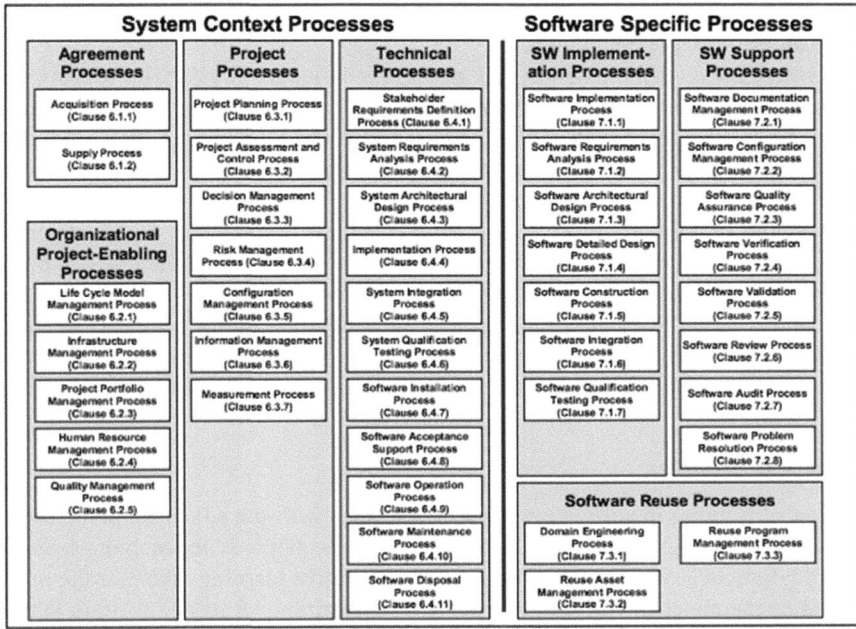

Fig. 1. Life cycle processes of ISO/IEC 12207[8].

or product into seven process groups. Each of the life cycle processes within those groups is described in terms of its purpose and desired outcomes.

2.2 Software Process Education

Software Engineering is the study and application of engineering principles to the design, development and maintenance of software. Its main objective is to create software systems, services or products with quality, taking into account the time and cost constraints [9]. To achieve this goal, software development activity normally is supported by standards such as ISO/IEC 12207 [8]. These standards provide a set of software processes that allow covering all the software life cycle and define the activities needed to conceive, develop, deploy, and maintain a software system, product or service.

Software engineering practices and software lifecycle processes are of crucial relevance on the road to success in the development of software systems, products or services. Therefore, equal importance should be given to the training that future software engineers receive in those areas of knowledge. However, this training usually consists of lectures along with a small software project [10] or blackboard activities, where software process is often treated separately from the software development activities and learners acquire knowledge in a theoretical environment. This causes learners to lose interest in this crucial area and. What is more important, that software engineering professionals start gaining experience *only* by working with real projects. In a real project, the effects of a bad decision can lead to product or service failure, or the loss of significant profit to the companies.

The theoretical teaching of software process is no longer suitable. Industrial professionals and well-known organizations demand for a training where learners can test their knowledge, in a highly practical way, with real-life scenarios during their studies, and theoretical and practical parts of the software process education are treated at the same time [3].

Given the importance of software process education, Heredia et al. presented a systematic mapping study to structure and characterize the state of the practice on software process education [2]. This work helps identify best practices and find new challenges in this area [2]. In their findings, the authors highlight the necessity of making the education of software process an interesting topic, because, among other factors, the success of software processes depends on the training of the people involved [2].

2.3 Serious Games

The need of training in software processes, together with the advances in technology, move trainers towards the development and use of new methods and techniques to teach in a highly practical way, promote active and interactive learning, increase the motivation and engagement of learners and design new training strategies to train software process practitioners as skilled and qualified professionals. Serious games, also called training or educational games, are games designed for a primary purpose other than mere entertainment. The "serious" adjective indicates that its goal is more than just fun and that they are designed to educate, train or inform users. This concept was defined by Clark Abt as follows: "Reduced to its formal essence, a game is an activity among two or more independent decision-makers seeking to achieve their objectives in some limiting context. A more conventional definition would say that a game is a context with rules among adversaries trying to win objectives. We are concerned with serious games in the sense that these games have an explicit and carefully thought-out educational purpose and are not intended to be played primarily for amusement" [11].

In [11], the author focused on card and board games, however, the definition of serious game can be generalized to all kinds of games designed for training. Nevertheless, Michael Zyda gives a more current definition that defines a serious game as "a mental contest, played with a computer in accordance with specific rules that uses entertainment to further government or corporate training, education, health, public policy, and strategic communication objectives" [12].

Serious games are powerful learning tools that allow participants to experiment, learn from their own mistakes and acquire experience, in a safe way within risk environments. The main goal of serious games is to create learning environments that allow to experiment with real-life problems. The idea is that a good design of the game can help to experiment and try out multiple solutions, explore and discover information and new knowledge without fear of making mistakes, since the play decision making has no risks or consequences in real life.

The majority of games incorporate the ability to play with multiple participants, which also facilitates resolution of problems in groups, collaboration, and the development of negotiation skills. You learn from the game *and* from the actions, ideas and decisions of other participants. Moreover, these games are being developed under multiple platforms to provide access and give meaning and educational value to the use of smartphones, game consoles, media players and other devices that are part of our daily lives. This allows us to transfer the innate characteristics of the games to the field of education.

A few initiatives of using serious games in the field of software process training can be found in the literature. DesignMPS [13] is a computer game designed to support teaching of software process modelling by reinforcing relevant concepts and providing software process modelling exercises, in where, learners play the role of a process engineer who must model a process. Problems and Programmers [10] is an educational serious card game to teach learners about the software engineering process, which is designed as a competitive game where participants try to finish a software project. Finally, Aydan, Yilmaz and O'Connor [4] investigate the need of a serious game to teach software process within an industrial scope, and as a result, they propose a 3D serious game with the aim to improve the ability of learners of ISO/IEC 12207 standard. Their idea of serious game need to simulate an office landscape to provide realistic virtual environment to ensure that the training will be based in real-life scenarios [4].

2.4 Gamification

Another concept related with training enrichment is the emerging phenomenon of gamification, which "seeks for improvement of the user's engagement, motivation, and performance when carrying out a certain task, by means of incorporating game mechanics and elements, thus making the task more attractive" [14]. Gamification is "the use of game elements and game design techniques in non-game contexts" [15]. It has become "an increasingly popular approach to increasing end-user engagement in many contexts, including employee productivity, sales, recycling, and education" [16].

In order to provide a more interesting education in software process, the design and use of gamification strategies for teaching is another solution to take into account. We can find several works that encourage the use of gamification in the field of software engineering as Pedreira, García, Brisaboa, and Piattini show in their systematic mapping study of the literature [14]. However, these authors conclude that the current studies on gamification applied to software engineering are very preliminary or even immature, and few of them provide empirical evidence of the impact of their proposals on user engagement and performance. Moreover, these authors show that the main software processes in which gamification is applied are software development processes, followed by some of the activities of software requirements, project management and configuration management, but these authors highlight that their exist important software process areas in which is needed to study the use of gamification in a thorough way.

In spite of the existence of many studies about the use of gamification in the area of software engineering, there does not seem to be any relevance research linked to software process education or training, as Heredia and his colleagues conclude in their systematic mapping study [2]. Their findings are a bit surprising especially when there is much positive evidence about applying gamification in education in the literature [17, 18]. The existence of this positive evidence means that the use of gamification strategies does improve the learning process. Through using game mechanics to drive game-like player behavior during the learning process, we have the possibility of injecting fun, recognition and/or competition into the knowledge acquisition process, and this promotes game thinking and engagement, thus motivating learners to reach their goals [5]. Hence, gamification can be used in university and corporate training and education as an intensely motivational method [19].

Gamification shares similar features with serious games though they are different approaches. Serious games use game environments, techniques, mechanics and thinking to train or educate users, as we have mentioned in the previous sub-section. Hence, the use of serious games within gamification strategies complement each other helping to expand game thinking and mechanics into non-game environments, such as the classroom or everyday life. In our work, we propose to take advantage of all the benefits that serious games and gamification offer, in order to improve the software process education and help learners to acquire professional experience to produce quality software.

3 ProDec and ISO/IEC 12207

ProDec [20] is a simulation-based serious game to teach, assess and motivate learners in software project management that allows them to acquire experience in a risk-free environment and improve their skills as project leaders in their professional life. Among its main features we can highlight that:

- ProDec helps learners to acquire practical experience in software project management. It allows learning in software project management before, during and after playing: Before, because learners need to know and understand the knowledge about software project management to play; during, because they use their knowledge to manage a project during the play with the goal of win; and after, because they can analyze the games played and acquire new knowledge.
- ProDec helps trainers to assess the learners learning process. It is a pioneer serious game in learner assessment. Through the data recorded during the play and the assessment criteria provided by instructors, ProDec generates an assessment report that learners can use to evaluate their own experience and trainers to assess and analyze the learning of the learners.
- ProDec gives the option to play in teams or individually. However, it is recommended to play in teams to involve learners in a social process where feelings and emotions are naturally linked to the learning experience.
- ProDec automatically generates a simulation model to simulate the project execution, together with the game's user interface, customized to the project provided by the player. This feature allows players make their own project plans to play with. Therefore, it allows players to have more than one scenario for simulation, something that is not provided by the same kind of games in this field [21].

In the rest of the section, we discuss the functionality associated with each stage of the game play's lifecycle and the level of coverage of the software lifecycle processes according with ISO/IEC 12207.

3.1 Game Play's Lyfecycle

ProDec can be used in two different modes namely Quick Play and Full Play. The aim of both modes is to successfully manage a software project. This involves completing the project in the planned time and within the allocated budget. Consequently, players follow a three-stage process that allows them to meet several processes relating to the software life cycle (see Fig. 2). Within the game, the three main stages of a game play's lifecycle are: Onset, Execution and End stages.

If the players select to play a quick game, they only practice their decision-making and project monitoring and controlling skills. On the other hand, if players select to play a full game, they follow a process that guides them in making the software project plan. So, in a full game, the Onset stage of a game play's life cycle has five sequential sub-stages which are: project information, size estimation, project team definition, tasks definition and risks analysis. These sub-stages allow players to provide all the data needed to create a new software project plan.

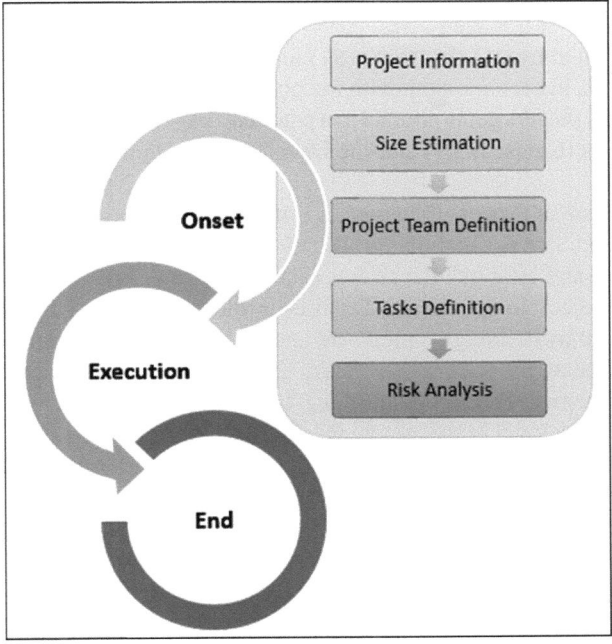

Fig. 2. ProDec game play's lifecycle.

3.2 Onset Stage

ProDec's *Onset stage (S1)* is the first contact that players have with the game. In Onset stage, players follow a process that guides them to create from scratch the project plan. This process, as commented above, is made of five sequential sub-stages which are the following:

- *Project Information (S1.1)*. In this sub-stage, players provide the general information of the project about its scope and features, such as the salary of the workers, the length of the project, the number of use cases, etc., that are necessary to begin the size estimation stage.
- *Size Estimation (S1.2)*. In this sub-stage, players make the size estimation of the project using Albrecht's method [22] of function points-base estimation.
- *Project Team Definition (S1.3)*. In this sub-stage, players define their project team. For this, they have to select their past work experience and some features for their personality based on the sixteen personality factors described by Cattell [23].
- *Tasks Definition (S1.4)*. In this sub-stage, players define the tasks of the project based on PERT diagram [24], and enter, for each of them, the time data, the budget allocated, and its predecessor tasks. Moreover, players have to allocate the personnel for each task.
- *Risk Analysis (S1.5)*. In the last stage of the process, players make a quantitative risk analysis.

As mentioned above, in this stage (S1) learners follow a set of sub-stages, making the best decisions in each moment with the goal of creating the project plan. Therefore, during this stage, players get in contact in a practical way with the activities of the Project Planning Process (Clause 6.3.1) and the Decision Management Process (Clause 6.3.3) of the standard.

The Measurement Process (Clause 6.3.7) is involved in the sub-stages Project Information (S1.1) and Size Estimation (S1.2), in which, learners have to provide the needed data to calculate and establish the size of each case of use, in order to get the size estimation of the project. In the Project Team Definition sub-stage (S1.3), learners design their project team by defining its members and in the Tasks Definition sub-stage (S1.4) they have to allocate the staff to each task, so learners can be educated in the Human Resource Management Process (Clause 6.2.4) of the standard.

The Life Cycle Model Management Process (Clause 6.2.1) and all the processes that are involved into the Technical Processes, the Software Implementation Processes and the Software Support Processes of the standard are covered by the Tasks Definition sub-stage (S1.4), where learners have to define all the activities and tasks needed in the development process of the project. For that reason, learners need to decide the life cycle model of the software development process, as well as, all the tasks involved from the initiation to the end of the project. The last sub-stage of the Onset stage is the Risk Analysis (S1.5), through this sub-stage learners can be educated in the risk analysis process of a project covering the Risk Management Process (Clause 6.3.4) of the standard.

3.3 Execution Stage

In the Execution stage (S2), the simulation of the project execution takes place. In this stage, learners practice two main concepts. First, they put into practice their knowledge about the Earned Value Analysis for monitoring the progress of the project. Second, learners practice their decision-making skills by correcting the potential deviations of the progress of the project with the goal of ending the project within time and budget. Moreover, during this stage, among the control decisions and activities that learners could need to perform, we can highlight the analysis of the monitoring indicators, the control of the appearance of not planned risks or planned risks, and the team member and tasks management where learners can hire/fire a team member or reorganize the project tasks. Therefore, through this stage, the game cover the Project Assessment and Control Process (Clause 6.3.2) and allow to complete the coverage of the Decision Management Process (Clause 6.3.3), the Human Resource Management Process (6.2.4), the Measurement Process (6.3.7) and the Risk Management Process (6.3.4). Table 1 summarizes the coverage of the life cycle processes of ISO/IEC 12207 by the Onset and Execution stages of ProDec game play's life cycle.

Table 1. Coverage of ISO/IEC 12207 processes by ProDec game play's lifecycle.

ProDec game play's lifecycle stages		ISO/IEC 12207 processes
Onset (S1)		• Project Planning Process (Clause 6.3.1) • Decision Management Process (Clause 6.3.3)
Onset (S1)	Project Information (S1.1)	Measurement Process (Clause 6.3.7)
	Size Estimation (S1.2)	
	Project Team Definition (S1.3)	Human Resource Management Process (Clause 6.2.4)
	Tasks Definition (S1.4)	• Human Resource Management Process (Clause 6.2.4) • Life Cycle Model Management Process (Clause 6.2.1) • Technical Processes • Software Implementation Processes • Software Support Processes
	Risk Analysis (S1.5)	Risk Management Process (Clause 6.3.4)
Execution (S2)		• Project Assessment and Control Process (Clause 6.3.2) • Decision Management Process (Clause 6.3.3) • Human Resource Management Process (Clause 6.2.4) • Measurement Process (Clause 6.3.7) • Risk Management Process (Clause 6.3.4)

3.4 End Stage

In the *End stage (S3)*, ProDec using the information records generated during the play and the assessment rubric provided by the instructors through the administration tool concludes with the generation of a detailed report. Hence, in this stage, learners get the lessons learned from their performance during the game. These lessons help learners learn from their own mistakes and can analyze the events occurred along the game to get new knowledge, generate new ideas for future plays or improve the life cycle process of the project and the decision-making. Then, this last stage helps learners to take contact with the ISO/IEC 33014 that provides informative guidance on using process assessment as part of a complete framework and method for performing process improvement. This information guidance allows a continual improvement activity [25]. Moreover, this last stage also helps to take contact with the ISO/IEC 15504 Information technology–Process assessment [26], which was initially derived from process lifecycle standard ISO/IEC 12207 [8].

4 Conclusions and Further Works

Software process education is a relevant topic to take into account in software engineering studies in order to provide a better education for future practitioners, regarding not only the theoretical aspects but also the practical aspects of their knowledge acquisition. According to many authors, we consider that the use of games and simulation-based experiences help us to teach software process in a practical way within a risk-free environment. ProDec, a simulation-based serious game for software project management training, can be use during the course not only to teach and practice the principles of software project management but also to educate learners and professionals in software process.

For this purpose, we have analyzed how ProDec covers the different software life cycle process groups of the standard ISO/IEC12207. The idea of using ProDec for software process education has been exposed and evaluated by ten university professors (n = 10) that served as experts in teaching courses in software engineering processes and management. The Delphi method was selected to perform this study since it works well when: (a) the goal is to improve our understanding of problems, opportunities and solutions, and (b) the sample is homogeneous and the size is small [27]. The experts concluded that the use of ProDec during the course can help learners acquire practical knowledge in the software process area, gaining practical experience with 33 out of 43 processes of the ISO/IEC 12207 software life cycle process standard. The use of ProDec also allows learners to learn software process, at the same time, that they acquire software project management knowledge. However, they also stated that ProDec can be considered only as a support tool. This means that ProDec helps learners to *apply* their knowledge and acquire experience in a practical environment, but learners need to acquire the main principles of software processes by other means such as lectures.

Taking into account the opinions of the experts and the analysis of the coverage of the ISO/IEC 12207 standard, we are confident that the use of ProDec is beneficial for learners and helps them to consolidate their knowledge in software process and software project management. In addition, we intend to use ProDec as an element within a framework conceived to design and deploy gamification strategies to support software process education and to engage and motivate learners from both industrial and university domains.

Our aim is to create a tool to support the effective practical training of the processes of software project management and, at the same time, a tool to educate in the software life cycle processes of ISO/IEC 12207. For this reason, we are studying to add new features to the game regarding software processes and software project management such as configuration management, quality management, and different methodologies of software development, among others.

Acknowledgements. This work has been partially supported by the Spanish Ministry of Science and Technology with ERDF funds (grant TIN2013-46928-C3-2-R) and the Andalusian Plan for Research, Development and Innovation (grant TIC-195).

References

1. The Standish Group: CHAOS MANIFESTO 2013. Think Big, Act Small (2013)
2. Heredia, A., Colombo-Palacios, R., Amescua-Seco, A.: A sytematic mapping study on software process education. In: Proceedings of the International Workshop on Software Process Education, Training and Professionalism, Gothenburg, Sweden (2015)
3. ACM/IEEE-CS Joint Task Force on Computing Curricula, Computer Science Curricula 2013, ACM Press and IEEE Computer Society Press (2013)
4. Aydan, U., Yilmaz, M., O'Connor, R.V.: Towards a serious game to teach iso/iec 12207 software lifecycle process: an interactive learning approach. In: Rout, T., O'Connor, R.V., Dorling, A. (eds.) SPICE 2015. CCIS, vol. 526, pp. 217–229. Springer, Heidelberg (2015)
5. Dorling, A., McCaffery, F.: The gamification of SPICE. In: Mas, A., Mesquida, A., Rout, T., O'Connor, R.V., Dorling, A. (eds.) SPICE 2012. CCIS, vol. 290, pp. 295–301. Springer, Heidelberg (2012)
6. Susi, T., Johannesson, M., Backlund, P.: Serious games: an overview (2007)
7. ASTD Research, Playing to Win: Gamification and Serious Games in Organizational Learning (2014)
8. ISO/IEC, ISO/IEC 12207:2008- Systems and software engineering—Software life cycle processes (2008)
9. Humphrey, W.S.: A Discipline for Software Engineering. Addison-Wesley Longman Publishing Co., Boston (1995)
10. Baker, A., Oh Navarro, E., Van Der Hoek, A.: An experimental card game for teaching software engineering processes. J. Syst. Softw. Softw. Eng. Educ. Train. **75**, 3–16 (2005)
11. Abt, C.: Serious Games. University Press of America, Lanhan (2002)
12. Zyda, M.: From visual simulation to virtual reality to games. Computer **38**, 25–32 (2005)
13. Chaves, R.O., von Wangenheim, C.G., Furtado, J.C.C., Oliveira, S.R.B., Santos, A., Favero, E.L.: Experimental evaluation of a serious game for teaching software process modeling. IEEE Trans. Educ. **58**(4), 289–296 (2015)
14. Pedreira, O., García, F., Brisaboa, N., Piattini, M.: Gamification in software engineering-a systematic mapping. Inf. Softw. Technol. **57**, 157–168 (2015)
15. Werbach, K., Hunter, D.: For the win: how game thinking can revolutionize your business. Digital Press, Wharton (2012)
16. Sheth, S.K., Bell, J.S., Kaiser, G.E.: Increasing Student Engagement in Software Engineering with Gamification (2012)
17. Von Wangenheim, C., Thiry, M., Kochanski, D.: Empirical evaluation of an educational game on software measurement. Empirical Softw. Eng. **14**(4), 418–452 (2009)

18. Domínguez, A., Saenz-de-Navarrete, J., De-Marcos, L., Fernández-Sanz, L., Pagés, C., Martínez-Herráiz, J.J.: Gamifying learning experiences: practical implications and outcomes. Comput. Educ. **63**, 380–392 (2013)
19. Kapp, K.M.: The Gamification of Learning and Instruction: Game-based Methods and Strategies for Training and Education. Wiley, San Francisco (2012)
20. Calderón, A., Ruiz, M.: ProDec: a serious game for software project management training. In: Proceedings of the 8th International Conference on Software Engineering Advances, Venice, Italy (2013)
21. Calderón, A., Ruiz, M.: Bringing real-life practice in software project management through a simulation-based serious game. In: Proceedings of the 6th International Conference on Computer Supported Education, Barcelona, Spain (2014)
22. Albrecht, A.: Measuring application development productivity. In: Proceedings of the joint SHARE, GUIDE and IBM Application Development Symposium, Monterey, California (1979)
23. Cattell, R., Eber, H., Tatsuoka, M.: Handbook for the sixteen personality factor questionnaire (16PF), Insitute for Personality and Ability Testing (1988)
24. Moder, J.J.: Project management with CPM, PERT, and precedence diagramming, 3rd edn. Van Nostrand Reinhold, New York (1983)
25. ISO/IEC, ISO/IEC TR 33014:2013 Information technology – Process assessment – Guide for process improvement (2013)
26. ISO/IEC, ISO/IEC 15504-4:2004 Information technology – Process assessment – Part 4: Guidance on use for process improvement and process capability determination (2004)
27. Skulmoski, G.J., Hartman, F.T., Krahn, J.: The delhi method for graduate research. J. Inf. Technol. Educ. **6**, 1–21 (2007)

A Gamification Approach to Improve the Software Development Process by Exploring the Personality of Software Practitioners

Mert Yilmaz[1,2], Murat Yilmaz[1,2(✉)], Rory V. O'Connor[3], and Paul Clarke[3]

[1] Virtual Reality Research and Development Laboratory, Çankaya University, Ankara, Turkey
merty89@hotmail.com
[2] Department of Computer Engineering, Çankaya University, Ankara, Turkey
myilmaz@cankaya.edu.tr
[3] School of Computing, Dublin City University, Dublin, Ireland
roconnor@computing.dcu.ie, paul.m.clarke@dcu.ie

Abstract. Although there are various kinds of processes designed to manage the complexities of software development, it is still a challenging endeavor. Recently, a significant number of researchers have started to investigate social problems such as incompatibilities with respect to personality that is likely to be encountered in all stages of the software development process. However, there is no computer-based artifact to reveal the personality types of software practitioners. To bridge this gap, a virtual 3D assessment environment is developed with the ability to immerse individuals similar to a realistic model of the assessment. The interactive questionnaire is based on previous interactive personality assessment framework, which was specifically designed for software engineers. Based on the developed tool, a study was conducted on software practitioners. The data gathered via a survey study from software practitioners is analyzed to observe the difference between the results of paper-based and interactive versions of the same assessment. The analysis of this research states that there is a significant difference between the results of participant's survey scores. Overall, these results indicate that proposed tool is relevant to help software professionals to improve the software development process when personality types are in consideration.

Keywords: Software process improvement · Team process · Gamification · Interactive assessment · Personality

1 Introduction

Software engineering is a discipline that encompasses a systematic design, production and maintenance of a software product. Development of new technologies, software and hardware improvements and affordable technological devices made this field of business more valuable. As new technologies emerge, branches inside software development started to blossom e.g. web development, embedded system development, etc. Video game development is one of those branches that is developed as a sub-field of software development, which requires a process for developing digital (video) games. Just like other software, digital (video) games also require scripted instructions. Moreover, other than the end-product and methodology, software and game development has no other differences.

The popularity of game industry has pioneered new approaches such as gamification. Gamification is a new field of research, which can improve any business process by adding game elements in a non-game context [1]. Gamification relies on autonomy of an individual as well as the experience that is captured in video games [2]. For this reason, through gamification it is possible to have people to participate in certain activities e.g. taking a poll or quiz. In addition, gamification and video games have also assisted the way to identify personality type (theory of psychological identification of an individual's preferred to be) of an individual.

The term personality comes from Greek word persona, which is seen in Greek comedies and tragedies in about year 200 [3]. From its origin to today, personality is still a valid social construct [4]. Today, personality types are mostly used on job interviews. The meaning of personality described as reference of different individuals responses for the different situations or events through psychological tendencies such as behaviors or traits [4]. MBTI is a one of the common ways to reveal personality types of individuals. It is based on Jung's theories about personality types and it summarizes them in 16 different types. However, none of these 16 types has a direct advantage over any other defined types [5]. Therefore, in this study the MBTI-like approach is utilized to reveal personality type of software developer practitioners. Rather than using MBTI traditionally, it is going to be used in an interactive assessment environment because of disadvantages of traditional personality assessments (e.g. extra costs and an effort to complete).

2 Background

2.1 Definition of Personality

From earliest times, a number of attempts were developed to create a system of typology to indicate among numerous functions and behavioral pattern have lead to born of personality types [4]. Types are a rating system that based upon observations on emotional and behavioral patterns as well as experiences and preferences of an individual [6]. Personality types have different opposite four bipolar categories that classify a person, from this a set of categories (e.g. an individual cannot be both consecutively) personality prediction seems possible as research indicates that personality types are unique defining characteristics of personality [7]. Therefore, personality refers to a significant form of information about an individual's social characteristics.

The situation leads to various definitions of personality among the literature. Funder [8] states that personality is the combinations of psychological mechanism and a person's characteristic patterns of thought, behavior, and emotion. In addition, Larsen and Buss [9] describe personality as a set of psychological types and mechanism of a person that are organized by interactions of intrapsychic[1], physical and social environments. Larsen [10] refer personality as an individual's characteristics clarified by certain patters such as feeling, thinking, and behaving.

2.2 The Myers-Briggs Type Indicator (MBTI)

Myers-Briggs type indicator is an extension of Carl Jung's theories over human personality that was published in 1921. Jung's theory of personalities consists of 8 personalities (two attitudes paired with four mental functions) [11]. Katherine Briggs and her daughter Isabel Myers have added a new dichotomous pair and published MBTI firstly in 1962 and it became widely used tool for identifying an individual's personality type [5]. MBTI has four dichotomous pairs as shown in Table 1.

Table 1. Dichotomies (the four opposite pairs of preferences)

Extroversion (E)	(I) Introversion
Sensing (S)	(N) iNtuition
Thinking (T)	(F) Feeling
Judgment (J)	(P) Perception

Extroversion vs. Introversion (E-I): In literature, the usage of these terms is defined by Jung himself. Extroversion means "outward" whereas Introversion means "inward". Jung's theory on personality type states that there are two worlds for a person's to focus his/her mind out world and in world. Extrovert people are talkative, outgoing and initiators while Introverts are quiet and reserved.

Sensing vs. Intuition (S-N): MBTI defines Sensing as a reality driven and Intuition as abstract driven function. Sensing people like to live in real and actual whereas Intuitive people like to look towards future and possibilities.

Thinking vs. Feeling (T-F): MBTI scale defines Thinking as a logical way of making decisions by using reasonable, logical and consistent given set of rules. Feeling on the other hand is defined as using emotions and "inside" feelings to come up with a decision.

Judging vs. Perceiving (J-P): Judging and Perceiving is coined by Briggs-Myers. Judging is tendency of being extremely strict and disciplined whereas Perceiving is being flexible and spontaneous.

---

[1] A psychological term referring to systematic thinking of the individual within mind or psyche.

Combination of these 4 different dichotomous pairs creates 16 different types of personalities and each of 16 different types namely; ISTJ, ISFJ, INFJ, INTJ, ISTP, ISFP, INFP, INTP, ESTP, ESFP, ENFP, ENTP, ESTJ, ESFJ, ENFJ and ENTJ.

2.3 Definition of a Game and Gamification

Games are essential part of human existence as well as ancient as human history [2]. Yet the controversies occur when one tries to seek the definition of games. Abt [12] defines games as an activity that having two or more participants to achieve certain goal using decision making. He then goes deep and adding games are activities within certain rules that adversaries trying to win or achieve a goal. Costikyan [13] indicates that game is form of art that participants called player pursuits the goal by in-game resource management (game tokens) as well as decision-making. Suits [14] defines games as a voluntary effort to get through unnecessary/artificial obstacles. Similarly, Avedon [15] also define games as a voluntary effort, they go further and adding games are embodiment of player conflict, which consists of rules to produce a disequilibral outcome. At this point, it is clear that games have many things in common, e.g. voluntarism, predefined rules and goals, and an artificial conflict. Salen and Zimmerman [16] define games as system that having participants as players to engaging an artificial conflict to achieve a quantifiable outcome within given set of rules. Quantifiable outcome in this context means that when the game is over player wins or loses or gets numerical representation of his or her effort such as score or rating. Game mechanics refers to rules, techniques and methods whereas dynamics refers to mechanics that depending on player's interaction and components refers to responses that game provides to player according to player's actions [17].

Gamification is a newly introduced area of research that combines certain elements of games to create an expression between rewards and games [18]. It is firstly introduces at 2008. However, it has become notable in 2010 [19]. Although, gamification has been introduced recently in many businesses domains, have been using gamification for a long time e.g. employee of the month, flight miles, etc.

Gamification has various types of definitions and the variety of definitions creates confusions between similar but different concepts like serious games [20]. The variety of definitions is also causing incompetent design and implementation of gamification [21]. The purpose of gamification is to engage and motive the people by combining intrinsic behavior with extrinsic reward such as points, badges, and leaderboards [22]. Intrinsic behavior is the drive for to do something without an external reason, and extrinsic reward is tangible re-ward that visible to everybody [18]. For instance, loyalty rewards that airlines and hotels providing to customers. In order to serve its purpose gamification uses main features of video game elements - player, environment, rule, challenge, goal, interaction, emotional experience, outcome and consequences - into context defined as nongame. Thus, this indicates that game which has all of the game elements, cannot be involved to be gamification process. Therefore, gamification is defined as a process of integrating game elements (badges, scores) into non-game context in order to create motivation and engagement [18,22].

To date, a number of studies have demonstrated that gamification is an important asset to improve the software development process [23,24].

3 Methodology

This study aimed to identify personality types of software practitioners by using a computer-based interactive assessment tool, which was developed to conduct this study. Based on a previous research [25], the personality types were extracted and the results was presented by using the MBTI typology. Our objective was to explore the usability of the proposed game-based approach. Next, results will be reviewed and the difference between a paper-based test and an computer-based version was analyzed.

The descriptive statistics and game play scale were used to conduct this study. In addition, we asked gender, age, education level of participants demonstrating demographics of individuals.

Game play scale [26] is a 5-point likert scale consists of 12 questions such as "I like the graphics in the game" and modified for both assessments to be able to rate the both of them. The modified version of this scale contains questions such as "Aesthetically, the assessment was satisfactory". In addition, the answers to these 12 questions have five choices ranging from "strongly disagree" to "strongly agree".

3.1 Personality Revealing Questions

To reveal the personality type of software development personnel, a computerized personality assessment environment was developed. Similar to Keirsey temperament sorter it contains 70 questions [25]. The personality related questions that were used in this interactive assessment was obtained from previous research [25], which aims to utilize a content specific (paper-based) personality revealing approach especially for software practitioners

For this study, a computerized personality assessment environment is created to observe, the more positive experience of the users of interactive assessment provided than paper-based assessment. In order to test this, the study utilized from user experience evaluation techniques. Basically, user experience study refers to a set of methods to measure the experience when a person interacts with a system, product or service in specific condition. This set of methods contains ways such as interviewing, eye tracking and surveying, etc.

In this context, survey study was chosen for this research and Game-play scale adopted and modified for both interactive and paper-based assessments. The modified scale was issued to participants after each participant done with both of the assessments in order to make comparison to determine the differences between results of questionnaires for each participant via analytical tools.

Figure 1 shows the steps of the procedure.

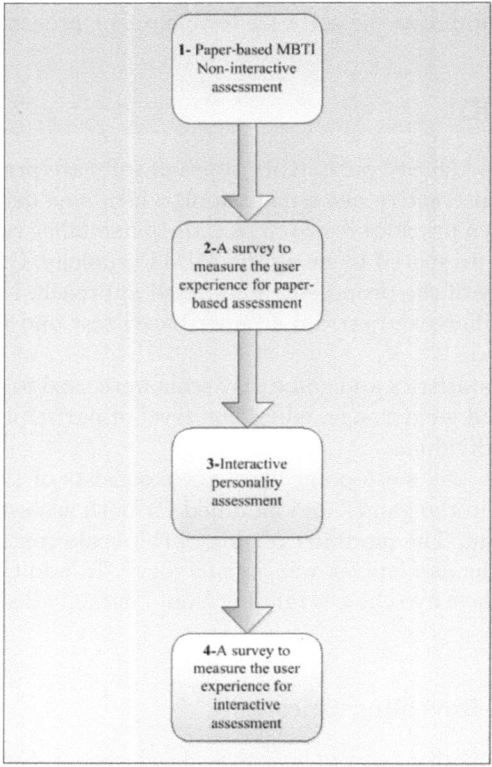

Fig. 1. The research process

1. The procedure of data collection begins with the distribution of paper version of personality revealing questions and participants were asked to fill the paper version of personality revealing questions at first.
2. After they filled the paper version of personality questions, they were given a questionnaire that adopted and altered version of game play scale to rate the experience they have while filling the paper version of the assessment.
3. Participants were introduced with a computerized personality assessment environment that designed and developed solely for this study. PC version of the environment is used for this research. Participants played the interactive assessment and answered the questions in the interactive environment.
4. Once the play session is over participants were guided to fill the same questionnaire as in part one that contains adopted and modified version of game-play scale. The steps of the procedure are repeated for each of the participants.

A Gamification Approach to Improve the Software Development Process 77

Fig. 2. A Screenshot from a personality assesment conducted on the virtual 3D enviroment

3.2 Interactive Assessment

The 3D interactive assessment environment has two main scenes, i.e. office and game over scene. It contains an office scene where the player is tasked to have an interview for software developer position. When the game starts player is given an objective indicating that he/she needs to speak the lady in reception for further instructions. Figure 2 shows a screen-shot from the interactive assessment.

In conversation, the non-playable character is telling the player that the interview will start whenever the player reaches the designated location, which in this case *meeting room*. When the player goes to the designated location, kind of disclaimer window that contains written information about the situation becomes visible. The interview starts after the player reads the information on the screen and agrees with it. During the interview, players can only look around by mouse and mouse-click the answers of the prompted questions, they cannot move from the position they standing. As soon as the interview starts, the first question and its voice recording become noticeable. Players cannot answer the questions until the voice record of the corresponding questions stops and the interview process goes through like this for all 70 questions. When the all of the questions are answered by players, the game skips to the next scene - Game Over Scene- to examine his or her personality.

The empirical part of the study took place in METU Technopolis between 16.12.2015 to 21.12.2015. Participants of this study were the software practitioners who worked in different companies that resided in METU Technopolis area.

4 Results and Analysis

This section illustrates statistical evidence based on the collected data for paper-based test and the test conducted in 3D interactive environment. Ultimately, ther goal is the show empirical evidence for showing the difference between two assessments. This section presents frequencies of detected personality from the participants.

There were 21 people who participate to this study, 16 (76.2 %) of them were man, and 5 (23.6 %) of them were woman. In descriptive part of the study, age of the participants was asked and age information is categorized under 4 sections. The first section was "18–25" and 5 (23.8 %) participants who fall in this category. The second section was "26–30" and 12 (61.9 %) participants were fall in this category. Similarly, section three was "31–35" and 1 (4.8 %) participant was categorized under this section. Lastly, fourth section was "> 40" (older than 40) and 2 (9.5 %) participants were fall in this section.

In last part of the descriptive statistics, education status of the participants was asked. Among this 21 participants 1 (4.8 %) of them were "High School" graduate, 16 (76.2 %) of them were "University" graduate and 4 (19.0 %) of them were "Master's Degree" graduate. Although, education status scale contains primary school, junior high and doctoral degree, the output is omitted because there were no data for these choices. The personality of participants were also recorded by paper based assessments and in-game assessment. The personality data obtained from 21 participants via both of the assessment methods resulted that; 3 (14.3 %) ENFJ, 2 (9.5 %) ENFP, 3 (14.3 %) ENTP, 2 (9.5 %) ESFJ, 1 (4.8 %) ESTJ, 1 (4.8 %) ESTP, 4 (19.0 %) INFJ, 3 (17.6 %) INFP and 2 (11.8 %) ISFP.

A straightforward approach has used to score the questionnaire. Since the questionnaire was a 5-point likert scale from "strongly disagree" (value = 1) to "strongly agree" (value = 5) values of each element were summed to reach a result. However, the questionnaire were containing 2 negative questions (question 3 and 5) so for those questions the scale were reversed "strongly disagree" (value = 5) to "strongly agree" (value = 1) to avoid statistical error. There were 12 questions in the questionnaire so the highest score was 60 whereas lowest score was 12 and the mid score was 36.

The purpose of this research is to observe the more positive experience that users of the interactive game assessment receive over paper-based version. In order to test this, the participants were took the modified version of game-play scale twice. Since, a participant was tested twice paired sample t-test or t-test for two related samples required to make the analysis

In this context, the hypothesis of this research is;

- H_0: The experience that the participants receive from both of the assessment methods has no difference.
- H_1: The experience that the participants receive from both of the assessment methods has a difference.

In order to calculate paired sample t-test IBM SPSS 20 portable version is used. For this test, level of significance selected as 0.05 (95%) ($\alpha = .05$). Since there were 21 participants the degree of freedom calculated as 20 (df = n - 1). Hence, the critical value is 2.080. In light of these, paired sample t-test value is 7.131. The calculation of paired samples t-test were performed using a computer, and the significance level were calculated as zero (p= .000), i.e. the probability was so small that computer rounds the number into zero. In situations such as this, the probability value shall be written as $p < .001$.

The calculated t-test indicates that the null hypothesis (H_0) is rejected and according to Cohen's d and percentage of variance (r^2) are required for calculating the effect size. For paired sample t-test, Cohen's d formula;

$$\text{Estimated d} = \frac{\text{sample mean difference}}{\text{sample standard deviation}} = \frac{M_D}{s} \quad (1)$$

M_D is calculated as difference between "second survey score" and "first survey score" over sample size (n), which was calculated as 9.85 and standard deviation (s) calculated as 6.335 and Cohen's d was 1.55[2]. Since it is calculated that the d equals 1.55 the effect size of this study was large.

The formula for percentage of variance (r^2) is;

$$M_D = \frac{\text{difference}}{\text{sample size}} = \frac{\sum D}{n} \quad (2)$$

Therefore, r^2 is calculated as 0.70 (70%) and r^2 states that any value greater than 0.25 is considered as large effect. Similar to Cohen's d the obtained data shows very large effect size. Alternative to paired sample t-test there is another test called Wilcoxon test, which uses data obtained from same subjects to observe difference between two specific conditions. Parameter for Wilcoxon test were the same as the paired sample t-test above (level of significance ($\alpha = .05$). Therefore, just like the results of the paired sample t-test, Wilcoxon test were also states that the null hypothesis of this research required to be rejected because $p < .0001$.

Validation Interviews

In order to support the findings of quantitative data, validation interviews for the interactive assessment environment were also conducted. In these interviews, 3 questions were asked to experts to receive opinion about the interactive assessment. The questions are listed as follows;

- What do you think about the generic functionality of the software product?
- What kind of improvements would you suggest?
- Do you think there are advantages of interactive assessment environment over paper-based assessment?

---

[2] Cohen's d any value greater than 0.80 is considered to be large effect.

For the first question, participants of validation interviews stated that the software product helped to reveal the personalities of software practitioners such an approach might reduce the problems that "human factor" causes. In addition, the software product was useful to software team forming and it helped to improve the software development processes when the personalities of practitioners were in consideration. In fact, one of the participants of the interviews stated that

> **Interview quotation:** *"The software product maintains the general activities of finding the true route of personality test and has a potential to compose more interactivity to expose to the user."*

However, he also mentioned that some bugs such as some buttons were do not work or the problems with sound records etc. For improvements, *"There should be continuously improvement in interactive assessment environment to engage users"* and one participant also mentioned that repetitive nature of the interactive assessment needs to be altered to avoid being boring and the time that takes to complete the interactive assessment needs to be adjusted for the same reason.

Some of the participants mentioned that the graphics or the visuals requires improvement and background music along with new sound effects and new ways of interactivity should be added to the interactive assessment environment. Lastly, depending on the release of the product the mobility or mobile support of the interactive environment can be considered as an advantage.

One of the interviewees suggested that

> **Interview quotation:** *"Based on the ambition, which is maintained by the software product, helps to make advantageous points over the paper based version certainly. One of them - probably the most obvious and important - one is that creating a graphical environment for the user to involve the activity rather than traditional reading and filling a survey."*

In addition, the feedback mechanism, the visual and the sound elements reside in the software product were considered as an advantage by majority of the interviewees.

5 Conclusion and Future Work

The main purpose of this research was to propose a 3D interactive approach to reveal personality types of software practitioners. Consequently, it addressed problems that can cause by personality type incompatibilities to improve the quality of team formation in software development. Literature review indicated that the software development process has various challenging tasks that developers need to tackle. These tasks however can become more complex because of the human factors. Therefore, an interactive assessment environment was designed to lift some of the burden from software developers. The analysis showed that there was significant difference between the results of first survey and the second. This indicated that the proposed method worked as it was intended. Furthermore, similar to the results of the analysis, the validation interviews also indicated that the interactive personality assessment environment was helpful to improve the software development processes for revealing personalities of software practitioners. Although, this marks the end of this research there were still various improvements should have been done as a future work.

The proposed method, in its currents state can be seen as a prototype of a software product. Like many other software products that released or developed, it has some deficiencies. The survey showed that in some cases participants were disagree or neutral about the survey question 3 for interactive assessment version. This situation was also mentioned in the validation interviews. This showed that interactive assessment should include more entertaining dialogues that all game-like approaches should have. Future releases will have features such as; (i) 3D environments with more office like interactivity, (ii) theme based animations, graphics and improved sound effects, (iii) rather than asking directly, the questions can be embedded into a story.

In addition, the time required to complete the interactive assessment needs to adjusted well to avoid being repetitive and boring according to validation interviews. The current state of the interactive assessment environment runs only desktop computers. Future mobile releases of the system can reach more people to gather more data. However, in a possible mobile release the interactive assessment requires optimization to work on mobile devices because the mobile devices have less computational capability than today's computers.

In order to optimize the developed assessment environment;

- The every 3D model including characters required to have fewer polygons to work on a mobile platform. To achieve this, 3D models in the interactive assessment required to be modeled again with fewer polygons.
- Frames of animations in the interactive assessment might require being less than the current form for mobile platforms.
- Some optimization techniques used by big budget games such as voxelization[3], and occlusion culling[4] that may require to be used in the interactive assessment environment.
- Lastly, a possible addition of new characters, environments, animations need to be created with the consideration of mobile involvement.

During this study, new technologies continued to emerge and some of them such as virtual reality (VR) were noted for future improvements. Virtual reality has become a huge phenomenon in recent years and poses great potential for scientific research with its interactive and immersive features. Therefore, further research in this field would be of great help for improving the proposed approach.

---

[3] Voxelization is a technique of transforming 2D or 3D data into voxel data for achieving better render results.

[4] Occlusion Culling is a technique of changing the rendering option of 3D object when camera frustum is not looking at that specific object for better performance.

References

1. Deterding, S., Khaled, R., Nacke, L., Dixon, D.: Gamification: toward a definition. In: Proceedings of the 2011 Annual Conference Extended Abstracts on Human Factors in Computing Systems. ACM, New York (2011)
2. McGonigal, J.: Reality is Broken: Why Games Make Us Better and How They Can Change the World. Penguin PR, New York (2011)
3. Nicholson, S.: A recipe for meaningful gamification. In: Gamification in Education and Business, pp. 1–20. Springer (2015)
4. Matthews, G., Deary, I.J., Whiteman, M.C.: Personality Traits, 3rd edn. Cambridge University Press, Cambridge (2009)
5. Myers, I., McCaulley, M., Quenk, N., Hammer, A.: MBTI manual. Consulting Psychologists Press (1999)
6. Capretz, L.: Personality types in software engineering. Int. J. Hum. Comput. Stud. **58**, 207–214 (2003)
7. Hardiman, L.: Personality types and software engineers. Computer **30**, 10 (1997)
8. Funder, D.C.: The Personality Puzzle: Seventh International Student Edition. WW Norton & Company, New York (2015)
9. Larsen, R.J., Buss, D.M.: Personality psychology. Naklada Slap, Jastrebarsko (2008)
10. Larsen, R., Buss, D.: Personality psychology: Domains of knowledge about human behavior (2002)
11. Jung, C., Baynes, H., Hull, R.: Psychological types. Routledge (1991)
12. Abt, C.: Serious games. University Press of America (1987)
13. Costikyan, G.: I have no words 8: I must design. The game design reader: A rules of play anthology (2005)
14. Suits, B.: What is a game? Philos. Sci. **34**(2), 148–156 (1967)
15. Avedon, E.: The structural elements of games. The psychology of social situations. Selected readings, pp. 11–17 (1981)
16. Salen, K., Zimmerman, E.: Rules of play: Game design fundamentals. MIT press, Cambridge (2004)
17. Fullerton, T.: Game design workshop: a playcentric approach to creating innovative games. CRC Press (2014)
18. Zichermann, G., Cunningham, C.: Gamification by Design: Implementing Game Mechanics in Web and Mobile Apps. O'Reilly Media, Newton (2011)
19. Groh, F.: Gamification: State of the art definition and utilization. Institute of Media Informatics Ulm University, p. 39 (2012)
20. Loh, C.S., Sheng, Y., Ifenthaler, D.: Serious Games Analytics: Methodologies for Performance Measurement, Assessment, and Improvement. Springer, New York (2015)
21. Kapp, K.M.: The gamification of learning and instruction: game-based methods and strategies for training and education. John Wiley & Sons, New York (2012)
22. Werbach, K., Hunter, D.: For the Win: How Game Thinking Can Revolutionize Your Business. Wharton Digital Press (2012)
23. Herranz, E., Palacios, R.C., de Amescua Seco, A., Yilmaz, M.: Gamification as a disruptive factor in software process improvement initiatives. J. UCS **20**(6), 885–906 (2014)
24. Yilmaz, M., O'Connor, R.V.: A scrumban integrated gamification approach to guide software process improvement: a turkish case study. Tehnički Vjesnik **23**, 237–245 (2016)

25. Yilmaz, M.: A software process engineering approach to understanding software productivity and team personality characteristics: an empirical investigation. Ph.D. thesis, Dublin City University (2013)
26. Felicia, P.: Handbook of Research on Improving Learning and Motivation through Educational Games: Multidisciplinary Approaches. IGI Global (2011)

A Simulation and Gamification Approach for IT Service Management Improvement

Elena Orta[(✉)] and Mercedes Ruiz

Department of Computer Science and Engineering, University of Cadiz,
Avda. de la Universidad de Cádiz, 11519 Puerto Real (Cádiz), Spain
{elena.orta,mercedes.ruiz}@uca.es

Abstract. This paper proposes a conceptual framework for improving Information Technology Service Management (ITSM) processes that is based on as follows: (a) to build a simulation model of the process to improve that enables IT managers to assess the process performance and analyze the effects of changes in the process before their implementation in the organization; and (b) to gamify the model simulation experimentation to increase IT managers motivation and engagement, and drive their behavior through model simulations to meet the established objectives. To illustrate the usefulness of the framework, an application case in the context of the ITIL service capacity management process is summarized.

Keywords: Gamification · Simulation modeling · IT service management · Process improvement

1 Introduction

IT Service Management (ITSM) is a discipline that focuses on the implementation and management of quality IT services that meet the needs of the business. ITSM is performed by IT service providers through an appropriate mix of people, process and implementation technology. Thus, it is a process-oriented discipline that provides a framework that allows IT organizations to deliver IT services to meet business objectives [1].

Nowadays, the IT service industry is one of the most relevant industries. Given the growing importance for organizations to manage adequately their services, several ITSM-related standards and management frameworks that provide process models and best practices for ITSM have been developed [2, 3]. Some of the most internationally accepted are ISO/IEC 20000 [4, 5], CMMI for Services [6] and ITIL [7]. Although the adoption of these reference models in real-life organizations provide important benefits [1, 8, 9] and continues to increase, a Gartner study [10] shows that the main IT service failures are the result of processes failures, and lack of employee skills and competence. Thus, organizations should focus on the process improvement [11, 12] and the human aspects.

To decide what changes perform to improve ITSM processes, IT managers have to know the business objectives [7, 11] and to assess the processes performance [13]. Besides, they need to dispose of tools [14] that allow the evaluation of the processes business impact and the established objectives compliance. Simulation models are powerful tools that support decision-making in this context because they facilitate the experimentation of different decisions and observing the results before their implementation in the organization [15].

To make successfully changes in ITSM processes, also it is necessary that all the people in the organization change their attitude, and acquire and practice new behaviors and skills aimed at improvement and better performance. Attitude towards change is one of the crucial human aspects addressed in process improvement approaches [16]. Besides, to increase the motivation and commitment of managers are very important for the success of process improvement initiatives [16]. Gamification could be helpful in this field because it has been identified as a tool that leads motivation and commitment in diverse functional areas [17, 18]. Moreover, gamification helps adapt people's works behavior simply by being clear about what the organization wants from them and promoting the desired behavior on them [19].

This research paper links these two knowledge areas, simulation modeling and gamification, and introduces a conceptual framework for ITSM processes improvement based on the following: (a) the building of a simulation model of the process to improve that allows IT managers to assess the process performance by varying the process configuration; and (b) the gamification of the simulation model experimentation to motivate IT managers and drive their behavior through model simulations.

The rest of the paper is structured as follows. Next section presents the foundations of simulation modeling and gamification, and related works. Section 3 describes a conceptual framework proposed for ITSM improvement. An application case of this framework is explained in Sect. 4. Finally, Sect. 5 contains our conclusions and indicates further work to realize in this area.

2 Foundations and Related Works

2.1 Simulation Modeling and IT Service Management

A simulation model is an abstraction or simplified representation of a real system that represents only the parts of the system that the developer considers especially important to the issues and questions the model helps address. Common purposes of simulation models are to provide mechanisms for experimentation, to predict system behavior, to answer questions such as "what if", and learning more about the system represented. These models facilitate the experimentation of different decisions and analysing the results in systems where the cost, time or risk of experimentation with real systems could be high [15].

Simulation modeling can help in decision-making in the field of process improvement because a process simulation model allows managers to understand how the process behaves over time and to compare their performance under different conditions. Thus, it enables the prediction of the impact of changes in the process before their implementation in the real process.

These techniques have been widely used to support the process improvement in a variety of disciplines, such as the area of software development [20–22]. The authors of [23–25] present simulation models developed in the context of software process improvement models.

The application of simulation modeling techniques in the field of ITSM is gaining increasing interest among academic researchers and practitioners. In [26], a detailed analysis of published research articles that apply these techniques in the context of ITIL processes is presented. The study results show that simulation modeling techniques are widely used in this context to improve mainly the following processes: strategy management, financial management, change management, capacity management, incident management, service level management, security management and availability management. It is observed that the analyzed works focus mainly on the assessment and improvement of as follows: (a) service management strategies, (b) process key performance indicators, (c) service cost, (d) degree of service level objectives compliance, and (e) process configuration.

2.2 Gamification and IT Service Management

Gamification is the application of game elements in non-game contexts to solve business problems [18]. It means incorporate game elements into existing business processes to modify and influence the behavior of the people [27]. Gamification can increase the motivation and commitment of the personnel involved in the process that will implicate an improvement in their productivity, skills and performance [17, 27, 28]. Besides, gamification can encourage participation and enhance the engagement in the process [17, 27, 29, 30].

There are three fundamental game elements: dynamics, mechanics and components [27]. Game dynamics are the most abstract game elements, and are related to the human needs and issues that motivate people intrinsically. A gamified system should include dynamics than enhance emotions, narrative, sense of progression and achievement, and relationships [27]. Game mechanics are the basic actions that motivate and engage user, and drive their behavior through incentive systems, feedback and competition, among others [27]. Finally, game components are the specific instantiations of game dynamics and mechanics. Though there are many game components, the most usual are points, badges and leaderboards [27]. Using the appropriate game mechanism and components, it is possible to create an experience that drives behavior by satisfying the game dynamics.

Although the technology is very important in a gamification project, many of them fail because they jump forward to a toolset implementation before the foundations are in place [28]. The key to success is to start analyzing the problem to solve, identifying the behaviors to promote, and applying some mechanism to engage and motivate the people [27].

Initially gamification was only used for marketing [31], but in the last years gamification is being applied to the process improvement in diverse business areas, such as, software engineering [19, 32–36] and ITSM. We have found few published works in the context of the ITSM, and the most of them apply gamification for improving the Service Desk performance and engagement [37–39].

Given the human nature of ITSM, change initiatives require significant effort to change people's behavior. Gamification can help increase the IT personnel motivation and provides an opportunity to engage individuals and reinforce individual behavior. Gamification drive IT managers behavior for improving ITSM processes because they engage and become focused in situations with defined goals, a measurable sense of progress leading to the goals, a notion of status as a result of achieving the goals, and meaning rewards for reaching the goals [40].

Next section describes a novel conceptual framework proposed to the ITSM processes improvement based on simulation modeling and gamification.

3 A Conceptual Framework for ITSM Processes Improvement

Figure 1 shows the conceptual framework proposed to improve ITSM processes which is based mainly on the following:

(a) The building of a simulation model of the process to improve which enables the process performance assessment and the analysis of process changes effects before their implementation in the organization.
(b) The gamification of the simulation model experimentation to increase the IT managers' motivation, and promote in them the behavior necessary to perform successfully model simulations that enable them to make better decisions to the process improvement.

In the following sections the key activities of the conceptual framework are described.

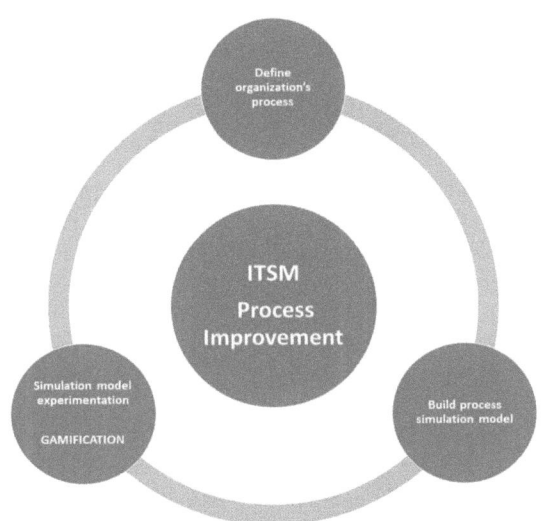

Fig. 1. Conceptual framework to improve ITSM processes

3.1 Define an Organization's Process

The purpose of this activity is to identify an organization process that needs improvements, and to describe it in detail: (a) process description, (b) management policies, (c) activity sequence, (d) resources, (e) inputs/outputs, (f) process metrics (KPIs, Key Performance Indicators), and (g) process objectives (SLOs, Service Level Objectives).

To describe successfully the process, it is fundamental to take into account the recommendations of an ITSM model reference such as ITIL [7], and adapt the process to the particular characteristics of the organization. We propose to use ITIL because is one of the ITSM reference models most used in organizations and has been accepted in the industry as the de *facto* standard for ITSM [1, 8]. Moreover, ITIL recommends using simulation modeling to support decision-making in the processes continual improvement [11].

3.2 Build a Process Simulation Model

This activity consists on perform a process prototype through a simulation model. For this, the following tasks will be conducted [26]: (a) build the simulation model, (b) identify and collect data, and (c) calibrate and test the simulation model.

The main aim of the simulation models is to allow IT managers to assess the process performance and the objectives compliance degree varying the process configuration. The simulation model elements are as follows: (a) *model input parameters* represent the process objectives (SLOs) and the process configuration parameters; (b) *model output variables* represent the process metrics (KPIs) and the degree of SLOs compliance; and (c) *conceptual model* represents the behavior of both the process and the management strategies.

The simulation model will be implemented with a tool that allows the gamification of the simulation model experimentation activity.

3.3 Gamify the Simulation Model Experimentation

Model simulations are conducted configuring different simulation scenarios through the user interface (model input parameters values) and running the model. Simulation results (model output variables values) allow IT managers to evaluate the process performance and the process objectives compliance degree with the process configuration considered in the simulation scenario. Thus, varying the simulation scenario configuration, IT managers can simulate the effects of changes in the process before their implementation in the organization, and make better decisions to the process improvement.

To motivate and engage IT managers, and drive their behaviors through model simulations we propose gamify this activity. In the following paragraphs the activities of the methodology proposed to gamify the simulation models experimentation are described. This methodology is based on the gamification methodology proposed by Werbach and Hunter in [27].

(1) *Defining the business objectives*

The business objectives to meet with the gamification of the simulation model experimentation are as follows: (1) improve IT managers' knowledge about the modeled process, and help them assess the process performance and make decisions to the process improvement; and (2) engage and motivate IT managers, and drive their behaviors through the model simulations to meet the established objectives.

Table 1. Target behavior for IT managers and metrics

Behavior	Metric
Create an account in the gamified system.	Number of accounts created.
Enter in the gamified system.	Number of entries in the system.
Read the simulation model experimentation instructions.	Number of instructions readings.
Perform a test of the instructions.	Score on the test.
Perform model simulations with different process configurations.	Number of model simulations conducted with different process configurations.
Find a process configuration which improves the process results and meets the objectives.	Number of improved process configurations found.
Perform model simulations frequently.	Number of model simulations conducted daily.
Know the progress in the gamified system.	Total score obtained.
Share accomplishments with other users.	Rank position in the leaderboard.
Learn about the process.	Score of the final process quiz.
Perform a satisfaction survey.	Results of the satisfaction survey.

(2) *Delineating target behaviors*

Table 1 shows the target behavior for IT managers and the metrics to measure such behavior.

(3) *Describing users*

The users (players) of the gamified simulation model will be IT managers. The knowledge of the process objectives and the gamification of the simulation model experimentation will increase the IT managers' motivation and will drive their behavior through model simulations.

(4) *Devising the activity cycles*

This activity consists on devising the engagement loops (player actions that in return produce feedback in the form of responses from the system) and the progression stars (description of the users' progress through the gamified system).

The IT managers' actions in the gamified system have been grouped in four different evolution levels. During each of them some of the IT managers' needs are satisfied. In the first level, IT managers create an account in the system, read the simulation model experimentation instructions and perform a test about these instructions. IT managers will pass to the second level when the number of test questions answers correctly is greater than or equal to 75 %. In the second level, IT managers perform model simulations with an initial process configuration, and evaluate the process KPIs and the process SLOs compliance degree. Once IT managers have learned how to conduct model simulations and have assessed the process performance with an initial process configuration, they will pass to the third level. In this level, IT managers perform model simulations by varying the process configuration to find the best one that improves the process KPIs and meets the SLOs. Finally, in the last level IT managers conduct a final process test and a satisfaction survey. Table 2 shows the evolution levels and the main actions that the IT managers perform in each of them.

Table 2. IT managers' actions and evolution levels

Level	Action
1	A1. Create an account in the gamified system.
	A2. Enter in the gamified system (this activity is performed in all the levels)
	A3. Read the instructions of the simulation model experimentation.
	A4. Perform a test about the instructions of the simulation model experimentation.
2	A5. Define the process objectives (model input parameters values)
	A6. Perform model simulations with an initial process configuration (model input parameters values) and asses the process results (model output variables values).
3	A7. Perform model simulations by varying the process management policies configuration (model input parameters values) and asses the process results (model output variables values).
	A8. Perform model simulations by varying the process configuration (model input parameters values) and asses the process results (model output variables values).
4	A9. Perform a final process test.
	A10. Perform a satisfaction survey.

(5) *Incorporating fun*

In order to make the gamified system more engage, we propose to include in the simulation model experimentation a game to find a treasure. IT managers will take quizzes and will conduct model simulations to meet concrete objectives for each stage in the IT manager's life cycle. For each objective met, IT manager will obtain a new clue that will drive his behavior through model simulations to find the treasure. The specific clues to include will depend on the process characteristics and the objectives to be achieved.

(6) *Deployment the appropriate tools*

The last activity consists on determining which game elements to include into the simulation model experimentation and codifying them. Given that this work proposes a conceptual framework and does not include the tool implementation, only the game elements are described below.

According to their abstraction level, the game elements can be categorized as dynamics, mechanics and components [27]. Game components are the specific manners to carry out the game dynamics and mechanics previously established [27]. Tables 3, 4 and 5 show the game dynamics, mechanics and components selected for gamifying the simulation model experimentation.

Table 3. Game dynamics

Dynamic	Description
Emotions	IT managers experience emotions such as engagement, motivation competitiveness, feeling of progression and desire for status.
Progress	IT managers improve their skills to manage the process and make decisions to the process improvement.
Relationships	Relationships and communication between IT managers improve.

Table 4. Game mechanics

Mechanic	Description
Challenges	Through model simulations IT managers overcome the following challenges: (1) learn how to manage the process, (2) make decisions to the process improvement, (3) identify the process parameters that most influence on the process results and (4) obtain the required score in the tests.
Chance	IT managers receive unexpected rewards during the simulation model experimentation.
Feedback	IT managers receive feedback to every activity they complete and every object they meet. Thus, they can evaluate their behavior and decisions, and improve their motivation and skills through the simulation model experimentation.
Rewards	IT managers receive positive rewards for the completed activities and reached objectives.
Win states	IT managers achieve win states when they meet the objectives established.

4 Case Study

This section presents an application case of the framework proposed in the context of the ITIL Capacity Management process. The simulation model built and the gamification of the simulation model experimentation are summarized below.

4.1 Service Capacity Management Simulation Model

The ITIL Capacity Management process comprises three sub-processes [41]: (a) Business Capacity Management, (b) Service Capacity Management, and (c) Component Capacity Management. This work focuses on the Service Capacity Management

Table 5. Game components

Component	Description
Achievements	The objectives (Oi) are introduced in points, badges and trophies descriptions.
Points	IT managers receive points when they complete the actions indicated in Table 2 and meet the following objectives: (O1) success percentage of instructions test > = 75 %; (O2) find a process configuration that improve some process KPIs; (O3) find a process configuration that meets some process SLOs.
Badges	IT managers obtain badges (gold, silver or bronze) if they find a process configuration that meet all the SLOs and improve all the process KPIs (O4). Additionally, an IT manager obtains a badge if as follows: (a) he is the first user that finds that process configuration (O5), (b) he is the user that performs the fewest model simulations to find that process configuration (O6), and (c) he is the user that takes the shortest time to find that process configuration (O7).
Trophies	An IT manager receives trophies if he meets the following objectives: (O8) he finds the process configuration that obtains the best process KPIs and comply all the process SLOs; and (O9) he finds the highest number of process configurations that improve the process results.
Stars	IT managers receive 1, 2 or 3 stars depending on how many questions they have answered correctly in the final test.
Levels	The different user levels in the system are described in Table 2.
Leaderboard	IT managers can see their progress with respect to others users on the leaderboard.
Progress bar	IT managers can visualize their progress in the system (completed activities versus total activities, and completed levels).

sub-process whose main aim is to manage the service capacity in order to meet SLAs that service providers agree with their clients.

The simulation model built in the context of the Service Capacity Management sub-process has been presented and described in [26, 42]. Only the simulation model elements necessary to explain the gamification of the simulation model experimentation are summarized below.

For the model construction, a banking validation service provider and an e-commerce company that sells their products through its web portal have been considered. The banking validation service provider provides the company a service that validates credit card details, and verifies that the company's customers possess enough credit to realize the purchase. The conditions under which the service must be provided (SLOs) are documented in the SLA signed with the company. The SLA parameters are as follows: (a) service capacity contracted by the company, (b) agreed service response times, (c) target service performance, and (d) penalties for non-compliance the service response times. In this context, service providers can implement different service capacity management strategies (the manner in which the service provider assigns the service capacity to validate the client's credit card) which have different effects on the service performance and the SLA compliance degree.

The main purpose of the simulation model built is to help service providers make decisions to properly manage service capacities assigned to their clients, and ensure compliance with SLAs. The model input parameters represent the process configuration parameters and the process objectives: (a) *client configuration* (SLA parameters and trend of the received service requests); and (b) *service capacity configuration* (service capacity assigned to the company and configuration of the service capacity management strategy). The *model output variables* represent the process KPIs and the SLOs compliance degree: (a) *service behavior* (service requests received, service requests validated within the agreed response times, and service requests abandoned); and (b) *service performance* (degree of SLA performance parameters non-compliance and penalization for not meet the agreed response times).

4.2 Gamification of the Service Capacity Management Simulation Model Experimentation

The service capacity management model simulations allow IT managers to analyze the service performance and the SLA compliance by varying both the service capacity assigned to the company and the service capacity management strategy configuration.

This activity has been gamified applying the methodology proposed in Sect. 3.3. Table 6 shows the rewards that IT managers receive when they complete the defined actions or meet the established targets.

Table 6. Study case rewards

Action	Reward
A1. Create an account in the gamified system.	5 points
A2. Enter in the gamified system.	1 point
A3. Read the simulation model experimentation instructions.	5 points
A4. Perform a test of the instructions.	
(a) Success percentage < 75 %	1 point
(b) Success percentage >=75 %	5 points
A5. Define the process objectives (SLOs).	2 points
A6. Perform model simulations with an initial process configuration (contracted service capacity and a particular capacity management strategy).	1 point
A7. Perform model simulations with the contracted service capacity and by varying the capacity management strategy.	2 points
A8. Perform model simulations with a service capacity < contracted service capacity and by varying the capacity management strategy.	4 points
A9. Perform a final process test.	1 point
(a) Success percentage > = 90 %	3 stars
(b) Success percentage is between 75 % and 90 %	2 stars
(c) Success percentage is between 50 % and 75 %	1 star
A10. Perform a satisfaction survey.	5 points

(*Continued*)

Table 6. (*Continued*)

Objective	Reward
O1. Success percentage of test > = 75 % the first time manager performs it.	10 points
O2. Find a process configuration that improves some service KPIs.	1 point/KPI
O3. Find a process configuration that meets some service SLOs.	1 point/SLO
O4. Find an improved process configuration (with the *contracted service capacity*) that meets the SLOs and improves the service KPIs.	10 points
O5. First manager that finds it.	bronze badge
O6. Manager that performs the fewest number of model simulations to find it.	bronze badge
O7. Manager that takes the shortest time to find it.	bronze badge
O4. Find an improved process configuration (with a *service capacity* < *contracted service capacity*) that meets the SLOs and improves the service KPIs.	10 points
O5. First manager that finds it.	silver badge
O6. Manager that performs the fewest number of model simulations to find it.	silver badge
O7. Manager that takes the shortest time to find it.	silver badge
O4. Find the process configuration that with the *lowest service capacity* meets the SLOs and improves the KPIs.	gold badge
O8. Find the process configuration that meets the SLOs and obtains the best KPIs	trophy
O9. Find the highest number of process configurations that meet the SLOs and improve the KPIs.	trophy

5 Conclusions

IT service industry is nowadays one of the most relevant industries, and in recent years have emerged several ITSM-related standards and management frameworks that offer process models and best practices for ITSM. Though organizations obtain important benefits with the adoption of these reference models, the main IT services failures are due to processes failures and lack of IT personnel skills. This paper focuses on these two issues, and proposes a conceptual framework to improve ITSM processes based on simulation modeling and gamification. The main activities of this framework are as follows: (a) to build a simulation model of the process to improve; and (b) to gamify the simulation model experimentation. Given that in [26] we introduce a methodology to build simulation models to improve ITSM processes, this work focuses on the gamification of these simulation models experimentation.

The experimentation of an ITSM process simulation model enables IT managers to assess the process performance varying the process configuration through the model input parameters. Thus, they can know the effects of process changes on the process results before their implementation in the organization, and make better decisions to the process improvement. The gamification of the experimentation of these simulation models on the one hand increases IT managers' motivation because the goals to meet are clearly defined and IT managers know their progress and receive rewards for reaching the goals. On the other hand, gamification drives IT managers' behavior through model simulations and help them to find an optimal process configuration that improves the process KPIs and meets the SLOs.

To illustrate the usefulness and applicability of the framework proposed, an application case in the context of ITIL service capacity management process is introduced. The gamification of the experimentation of the simulation model built in the context of this process motivates service providers and helps them decide what service capacity strategy to adopt for improving the service response times and ensure the service level objectives compliance.

Finally, our further work in this field will be focused on the implementation of the game elements into the simulation model of the capacity management process, and the validation of the gamified simulation model with users. Besides, we will applicate the proposed framework in the context of other ITSM processes.

Acknowledgments. This research paper has been supported by the Spanish Ministry of Science and Technology with ERDF funds under grants TIN2013-46928-C3-2-R.

References

1. Mesquida, A.L., Mas, A., Amengual, E., Calvo-Manzano, J.A.: IT service management process improvement based on ISO/IEC 15504: a systematic review. Inf. Softw. Technol. **54**, 239–247 (2012). doi:10.1016/j.infsof.2011.11.002
2. Mora, M., Raisinghani, M., O'Connor, R.V., Gomez, J., Gelman, O.: An extensive review on IT service design in seven international ITSM processes frameworks (part 1). Int. J. Inf. Technol. Syst. Approach **7**(2), 85–109 (2014). doi:10.4018/ijitsa.2014070105
3. Mora, M., Raisinghani, M., O'Connor, R.V., Gomez, J., Gelman, O.: An extensive review on IT service design in seven international ITSM processes frameworks (part II). Int. J. Inf. Technol. Syst. Approach **8**(1), 69–90 (2015). doi:10.4018/ijitsa.2015010104
4. ISO/IEC 20000-1:2011. Information technology– Service management– Part 1: Service management systems requirements
5. ISO/IEC 20000-2:2012. Information technology– Service management – Part 2: Guidance on the application of service management systems
6. Capability Maturity Model Integration for Services (CMMI). http://www.sei.cmu.edu/reports/10tr034.pdf. (consulted in February of 2016)
7. ITIL 2011. http://www.itil-officialsite.com/. (consulted in February of 2016)
8. Iden, J., Eikebrokk, T.R.: Implementing IT service management: a systematic literature review. Int. J. Inf. Manage. **33**, 512–523 (2013). doi:10.1016/j.ijinfomgt.2013.01.004
9. Marrone, M., Kolbe, L.M.: Impact of IT service management frameworks on the IT organization. An empirical study on benefits, challenges and processes. Bus. Inf. Syst. Eng. **3**(1), 5–18 (2011). doi:10.1007/s12599-010-0141-5
10. Gartner study. In: Cox, R., Marriot, I., Seabrook, D. The Gartner Group, Stamford, April 2003
11. Office of Government Commerce (OGC), ITIL® Continual Service Improvement (2011)
12. Renault, A., Cortina, S., Barafort, B.: Towards a maturity model for ISO/IEC 20000-1 based on the TIPA for ITIL process capability assessment model. In: Rout, T., O'Connor, R.V., Dorling, A. (eds.) SPICE 2015. CCIS, vol. 526, pp. 188–200. Springer, Heidelberg (2015)

13. Jäntti, M., Rout, T., Wen, L., Heikkinen, S., Cater-Steel, A.: Exploring the impact of IT service management process improvement initiatives: a case study approach. In: Woronowicz, T., Rout, T., O'Connor, R.V., Dorling, A. (eds.) SPICE 2013. CCIS, vol. 349, pp. 176–187. Springer, Heidelberg (2013). doi:10.1007/978-3-642-38833-0_16
14. Cater-Steel, A., Tan, W.-G., Toleman, M., Rout, T., Shrestha, A.: Software-mediated process assessment in IT service management. In: Woronowicz, T., Rout, T., O'Connor, R.V., Dorling, A. (eds.) SPICE 2013. CCIS, vol. 349, pp. 188–198. Springer, Heidelberg (2013). doi:10.1007/978-3-642-38833-0_17
15. Kellner, M.I., Madachy, R.J., Raffo, D.M.: Software process simulation modeling: why? what? how? J. Syst. Softw. **46**(2/3), 91–105 (1999). doi:10.1016/S0164-1212(99)00003-5
16. Korsaa, M., Johansen, J., Schweigert, T., Vohwinkel, D., Messnarz, R., Nevalainen, R., Biro, M.: The people aspects in modern process improvement management approaches. J. Softw. Evol. Process **25**(4), 381–391 (2012). doi:10.1002/smr.570
17. Gartner. Gamification 2020: What Is the Future of Gamification? 5 November 2012
18. Deterding, S., Dixon, D., Khaled, R., Nacke, L.: From game design elements to gamefulness: defining gamification. In: Proceeding of the 15th International Academic MindTreck Conference: Envisioning Future Media Environments, pp. 9–15 (2011). doi:10.1145/2181037.2181040
19. Herranz, E., Colomo-Palacios, R., Amescua, A., Yilmaz, M.: Gamification as a disruptive factor in software process improvement initiatives. J. Univ. Comput. Sci. **20**(6), 885–906 (2014). doi:10.3217/jucs-020-06-0885
20. Zhang, H., Kitchenham, B., Pfahl, D.: Reflections on 10 years of software process simulation modeling: a systematic review. In: Wang, Q., Pfahl, D., Raffo, D.M. (eds.) ICSP 2008. LNCS, vol. 5007, pp. 345–356. Springer, Heidelberg (2008). doi:10.1007/978-3-540-79588-9_30
21. Zhang, H., Kitchenham, B., Pfahl, D.: Software process simulation modeling: an extended systematic review. In: Münch, J., Yang, Y., Schäfer, W. (eds.) ICSP 2010. LNCS, vol. 6195, pp. 309–320. Springer, Heidelberg (2010)
22. Ahmed, R., Hall, T., Wernick, P., Robinson, S., Shah, M.: Software process simulation modelling: a survey of practice. J. Simul. **2**, 91–102 (2008). doi:10.1057/jos.2008.1
23. Ruiz, M., Ramos, I., Toro, M.: A dynamic integrated framework for software process improvement. Software Qual. J. **10**, 181–194 (2002). doi:10.1023/A:1020580008694. Kluwer Academic Publishers
24. Raffo, D., Kellner, M.: Modeling software processes quantitatively and evaluating the performance of process alternatives. In: Elements of Software Process Assessment and Improvement, IEEE Computer Society Press (1999), chapter 16
25. Crespo, D., Ruiz, M.: Decision making support in CMMI process areas using multiparadigm simulation modeling. In: Proceedings of the Winter Simulation Conference (WSC 2012), pp. 1–12. doi:10.1109/WSC.2012.6464994
26. Orta, E., Ruiz, M., Hurtado, N., Gawn, D.: Decision-making in IT service management: a simulation based approach. Decis. Support Syst. **66**, 36–51 (2014). doi:10.1016/j.dss.2014.06.002
27. Werbach, K., Hunter, D.: For the win: how game thinking can revolutionize your business. Wharton Digital Press, Philadelphia (2012)
28. Gartner (2012). http://www.gartner.com/newsroom/id/2251015
29. Cognizant Reports. Gamifying business to drive emproyee engagement and performance (2013)
30. Robson, K., Plangger, K., Kietzmann, J.H., McCarthy, I., Pitt, L.: Game on: engaging customers and employees through gamification. J. Bus. Horiz. **59**(1), 29–36 (2016). doi:10.1016/j.bushor.2015.08.002

31. Burkie, B.: Gamification trends and strategies to help prepare for the future. Gartner, Paris (2012)
32. Pedreira, O., García, F., Brisaboa, N., Piattini, M.: Gamification in software engineering- A systematic mapping. J. Inf. Softw. Technol. **57**, 157–168 (2015). doi:10.1016/j.infsof.2014.08.007
33. Dorling, A., McCaffery, F.: The gamification of SPICE. In: Mas, A., Mesquida, A., Rout, T., O'Connor, R.V., Dorling, A. (eds.) SPICE 2012. CCIS, vol. 290, pp. 295–301. Springer, Heidelberg (2012). doi:10.1007/978-3-642-30439-2_35
34. Herranz, E., Colomo-Palacios, R., de Amescua Seco, A.: Gamiware: a gamification platform for software process improvement. In: O'Connor, R.V., et al. (eds.) EuroSPI 2015. CCIS, vol. 543, pp. 127–139. Springer, Heidelberg (2015). doi:10.1007/978-3-319-24647-5_11
35. Medeiros, D.B., Dos Santos Neto, P., Passos, E.B., de Souza Araújo, W.: Working and playing with Scrum. Int. J. Softw. Eng. Knowl. Eng. **25**(06), 993–1015 (2015)
36. Unkelos-Shpigel, N., Irit Hadar, I.: Gamifying software engineering tasks based on cognitive principles: The case of code review. In: Proceeding of IEEE/ACM International Workshop on Cooperative and Human Aspects of Software Engineering (2015). doi:10.1109/CHASE.2015.21
37. Yuan, Y., Qi, K.K., Marcus, A.: Gamification and persuasion of HP IT service management to improve performance and engagement. In: Fui-Hoon Nah, F., Tan, C.-H. (eds.) HCIB 2015. LNCS, vol. 9191, pp. 550–562. Springer, Heidelberg (2015). doi:10.1007/978-3-319-20895-4_51
38. Conger, S.: Gamification of service desk work. In: Lee, J. (ed) The impact of ICT on work, pp. 151–172. doi:10.1007/978-981-287-612-6_8
39. Conceicao, F., Silva, A., Filho, A., Cabral, R.: Toward a gamification model to improve IT services management quality on service desk. In: Proceedings of the International Conference on the Quality of Information and Communications Technology, pp. 255–260 (2014). doi:10.1109/QUATIC.2014.41
40. Bunchball. Using gamification to engage employees (technical report) (2014)
41. Office of Government Commerce (OGC), ITIL® Service Operation (2011)
42. Orta, E., Ruiz, M., Toro, M.: A system dynamics approach to web service capacity management. In: IEEE European Conference on Web Service, pp. 109–117 (2009). doi:10.1109/ECOWS.2009.20

Towards a Manifesto for Software Process Education, Training and Professionalism

Jørn Johansen[1], Ricardo Colomo-Palacios[2(✉)], and Rory V. O'Connor[3]

[1] Whitebox, Horsholm, Denmark
jj@whitebox.dk
[2] Ostfold University College, Halden, Norway
Ricardo.colomo-palacios@hiof.no
[3] Dublin City University, Dublin, Ireland
Rory.OConnor@dcu.ie

Abstract. In June 2015 a group of experts in Software Process Improvement (SPI) and Education from all over the world gathered at the 1st International Workshop on Software Process Education, Training and Professionalism held in connection with 15th International Conference Software Process Improvement and Capability Determination. Discussions with key players in the relevant professional and personal certification fields, as well as experienced educators led to a consensus that it is time for the industry to rise to the new challenges and set out in a manifesto a common vision for educators and trainers together with a set of recommendations to address the challenges faced. At the workshop 14 "experts" from education and industry presented and discussed their "wisdom and experience" of the challenges faced for software process education, training and professionalism, especially with the background of the new modes of learning and teaching in higher education. Based on the presentations, 32 workshop participants brainstormed core values and principles specifically addressing the needs of software process education, training and professionalism. Via affinity analysis and group thinking exercises we identified an initial manifesto, consisting of 10 values and 4 principles. It is expected that this draft manifest will give expression to state-of-the-art knowledge on software process education, training and professionalism. It is based on hundreds of person-years of practice and experience from educators and industry professionals globally. Further work is currently being undertaken to extend and validate this draft manifesto with a view to publishing in its entirety by 2016.

Keywords: Software process · Education · Training · Professionalism

1 Introduction

Within the broad field of software engineering, and according to SWEBOK [1], software engineering processes or software processes in short are concerned with work activities accomplished by software engineers to develop, maintain, and operate software, such as requirements, design, construction, testing, configuration management, and other software engineering processes. Software Process is one of the fifteen knowledge areas

(KA) defined in SWEBOK 3.0 [1] and was also one of the ten KAs defined in the previous version of this body of knowledge.

The software process is concerned with software process definition, software life cycles, software process assessment and improvement, software measurement, and software engineering process tools. Software process is inherent to software practice. In working scenarios, software practitioners are often unfulfilled with their level of preparation when they start their careers [2]. Literature pointed out that, among other aspects, this problem lies in the way software process is typically taught at universities [3]. These courses present constraints inherent in an academic setting including depth and time limitations. These restrictions lead to inefficient training in the many facets of the software lifecycle [4].

However and in spite of these recent and disappointing studies, the topic is covered in current curricular efforts in the fields of software engineering. In the field of undergraduate degree programs, according to the Curriculum Guidelines for Undergraduate Degree Programs in Software Engineering [5], software process is one of the 10 knowledge areas of the curriculum. In this publication, authors identify 467 h of course contents and 10 courses or knowledge areas. Software Process course is presenting a teaching load of 33 h covering various process models that support individual and team experiences with one or more software development processes, including planning, execution, tracking, and configuration management. Moreover, one of the guidelines in the curriculum definition claims, "Software process should be central to the curriculum organization and to students' understanding of software engineering practice". In the field of graduate degree programs, the equivalent effort is the Curriculum Guidelines for Graduate Degree Programs in Software Engineering launched back in 2009 [6]. In this case, Software Process is one of the 8 knowledge areas in the Software Engineering section of the body of knowledge. In a nutshell, the difference between the undergraduate and graduate curricular effort in the software process arena is rooted on the fact that in the first the topic is addressed only at Bloom's Taxonomy levels 1 and 2 while in the second it is covered at levels 2 and 3.

Although the coverage of software process education is established in curriculum initiatives, increasing its coverage in educational settings is still challenging. The complexity of the subject together with the need of a good background of the discipline is normally pushing subjects into master programs, while personal and team software approaches are mostly present in bachelor curricula [7]. Further as has been noted by Prof. Margaret Ross, the UKs most influential software quality educator and commentator, there is a lack of relevant knowledge and experience of teachers and lecturers coupled with the problems of pressures by other topics on academic course [8]. Further she states that most syllabuses are already very full on these courses, with constant pressure to introduce additional topics. Dedicated units on quality and process improvement are not usual.

An associated aspect of software process education and professionalism is related to the teaching and usages of international standards in educational settings. Whilst there have been limited attempts to teach international software process standards to students [15] and engage professionals [16, 19] alike, these have met with limited success [18].

Quite apart from the issues of education and training, it has been well established that there are business benefits to the adoption of SPI practices in an industrial setting, although some practice issues remain in some areas such as SME sector [5, 6, 17]. Moreover, recent studies e.g. [9] showed up gaps in software process competence in samples of software professionals. It is therefore considered both appropriate and necessary to expand the remit of an SPI education manifesto beyond the realm of education and training and to include professionalism from an industry practitioner perspective as well.

As a result of this need, a set of software process consultant and practitioners along with a group of academics on the topic detected this gap and decided to launch a manifesto for software process education, training and professionalism. This paper is devoted to illustrate the initial steps taken by these set of experts towards this goal. The remaining of the paper is structured as follows. In Sect. 2, authors present the initiative and initial results along with ongoing works. Section 3 is aimed to wrap up the paper and to portray main future works.

2 A Manifesto for Software Process Education, Training and Professionalism

According to the Merriam Webster dictionary, a manifesto is a written statement declaring publicly the intentions, motives, or views of its issuer. The etymological origin of the word, according to Oxford dictionaries can be rooted in the Italian (mid-17th century) from *manifestare* that is also from Latin, 'make public', from *manifestus*. Manifestos are quite common in the technological arena. Maybe the most popular of them is the Manifesto for Agile Software Development [10] while there are other with less repercussion like, for instance, the Manifesto for Software Craftmanship [11] or the SPI Manifesto [12].

Following the path previously followed by these initiatives, in this section authors explain the process, structure and initial results for the Manifesto for Software Process Education, Training and Professionalism.

2.1 The Process

In June 2015 a group of 32 experts in Software Process Education, Training and Professionalism from 15 different countries and 3 continents gathered in connection with the SPICE 2015 Conference [13] for a workshop at Gothenburg University in Sweden. This workshop was the 1st International Workshop Software Process Education, Training and Professionalism (SPEPT 2015) [14]. The initial aim for the workshop was to present a set of works on the topic but, taking into account the importance of the topic and previous feedback from scientific and professional arenas, it was aimed to develop a manifesto for Software Process Education, Training and Professionalism. The overall structure of the manifesto is based on previous initiatives on the topic and more precisely, the SPI Manifesto, launched by the EuroSPI community by 2009 [12]. In what follows, the main aspects of the process of the definition of the manifesto is presented.

A. Before the workshop, facilitator performed a set of tasks to support the definition of the manifesto:
   I. Workshop facilitator extracted 7 preliminary values and 139 principles derived from 10 background papers describing the problems and barriers in SE and SPI education and learning presented in the workshop.
   II. These principles were group into 24 different topics.
   III. The 24 topics was allocated to 4 working groups: Method and Delivery; Certification and Training; Links between Management and SE/SPI and, finally, SPI.

As a final remark, authors want to underline that it took much more time than planned to identify the preliminary values and principles from the papers, and bring it to a form, which enabled it for the workshop as basis material.

B. During the workshop:
   IV. In the morning session ten live presentations on the topic were scheduled and a set of recorded videos supporting the initiative were displayed.
   V. In the evening session, a short description of the workshop tasks was presented to workshop attendants by workshop facilitator.
   VI. The set of materials to develop the task were presented. Materials include stickers, wall papers, pens, postIts, labels with the 7 values, labels with the allocated principles.
   VII. Participants were divided into four different groups to develop values and practices along as identifying supporting actions according to the 4 working groups defined earlier. Each group presented a moderator.
   VIII. The groups first discussed the initial values. It was allowed to come up with new values.
   IX. Than the groups sorted and grouped the allocated principles. It was allowed to remove and to come up with new principles.
   X. The grouped principles was dot voted and the most important were linked to the values.
   XI. Apart from the set of values and principles, all groups also proposed a set of supporting actions for the initiative.
   XII. Once defined, a short presentation on the outcomes of each group was provided, which was recorded on video.
   XIII. Facilitator documented the process and presented an overall preliminary result of the workshop at the end of the conference.

C. After the workshop.
   XIV. The editorial board for the manifesto is designed and contributors join editors in specific areas.
   XV. A template of the manifesto, the background papers, the initial values and principles as well as the documentation from the workshop were sent to the editorial board.
   XVI. Editors and contributors develop editorial content.
   XVII. A number of iterations of writing, reviewing, commenting and rewriting took place.

XVIII. Expert reviews are provided and the document was updated.
XIX. Final document is edited and distributed.

The whole process is scheduled to be complete by 2016.

2.2 The Structure

As stated before, the structure of the manifesto is based on the SPI Manifesto [12]. Consequently, the manifesto adopts the approach based on values and principles.

Value or Values present several entries in dictionaries, but focusing in the intended meaning for this document, values are principles or standards of behavior; one's judgement of what is important in life, according to the Oxford Dictionary. In the Cambridge dictionary, the term is defined as the beliefs people have, especially about what is right and wrong and what is most important in life, that control their behavior. For the aims of the manifesto values represent the core priorities in an education culture, including what drives priorities and how you truly act when doing education. In other words, a value is something that deserves to be in focus because of its importance or worth. The identified values is core for Software Engineering and Software Process Improvement are the values that we have prioritized.

Principle presents also different meanings. According to Merriam-Webster dictionary, a principle is a moral rule or belief that helps you know what is right and wrong and that influences your actions. Oxford dictionaries offer a definition of the term as follows: a fundamental truth or proposition that serves as the foundation for a system of belief or behavior or for a chain of reasoning. Again, for the sake of this manifesto, a principle is a basic generalization that is accepted as true and that can be used as a basis for education reasoning or education behavior. A principle is something that can serve as a foundation for action to reach the value. You can use the principles to govern your personal behavior in relation to reach the necessary competences for Software Engineering and Software Process Improvement work.

Finally, practices are specific supporting actions for principles and values.

2.3 Initial Results

It is important to note that, although process was defined and explained to participants, the documentation of the work differed to some degree among groups. This difference introduce some extra work for the editors while writing the parts of the manifesto – the complete overview was difficult to keep when going into detail of the documentation of the workshop.

Results from the workshop with regards to groups, 10 values, 15 principles and supporting actions are as follows:

VALUES:

1. Professional achievement: Experience a feeling of accomplishment for job well done, that you have made a contribution, sense of competence.
2. Knowledge management: Feel what you do makes a difference, provides new knowledge, enhances existing systems, provides development of others.

3. Personal competence: Engage in work that offers opportunity to learn and grow as a person, room for retrospective.
4. Universal recognition: Have others look up to you, admire your skill and expertise, be seen as admirable and successful, have a sense of knowledge and prestige.
5. SPI as profession: The conduct, aims, or qualities that characterize or mark a profession or a professional person"; and it defines a profession as "a calling requiring specialized knowledge and often long and intensive academic preparation.
6. Innovative: Focused on constant improvement and being at the forefront of change and innovation in education and training.
7. Accessibility: Providing a framework of flexible learning opportunities, proactive support mechanisms and administrative processes facilitating and simplifying access for students at all levels and facilitating the transferability of credits.
8. Value: Value to the business according to customers.
9. Inspiring: No consensus was reached on its definition. Final definition will be provided in future steps.
10. Collaboration: No consensus was reached on its definition. Final definition will be provided in future steps.

PRINCIPLES:

During the workshop, 3 to 4 principles per group were defined. These principles are in writing at the moment, but the link between group and principles is as follows:

1. Link between management and SE/SPI: Evaluation; Content; Form.
2. Method and delivery: Technical approaches; Industry collaboration; tools; Learning approaches.
3. Certification and training: Value added; Holistic; Innovation; Just good enough.
4. SPI: Content; Lean by doing; Form; Model.

SUPPORTING ACTIONS:

- Get professional societies unified
- Create Body of Knowledge
- Develop a SPI Book of Knowledge
- Link to professional association (IEEE, ICM, ISTQB)
- Consult with Certification Scenes (e.g. ARCS, ECQA, ISTQB)
- Link to HR associations/Skills (ECTS)
- Investigate systems that measure experience levels

3 Conclusions

The development of a Manifesto for Software Process Education, Training and Professionalism has the ability to assist with addressing many of he identified issues and gaps facing both educators and the software profession today

As there is always pressure to include new topics on courses, the professional bodies, they could specify that process improvement should be included in any degree course to be accredited by that body. The governments, through their financial power, could play a major role in encouraging the professional bodies and the universities and colleges to give a higher priority to relevant courses and in particular to quality and process improvement

To assist the lecturers to inspire their students, in addition to helping with suitable material, opportunities could be provided for lecturers and teachers to gain real life experience by shadowing process improvement professionals, possibly with Certification Bodies, subject to their clients' agreement, and in organisations with quality and process improvement sections. This would enable the lecturers to introduce some real world, even though limited, experience to their discussions with students.

From a professional perspective, there are limited numbers of professionals with adequate experience and knowledge of process improvement, to be able to influence the majority of organisations. In many cases, there is little opportunity of gaining practical experience, especially if they are employed by SMEs. Individual (professionals) could address these problems by attending professional training and University courses.

Software process improvement is considered one of the most important fields in the software engineering discipline. However, and in spite of its importance, increasing its coverage in educational settings is still challenging. By influencing the syllabus for these courses, and other degree courses, to include quality and process improvement, the future professionals, on entering the various Industries, could act as ambassadors for process improvement for the future. Ultimately, it is the hope of the champions behind the development of the Manifesto for Software Process Education, Training and Professionalism that it can address some of these needs.

Acknowledgments. Authors would like to thank all workshop participants and manifesto reviewers and editors for their support to the initiative.

References

1. Abran, A., Fairley, D.: SWEBOK: guide to the software engineering body of knowledge version 3. IEEE Computer Society (2014)
2. Exter, M.: Comparing educational experiences and on-the-job needs of educational software designers. In: Proceedings of the 45th ACM Technical Symposium on Computer Science Education, pp. 355–360. ACM, New York, NY, USA (2014)
3. Bin Ali, N., Unterkalmsteiner, M.: Use and evaluation of simulation for software process education: a case study. In: Proceedings of the European Conference Software Engineering Education, pp. 59–73. Shaker Verlag, Seeon Monastery, Germany (2014)
4. Kohwalter, T.C., Clua, E.W.G., Murta, L.G.P.: Reinforcing software engineering learning through provenance. In: 2014 Brazilian Symposium on Software Engineering (SBES), pp. 131–140 (2014)
5. LeBlanc, R.J., Sobel, A.: Software engineering 2014: curriculum guidelines for undergraduate degree programs in software engineering. IEEE Computer Society (2014)
6. Adcock, R., Alef, E., Amato, B., Ardis, M., Bernstein, L., Boehm, B., Bourque, P., Brackett, J., Cantor, M., Cassel, L., et al.: Curriculum guidelines for graduate degree programs in software engineering. Stevens Institute of Technology (2009)

7. Heredia, A., Colomo-Palacios, R., Amescua-Seco, A.: A systematic mapping study on software process education. In: Proceedings of 1st International Workshop on Software Process Education, Training and Professionalism, pp. 7–17. Ceur Workshop Proceedings, Gothenburg, Sweden (2015)
8. Ross, M.: Process improvement - barriers and opportunities for teaching and training. In: Proceedings of 1st International Workshop Software Process Education, Training and Professionalism (SPEPT 2015), EUR Workshop Proceedings Series, vol. 1368 (2015)
9. Colomo-Palacios, R., Casado-Lumbreras, C., Soto-Acosta, P., García-Peñalvo, F.J., Tovar-Caro, E.: Competence gaps in software personnel: a multi-organizational study. Comput. Hum. Behav. **29**, 456–461 (2013)
10. Beck, K., Beedle, M., Van Bennekum, A., Cockburn, A., Cunningham, W., Fowler, M., Grenning, J., Highsmith, J., Hunt, A., Jeffries, R., et al.: Manifesto for agile software development (2001)
11. Ambler, S.: The Manifesto for Software Craftsmanship. http://manifesto.softwarecraftsmanship.org/
12. Pries-Heje, J., Johansen, J.: SPI Manifesto (2010). http://www.madebydelta.com/imported/images/DELTA_Web/documents/Ax/SPI_Manifesto_A.1.2.2010.pdf
13. Rout, T., O'Connor, R.V., Dorling, A. (eds.): Proceedings of the 15th International Conference on Software Process Improvement and Capability Determination, SPICE 2015, Gothenburg, Sweden, 16–17 June 2015. CCIS vol. 526. Springer, Heidelberg (2015)
14. O'Connor, R.V., Mitasiunas, T., Ross, M.: Proceedings of 1st International Workshop Software Process Education, Training and Professionalism. EUR Workshop Proceedings Series, vol. 1368 (2015)
15. Laporte, C.Y., O'Connor, R.V.: Software process improvement in graduate software engineering programs. In: Proceedings of 1st International Workshop Software Process Education, Training and Professionalism (SPEPT 2015), vol. 1368 pp. 18–24, CEUR Workshop Proceedings, Gothenburg, Sweden (2015)
16. Laporte, C., O'Connor, R., Garcia Paucar, L., Gerancon, B.: An innovative approach in developing standard professionals by involving software engineering students in implementing and improving international standards. J. SES (The Society for Standards Professionals) **67**(2), 2–9 (2015)
17. Larrucea, X., O'Connor, R.V., Colomo-Palacios, R., Laporte, C.Y.: Software process improvement in very small organizations. IEEE Softw. **33**(2), 85–89 (2016)
18. O'Connor, R.V.: Developing software and systems engineering standards. In: Proceedings of the 16th International Conference on Computer Systems and Technologies, pp. 13–21. ACM (2015)
19. O'Connor, R.V., Laporte, C.Y.: An innovative approach to the development of an international software process lifecycle standard for very small entities. Int. J. Inf. Technol. Syst. Approach **7**, 1–22 (2014)

SPI in Agile and Small Settings

A Maturity Model for Integrating Agile Processes and User Centred Design

Dina Salah[1(✉)], Richard Paige[2], and Paul Cairns[2]

[1] Sadat Academy for Management Science, Cairo, Egypt
dina.salah.nasr@gmail.com
[2] The University of York, York, UK
{richard.paige,paul.cairns}@york.ac.uk

Abstract. This paper presents a lightweight, descriptive maturity model for integrating Agile processes and User Centred Design. The maturity model addresses the specifics, activities, success factors and challenges identified within the Agile User Centred Design Integration domain. The model provides a set of dimensions, processes, and practices that act as a road map for successful AUCDI as well as a diagnostic tool to assess an organisation's capability to integrate Agile processes and UCD. The paper provides details on the model's evaluation and evolution as a result of expert reviewers feedback.

Keywords: Agile · User Centred Design · Maturity models · Agile User Centred Design Integration (AUCDI) maturity model

1 Introduction

Agile processes and User Centred Design (UCD) integration is gaining increased recognition due to three reasons: first, UCD pros of providing developers with deeper understanding of prospective users' activities, needs and goals. Second, the deficiency of Agile practices and principles that are used for elicitation of user requirements and evaluation of Agile systems for user experience and usability [12, 14]. Third, the presence of principled differences between UCD and Agile methods that poses challenges on the integration process [25, 27]. User Centred Design is a set of methods, techniques, processes, and a philosophy that aim to satisfy users via producing usable products as a result of the methodical UCD effort throughout the development process [8].

In the 1990s a number of Usability Maturity Models (UMMs) emerged that aimed to assess the organisation's UCD capability and/or performance. Usability capability is defined as "A characteristic of a development organisation that determines its ability to consistently develop products with high and competitive level of usability [10]". These UMMs aim to assist organisations in conducting a systematic current state analysis of the organisation's ability to consistently develop products with high usability level via assessing the organisation's strengths and weaknesses in regards to UCD aspects and accordingly plan for improvement [10].

The rest of this paper is organized as follows: Sect. 2 discusses related work. Section 3 details the research method. Section 4 discusses the knowledge base.

Section 5 discusses AUCDI dimensions. Section 6 discusses the maturity model. Section 7 discusses the model's evaluation and evolution and Sect. 8 discusses the conclusion and future work.

2 Related Work

In the past decade there has been an increased industrial and research interest in the integration of agile processes and UCD. This was reflected by a number of dedicated workshops, panels, tutorials, seminars, discussion groups and publications. A systematic literature review and a systematic mapping study were conducted [25, 27] in which agile user centred design integration studies were classified according to their integration approach. The aim behind this classification was to identify the current state of research in regards to the different integration approaches. This study revealed the presence of eight different categories of integration approaches

1. Integrating Agile and UCD as two separate processes
2. Incorporating UCD techniques into Agile
3. Adapting or extending Agile practices to take UCD into account
4. Adapting or extending organisational practices to suit AUCDI
5. Adapting or extending UCD techniques to suit Agile development process
6. Proposing a tool support for the integration
7. Introducing new team roles
8. Investigating developers and UCD practitioners engagement

Agile and UCD Integration research provides a plethora of methods and techniques, however, the mapping study revealed that non of the available research take into consideration the organizational capabilities as a factor that may facilitate or hinder the utilisation of any of those recommended methods or techniques interest [28]. Although AUCDI research is growing, nevertheless, the maturation process of Agile development processes and UCD and its constituents has not been directly approached [27]. There is an absence of an AUCDI maturity model that can allow organisations to conduct an analysis of the current state in order to: pinpoint its weaknesses and strengths in deploying Agile processes and UCD, determine whether the organisation is sufficiently mature for AUCDI, and identify the potential difficulties that could develop during the AUCDI process in order to mitigate them beforehand [27].

3 Research Method

From 2008 till 2014 the researchers investigated the suitability of utilizing maturity models in the context of Agile processes. A series of studies [22–28] were conducted and published as a foundation for developing the maturity model proposed in this paper: first, A Systematic Literature Review (SLR) [25] that identified and classified AUCDI challenges and explored the proposed practices to deal with them. Second, an interview study of industrial AUCDI attempts that identified the AUCDI difficulties and integration methods [24]. Third, an interview study [22, 26, 27] that evaluated the suitability of two Usability Maturity Models (UMMs): Nielsen model [18, 19] and Usability Maturity Model-Human Centrdness Scale (UMM-HCS) [6] for utilization in assessing usability maturity levels in the context of Agile projects. The results of the SLR [25] and the empirical studies [22, 24, 26] were utilised in developing a set of dimensions that represent fundamental elements that affect the AUCDI process. These dimensions were used in the development of a lightweight descriptive maturity model for integrating agile processes and UCD. Descriptive maturity models are used as a diagnostic tool to assess the current capabilities of the examined entity against specific criteria [2]. The AUCDI Maturity model addresses the AUCDI activities, success factors, and challenges [27].

4 Knowledge Base

AUCDI dimensions represent fundamental elements that affect the integration of Agile development processes and UCD. The knowledge base used for constructing the AUCDI dimensions included theoretical sources, literature reviews and empirical sources as illustrated below.

Theoretical Sources: Since the aim was to provide AUCDI dimensions that does not conflict with both Agile values and principles and UCD principles thus two theoretical sources were utilised. These sources were: first, the Agile Manifesto to ensure that none of the proposed processes or practices for integration conflict with Agile values and principles. Second, a number of sources for describing UCD principles and activities so as to ensure concrete guidance in regards to integrating UCD into the overall project plan and all phases in the product development life cycle via clear milestones for UCD activities along the software development process. Thus UCD principles and activities discussed in ISO 13407, and UCD Processes from KESSU 2.2 [11] were considered.

Literature Reviews: A number of issues were taken into consideration to formulate the AUCDI dimensions. First, Agile and UCD differences and commonalities since they represent divergence and convergence points that can hinder or enhance the integration. Second, AUCDI integration success factors in order to include them as integration processes or practices in the proposed dimensions. Thus two literature reviews were conducted, the first, a systematic literature review to investigate AUCDI challenges, strategies and success factors [25, 27] that included a total of 71 AUCDI experience reports, lessons learned, and success and failure AUCDI case studies. This SLR resulted in identifying the differences and commonalities between Agile and UCD, AUCDI challenges, success factors and practices. The second literature review focused on usability maturity models. The results of the UMMs literature review revealed the UMMs deficiencies in the quantity of published research in the public domain in general and on empirical validation in particular and lack of a UMM that is initially created for use in the context of Agile processes [27].

Empirical Sources: Two empirical studies were conducted and their findings provided insights for the proposed AUCDI dimensions. These empirical sources were: first, an interview study that involved 14 participants from 11 companies in five different countries to investigate industrial AUCDI practices [24]. This empirical study investigated the difficulties that hinder AUCDI attempts, the integration methods, and practices utilised by industrial practitioners to tackle those difficulties. Second, an interview study whose purpose was two-fold: to investigate the relationship between the success of AUCDI attempts and usability maturity level and to investigate the suitability of UMMs for utilisation in the context of Agile processes. This study utilised Nielsen Model [18, 19] and UMM-HCS [6] in assessing the usability maturity level of five AUCDI case studies and was reported in [22, 26]. The findings from Nielsen model and UMM-HCS revealed their deficiencies in addressing the specifics, activities, success factors and challenges identified within the AUCDI domain. Moreover, both Nielsen model and UMM-HCS were found to be deficient in their theoretical foundations with respect to maturation, scoring scheme, advice on the assessment of criteria, terminology used and accuracy of some practices [22, 26].

5 AUCDI Dimensions

The objective of this section is to discuss a set of dimensions that represent fundamental elements that affect the integration of Agile processes and UCD. These dimensions will act as the foundation for developing a descriptive multidimensional AUCDI maturity model. This section argues that AUCDI is dependent on four main dimensions: UCD infrastructure; AUCDI process; people involved in the integration process; and UCD continuous improvement.

5.1 Dimension 1: UCD Infrastructure

Usability research is situated in an organisational context, requires organisational knowledge, and depend on organisational involvement and can motivate organisational changes [30]. UCD infrastructure involves a number of organisational elements that need to be available in order to achieve successful integration of Agile processes and UCD. The importance of UCD infrastructure is that it signifies a high maturity for AUCDI since in the absence of this infrastructure AUCDI will be dependent on the usability champion's efforts or development team members in achieving the integration. As a result the integration will occur on per project basis based on the availability of development team skills and interest rather than on an organisational policy that encourages and enforces AUCDI throughout all projects. UCD infrastructure as a component is composed of a number of sub-components: funds, staff, tools, methods, management support, training, utilisation of standards, patterns and style guides and colocation of developers and UCD practitioners.

5.2 Dimension 2: AUCDI Process

The second dimension is the presence of an AUCDI process that takes into consideration the iterative and incremental nature of Agile processes. This AUCDI process focuses on the planning and implementation of UCD activities and principles into the Agile development life cycle so as to achieve the integration. This involves the following issues: planning for the inclusion of UCD activities in the project plan, providing both developers and UCD practitioners with a road map on their roles and responsibilities, executing UCD activities throughout the Agile cycles and synchronizing the efforts of UCD practitioners and developers, etc.

The AUCDI process integrates UCD related activities throughout the Agile development life cycle via milestones for UCD activities along the development process. This is achieved via the inclusion of detailed activities of user requirement gathering, feedback and design evaluation as well as explicating integration work products, work flows, roles, and responsibilities. It is based on the ISO 13407 UCD activities and UCD processes of KESSU 2.2 [9]. However, the AUCDI process extends those founding UCD processes and activities by addressing the AUCDI activities, success factors, and challenges.

The AUCDI process is based around a number of processes that are achieved through the implementation of a set of practices that can be perceived as sub-processes of a process. These processes are: planning the UCD process, user analysis, task analysis, identification and understanding of user requirements, identification and understanding of user interface design requirements, lightweight documentation, synchronization efforts between UCD practitioners and developers, coordination and effective scheduling of UCD practitioners and developers activities, interaction design, user task design, usability evaluation. Each of these processes has a set of subsequent practices. Processes and their associated practices utilise and produce associated work products that take the form of designs, documents, prototypes, working code, training courses, or individual awareness, etc. The AUCDI process adopts parallel tracks [16] for coordinating the work of developers and UCD practitioners. Parallel tracks involves performing the implementation and design as two equal and highly interrelated tracks. The parallel track is organised around a number of cycles: cycle 1, involves work by designers on designing interfaces for features to be implemented by developers in cycle 2. Then low or high fidelity prototypes are built to test the design. Design problems that were revealed during the usability tests are corrected, fixed in the prototypes and retested. This cycle continues until the designs achieve their design goals. Developers use cycle 1 in working on features with high development costs and little user interface. Figure 1 presents the main AUCDI processes and practices.

5.3 Dimension 3: People

The AUCDI process involves customers, users, developers, UCD practitioners and XP coach in case of XP, Scrum master and product owner in case of Scrum.

Customers. Agile approaches require development teams to include customer representatives. In XP, the customer is a fundamental part of the development team and is expected to be responsible of a set of tasks, for example, generation of requirements and acceptance tests, answering queries of developers, discussing user stories, setting product priorities, providing feedback on iterations and facilitating emergent

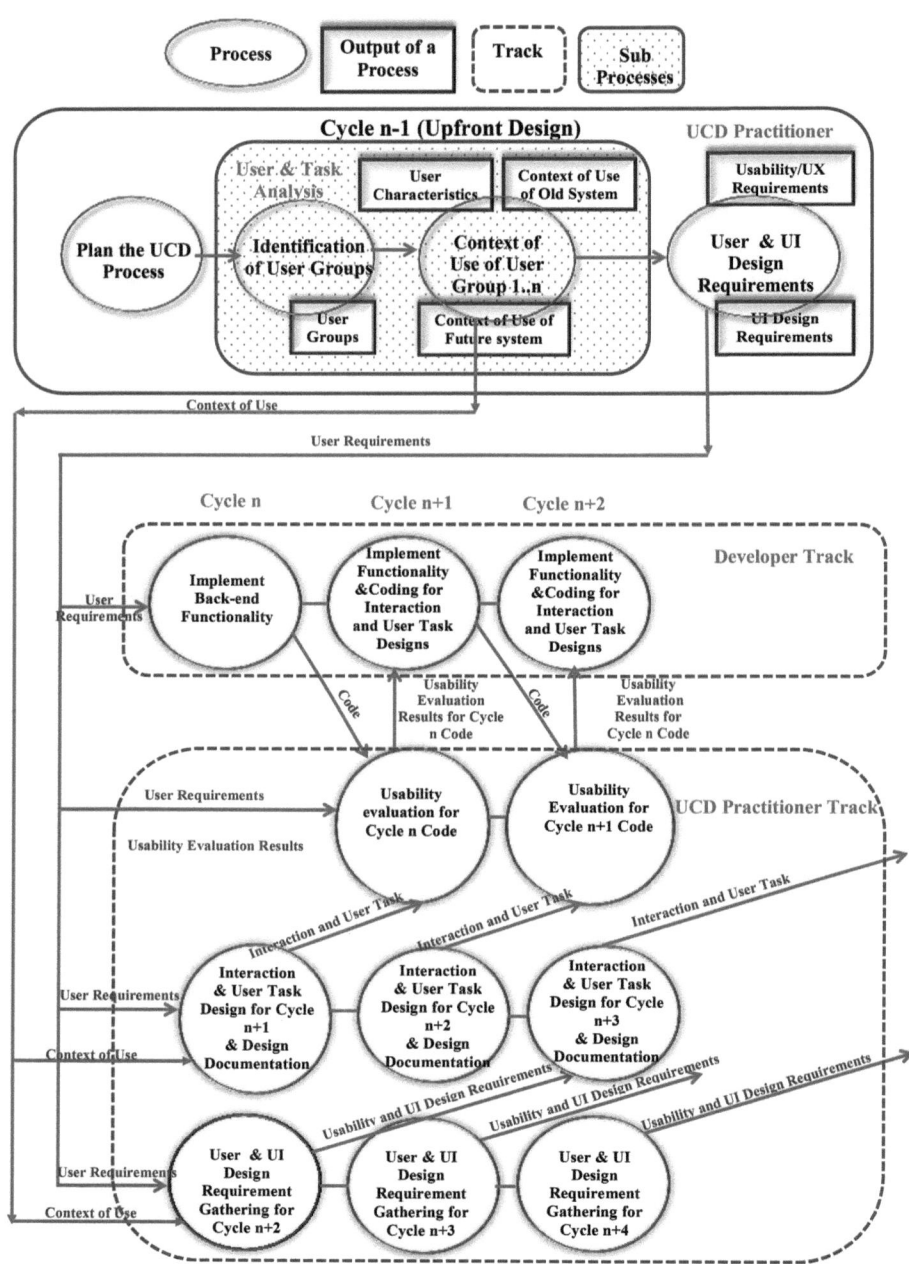

Fig. 1. AUCDI process

requirements [1]. The important issues that are related to customers in order to achieve AUCDI are: awareness of Agile and UCD principles and activities, attitude, and early and continuous involvement.

Users. Software engineering emphasizes the importance of identifying users, understanding their goals and priorities and actively involving them in uncovering requirements [13]. Understanding users is important but user involvement in the development process is also important and this entails early and continuous involvement of users who represent the larger user population [29]. Agile processes rarely differentiate between customers and users. This resulted in Agile approaches paying little attention to users and their roles in the development process [3]. However, XP focuses on users since the on-site customer is supposed to be a potential user [29]. Nevertheless, there is little research on their number and selection method [20] although they are responsible for prioritising requirements and choosing what goes in or out of an iteration [29]. The practices that are related to users in order to achieve successful AUCDI are: identification and selection of users, and early continuous involvement.

UCD Practitioners. Agile teams' structure varies; some teams have a dedicated UCD practitioner and others do not. This can negatively impact the quality of product's usability or user experience. The interface designer place on Agile teams is ill defined [4]. There is a scarcity of a specialized role in Agile teams with the skills and responsibility to coordinate the work of interaction design [3]. As a result usability and design lies in the hands of the customers or developers and users [3]. Thus customers or users are held responsible to define product features they want, prioritize them, and communicate them to developers [3]. The important practices that are related to UCD practitioners in order to achieve successful Agile and UCD integration are: competence, awareness, and attitude.

Developers. Successful integration of the UX team requires full collaboration and cooperation with cross functional team members [17]. Agile development strongly emphasizes team interaction between people. Developers' and UCD practitioners' interaction in Agile teams occur at different times with different forms. This interaction could occur in the form of communication, collaboration or cooperation. The important practices that are related to UCD practitioners in order to achieve Agile and UCD integration are: awareness, and attitude.

5.4 Dimension 4: UCD Continuous Improvement

This dimension has a number of practices as follows:

- A UCD monitoring process across projects.
- A systematic improvement process for UCD activities, methods, and skills.
- Benchmarking product's usability and/or user experience against competitive products' usability and/or user experience.
- Product decisions emerge from end user and customer studies and are targeted to meet users needs and expectations.

6 A Maturity Model for Integrating Agile Development Processes and User Centred Design

The AUCDI Maturity Model utilised the proposed dimensions in the development of a lightweight multidimensional descriptive maturity model for integrating Agile processes and UCD that contributes to provision of structure of AUCDI efforts via providing organisations with a set of dimensions, processes, and practices that act as a road map for successful AUCDI thus it can be used by organisations for both process definition and process assessment.

6.1 Maturity Stages for AUCDI Model

Maturity stages are evolutionary successive stages or levels that signify step by step patterns of evolution and change designating the desirable or current organizational capabilities against a specific class of entities [21]. The maturity stages for AUCDI maturity model are shown in Table 1.

Table 1. Maturity stages for AUCDI maturity model

Stage	Definition
Level 0: Not Possible	AUCDI is discouraged. There is a general unwillingness to integrate UCD into the Agile development process. Management and development teams do not seem to value or understand UCD
Level 1: Possible	AUCDI is not discouraged. There exists a general willingness to perform it. One or few development team members understand the value and meaning of UCD and the benefits of AUCDI
Level 2: Encouraged	Organisational culture encourages AUCDI. Value, benefits and meaning of UCD is recognised. AUCDI is achieved in some projects
Level 3: Enabled/Practiced	AUCDI is practiced. UCD methods, tools, workspace and qualified staff exist to enable the integration activities. Management supports and promotes the integration of Agile and UCD
Level 4: Managed	Employees are expected to perform AUCDI. Training is available. AUCDI activities are part of the development life cycle. UCD methods, tools, workspace, cycles and qualified staff for supporting AUCDI activities are available. Team Leaders exhibit awareness and commitment to UCD and provide a strategy for achieving Agile UCD integration throughout all development projects. Development team exhibits awareness and commitment to AUCDI. Customer(s) exhibits awareness and commitment to AUCDI
Level 5: Continuous Improvement	AUCDI processes are reviewed for assessing the status-quo and plan for improvement. UCD methods, tools, guidelines, workspace and qualified staff are widely accepted, regularly monitored and continuously improved

6.2 AUCDI Maturity Model Domain Components and Sub-components

A domain component is a major, independent aspect that is significant to a particular domain maturity e.g. critical success factors, barriers to entry [7]. Whereas domain sub-components assist in the development of assessment questions used in the maturity questionnaire, enable richer analysis of maturity results, represents specific capability areas that enable targeted maturity level improvements, and improve the ability to present maturity results in order to meet the needs of target audience. The goal is to attain domain components and sub-components that are collectively exhaustive and mutually exclusive [7]. Figure 2 represents domain components/dimensions and sub-components identified for the AUCDI maturity model. The AUCDI maturity model is composed of three components: first, a multidimensional reference model that has a set of fundamental elements that affect AUCDI and thus should be reflected in the model and examined in an assessment. Second, a performance scale to rate the project's and organisation's performance in the assessed elements included in the AUCDI reference model. Third, an assessment procedure to provide practical guidance for performing the assessment. Further details on these components are discussed below and full details are discussed in [27]:

Multidimensional AUCDI Reference Model: The multidimensional AUCDI reference model. This reference model is composed of a set of dimensions that represent fundamental elements that affect the integration of Agile development processes and UCD and thus should be examined in an assessment. These elements are included in the AUCDI reference model. The results of the assessment can help organisations assess their current status and all the factors that impact AUCDI process and pinpoint weaknesses and strengths in order to pinpoint improvement areas. Those dimensions were discussed earlier in Sect. 5. Further details on these dimensions are included in [27].

Performance Scale: The performance scale (scoring scheme) helps the assessors to rate organisational performance in regards to the examined AUCDI elements included in the AUCDI reference model. The closer the organisation achieves the AUCDI reference model requirements, the higher its ratings.

Assessment Procedure: The assessment procedure provides guidance to AUCDI assessors to assess the organisation's and project's capability to integrate Agile and UCD. The assessment procedure is composed of the following:

1. **Maturity Recording Sheet:** This is used to provide assessors with a template to record their assessment of the different AUCDI processes and practices.
2. **Maturity Levels Performance Rating:** Assessors can use the performance rating of the AUCDI maturity levels to compare the recorded scoring in the maturity recording sheet with the performance rating of the AUCDI maturity levels to determine the organisation's AUCDI maturity level.
3. **Typical Quotes:** A number of typical quotes were put together that signify each AUCDI maturity level. These quotes provide assessors with a benchmark to compare their maturity level and the assessor can use these quotes to ensure that he has

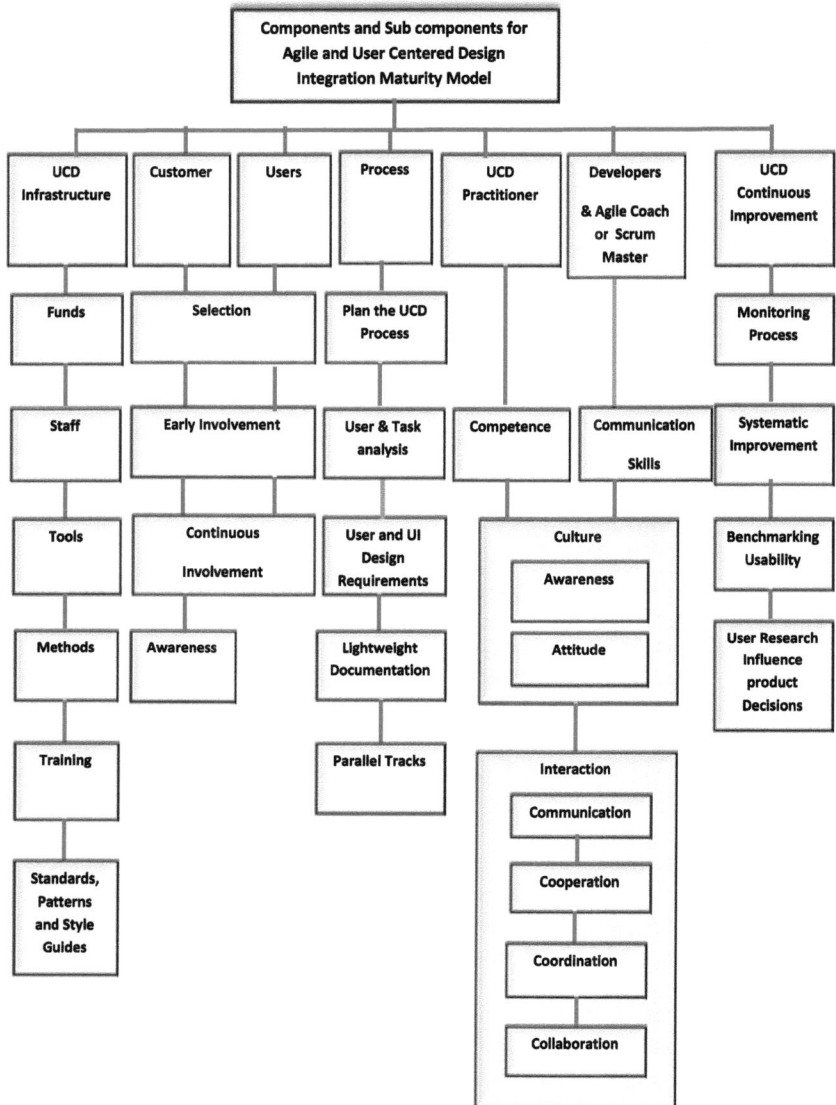

Fig. 2. Domain components and sub-components for the AUCDI maturity model

correctly assessed the organisational AUCDI maturity level. The inclusion of typical quotes as a guideline for assessors was used in Crosby [5], Earthy [6] in Quality Maturity Grid and UMM-HCS respectively.

4. **Assessment Guidelines:** A set of assessment guidelines were put together in order to provide assessors by a clear road map for conducting the assessment.

The assessment results are utilised in generating an assessment report that includes an executive summary with the maturity level and an AUCDI maturity profile. The AUCDI maturity profile indicates the degree of satisfaction of practices and whether it is unsatisfied or needs improvement. Full details on all components and sub-components can be found in [27].

7 AUCDI Maturity Model Evaluation and Evolution

7.1 Evaluation of the AUCDI Maturity Model

Maturity models' testing should focus on two aspects: the model's construct and the model instruments [7]. Content validity is assessed as to how domain representation is complete. The literature review extent and breadth of the covered domain provides a measure of content validity [7]. Content validity was addressed via conducting a SLR on the AUCDI domain [25] to ensure that the model's theoretical basis is sound. Face validity is assessed by the achievement of good translations of the constructs. Populating the model via complementary methods assist in achieving face validity [7]. Face validity was addressed in the AUCDI maturity model via a set of complementary methods that involved theoretical sources, literature reviews and empirical sources and was reported in Sect. 4. Moreover, maturity model constructs should be tested for simplicity, completeness, ease of use, understandability, operationality, efficiency and impact on the environment and users [15]. Whereas the model instruments need to be tested for validity to ensure they measure what it was intended to measure and reliability to verify that obtained results are repeatable and accurate [15]. Thus an evaluation form was designed [23] in order to evaluate the various aspects related to the model construct and instruments via expert reviewers.

The evaluation of the AUCDI maturity model so far included an expert evaluation of the model. The domain expert evaluation process involved a number of steps: choosing domain experts, inviting them to evaluate the model, and evaluating the model. The evaluation results resulted in the models evolution into subsequent versions.

Choosing Domain Experts. Choosing an expert panel was facilitated by the SLR results, which gave an overview of the key domain experts whether from industry or from academia. The selection of the AUCDI domain expert panel occurred via preparing a preliminary list of potential candidates who are experts in the domain of integrating Agile and UCD.

Inviting AUCDI Domain Experts. An email was sent to the chosen AUCDI domain experts with two attachments: an informed consent form and the AUCDI maturity model documentation. The AUCDI domain expert evaluation form that was designed in order to be used to conduct the evaluation was published in [23]. The members of the AUCDI domain expert panel were encouraged to elaborate on their answers and to suggest any justified updates or improvements. The result of the AUCDI maturity model expert evaluation led to the evolution of the original AUCDI maturity model into a number of subsequent versions as shown in Sect. 7.2.

7.2 AUCDI Maturity Model Evolution

This section discusses the AUCDI maturity model's evolution into subsequent versions as a result of expert evaluation. The changes to the model and the reasons behind these changes were recorded and analysed. The valuable evaluation that was received from expert reviewers were used to refine the model as follows:

Version 1.0: Dr. Paul Cairns feedback led to transferring the questions in AUCDI domain expert evaluation form into statements, using simpler terms in question wording, and adding questions to elaborate on reviewer's answers.

Version 2.0 to 2.2: Based on AUCDI domain experts' feedback the following changes were made:

- Maturity level 5 description was updated to include a process for reviewing and assessing guidelines.
- Training practices were updated to include UCD awareness training to product owner. Further product owner features were added to the people dimension. Those included understanding of UCD and UCD practitioner role.
- The description of standards, patterns, and style guides was edited to indicate their role in ensuring consistency across products and re-usability and their importance in improving projects developed by small agile teams.
- Early work phase description was edited to refer to the communication between UCD practitioners and architects to check the project's technical feasibility. Moreover, the description was edited to include its utilisation in acquiring feedback from management and sales department (Table 2).

Table 2. Evolution of AUCDI maturity model

Version	Date	Reviewer
1.0	7/3/2013	Dr. Paul Cairns
2.0	21/4/2014	Mona Singh
2.1	23/4/2014	Jim Ungar
2.2	30/4/2014	Jason Chong Lee

8 Conclusion and Future Work

This paper reported on the development of a lightweight, descriptive maturity model for integrating agile development processes and UCD. The maturity model addresses the specifics, requirements, activities, success factors, and challenges identified within the AUCDI domain. This AUCDI maturity model can be used for both process definition and process assessment. Process definition is embodied via providing organisations with a set of dimensions, processes, and practices that act as a road map for successful AUCDI. This AUCDI maturity model provides organisations with a profound and thorough understanding of AUCDI specifics, activities, roles, timing, responsibilities, success factors, and challenges. Process assessment focuses on providing organisations with a diagnostic tool to assess both the capability and performance for AUCDI. The process assessment results in identifying AUCDI weaknesses and strengths. The results of this assessment can be communicated to: first, management to provide them with a better understanding of the issues involved in consistently developing products with high and competitive usability level as well as pinpoint AUCDI hindrance. Second, developers to provide them with a better understanding of usability and UCD. Third, UCD practitioners by pinpointing areas that require improvement in usability processes and practices.

Future work involves utilising the model in a number of case studies to assess the current AUCDI capability, identify the strengths and weaknesses related to AUCDI and provide guidance for the improvement actions of the organisation.

Acknowledgment. Thanks to Professors Helen Sharp and Tim Kelly, Dr. Mona Singh, Dr. Jim Ungar and Dr. Jason Lee Chong for their feedback that led to the model's improvement.

References

1. Beck, K.: Extreme Programming Explained. Embrace Change, 2nd edn. Addison Wesley Longman Publishing, Boston (2004)
2. Becker, J., Knackstedt, R., Poppelbus, J.: Developing maturity models for IT management. Bus. Inf. Syst. Eng. **1**, 213–222 (2009)
3. Blomkvist, S.: Towards a model for bridging agile development and user-centered design. In: Seffah, A., Gulliksen, J., Desmarais, M. (eds.) Human-Centered Software Engineering - Integrating Usability in the Software Development Lifecycle. Human-Computer Interaction Series, vol. 8, pp. 219–244. Springer, Netherlands (2005)
4. Brown, J., Lindgaard, G., Biddle, R.: Collaborative events and shared artefacts: agile interaction designers and developers working toward common aims. In: Agile Conference (AGILE), pp. 87–96, August 2011
5. Crosby, P.: Quality is Free: The Art of Making Quality Certain. McGraw Hill, New York (1978)
6. Earthy, J.: Usability maturity model: human centredness scale: INUSE project deliverable D5.1.4(s) Version 1.2. Technical report, Llyod's Register (1998)
7. DeBruin, T., Freeze, R., Kaulkarni, U., Rosemann, M.: Understanding the main phases of developing a maturity assessment model. In: Australian Conference on Information Systems, New South Wales (2005)
8. Detweiler, M.: Managing UCD within agile projects. Interactions **14**(3), 40–42 (2007)
9. Jokela, T.: Evaluating the user-centredness of development organisations: conclusions and implications from empirical usability capability maturity assessments. Interact. Comput. **16**(6), 1095–1132 (2004)
10. Jokela, T., Abrahamsson, P.: Usability assessment of an extreme programming project: close co-operation with the customer does not equal to good usability. In: Bomarius, F., Iida, H. (eds.) PROFES 2004. LNCS, vol. 3009, pp. 393–407. Springer, Heidelberg (2004)
11. Jokela, T.: Making user-centred design common sense: striving for an unambiguous and communicative UCD process model. In: Proceedings of the Second Nordic Conference on Human-Computer Interaction, NordiCHI 2002, New York, pp. 19–26. ACM (2002)

12. Kane, D.: Finding a place for discount usability engineering in agile development: throwing down the gauntlet. In: Proceedings of the Conference on Agile Development, ADC 2003, Washington, DC. IEEE Computer Society (2003)
13. Kotonya, G., Sommerville, I.: Requirements Engineering: Processes and Techniques. Wiley, Sussex (1998)
14. Lee, J.C., McCrickard, S., Stevens, T.: Examining the foundations of agile usability with eXtreme scenario-based design. In: Agile Conference, August 2009
15. March, S., Smith, G.: Design and natural science research on information technology. Decis. Support Syst. **15**, 251–266 (1995)
16. Miller, L.: Case study of customer input for a successful product. In: Proceedings of the Agile Development Conference, ADC 2005, Washington, DC, pp. 225–234. IEEE Computer Society (2005)
17. Najafi, M., Toyoshiba, L.: Two case studies of user experience design and agile development. In: Proceedings of the Agile 2008, AGILE 2008, Washington, DC. IEEE Computer Society (2008)
18. Nielsen, J.: Neilsen's Alertbox: Corporate Usability Maturity: Stages 1-4 (2006)
19. Nielsen, J.: Neilsen's Alertbox: Corporate Usability Maturity: Stages 5-8 (2006)
20. Rittenbruch, M., McEwan, G., Ward, N., Mansfield, T., Bartenstein, D.: Extreme participation - moving extreme programming towards participatory design. In: Proceedings of the Seventh Biennial Participatory Design Conference (2002)
21. Rosemann, M., deBruin, T.: Towards a business process managemet maturity model. In: European Conference on Information Systems, Germany (2005)
22. Salah, D., Paige, P., Cairns, P.: Observations on utilizing usability maturity model-human centrdness scale in integrating agile development processes and user-centred design. In: Rout, T., O'Connor, R.V., Dorling, A. (eds.) SPICE 2015. Communications in Computer and Information Science, vol. 526, pp. 159–173. Springer, Switzerland (2015)
23. Salah, D., Paige, R., Cairns, P.: An evaluation template for expert review of maturity models. In: Jedlitschka, A., Kuvaja, P., Kuhrmann, M., Männistö, T., Münch, J., Raatikainen, M. (eds.) PROFES 2014. LNCS, vol. 8892, pp. 318–321. Springer, Heidelberg (2014)
24. Salah, D., Paige, P., Cairns, P.: A practitioner perspective on integrating agile and user centered design. In: The British HCI Conference (HCI 2014) (2014)
25. Salah, D., Paige, P., Cairns, P.: A systematic literature review for agile development processes and user centred design integration. In: The International Conference on Evaluation and Assessment in Software Engineering, London (2014)
26. Salah, D., Paige, R., Cairns, P.: Integrating agile development processes and user centred design- a place for usability maturity models? In: Sauer, S., Bogdan, C., Forbrig, P., Bernhaupt, R., Winckler, M. (eds.) HCSE 2014. LNCS, vol. 8742, pp. 108–125. Springer, Heidelberg (2014)
27. Mostafa, D.: Maturity models in the context of integrating agile development processes and user centred design. Phd thesis. The University of York, York (2013)
28. Salah, D.: A framework for the integration of user centered design and agile software development processes. In: 33rd International Conference on Software Engineering (ICSE), May 2011
29. Sharp, H., Robinson, H., Segal, J.: Integrating user-centred design and software engineering: a Role for eXtreme programming? In: BCS-HCI Group's 7th Educators Workshop: Effective Teaching and Training in HCI (2004)
30. Uldall-Espersen, T., Frokjaer, E., Blandford, A., Jokela, T.: Increasing the impact of usability work in software development. In: CHI 2007 Extended Abstracts on Human Factors in Computing Systems, CHI EA 2007, New York, pp. 2873–2876. ACM (2007)

Analysis of Tools for Assessing the Implementation and Use of Agile Methodologies in SMEs

Mirna Muñoz[1(✉)], Jezreel Mejia[1], Brisia Corona[1],
Jose A. Calvo-Manzano[2], Tomas San Feliu[2], and Juan Miramontes[1]

[1] Centro de Investigación en Matemáticas, Av. Universidad no 222,
98068 Zacatecas, Mexico
{mirna.munoz,jmejia,brisia.corona,
juan.miramontes}@cimat.mx

[2] Escuela Técnica Superior de Ingenieros Informáticos, UPM,
Campus de Montegancedo S/N, 28660 Madrid, Spain
{joseantonio.calvomanzano,tomas.sanfeliu}@upm.es

Abstract. Nowadays, small and medium enterprises are using agile methodologies as an effort to produce software to meet the time requested by the market. However, the lack of knowledge on how to use them adequately results in their empirical adoption with an inefficient software development. In this context, a set of software tools that pretend to help SMEs in the implementation of an agile methodology have been developed. Unfortunately, most of them list a set of questions without providing the expected support. This paper aims to analyze a set of the most used software tools found in the literature in order to identify which elements are covered and focused by the software tools. Besides, this analysis allowed us to identify deficiencies in the actual tools and a set of key elements that should be taken into account to help SMEs in the correct implementation and the achievement of maturity on the use of an agile methodology.

Keywords: Agile assessing tools · Agile methodologies · Small and medium enterprises · SMEs · Agile methodologies implementation and use

1 Introduction

In recent years the growth in the importance of software development provides the opportunity for small and medium enterprises (SMEs) to produce software products and services in order to satisfy the market needs. Due to this situation, in Latin America around 99 % of businesses are composed of SMEs [1, 2].

In this context, SMEs have a continuous need for improving their development processes in order to stay in the market and to achieve a steady growth. Then, SMEs are implementing agile methodologies in an effort to deliver software as quickly as it is required by the market and to increase their productivity.

Unfortunately, most of time, the implementation of an agile methodology is based on the benefits that have occurred in other organizations [3, 4]. As a result, SMEs adopt them in an empirical way resulting in an inefficient software development. Moreover, according to [4] the organizations that are implementing an agile methodology, have a critical period to decline its use that happens between the first and the second year.

This situation is because there is a lack of knowledge in the correct implementation of an agile methodology, even when the Agile Manifesto [5] provides principles that could serve as a guide in the implementation of the agile methodology.

This paper aims to analyze a set of the most used software tools found in the literature in order to identify which elements are covered and focused by the software tools, it is also focused on assessing if an organization has adopted and used in a correct way the agile methodology.

Moreover, this analysis allows us to identify the key elements that should be taken into account to provide a complete support to SMEs in the right implementation of an agile methodology as well as in the maturity on the use of the agile methodology.

After the introduction, the rest of the paper is organized as follows: Sect. 2 presents background of this research paper; Sect. 3 shows the procedure established to perform the analysis; Sect. 4 shows the results of the analysis, and finally, Sect. 5 shows the conclusions and future work.

2 Background

According to Highsmith in [6] "the agility is the ability of both to create and to respond to change in order to profit in a turbulent business environment".

In this context, the Agile Manifesto [5] provides the principles and values that should be reflected in the use of an agile methodology to address a rapid development of software and to face the problems of the different steps of software development in an agile way.

However, not all organizations that adopt an agile methodology achieve the use of it successfully. Therefore, the background of this paper is a research work that has been raised based on the next assumptions:

- Most of the time the implementation of an agile methodology is based on the benefits that occur in other organizations and not following a guide to implement it in a correct way.
- There exists a critical period in an organization that implements an agile methodology to decline its use, between the first and second year, this is due of the lack of knowledge on how to implement and mature its use.
- The lack of knowledge of how to implement an agile methodology in a correct way is reflected in an inefficient software development.

Taking into account the assumptions listed before, this research work aims to provide a method that helps SMEs to evaluate the use of an agile methodology and to evolve toward increasing the maturity in its use.

To achieve that, as first step, we performed a systematic literature review following the protocol of Kitchenham [7]. The systematic review was focused on establishing the state of art of frameworks, methods and methodologies to assess the implementation and use of agile methodologies in SMEs, because we think organizations need to know what they are doing as "agile methodology" in order to improve the use of the agile methodology, and therefore, to get an efficient software development.

To perform the systematic review, three questions were defined:

- (RQ1). What models, methodologies or standards are used in SMEs?
- (RQ2). What is the percentage of SMEs in Latin America that use agile methodologies?
- (RQ3). Are there frameworks, methods, or methodologies for assessing or evaluating agile methodologies in SMEs?

The complete systematic review of this research, which includes both the developed protocol and the obtained results, was reported in [8].

Then, the scope of this paper is derived from the results obtained of the third question, where 18 papers that present proposals to assess agile methodologies were identified (see Table 1).

As Table 1 shows, after analyzing the tools paper[1], it was found a list of 41 proposal tools that aim to provide support to the SMEs assessment of an agile methodology. Therefore, "tools" with 41 proposals became the most used evaluation type due to the number of proposals.

Then, information regarding the 41 tools was collected and analyzed in order to identify which elements are covered and focused by software tools, which is the goal of this paper.

Table 1. Proposals developed to assess agile methodologies.

Evaluation type	Quantity of papers	Number of proposals
Survey	6	6
Checklist	1	1
Evaluation methodology	2	2
Framework	5	5
Evaluation model	3	3
Tools	1	41

3 Analysis Procedure

This section shows the procedure established to perform the analysis of software tools to achieve the goal of this paper.

It is important to mention that a "tool" for this research is a software tool developed to help SMEs in the assessment of the implementation of an agile methodology in order to provide support to the organizations to improve the use of the agile methodology to achieve an efficient software development.

---

[1] M. Steven Palmquist; Mary Ann Lapham; Suzanne Miller; Timothy Chick; Ipek Ozkaya. Parallel Worlds: Agile and Waterfall Differences and Similarities. SEIR, 1, 101. (2013).

To address the analysis two questions were established: (1) which is the most common kind of software tool used for assessing agile methodologies? and (2) what are the aspects focused by the software tools in the assessment of an agile methodology?

Then, two aspects were established: (A) the analysis procedure and (B) a set of criteria to be applied.

A. Analysis Procedure. Two different analyses were performed according to the goals of this research:

(1) *Kind of tool*: this analysis is focused on classifying the tools according to the kind of tool; that could be: checklist, surveys, questionnaires, test, toolkit and others. The kind of tools is briefly described below:

- *Checklist*: tool focused on assessing the agile methodology providing *"a list of things to be checked or done"*. It helps to ensure if a set of tasks is been carried out in a complete way reducing failures associated to human memory and attention.
- *Surveys*: tool focused on assessing the agile methodology providing a set of short questions to be answered and providing a set of short option answers. It helps to ask many people a set of questions in order to gather information about what most people do or think about something.
- *Questionnaires*: tool focused on assessing the agile methodology by providing a set of questions to be answered and providing spaces for collecting open and large answers. It helps to collect facts or opinions about something. An expert should analyze the answers.
- *Test*: tool focused on assessing the agile methodology providing a set of no more than 10 questions for measuring someone's skills, knowledge, or abilities. The questions should be answered through selecting an answer from a set of short sentences or words with an associated value.
- *Toolkit*: tools focused on assessing the agile methodologies by providing software designed to evaluate agility through excel, word or online applications that allow collecting data regarding agile methodologies.
- *Others*: tools focused on providing professional consulting.

(2) *Aspects focused:* this analysis is focused on applying the established criteria to each kind of tools in order to identify those aspects focused on the assessment.

B. Established Criteria. In order to achieve an unbiased analysis of the 41 tools, a set of criteria were established. The list of the established criteria is showed in Table 2.

4 Analysis Results

This section shows the analyses performed and their results.

4.1 Kind of Tool

This analysis shows the classification of the 41 assessment tools according to the kind of tool conferring to the classification listed in the "procedure" of Sect. 3. Figure 1 shows a graphic with the classification of the 41 tools by type.

Table 2. Established criteria

Criteria	Description
Assessed methodology	The agile methodology assessed by the tool such as XP, Scrum or others, which include other agile methodologies such as FDD, crystal, kanban, among others
Focus	If the tool is focused on assessing the agile methodology implementation, adoption or both • *Adoption*: the tool is focused on assessing the level of adoption and acceptation of the agile methodology. • *Implementation*: the tool is focused on assessing the set of activities toward the implementation of the agile methodology
Target	What is the scope of the tool, it is generating a discussion or providing a guide
User support	If the tool has a set of instructions to use it
Agile principles	If the tool applies the agile principles
Score	If the tool is based on a specific score to assess the agile methodology

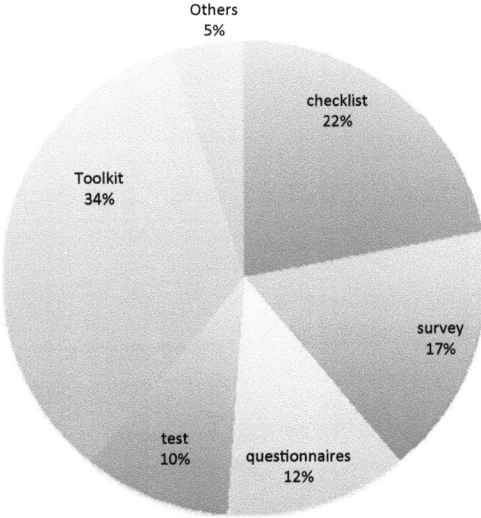

Fig. 1. Tools classified by type.

As Fig. 1 shows, most of tools are based on toolkits and checklists, therefore this data its important in order to understand what kind of tool has better acceptation in an agile environment.

4.2 Aspects Focused

This section shows the results of applying the set of criteria showed in Table 2 of Sect. 3. This analysis aims to identify which aspects are focused by the tools. Next sections provide the analysis by kind of tool and a discussion of the results.

It is important to mention that after collecting the information of the 41 tools, four criteria were applied: (1) tools that have available information in any source; (2) tools that provide a software tool focused on SMEs; (3) tools that provide a software tool to assess an agile methodology and (4) tools that explain clearly how agile principles are applied.

After applying the criteria they were selected those software tools that met at least three of four criteria. Then, 27 tools were selected to perform the analysis.

4.2.1 Checklist Software Tools

The analysis of applying the criteria to the checklist software tools is showed in Table 3.

Table 3. Checklist software tools analysis.

Tool	Assessed methodology	Focus[a]	Target	User support	Agile principles	Score[b]
The unofficial scrum checklist [9]	Scrum	IM	Generates a discussion	Instructions	Yes	NA
Questions for transitioning to agile [10]	Others	IM	Assess	Instructions	Yes	NA
Scrum checklist framework [11]	Scrum	IM	Assess	Instructions	Yes	NA
Corporate agile 10-point checklist [12]	Others	IM	Provides a guide	No	No	NA
Joe's unofficial scrum checklist [13]	Scrum	IM	Generates a discussion	Instructions	Yes	NA
How to measure team agility [14]	Others	IM	Assess	Instructions	Yes	0–4
Open assessments [15]	Scrum	IM	Provides a guide	Instructions	Yes	NA
An organizational transformation checklist [16]	Others	IM	Provides a guide	Instructions	Yes	NA
The InfoQ minibook scrum hard facts: roles. artifacts. All meetings [17]	Others	IM	Provides a guide	No	Yes	NA

[a]Column b values could be: (IM) implementation or (AD) Adoption.
[b]NA means not available.

As Table 3 shows, after applying the established criteria the obtained results are: (a) *assessed methodology*: most of the tools assess other methodologies; (b) *focus*: all of them focus on the implementation of the methodology; (c) *target*: most of them focus on providing a guide for the introduction in an agile environment and only three of them focus on assessing the agile methodology; (d) *user support*: most of them provide instructions for the user on how to use it; (e) *agile principles*: most of them address the agile principles and (f) *score*: none of them has a score to make the assessment.

4.2.2 Surveys Software Tools

The analysis of applying the criteria to the surveys software tools is showed in Table 4.

As Table 4 shows, after applying the established criteria the obtained results are: (a) *assessed methodology*: the half of the tools assess the scrum methodology and the other half of the tools assess other agile methodologies such as Kanban, Dynamic Systems Development Method (DSDM) and Feature Driven Development (FDD); (b) *focus*: most of them focus on the implementation of the methodology; (c) *target*: most of them focus on assessing the agile methodology; (d) *user support*: all of them provide instructions to support the user on how to use it; (e) *agile principles*: Only three of them addresses the agile principles; and; (f) *score*: most of them have a score to make the assessment.

Table 4. Survey software tools analysis.

Tool	Assessed methodology	Focus[a]	Target	User support	Agile principles	Score[b]
42 point test: how agile are you [18]	Scrum & Others	AD	Assess	Instructions	No	1/0
Team barometer [19]	XP	Focus on the relationship among the team	Generates a discussion	Instructions	No	NA
Agile maturity self assessment [20]	Others	AD	Assess	Instructions	No	1/0
Comparative agility [21]	Scrum & XP	IM	Assess	Instructions	Yes	1/0
Agile enterprise [22]	Others	IM	Assess	Instructions	Yes	1/0
Enterprise agility maturity matrix [23]	Scrum, Xp & Others	IM	Assess	Instructions	Yes	NA

[a]Column b values could be: (IM) implementation or (AD) Adoption.
[b]NA means not available.

4.2.3 Questionnaire Software Tools

The analysis of applying the criteria to the checklist tools is showed in Table 5.

As Table 5 shows, after applying the established criteria the obtained results are: (a) *assessed methodology*: both tools assess other agile methodologies such as Kanban, Dynamic Systems Development Method (DSDM) and Feature Driven Development (FDD); (b) *focus*: one focuses on the implementation and the other focuses on the adoption; (c) *target*: both tools focus on assessing the agile methodology; (d) *user support*: both tools provide instructions to support the user on how to use them; (e) *agile principles*: only one addresses the agile principles and (f) *score*: only one has a score to make the assessment.

Table 5. Questionnaire software tools analysis.

Tool	Assessed methodology	Focus[a]	Target	User support	Agile principles	Score[b]
Questionnaire for assessing your client's agility [24]	Others	AD	Assess	Instructions	Yes	1/0
Depth of kanban [25]	Others	IM	Assess	Instructions	No	NA

[a]Column b values could be: (IM) implementation or (AD) Adoption.
[b]NA means not available.

4.2.4 Test Software Tools

The analysis of applying the criteria to the checklist software tools is showed in Table 6.

As Table 6 shows, after applying the established criteria the obtained results are: (a) *assessed methodology*: both tools assess scrum methodology; (b) *focus*: both tools focus on the implementation; (c) *target*: one focuses on providing a guide to the introduction in an agile environment and the other focuses on assessing the agile methodology; (d) *user support*: both tools provide instructions to support the user on how to use them; (e) *agile principles*: both tools address the agile principles; and; (f) *score*: both tools have a score to make the assessment.

Table 6. Tests software tools analysis.

Tool	Assessed methodology	Focus[a]	Target	User support	Agile principles	Score[b]
ScrumButt test aka the nokia test [26]	Scrum	IM	Provides a guide	Instructions	Yes	1/0
Borland agile assessment [27]	Scrum	IM	Assess	Instructions	Yes	1/0

[a]Column b values could be: (IM) implementation or (AD) Adoption.
[b]NA means not available.

4.2.5 Toolkit Software Tools

The analysis of applying the criteria to the toolkit software tools is showed in Table 7.

As Table 7 shows, after applying the established criteria the obtained results are: (a) *assessed methodology*: most of the tools assess other agile methodologies such as Kanban, Dynamic Systems Development Method (DSDM) and Feature Driven Development (FDD); (b) *focus*: most of them focus on both the implementation and the adoption; (c) *target*: most of them focus on assessing the agile methodology; (d) *user support*: all of them provide instructions to support the user on how to use them; (e) *agile principles*: all of them address the agile principles and (f) score: half of them have a score to make the assessment.

Table 7. Tookit software tools analysis.

Tool	Assessed methodology	Focus[a]	Target	User support	Agile principles	Score[b]
Enterprise agile practice assessment tool [28]	Others	AD	Assess	Instructions	Yes	NA
Readiness & fit analysis [29]	Others	AD	Provides a guide	Instructions	Yes	NA
Agile journey index [30]	Others	AD & IM	Provides a guide	Instructions	Yes	1/0
Agile maturity matrix in JIRA[31]	Scrum	AD & IM	Assess	Instructions	Yes	1/0
IBM DevOps practices self assessment [32]	Others	AD & IM	Assess	Instructions	Yes	NA
Ready for agile part 1 and part 2 [33]	Scrum & Others	AD & IM	NA	Instructions	Yes	0-4
Agile health radar [34]	Others	AD & IM	Provides a guide	Instructions	Yes	0-4
Agile essentials (card game) [35]	Others	AD	Provides a guide	Instructions	Yes	NA

[a]Column b values could be: (IM) implementation or (AD) Adoption.
[b]NA means not available.

4.2.6 Best Tools

After analyzing the tool we select those tools that for us are the best tools because they cover the next aspects: (a) they provide instructions to support the user on how to use them; (b) they provide a start point and end of each section they assess and they provide monitoring to the progress through its levels; (c) they have a score to assess the agile methodology; (d) they provide results but do not force the user to pay the consulting to see their results. Table 8 shows the analysis performed to the best tools to identify the aspects covered regarding an agile methodology. Besides, taking into account that six of nine tools are based on assessing scrum methodology, the roles and artifacts of scrum were taken as base to perform the analysis.

Table 8. Analysis of the best tools

Tool	Agile roles focused by the tool	Methodology artefacts
Scrum checklist framework	Product owner, scrum master and scrum team	Product backlog, sprint planning meeting; sprint backlog; daily scrum meeting; sprint execution; sprint review; sprint retrospective and Burndown
Open assessment	Product owner, scrum master and scrum team	Sprint planning meeting; sprint backlog; sprint execution; sprint review, sprint retrospective
42 point test: how agile are you	Product owner and scrum team	Product backlog, sprint planning meeting; sprint backlog; daily scrum meeting; sprint review and sprint retrospective
Enterprise agility maturity matrix	Product owner, scrum master and scrum team	Product backlog; sprint backlog; daily scrum meeting; sprint execution; sprint review, sprint retrospective
Questionnaire for assessing your clients agility	Product owner, scrum master and scrum team	Sprint planning meeting; sprint backlog; daily scrum meting; sprint review and burndown
Enterprise depth of kanban	Scrum team	Product backlog, sprint planning meeting; sprint backlog; sprint review, sprint retrospective and daily scrum meeting
ScrumButt test aka the nokia test	Product owner	Product backlog, sprint planning meeting; sprint backlog; daily scrum meeting; sprint execution; sprint review; sprint retrospective and Burndown
Agile journey index	Scrum master and scrum team	Product backlog; sprint backlog; daily scrum meeting; sprint review, sprint retrospective and burndown

5 Conclusions and Next Steps

Nowadays, there has been an increasing interest of SMEs in the adoption and the implementation of agile methodologies in an effort to achieve an efficient development of software. Unfortunately, the lack of knowledge in the correct implementation of agile methodologies results in an inefficient development of software or even in the decline of use of the agile methodology.

The most common way currently used to assess the use of an agile methodology in SMEs is measuring the use of the methodology based on two aspects: the years that the agile methodology has been continuously incorporated within the organization and the level of individuals using it and the size of the project in which it has been applied. However, this way does not warrant the success in the implementation of an agile methodology.

Therefore, this paper analyzed a set of software tools that aim to support SMEs in the implementation of an agile methodology. However, the results of the analysis showed that the tools do not offer a complete support for SMEs including the assessment, the analysis of the results and the suggested actions according to the results covering both the implementation and use of the agile methodology. Besides, it was identified that in order to provide a complete support to SMEs it is necessary to cover two main aspects: on the one hand it is important to focus on the knowledge regarding the agile methodology such as activities, techniques, tools and metrics; on the other hand it is necessary to focus on the expected behavior of the team members throughout the different activities proposed by the methodology.

As future work, we are developing a method to assess the use and evolution of the use of agile methodologies taking into account the findings of the analysis performed in this paper, focusing on the elements not covered by the software tools as well as the key aspect identified. The method should help the SMEs to identify problems regarding the behavior and the use of artifacts and to provide the findings as well as a guide to improve the use of the agile methodology. To achieve that, the method will provide a software tool to facilitate its use.

References

1. Gasca-Hurtado, G., Manzano, J.C., Giraldo, L.M., Arias, J.A.: Statistical analysis of the implementation for best practices in software development organizations. In: 2013 8th Iberian Conference on Information Systems and Technologies (CISTI), pp. 1–8 (2013)
2. Gómez, G.E., Aguileta, A.A., Ancona, G.B., Gómez, O.S.: Advances in software developments SMEs: a systematic review. Latino Am. J. Softw. Eng. **1**, 7 (2014)
3. VersionOne © 2014. 8th annual state of agile survey. VersionOne, 8, 17 (2014)
4. VersionOne © 2015. 9th annual state of agile survey. VersionOne, 9, 16 (2015)
5. Beck, K., Beedle, M., van Bennekum, A., Cockburn, A., Cunningham, W., Fowler, M., Grenning, J., Highsmith, J., Hunt, A., Jeffries, R., Kern, J., Marick, B., Martin, R.C., Mellor, S., Schwaber, K., Sutherland, J., Thomas, D: Manifesto for agile software development (2001). www.agilemanifesto.org/
6. Chetankumar, P., Ramachandran, M.: Agile maturity model (AMM): a software process improvement framework for agile software development practices. Int. J. Softw. Eng. **2**(1), 3–28 (2009)
7. Kitchenham, B., Charters, S.: Guidelines for Performing Systematic Literature Reviews in Software Engineering, vol. 2 (2007)
8. Corona, B., Miramontes, J., Muñoz, M.: Establishing the state of art of frameworks, methods and methodologies to assess the implementation and use of agile methodologies in SMEs: a systematic review. In: Mejia, J., Muñoz, M., Carrillo, Y., Mitre, H., Mora, J.A. (eds.) Software Engineering Tendencies, 2015 International Conference of Software Process Improvement (2016). CIMAT. ISBN: 978-607-96212-6-1
9. Kniberg, H.: The unofficial scrum checklist (2010). https://goo.gl/D6whaJ
10. Rothman, J.: Questions for transitioning to agile (2013). http://goo.gl/cR3meH
11. Gloger, B.: Scrum checklist (2013). http://goo.gl/4lYspl
12. Yatzeck, E.: Corporate agile 10-point checklist (2012). http://goo.gl/bFrjkY
13. Little, J.: Joe's unofficial scrum checklist (2016). http://goo.gl/z83cyY. Unofficial scrum checklist
14. Lagestee, L.: How to measure team agility (2012). http://goo.gl/fM3h9s
15. Scrum.org. Open assessments (2015). https://www.scrum.org/Assessments/Open-Assessments

16. Sahota, M.: An organizational transformation checklist (2012). http://goo.gl/CPRfyU
17. Sahota, M.: The InfoQ minibook an agile adoption and transformation survival guide (2012). http://goo.gl/yYyWWv
18. Waters, K.: 42 point test: how agile are you (2008). http://goo.gl/VgKF7q
19. Janlén, J.: Team barometer (2014). http://goo.gl/2zLf8V
20. Iver, R.M.: Agile maturity self assessment (2010). http://goo.gl/GkyjVc
21. Rubin, K., Cohn, M.: Comparative agility (2008). https://goo.gl/I039oe
22. Storm-Consulting. Agile enterprise survey (2016). http://goo.gl/uBTdlw
23. DrAgile. Enterprise agile practice assessment tool (2015). http://www.dragile.com/
24. The Digital Business Analyst. Assessing your client's agility - an agility questionnaire (2014). http://goo.gl/g53VCZ
25. Lean-Agile Software Development. Depth of kanban - a good coaching tool (2013). http://goo.gl/gG8pQr
26. Scruminc. ScrumButt test aka the Nokia test (2015). https://goo.gl/2VNsku
27. From the Agile Transformation Trenches. Assessment, borland agile. (2009). http://goo.gl/k71DXm
28. Miller, S.: Is your organization ready for agile? - part 1 (2012). https://goo.gl/gK54Pc
29. Agile Dimensions LLC. Assess – agile journey index (2012). http://goo.gl/hL7VJs
30. Schenck, M.: Agile maturity – how agile is your organization? (2015). http://goo.gl/MjO8SD
31. IBM Corporation. DevOps practices self-assessment (2015). http://goo.gl/bJYFvY
32. Sidky, S.E.: Based on research by A. Ready for agile demo part 2–part1 (2012). http://safeshare.tv/w/HWCJuBVueB
33. Agilityhealth. Agile health radar (2015). http://goo.gl/drl916
34. Jacobson, I.: Agile essentials starter pack | agile practices (2015). https://goo.gl/BFHDtN
35. Schenck, M.: Agile maturity matrix in JIRA (2013). http://goo.gl/weQC4t

Evaluation of Agility Assessment Tools: A Multiple Case Study

Onat Ege Adalı^(✉), Özden Özcan-Top, and Onur Demirörs

Informatics Institute, Middle East Technical University, 06800 Ankara, Turkey
onategeadali@gmail.com, ozdentop@gmail.com, demirors@metu.edu.tr

Abstract. Agile software development has been one of the most important paradigms of software engineering community. Agile methods that are shaped around Agile Manifesto and principles, provide promising results when applied properly in software organizations. Agile assessment models and tools have potential to indicate agile adoption problems at project level or organization level. In the scope of this study, we identified 37 agility assessment tools. Among those tools, we evaluated 11 agility assessment tools based upon 9 criteria within a multiple case study. The purpose of this study is to evaluate existing agility assessment tools to provide an overview about potential uses, advantages and drawbacks. The results of the case study indicate that none of the 11 tools are eligible to fully achieve the 9 criteria.

Keywords: Agile software development · Agility assessment tools · Agile assessments · Agility assessments · Multiple case study

1 Introduction

Agile software development methods have gained widespread popularity [1]. 2014 State of Agile™ survey remarks that 94 % of the organizations surveyed develop software using agile methods [2]. As agile adoption process is not straightforward [3, 4], it is important for organizations to understand their agility levels and gaps towards agility. The best way to that is to evaluate software processes and apply improvement actions continuously. Such a continuous evaluation and improvement need lead researchers to develop different forms of agility assessment approaches. These approaches include; agility assessment models, agility checklists, agility surveys, and agility assessment tools [5]. When agility assessment is performed based upon structured assessment models, assessment findings would clearly indicate where projects stand in terms of agility and which areas of the adopted agile methods need improvement.

There has been significant amount of research based on developing agile assessment models, agile checklists and agile surveys but there hasn't been much research about agile assessment tools guiding the application of these models, checklists, and surveys. In the scope of this study, the term tool is used for templates or software programs that automate and guide the assessment process.

The main objective of this study is to review and evaluate existing agility assessment tools to determine their suitability for agility assessment. In order to achieve this purpose, we defined a research question:

RQ1: To what extent are the current agility assessment tools sufficient to meet the expected criteria?

To answer the research question, we conducted a multiple case study in a software organization that includes 11 assessments each of which refers to evaluated agility assessment tools.

The rest of this paper is organized as follows: In Sect. 2, we refer to the related research on comparison of agility assessment tools and provide a survey of existing agility assessment tools. In Sect. 3, we present the quality criteria to evaluate and compare the assessment tools. In Sect. 4, we give details of the case study. In Sect. 5, we present the results of the case study and give a discussion on the comparison of the tools. Finally in Sect. 6, we provide conclusion and future work.

2 Related Research and Survey of Agility Assessment Tools

This section presents related research on comparison of the agility assessment tools and provides a discussion on the conducted research studies. Also we provide a brief introduction to the agility assessment tools that are subject to our evaluation. It was observed that only a few studies have been conducted on comparison of the agility assessment tools.

In one of their research, Soundararajan and Arthur [5] have reviewed Comparative Agility [6], and Thoughtworks Agile Assessment [7] tools. They compared the tools according to their ability to measure agility. Soundararajan and Arthur concluded that these agility assessment tools "primarily focus on the presence or absence of practices" and they have stated that presence or absence of practices is not sufficient to "indicate an organization's ability to implement an agile method or the effectiveness of an agile method" [5].

In another study [8] Gandomani and Nafchi again reviewed Comparative Agility and Thoughtworks Agile Assessment Tools. They have agreed the findings of Soundararajan and Arthur on Comparative Agility and they added that the Thoughtworks Assessment Tool does not include the identification of effectiveness of the Agile methods and twenty practices included in the tool is not sufficient.

Considering the shortage of related research work and their limited scope, we intend to conduct an in-depth review and comparison of agility assessment tools with a broader scope to better evaluate their capabilities.

Our literature and web research on agility assessment tools have resulted with 37 assessment tools listed on the Table 1. For this study, only the tools that have a degree of ability to automate the assessment process were included in the evaluation. Therefore, 16 tools, which are basically text-based checklists, questionnaires, and frameworks, are excluded from the scope of this study. Furthermore, additional 10 tools are also excluded from the scope due to being paid services or due to their unavailability. This left us with 11 tools that we briefly introduce in the alphabetical order on the remaining of this Section.

Table 1. The complete list of agility assessment tools

	Name	Owner	Type	Availability
1	A Corporate Agile 10-point Checklist	Elena Yatzeck	Text based	A
2	abetterteam.org	Sebastian Hermida	Web tool	NA
3	Agile 3R Model of Maturity Assessment	Phani Thimmapuram	Text based	A
4	Agile Assessment	Toughtworks	Web tool	NA
5	**Agile Enterprise Survey**	**Storm-Consulting**	**Web tool**	**A**
6	Agile Health Assessment Tool	Agile Transformation Inc.	Unknown	NA
7	**Agile Health Dashboard**	**Len Lagestee**	**Sheet tool**	**A**
8	**Agile Journey Index**	**Bill Krebs**	**Sheet tool**	**A**
9	Agile Maturity Matrix in JIRA	Atlassian	Web tool	Paid service
10	Agile Maturity Self Assessment	Robbie Mac Iver	Text based	A
11	Agile Maturity Self-Assessment Survey	Eduardo Ribeiro	Text based	A
12	**Agile Process Assessment Tool**	**Info Tech Research Group**	**Sheet tool**	**A**
13	**Agile Self Assessment**	**Cape Project Management**	**Web tool**	**A**
14	Agile team evaluation	Eric Gunnerson	Text based	A
15	**Agility Questionnaire**	**Marcel Britsch**	**Sheet tool**	**A**
16	AGIS	Santiago Matalonga	Text based	A
17	Borland Agile Assessment	Borland	Text based	A
18	CAMT (Comprehensive Agility Measurement Tool)	Ameya S. Erande, Alok K. Verma	Unknown	NA
19	Checklist for Change Agents	Michael Sahota	Text based	A
20	**Comparative Agility Tool**	**Mike Cohn and Kenny Rubin**	**Web tool**	**A**
21	**Depth of Kanban**	**Christophe Achouiantz**	**Chart tool**	**A**
22	Enterprise Agile Practice Assessment Tool	DrAgile	NA	Paid service
23	**Enterprise Agility Maturity Matrix**	**Eliassen Group**	**Sheet tool**	**A**
24	Forrester's Agile Testing Maturity Assessment Tool	Diego Lo Giudice, Margo Visitacion, Phil Murphy, Rowan Curran	NA	Paid service
25	**GSPA: A GENERIC SOFTWARE PROCESS ASSESSMENT TOOL**	**Ozan Raşit Yürüm**	**Desktop tool**	**A**
26	How Agile Are You?	Kelly Waters	Text based	A
27	**IBM DevOps Practices Self Assessment**	**IBM**	**Web tool**	**A**
28	Joe's Unofficial Scrum Checklist	Joe Little	Text based	A
29	Lean Enterprise Self Assessment Tool	LAI	NA	NA
30	Maturity Assessment Model for Scrum Teams	Marmamula Prashanth Kumar	Text based	A
31	Net Objectives Lean-Agile Roadmap for Achieving Enterprise Agility	Net Objectives	NA	NA

1. Agile Enterprise Survey. Agile Enterprise Survey [9] is a web-based online survey designed by Storm Consulting to assess enterprise agility. The survey presents different sets of statements and asks the assessor to specify how well these statements reflect his or hers organization. The statements are placed under 16 questions that are categorized into five distinct parts namely: Values and Practices, Working Environment, Capabilities, Activities, Blue Sky thinking, and Organization Background. The survey can be run externally and is anonymous. No names or email addresses are stored with the survey data.

2. Agile Health Dashboard. Agile Health Dashboard [10] is a tool designed to measure the team agility. The tool consists of following parts: Completed/Committed Stories, Team Composition, Team Size, Team Member Dedication, and Family Fun. These parts are updated after every sprint to observe the current team health. The tool comes in a spreadsheet format with pre-defined features and metrics to reflect the team agility.

3. Agile Journey Index. Agile Journey Index [11] is an agility assessment model that aids organizations to improve their agility. The index is constructed around 19 questions in 4 distinct groups. "Questions are related to 19 key agile practices and groups include the following: Planning, Do, Wrap, and Program Organization Criteria" [12]. "Each practice is rated on a scale of 1–10, with specific criteria for each number" [12]. The tool is available for use in a spreadsheet format and provided with supplementary documentation.

4. Agile Process Assessment Tool. The Agile Process Assessment Tool [13] which was developed by Info-Tech Research Group analyzes "how well an organization is lined up with the agile ideal across different process issues" [13]. The tool includes 67 questions in six different categories. These categories are: Configuration Management, Change Management, Release Management, Comprehensive Testing, Automation, and Compliance. The tool is available in spreadsheet format and it includes instructions encapsulated in the spreadsheet as well.

5. Agile Self Assessment. Agile Self Assessment [14] tool developed by Cape Project Management, Inc. is a web based online survey that is built upon the Scrum Checklist [15]. The tool reflects the results of the checklist onto an agility maturity matrix [14] that has five different levels of agility. There are 60, agree and disagree questions. "The scoring of the questions are based upon the overall importance of the answer" [14]. After answering the questions, the tool calculates the scores and indicates the agility level according to the agility maturity matrix.

6. Agility Questionnaire. Agility Questionnaire [16] allows "establishing a holistic view of organizational, team and project related factors, thus creating an Agility Profile which provides the necessary insight to make the right decision towards delivery methodology and more importantly areas of the methodology that require tailoring to optimize for the specific case at hand". "The questionnaire consists of two parts: Agility, and Project Profile. The questions under Agility are used to assess the capability to be Agile and the questions under Project Profile, indicates the characteristics of a particular project that may be used for tailoring methodologies" [16]. The tool comes in a spreadsheet format and enables answering questions and identifying agile capability.

7. Comparative Agility. The main idea behind Comparative Agility [17, 18] is assessing an organizations' agility by comparing it to its competitors. "Rather than guiding organizations to a perfect score or level of agility, it presents a comparison of results" [19]. The accompanying agility assessment tool is a web based online survey that is designed for self-assessments. The assessment includes 100 questions that are divided into seven dimensions. The dimensions are: teamwork, requirements, planning, technical practices, quality, culture, and knowledge creation [19]. Each dimension includes three to six characteristics and each characteristic has distinct questions related to it.

8. Depth of Kanban. Depth of Kanban [20] is a coaching tool for assessing the depth of a Kanban [21] implementation. The tool is a spider graph that is structured around seven axes that are based on Kanban principles. The principles are: Visualize, Limit Work in Progress, Manage Flow, Make Policies Explicit, Implement Feedback Loops, Improve, and Effects. Each axe includes different numbers of yes/no questions to answer and the depth of the implementation (the level of agility) is determined by the positive answers given.

9. Enterprise Agility Maturity Matrix. The primary goal of Enterprise Agility Model is to "encapsulate and document the well-known best practices for transforming an Enterprise to Agile as simply as possible, inventing as little new as possible" [22]. The model is structured according to the principles of Agile Manifesto and the Enterprise Agility Maturity Matrix tool is provided with the model. "The tool is mainly used for setting transformation goals, monitoring progress, and getting everybody on the same page regarding Agile including: Agile Coaches, team members, managers, and senior leadership" [23]. The tool is in the spreadsheet format and comes in a compressed file including supplementary documentation about both Enterprise Agility Model and the Enterprise Agility Maturity Matrix tool. The matrix is also integrated to the JIRA Software [24] project management tool but since it's a paid-service, it's excluded from the scope of this study.

10. GSPA: A Generic Software Process Assessment Tool. GSPA is an offline process assessment tool that enables making process assessments with a wide range of process assessment models including the agility assessment models. The tool employs a metamodel that combines common structures of most common process assessment models: CMMI [25] and ISO 15504 [26]. By using the meta-model, any kinds of assessment models can be introduced into the tool. Since the tool does not include a predefined agility assessment model or survey, we have used tool's meta-model to integrate one of the structured and complete agility assessment models, AgilityMOD [27, 28] that guides organizations on their way to become agile into the tool and performed our evaluation according to it.

11. IBM DevOps Practices Self-Assessment. The IBM DevOps Practices Self-Assessment is developed to "evaluate the state of an organization's software delivery approach" [29]. The aim is to improve agility with adoption paths and proven practices. Web based online tool enables assessors choose an adoption path and assess the organization according to the practices related to the chosen path.

3 Criteria to Evaluate Tools

In order to evaluate and compare the current agility assessment tools, we defined nine quality criteria. The criteria are based on our previous research studies on software process improvement tools [30]. These include coverage, availability, guidance capability, assessment recording, automated reporting, comparability, different modes of usage, different scopes and extensibility. These criteria were defined based upon the functions expected from a fully functioning agility assessment tool. What guided us on specifying these criteria were our experiences and studies that had been performed on evaluating agility assessment models [31] and process assessment tools [30].

Coverage. Agility assessment tools should address all twelve agile principles stated in the Agile Manifesto [32], in order to perform a comprehensive and complete agility assessment. Agile principles and values construct a foundation of agile sense together and explain how agile practices work in practice [33], therefore full coverage of these values and principles are mandatory for agile assessment tools. We rated this criterion based on tools' coverage of 12 agile principles using a four-point ordinal (N-P-L-F) scale. The details of the rating are given below:

- Not Achieved: 0–2 principles are covered
- Partially Achieved: 2–6 principles are covered
- Largely Achieved: 6–11 principles are covered
- Fully Achieved: 12 principles are covered

Availability. In order to provide equal access and equal opportunity for majority, an agility assessment tool should be universally reachable. Therefore, tools are expected to be online and web-based applications. This criterion is evaluated with a dichotomous (Web-Based/Not Web-Based) scale.

Guidance Capability. Agility assessment tools are expected to provide guidance for assessors who are not experts on agile software development. In this manner, tools should include guiding facilities such as help menus, example cases and responses, tips, and samples to guide assessors both beforehand and during the assessment. This criterion is evaluated with a four-point rating (N-P-L-F) scale according to the three categories of guidance capability expected from the tools. The categories are: providing guidance before assessment, providing guidance during the assessment, and providing guidance after the assessment. The details of the rating are given below:

- Not Achieved: None of the guidance capabilities is provided
- Partially Achieved: Only one type of guidance capability is provided
- Largely Achieved: Two types of the guidance capabilities are provided together
- Fully Achieved: All Three types of the guidance capabilities are provided together

Assessment Recording. Agility assessment tools are expected to provide recording capabilities to store both agility assessment findings and the resulting reports for further modifications, analysis, and comparison. This criterion is evaluated with a dichotomous (yes/no) scale.

Automated Reporting. Agility assessment tools are expected to include an automated reporting function that generates reports for the presentation of the results of the performed assessment. Assessment findings, which are supported by graphics and tables would be valuable for the interpretation of the results. This criterion is evaluated with a dichotomous (yes/no) scale.

Comparability. Agility assessment tools are expected to enable comparison between the reports of previously performed assessments. Continuous learning is a significant part of agile philosophy. It is obvious that agile teams would benefit comparison of their progress which are held within retrospective meetings mostly. An agility assessment tool needs to allow comparison of previous appraisal within the team itself. Here is to mention that assessment results would be valuable for the team itself indicating the challenged points. Therefore, parameters like velocity shouldn't be compared between agile teams. This criterion is evaluated with a dichotomous (yes/no) scale.

Different Modes of Usage. Agility assessments can be performed by single individuals and/or multiple individuals in teams, in departments, or in groups. Hence, tools are expected to support different usage mods for individuals and multiple users, and provide parallel assessments for simultaneous assessments. This criterion is evaluated with a four-point rating (N-P-L-F) scale based upon three types of usage categories. These types are single user assessment mode, multi-user assessment mode and parallel assessment mode. The details of the rating are given below:

- Not Achieved: None of the usage modes is provided
- Partially Achieved: Only one type of usage mode is provided
- Largely Achieved: Two types of the usage modes are provided together
- Fully Achieved: All Three types of the usage modes are provided together

Different Scopes. An agility assessment may be performed on from different perspectives. Assessments may target projects, teams, and/or organizations. Therefore, Agility assessment tools are expected to be able to support different types of scopes to provide different types of agility assessments. This criterion is evaluated with a four-point rating (N-P-L-F) scale according to the three types of scopes: project, team, and organization. The details of the rating are given below:

- Not Achieved: None of the scope types is supported
- Partially Achieved: Only one type of scope is supported
- Largely Achieved: Two types of the scopes are supported together
- Fully Achieved: All Three types of the scopes are supported together

Extensibility. Performing agility assessments on different contexts may require adaptation and extension of the agility assessment models. Therefore, tools are expected to provide a means of extensibility on model features to meet emerging needs of different types of contexts. This criterion is evaluated with a dichotomous (yes/no) scale.

4 Case Study

For evaluation of the capability of the agility assessment tools according to the defined criteria, we conducted a multiple case study on a software development organization that employs an established agile software development methodology, namely Scrum. Within the scope of the case study we performed 11 agility assessments by using each one of the 11 agility assessment tools. Each assessment is conducted according to the target scope established by the accompanying tool. Therefore assessments were subject to different extends of the organization such as project, team and/or whole organization.

The selected organization for the case study is currently developing mobile and web applications with two dedicated self-organizing teams, each consisting of 5 team members. For the project level assessments, the selected project for the study was a web application, which was completed within six weeks with a fixed budget. And for the team level assessments, the same team that developed the project was selected. The selected team consisted of 1 project manager, 3 software developers and a user experience designer. The team has an experience of employing agile software development practices for 4 years.

The case study was conducted by the project manager of the selected team who is also one of the authors of this paper. After the assessments were completed, the results were reviewed with other team members to better objectify the results. Finally, during and after the assessments, each tool has been rated by project manager according to its capabilities on meeting the 9 criteria described in the Sect. 3.

4.1 Agility Levels of the Assessed Project Based on 11 Agility Tools

In this subsection, the results of the agility assessments that were performed with 11 tools to identify agility level of the software project, team, and/or organization are given. Below, each paragraph describes the assessment scope and approach of the agility assessment made and resulting agility level indication obtained by using the respective tool. The only tool that we did not manage to get a report was the *Agile Enterprise Survey*. Therefore the assessment results for *Agile Enterprise Survey* is not included in this section.

Agile Health Dashboard indicates agility by assessing a given team's health according to sprint characteristics. After data entry about sprints the dashboard indicated that the assessed team's sprint planning, sprint velocity and team flow health is at the highest level: Excellent.

Agile Journey Index indicates agility on four different categories Planning, Do, Wrap, and Program Organization Criteria. However the tool includes only assessment of first three categories. Each category includes related practices that are rated on a 10-point scale while 1 being the lowest level of agility and 10 being the highest level of agility. The assessment results of the index for the three categories are as follows: Plan: 5.9, Do: 5.0 and Wrap: 3.7.

Agile Process Assessment Tool assesses an organization's readiness for agile adoption. It evaluates six different categories that include various statements to rate on a Yes/No or six-point agree/disagree type of scale. The readiness results for agile adoption according to the each one of the six categories is shown on a four-point scale Very Low, Low, High, and Very High. The assessment results for the categories are as follows: Configuration Management: Low, Change Management: Low, Release Management: Low, Testing Protocols: Very Low, Automation: Very Low and Compliance: Not Available. The compliance category was not available for the organization that was subject to the case study.

Agile Self Assessment tool uses an agile maturity matrix that consists of five levels to indicate agility. The levels are Level 1: Ad Hoc Agile, Level 2: Doing Agile, Level 3: Being Agile, Level 4: Thinking Agile and Level 5: Culturally Agile while Level 1 indicating lowest level of agility and level 5 indicating highest level of agility. After completing 60 questions, the assessment results indicated that the assessed organization is at Level 3: Being Agile.

Agility Questionnaire includes two different parts: Agility and Project Profile. The Agility part indicates the assessed organizations agility level and project profile part brings out the characteristics of the project for tailoring agile methodologies. For the case study only the Agility part of the questionnaire is used. The Agility part includes 6 areas that indicate agility on a −10 to 10 scale while −10 being the lowest agility level and 10 being the highest agility level. The results for each area is as follows: Value Focus: 5, Ceremony: 4, Collaboration: −2, Decisions and Information: 2, Responsiveness: 6 and Experience: 4.

Comparative Agility indicates an organization's level of agility in comparison to other organizations that have taken the survey. The results are displayed in a form of standard deviations that shows how given answers differ from the answers given by the competitors. Therefore positive standard deviations indicate better level of agility and negative standard deviations indicate worse level of agility than competitors. The resulting report includes two graphs: the first one displays the dimension analysis and second one displays characteristic analysis. The tool includes seven dimensions and dimensions are made up of three to six characteristics. Here, only the dimension results are given due to space concerns. The results are as follows: Teamwork: 0.43, Requirements: 0.15, Planning: 0.55, Technical Practices: 0.15, Quality: −0.05, Culture: −0.03, Knowledge Creating: −0.27 and Outcomes: −0.45.

Depth of Kanban, assesses the agility by identifying the depth of a Kanban implementation. The tool is basically a radar chart that includes seven dimensions. Each dimension includes three different colored areas: red, yellow, light green and dark green. The areas are described from red to dark green as No Improvement, Sustainable Improvement, Excellence and Lean. Each dimension includes different questions and scales. The assessment results for each of the dimensions are in light green: Excellence and the ratings for each dimension is as follows: Visualize: 11, Limit Work in Progress: 3,

Manage Flow: 8, Make Policies Explicit: 10, Implement Feedback Loops: 5, Improve: 6, and Effects: 8.

Enterprise Agility Maturity Matrix includes two different levels: organizational level practices and team level practices. The tool includes five-point scale to indicate the levels of agility. The scale is defined as: 0-Impeded, 1-In Transition, 2-Sustainable, 3-Agile and 4-Ideal while Impeded indicating the lowest level and the Ideal indicating the highest level of agility. The assessment results suggest that on organizational level practices, 10 out of 14 practices are at 3-Agile level and remaining four practices are at 1-In Transition level and on team level 16 out of 35 practices are at 4-Ideal level, 17 out of 35 practices are at 3-Agile level and remaining two practices are at 1-In Transition level.

GSPA tool has been built upon the AgilityMod, software agility assessment reference model. AgilityMod includes two dimensions: Agility and Aspect Dimensions. Agility Dimension includes four levels of agility: Not Implemented, Ad Hoc, Lean and Effective. Aspect Dimension includes four aspects: Exploration, Construction, Transition and Management. AgilityMod provides guidance for agility assessment of projects and the agility level of a project is determined according to the project teams' ability to perform certain practices defined under each aspect. Teams are given a rating on a four-point rating (N-P-L-F) scale for each aspect. The agility levels of the project based on AgilityMod are as follows: Exploration Aspect: Effective level, Construction Aspect: Lean level, Transition Aspect: Lean level and Management Aspect: Lean level.

For *IBM DevOps Practices Self-Assessment,* an assessment based on the predefined Develop/Test adoption path is performed. The tool employs four levels: Practiced, Consistent, Reliable and Scaled to indicate agility of the each assessed practice. The result of the assessment includes a Blue Border, which indicates a level fully achieved and a Yellow Border, which indicates a level partially achieved. The results of our assessment for each practices assessment in the Develop/Test adoption path are as follows: Design: *Blue Border: Reliable & Yellow Border: Scaled*, Construct: *Blue Border: Practiced & Yellow Border: Consistent*, Build: *Yellow Border: Practiced*, Configuration Management: *Yellow Border: Practiced*, Assess Quality: *Blue Border: Reliable & Yellow Border: Scaled*, Test: *Blue Border: Practiced & Yellow Border: Consistent*.

Each one of these 11 agility assessment tools has different assessment approaches that yield various different results concerning the agility of the assessed target. Also tools are mainly developed for assessing agility in certain conditions such as the beginning of an agile adoption process or certain implementations such as a Kanban implementation. Therefore the results of these assessments are inconsistent with each other and comparing the results of these assessments will be irrelevant.

5 Case Study Results and Comparison of the Tools

Table 2 below summarizes the results of the evaluation of the tools and gives the comparison of the tools according to nine criteria discussed in details below.

Table 2. Evaluation results of the agility assessment tools

#	Tool/Quality Criteria	Coverage	Availability	Guidance Capability	Assessment Recording	Automated Reporting	Comparability	Different Modes of Usage	Different Scopes	Extensibility
1	Agile Enterprise Survey	LA	Web-Based	PA	No	No	No	NA	NA	No
2	Agile Health Dashboard	LA	Not Web-Based	FA	Yes	Yes	Yes	NA	NA	Yes
3	Agile Journey Index	FA	Not Web-Based	FA	Yes	Yes	Yes	NA	NA	No
4	Agile Process Assessment Tool	LA	Not Web-Based	PA	Yes	Yes	No	NA	NA	No
5	Agile Self Assessment	FA	Web-Based	LA	Yes	Yes	No	LA	NA	No
6	Agility Questionnaire	LA	Not Web-Based	LA	Yes	Yes	No	NA	FA	Yes
7	Comparative Agility	FA	Web-Based	FA	Yes	Yes	Yes	NA	NA	Yes
8	Depth of Kanban	LA	Not Web-Based	PA	N/A	No	No	NA	NA	Yes
9	Enterprise Agility Maturity Matrix	FA	Not Web-Based	LA	Yes	Yes	No	NA	LA	No
10	GSPA	FA	Not Web-Based	LA	Yes	Yes	No	LA	LA	Yes
11	IBM DevOps Practices Self Assessment	LA	Web-Based	LA	Yes	Yes	No	NA	NA	No

Findings of the case study revealed that *Agile Health Dashboard*, *Agile Journey Index*, *Agile Process Assessment Tool*, *Agility Questionnaire*, *Enterprise Agility Matrix*, and *IBM DevOps Practices Self-Assessment* are developed with questions based upon commonly accepted agile practices and applications of these practices. Although commonly accepted practices are compatible with the agile principles and provide some degree of evaluation, a comprehensive set of practices is essential for full coverage of the context. *Comparative Agility* and *Agile Self-Assessment* tools enable assessment based upon Scrum method and these two provide full coverage among other tools assessed. The *Depth of Kanban* is based upon Kanban method and since it's aimed to assess the depth of a Kanban implementation, it lacks the coverage of some agile principles. The Enterprise Agility Survey tool is aimed to assess the organizational agility and it has a higher perspective of agility. This higher perspective gives an abstract coverage of agile principles. The only tool that provides a structured agile assessment approach is the *GSPA* tool that relies upon AgilityMOD (Agility Assessment Reference Model) [27, 28] it manages to provide a full coverage.

The majority of the tools are not web-based tools. Some of these tools are available in spreadsheet format, these are: *Agile Health Dashboard*, *Agile Journey Index*, *Agile Process Assessment Tool*, *Agility Questionnaire*, *Enterprise Agility Matrix*. *Depth of Kanban* tool is available in printable format. *GSPA* tool is available as an executable JAR file and it is not a web-based application. The web-based tools are *Agile Enterprise Survey*, *Agile Self Assessment*, *Comparative Agility*, and *IBM DevOps Practices Self-Assessment*.

All of the tools are able to provide some degree of guidance for assessment process. *Agile Enterprise Survey* includes clear questions with explanatory notes providing guidance on the top of each question. *Agile Health Dashboard* includes clearly defined data entry fields with explanatory notes attached to them. It also includes example cases and an instruction sheet that includes examples and explanations on how to use the tool.

Agile Journey Index includes columns that houses guiding notes, examples, explanations, and definitions related to the practices. It also includes sheets that provide example cases. *Agile Process Assessment* tool includes an introduction sheet about the tool and how to use it. *Agile Self-Assessment* survey has an introduction about the structure of the survey and includes a panel that provides navigation to all of the questions. *Agility Questionnaire* includes explanatory columns attached to the each question and at the summary section. *Comparative Agility* includes tips and warnings on the top of the questions. It also includes explanatory pop-ups and progress bar that informs the assessor about the state of the assessment. *Depth of Kanban* includes explanatory statements in questions but it does not have any means of instructions or introduction embedded in the tool. *Enterprise Agility Maturity Matrix* includes clear statements but it has a very limited glossary that houses a single item. *GSPA* includes fields that provide steps about how to use the tool and includes explanatory fields for the models that are used for the assessment. *IBM DevOps Practices Self-Assessment* includes an introductory page and provides warnings and explanations throughout the assessment.

Except for the *Agile Enterprise Survey*, all the other tools satisfy the assessment recording criterion. This quality criterion is not applicable to *Depth of Kanban* since it's provided in a printable format.

Two of the tools do not provide automated reporting, these are: *Agile Enterprise Survey* and *Depth of Kanban*. All the other tools provide automated reporting functionality with commentary for analysis that is supported with graphical elements such as radar charts, status lights, tables, and bar charts.

Agile Health Dashboard, *Agile Journey Index*, and *Comparative Agility* are the only tools that are able to satisfy the comparability criterion. Agile Health Dashboard enables comparison between different teams, *Agile Journey Index* enables comparison with samples, and *Comparative Agility* provides comparison between a database of surveys.

Only *Agile Self-Assessment* and *GSPA* provide different modes of usage for multi-users. However, both of the tools fail to provide parallel assessments for simultaneous assessments and could only provide multi-users by aggregating the results.

Only *Agility Questionnaire* fully provides all three types of different scopes for assessments. Apart from that, *Enterprise Agility Maturity Matrix* and *GSPA* can also provide different scopes for assessments but not completely. *Enterprise Agility Maturity Matrix* provides assessments at organizational and at team levels and *GSPA* provides assessments at project and organization levels.

In general, web-based tools do not provide any means of extensibility. The only exception is that *Comparative Agility* provides customized surveys by request. Amongst the tools in spreadsheet format only *Agile Health Dashboard* and *Agility Questionnaire* provides explicit extensibility with predefined sections for configuring and extending the tools. *Depth of Kanban* is extensible in any manner and *GSPA* provides extensibility on process assessment models by its meta-model.

6 Conclusion and Future Work

In this study, our objective was to review and evaluate agility assessment tools to answer a research question: (RQ1) "To what extent are the current agility assessment tools sufficient to meet the expected criteria?" To be able to address the question, we conducted a multiple case study and evaluated 11 tools based on nine criteria that we have defined. These criteria are: (a) coverage, (b) availability, (c) guidance capability, (d) assessment recording, (e) automated reporting, (f) comparability, (g) different modes of usage, (h) different scopes and (i) extensibility. As a result, of our evaluation, none of the current agility assessment tools was able to meet all of the criteria. The tool that is able to meet the most of the criteria, was the *Comparative Agility*, with completely satisfying seven (a, b, c, d, e, f, and i) out of nine criteria. However, some tools proved themselves useful for special contexts. For example, *Depth of Kanban* is useful for assessing Kanban implementations, *Enterprise Agility Maturity Matrix* is useful for during agile transformations, *Agile Health Dashboard* is useful for monitoring health of agile teams on a sprint basis, and *IBM DevOps Practices Self-Assessment* is useful to adopt a predefined agile adoption path.

As a result of our evaluation, we concluded that the main requirement for an agility assessment tool is, the ability to reduce the amount of time and effort required for agility assessments. During our case study, we observed that tools are mostly focused on conducting the assessment but lacking the support for other important parts of the assessment process such as planning and data validation. Therefore, in addition to fully satisfying our nine criteria, the tools are expected to have features that facilitate and automate the whole assessment process including planning, conducting, and reporting the agility assessments.

Furthermore, we also observed that majority of the tools use a set of agile practices to indicate the level of agility. While these practices are crucial for specific implementations of agile methods, the mere absence or presence of these practices is not sufficient to indicate the success of the adopted agile method. In addition to that, majority of the tools do not provide an indication of agility levels or the possible improvement areas towards agility. One way to overcome these deficiencies is to build tools that have the capability to support the use of structured agility assessment models that provide clearly defined agility levels and possible improvement areas.

To conclude, this study has demonstrated that the current agility assessment tools are not fully sufficient to aid agile adopters to increase their agility. For future work, we intend to develop an agility assessment tool that fully satisfies the criteria specified above, and will have the capabilities of supporting the agility assessment process as a whole with additional support for the use of structured agility assessment models.

Acknowledgement. This research is supported by Scientific and Technological Research Council of Turkey (TÜBİTAK), grant number 113E528.

References

1. Misra, S.C., Kumar, V., Kumar, U.: Success factors of agile software development. In: Software Engineering Research and Practice, pp. 233–239, June 2006
2. VersionOne, 9th Annual State of Agile™ (2014). https://www.versionone.com/pdf/state-of-agile-development-survey-ninth.pdf
3. Fraser, S., Boehm, B., Järkvik, J., Lundh, E., Vilkki, K.: How do Agile/Xp development methods affect companies? In: Abrahamsson, P., Marchesi, M., Succi, G. (eds.) XP 2006. LNCS, vol. 4044, pp. 225–228. Springer, Heidelberg (2006)
4. Gandomani, T.J., Zulzalil, H., Ghani, A., Azim, A., Sultan, A.B.: Important considerations for agile software development methods governance. J. Theor. Appl. Inf. Technol. **55**(3), 345–351 (2013)
5. Soundarajan, S., Arthur, J.D.: A structured framework for assessing the "goodness" of agile methods. In: 18th IEEE International Conference and Workshops on Engineering of Computer-Based Systems (2011)
6. Williams, L.: Comparative Agility. http://comparativeagility.com/
7. Toughtworks. Agile Assessments. http://www.agileassessments.com/
8. Gandomani, T.J., Nafchi, M.Z.: Agility assessment model to measure agility degree of agile software companies. Indian. J. Sci. Technol. **7**(7), 955–959 (2014)
9. Storm-Consulting Agile Enterprise Survey. http://www.storm-consulting.com/agile-enterprise-survey/
10. Lagestee, L.: Agile Health Dashboard (2012). http://illustratedagile.com/2012/09/25/how-to-measure-team-agility/
11. Krebs, W., Morgan, P., Ashton, R.: Agile Journey Index. http://www.agiledimensions.com
12. Krebs, W.: Level up Your Agile with the Agile Journey Index (2013)
13. Group, I.-T.R. Agile Process Assessment Tool. http://www.infotech.com/research/ss/it-deploy-changes-more-rapidly-by-going-agile/it-agile-process-assessment-tool
14. Management, C.P.: Agile Self Assessment. http://www.agileprojectmanagementtraining.com/agile-self-assessment/
15. Kniberg, H.: Scrum Checklist. http://www.crisp.se/gratis-material-och-guider/scrum-checklist
16. Britsch, M.: Agility Questionnaire (2014). http://www.thedigitalbusinessanalyst.co.uk/2014/07/Agile-Questionnaire.html
17. Comparative Agility. https://comparativeagility.com/surveys/start
18. Doyle, M., Williams, L., Cohn, M., Rubin, K.S.: Agile software development in practice. In: Cantone, G., Marchesi, M. (eds.) XP 2014. LNBIP, vol. 179, pp. 32–45. Springer, Heidelberg (2014)
19. Comparative Agility Overview. https://comparativeagility.com/overview
20. Achouiantz, C.: Depth of Kanban (2013). http://leanagileprojects.blogspot.se/2013/03/depth-of-kanban-good-coaching-tool.html
21. Anderson, D.: Kanban - Successful Evolutionary Change for your Technology Business. Blue Hole Press, Sequim (2010)
22. Group, E.: Enterprise Agility Guide (2013)
23. Group, E.: Introducing the Agility Maturity Matrix (2013). http://www.eliassen.com/agile-blog/introducing-the-enterprise-agility-maturity-matrix
24. Atlassian: Jira Software. http://www.atlassian.com/software/jira
25. Kneuper, R.: CMMI: Improving Software and Systems Development Processes Using Capability Maturity Model Integration, p. 224. Rocky Nook, Santa Barbara (2008)

26. (IEC), I.O.f.S.I.a.I.E.C., ISO/IEC 15504-2:2003 Information technology – Process assessment – Part 2: Performing an assessment (2003)
27. Ozcan-Top, O., Demirors, O.: A reference model for software agility assessment: AgilityMod. Middle East Technical University (2014)
28. Ozcan-Top, O., Demirörs, O.: A reference model for software agility assessment: agilitymod. In: Rout, T., O'Connor, R.V., Dorling, A. (eds.) SPICE 2015. CCIS, vol. 526, pp. 145–158. Springer, Heidelberg (2015)
29. IBM. IBM DevOps. http://www.ibm.com/ibm/devops/us/en/
30. Yürüm, O.R.: GSPA: A Generic Software Process Assessment Tool. The Graduate School of Informatics, Middle East Technical University (2013)
31. Ozcan-Top, O., Demirörs, O.: Assessment of agile maturity models: a multiple case study. In: Woronowicz, T., Rout, T., O'Connor, R.V., Dorling, A. (eds.) SPICE 2013. CCIS, vol. 349, pp. 130–141. Springer, Heidelberg (2013)
32. Agile Manifesto (2001). www.agilemanifesto.org
33. Ambler, S.W., Lines, M.: Disciplined Agile Delivery: A Practitioner's Guide to Agile Software Delivery in the Enterprise, p. 544. IBM Press, Indianapolis (2012)

Exploring Processes in Small Software Companies: A Systematic Review

Nirnaya Tripathi[(✉)], Elina Annanperä, Markku Oivo[(✉)], and Kari Liukkunen

M3S Research Unit, University of Oulu, Oulu, Finland
{Nirnaya.Tripathi,Elina.Annanpera,
Markku.Oivo,Kari.Liukkunen}@oulu.fi

Abstract. Context: To attain an advantage over competitors, small software companies (SSCs) need to have an efficient software development process. However, systematic review studies that have examined the software development process within the context of SSCs are limited. Objective: Therefore, the objective of this paper is to rigorously assess the current state of practice of the software development process of SSCs using ISO/IEC 12207 standard as an analyzing framework. Method: A systematic literature review was conducted to analyze relevant papers published between 2004 and 2014. The selected papers were categorized according to the empirical technique used. A total of 41 primary papers focusing on various aspects of the software development process of SSCs were discovered out of 3841 papers. Results: Based on the evidence found in primary papers, requirement engineering, project planning, life cycle model management and configuration management are the frequently considered processes for improvement when software process improvement (SPI) programs are conducted in SSCs. In addition, understanding the collected requirements and communication barriers between product management and the rest of the work team were among the challenges observed and experienced by SSCs during the software development process.

Keywords: Software process · Small software company · Systematic literature review · ISO/IEC 12207

1 Introduction

In the global economy, the most rapidly growing sector is the software industry, which has emerged as one of the key economic drivers for many nations [1]. Another significant entity that contributes to driving the world economy is the small software company (SSC). SSCs play an important role in their nations' economies because of their ability to capture the kinds of markets that larger companies are incapable of reaching or have rejected. SSCs typically consist of less than 50 employees, and their aim is to create one or a few software products for their customers [2]. They also develop components for larger systems produced by other companies or offer maintenance services for the software products created by other firms [3].

To maintain their competitiveness in their target markets and to sustain a healthy relationship with their customers, SSCs need to supply increasingly faster and cheaper software products [4]. To develop such software products, these companies need to have efficient software development processes [5]. SSCs definitely need all the assistance in seeking the relevant information to make their software development processes efficient, but they often lack systematic process knowledge for determining which type of processes are more relevant to their context [3, 6]. One way to analyze software process knowledge is by systematically examining the existing literature on SSCs. Some systematic literature reviews (SLRs) have focused on analyzing the existing approaches toward software process improvement (SPI) in small and medium enterprises (SMEs). For example, Pino et al. [7] concluded that models such as Capability Maturity Model Integration (CMMI) and Software Process Improvement and Capability Determination (SPICE) are not suitable for SPI programs in SMEs and instead proposed the use of lighter-weight models. Sulayman and Mendes [8] concluded that very few studies have explicitly focused on SPI for Web companies. Paternoster et al. [9] and Klotins et al. [10] described the software development of start-ups. However, systematic review studies in the context of SSCs and their software development processes are limited [11]. Therefore, there is a need for systematic review studies in the SSC context with the goal to explore the state-of-practice of software processes and the types of challenges associated with it.

In this paper, we present a systematic review of the literature, with the aim of identifying the software processes utilized in SSCs. We have used the ISO/IEC 12207 [12] processes as an analyzing framework to describe both the current state-of-practice and challenges present in the software development processes. The paper proceeds as follows. In Sect. 2, the background and motivation are described. In Sect. 3, the systematic review is presented. Section 4 presents the results from the review, followed by a discussion of the research questions presented and our conclusions.

2 Background and Motivation

SSCs are considered as an important entity in the software industry and they represent up to 85 % of all software companies [13, 2]. They often face vicious competition from their competitors in developing quality software products on a strict deadline to fulfill customer requirements [2]. Their software development activity is generally in casual state [14]. Therefore, in order to improve their productivity, they need to improve their software development processes [15]. However, SSCs typically avoid process improvements [15]. This avoidance mainly appears due to the lack of financial and human resources [14]. To help SSCs, it is important for the software engineering research community to explore software processes in detail. Doing this will provide added value to the practitioners operating in the small-scale context.

There are some SLRs that have focused on the improvement of software development processes in SMEs. For example, Pino et al. [7] analyzed the existing approaches toward SPI in SMEs. They concluded that proper SPI programs based on models such as CMMI and SPICE are not suitable for SMEs and proposed the use of lighter-weight models. They also observed in their study that frequently improved processes in SPI programs are project management, documentation, requirement change management, process establishment, configuration management, and requirement elicitation. Sulayman and Mendes [8] conducted a systematic review study to determine the current state of research in SPI models and techniques used by small and medium Web development companies. They found that very few studies have explicitly focused on SPI for Web companies despite the large number of Web companies across the globe. Paternoster et al. [9] conducted a mapping study to explore the state of art of software development in start-ups. Their conclusion was that software engineering work practices are chosen based on the start-up context. Klotins et al. [10] also conducted a mapping study, in which they focused on the software engineering aspect of start-ups. They found that very few research papers have provided concrete evidence of software engineering knowledge areas in start-up companies.

However, systematic review studies in the particular field of SSCs focusing on the software development processes are limited [11]. To the best of our knowledge, an in-depth analysis of the studies reported in this context that describes the state-of-practice and the associated challenges with it does not appear to exist. To address this gap in the literature, we therefore decided to conduct a systematic review of the literature that focuses on software development processes in SSCs to explore this topic area. To analyze the software development processes in SSCs within a standardized framework, we decided to follow the classification of processes as defined in ISO/IEC 12207 [12]. ISO/IEC 12207 includes a process reference model that categorizes the processes related to software system into seven groups: agreement processes, organizational project-enabling processes, project processes, technical processes, software implementation processes, software support processes, and software reuse processes [12]. We did not consider ISO/IEC 29110 [16] as our analyzing framework since the standard is applicable to very small entities (up to 25 people), whereas our study focus is on SSCs (up to 50 people).

3 Research Methodology

Our literature review is based on the guidelines provided by Kitchenham and Charters [17]. We also used a software tool (StArt) to support our systematic review [18].

3.1 Research Question

The main goal of our review is to find all the research studies that relate to the software development processes of SSCs and that describe the key processes used and any related challenges. To achieve this goal, the following research questions (RQs) are defined:

> RQ1: *What is the state-of-practice in terms of the use of processes in small software companies?* The outcome of this question is the current state of the processes used in SSCs. The state-of-practice is analyzed using the ISO 12207:2008 life-cycle processes.

RQ2: *What are the challenges that small software companies face in the processes?* The outcome of this question is the discovery of the challenges associated with the software development processes in SSCs.

3.2 Search Strategy and Data Retrieval

The initial sets of keywords for SSCs were taken from the work of Pino et al. [7]. Pilot searches in the key software engineering research domain databases were conducted, and new keywords were added to better target the searches to the desired data set. In the end, the search strings were formulated by combining the terms representing the population AND intervention. It can be summarized as follows: (X1 OR X2...OR Xn) AND (Y1 OR Y2...OR Yn), where X represents the population and Y represent intervention. The population (X) is represented as {software engineering process, software process, software engineering}, whereas intervention (Y) is represented as {small company, small enterprises, small organizations, small team, and small settings}. During the data retrieval process, the publication period was set to 2004 to 2014, with the purpose of summarizing the most recent related work. We used a total of four databases in our study:

- Scopus (http://www.scopus.com/)
- IEEE Xplore (http://ieeexplore.ieee.org)
- Science Direct (http://www.sciencedirect.com/)
- Web of Science (http://www.webofknowledge.com).

3.3 Study Selection and Data Extraction

The database searches resulted in identifying 7967 papers, out of which 4022 were duplicates. The remaining 3945 papers were screened and assessed by two researchers. The inclusion/exclusion criteria were determined based on title, abstract, and keywords, implicitly or explicitly (see Table 1). The papers were categorized as "accepted", "rejected" or "can't decide" (in StArt terms, "unclassified" is used to the same extent). The "can't decide" papers were discussed, and issues were resolved between the first and second author. After that, 104 papers were selected for full text reading. Thus, 41 studies were finally selected as the primary study papers. For quality assessment, we used the systematic and validated model [19] to assess the scientific rigor and industrial relevance of each primary study. For scientific rigor, we considered the following aspects: context, study design, and validity. For industrial relevance, we considered the following aspects: subjects, context, scale, and research method. More details about the papers, based on scientific rigor and industrial relevance, are shown in Fig. 1. Data extraction and analysis was done through qualitative data analysis using the NVivo software. We used the deductive approach for coding the primary studies [20].

Table 1. Inclusion/exclusion criteria

Inclusion criteria	Exclusion criteria	Articles
(1) Reports an empirical study and/or (2) reports a study on small software companies and the software development process	Title, Abstract, Keywords: (1) The main focus was not on the small software companies and/or the software development process; or (2) the paper was not available; or (3) it was not in English; or (4) the paper was a letter, editorial, or position paper	104
	Full Text Read: (1) No reported result or (2) same content as other studies (extended papers, summaries)	41

3.4 Validity Discussion

In this section, we discuss the validity of our study in terms of construct validity, internal validity, external validity, and reliability [21]. Construct validity deals with whether the primary study papers focused on the software development processes and SSCs. During the search process, search strings were designed in such a way that they would collect a wide variety of papers related to this topic. To collect the papers, databases that are frequently used for accessing software engineering literature were used. During the full-text selection phase, manual screening was conducted twice to ensure that only papers relevant to the research questions were included. Reliability concerns whether the study can be repeated by the other researchers. Our study was based on a systematic review process protocol with well-defined search strings in the most common databases through the use of the SLR tool. Therefore, our review process can easily be reproduced by other researchers. The inclusion and exclusion criteria were piloted and followed during the review process. Internal validity refers to problems in the analysis of the data. During the execution phase, some primary study candidate papers did not show clear objectives and results, which made inclusion/exclusion criteria difficult. To overcome this situation, several meetings were arranged between the authors to evaluate the discrepant papers and eliminate the ones that did not match the inclusion/exclusion criteria. External validity concerns whether the results of an SLR can be generalized. In this situation, the results from this study were limited to the SSC context; therefore, both researchers and industrial communities interested in the software development processes of SSCs can benefit from our findings.

4 Results

As a result of the systematic review, a total of 41 primary studies were found to be relevant to the RQs. The descriptions of the 41 papers are shown in Table 2. In the following section, we give an overview of the primary studies. We then explore the state-of-practice and challenges associated with SSCs' processes. To investigate the software development processes of SSCs in a systematic way, we classified the processes as defined in the ISO/IEC 12207 [12].

Table 2. List of primary studies

ID	Source	Year	Method	ID	Source	Year	Method
[3]	Scopus	2006	Case study (CS)	[22]	Scopus	2012	Ethnography
[4]	Scopus	2008	Case study	[23]	Scopus	2007	Case study
[6]	IEEE	2012	Case study	[24]	Scopus	2014	Case study
[25]	Scopus	2008	Case study	[26]	Scopus	2010	Case study
[27]	Scopus	2010	Case study	[28]	Scopus	2007	Experiment
[29]	Scopus	2010	Case study	[30]	IEEE	2012	Experiment
[13]	Scopus	2013	Action research	[31]	Scopus	2006	Case study
[32]	Scopus	2006	Case study	[33]	Scopus	2010	Survey
[14]	Scopus	2010	CS/Survey	[34]	Scopus	2009	Case study
[15]	IEEE	2009	Experiment	[35]	IEEE	2008	Case study
[36]	Web of science	2008	Survey	[37]	Web of science	2008	Experiment
[38]	Scopus	2013	Action research	[39]	Scopus	2005	Case study
[40]	WOS	2008	Case study	[41]	Scopus	2004	Survey
[42]	Scopus	2013	Case study	[43]	Scopus	2004	Case study
[44]	Scopus	2005	Case study	[45]	Scopus	2009	Case study
[46]	Scopus	2013	Survey	[47]	Scopus	2011	Case study
[48]	Scopus	2012	Case study	[49]	Scopus	2010	Case study
[50]	IEEE	2010	Case study	[51]	IEEE	2007	Case study
[52]	WOS	2004	Survey	[53]	Scopus	2012	Case study
[54]	IEEE	2006	Case study	[55]	Scopus	2011	Survey
[56]	Scopus	2009	Experiment				

4.1 Overview of the Studies

Rigor and Relevance. The quality of the primary studies was evaluated according to rigor and relevance, as discussed in Sect. 3.3. As can be seen in Fig. 1, thirteen studies are in the upper-right quadrant (Rigor: High, Medium and Relevance: High, Medium) in the most appropriate region. Sixteen studies exhibited high industry relevance (Relevance: High), out of which ten showed low scientific rigor. Twenty-five studies exhibited moderate industry relevance, out of which seven demonstrated medium rigor and eighteen demonstrated low rigor. Based on this evaluation, we established the fact that most of the identified studies were conducted in cooperation with an actual SSC, thus scoring medium or high on the relevance scale. However, many of these studies had low rigor.

Research Methodology. Most of the studies focused on empirical evaluations of theoretical concepts related to the software development processes and were applied in an SSC context, with the overall goal of assessing and/or improving software development processes. In Fig. 1, it can be seen that the majority of the primary studies are listed in the case study category. The other common methods were surveys and experiments. Also, looking at the left-lower quadrant in Fig. 1, it can be seen that the majority of the papers (28; 18 case studies, 5 surveys, 4 experiments, and 1 ethnographic study) fell in the low rigor category. Therefore, generalizability of the results of the given studies is low.

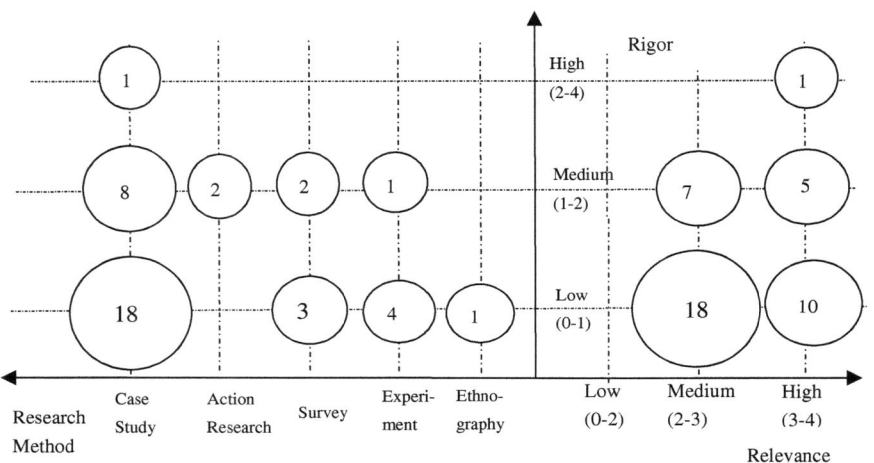

Fig. 1. Overview of research method, rigor, and relevance distribution of papers

4.2 Processes

A detailed overview of processes as defined in the ISO/IEC 12207 and relevant primary study papers are shown in Table 3.

SW Implementation Processes. Processes related to requirements are often considered critical processes for improvement since SSCs aim to quickly deliver what their customers want using their own practices rather than including customer commands in their development process [15]. Generally, functional requirements are the main focus during the requirement gathering of the software product [52]. One challenge that SSCs experience is understanding what the collected requirements really mean. The gathered information needs to be clearly understood to change it into clear product requirements. Clear understanding is crucial because it is important to determine which requirements match the business goal. Without a clear understanding, it is difficult to determine which product requirements need to put into which release plan to meet the business goals. [27] In respect to software qualification testing, some studies have reported that some companies have had troubles with testing their products [24, 25]. One problem was related to a deficiency of testing knowledge in the company. This lack of knowledge results in a lack of test plans, which causes uncertainty in companies during the testing process [25]. This lack of knowledge can be due to the absence of defined process descriptions or the quality of instructional manuals. However, Clarke and O'Connor [46] found that a majority of companies report general improvements in testing, including a periodic increase in test suites, the creation of a standardized testing process, and more emphasis on performance testing. Another improvement reported was measuring more code coverage of the automated tests [46].

SW Support Processes. In regard to the software quality assurance (QA) process, Wilkie et al. [44] surveyed six companies and found that they each defined QA differently. For some, QA means testing, while for others, it is an instrument to assess a software product [44]. This confusion may be due to a lack of proper process knowledge. Regarding software configuration management (CM), one study [52] found that SSCs are able to perform basic CM tasks (i.e., version control, change management, and release management). One strength of the CM process in most of the companies was the code version control [52]. Some challenges with CM were also reported, such as uncertainty surrounding which work products should be with what version control and the lack of appropriate guidelines for CM [52].

Table 3. Processes and relevant papers

Life cycle processes	Primary study and frequency percentage	
Software specific processes		
SW implementation processes		
Software implementation	–	
Software requirements analysis	[4, 15, 22–24, 26, 31, 32, 37, 39–46, 51, 56, 27]	49 %
Software architectural design	[24]	2 %
Software detailed design	[32, 43, 56]	7 %
Software construction	[3, 24, 37, 38, 41, 43, 56]	17 %
Software integration	[43]	2 %
Software qualification testing	[23–25, 31, 37, 38, 43, 46, 56]	22 %
SW support processes		
Software documentation management	[23, 25, 49]	7 %
Software configuration management	[22, 24, 26, 41, 43, 44, 49, 51, 52]	22 %
Software quality assurance	[22, 24, 26, 39, 41, 43, 44]	17 %
Software verification, validation	–	

(*Continued*)

Table 3. (*Continued*)

Life cycle processes	Primary study and frequency percentage	
Software specific processes		
Software review, audit	–	
Software problem resolution	[41, 43, 3, 15, 31, 46, 49]	17 %
Software reuse processes	–	
Domain engineering	–	
Reuse asset management	–	
Reuse program management	–	
System context processes		
Agreement processes		
Acquisition process	–	
Supply process	[3, 31, 46, 27]	10 %
Organizational project-enabling processes		
Life cycle model management	[11, 27, 37, 48, 49, 4, 6, 14, 16, 24, 47, 50, 51, 55, 22, 25, 32–34, 39, 42, 45, 53]	56 %
Infrastructure management	[46, 49]	5 %
Project portfolio management	–	
Human resource management	[37, 49, 55]	7 %
Quality management	[37, 52]	5 %
Project processes		
Project planning	[6, 15, 22–24, 26, 37, 39, 40, 43–46, 50, 51, 54]	39 %
Project assessment and control	[15, 24, 26, 39, 40, 44, 45, 51]	20 %
Decision management	–	
Risk management	[41, 43]	5 %
Configuration management	–	
Information management	–	
Measurement	[26, 34, 39, 44, 53]	12 %
Technical processes		
Stakeholder requirements definition	–	
System requirements analysis	[43]	2 %
System architectural design	[50]	2 %
Implementation	–	

(*Continued*)

Table 3. (*Continued*)

Life cycle processes	Primary study and frequency percentage	
Software specific processes		
System integration	[43]	2 %
System qualification testing	[43]	2 %
Software installation	[3, 31, 46, 49]	10 %
Software acceptance support	–	
Software operation	[3, 30, 31, 43]	10 %
Software maintenance	[24, 30, 34, 43, 46]	12 %
Software disposal	[46]	2 %

Agreement Processes. In the case of SSCs, no study has explicitly reported the use of processes within the acquisition process. The reason could be that SSCs are usually the ones who initially approach the customer. Since the amount of customers of SSCs is limited, this aspect is not well defined or of much interest. Regarding the supply process, Wangeheim et al. [3] found in their case study that this was one of the priority processes for improvement. In their other study [31] with eight companies, they found out that some of the companies had established systematic supply processes and had developed contract templates to improve relationships with their customers. Clarke and O'Connor [46], in their survey of 15 SMEs, found that those companies had made extensive improvements, specifically in the area of tendering, as well as in negotiating with customers.

Project Processes. On the subject of project processes, two studies [3, 32] that assessed SSCs reported that project management is considered a high-priority process. Saastamoinen and Tukiainen [52] pointed out that project planning is an important aspect in SSCs. In addition, within the project plan, the development approach should be clearly described. For SSCs, a project is managed in an iterative or incremental way, tending to follow the waterfall model. A project's work capacity and time approximation are usually calculated based on the project manager's experience.

Organizational Project-Enabling Processes. In relation to process establishment within life cycle model management, O'Connor et al. [29] explained that process establishment in SSCs is based on two categories: software development manager work background and market requirements [29]. From the perspective of an SSC, the benefits provided by a more standardized process could include increased competitiveness, superior customer satisfaction, and greater product quality [36]. Regarding process assessments, one study [14] reported that SSCs usually avoid the adoption of any process standards in their software development process. This may be due to the opinion that process standards are overly complex. However, in the context of process improvement, the objective for SSCs is to improve efficiency within the organization, improve productivity, and reduce development time [43]. SSCs tend to have problems with effectively improving their software processes [13], and the major difficulty could be a struggle to change [54]. In the context of knowledge management (KMP) within the human resource management process, Basri and O'Connor [55] stated that SSCs have clear KMPs within their organizations. They pointed out that knowledge waste is not a serious problem in a small-scale context. Also, informal communication and macro management can assist in creating team dynamics, which can further heighten KMP [55, 49]. Concerning quality management, requirements for ensuring that SSCs meet a certain level of quality are lacking. To improve the quality of their products, a clear definition of quality is needed, and goals for quality management need to be set. These quality goals can be altered based on the project [52]. In the context of software maintenance within technical processes, one study observed that software maintenance is poorly implemented in some companies and needs to be a priority for further improvement [24]. A number of companies have reported that they have amplified the refactoring level to reduce future support and maintenance costs [46].

Challenges in Process. Some challenges were also observed in the primary study papers. A list of the challenges observed and experienced by SSCs within the processes is presented in Table 4. The challenges are mostly related to the following processes: software requirements analysis, software qualification testing, software quality assurance, software documentation management, software configuration management, and life cycle model management.

Table 4. Challenges in processes

Process	Challenge	Description
Software requirements analysis	Understanding gathered information	The gathered information needs to be clearly understood to determine its business value and to further develop it into an explicit product requirements for release plan [27]
	Communication gaps	This is difficulty in sharing information between the customers, product management team, and the rest of the organization [27]
	Nonfunctional requirements	Nonfunctional requirements such as performance and the usability of software products are hardly documented. The focus is more on collecting functional requirements [52]
Software qualification testing	Testing knowledge	This refers to the lack of proper testing knowledge [25]. This may be due to undefined process descriptions or quality manuals in small companies. This results in uncertainty regarding when and what to test
Software quality assurance	QA definition	The meaning of *QA* differs between companies [44]. The lack of proper process knowledge and a clear definition of QA may be the cause for this
	QA as overhead	Due to a smaller number of employees and resources, small companies consider QA activities as a burden [26]

(*Continued*)

Table 4. (*Continued*)

Process	Challenge	Description
Software documentation management	No documentation	The information is often transferred in discussions without documenting it. Due to this, scheduling a meeting at a specified time is a challenge in SSCs [25]
Software configuration management	CM guidelines.	Due to a lack of proper CM guidelines, there is uncertainty about which work products should be with version control [52]. This is due to an undefined process description or the lack of quality manuals in SSC
Life cycle model management	Avoid process adoption	SSCs usually avoid the adoption of any process standards in their software development process [14]. The reason could be due to that SSCs' consider process assessments and improvement as overly complex or think that they could raise project costs and delay project delivery

5 Discussion and Conclusion

In this paper, we have applied a systematic review method to analyze the literature related to processes within the SSC context, with the goal of exploring the state of the practice of the software development processes and the challenges associated with them.

In regard to RQ1: What is the state-of-practice in terms of the use of processes in small software companies? The current state of the practice related to the software development processes in SSCs can be seen in Table 3. It shows that software requirements analysis (49 %) within software implementation processes, project planning (39 %) within project processes, configuration management (22 %) in software support processes, and life cycle model management (56 %) in organizational project-enabling processes are the frequently considered processes for improvement when software process improvement (SPI) programs are conducted in SSCs. This suggests that SSC are mostly attracted to the above processes. The reason for the significant frequency of software requirement may be that requirements are considered an obligatory process and are often fundamental to any software company's success [51]. Therefore, it is considered to be a critical process for further improvements since SSCs wish to quickly deliver what their customers want to remain competitive in a dynamic market and to maintain a healthy relationship with their customers [15]. Thus, focusing more on requirement engineering seems to be legitimate, based on the nature of SSCs.

In regard to RQ2: What are the challenges that small software companies face in the processes? Several challenges were also found in the context of processes, such as a lack of understanding in terms of what collected requirements really mean, a lack of testing knowledge, and a lack of CM guidelines (see Table 4). The reported challenges mostly fall under the frequently reported processes in Table 4. Typically, SSCs do not implement the necessary SPI programs for improving the process [15, 7]. In fact, most SSCs lack the required knowledge [14]. This could be a possible root cause for the many challenges revealed in the primary study papers.

Our observation from this review is that most of the studies we analyzed were conducted in collaboration with SSCs and that some also included medium-sized companies. Some papers referred to the SPI program based on models such as CMMI and SPICE within SSCs. We also observed that the SPI efforts carried out in SSCs are significantly reported in the literature, while descriptions of software processes in SSCs have received surprisingly little attention. An exploration of the empirical methods used in the primary studies showed that the majority of the studies were case studies. However, based on a systematic and validated model [19], our analysis shows that the majority of these papers fall under the low-rigor category (i.e., most of the studies lacked an adequate description of the study context, study design, and/or study validity). Therefore, further rigorous empirical studies within the context of software processes and SSCs are required. Various challenges were also found during the review that should be validated empirically in future research.

Acknowledgments. This research is supported by HILLA and ICT SHOK N4S (Need for Speed) programs funded by TEKES (Finnish Funding Agency for Technology and Innovation).

References

1. Arora, A., Gambardella, A.: The globalization of the software industry: perspectives and opportunities for developed and developing countries (2004)
2. Richardson, I., von Wangenheim, C.G.: Why are small software organizations different? IEEE Softw. **24**, 18–22 (2007)
3. Von Wangenheim, C.G., Weber, S., Hauck, J.C.R., Trentin, G.: Experiences on establishing software processes in small companies. Inf. Softw. Technol. **48**, 890–900 (2006)
4. Pettersson, F., Ivarsson, M., Gorschek, T., Öhman, P.: A practitioner's guide to light weight software process assessment and improvement planning. J. Syst. Softw. **81**, 972–995 (2008)
5. Fuggetta, A., Di Nitto, E.: Software process. In: Proceedings of the on Future of Software Engineering - FOSE 2014, pp. 1–12. ACM Press, New York, USA (2014)
6. De Castro, R.M., Braga, J.L., Soares, L.S., Oliveira, A.D.P.: Selection of software development good practices in micro and small enterprises: an approach using knowledge-based systems. In: 2012 31st International Conference on Chilean Computer Science Society, pp. 12–20 (2012)
7. Pino, F.J., García, F., Piattini, M.: Software process improvement in small and medium software enterprises: a systematic review. Softw. Qual. J. **16**, 237–261 (2008)
8. Sulayman, M., Mendes, E.: A systematic literature review of software process improvement in small and medium web companies. In: Ślęzak, D., Kim, T.-H., Kiumi, A., Jiang, T., Verner, J., Abrahão, S. (eds.) ASEA 2009. CCIS, vol. 59, pp. 1–8. Springer, Heidelberg (2009)

9. Paternoster, N., Giardino, C., Unterkalmsteiner, M., Gorschek, T., Abrahamsson, P.: Software development in startup companies: a systematic mapping study. Inf. Softw. Technol. **56**, 1200–1218 (2014)
10. Klotins, E., Unterkalmsteiner, M., Gorschek, T.: Software engineering knowledge areas in startup companies : a mapping study. In: Fernandes, J.M., Machado, R.J., Wnuk, K. (eds.) ICSOB 2015. LNBIP, vol. 210, pp. 245–247. Springer, Heidelberg (2015)
11. Zhang, H., Ali Babar, M.: Systematic reviews in software engineering: an empirical investigation. Inf. Softw. Technol. **55**, 1341–1354 (2013)
12. ISO/IEC/IEEE Standard for Systems and Software Engineering - Software Life Cycle Processes (2008)
13. Espinosa-Curiel, I.E., Rodríguez-Jacobo, J., Fernández-Zepeda, J.A.: A framework for evaluation and control of the factors that influence the software process improvement in small organizations. J. Softw. Evol. Process. **25**, 393–406 (2013)
14. Basri, S., O'Connor, R.V.: Understanding the perception of very small software companies towards the adoption of process standards. In: Riel, A., O'Connor, R., Tichkiewitch, S., Messnarz, R. (eds.) EuroSPI 2010. CCIS, vol. 99, pp. 153–164. Springer, Heidelberg (2010)
15. Tosun, A., Bener, A., Turhan, B.: Implementation of a software quality improvement project in an SME: a before and after comparison. In: 2009 35th EUROMICRO Conference on Software Engineering and Advanced Applications, SEAA 2009, pp. 203–209 (2009)
16. O'Connor, R.V., Laporte, C.Y.: Using ISO/IEC 29110 to harness process improvement in very small entities. In: O`Connor, R.V., Pries-Heje, J., Messnarz, R. (eds.) EuroSPI 2011. CCIS, vol. 172, pp. 225–235. Springer, Heidelberg (2011)
17. Kitchenham, B., Charters, S.: Guidelines for performing systematic literature reviews in software engineering. Engineering **2**, 1051 (2007)
18. StArt — LaPES - Laboratório de Pesquisa em Engenharia de Software. http://lapes.dc.ufscar.br/tools/start_tool
19. Ivarsson, M., Gorschek, T.: A method for evaluating rigor and industrial relevance of technology evaluations. Empir. Softw. Eng. **16**, 365–395 (2011)
20. Cruzes, D.S., Dyba, T.: Recommended steps for thematic synthesis in software engineering. In: 2011 International Symposium on Empirical Software Engineering and Measurement, pp. 275–284 (2011)
21. Yin, R.K.: Case Study Research: Design and Methods. Sage Publications, Thousand Oaks (2009)
22. Hidayah, I., Wahyuni, W., Nugroho, L.E.: Process model and software process improvement for small software organization: an ethnographic study in Indonesia. **2**, 852–856 (2012)
23. Savolainen, P., Sihvonen, H.-M., Ahonen, J.: SPI with lightweight software process modeling in a small software company. Softw. Process Improv. **4764**, 71–81 (2007)
24. Ayalew, Y., Motlhala, K.: Software process practices in small software companies in Botswana. In: 2014 14th International Conference on Computational Science Its Applications, pp. 49–57 (2014)
25. Valtanen, A., Ahonen, J.J.: Big improvements with small changes: improving the processes of a small software company. In: Jedlitschka, A., Salo, O. (eds.) PROFES 2008. LNCS, vol. 5089, pp. 258–272. Springer, Heidelberg (2008)
26. Lester, N.G., Wilkie, F.G., Mcfall, D., Ware, M.P.: Investigating the role of CMMI with expanding company size for small- to medium-sized enterprises. J. Softw. Maint. Evol. Res. Pract. **22**, 17–31 (2010)
27. Jantunen, S.: Exploring software engineering practices in small and medium-sized organizations. In: Proceedings of the 2010 ICSE Workshop on Cooperative and Human Aspects of Software Engineering - CHASE 2010, pp. 96–101 (2010)

28. Yilmaz, L., Phillips, J.: The impact of turbulence on the effectiveness and efficiency of software development teams in small organizations. Softw. Process Improv. Pract. **12**, 247–265 (2007)
29. O'Connor, R.V., Basri, S., Coleman, G.: Exploring managerial commitment towards SPI in small and very small enterprises. In: Riel, A., O'Connor, R., Tichkiewitch, S., Messnarz, R. (eds.) EuroSPI 2010. CCIS, vol. 99, pp. 268–279. Springer, Heidelberg (2010)
30. Jezreel, M., Mirna, M., Pablo, N., Edgar, O., Alejandro, G., Sandra, M.: Identifying findings for software process improvement in SMEs: an experience. In: Proceedings of the 2012 9th Electronics, Robotics and Automotive Mechanics Conference CERMA 2012, pp. 141–146 (2012)
31. von Wangeheim, C.G., Anacleto, A., Salviano, C.F.: Helping small companies assess software processes. IEEE Softw. **23**, 91–98 (2006)
32. von Wangenheim, C.G., Varkoi, T., Salviano, C.F.: Standard based software process assessments in small companies. Softw. Process Improv. Pract. **11**, 329–335 (2006)
33. Basri, S., O'Connor, R.: Organizational commitment towards software process improvement an irish software VSEs case study. In: Proceedings of 4th International Symposium on Information Technology 2010 (ITSim 2010), Malaysia, June 2010
34. Pino, F.J., Garcia, F., Piattini, M.: Key processes to start software process improvement in small companies. In: Proceedings of the 2009 ACM Symposium on Applied Computing, pp. 509–516 (2009)
35. Del Maschi, V.F., Spinola, M.M., Costa, I.A., Esteves, A.L., Souza, L.S., Vendramel, W., Pirola, J.: Practical experience in customization for a software development process for small companies based on RUP process and MSF. In: Software Process Improvement for Small and Medium Enterprises: Techniques and Case Studies, pp. 71–93 (2008)
36. Laporte, C.Y., Alexandre, S., O'Connor, R.: A software engineering lifecycle standard for very small enterprises. In: O'Connor, R.V., Baddoo, N., Smolander, K., Messnarz, R. (eds.) EuroSPI 2008. CCIS, vol. 16, pp. 129–141. Springer, Heidelberg (2008)
37. Habra, N., Alexandre, S., Desharnais, J.M., Laporte, C.Y., Renault, A.: Initiating software process improvement in very small enterprises: experience with a light assessment tool. Inf. Softw. Technol. **50**, 763–771 (2008)
38. Nilsson, A., Castro, L.M., Rivas, S., Arts, T.: Assessing the effects of introducing a new software development process: a methodological description. Int. J. Softw. Tools Technol. Transf. **17**, 1–16 (2013)
39. McCaffery, F., McFall, D., Wilkie, F.G.: Improving the express process appraisal method. In: Bomarius, F., Komi-Sirviö, S. (eds.) PROFES 2005. LNCS, vol. 3547, pp. 286–298. Springer, Heidelberg (2005)
40. Hauck, J.C.R., von Wangenheim, C.G., de Souza, R.H., Thiry, M.: Process reference guides – support for improving software processes in alignment with reference models and standards. In: O'Connor, R.V., Baddoo, N., Smolander, K., Messnarz, R. (eds.) EuroSPI 2008. CCIS, vol. 16, pp. 70–81. Springer, Heidelberg (2005)
41. Cater-Steel, A.P.: Low-rigour, rapid software process assessments for small software development firms. In: Proceedings of the Australian Software Engineering Conference, ASWEC 2004, pp. 368–377 (2004)
42. Hurtado, J.A., Bastarrica, M.C., Ochoa, S.F., Simmonds, J.: MDE software process lines in small companies. J. Syst. Softw. **86**, 1153–1171 (2013)
43. Tuffley, A., Grove, B., McNair, G.: SPICE for small organisations. Softw. Process Improv. Pract. **9**, 23–31 (2004)
44. Wilkie, F.G., McFall, D., McCaffery, F.: An evaluation of CMMI process areas for small - to medium-sized software development organisations. Softw. Process Improv. Pract. **10**, 189–201 (2005)

45. Diaz, J., Garbajosa, J., Calvo-Manzano, J.A.: Mapping CMMI level 2 to scrum practices: an experience report. In: O'Connor, R.V., Baddoo, N., Cuadrago Gallego, J., Rejas Muslera, R., Smolander, K., Messnarz, R. (eds.) EuroSPI 2009. CCIS, vol. 42, pp. 93–104. Springer, Heidelberg (2009)
46. Clarke, P., O'Connor, R.V.: An empirical examination of the extent of software process improvement in software SMEs. J. Softw. Evol. Process **25**(9), 981–998 (2013)
47. Caballero, E., Calvo-Manzano, J.A., San Feliu, T.: Introducing scrum in a very small enterprise: a productivity and quality analysis. In: O`Connor, R.V., Pries-Heje, J., Messnarz, R. (eds.) EuroSPI 2011. CCIS, vol. 172, pp. 215–224. Springer, Heidelberg (2011)
48. O'Connor, R.V.: Evaluating management sentiment towards ISO/IEC 29110 in very small software development companies. In: Mas, A., Mesquida, A., Rout, T., O'Connor, R.V., Dorling, A. (eds.) SPICE 2012. CCIS, vol. 290, pp. 277–281. Springer, Heidelberg (2012)
49. Ribaud, V., Saliou, P., O'Connor, R.V., Laporte, C.Y.: Software engineering support activities for very small entities. In: Riel, A., O'Connor, R., Tichkiewitch, S., Messnarz, R. (eds.) EuroSPI 2010. CCIS, vol. 99, pp. 165–176. Springer, Heidelberg (2010)
50. Allison, I.: Organizational factors shaping software process improvement in small-medium sized software teams: a multi-case analysis. In: Proceedings of the 7th International Conference on Quality of Information and Communications Technology, QUATIC 2010, pp. 418–423 (2010)
51. McCaffery, F., Taylor, P.S., Coleman, G.: Adept: a unified assessment method for small software companies. IEEE Softw. **24**, 24–31 (2007)
52. Saastamoinen, I., Tukiainen, M.: Software process improvement in small and medium sized software enterprises in eastern finland: a state-of-the-practice study. In: Dingsøyr, T. (ed.) EuroSPI 2004. LNCS, vol. 3281, pp. 69–78. Springer, Heidelberg (2004)
53. Zhang, Y., Zhao, X., Zhang, X., Zhang, T.: Test effectiveness index: integrating product metrics with process metrics. In: 2012 IEEE International Conference on Cyber Technology in Automation, Control, and Intelligent Systems, CYBER 2012, pp. 54–57 (2012)
54. Alexandre, S., Renault, A., Habra, N.: OWPL: a gradual approach for software process improvement in SMEs. In: Proceedings of the 32nd EUROMICRO Conference on Software Engineering and Advanced Applications, SEAA 2006, pp. 328–335 (2006)
55. Basri, S., O'Connor, R.V.: Towards an understanding of software development process knowledge in very small companies. In: Abd Manaf, A., Sahibuddin, S., Ahmad, R., Mohd Daud, S., El-Qawasmeh, E. (eds.) ICIEIS 2011, Part III. CCIS, vol. 253, pp. 62–71. Springer, Heidelberg (2011)
56. Suula, M., Makinen, T., Varkoi, T.: An approach to characterize a software process. In: 2009 Portland International Conference on Management of Engineering and Technology, PICMET 2009, pp. 1103–1109 (2009)

SPI and Assessment

Developing Process Definition for Financial and Physical Resource Management Process in Government Domain

Ebru Gökalp[✉] and Onur Demirörs

Informatics Institute, Middle East Technical University, Ankara, Turkey
{egokalp,demirors}@metu.edu.tr

Abstract. Public Financial and Physical Resource Management (PFPRM) is becoming a core competency critical to a government organization's competitive advantage. Recent studies have shown that organizations with established PFPRM are able to generate millions of dollars in additional savings and have a distinct competitive advantage. Our literature review showed that there is also a lack of a guideline for process capability determination and improvement of PFPRM. On the other hand, after observing benefits in software organizations, The ISO/IEC 15504 is used as a baseline to generate capability/maturity models for different specific domains/sectors. Accordingly, the same approach is utilized in the government domain, and process definition of PFPRM based on the requirements of ISO/IEC 15504 is developed. Therefore, PFPRM can be assessed based on ISO/IEC 15504 to be consistently applied, managed, and controlled across governmental agencies. A case study, including the assessment of an organization's PFPRM capability level is performed. The assessment results are used to develop a road-map for implementing process improvement in the study. The initial findings show the applicability and adequacy of the proposed approach.

Keywords: Financial management · Physical resource management · Procurement management · Process improvement · Process definition

1 Introduction

The governments are under pressure to improve the service performance with limited budget. A key government priority is to substantially reduce costs and achieve better Value for Money (VFM) through reforming public financial and physical resources management (PFPRM) process. While attempting to adopt and comprehend effective, transparent, and contributory administration measures, they are faced with the challenge of transformation and the need to reengineer governmental processes and systems [1]. In the wake of the financial problems confronted by the government during the 2000s, the necessity of transformation for effective and efficient management of PFPRM process has become increasingly important in the governmental organizations.

As the government organizations continue to focus on core competencies and outsource non-core, yet critical functions, these organizations are relying on PFPRM process as a key to achieve and to maintain. Today's government organizations must now manage an increasing number of contractors and suppliers who are performing mission-critical functions for their organizations. Thus, public sector organizational core competencies now include the PFPRM processes. As stated in [2], public sector organizations should be focusing their attention on measuring the performance of their PFPRM processes in order to improve its core competencies.

The capability maturity models have been used in many organizations to assess the level of capability of their most critical processes. There are well-accepted Process Capability/Maturity Models (PCMMs), such as ISO/IEC TS 15504 [3–6], CMMI-DEV (Capability Maturity Model Integration for Development) model [7]. The ISO/IEC TR 15504 standard has recently entered a revision cycle. It will be gradually replaced by a new series of standards: the ISO/IEC 33000 series [8]. These models are used as an evaluative and comparative basis for process improvement and/or assessment, assuming that higher process capability or organizational maturity is associated with better performance. As a result of the observed benefits of these models, the extensions the use of them to other sectors/ domains are made available. i.e.: Automotive SPICE [9], Medi SPICE [10], Enterprise SPICE [11], etc.

We intend to utilize the same approach for the government domain by developing the Government Process Capability Determination Model (Gov-PCDM) based on ISO/IEC15504 standard [3–6]. The aim of Gov-PCDM is providing the base for improving the processes of governmental organizations. It pursues a structured and standardized approach by assessing relevant processes in order to perform quality improvement initiatives in a consistent, repeatable manner, assessed by adequate metrics with guidance on what to do to increase quality in government institutions.

The model is aimed to fulfill four high-level requirements as followings: enabling each public agency to evaluate its processes in detail; identifying the current state of its process capability; comparing itself against other agencies evaluated with the same model; and achieving feasible improvement roadmap to follow for improving their process capability levels.

The research question of the model is that how can a government organization improve its processes by assessing its process capability in a structured way?

We performed an exploratory case study to check if customization of ISO/IEC 15504 for government domain is applicable. The study was presented at the Spice Conference in 2014 [12]. Public investment management process performed in the Ministry of Development in Turkey was defined in an ad-hoc fashion, assessed its capability level, and a road-map to improve the process capability level was derived in the study. As a result of the study, although initial findings indicated the usefulness and adequacy of the proposed approach; the necessity of a methodology incorporating guidelines for government specific process definition was determined. In order to satisfy this determined necessity, the methodology was developed. The corresponding study of proposing an ISO/IEC 15504 based process improvement method for the government domain was presented at the Spice Conference in 2015 [13].

In the scope of this study, we analyze the PFPRM process performed in government organizations and we develop a process definition of PFPRM process, including level 1 process performance indicators as outcomes, base practices and work products. The research methodology of how to develop the process definition of PFPRM is described in detail in this study. Additionally, a case study is performed in order to check the usefulness and adequacy of the proposed approach.

This paper is divided into six sections. In the Sect. 2, a brief literature review about PFPRM process improvement is given. Research methodology of the study is discussed in the Sect. 3. Process definition of PFPRM is given in the Sect. 4. In the Sect. 5, the case study performed in the Ministry of Development in Turkey is covered and the results of the case study are analyzed and the derived road-maps to improve the process in the organization are given. The study is concluded and future studies are summarized in the final section.

2 Literature Review

As stated in [14], the literature reflects an increasing flow in the research stream of public sector performance assessment and benchmarking. Hong et al. [15] also identified a growing need for assessment and benchmarking studies of complex business practices and increased research in the area of public sector processes. Fettke et al. [16] demonstrated the use of a business process maturity model to improve service response efficiency and effectiveness in public administration.

The use of maturity models for PFPRM process, such as contracting and procurement sub-processes, has seen some, but limited, application in the public sector. Raymond [17] stated that the necessity for PFPRM process best practices is increasing, especially in the areas of value for money, ethics, competition, transparency, and accountability. Redon [18] developed Contract Management Maturity Model to assess and measure a US Air Force contracting agency's procurement process and identified process improvement initiatives. Møller et al. [19] developed and applied a public procurement maturity model for the Denmark government. The use of their model will improve standardization, consistency, and transparency of Danish public procurement organization practices. Waterman and Knight [20] explored using a capability maturity model for conducting self-assessments in a case study on UK government procurement departments. Concha et al. [21] introduced the e-Government Procurement Observatory Maturity Model (eGPO-MM) to measure government e-procurement portals status across the Latin American region and to enable development of an improvement road map for eGP in each participating country.

The literature review can be summarized by concluding that there is a growing research stream in the benefits and challenges of measuring PFPRM process. Additionally, the literature review identified a research gap in that there is limited research in the use of maturity models for assessing PFPRM process. Of the research identified in the review, no study was based on the Turkish government, additionally, the maturity models identified in the review were not based on key PFPRM process base practices, but on other procurement and contracting functions. The research in this study aims to fill this gap by assessing PFPRM process performed in the Turkish government.

The research methodology, including the method of the process definition of PFPRM and the assessment is given in the next section.

3 Research Methodology

3.1 Process Definition

The development of the process definition of PFPRM is illustrated in Fig. 1. As a first step, documents related to policies & business rules of the government for the PFPRM, and existing quality improvement models and standards are investigated. The process definition of PFPRM is developed by harmonizing existing quality improvement models and standards as FEAF (Federal Enterprise Architecture Framework) [22], APQC (American Process Qualification Center) [23], ISO/IEC 15504 [3–6], CMMI-SVC [24] based on the policies and business rules of the PFPRM. The draft version of PFPRM definition is established by one of the authors. The process definition draft is formally reviewed by five PFPRM owners who are working in the finance department in government agencies. They are requested to provide verbal and written feedback on the following questions:

(1) Are the major elements of the process definition of PFPRM; such as, outcomes, base practices, and work products are well defined and articulated?
(2) Is there any information you want to add in the process definition of PFPRM?

The feedbacks are used to refine and revise the model. The revised version of the process definition of PFPRM is reviewed and approved by the management with executive responsibility within two different governmental organizational units by 2

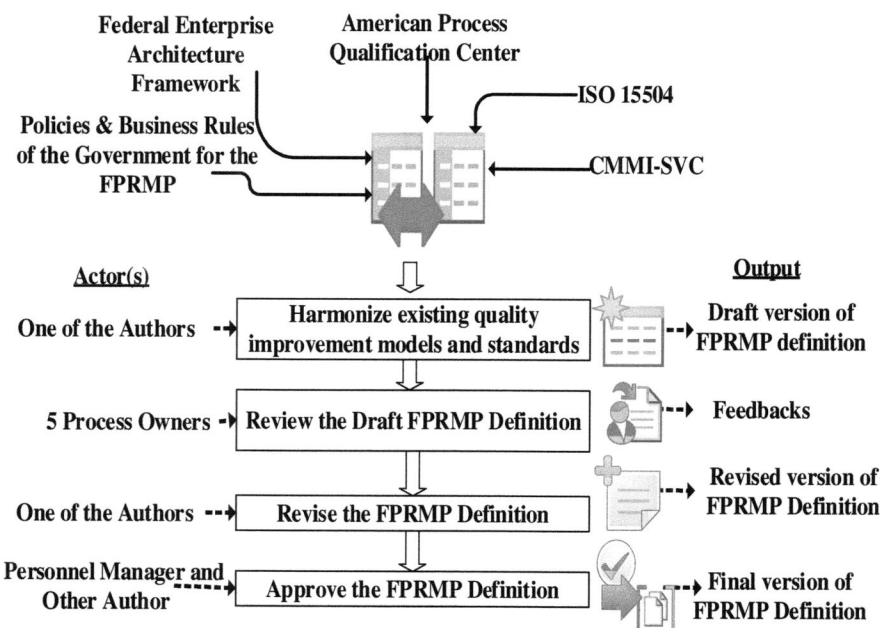

Fig. 1. The development of process definition of PFPRM

people and one of the authors who has both professional and academic experience in using ISO/IEC 15504. Consequently, the final version of the process definition of PFPRM which is given in Sect. 4 is achieved.

The process definition of the PFPRM is developed to perform assessment of Level-1. The process practice indicator of the PA 1.1. (Process Performance Attribute), seen in Fig. 2, is achieving outcomes defined in the process definition. The developed process definition of PFPRM is used to assess if the process is performed. The process definition is characterized by process purpose statements which are the essential measurable objectives of a process; process outcomes, base practices, and work products.

- *The purpose* describes the goal of performing the process;
- *The outcomes* express the observable results expected from the successful performance of the process;
- *The base practices* are a list of actions that may be used to achieve the outcomes;
- *The work products* are separately identifiable bodies of information produced and stored for human use during a system life cycle.

3.2 Process Assessment

The assessment procedures related to details of activities such as planning, briefing of the participants, data collection and validation and reporting are based on ISO/IEC 15504-3 [4]. Process Capability is classified into six levels in ISO/IEC 15504-2 [3]; as Level 0: Incomplete; Level 1: Performed; Level 2: Managed; Level 3: Established; Level 4: Predictable; Level 5: Optimizing.

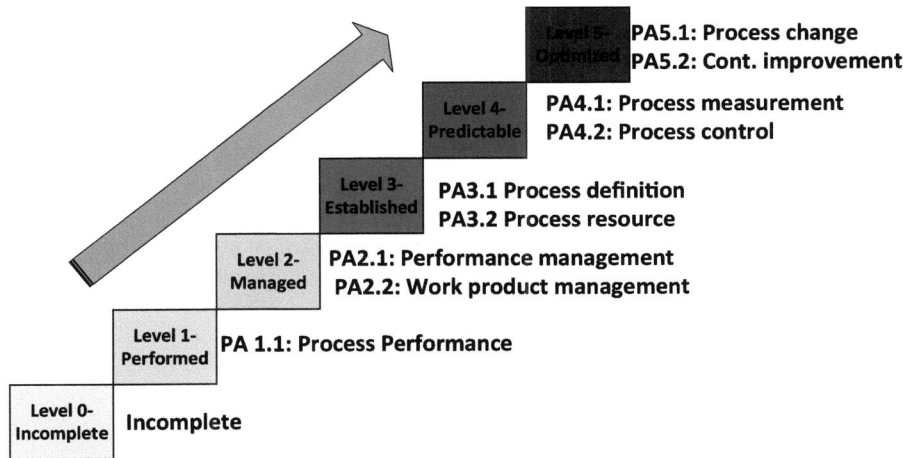

Fig. 2. Process capability levels

The measure of capability is based upon a set of process attributes (PA). Process capability indicators are the means of achieving the capabilities addressed by the considered process attributes. Evidence of process capability indicators supports the judgment of the degree of achievement in the PA.

The PA of Level 1 is Process Performance attribute which is a measure of the extent to which the process purpose is achieved. Developed process definitions are used for Level 1 assessment. For the assessments of levels 2 to 5, we use exactly the same 'generic practices indicators', 'generic resources indicators' and 'generic work products indicators' as the exemplar PAM provided by the ISO/IEC 15504-5 [6].

The capability level of each process instance is determined by rating process attributes. For example, to determine whether a process has achieved capability level 1 or not, it is necessary to determine the rating achieved by PA1.1 (Process performance attribute). A process that fails to achieve capability level 1 is at capability level 0. Each process attribute is measured by an ordinal rating F (Fully), L (Largely), P (Partially), or N (Not) achieved that represents the extent of achievement of the attribute. A process instance is defined to be at capability level k if all process attributes below level k satisfy the rating F and the level k attribute(s) are rated as F or L, as defined in ISO/IEC 15504-2 [3].

4 Financial and Physical Resource Management Process Definition

The developed process definition of FPRMP is given in Tables 1 below.

Table 1. The process definition of financial and physical resource management process

Purpose
The purpose of financial and physical resource management is to deploy and use the government's resources, facilities and assets.
Outcomes
As a result of successful implementation of the financial and physical resource management process;
1. Financial and physical resource strategy and policies are established.
2. The detailed financial plan (budget) containing cost estimates for consumed resources and, where applicable, revenue projections for fees[a] received is generated.
3. Procurements of goods, services or works are performed based on public procurement law.
4. Finance and accounting transactions are handled for procured goods/services or works and receiving where applicable.
5. Physical resources are acquired, constructed and disposed.
6. Warehouse used for storing tangible physical resources is managed.
7. Reports including internal and external financial information are generated.
8. Internal and external audits are conducted.

(*Continued*)

Table 1. (*Continued*)

Base Practices
MGRSP3.BP1: Establish and maintain a strategy and policies for financial and physical resource management: Establish and maintain a strategy and policies for financial and physical resource management. [Outcome: 1]
3.1.1 Build a strategic plan to support business objectives
3.1.2 Design capital structure
MGRSP3.BP2: Perform budgeting: Prepare periodic detailed budgets and plans and financial forecasts, according to established strategy and policies.[Outcome:1,2]
3.2.1 Develop annual budget proposal
3.2.2 Get approve for the budget from ministry of finance
3.2.3 Develop periodic detailed financial plan/budgets and forecasts based on the approved budget
3.2.4 Allocate resources
3.2.5 Manage financial risk
3.2.6 Manage fee administration, where applicable
MGRSP3.BP3: Procure goods/services or works: Purchase goods/services or works based on the public procurement law [Outcome:1,2,3]
3.3.1 Recognize need and requirements.
3.3.2 Prepare technical contract.
3.3.3 Conduct market research to calculate the approximate cost.
3.3.4 Determine tender procedure.
3.3.5 Prepare documents related to tender including proposal evaluation criteria.
3.3.6 Obtain approval for the tender.
3.3.7 Define tender committee.
3.3.8 Publish invitation for bid.
3.3.9 Review tender documents.
3.3.10 Receive tender proposals.
3.3.11 Apply evaluation criteria to select a provider, negotiate contract terms and conditions to resolve open items and select the contractor.
3.3.12 Invite the selected contractor to sign the contract.
3.3.13 Monitor contractor performance.
3.3.14 Close the contract after ensuring that each party's performance meets contractual requirements.
MGRSP3.BP4: Process finance and accounting transactions: Process all the transactions related to purchasing products/services, paying, and receiving. [Outcome: 1,3,4]
3.4.1 Process accounts payable
3.4.2 Process accounts receivable, credit, and collections
MGRSP3.BP5: Manage physical resources: Establish requirements and standards for physical items which are acquired, constructed and disposed. [Outcome: 1,5]
3.5.1 Acquire and redeploy assets
3.5.2 Manage facilities
3.5.3 Manage physical risk
3.5.4 Dispose nonproductive physical assets

(*Continued*)

Table 1. (*Continued*)

MGRSP3.BP6: Operate Warehousing Collect, receive, and store assets, according to established strategy and procedures. [Outcome: 1,6]	
3.6.1 Track inventory deployment	
3.6.2 Receive, inspect, and store deliveries	
3.6.3 Track product availability	
3.6.4 Record taking out of store	
3.6.5 Track inventory accuracy	
3.6.6 Track third-party logistics, storage and shipping performance	
3.6.7 Manage physical finished goods inventory	
MGRSP3.BP7: Report information: Report transactions to accounting department (internal) and court of accounts (external). [Outcome: 1,7]	
3.7.1 Provide external financial information	
3.7.2 Provide internal financial information	
MGRSP3.BP8: Conduct internal and external audits: Determine compliance of performed process with the requirements, plans, laws and procedures, as appropriate. [Outcome: 8]	
3.8.1 Develop and implement audit strategy	
3.8.2 Plan an audit	
3.8.3 Perform Auditing	
3.8.4 Identify corrective actions from the audit report	
3.8.5 Track actions for audit report	
Work Products	
Inputs	**Outputs**
Public Financial Management and Control Law [Outcomes: 1,8]	
Budget Preparation Guideline [Outcomes: 2]	
Public Procurement Law [Outcomes: 3]	
Public procurement Contracts Law [Outcomes: 3]	
Asset Legislation [Outcomes: 5,6]	
Regulation on Prepayment Procedures and Principles [Outcomes: 2,3,4]	
Regulation on the Principles and Procedures of Internal Control and Preliminary Financial Control [Outcomes: 7,8]	
	Budget Proposal [outcome:2]
	Detailed financial plan [outcome:2]
Payment Order Document [outcome:4]	
	Warehouse Documents for (asset request stock-in, stock out, inspection and acceptation) [outcome:6]
	Appropriation Transfer Document [outcome:7]
	Audit Report [outcome 8]

[a]Many government services issue licenses and permits and collect an associated fee.

5 Case Study

A case study is performed in the Ministry of Development of Turkey in order to evaluate the adequacy of the proposed approach.

The Ministry of Development in Turkey is an expert based organization which plans and guides the country's development process in a macro approach and focuses on the coordination of policies and strategy development. It has 38 departments, 818 employees. An information system, named as E-budget, integrated with the Ministry of Finance and Public Contract Institute is used to coordinate the financial activities. The finance department is responsible for carrying out all works related to procurement, contracting, and physical resources management.

The result of the PFPRM process assessment that the capability level of the process performed in the Ministry of Development is Level 2 with the following rationale based on collected and validated evidence in Table 2. More details of the assessment are given in the technical report [25].

Table 2. Financial and physical resource management process assessment result

Attribute	Evidences	Assessment value
1.1. Process Performance	The process clearly achieved its purpose by maintaining financial and physical resource management	Fully Achieved
2.1. Performance Management	Reviews of the process work products are not planned. The performance is planned and managed informally, but they are not adjusted. Performance quality criteria are not defined and not monitored. There is no evidence of meeting, reviews and corrective actions. The e-budget system is used to manage the interfaces	Largely Achieved
2.2. Work Product Management	Work products are defined, revisions of the work products are stored in information systems but their appropriate review and approval criteria are not identified. Additionally, they are not reviewed	Largely Achieved

In order to improve the capability level of the PFPRM Process to Level 3, assessment values of the process attributes should be as follows; Performance and Work Product Management attributes: Fully Achieved, Process Definition and deployment attributes: Largely or Fully Achieved.

5.1 Guideline for Improvement Capability of the Process

The roadmap to improve the capability level of the processes is derived from the assessment evidences in the technical report [25]. The aim is to turn negative evidences into positive evidences of process capability indicators supporting the judgment of the degree of achievement of the process attribute. For example; for performance management attribute; the second indicator (Generic Practice 2.1.2) is to plan and monitor the performance of the process to fulfill the identified objectives. Negative evidence, observed while interviewing with process owners for this indicator is that the risk is not taken into consideration. Thus, necessity of reviewing work products is indicated in the guideline as follows:

- Work-product Management
  - Define requirement of work product
  - Define quality criteria
  - Define appropriate review and approval of work products. And also, review the work products based on this definition.
  - Define relations between work products
- Configuration Management
  - Assign versions of the work products to product configurations as applicable.
  - Change control of the work products (keep version status, etc.)
- Workflow Management
  - A workflow management system to define activities, tasks, responsible employees and authorities and also sequence and interaction between processes.
- Process Management
  - Verify the conformance of defined process with standard process requirements officially.
  - Monitor and adjust the process performance indicators if necessary
- Risk Management System
  - Define risks related to fulfill the objective of the process.
  - Develop problem and issue management mechanism
  - Define how to adjust the objective when needed

5.2 Interviews with the Stakeholders

In order to check usefulness and adequacy of the proposed approach, interviews were conducted with stakeholders. The open-ended structured questionnaire below is utilized.

- Are measuring process capability and obtaining guideline for improvement useful?
- Do you think that applying these suggestions will improve the process performance?
- Is there any information you want to add to the PFPRM process definition?
- Is there any missing item in guideline for improvement list?

Interviews are conducted with six process owners, four of them have more than five years work experience. The rest of them has under 3 years' work experiences. The findings in the conducted interviews support our proposed approach. All of the answers for the first two questions are positive. They think that achieving a road map to guide what to do for increasing process capability is useful, all of the suggestions indicated in the guideline will improve the process performance of the PFPRM process. They stated that the biggest contribution to the improvement of the process is provided by developing risk management system and monitoring the effectiveness and suitability of the process. They also confirm the PFPRM process definition covers all outcomes of the process.

6 Conclusion

The process improvement of PFPRM process has the key government priority. Since government organizations are under the pressure to limit the budgets and to achieve effective, transparent, and contributory administration measures. In accordance with this purpose, we propose an approach to determine the capability level of the PFPRM process and achieve a road-map to improve the PFPRM process capability level based on ISO/IEC 15504.

Financial and Physical Resources Management process, performed in the government domain, is defined based on the requirements stated in ISO/IEC 15504-2 [3]. The definition of the PFPRM is described in detail in the study. Additionally, a case study is performed to check the usability of the approach. ISO/IEC 15504-3 [4] is used as a guideline to perform a conformance assessment. ISO/IEC 15504-4 is used as a guideline for developing the proposed roadmap for process capability improvement. ISO/IEC 15504-5 is used to identify indicators for levels 2 to 5. As a result of the case study it is indicated the usefulness and adequacy of the proposed approach of the process assessment of PFPRM.

Future studies include the validation of the proposed approach by performing different case studies in diversified government institutions. The findings from the case study shows that the approach is equally applicable in the wider government sector context.

References

1. Ertürk, A.: Influences of HR practices, social exchange, and trust on turnover intentions of public IT professionals. Publ. Pers. Manage. **43**(1), 140–175 (2014)
2. Burt, D.N., Dobler, D.W., Starling, S.L.: World Class Supply Management: The Key to Supply Chain Management. McGraw-Hill/Irwin, New York (2003)
3. ISO, ISO/IEC 15504-2: Information technology - Process assessment - Part 2: Performing an assessment (2003)
4. ISO, ISO/IEC 15504-3: Information technology – Process assessment – Part 3: Guidance on performing an assessment (2004)
5. ISO, ISO/IEC 15504-4: Information technology – Process assessment – Part 4: Guidance on use for process improvement and process capability determination (2004)
6. ISO, ISO/IEC 15504-5: Information technology - Process assessment - Part 5: An exemplar Process Assessment Model (2012)
7. Software Engineering Institute (SEI): CMMI Product Team, CMMI® for Development, Version 1.3, Improving processes for developing better products and services (2010)

8. ISO/IEC 33000 – Information Technology – Process Assessment, International Organization for Standardization (2014)
9. Automotive SIG. Automotive SPICE - Process Assessment Model (2007). http://www.itq.ch/pdf/AutomotiveSPICE_PAM_v23.pdf
10. Mc Caffery, F., Dorling, A.: Medi SPICE development. J. Softw. Maintenance Evol. Res. Pract. **22**(4), 255–268 (2010)
11. Ibrahim, L.: Improving process capability across your enterprise. In: 4th World Congress on Software Quality (4WCSQ), Bethesda, USA (2008)
12. Gökalp, E., Demirörs, O.: Government process capability model: an exploratory case study. In: Mitasiunas, A., Rout, T., O'Connor, R.V., Dorling, A. (eds.) SPICE 2014. CCIS, vol. 477, pp. 94–105. Springer, Heidelberg (2014)
13. Gökalp, E., Demirörs, O.: Proposing an ISO/IEC 15504 based process improvement method for the government domain. In: Rout, T., O'Connor, R.V., Dorling, A. (eds.) SPICE 2015. CCIS, vol. 526, pp. 100–113. Springer, Heidelberg (2015)
14. Maheshwari, D., Janssen, M.: Measurement and benchmarking foundations: providing support to organizations in their development and growth using dashboards. Gov. Inf. Q. **30**, S83–S93 (2013)
15. Hong, P., Hong, S.W., Jungbae Roh, J., Park, K.: Evolving benchmarking practices: a review for research perspectives. Benchmarking Int. J. **19**(4/5), 444–462 (2012)
16. Fettke, P., Zwicker, J., Loos, P.: Business process maturity in public administrations. In: vom Brocke, J., Rosemann, M. (eds.) Handbook on Business Process Management 2, pp. 485–512. Springer, Berlin (2015)
17. Raymond, J.: Benchmarking in public procurement. Benchmarking Int. J. **15**(6), 782–793 (2008)
18. Rendon, R.G.: Procurement process maturity: key to performance measurement. J. Publ. Procurement **8**(2), 200 (2008)
19. Møller, M., Hedegaard, J., Petersen, K., Vendelbo, A., Jakobsen, S.: Development model for public procurement in a Danish context. In: Proceedings from 4th International Public Procurement Conference, Part 18, vol. 1 (2006)
20. Waterman, J., Knight, L.: Achieving continuous improvement through self-assessment. In: International Public Procurement Conference (2010)
21. Concha, G., Astudillo, H., Porrúa, M., Pimenta, C.: E-government procurement observatory, maturity model and early measurements. Gov. Inf. Q. **29**, S43–S50 (2012)
22. C.I.O. Council. Federal Enterprise Architecture Consolidated Reference Model Document. Version 2.3 (2007)
23. American Productivity & Quality Center (APQC). Process Classification Framework, APQC, Washington, DC (2012). http://www.apqc.org/free/framework.htm
24. C.P. Team. CMMI for Service, Version 1.2, CMMI-SVC v1. 2. CMU/SEI-2009-TR-001. Technical report, Software Engineering Institute (2009)
25. Gokalp, E.: Technical Report of Financial and Physical Resource Management Process Assessment in Ministry of Development in Turkey (2016). http://smrg.ii.metu.edu.tr/smrgp/index.php?option=com_jresearch&view=publication&task=show&id=741&Itemid=54

A Nominal Group Interview Technique to Support Lightweight Process Assessments: Description and Experience Report

Eduardo Miranda[✉]

Institute for Software Research, Carnegie Mellon University,
Pittsburgh, PA, USA
mirandae@andrew.cmu.edu

Abstract. This paper describes a group interview technique designed to support lightweight process assessments while promoting at the same time collaboration among assessment participants. The method was successfully used in one consulting assignment were it got previously discording participants, talking to each other and agreeing on the issues. The technique borrows from agile software development the concept of user stories to cast CMMI's specific practices in concrete terms and the Planning Poker technique, instead of document reviews and audit like interviews, for fact finding and corroboration.

Keywords: Process assessment · Planning Poker · Lightweight assessment · CMMI · SCAMPI

1 Introduction

The group interview technique presented in this paper was developed by the author to support the assessment portion of a process improvement initiative launched by the management of a research agency which, as part of its mandate, develops and maintains a very sophisticated application used by more than 2,000 scientists all over the world. The organization was aware of its two main problems concerning this application: the accumulation of technical debt resulting from the development of features over a period of ten years without much architectural oversight and little refactoring, and the lack of a common development process fueled by the internal dissent of highly specialized and almost irreplaceable specialists. A previous attempt to address these problems had backfire due to the heavy handed approach followed by the person responsible for the improvement initiative. In requesting an assessment of their current ways of working, management had two objectives in mind: pinpointing specific problems by means of a recognized best practices framework and getting the development group to buy-in into the initiative. The development group for its part, was skeptical of what was perceived as a bureaucratic exercise getting in the way of doing the work.

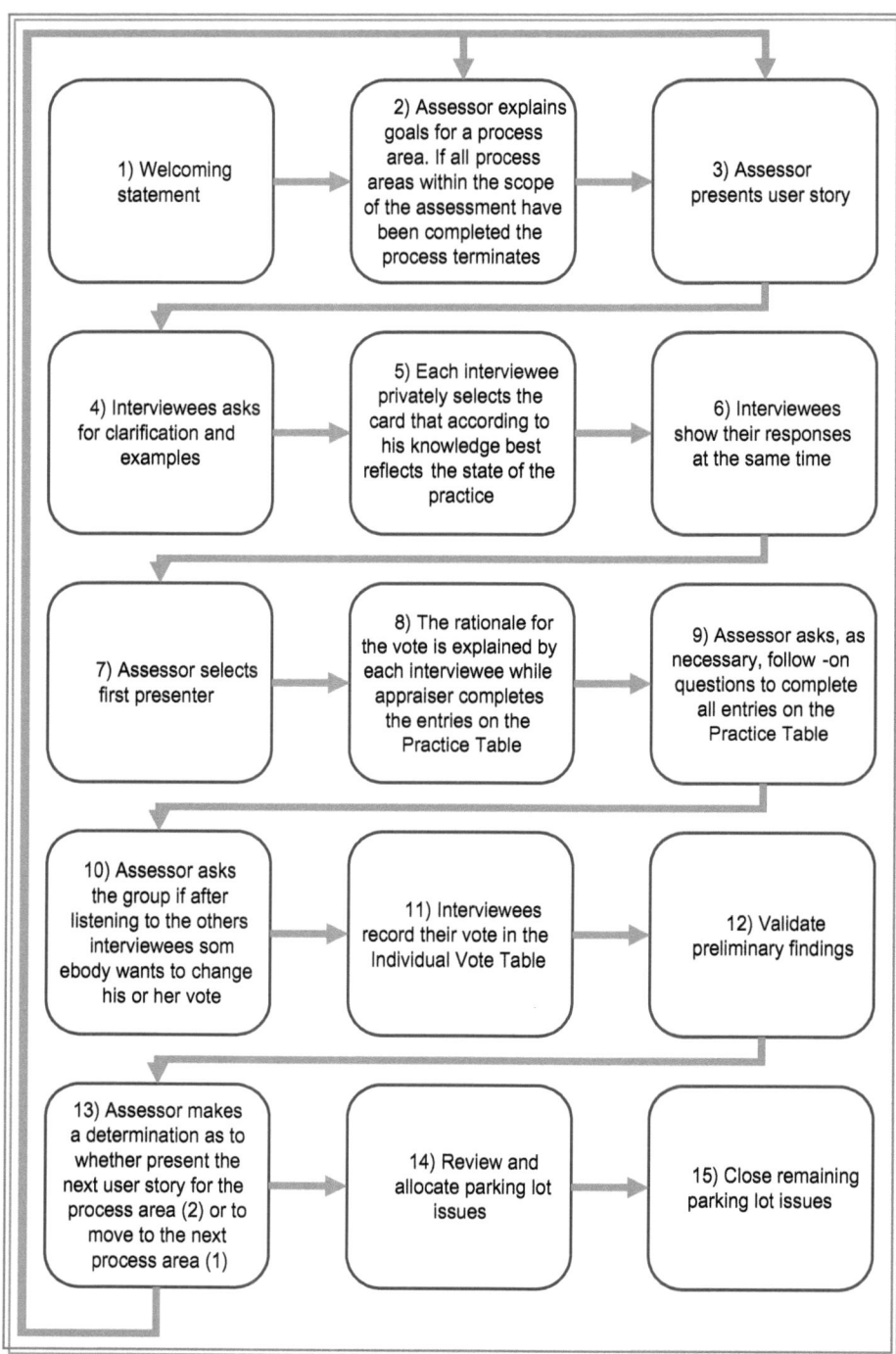

Fig. 1. Group interview process

In this context, a SCAMPI[1] like assessment based on document reviews and audit-like interviews was out of the question. In the opinion of the author, this approach would not only had met with the passive resistance of those involved but would have further convinced them, that they were right in their rejection of the whole process.

Through his teaching activities in the Master of Software Engineering at Carnegie Mellon University, the author had learned first-hand about the power of user stories to synthesize a lot of information in a concise format and that of the Planning Poker to get people talking and helping them to arrive to a consensus. So he thought to himself: why not use them for fact finding and corroboration? Both techniques looked apt for the job and would give the assessment a much needed fresh look in the eyes of the developers.

The assessment comprised individual interviews with managers and a group interview with practitioners. Figure 1 depicts the group interview process, the focus of this experience report. The interviews with managers had for purpose finding out what were the pain points, the improvement goals, the degree of support for the initiative and the impediments they saw moving forward. The group interview with practitioners focused on the state of the practice within the group vis-à-vis all level 2 and some level 3 process areas of the CMMI, the issues from the practitioners' point of view and whether the group had a congruent view of the problem and its possible solution.

The rest of the paper is organized as follows: Sect. 2 explains why and how to express specific practices as user stories. Section 3 discusses the modified Planning Poker technique used in the assessment of the current practice. Section 4, describe the preparation of the final findings documents, Sect. 5 briefly describes management interviews and Sect. 6 the experience applying the method.

2 Expressing Specific Practices as User Stories

Assessing the group's way of working against the process areas of the CMMI requires verifying whether the practices defined by it are performed or not and in the affirmative they do so in an effective and efficient manner. To do this, the group interview process presented in the next section walks assessment participants through all the practices in scope, asking them whether the practice is implemented or not, and whether they find it valuable. The participants' answers and more importantly, their buy-in into the process depends a lot on how the question is formulated (Dutton and Ashford 1993). For example, while few people will argue that connecting test cases to the functionality they verify is an important quality of a software development process, asking them if they *"maintain bidirectional traceability among requirements and work products"* would rise quite a number of eyebrows.

Of course the two phrases are not equivalent, the first is an instance of the second and is limited to a single work product. The point here is that while the CMMI rightly

---

[1] Standard CMMI Appraisal Method for Process Improvement (SCAMPI) is a family of appraisal methods developed by the Software Engineering Institute (SCAMPI Upgrade Team 2011).

aims for generality, response accuracy, buy-in and the development of a shared understanding about the problems is built around specific and not abstract constructs. The situation has been cleared described by Arent (2000) in the recount of their experience at Ericsson: *"The problem was that the project managers didn't understand the reasons for using CMM until they had actually tried to use it, and they didn't use it because they didn't understand the reasons for it. It was a vicious circle, making it difficult to succeed"*.

To make CMMI specific practices concrete, we use a slightly modified user story format: "As a <role> <personal pronoun> <practice instance> so <benefit>". This is a good vehicle for moving from the abstract to the concrete not only because most developers are already familiar and well predisposed to them but because they include who does it or who benefits from the practice: the <role>, what is done: the <practice instance> and the reason for doing it: the <benefit>. The <personal pronoun> is just that, its function is to make the user story grammatically correct.

The user stories are crafted by the assessor using his or her knowledge of the CMMI, some knowledge about how the organization works and their vocabulary. Table 1 below provides some examples as to how this is done.

Notice that there could be more than one <role> or <benefit> associated with a single <practice instance>, for example a <practice instance> could benefit or be performed by developers and testers and/or there could be multiple <benefit>s accruing from it, but in order to keep things simple we circumscribe the user story to direct performers and beneficiaries or, if already in use by the organization, a more encompassing category such as "team member", but we do not create artificial roles for the sake of economy of expression. Similarly we limit the description of the user story to one or two direct benefits since these are all it is needed to justify a practice. Conversely, if we could not find any beneficiary for doing something, we should consider dropping the practice from the assessment, otherwise seems like the organization has to do things for the sake of the model and not for the quality of the product or to better their way of working.

The more abstract a concept is, the higher the level of interpretation required and in consequence the higher the variability in the understanding of the same (Flesch 1962). This makes the choice of <practice instance> to be used in lieu of the corresponding CMMI abstract practice, a critical issue in eliciting definite answers from the assessment participants. Continuing with the idea of making things obvious, a simpler practice is preferred to a more complex one. In general, if the organization is not doing those things that give more bang for the buck it is unlikely they will do those that are at the fringes. Including a simpler practice in the user story when the organization is doing something more elaborate, is not a problem because one or more participants in the interview are likely to recognize the intent of the practice and answer correctly while at the same time volunteering good information.

The previous discussion deals with specific practices, but what about, CMMI's generic goals and practices? A CMMI generic goal is one that applies to multiple process areas in the model. These goals and their associated practices deal with the institutionalization of the specific processes that is whether the organization follows them routinely as part of doing business or not.

In the proposed method, the institutionalization of the process is assessed via the consistency of the interview responses and by the comments made by the interviewees. This will be explained in detail in the next section.

Table 1. Recasting CMMI's specific practices as user stories. Selected examples.

Reference	CMMI practice	User story
REQM 1.3 L2	Manage changes to requirements as they evolve during the project	As a team member I can find how user stories have evolved over time as well as their current status so I can better understand stakeholders' needs and avert "he said, she said" situations
PP 1.2 L2	Establish estimates of work product and task attributes	As a team we establish estimates for user stories and tasks so that we can make commitments to our stakeholders and plan our work
RSKM 1.1 L3	Determine risk sources and categories	As a team we have at our disposal a list of risks sources that can help us identify what might go wrong in a project and decide what to do about it
RSKM 2.1 L3	Identify and document risks	As a team we make a conscious effort to identify and document potential problems so we don't overlook them
TS 1.1 L3	Develop alternative solutions and selection criteria	As a team we discuss the characteristics a good software solution should possess and evaluate different solutions against them to avoid following a dead end path
VER 2.2 L3	Conduct peer reviews	As developers we review each other code with the purpose of identifying bugs and non-compliances with our coding guidelines

3 The Group Interview Technique

Figure 1 above, describes the workflow used in the practitioners interview. The process is based on the nominal group technique proposed by Delbecq et al. (1975) and on the Planning Poker (Grenning 2002; Cohn 2005), from which we borrow the idea of using cards to answer the interview questions, see Fig. 2.

The two key activities in the nominal group technique are the private voting and the round–robin explanation mechanism. Both activities synergistically promote frankness, participation and engagement. Because private voting precludes people from knowing how the others will vote, people cannot piggyback on somebody else's explanations forever while maintaining some kind of intellectual consistency over the course of the assessment, so most participants would choose to be candid in their votes and explanations. The stipulation that all voting cards must be turned at the same time reduces conformity effects. The round robin mechanism promotes engagement by either giving the opportunity or by forcing everybody to speak about their vote and in turn, listen to the explanations provided by others. In the words of Delbecq et al. (1975), the inventors of the method, *"The rather mechanical format of going to each member in turn to elicit ideas establishes an important behavior pattern. By the second or third round of idea giving, each member is an achieved participant in the group"*. We observed a similar pattern that is discussed in Sect. 5.

The selection of participants for the assessment is key to the credibility of findings and recommendations. The selection must ensure discipline coverage; balancing experienced personnel, who understand the organization well, with new comers, who face the challenge of getting on board. Having a wide spectrum of participants also ensures domain coverage. To promote openness management shall be excluded from participation in these interviews. Since the method relies on the agreement or disagreement of the interviewees it is very important to have at least two representatives from the main development areas. The number of participants should be kept under ten in the interest of time. The following paragraphs detail each of the workflow steps.

1. Welcoming statement

The assessor welcomes the participants, explain the process, its purpose, and objectives. Participants are also informed about the reason for their selection, highlighting the need for everybody's contribution despite differences in roles and seniority. During the welcoming statement participants are provided with the deck of cards, see Fig. 2, they will use to take votes and made aware of the basic appraisal rules: no attribution of votes and comments, no right or wrong answers, that interviewees should answer to the best of their knowledge, and that questions might be skipped if it becomes obvious from previous responses that no new insights will be gained by asking them. On a more mundane note, the assessor will inform participants about breaks and other logistics. The author has also found that cookies, coffee and a brief words by a senior manager concerning the importance of the initiative, will go a long way towards a successful meeting.

2. Assessor explains the goals of the process area

The assessor explains the intent of the process area the group is about to aboard. During this activity the assessor will explain the overall intent of the process area and that he will be using scenarios, in the form of user stories, to exemplify specific practices but that the organization might be achieving the same through some other mechanism and for that reason is very important to keep an open mind.

3. Assessor presents a user story

The assessor presents a user story to the group and after explaining it asks if clarification is required. User stories for each process area are presented one at a time. The assessor will first put a slide with the user story text that will remain up until the next one is presented and read it aloud. During the presentation the assessor might remind the group that the <practice instance>, as well as the <role> and the <benefit>s presented are just an exemplar and that there might exist other <role>s performing it or other <benefit>s derived from it. The assessor ends the presentation by asking if the user story is understood or if further clarification is required.

4. Interviewees ask for clarification

During this step the assessment participants ask questions with regards to the practice. Typical questions include the practice implementation, its goals and the protagonists. In responding, the assessor might resort to the original text of the specific CMMI practice to widen the perspective of the group in considering it. Time-boxing this period helps keep the conversation on point and minimizes wasted time. A good technique to prevent the conversation from drifting while remaining respectful of the speaking participant, is to acknowledge the argument and explain the point will be addressed on a coming process area or ask the group if the issue can be put in a parking lot to deal with it later.

5 & 6. Interviewees vote.

Interviewees privately select the card that according to their knowledge best reflects the state of the practice. Once everybody has selected his or her answer, they all show them up at the same time. After answering the interviewee's questions, the assessor will direct the assessment participants to take a preliminary vote on whether the practice is always followed, often followed, seldom followed, never followed or to indicate they don't know using cards like the ones show in Fig. 2. During this activity each assessment participant privately selects from the deck of cards the one that, to the knowledge of the interviewee, best reflects the state of the practice.

When the assessor notices that everybody has selected his or her card, he will ask the interviewees to show their votes at the same time. The assessor shall allow an adequate time for thinking and reflection before the vote.

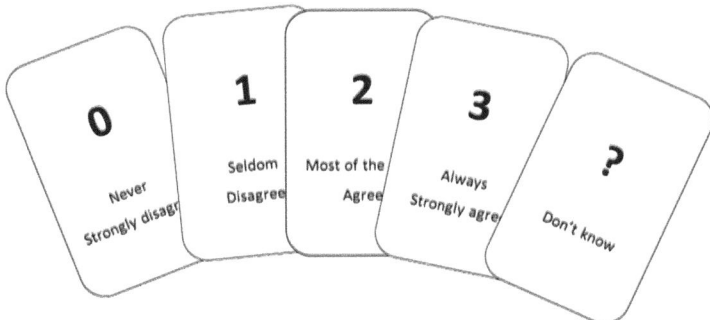

Fig. 2. Voting cards. Notice the cards do not include a neutral option. This was purposefully designed to force participants to take a stand on one side or other of the scale

7. Starter selection

The assessor select the first participant to start the explanation round. This might seem as a trivial step, but in order to avoid primacy and recency effects and for preventing a more extrovert personality to unduly dominate the meeting with his or her explanations or to liberate shy individuals from the stress of always being the first, it is important to choose a different starting participant for each round of explanations.

Sometimes it might be the person that was second to the first in the previous round some other times it could be somebody with a dissenting or extreme vote, because as much as the private vote mitigates conformity effects, hearing a couple of their colleagues say the opposite, might weaken the sound of a lonely voice. To avoid having participants misinterpreting this move as an affront or disrespect for their opinions it is very important to explain this during the welcoming statement.

8. Explanations

Each interviewee explain his vote. No interruptions are allowed during the exposition. During this step the interviewees take turn to explain the rationale for their vote. It is key that participants feel free to express varying points of view or to disagree. At this time the assessor has three responsibilities: pace the group in order to give time to everybody to talk, avert side conversations and excessive argumentation among participants and take notes. Notice that during this step the assessor does not attempt to clarify or seek additional information. Doing so might bias the explanations in a certain direction, when the goal is to cast a wide net. If at some point the explanations start to repeat and the remaining votes coincide, the assessor might ask the participants if somebody has anything new to add and otherwise go to the next step in order to save time.

For capturing the information in a structured manner and ensure completeness the author has used the list shown in Fig. 3 and referred to as "Practice Table" in the workflow.

- Is the practice being performed? Requires majority of respondents to agree or strongly agree
- Brief description if alternative practice
- Is it relevant? Adds value? If it were not executed something would not be accomplished, would cost more, etc.
- Efficient? The achievement of the goal requires an effort commensurate with the value of the outcome. The practice does not overlap or interfere with other practices
- Institutionalized? Does the staff receive training to perform it? Are adequate resources provided for performing it? Whenever a project is late, does the organiztion shortcut the practice with the excuse of saving time?
- Documented? Is there a document that mandates or describes the practice?
- Are there any noticeable strengths or weaknesses?
- Assuming that it makes sense, what prevents the practice from being implemented?
- Can anybody remember a problem in a project that can be traced back to deficiencies/lack of practice being performed?
- Additional comments

Fig. 3. Practice Table

9. Follow-on questions

If necessary the assessor asks follow-on questions. After all participants have provided their votes' explanation the assessor might ask follow on questions or seek clarification to some answers. In interest of time, the assessor should keep this short. The completion of all entries in the Process Table serves as exit criteria for the task. If there are items in which the assessor wants to go deeper, the assessor should make a note to retake the conversation at a later time and move on.

10. Definitive vote

At this point the assessor will ask participants if after listening to their colleagues they would like to change their vote.

11. Vote recording

Participants record their vote in the Vote Table, see Fig. 4. Each participant has its own form to vote and, of course, the forms are not attributable to a particular participant. The purpose of recording the votes is twofold: (1) to have a backup if any of the findings is challenged and (2) to provide an indication of the validity and strength of the findings to those that did not take part in the interview. For example, a finding where 90 % of the interviewees voted "seldom done" or "never" it is easier to accept and would trigger different improvements actions, than one where 80 % of the participants say it is practiced "most of the time" and the other 20 % say they "don't know".

12. Validate preliminary findings

The assessor communicates to the group his understanding of the state of the practice. If something had been misinterpreted the assessor corrects or clarifies the mistake. In case of disagreement the item is sent to a parking lot and the group moves forward. Instead of waiting until the end of the interview or later, to confirm a batch of preliminary findings like prescribed in the SCAMPI approach, the proposed interview

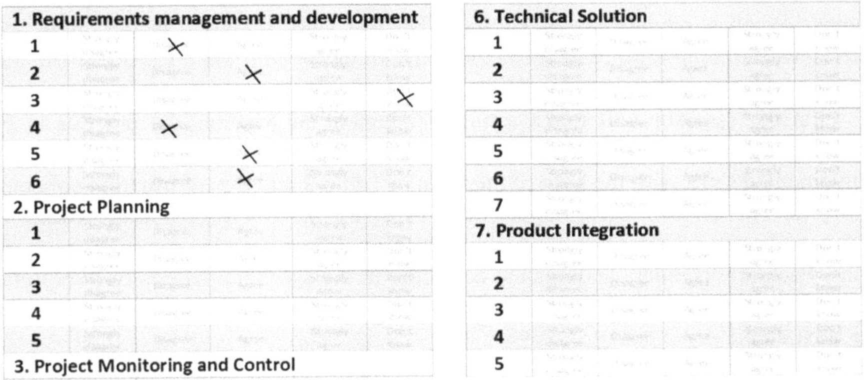

Fig. 4. Vote Table. Each row corresponds to a user story/specific practice in the respective process area

Table 2. Vote interpretation rules

Scenario	Rating	Reasoning
All the participants vote "Always" or "Most of the time" ("Strongly Agree" or "Agree")	Fully Implemented (FI)	All the participants know about the practice and they all perform it to some extent under most circumstances
All participants vote "Never" or "Seldom" ("Strongly Disagree" or "Disagree")	Not Implemented (NI)	One or more participants could have tried the practice, the "seldom" votes, in the past or through individual efforts but the practice is not being performed
A majority of the participants vote "Always" or "Most of the time" ("Strongly Agree" or "Agree"). The dissenting votes are "Don't know"	Largely Implemented (LI)	Most of the participants are performing the practice and those that don't is because they didn't seem to be aware of them. This could be due to lack of training, weaknesses in the onboarding process or lack of an organizational level policy
A majority of the votes fell in the "Seldom", "Most of the time" and "Don't know" categories	Partially Implemented (PI)	This clearly points to a practice that is carried out through individual efforts with some success, the "most of the time" votes, but is not institutionalized as indicated by the "seldom" and "Don't know" votes
Other	Assessor judgment	

process includes a quick validation step at the end of each iteration to validate the assessor understanding of the state of the practice. Because this takes place in the context of what is being discussed and what was said still vivid in the minds of the interviewees the possibility of misreading the situation with the consequent frustration and rework is avoided.

First the assessor will make a quick judgment of whether the practice is Fully Implemented (FI), Largely Implemented (LI), Partially Implemented (PI), or Not Implemented (NI), with the help of the rules in Table 2 and the information collected in the form. The assessor then his judgment using the reasoning behind the voting rules and paraphrasing the information gathered through explanations and follow-on questions. Factual misunderstandings are corrected in the spot and matters of interpretation are put on a parking lot for further discussion at a later time. The group then moves to the next step.

13. Assessor makes a determination about what to do next

The assessor decides if it is worth continue exploring the same process area or move to the next. Normally the assessment will move from one user story to the next within the same process area and once all user stories have been assessed, to the next process area. Sometimes however, after the exploration of a few user stories, it might become obvious the assessed organization does not meet the intent of the process area, and is of no use and almost demeaning to continue asking questions to which we already know the answer. At this point, the assessor should ask the group whether it is worth continuing with the current process area or move to the next.

14. Review and allocate parking lot issues

To conclude the group interview, participants review items put in the parking lot. Some of those would have probably resolved themselves through explanations following the decision that put them there in the first place. Unresolved issues, are assigned to specific participants to gather additional evidence, most likely in the form of work products or descriptions of alternate practices. A meeting with the group is scheduled for the next day.

15. Close remaining parking lot issues

All outstanding parking lot issues are closed. Some items might not have a single best answer and in this case to avoid damaging the relation between the assessor and the interviewees the second best alternative is to agree to disagree. If consensus cannot be reached, the assessor in his character of expert has the last word on the disposition of the item but has to leave established that consensus was not reached.

4 Final Findings

The assessor rates the specific goals, determines whether each process area is satisfied or not and derives strengths and weaknesses from the practitioners and management affirmations and his own observations[2]. Optionally an unofficial maturity level might be reported.

Final findings are goal-level statements that summarize the gaps in process area implementation (Kulpa and Johnson 2008). Strengths are enablers of organizational development. Implementations worth highlighting might be included in the final findings as long as they don't seem to be there just to have something to say on the "bright side". Weaknesses are inefficient implementations of a key practice or hurdles to be overcome to make the improvement initiative successful.

The judgments made about goal satisfaction are driven by the validated preliminary findings and the observations of the assessor. When a goal is not satisfied, it is

---

[2] In this we differ from SCAMPI which tries to be totally data driven. We believe the experience of the assessor is relevant especially in a process improvement setting.

important to be able to describe how the set of documented weaknesses or the extent of implementation of the associated practices led to this rating. It is also important to link this rating to one or more problems experienced by the organization to make, a compelling case for improvement.

5 Management Interview

Management interviews encompass senior and middle level managers. The focus of these interviews is not on the ways of working but rather the improvement goals from a managerial perspective, the organization culture, the political situation and the consensus about the improvement initiative. The questionnaire shown in Fig. 5 was used during the interviews.

6 Experience

The group interview technique described here was employed twice in the course of assessing the organization which has development sites at two different locations. In both cases the reaction to it was much the same which gives the technique some extra credibility over the single data point case.

Each assessment was conducted on two sessions of three and a half hours each. In one case the sessions were scheduled in two different days, in the other we had a morning and afternoon session. During the sessions there were little or no signs of fatigue. The use of the cards created a lively environment which was marked by the anticipation of knowing how the others would vote after each user story was presented.

Everybody present at the interview participated, even those that because of personality or opinion, were reluctant in the beginning. In this regard, I just can speculate as to the why. For those normally withdrawn, the engagement was perhaps the result of having the opportunity to talk and be listened to. For others the possibility of change that the assessment opened up. Those that thought the assessment was a bad idea, were put in an uncomfortable position by the round-robin mechanism which left them with no choice but to decline to talk and be perceived as negative and childish or participate. Participating when you did not believe in it though, would trigger a feeling of dissonance which could, unconsciously, be resolved by saying to oneself that this type of assessment was not so bad, and fostering engagement.

Whatever the reason, engagement was achieved within a couple of voting rounds and maintained through the assessment. These observations are not only consistent with those already mentioned of Delbecq et al. (1975) but also with those reported by Gresham (1986) in his dissertation "Expressed Satisfaction with the Nominal Group Technique Among Change Agents" and Haugen (2006) in his study of the Planning Poker.

> Current situation
> - What is your organization responsibility with regards to software development?
> - The 2013 User Committee Report identified a number of problems: communications with user, prioritization, performance and usability, lack of predictability, third party participation. Some of the same problems repeat in the 2014 Report. Do you agree with these problems?
> - Do these problems affect your funding, the survival of the organization, why is important to solve them?
> - Are there other pain points not mentioned in the reports?
> - What do you think is the root cause of these problems?
> - What do you see as impediments to solve this problems?
> - Do other members of the management team share your assessments?
>
> Environment
> - What are your improvement goals? How would you know you have reached them?
> - If you were to establish development processes or ask team members to report time or status, how do you think they would react to that?
> - Is there any organizational policy mandating software development, project management, quality assurance? Why not?
> - Does management provide adequate funding, physical facilities, skilled people, training and appropriate tools to perform the processes?
> - Do you assign responsibility and authority for performing the process, for example through job descriptions?
>
> Closing
> - Before we close the interview, is there anything you would like to add, any points we missed and you would like to comment on?

Fig. 5. Management interview questionnaire

7 Conclusion

Many process improvement methods resort to assessments for the purpose of determining the gap between a "best practices" framework, such as the Capability Maturity Model Integrated (CMMI) (CMMI Product Team 2010), the Information Technology Infrastructure Library (ITIL) (Cartlidge et al. 2011) or the new ISO/IEC 33000[3] and the way the assessed organization works to decide what needs to be improved and, depending on the type of assessment, how.

During the assessment, the assessors examine project and organizational practices to see whether they support the best practices included in the framework or not. The determination is done by reviewing work products and interviewing personnel and comparing the findings to the prescriptions of the framework. One of the problems with this audit like type of assessment, is that it automatically sends interviewees into a

---

[3] ISO/IEC 33000 is a new series of standards for software process assessment that replaces the 15504 series published by the International Organization for Standardization.

defensive mood and that it reinforces the perception of the process approach as an attempt to curtail creativity and collaboration by part of the management establishment. This is just the opposite of what is needed when you are about to embark in an organizational process improvement initiative.

The assessment method presented here takes a totally different approach. It is based on the Planning Poker, a well-known nominal group technique used for estimation purposes, which favors consensus building while mitigating common phenomenon like conformity effects and groupthink. The technique was successfully put into practice in two group interviews of the same organization. The method application was successful in the sense that not only correctly identified the organizational problems it was supposed to identify but also played a reconciliation role among groups with different views and people that was against the initiative ended up being very supportive.

Compared to a conventional SCAMPI-B or C (SCAMPI Upgrade Team 2011), the proposed method is economical and its light ceremony makes it palatable to the agile practitioners.

References

Cartlidge, A., et al.: An Introductory Overview to ITIL 2011. itSmf, London (2011)
CMMI Product Team: CMMI for Development, Version 1.3. Software Engineering Institute, Pittsburgh (2010)
Cohn, M.: Agile Estimating and Planning. Prentice Hall, Stoughton (2005)
Delbecq, A., Van de Ven, A., Gustafson, A.: Group Techniques for Program Planning: A Guide to Nominal Group and Delphi Processes. Scott, Foresman and Company, Glenview (1975)
Dutton, J., Ashford, S.: Selling issues to top management. Acad. Manage. Rev. **18**(3), 397–428 (1993)
Flesch, R.: The Art of Clear Thinking. Collier Books, New York (1962)
Grenning, J.: Planing Poker or how to avoid analysis paralysis while release planning (2002). http://renaissancesoftware.net/files/articles/PlanningPoker-v1.1.pdf. (Accessed 2012)
Gresham, J.: Expressed satisfaction with the nominal group technique among change actors. Texas A&M University (1986)
Haugen, N.: An empirical study of using Planning Poker for user story estimation. In: AGILE 2006 (2006)
Arent, J.: Project assessments: supporting commitment, participation, and learning in software process improvement. In: Proceedings of the 33rd Annual Hawaii International Conference on Systems Sciences, Hawaii (2000)
Kulpa, M., Johnson, K.: Interpreting the CMMI: A Process Improvement Approach, 2nd edn. CRC, Boca Raton (2008)
SCAMPI Upgrade Team: Standard CMMI Appraisal Method for Process Improvement (SCAMPI) A, Version 1.3: Method Definition Document. Software Engineering Institute, Pittsburgh (2011)

The Issue of Reliability in Software Mediated Process Assessments

Anup Shrestha, Aileen Cater-Steel^(✉), Mark Toleman,
Terry Rout, and Suren Behari

University of Southern Queensland, Toowoomba, Australia
{Anup.Shrestha,Aileen.Cater-Steel,Mark.Toleman,
Terry.Rout,Suren.Behari}@usq.edu.au

Abstract. This paper reports on a reliability analysis of a Software-mediated Process Assessment (SMPA) decision support tool as it was used at three sites. The tool was used at two sites as part of its development process. Following its evaluation, further development included the formulation of assessment questions and knowledge items to complete the requirements for all ISO/IEC 20000 processes. The SMPA was deployed at a third site, a large financial services firm. These three case studies brought up the issue of the reliability of the capability ratings and the value of the reliability measure (coefficient of variation) incorporated in the SMPA. Further data collection when undertaking assessments is required to have better assurance of the results given the variability of subjects. In addition the future of ISO/IEC 15504/ISO/IEC 330xx and ISO/IEC 20000 and how the SMPA will need to change to maintain alignment is raised.

Keywords: Reliability · ITSM process assessment · ISO/IEC 15504 · ISO/IEC 330xx · Evaluation · IT Service Management · Process improvement · ITIL · ISO/IEC 20000

1 Introduction

The service philosophy in IT management commenced when the UK Government developed a set of service-oriented recommendations in response to the growing importance of IT for the government in the 1980s. Since then, governments and businesses have gradually promoted the service view in IT operations and strategies leading to the discipline of IT Service Management (ITSM). A major contribution to date in the ITSM knowledge area is the development and worldwide adoption of a collection of books on ITSM best practices built around a process approach to manage IT services. These books are known as the IT Infrastructure Library (ITIL®). Since its initial development in 2005, the international standard for ITSM, ISO/IEC 20000 [1] has evolved based on the ITIL framework [2]. Recent research suggests increasing relevance of ITSM processes, particularly for smaller organisations in the coming years [3].

Akin to any process-based management systems, ITSM promotes continuous improvement of its processes. Improvements in ITSM processes require periodic review of process activities against an established benchmark such as the ISO/IEC 20000 standard or the ITIL framework. Measurement of process improvement can be undertaken through a formal compliance audit or by conducting regular process assessments. Assessments of ITSM processes are typically performed by expert assessors following guidelines from the international standards for process assessment, ISO/IEC 15504/ISO/IEC 330xx [4], and the SCAMPI method [5], among others. This research team developed and evaluated a software-mediated process assessment (SMPA) approach based on ISO/IEC 15504 (the Standard in use at the time), ISO/IEC 20000 and ITIL at two IT service providers. The SMPA uses a Decision Support System (DSS) tool to offer a transparent and efficient approach to assess the capability of ITSM processes. The initial deployment included assessment of four processes: change, problem, configuration, and service level management.

An explanation of a sound logic of process measurement can lead to increased satisfaction and trust in the SMPA approach by process managers. Since the DSS automatically derives the process capability scores using the arithmetic mean of all valid responses in the SMPA approach, it is critical to explain the logic of measuring such scores to promote transparency and reliability of the assessment. We have also developed the reliability scores using the statistical measure of coefficient of variation (CoV) to highlight the spread of responses that may lead to determination of a particular process capability score. Using the reliability metric while presenting the process profiles can boost confidence to accept the assessment results. The mean and the CoV are statistical measures to understand what the critical mass of assessment respondents think about the processes being assessed. The SMPA approach has used these simple calculations and is being continuously evaluated to determine process strengths and weaknesses in a transparent and efficient way.

Motivated by ongoing evaluation of the SMPA approach, this paper addresses the research question: *how can a measure of reliability be calculated for process attribute scores?*

The next section reviews literature on the standards for ITSM process assessment, and briefly explains relevant reliability measurement. The background and structure of the SMPA approach is then described with a detailed explanation of the calculation of the reliability of the process capability score. After a brief description of the methodology, the results of the assessments are provided with a discussion focused on the reliability measures. The final section summarises the paper, identifies limitations and highlights future developments in the SMPA and its underlying standards.

2 Literature Review

2.1 Standards for ITSM Process Assessment

The literature associated with ITSM process assessment is rooted in the concept of service and quality. Existing work on IT service quality has looked to the service marketing literature and focused on adapting the SERVQUAL instrument [6] to the context of IT service. Research on IT service quality has largely focused on user satisfaction measures while there is limited research related to processes [7].

It is a widely-agreed concept that service quality is ultimately determined by what the customer perceives. Nevertheless, there is little doubt that service providers should strive to improve their processes. Organisations can conduct customer satisfaction surveys to assess the outcome of the service provision. However customer satisfaction surveys do not provide descriptive information to service providers for improving their processes [8]. Therefore IT organisations need to find ways to improve their ITSM processes for better IT service quality [7]. Existing literature on IT service quality in terms of processes has shown a lack of research on this topic [9].

Measuring IT services is a challenging feat that requires both quantitative and qualitative metrics based on diverse service quality measures such as IT service quality, information systems quality, process quality, customer satisfaction, service value and service behaviour [7]. Few studies provide methodological guidance on an approach to determine process quality measures. The ITSM industry has defined widely popular best practice guidelines for process improvement and compiled them in the IT Infrastructure Library (ITIL) library. ITIL process best practices and the international standard for ITSM, ISO/IEC 20000, have been extensively used for ITSM process assessments. Non-ITIL approaches such as CMMI® for Services or eSCM for service providers have transparent models and frameworks but lack a consistent method to conduct process assessments.

The method for process assessment, as a mechanism for evaluating the implementation of effective processes in an organisation, derives from the pioneering work of Radice and his colleagues in IBM [10] and was further developed by Watts Humphrey [11]. The increasing commercial significance of the method resulted in the development of an international standard to prescribe consistent ways to conduct process assessments, resulting in the publication of the international standard for process assessment, ISO/IEC 15504 [12]. A key factor in the development of this standard was the application of empirical studies to validate the elements of the standards framework [13]. The standard initially comprised five parts, but with increasing use and application, further parts were added, to a total (for ISO/IEC 15504) of 10 parts. In order to address this a revision of the standard was undertaken to transform it from a single, multi-part standard to a set of related standards using a defined numeric range, the ISO/IEC 330xx series [14]. This transformation is resulting in an expanded range of application, and to a significantly more open standards framework. The revised requirements for the standard envisage that it will address the assessment of other process characteristics beyond that of process capability, which has been the focus of attention to date. The scope also makes possible the extension of assessment to fields outside the ICT domain [15].

Using ITIL processes and ISO/IEC 15504, evidence of repeatable and objective improvement in IT service quality has been reported [16]. Extensive work on the combination of ITIL and ISO/IEC 15504 led to the development of a popular ITSM process assessment approach called Tudor's IT Process Assessment (TIPA) [17]. TIPA has been promoted as a commercial framework for ITSM process assessment [18].

Even though international standards and best practices exist to assist in ITSM process assessments, inconsistent outcomes from different assessment services hinder comparisons and benchmarking due to proprietary assessment methods. Consequently, the lack of transparency still persists in ITSM process assessments due to disparate assessment methodologies. Addressing transparency is a major challenge of process assessments [19].

2.2 Reliability of Measures

All measures have errors. The literature is replete with studies arguing that errors in construct measurement are not accounted for adequately by researchers (e.g. [20, 21]) and there are continued calls for more rigour. Classical test theory or so-called true score theory [22] splits an observed score into two components, a true score and an error term. Now this error term may be completely random (which relates to reliability) and/or it might have a systematic component (which relates to the validity of the measure). Our interest here is on reliability and its measurement. Much of the literature on reliability is concerned with multidimensional constructs (typically psychological or behavioural constructs) and the various, sometimes complex measures of reliability (e.g. Cronbach's alpha). With one-dimensional measures simpler measures of reliability include the sample variance or permutations of that statistic. This is the approach applied in the SMPA, i.e. coefficient of variation is used. The reliability of the approaches defined in ISO/IEC 15504 have been studied extensively in the SPICE Trials, and generally high levels of agreement in rating process capability has been shown [13].

3 SMPA Approach and Reliability Measures

3.1 Background of SMPA Approach

From 2012 to 2014, our team developed and evaluated the *Software-mediated Process Assessment (SMPA)* approach. The SMPA is a standards-based process assessment approach that can be used by IT service providers to self-assess their processes. It employs a decision support system (DSS) tool to determine process capabilities. The DSS tool facilitates the SMPA approach to collect data for process assessments and analyses process capabilities to recommend process improvements.

To lend objectivity and consistency to the SMPA approach, its activities are aligned with the international standard for process assessment: ISO/IEC 15504 [23]. The application of the standard in ITSM is relatively new [18]. An exemplar process assessment model for ITSM has been published as a part of the international standard for process assessment [24].

Details of the design and architecture of the SMPA approach were previously published [25]. SMPA advocates best practice IT service processes based on the IT Infrastructure Library (ITIL®) and the international standard for ITSM ISO/IEC 20000.

While most of the existing process assessment methods rely on process-specific indicators that demonstrate objective evidence of process capabilities, the SMPA approach facilitates a top-down approach where assessment at each level of process capability is conducted through online surveys. In the SMPA approach, explicit questions based on the standard indicators are presented. Every question is rated using the scale: "Not", "Partially", "Largely", "Fully" and "Not Applicable" as defined in the standard. All responses for survey questions are stored in order to calculate scores for the nine process attributes as defined in ISO/IEC 15504:

PA1.1 Process Performance
PA2.1 Performance Management
PA2.2 Work Product Management
PA3.1 Process Definition
PA3.2 Process Deployment
PA4.1 Process Measurement
PA4.2 Process Control
PA5.1 Process Innovation
PA5.2 Process Optimisation.

Rather than the assessment team making a subjective choice of the testimony of process stakeholders, the online survey collects and objectively measures [26] feedback from the process stakeholders directly from the responses to the questions. The approach of asking questions directly in a web-based survey environment represents a faster and more efficient data collection method compared to assessment interviews [26]. Figure 1 shows the structure of the SMPA approach.

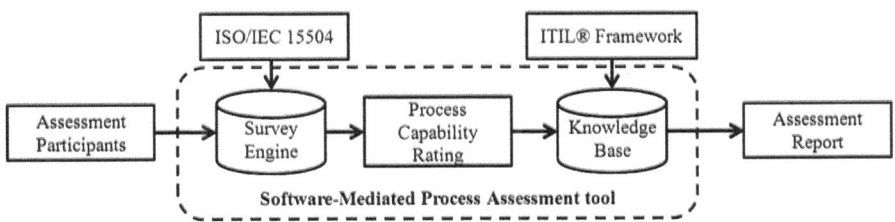

Fig. 1. Structure of SMPA approach

3.2 Calculation of Process Attribute Scores

Based on the online survey responses to the assessment questions, the process attribute scores are calculated as follows:

1. Since each of the four responses for a question (NPLF) are mapped to the rating scale, the mean value of a response (x) is determined based on Table 1.
2. For all responses belonging to one question, the arithmetic mean of x is calculated. The reliability of the process attribute score increases when there is a large number of responses for a process.
3. The NPLF rating scale as defined in Table 1 is used to normalise the arithmetic mean of x.
4. For all questions belonging to one process attribute, the arithmetic mean of the normalised mean of x is calculated. All questions contribute equal weight to the process attribute as they relate to assessment indicators defined by the ISO/IEC 15504 standard.

5. The NPLF rating scale as defined in Table 1 is used again to normalise the final mean result, which is the process attribute score for the process.

Table 1. NPLF rating scale based on the ISO/IEC 15504 standard

Answer option	Rating score	Scale %	Mean value of response (x)
No, never	N	0–15	7.5
Yes, but only sometimes	P	>15–50	32.5
Yes, most of the time	L	>50–85	67.5
Yes, always	F	>85–100	92.5

3.3 Calculation of Reliability of Process Attribute Score

The coefficient of variation (*CoV*) is computed to analyse the reliability of the process attribute score based on data dispersion. A lower *CoV* suggests low variability in the responses which boosts the degree of confidence of the score and vice versa. The *CoV* measure therefore checks the spread of the responses to determine a corresponding reliability score for the process attribute score.

The following steps calculate the process attribute reliability score:

1. Since each of the four responses for a question (NPLF) are mapped to the rating scale, the mean value of a response (x) is determined based on Table 1.
2. For all responses to questions of a process attribute, the arithmetic mean of x is calculated. The reliability of the process attribute score increases when there is a larger number of responses for a process.
3. For all responses to questions of a process attribute, the standard deviation of x is also calculated. The standard deviation shows the dispersion from the arithmetic mean of x.
4. Coefficient of variation (*CoV*) is calculated using the standard deviation and the arithmetic mean. *CoV* is expressed as an absolute value percentage (relative standard deviation), i.e. the standard deviation of x divided by the arithmetic mean of x.
5. The reliability score (*CoV'*) is determined based on the percent value of *CoV* and the range of acceptable variation of responses. The *CoV* value is grouped into one of three categories based on a scale of dispersion of responses. The research team confirmed the logic to cluster *CoV* value of less than 30 percent as a "high" reliability score, *CoV* value of over 50 percent as a "poor" reliability score and anything in between as a "moderate" reliability score:

    a. If CoV < 30%, CoV' = "HIGH"
    b. If CoV between 30% and 50%, CoV' = "MODERATE"
    c. If CoV > 50%, CoV' = "POOR"

The use of arithmetic mean and coefficient of variation are a simple yet effective statistical measure to understand what the critical mass of the assessment respondents think about the processes. The assessment report provides the assessment profile that includes all the process attributes scores and their reliability scores along with the rationale for the ratings [27].

3.4 Initial Evaluation of SMPA

Trials of the SMPA were conducted at two large IT service providers – Case A and Case B - based on the evaluation strategy advocated by Pries-Heje, Baskerville and Venable [28]. The DSR guidelines proposed by Hevner et al. [29] were also followed in an ex-post, naturalistic evaluation conducted at an IT service organisation. In order to assess if the SMPA approach has utility in a real organisation, it was essential to ensure that the survey approach was usable. The concept of usability as defined in ISO/IEC 25010 software quality in use model [30] was applied to evaluate five quality factors of the online survey: effectiveness, efficiency, usefulness, trust and comfort.

Focus groups and interviews were held at Case A and B to evaluate the usability of the online survey phase in the SMPA approach. The discussion with participants was recorded and later transcribed to enable qualitative data analysis. Since all participants of the focus group discussion had completed the assessment surveys, it was interesting to note the inconsistencies and variations that existed among the participants in terms of their experiences and attitudes towards the usability of the online survey.

4 Methodology

The methods used to design the SMPA and the evaluation results from Case A have been detailed in previous publications [31]. Assessment questions and knowledge items for four processes were included in the trial at Case A and Case B: problem, change, configuration and service level management. After the results of the trial were considered, we updated the wording of some of the level two questions.

In 2015, an opportunity arose to deploy the SMPA as part of an ITSM improvement project conducted in Case C, a global financial services firm in North America. An initial baseline assessment of three processes (problem, change and incident management) has been completed and two more checkpoint assessments are planned. This action research project contributes to the requirements of a doctoral qualification for a senior IT manager at the firm.

In this paper, we draw on the assessment results from the three cases. We compare the reliability of the process attribute scores in light of feedback from participants. Rather than focus on the capability ratings, we focus on the reliability scores.

5 Findings and Discussion

5.1 SMPA Approach Deployment

In this section, the process profiles for the three cases are presented with a discussion of the reliability of the process attribute score. Table 2 summarises the processes and capability levels assessed at each Case organisation.

Table 2. Processes assessed at each Case organisation

Process Assessed	Case A	Case B	Case C
Problem Management	✓	✓	✓
Change Management	✓		✓
Configuration Management	✓	✓	
Service Level Management		✓	
Incident Management			✓
Highest capability level assessed	*5*	*4*	*3*

5.2 Case A

Case A is an IT service department of an Australian local government authority. Case A relies on ICT tools to support the delivery of services 24/7. Case A had identified a number of initiatives in its ICT Strategic Plan such as customer contact management; unified communications; eBusiness solutions for improved online accessibility; spatial information services; and business architecture improvements.

With the help and support from the assessment facilitators and assistance from the survey tracking functionality of the DSS tool, assessment data collection using surveys was completed and the assessment report was provided to Case A. The evaluation was performed with focus groups and interviews of Case A staff.

Three IT service processes were assessed at Case A: Problem Management, Change Management and Configuration Management. The scope of the assessment included the full range of process attributes up to level five. The assessment profile is provided in Table 3. Each attribute received 9 or 10 survey responses.

Table 3. Case A process assessment profile

Profile	Level 1	Level 2		Level 3		Level 4		Level 5	
	PA1.1	PA2.1	PA2.2	PA3.1	PA3.2	PA4.1	PA4.2	PA5.1	PA5.2
Problem Management – 10 responses – Capability Level 1									
Process attribute	L	P	P	P	P	P	N	P	P
Reliability	HIGH	MOD	POOR	POOR	MOD	MOD	MOD	MOD	MOD
Change Management – 9 responses - Capability Level 0									
Process attribute	P	P	P	P	L	P	P	P	P
Reliability	MOD	MOD	MOD	POOR	HIGH	MOD	MOD	MOD	MOD
Configuration Management – 9 responses - Capability Level 0									
Process attribute	P	P	P	P	P	P	P	P	P
Reliability	POOR	MOD	POOR	POOR	HIGH	MOD	MOD	MOD	MOD

As shown in Table 3, the majority of the rating scores for all processes at Case A demonstrated a weak reliability score (six "Poor", 18 "Moderate" and only three "High" reliability scores). This meant that survey respondents were not consistent in their answers and responses were varied. Interviews with the assessment facilitator and process managers to discuss the assessment results revealed that high staff turnover and the lack of ITIL training might have contributed to the highly dispersed responses. Moreover Case A participants did not engage in the facilitated workshops offered by the researchers to explain the SMPA approach. Additionally, there was no response from the assessment facilitator during the assessment period regarding the experience of respondents despite repeated requests for feedback. Likewise, the process stakeholders undertook multiple process roles and answered questions up to capability level 5 – leading to information overload and exposure to assessment questions that were not really relevant to their organisation. It was apparent that this trial was conducted due to a top management "push" rather than a genuine effort from the process stakeholders to improve processes.

5.3 Case B

Case B is a state government entity in Australia that manages a range of ICT services for the government, including a major consolidation of data centers, the implementation of consolidated network connectivity and internet service provision. Case B has over 400 staff and operates as both an internal and external service provider with a geographic spread across Australia.

Three IT service processes were assessed at Case B: Problem Management, Service Level Management and Configuration Management. The scope of the assessment included up to process capability level 4. The assessment profile is provided in Table 4. Each attribute received 4 or 5 survey responses.

As shown in Table 4, the majority of the rating scores for all processes at Case B demonstrated a very strong reliability score (19 "High" against only one "Moderate" and one "Poor" reliability score). This meant that survey respondents predominantly agreed on their ratings. Interviews with the assessment facilitator and process managers to discuss the assessment results concluded that all processes under assessment had dedicated process owners, low frequency of staff appointments across the organisation and a significant level of awareness of the ITIL framework (over 75 % had formal ITIL certification) contributed to the consistency of results. Moreover, case B participants, facilitated by an active and enthusiastic process facilitator, engaged in several informal and formal discussions surrounding the SMPA approach and the assessment questions.

5.4 Case C

Case C is a global financial services company with over 200 employees, headquartered in North America, with offices in New York, London, Singapore, Tokyo and Bangalore. Case C has about 70 IT staff who attend to incidents, problems and changes on a daily basis.

Table 4. Case B process assessment profile

Profile	Level 1	Level 2		Level 3		Level 4		Level 5	
	PA1.1	PA2.1	PA2.2	PA3.1	PA3.2	PA4.1	PA4.2	PA5.1	PA5.2
PROBLEM MANAGEMENT – 4 responses - Capability Level 1									
Process attribute	L	L	L	L	L	L	P		
Reliability	HIGH	HIGH	HIGH	HIGH	HIGH	HIGH	POOR		
SERVICE LEVEL MANAGEMENT – 5 responses - Capability Level 1									
Process attribute	L	L	L	L	L	P	L		
Reliability	HIGH	HIGH	HIGH	HIGH	HIGH	MOD	HIGH		
CONFIGURATION MANAGEMENT – 5 responses - Capability Level 1									
Process attribute	L	L	L	L	L	L	F		
Reliability	HIGH	HIGH	HIGH	HIGH	HIGH	HIGH	HIGH		

Case C began to scrutinize its IT group's performance to ensure that it was in line with the overall business performance and contributed to the business's bottom line. Case C embarked on implementing three of the 26 ITSM processes: Incident Management, Problem Management and Change Management, and are now looking to improve these processes to lower costs, improve efficiency and offer higher service levels. The business drivers for process improvement are service availability and reliability, and continual improvement of services. The motivation to use the SMPA tool was for its transparency and convenience. The assessment profile for Case C is provided in Table 5.

As shown in Table 5, the majority of the rating scores at Case C demonstrated a very strong reliability score (12 "High"; one "Moderate" and two "Poor" reliability scores). This meant that survey respondents predominantly agreed on their ratings.

A focus group discussion was held at Case C with senior staff to discuss the results of the SMPA assessment. The results for Problem and Change Management were deemed inconsistent with the views held by the focus group participants about the capability of these processes. However, the results for Incident Management were in line with Case C expectations. After some probing questions, the researcher discovered that five different work groups were performing the three assessed processes. Two of the work groups are based at Case C's head office, while the other three groups are located in different countries. The focus group discussed how the SMPA report results may have been influenced by the specific characteristics of the five groups of staff.

Table 6 shows the distribution of the number of participants by organisation work group per process assessed.

Table 5. Case C process assessment profile

Profile	Level 1	Level 2		Level 3		Level 4		Level 5	
	PA1.1	PA2.1	PA2.2	PA3.1	PA3.2	PA4.1	PA4.2	PA5.1	PA5.2
PROBLEM MANAGEMENT – 21 responses - Capability Level 1									
Process attribute	L	P	P	P	P				
Reliability	HIGH	POOR	HIGH	HIGH	MOD				
CHANGE MANAGEMENT – 45 responses - Capability Level 1									
Process attribute	L	L	L	L	L				
Reliability	HIGH	HIGH	HIGH	HIGH	POOR				
INCIDENT MANAGEMENT – 26 responses - Capability Level 1									
Process attribute	L	L	L	L	L				
Reliability	HIGH	HIGH	HIGH	HIGH	HIGH				

Table 6. Number of responses by work group for each process

Work group	Location	Change management	Incident management	Problem management
Business Support	US, UK, Singapore	3	9	3
Operations	US, Bangalore	12	12	0
Trading Solutions	US, UK, Singapore, India	19	0	0
Execution Services	US	7	1	1
Engineering	US, India	0	0	14
Stakeholders	US	4	4	3

Although all work groups use the same process management tool (Zendesk), each group follows its own set of procedures and workflows. Only two groups, Business Support and Operations follow the same procedures and workflows.

The Executive Management at Case C is very aware that Change Management is the most immature process and it frequently causes financial loss and customer dissatisfaction. It was surprising that the survey results gave Change Management a rating score of "Largely" for all five process attributes, with a high reliability score for all the process attributes except for PA3.2 (Process Deployment) which scored "Poor" reliability.

Feedback after the assessment revealed that some of the participants were allocated three surveys and they were unsure if they were responding on behalf of their work group or the entire organisation. One of the participants mentioned that because some of the questions seemed to be the same, he provided the same response without thinking about it – so one can question the reliability in this case. Here is an example of two similar questions: *Do you know if requests for change (RFCs) are assessed to identify new or changed information security risks?* and *Do you know if requests for change (RFCs) are assessed to identify potential impact on the existing information security policy and controls?*

The same respondent felt that if he had printed all the questions, he would have had a better understanding of what was being assessed and some questions may have helped him understand others.

When processes are performed by multiple groups within an organization, each group may have a very different perspective on its process capability, especially if there is no consistency in the procedures and workflows followed. This may result in disparate results when assessing the organization as a whole. The focus group members expressed the view that capability level of 1 for Change Management may not be accurate, as the largest group (Trading Solutions) may have biased the result by being overly positive in their responses. The focus group members suggested that overall PA1.1 (Process Performance) was only partly attained. Similar views were expressed for Problem Management, where the Engineering group made up the largest response group, and this may have swayed the results for this process.

6 Conclusion

We have answered the research question: the calculation of a measure of reliability for process attribute scores has been explained. Furthermore, possible causes of unsatisfactory reliability were discussed. In summary, our initial analysis of these three cases indicates that the process attribute scores and corresponding maturity level should be considered in light of the reliability measures. Reliability may be influenced by many factors. At the individual level there are psychological and behavioural characteristics as well as respondents' work experience, motivation, knowledge of ITIL concepts and terminology. The organizational and national culture of the work group, and consistency of adoption of work practices may also influence how respondents answer the online survey questions.

In the future, the online survey could be extended to collect respondent demographics e.g. education, training, work group, experience in the specific role/process at the organisation. Rather than a static report, assessment results could be offered such that facilitators drill down into the collected data to identify outliers, and analyse responses across variables.

The SMPA approach takes a positivist view and although the tool allows for comments to be recorded, it does not provide qualitative analysis of these comments. In the future, sentiment analysis of comments may uncover motivations, agendas, cultural and political issues that bias results.

At the completion of the SMPA trial, we evaluated the work required to complete the population of the assessment questions database and knowledge base to cover all processes in ISO/IEC 20000-1:2011. Based on our analysis, the DSS was extended with the inclusion of 24 additional processes. To achieve this, 2,416 assessment questions were formulated and added to the assessment questions database. The knowledge base was expanded with 2,548 corresponding knowledge items derived from the ITIL guidelines.

With the functionality to assess any ISO/IEC 20000-1:2011 process, the SMPA approach can be applied to conduct assessments for specific ITSM processes or for organisations seeking ISO/IEC 20000 compliance. Cognisant of the work underway to update the underlying standards, we investigate the planned changes to the standards, and consider how the SMPA and DSS will need to be changed to accommodate such changes in the future.

The new suite of Standards (ISO/IEC 330xx) at present comprises four core normative standards, covering the overall performance of process assessment; a measurement framework for the evaluation of process capability; and a key guidance document on process improvement. In addition, Process Assessment Models for IT Security processes and for Enterprise processes have been approved; the latter of these was developed by the Enterprise SPICE Project and is published as a Publicly Available Specification (PAS) [32]. It is expected that the use of PAS will expand, with an assessment model addressing processes for sustainability (Green IT). The ISO/IEC 330xx approach has also been adopted by other Standards groups to develop domain specific assessment models for processes for Medical Device Software development, and for IT Outsourcing. Current plans include the development of further guidance documents, and of additional domain-specific assessment models. Application of formal Conformity Assessment to the performance of assessments, and the certification of results, is also under development.

In the future, the SMPA approach and underlying assessment questions database and knowledge base can be extended from ITSM processes to accommodate the new ISO/IEC 330xx Measurement Framework and processes for IT Security, Enterprise and Green IT processes when the process reference frameworks and assessment models have been approved.

Acknowledgements. This work is supported by an Australian Research Council (ARC) Linkage grant. We thank Mr. Paul Collins of Assessment Portal Pty. Ltd. for his involvement and support in providing the platform to implement the DSS tool. We also appreciate the opportunity provided by staff at the three case study organisations.

Note. ITIL® is a Registered Trade Mark of AXELOS Limited.
CMMI® is the Registered Trademark of Carnegie Mellon University.

References

1. ISO/IEC: ISO/IEC 20000-1:2011 – Information Technology – Service Management – Part 1: Service Management System Requirements. International Organisation for Standardisation, Geneva (2011)
2. OGC: ITIL Service Strategy. TSO for the Office of Government Commerce, London (2011)

3. Winkler, T.J., Wulf, J., Brenner, W.: The relevance of IT service management maturity for IT alignment and its strategy and organization size contingencies. In: First AIS-Journals Joint Author Workshop in ECIS. AIS Electronic Library (AISeL) (2014)
4. ISO/IEC: ISO/IEC 33001:2016 Information technology - Process assessment - Concepts and terminology. In: JTC IT-015 (ed.). International Organization for Standardization, Geneva (2015)
5. SCAMPI Upgrade Team: Appraisal Requirements for CMMI® Version 1.3 (2011)
6. Parasuraman, A., Zeithaml, V.A., Berry, L.L.: A conceptual model of service quality and its implications for future research. J. Mark. **49**, 41–50 (1985)
7. Lepmets, M., Cater-Steel, A., Gacenga, F., Ras, E.: Extending the IT service quality measurement framework through a systematic literature review. J. Serv. Sci. Res. **4**, 7–47 (2012)
8. Jia, R., Reich, B.H.: IT service climate—an essential managerial tool to improve client satisfaction with it service quality. Inf. Syst. Manage. **28**, 174–179 (2011)
9. Spath, D., Bauer, W., Praeg, C.-P.: IT service quality management: assumptions, frameworks and effects on business performance. In: Praeg, C.-P., Spath, D. (eds.) Quality Management for IT Services-Perspectives on Business and Process Performance, pp. 1–21. IGI Global, Hershey (2011)
10. Radice, R.A., Harding, J.T., Munnis, P.E., Phillips, R.W.: A programming process study. IBM Syst. J. **24**, 79–90 (1985)
11. Humphrey, W.S.: Managing the Software Process. Addison-Wesley, Reading (1990)
12. ISO/IEC: ISO/IEC 15504.1:2005 Information technology - Process assessment - Concepts and vocabulary (2005)
13. Rout, T.P., El Emam, K., Fusani, M., Goldenson, D., Jung, H.W.: SPICE in retrospect: developing a standard for process assessment. J. Syst. Softw. **80**, 1483–1493 (2007)
14. Rout, T.P.: A new framework for standardisation and certification for process assessment. Softw. Qual. Prof. **14** (2011)
15. Rout, T.P.: Critical design decisions in the development of the standard for process assessment. In: Woronowicz, T., Rout, T., O'Connor, R.V., Dorling, A. (eds.) SPICE 2013. CCIS, vol. 349, pp. 247–251. Springer, Heidelberg (2013)
16. Mesquida, A., Mas, A., Amengual, E., Calvo-Manzano, J.: IT service management process improvement based on ISO/IEC 15504: a systematic review. Inf. Softw. Technol. **54**, 239–247 (2012)
17. Barafort, B., Betry, V., Cortina, S., Picard, M., St-Jean, M., Renault, A., Valdès, O.: ITSM Process Assessment Supporting ITIL. Van Haren Publishing, Zaltbommel (2009)
18. Renault, A., Cortina, S., Barafort, B.: Towards a maturity model for ISO/IEC 20000-1 based on the TIPA for ITIL process capability assessment model. In: Rout, T., O'Connor, R.V., Dorling, A. (eds.) SPICE 2015. CCIS, vol. 526, pp. 188–200. Springer, Heidelberg (2015)
19. Lloyd, V.: ITIL Continual Service Improvement. The Stationery Office, London (2011)
20. Straub, D.W.: Validating instruments in MIS research. MIS Q. **13**, 147–168 (1989)
21. MacKenzie, S.B., Podsakoff, P.M., Podsakoff, N.P.: Construct measurement and validation procedures in MIS and behavioral research: integrating new and existing techniques. MIS Q. **35**, 293–334 (2011)
22. Lord, F.M., Novick, M.R.: Statistical Theories of Mental Test Scores. Addison-Wesley Publishing, Reading (1968)
23. ISO/IEC: ISO/IEC 15504-2:2004 – Information Technology – Process Assessment – Part 2: Performing an Assessment. International Organization for Standardization, Geneva (2004)
24. ISO/IEC: ISO/IEC TS 15504-8:2012 - Information Technology - Process Assessment - Part 8: An Exemplar Process Assessment Model for IT Service Management. International Organization for Standardization, Geneva (2012)

25. Shrestha, A., Cater-Steel, A., Toleman, M., Rout, T.: Towards transparent and efficient process assessments for IT service management. In: Mitasiunas, A., Rout, T., O'Connor, R.V., Dorling, A. (eds.) SPICE 2014. CCIS, vol. 477, pp. 165–176. Springer, Heidelberg (2014)
26. Deutskens, E., de Ruyter, K., Wetzels, M.: An assessment of equivalence between online and mail surveys in service research. J. Serv. Res. **8**, 346–355 (2006)
27. ISO/IEC: ISO/IEC TS 15504-9:2011 – Information Technology – Process Assessment – Part 9: Target Process Profiles. International Organisation for Standardisation, Geneva (2011)
28. Pries-Heje, J., Baskerville, R., Venable, J.R.: Strategies for design science research evaluation. In: 16th European Conference on Information Systems. (2008)
29. Hevner, A.R., March, S.T., Park, J., Ram, S.: Design science in information systems research. MIS Q. **28**, 75–106 (2004)
30. ISO/IEC: ISO/IEC 25010:2011 – Systems and software engineering – Systems and software Quality Requirements and Evaluation (SQuaRE) - System and software quality models. International Organisation for Standardisation, Geneva (2011)
31. Shrestha, A., Cater-Steel, A., Toleman, M., Rout, T.: Evaluation of software mediated process assessments for IT service management. In: Rout, T., O'Connor, R.V., Dorling, A. (eds.) SPICE 2015. CCIS, vol. 526, pp. 72–84. Springer, Heidelberg (2015)
32. ISO/IEC: FDIS 33071 - Information technology – Process assessment – An integrated process capability assessment model for Enterprise processes. International Organisation for Standardisation (2016)

Towards a Process Capability Assessment Model for Government Domain

Ebru Gökalp[(✉)] and Onur Demirörs

Informatics Institute, Middle East Technical University, Ankara, Turkey
{egokalp,demirors}@metu.edu.tr

Abstract. Government Process Capability Determination Model is developed based on ISO/IEC 15504 by the authors in order to assess the extent of the processes to be consistently applied, managed, and controlled across governmental agencies. Government Process Reference Model consists of definitions of common processes across all governmental agencies as well as a generic process definition for agency-specific governmental processes. This study covers the development of the generic process definition in detail. AWL introduced by Medina-Mora is taken as a starting point to develop the generic process definition. A capability dimension based on the capability dimension of 15504-2 is defined. The outcomes and BPs described are, however, considered to be the minimum necessary to meet ISO/IEC 15504 requirements. In order to explore the applicability of the proposed definition, case studies are conducted. Public investment management process definition, ad-hoc defined beforehand, compared to the generic process definition. Moreover, The Graduate Student Selection process performed in METU is assessed and capability level of the process is determined; correspondingly, a roadmap to improve process capability level is derived. The findings of the study indicate the usefulness and adequacy of the proposed approach.

Keywords: ISO/IEC 15504 · Government · Process assessment model · Process Capability Determination

1 Introduction

The government agencies are non-profit-oriented organizations, while their processes are commonly unstructured, and depend on the judgment of the employees. That results in some quality problems in the agencies as; inefficiency, citizen dissatisfaction, and high defect rates. Conversely, the government agencies are under increasing pressure to show that their services are customer-focused and that continuous performance improvement is being carried out. There are some quality improvement initiatives in the government domain, however, quality improvement in this domain is sometimes problematical because of its specific characteristics which are defined in [1, 2] as the necessity of being firmly based in-law of decisions, culture, multiple stakeholders for many processes, etc. While ICT has the potential for improvement of the governmental service quality, the automation practices in the agencies have not provided the expected efficiency improvements. The reason of that existing process defects is carried out to automate the process [3]. Whereas, the existing processes should be improved beforehand to perform successful ICT projects [4]. It is also stated in [5, 6] that, Enterprise Architecture (EA) in the government domain has to be transformed from being IT-centric to business-centric. Nevertheless, only a limited number of papers investigate the necessary changes of business processes in the government domain [7].

There are various well-accepted Process Capability/Maturity Models (PCMMs), such as ISO/IEC 15504 [8–11], CMMI (Capability Maturity Model Integration) [12]. The ISO/IEC 15504 standard has recently entered a revision cycle. It will be gradually replaced by a new series of standards: the ISO/IEC 33000 series [13]. These models are used as an evaluative and comparative basis for process improvement and/or assessment, assuming that higher process capability or organization maturity is associated with better performance. As a result of the observed benefits of these models, various process capability maturity models are generated based on these PCMMs, i.e.: Automotive SPICE [14], Medi SPICE [15], Enterprise SPICE [16], etc.

We propose to apply the same approach for the government domain by developing the Government Process Capability Determination Model (Gov-PCDM) based on ISO/IEC 15504 standard [8–11]. The purpose of Gov-PCDM is to offer the base to improve the governmental processes. It pursues a structured and standardized approach by assessing governmental processes in order to accomplish quality improvement initiatives in a consistent, repeatable manner, assessed by adequate metrics with guidance on what to do for increasing quality in the government organizations.

The Gov-PCDM is aimed to accomplish four upper-level requirements as followings: to enable each government organization to assess its processes in detail; to identify the current state of its processes capability; to compare itself against other government organizations assessed with the same model; and to achieve a guideline to improve the process capability level.

We performed an exploratory case study to control if the customization of ISO/IEC 15504 for government domain is applicable. The study was presented at the Spice Conference in 2014 [17]. Public investment management process performed in the Ministry of Development in Turkey was defined in an ad-hoc fashion, assessed its capability level, and a road-map to improve the process capability level was derived in the study. As a result of the study, although initial findings indicated the usefulness and adequacy of the proposed approach; the necessity of a methodology incorporating guidelines for government specific process definition was determined. In order to satisfy this determined necessity, the methodology was developed. The corresponding study of proposing an ISO/IEC 15504 based process improvement method for the government domain was presented at the Spice Conference in 2015 [18].

As a result of analyzing the governmental organizations, we classified governmental processes into two main groups; one of them is common processes performed across all governmental agencies; such as human resource management process. We named them as Management of Government Resources and Support Processes (MGRSPs). The second category consists of agency-specific processes performed only by an agency. For instance; curriculum development for primary education is just performed in ministry of education. Government Process Reference Model (Gov-PRM) is constructed based on these classifications. The process definitions of MGRSPs are defined. A generic process definition is developed for governmental agency-specific processes assessment. This study covers the generic process definition. Moreover, in order to explore the applicability of the proposed approach two case studies are conducted. One of them which consists of comparing generic process definition to the public investment management process definition which was defined in ad-hoc fashion in [17]. The second case study includes graduate student selection process, performed in Middle East Technical University (METU) which is a public university. The process is assessed and capability level of the process is determined, as well as a roadmap to improve process capability is also constructed. Interviews with process owners are conducted to check the validity of the results and if the proposed approach is useful and adequate.

The remainder of the paper includes a brief description of the proposed Gov-PCDM approach in the Sect. 2, then developed generic process definition is proposed, the explanation of the case studies performed is given in the Sect. 4, analysis of the case study results is discussed in the Sect. 5, finally the study is concluded.

2 Government Process Capability Determination Model

The Gov-PCDM is developed for capability level determination of processes performed in governmental organizations. The Gov-PCDM is based on the assumption that business service quality can be achieved by the means of process quality – process capability. High process capability level can be achieved by applying an iterative procedure of process capability assessments and improvement. The Gov-PCDM aims to provide benefits of well-known process improvement models (i.e.: CMMI, ISO/IEC 15504 etc.) by proposing a specific process assessment model for government domain. These aimed benefits are increasing in service quality, in customer and employee satisfaction, as well as decreasing in operating costs, as a result of improving process capability.

The aim of Gov-PCDM is providing the base for improving the processes of governmental organizations. It pursues a structured and standardized approach by assessing relevant processes. The structure of the Gov-PCDM is made up of two dimensions as seen in Fig. 1.

The process dimension consists of governmental business processes. This dimension is characterized by process purpose statements which are the essential measurable objectives of a process; process outcomes, base practices, and work products which are constructed based on the standard of ISO/IEC 15504- 2 [8].

The capability dimension, which is characterized by a series of process attributes, is applicable to any process, which represents measurable characteristics necessary to manage a process and improve its capability to perform. It is adapted from ISO/IEC 15504-part 5 [11].

2.1 Government Process Reference Model (Gov-PRM)

The process dimension of Gov-PCDM is composed of the processes from Gov-PRM with the inclusion of base practices and work products for each process. We classified

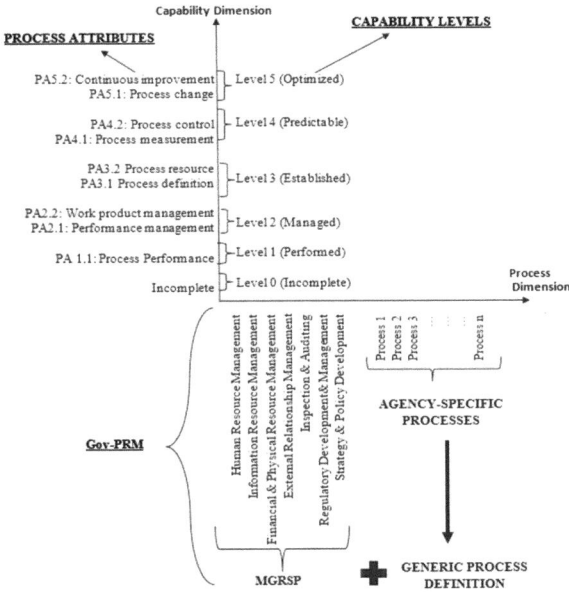

Fig. 1. Gov-PCDM structure

Governmental business processes into 2 main groups. One of them is Agency-Specific Process which is performed specifically for one institute, such as; birth, death and marriage registration process is performed just in the civil registry office. The generic process definition is developed for using level 1 assessment of agency-specific processes. The details of generic process definition are given in the Sect. 3. The second one is Management of Government Resources and Support Processes (MGRSPs), common processes across the governmental agencies, refer to the support activities that enable the government to operate efficiently, There are 7 main classes for management of government resources processes as human resource management, information resource management, financial & physical resource management, external relationship management, inspection & auditing, regulatory development and management, strategy & policy development. Gov-PRM includes the process definitions of these processes.

Process Definitions of MGRSPs are developed by harmonizing existing quality improvement models and standards as FEAF (Federal Enterprise Architecture Framework) [19], APQC (American Process Qualification Center) [20], ISO/IEC 15504 [8–11], CMMI-DEV [12], CMMI-SVC [21], People-CMM [22], etc. The details of process definitions of MGRSPs are not in the scope of this study. The generic process definition is established on the basis of process modeling diagrams of 40 different agency-specific processes performed in five different public agencies. The developed generic process definition is reviewed by 30 process owners working in 10 different departments.

All process definitions are formally approved by the management with executive responsibility within two different organizational units and one of the authors who has both professional and academic experience in using ISO/IEC 15504 after reviewing respective process definitions.

2.2 Government Process Assessment Model

A capability dimension based on the capability dimension of 15504-2 [8] is defined for Gov-PCDM. Assessment procedures related to details of activities such as planning, briefing of the participants, data collection and validation and reporting are based on ISO/IEC 15504-3 [9]. Process Capability is classified into six levels in ISO/IEC 15504-2 [8]; as Level 0: Incomplete; Level 1: Performed; Level 2: Managed; Level 3: Established; Level 4: Predictable; Level 5: Optimizing.

The measure of capability is based upon a set of process attributes (PA). Process capability indicators are the means of achieving the capabilities addressed by the considered process attributes. Evidence of process capability indicators supports the judgment of the degree of achievement in the process attribute.

Process Attribute of Level 1 is Process Performance attribute which is a measure of the extent to which the process purpose is achieved. Developed Process definitions are used for Level 1 assessment. For the assessments of levels 2 to 5, we use exactly the same 'generic practices indicators', 'generic resources indicators' and 'generic work products indicators' as the exemplar PAM provided by the ISO/IEC 15504-5 [11].

The capability level of each process instance is determined by rating PAs. For example, to determine whether a process has achieved capability level 1 or not, it is necessary to determine the rating achieved by PA1.1 (Process performance attribute). A process that fails to achieve capability level 1 is at capability level 0. Each process attribute is measured by an ordinal rating F (Fully), L (Largely), P (Partially), or N (Not) achieved that represents the extent of achievement of the attribute. A process instance is defined to be at capability level k if all process attributes below level k satisfy the rating F and the level k attribute(s) are rated as F or L, as defined in ISO/IEC 15504-2 [8].

3 Generic Process Definition

The generic process definition is developed to use capability determination of the agency-specific processes of governmental organizations. It is also including level 1 process performance indicators. The ISO/IEC 15504-2 [8] requires the process outcomes to be the minimum set of results to achieve the process purpose. This requirement excludes improvement activities from the process outcome list. Therefore, the Action Workflow Loop (AWL) is more appropriate for our study rather than BPM life-cycle. Thus, we propose to use the AWL introduced by Medina-Mora [23]. He created the AWL which breaks down the business process as a loop constituted of four generic phases: proposal, agreement, performance, and satisfaction as seen in Fig. 2.

- *Proposal:* The customer requests completion of a particular action according to some stated conditions of satisfaction.

- *Agreement:* The two parties come to a mutual agreement on the conditions of satisfaction, including the times by which further steps will be taken. This agreement is only partially explicit in the negotiations, resting on a shared background of assumptions and standard practices.
- *Performance:* The performer declares to the customer that the action is complete.
- *Satisfaction:* The customer declares that the completion is satisfactory.

In the context of our study, we customize this AWL for the government domain by

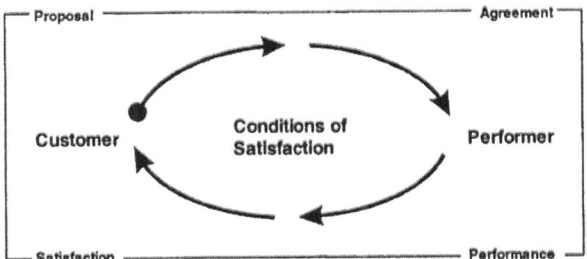

Fig. 2. Process phases by Medina-Mora [23]

defining outcomes and base practices for each phase to verify the process is completely defined. The customer is mainly higher level management, and performer is a public agency. The loop works in the government domain as follows;

Proposal: Higher level management request the particular action to perform by the way of publishing law, decree law etc. All processes performed in the government must be based on the specific law. Outcome 1 is defined for this phase.

Outcome 1: Politics/strategy is defined

Agreement: Some of the documents as regulation, legislation, or guidelines, including what to do for the process are published. The requirements of the process, such as maximum budget to use are derived and allocated to the process. Interactions are conducted for this phase, such as receiving information about derived requirement. Outcome 2, 3, and 4 are defined for this phase.

Outcome 2: Policies and guidelines are published
Outcome 3: Requirements are derived and allocated
Outcome 4: Interactions with involved parties is managed

Performance: The public agency communicates with other departments/agencies (if necessary) and apply technical methods to perform the work. How to perform the work differs according to the objective of the process. We classify process objectives in the government domain in 3 main groups as; generating a document, evaluating an application, and providing a service. Interactions are conducted while performing technical effort. Outcome 4 and 5 cover this phase.

Table 1. The generic process definition

Outcomes	1) Politics/strategy is defined 2) Policies and guidelines are published 3) Requirements are derived and allocated 4) Interactions with involved parties are managed 5) Technical effort is performed to obtain the result 6) Approval of the result is achieved 7) Results are made available to all related parties
Base Practices	**BP1. Develop a strategy for the process:** Produce Strategy document by higher level management of government. I.e.: law, decree law, etc. [Outcome:1] **BP2. Publish policies and guidelines:** Establish Policies and guidelines which include how work gets done. I.e.: Regulations, legislation etc. [Outcome:1,2] **BP3. Allocate requirements for the process:** Obtain requirements for performing the process from higher level management. These requirements can be amount of budget, maximum number of people, or maximum amount of resource, etc. [Outcome:2,3,4] **BP4. Establish interactive communication methodologies and structures with involved parties:** A communication mechanism for receiving/storing/sending information or documents (if there is) with involved parties is established. [Outcome:4] **BP5: Achieve approval for the result:** Establish and maintain and approval mechanism from inside the agency and the institutions the agency is dependent on (if necessary) [Outcome:2,4,6] **BP6: Share results with involved parties**: Establish and maintain an informing mechanism for sharing the results with all stakeholders. Publishing results on the web page of the agency, publishing in the official gazette, sending e-mail to involved parties can be some alternatives for sharing results. [Outcome:2,4,7]
Base Practices	A) <u>If the objective to perform the technical effort is to create a document:</u> **BP7A: Collect information**: Gather necessary information. It may occur in different ways as; requesting information from other departments/agencies, recording information from organized meetings, collecting information from intranet/internet, doing surveys/auditing/inspection. [Outcome:4,5] **BP8A: Analyze information**: Analyze/evaluate the collected information is analyzed by applying technical methods. [Outcome:5] **BP9A: Generate the document**: Create the document (report, plan, strategy etc.) based on analyzed information [Outcome:5]
Base Practices	B) **If the objective of performing technical effort is to evaluate an application:** **BP7B:Receive Application(s)** Receive applications together with required documents [Outcome:4,5] **BP8B: Evaluate Application(s)** Analyze the application(s) based on defined evaluation criteria by applying technical methods[Outcome:5] **BP9B: Document the result** Generate reports including the result, if necessary. [Outcome:5]
	C) **If the objective of performing technical effort is to provide a service:** **BP7C: Establish resource management capability:** Establish a structure for the management of the resource. It may include tools, equipment, resource, and procedures. [Outcome:5] **BP8C: Maintain the service management:** Collect, receive, store, and distribute the resource according to established strategy and procedures [Outcome:5] **BP9C: Support the service and solutions:** Collect complaint and compliments and manage to resolve [Outcome:4,5] **BP10C:Report information:** Generate reports for internal and external units if necessary [Outcome:5]

Outcome 4: Interactions with involved parties is managed
Outcome 5: Technical effort is performed to obtain the result

Satisfaction: Higher level management declares the satisfactory completion by approving it. Additionally, approved result should be informed to all stakeholders by using communication mechanisms. There are interactions in this phase as well, such as sending documents to approve. Outcome 4, 6, and 7 cover this phase.

Outcome 4: Interactions with involved parties is managed
Outcome 6: Approval of the result is achieved
Outcome 7: Results are made available to all related parties

Base practices (BPs) are activities that address the process purpose. Implementing the BPs of a process should achieve the basic outcomes that reflect the process purpose. BPs are defined for the defined 7 outcomes in the generic process definition. We classified base practices for outcome 5 into 3 main groups. It changes according to the objective of the process, as seen details in Table 1. For instance; if the process objective is generating a document, base practices classified into A section as BP7A, BP8A, and BP9A; if the objective is to evaluate an application, base practices classified into B section as BP7B, BP8B, BP9B; if the objective is to provide a service, base practices classified into C section as BP7C, BP8C, BP9C, BP10C should be used to check whether outcome 5 is achieved during the level 1 assessment. The other BPs are common for each objective.

The perspective of the generic process description is to enhance the government process description with a structured way to create processes and to write the process description. It specified describing at an abstract level the governmental processes and it is considered to be the minimum necessary to meet ISO/IEC 15504 requirements. Any organization may define their own processes by tailoring it in order to suit it to its specific environment and circumstances to conform their respective PRM and PAM.

4 Case Study

4.1 The Public Investment Management Process

Public investment management process performed in the Ministry of Development in Turkey was defined in an ad-hoc fashion and assessed as an exploratory case study to check if customization of ISO/IEC 15504 for government domain is applicable [17]. The process was not defined applying a generic process definition. As a result of the study, although initial findings indicated the usefulness and adequacy of the proposed approach; the necessity of a methodology incorporating guidelines for government specific process definition was determined.

Ad-hoc defined outcomes and base practices are below. When we apply the generic process definition approach to the same process, it is observed that there are some missing BPs in the definition although they are performed as seen in Table 2. Since the objective of technical effort is evaluating an application, BPs of 1, 2, 3, 4, 5, 6 and 7B, 8B and 9B are used.

Base practices of 5 and 9B are missing in the ad-hoc process definition, although accepted projects are documented as a report and the report is approved by three bureaucratic levels before the announcement.

As a result, it is observed that the generic process definition serves as a guideline to process owners to define their processes without any missing practice.

The next section includes application of Gov-PCDM to an agency-specific process to evaluate the proposed approach in a different institute.

Table 2. Ad-hoc defined base practices in [17] and their corresponds in developed generic process definition

Ad-hoc defined base practices in [17]	Corresponds in developed generic process definition
BP1: Create and manage public investment politics, policies and plans	**BP1:** Develop a strategy for the process
BP2: Evaluate pre-feasibility study by organizing meetings with public institutionsm	**BP4:** Establish interactive communication methodologies and structures with involved parties
BP3: Develop public investment policies and guideline	**BP2:** Publish policies and guidelines
BP4: Allocate budget to public agencies as high-level planning	**BP3:** Define requirements for the process
BP 5: Submit public investment projects.	**BP7B:** Receive Application
BP 6: Evaluate public investment projects	**BP8B:** Evaluate Application(s)
BP 7: Evaluate submitted as aggregated or bulk project	**BP8B:** Evaluate Application(s)
BP 8: Announce accepted projects	**BP6:** Share results with involved parties

4.2 The Graduate Student Selection Process

A case study is performed in a governmental-specific process in order to evaluate the adequacy of the proposed approach. As stated in [24], there are some quality problems in public universities; as slow response time, being no single "owner" responsible for ensuring that the process works efficiently and effectively, poor documentation with no standardized written instructions or employee training programs, failing to benefit from the insights and recommendations of process owners, etc. These problems are also observed in METU Informatics Institute. As a strategic decision, the institute authorities support process improvement initiative across the institute by applying Gov-PCDM.

Institutes' processes are derived by applying a top-down approach by one of the authors, who has both professional and academic experience in business process management domain as well as 4 years working experience as an academic staff in the institute, together with an administrative staff. Processes to be covered in process improvement initiative are selected by institute authorities. The graduate student selection process is one of the most critical process performed in the institute, since it is highly employee-intensive and slow. A massive volume of paper, including transcripts, test scores, and letter of recommendations further hampers the process. It is observed that there is a need to improve the process performance to achieve academic and operational excellence. Thus, the graduate student selection process is selected to improve process capability level with a guidance on what to do to increase quality.

Process Definition. Since the process is an agency-specific process, generic process definition, seen in Table 1, is used for assessing process attribute of Level 1, which is process performance attribute. Since the objective of technical effort is evaluating an application, BPs of 1, 2, 3, 4, 5, 6 and 7B, 8B and 9B are used.

The purpose of the graduate student selection process is to select masters' and PhD students with different knowledge bases for programs. It is performed as follows;

- *BP1. Develop a strategy for the process* → 2547 number higher education law is defined by the Higher Education Institute.
- *BP2. Publish policies and guidelines* → METU Education Regulation is published to include guideline of graduate student selection.
- *BP3. Define requirements for the process* → Maximum number of students to select for the graduate program is decided by the institutional academic committee.
- *BP4. Establish interactive communication methodologies and structures with involved parties* →
  – Announcement including application period and required qualifications is done through the web site.
  – Webpage for submitting application is activated when the application period comes.
  – Employees from student relations department control the submitted documents, inform appliers if there is a missing or incorrect after receiving the applications.
  – The finalized list is sent to the Head Student Relations Department of METU.
- *BP5: Achieve approval for the result* → Academic and management committees of the institute approve finalized accepted application list.
- *BP6: Share results with involved parties* →
  – Candidate list for call for interview is published on the institute web page.
  – The result is published on the webpage.
- *BP7B: Receive Application(s)* → Student candidates apply to the program. Fill the application form, collect necessary documents and send/submit them to student relations department of the institute.
- *BP8B: Evaluate Application(s)* →
  – Applications are evaluated by the determined criteria as CGPA, Test Scores, Recommendation letters etc. and candidates who get call for oral interview are determined by the academic committee.
  – The interview is performed.
  – The academic committee evaluates the interview results, and finalizes accepted application list.
- *BP9B: Document the result* → Finalized accepted application list is documented.

Process Assessment. Process Assessment is performed by the participants in the organization responsible for the quality assurance and by the authors, one of whom is a competent assessor formally certified by the INT-ACS (International ISO/IEC 15504 Assessors Schema). Accordingly, the assessment team follows the 'ISO/IEC 15504- 3: Guidance on Performing an Assessment' [9] as the documented procedural approach for conducting the assessment.

Process performance attribute of Level 1 assessment covers checking whether the process achieves its defined outcomes. During the assessment, it is observed that all base practices stated in the generic process description are fully achieved in the graduate student selection process.

Details of the assessment activities such as planning, briefing of the participants, data collection and validation, and reporting are put together into an assessment plan document and an assessment report in [25].

5 Analysis of the Results

The result of the application of the generic process definition to public investment management process and comparing results with ad-hoc defined process definition is that the generic process definition covers ad-hoc defined process definition. It serves as a guideline to process owners to define their processes without any missing practice.

The result of the graduate student selection process assessment based on Gov-PCDM is that the capability level of the graduate student selection process performed in the Informatics Institute in METU is Level 2 with the following rationale based on collected and validated evidence in Table 3. More details of the assessment are given in the technical report [25].

In order to improve the capability level of the graduate student selection process to Level 3, assessment values of the process attributes should be as follows; Performance and Work Product Management attributes: Fully Achieved, Process Definition and deployment attributes: Largely or Fully Achieved.

Table 3. Graduate student selection process assessment result

Attribute	Evidences	Result
1.1 Process Performance	The process clearly achieved its purpose by maintaining steady student selection	Fully Achieved
2.1 Perf. Management	Process work products' reviews are not planned. The performance is planned and managed informally, performance quality criteria are not defined and not monitored	Largely Achieved
2.2 Work Product Management	Work products are defined, but their appropriate review and approval criteria are not identified and they are not reviewed	Largely Achieved
3.1 Process Definition and Tailoring	The process modeling diagrams are produced, however, no evidence can be obtained for the definition of metric/methods/criteria, monitoring effectiveness and suitability of the process	Largely Achieved

(*Continued*)

Table 3. (*Continued*)

Attribute	Evidences	Result
3.2 Process Deployment	The deployment rules are known by the personnel. Required human, information, infrastructure resources are available, but there is no conformance/test to verify the defined process satisfies the requirements. Additionally, data required to understand the behavior, suitability and effectiveness of the defined process are not identified/collected	Partially Achieved

5.1 Guideline for Improvement Capability of the Process

The roadmap to improve the capability level of the processes is derived from the assessment evidences in the technical report [25]. The aim is to turn negative evidences into positive evidences of process capability indicators supporting the judgment of the degree of achievement of the process attribute. For example; for performance management attribute; the second indicator (Generic Practice 2.1.2) is to plan and to monitor the performance of the process to fulfill the identified objectives. Negative evidence, observed while interviewing with process stakeholders for this indicator is that process work product reviews are not planned. Thus, necessity of reviewing work products is indicated in the guideline as follows:

- Review of the work products should be planned and performed in accordance with the requirements.
- Performance quality criteria should be defined and performance of the employees should be monitored.
- Quality criteria of the work products should be identified.
- Quality criteria for reviewing and approving the content of the work products should be defined.
- HR qualification should be identified.
- Standardization for evaluation of oral interview should be applied. Interview criteria and their weights should be determined.
- Monitoring and reporting processes should be performed.
- Accepted applications list revisions should be controlled systematically. Resolving issues arising from work product reviews should be tracked systematically.
- Data required understanding the behavior; suitability and effectiveness of the defined process should be identified/collected and used for improvement.
- Internal audit and management review should be conducted.
- Metrics/methods/criteria should be defined for monitoring effectiveness and suitability of the process.

5.2 Interviews with the Stakeholders

In order to check usefulness and adequacy of the proposed approach, interviews were conducted with the process stakeholders. The open-ended structured questionnaire below is utilized.

- Are measuring process capability and obtaining the guideline for improvement useful?
- Do you think that applying these suggestions will improve the process performance?
- Is there any information you want to add in the generic process definition?
- Is there any missing item in the guideline for improvement?

Interviews are conducted with 4 process stakeholders, 3 of them have more than 5 years' work experiences. One of them has 3 years' work experiences. The findings in the conducted interviews support our proposed approach. All of the answers for the first two questions are positive. They think that achieving a road map to guide what to do for increasing process capability is useful, all of the suggestions indicated in the guideline will improve the process performance of the graduate student selection process. They thought that the biggest contribution to the improvement of the process is provided by defining quality criteria/metrics/methods and monitoring the effectiveness and suitability of the process. While answering the last question, they point out some possible improvement areas such as interoperability of involved parties as head of student relations department of METU, academic committee, management committee, and student relations of the institute. However, this is out of our scope and is primarily related to e-government initiatives. They also confirm that generic process definition covers all outcomes of the process.

6 Conclusion

Initial findings of the case study indicate the usefulness and adequacy of the proposed approach of using process assessment in the government domain.

Lessons learned from this case study as follows:

- The AWL proposed by Medina-Mora [23] is of great help for starting point of government-specific process definition.
- The generic governmental process can be defined using the requirements stated in ISO/IEC 15504-2 [8].
- The developed generic process definition includes level 1 process performance indicators.
- Exactly the same 'generic practices indicators', 'generic resources indicators' and 'generic work products indicators' as the exemplar PAM provided by the ISO/IEC 15504-5 can be used for the assessment of level 2 to 5.
- The exemplar documented process in ISO/IEC 15504-3 can be used by a competent assessor to perform a conformance assessment.
- ISO/IEC 15504-4 is used as a guideline for developing the proposed roadmap for process capability improvement.

Future studies include validation of the Gov-PCDM by performing different case studies in various government agencies. Additionally; it is planned to analyze the possible use of the generic process definition for Graduate Student Selection Process in another university and to compare the results. The findings from the case study will be shown to be equally applicable in the wider public sector context.

References

1. Teicher, J., Hughes, O., Dow, N.: E-government: a new route to public sector quality. Manag. Serv. Q. Int. J. **12**(6), 384–393 (2002)
2. Hutton, G.: Business process re-engineering–a public sector view. In: Armistead, C., Rowland, P. (eds.) Managing Business Processes–BPR and Beyond. Wiley, Chichester (1996)
3. Acar, M., Kumaş, E.: Türkiye'nin Dönüşüm Sürecinde Anahtar Bir Mekanizma Olarak e-devlet, e-dönüşüm ve Entegrasyon Standartları. 2. In: National Economoy Symposium (2008)
4. Stemberger, M.I., Jaklic, J.: Towards E-government by business process change—a methodology for public sector. Int. J. Inf. Manage. **27**(4), 221–232 (2007)
5. Isomäki, H., Liimatainen, K.: Challenges of government enterprise architecture work – stakeholders' views. In: Wimmer, M.A., Scholl, H.J., Ferro, E. (eds.) EGOV 2008. LNCS, vol. 5184, pp. 364–374. Springer, Heidelberg (2008)
6. Hjort-Madsen, K., Gøtze, J.: Enterprise architecture in government-towards a multi-level framework for managing IT in government. In: 4th European Conference on e-Government, Dublin Castle, Ireland, pp. 365–374 (2004)
7. Fong, E.N., Goldfine, A.H.: Information management directions: the integration challenge. ACM SIGMOD Rec. **18**(4), 40–43 (1989)
8. ISO: ISO/IEC 15504-2: Information technology - Process assessment - Part 2: Performing an assessment (2003)
9. ISO: ISO/IEC 15504-3: Information technology – Process assessment – Part 3: Guidance on performing an assessment (2004)
10. ISO: ISO/IEC 15504-4: Information technology – Process assessment – Part 4: Guidance on use for process improvement and process capability determination (2004)
11. ISO: ISO/IEC 15504-5: Information technology - Process assessment - Part 5: An exemplar Process Assessment Model (2012)
12. Software Engineering Institute (SEI): CMMI Product Team, CMMI® for Development, Version 1.3, Improving processes for developing better products and services (2010)
13. ISO/IEC 33000 – Information Technology – Process Assessment, International Organization for Standardization (2014)
14. Automotive SIG: Automotive SPICE - Process Assessment Model (2007). http://www.itq.ch/pdf/AutomotiveSPICE_PAM_v23.pdf
15. Mc Caffery, F., Dorling, A.: Medi SPICE development. J. Softw. Maintenance Evol. Res. Pract. **22**(4), 255–268 (2010)
16. Ibrahim, L.: Improving process capability across your enterprise. In: 4th World Congress on Software Quality (4WCSQ), Bethesda, USA (2008)
17. Gökalp, E., Demirörs, O.: Government process capability model: an exploratory case study. In: Mitasiunas, A., Rout, T., O'Connor, R.V., Dorling, A. (eds.) SPICE 2014. CCIS, vol. 477, pp. 94–105. Springer, Heidelberg (2014)
18. Gökalp, E., Demirörs, O.: Proposing an ISO/IEC 15504 based process improvement method for the government domain. In: Rout, T., O'Connor, R.V., Dorling, A. (eds.) SPICE 2015. CCIS, vol. 526, pp. 100–113. Springer, Heidelberg (2015)
19. CIO Council: Federal Enterprise Architecture Consolidated Reference Model Document. Version 2.3 (2007)
20. American Productivity & Quality Center (APQC), Process Classification Framework, APQC, Washington, DC (2012). http://www.apqc.org/free/framework.htm

21. CP Team: CMMI for Service, Version 1.2. CMMI-SVC v1. 2. Technical report, CMU/SEI-2009-TR-001, Software Engineering Institute (2009)
22. Curtis, B., Hefley, B., Miller, S.: People Capability Maturity Model (P-CMM) Version 2.0. No. CMU/SEI-2009-TR-003 (2009)
23. Medina-Mora, R., Winograd, T., Flores, R., Flores, F.: The action workflow approach to workflow management technology. In: ACM Conference on Computer-Supported Cooperative Work, pp. 281–288. ACM (1992)
24. Balzer, W.K.: Lean Higher Education: Increasing the Value and Performance of University Processes. CRC Press, Boca Raton (2010)
25. Gokalp, E.: Technical Report of Graduate Student Selection Process Assessment (2016). http://smrg.ii.metu.edu.tr/smrgp/index.php?option=com_jresearch&view=publication&task=show&id=740&Itemid=54

SPI and Project Management Concerns

Measuring Global Distance: A Survey of Distance Factors and Interventions

John Noll[✉] and Sarah Beecham

Lero, The Irish Software Research Centre, University of Limerick, Limerick, Ireland
{john.noll,sarah.beecham}@lero.ie

Abstract. Geographic separation, lack of timezone overlap, and cultural differences are widely recognized as factors that impede communication and collaboration of globally distributed software development teams.

While much research has been done into *how* these factors affect communication and collaboration, there needs to be a way of measuring *how much* effect they have. This research develops a *Global Distance Metric* that attempts to quantify global distance as the combination of three factors: geographic, temporal, and cultural distance. Thirty researchers and practitioners were asked to rate the degree to which distance factors affect collaboration. The responses were aggregated and used to calibrate a global distance metric.

The metric revealed some surprising insights into the perception of global distance among the teams. In particular, pairs of teams had different perceptions of the cultural distance with their peers, with native English speakers perceiving a lower value than non-native speakers.

Keywords: Global software development · Metrics · Empirical software engineering

1 Introduction

Global Distance – geographic separation, lack of timezone overlap, and cultural differences among distributed software development teams – impedes communication among distributed software teams. Global distance prevents the kind of informal communication that can fill-in the gaps in specifications, designs, plans, and other formal communications. Consequently, much research has been devoted to characterizing the effects of global distance on a global software development effort, and to finding ways to reduce global distance or mitigate its impact [10,14].

Factors such as culture, language, distance, and time all contribute to communication barriers that impede collaboration [16]. Consequently, in a global software development context, software process improvement must address global distance [18]. However, in order to prioritize process improvement interventions intended to reduce or mitigate global distance, it is important to not only identify *which* factors impede communication, but also to measure *how much* these various factors that comprise global distance affect communication and collaboration. For example, developers in a multi-site team working in San Francisco and Boston, will have relatively less difficulty collaborating than if they were located in Shanghai and Ireland.

How, then, can we measure the relative impact of these distance factors on a team's ability to collaborate? And, how can we measure the degree to which process interventions, designed to reduce the impact of global distance, do, in fact, improve communication and collaboration?

In order to provide empirically grounded values for global distance factors and interventions, we designed a survey to elicit researcher and practitioner opinions on the impact of distance factors and interventions. Thirty researchers and practitioners were asked to rate the impact of each factor or intervention on a five-point scale, ranging from "Hardly at all" to "Very much." The responses were then used to calibrate a metric [2] for assessing the Global Distance between software development teams. Finally, we asked three development teams, located in Spain, Germany, and the United Kingdom, to compute their global distances based on this metric.

The results revealed a agreement among researchers and practitioners on the effect of different distance factors and interventions, lending credence to the resulting metric. The trial reveals a surprising *disagreement* between teams on the size of the distance between them.

The impact of these results is threefold.

First, project managers and team leaders can use an empirically-calibrated metric to gauge the global distance between collaborating teams. This is useful for allocating tasks to reduce communication overhead, and for planning interventions to reduce distance between teams that must communicate.

Second, researchers can use the results to calibrate models, and to prioritize recommendations comprising process models for global software development. For example, we used these results to parameterize a project survivability model [2] for global software development projects.

Finally, the results make it possible to compare different interventions to reduce the effects of global distance.

In the next section we review some existing metrics related to global software development. Following that we present the method used to collect empirical data to calibrate the model. Then, we present a Global Distance metric that uses the empirical data to compute a value for Global Distance. Finally we discuss a case study of the model's application to a real-world situation, followed by conclusions and plans for future work.

2 Background

More than a decade of global software engineering research has yielded numerous insights into the problems organizations encounter when moving to globally distributed software development. These can be classified broadly into a handful of categories, as shown in Table 1 [4].

Table 1. Common Global Software Development issues.

Category	Example consequence
Global distance (geographic, temporal, cultural)	Lack of informal communication
Organization	Increased communication overhead
Management	Reporting delays; culturally inappropriate rewards
Process	Problems scaling co-located processes
Infrastructure	Tool mismatch among teams
Fear and Trust	Lack of communication

Research has revealed not only issues related to global software development, but also potential solutions [16]. For example, the Global Teaming Model [18] includes 70 practices based on empirical research that address management issues related to global software development. However, while the practices are known to be effective, based on evidence from case studies and other empirical investigation, the model does not include any metrics of how effective they are. As such, it is difficult to know how to prioritize implementation of practices. This is true of most process models related to global software development.

There have been some attempts to provide measures of effectiveness to aid in prioritizing process improvement efforts. For example, Aranda and colleagues [1] propose a selection strategy for choosing collaboration tools, based on the notion of "cognitive styles." Lasser and Heiss [12] developed a model that correlates collaboration maturity with an "offshoring cost barrier" that could be used to gauge an organizations' readiness to engage in global software development.

Espinosa and Carmel [8] present a model for predicting costs based on several factors including collaboration structure, timezone overlap, and communication infrastructure. However, their model was not validated with empirical data.

Herbsleb and colleagues characterized the relationship between geographic distance and communication delay in distributed software development [9]. Similarly, social network analysis [7,13,15] has been used to gain insight into how successful GSD projects communicate. For example, Bird and colleagues developed and approach to predict faults in source code [5].

Socio-technical congruence, a metric that has emerged from this line of research, measures the degree to which an organization's communication structure matches the architecture of the product it is developing [6]. Metrics have been developed for measuring socio-technical congruence [11], as well as tools for improving congruence [17].

In summary, while there exist software process models and frameworks that organize practices to address most or all of the categories shown in Table 1, there appears to be no corresponding metric or set of metrics to support prioritizing and measuring progress of implementation of those practices.

Toward that goal, we conducted an empirical study to address the following questions:

1. What is the *magnitude* of impact on communication and collaboration of factors that comprise global distance, such as geographic separation, lack of timezone overlap, and cultural differences?
2. What is the *magnitude* of mitigation resulting from interventions designed to reduce the impact of global distance?

In the next section, we describe our approach to answering these questions.

3 Approach

What values should be assigned to capture the impact of distance factors and interventions? Geographic and temporal distance can be measured accurately, but the *impact* of increasing distance, for example, is not necessarily proportional to the distance value; rather, the impact is related to the *effort* required to visit a remote site. For example, one can visit a remote site that is an hour's flight in a single day, while a three hour flight may require an overnight stay. Similarly, sites in adjacent timezones are much "closer" temporally than sites across a continent.

Cultural distance is by nature qualitative; we consider China and Ireland to be further apart culturally than North America and Ireland, this difference is based on a qualitative comparison rather than a measurement. Interventions are likewise qualitative; the impact of interventions can be compared, but the exact value of each impact is difficult to assess.

Nevertheless, we need to assign values to distance factors and interventions in order to compute values for Global Distance that can be compared. As such, we chose an ordinal scale comprising five values to characterize the degree to which a factor increases, or intervention decreases, distance: "Not at all," "A little," "Moderately," "A lot," and "Very Much." Then, we asked researchers and practitioners involved in Global Software Development to rate distance factors and interventions using this scale.

The method we used to conduct this survey, and the results of the survey, are presented in the next sections.

3.1 Method

First, we designed a survey instrument to elicit opinions on the impact of distance factors and interventions. The survey comprised three parts:

1. A set of three questions asking respondents to rate the degree to which thirteen factors related to geographic distance, degree of timezone overlap, and cultural differences, increase global distance. Respondents were asked to use the five-point scale ranging from "Not at all" to "Very much" as described above to perform their rating.
2. A set of three questions asking respondents to rate the extent to which fifteen interventions reduce the impact of geographic, temporal, and cultural distance, again using the same five-point scale.

3. A set of five demographic questions about the respondent's role, background, and experience.

The entire survey is included in the Appendix.

Next, we solicited volunteers from the attendees at the International Conference on Global Software Development, held in Shanghai in August, 2014, to complete the survey.

Subsequently, we asked participants in a two-day workshop on collaboration across distance to complete the survey. This workshop was organized for employees of a multinational company that provides analytic services, and has software development teams across Europe.

Finally, we aggregated the responses to obtain impact values for each distance factor and intervention.

4 Survey Results

4.1 Demographics

A total of 30 volunteers completed the survey; 15 researchers and practitioners attending ICGSE 2014 in Shanghai, and 15 participants in the collaboration workshop. Among the respondents, there were eleven academic researchers, four researchers working in industry, and fourteen practitioners. These figures are summarized in Table 2.

Table 2. Demographics of survey respondents.

Experience	Years
Average experience in GSD	7
Average total software engineering experience	14
Countries represented	10
(Pakistan, Brazil, New Zealand, Germany, USA, China, UK, Finland, Spain, France)	
Respondent Role	Number
Academic researcher	11
Industry researchver	4
Practitioner	14

4.2 Ratings

Table 4 shows the median and mode (most common) rating for the impact of distance factors on distance components.

Table 3 provides some useful insight into the effects of global distance. Respondents considered both transcontinental and intercontinental distance to increase geographic distance "very much," perhaps reflecting the fact that a flight longer than three hours is a full-day commitment requiring an overnight stay.

Table 3. Survey results.

Questions regarding *Distance Factors*	# Resp.	Median	Mode
How much do the following increase geographic distance?			
Different building on same campus	30	1	1
Different towns in same region (two hour drive)	30	2	2
Less than three hour flight (Frankfurt to Helsinki)	29	3	3
Transcontinental flight (New York to San Francisco)	30	4	4
Intercontinental flight (London to Shanghai)	30	4	4
How much do the following increase temporal distance?			
Transcontinental (five hour overlap)	30	1	0
Intercontinental (three or four hour overlap)	30	2	3
Global (one or two hour overlap)	30	3	4
No overlap	29	4	4
How much do the following increase cultural distance?			
Uneven language skills	28	2.5	3
East/West divide in culture	27	3	3
Different national culture	27	2	2
Different organizational culture	29	3	3
Questions regarding *Interventions*	# Resp.	Median	Mode
How much do the following reduce geographic distance?			
Face-to-face meetings (in-person or onsite)	30	4	4
Face-to-face meetings (via video)	30	3	3
Exchange program	27	3	4
Synchronous communication infrastructure	29	2	2
Support for video conferencing at all sites	27	2.5	3
Range of communication tools with different comm. modes	28	2	2
How much do the following reduce temporal distance?			
Relocate team(s) to adjacent time zones	24	2	2
Create bridging team(s)	19	2	2
Adopt Follow-the-Sun development	26	3	3
How much do the following reduce cultural distance?			
Face-to-face meetings (in-person or onsite)	30	3	4
Face-to-face meetings (via video)	30	2	2
Cultural Training	29	3	3
Cultural Liaison/Ambassador	28	3	3
Adopt low-context communication style	26	2	2
Reduce interaction between teams from different cultures	25	2	0

In other words, there may be a distance threshold where significantly greater commitment is required to hold a face-to-face meeting.

A similar threshold appears to exist in timezone overlap: responses indicate a five hour overlap has little or no impact on distance, but if the overlap is reduced to four, the impact increases to "a lot." Respondents considered two or less hours of overlap to have the same impact as no overlap at all, affecting temporal distance "very much."

With one exception, results indicate that cultural factors increase cultural distance "a lot." The exception, curiously, is differences in national culture; respondents considered that this factor only increases cultural distance "moderately." This may be a consequence of the fact that nearly two-thirds (19) of respondents were from Europe, where the European Union and Eurozone have promoted increasing trans-national integration.

Regarding interventions, the notable result is the value respondents place on face-to-face interactions to address geographic separation. In-person interactions are considered most effective, with video conferencing next. Other communication infrastructure besides video is rated less impactful.

Also, respondents favor cultural interventions involving face-to-face interaction, such as exchange programs and cultural ambassadors. In the case of culture, however, in-person interactions are rated much higher than video interactions. While the results indicate video-conferencing can mitigate geographic distance "a lot," and cultural distance "moderately," it appears there is no substitute for in-person interaction. Numerous studies recommend holding face-to-face meetings, especially as a project "kick-off"; our survey results support this recommendation as highly effective.

In summary, our survey results indicate that transcontinental or greater separation has a high impact; the most effective way to reduce this impact is to facilitate in-person, face-to-face interactions among team members, via meetings and exchange programs. These in-person meetings should be supplemented with video conferencing.

Comparing the median and mode (most popular answer) for each item in Table 3 shows that there is remarkable agreement among survey respondents as to the impacts of distance factors and interventions. In only eight of 28 items did the mode differ from the median, and in all but one case the mode was higher than the median. The most controversial item appears to be the intervention of reducing interaction among teams in order to reduce the impact of cultural differences. It appears that our survey respondents are divided about whether it is effective to sidestep this problem by keeping culturally different teams apart; possibly, this is a reflection of the population from which the respondents were drawn, a population, by virtue of attending events such as ICGSE, that appears to value cross-cultural interaction.

5 Example: A Global Distance Metric

As part of an effort to develop a model to predict how long it would take for a global software development project to recover from an adverse event [2,3], we developed a measure of global distance based on three distance dimensions: geographic, temporal, and cultural distance. The global distance between two sites is then the *Euclidean Distance* calculated from the three dimensions:

$$D_{global} = \sqrt{D_{geographic}^2 + D_{temporal}^2 + D_{cultural}^2} \quad (1)$$

where D_c is the value of distance dimension $c \in \{geographic, temporal, cultural\}$.

The global distance metric was used in the survivabilty model to calculate the probability that communication among teams facing an adverse event is adequate to deal with that event.

In Eq. (1), each dimension ($D_{geographic}$, $D_{temporal}$, and $D_{cultural}$) is, in turn, computed as the sum of the impacts of various distance factors such as degree of timezone overlap, language skills, cultural difference, and geographic separation:

$$D_c = \sum_{j \in \mathcal{D}_c} d_{c,j} \quad (2)$$

In this equation, $\mathcal{D}_c$ is the set of factors contributing to distance component c, where $c \in \{geographic, temporal, cultural\}$; $d_{c,j}$ is the impact value of a distance factor j along dimension c, such as geographic separation ($c = geographic$), degree of timezone overlap ($c = temporal$), extent of cultural differences ($c = cultural$), or competency in the project's *lingua franca* ($c = cultural$).

This metric has the potential to provide a way for a software project to assess the barriers between teams introduced by global distance, plan interventions to reduce those barriers, and measure the effect of improvement efforts intended to reduce global distance.

In order for the metric to be truly useful, however, the impact values should be based on empirical evidence, so that the resulting distance measure reflects current understanding of how distance, time, and culture affect collaboration.

Each distance factor has a value that reflects the degree to which the factor impedes communication and collaboration. We use the results of our survey to parameterize the global distance metric, by using the mode as the impact value for each factor; the result is shown in Table 4.

As an example, consider a multi-site team with developers in New York and London that work for the same company. This team would have intercontinental geographic distance ($d_{5,geographic} = 4$), intercontinental temporal distance ($d_{2,temporal} = 3$), different national cultures ($d_{3,cultural} = 2$), but would have a common language and organizational culture. Thus, we would compute the Global Distance between the sites as:

$$D_{global} = \sqrt{4^2 + 3^2 + 2^2} \quad (3)$$
$$= \sqrt{29} = 5.4$$

5.1 An Application of the Metric

To validate the usefulness of the Global Distance metric, we conducted a trial to compare the Global Distance among three teams.

Table 4. Factors contributing to distance ($\mathcal{D}_c$).

j	Factors affecting geographic distance	$(d_{j,geographic})$
1	Different building on same campus	1
2	Different towns in same region (two hour drive)	2
3	Less than three hour flight (Frankfurt to Helsinki)	3
4	Transcontinental flight (New York to San Francisco)	4
5	Intercontinental flight (London to Shanghai)	4
j	Factors affecting temporal distance	$(d_{j,temporal})$
1	Transcontinental (five hour overlap)	0
2	Intercontinental (three or four hour overlap)	3
3	Global (one or two hour overlap)	4
4	No overlap	4
j	Factors affecting cultural distance	$(d_{j,cultural})$
1	Uneven language skills	3
2	East/West divide in culture	3
3	Different national culture	2
4	Different organizational culture	3

Participants in the workshop on collaboration across distance described in Sect. 2 represented three teams from across Europe: one in Spain, one in Germany, and one in the United Kingdom. We asked them to form three comprising members of teams at the same location. The groups were then tasked with computing their Global Distance to each of the other two teams, using the formula specified in Eq. (1).

All teams determined that geographic distance affected them "Moderately" (2), and temporal distance affected them "A little" (1). The main differences were in the way each team perceived the impact of cultural differences.

The results, depicted in Fig. 1 are surprising in their asymmetry: the German team computed the same distance from both Spain and the UK; at 11.4 for each, this was the largest distance metric among the three. The Spanish team had the smallest distance to the UK, at 3.7; conversely, the British team computed their distance to the Spanish team at 5.5. The distance computed from the UK to Germany was 6.4, while the Spanish team put this value at 7.3.

Despite all team members being fluent English speakers, it's possible that the Spanish team felt closer to the UK team because one of the UK team members was a native Spanish speaker; this might mean they felt it was easier for them to communicate with the UK team, while the UK team had no such cultural "ambassador" on site in Spain.

The German team was part of a recent acquisition as so was new to the organizational culture. This might explain why they felt further apart culturally from their counterparts; the perception might have been from the opposite end that the German team was adapting well, while the German team might have perceived the transition as more difficult. It should be noted that one of the

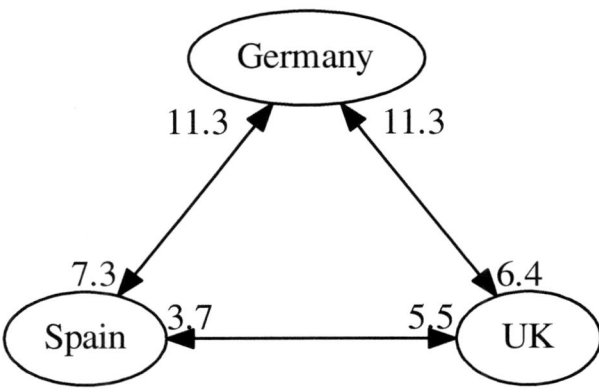

Fig. 1. Global distance among three distributed teams.

German team was a native English speaker, but language skills across the team were somewhat uneven.

Regardless of the root cause for the differences in perception, the fact that teams viewed their cultural distance differently is a signal for higher management that some interventions (such as the workshop the participants in this trial were attending) would be appropriate, to bring the teams closer together along the cultural dimension. An informal survey at the beginning of the workshop confirmed this: the overwhelming majority of attendees had meeting members of other teams as one of their objectives for the workshop.

6 Conclusions

In this paper, we presented the results of a survey designed to assess the impact of various factors that contribute to, or help reduce, global distance in software development projects. We used these results to calibrate a global distance metric, that provides a comparative measure of the impact of distance on communication and collaboration.

Project managers and team leaders can use this metric to measure the global distance between collaborating teams. As shown in Sect. 5.1, this metric can provide valuable insight into how teams perceive their counterparts; this insight would be invaluable when planning interventions to reduce distance between teams that must communicate and collaborate.

Second, researchers can use the results to calibrate models, such as the project survivability model proposed by Avritzer and colleagues [2]. Also, the values placed on different interventions can be used to prioritize recommendations comprising process models for global software development.

Finally, the results provide a way to compare the effect of different interventions an organization might take to reduce the effect of distance on a software development project. This is important because it allows an organization to assess the cost-effectiveness of different approaches to dealing with global distance.

Limitations

While our survey resulted in a significant number of responses (30 in total), the participants come from an "opportunistic" sample of conference and workshop attendees. While the respondents represent experienced researchers and practitioners with an interest as well as stake in issues related to global software development, there is the possibility of a hidden selection bias in the sample, since the respondents elected to attend each event voluntarily, and also participated in the survey voluntarily.

Nevertheless, based on their reported experience in software engineering in general, and global software engineering in particular, we feel respondents possess the necessary expertise to render informed opinions about the various factors and interventions.

Also, as noted in Sect. 4, Europe was disproportionately represented among the survey respondents; this might introduce an unidentified European bias to the results.

Finally, the metric presented in Sect. 5 provides a way to *rank* different scenarios involving global distance. However, the scale has not been calibrated, and so we cannot say with confidence *how much* greater one distance metric is over another.

Future Directions

As noted above, the global distance metric in Sect. 5 could be calibrated so that the values can be used to compare the actual differences between sites, rather than simply ranking them. This would be useful in the case presented in Sect. 5.1, where the metric could be applied before and after taking steps to reduce the perceived cultural distance of the German team. A calibrated metric would show not only that improvement occurred, but also how much.

In a similar vein, the effect of interventions on reducing global distance could be added to the global distance metric; this would aid in planning interventions.

The survey itself could be expanded to include more participants from outside Europe; North America and the Indian subcontinent, in particular, could have better representation in our sample.

Also, the number of factors and interventions could be expanded to include factors such as product architecture, organizational structure, and process.

Acknowledgments. We would like to thank the ICGSE 2014 attendees, and practitioners who participated in the global software development workshop, who completed our survey.

This work was supported, in part, by Science Foundation Ireland grants 10/CE/I1855 and 13/RC/2094 to Lero - the Irish Software Research Centre (www.lero.ie).

Survey: Measuring Global Distance

John Noll (john.noll@leroie), *Sarah Beecham* (sarah.beecham@lero.ie)

Geographic separation, lack of working day overlap, and cultural differences affect how well teams at different locations collaborate on a software development project. Taken together, we call these factors "Global Distance", which comprises three components: *geographic distance* (separation between sites), *temporal distance* (difference in timezones between sites), and *cultural distance* (difference in national, regional, and organizational culture between sites).

This survey has two objectives: 1. to assess the degree to which different factors increase Global Distance, and 2. to assess how different interventions reduce or mitigate Global Distance.

Please circle the number that best answers the question.

Distance Factors						
How much do the following increase geographic distance?	Not at all	A little	Moderately	A lot	Very much	Don't Know
Different building on same campus	0	1	2	3	4	X
Different towns in same region (two hour drive)	0	1	2	3	4	X
Less than three hour flight (Frankfurt to Helsinki)	0	1	2	3	4	X
Transcontinental flight (New York to San Francisco)	0	1	2	3	4	X
Intercontinental flight (London to Shanghai)	0	1	2	3	4	X
How much do the following increase temporal distance?	Not at all	A little	Moderately	A lot	Very much	Don't Know
Transcontinental (five hour overlap)	0	1	2	3	4	X
Intercontinental (three or four hour overlap)	0	1	2	3	4	X
Global (one or two hour overlap)	0	1	2	3	4	X
No overlap	0	1	2	3	4	X
How much do the following increase cultural distance?	Not at all	A little	Moderately	A lot	Very much	Don't Know
Uneven language skills	0	1	2	3	4	X
East/West divide in culture	0	1	2	3	4	X
Different national culture	0	1	2	3	4	X
Different organizational culture	0	1	2	3	4	X
Interventions						
How much do the following reduce geographic distance?	Not at all	A little	Moderately	A lot	Very much	Don't Know
Face-to-face meetings (in-person, onsite)	0	1	2	3	4	X
Face-to-face meetings (via video)	0	1	2	3	4	X
Exchange program	0	1	2	3	4	X
Synchronous communication infrastructure	0	1	2	3	4	X
Support for video conferencing at all sites	0	1	2	3	4	X
Range of communication tools with different comm. modes	0	1	2	3	4	X
How much do the following reduce temporal distance?	Not at all	A little	Moderately	A lot	Very much	Don't Know
Relocate team(s) to adjacent time zones	0	1	2	3	4	X
Adopt Follow-the-Sun development	0	1	2	3	4	X
Create bridging team(s)	0	1	2	3	4	X
How much do the following reduce cultural distance?	Not at all	A little	Moderately	A lot	Very much	Don't Know
Face-to-face meetings (in-person, onsite)	0	1	2	3	4	X
Face-to-face meetings (via video)	0	1	2	3	4	X
Cultural Training	0	1	2	3	4	X
Cultural Liaison/Ambassador	0	1	2	3	4	X
Adopt low-context communication style	0	1	2	3	4	X
Reduce interaction between teams from different cultures	0	1	2	3	4	X

Demographic Information
The following information will allow us to see how point-of-view (experience, culture, and role) affects opinion.

Your role (please circle one): Academic researcher   Industry researcher   Practitioner
Your nationality:
Years of GSD experience (research and/or practice):
Total years of Software Engineering research/practice experience, including GSD experience:
Did you see Alberto's presentation on Survivability Models?   Yes   No

References

1. Aranda, G.N., Vizcaino, A., Cechich, A., Piattini, M.: Technology selection to improve global collaboration. In: Proceedings of the IEEE International Conference on Global Software Engineering (ICGSE 2006), pp. 223–232. IEEE Computer Society, Florianopolis, Brazil, October 2006
2. Avritzer, A., Beecham, S., Britto, R., Kroll, J., Menasché, D.S., Noll, J., Paasivaara, M.: Extending survivability models for global software development with media synchronicity theory. In: IEEE 10th International Conference on Global Software Engineering (ICGSE). Ciudad Real, Spain, July 2015
3. Avritzer, A., Beecham, S., Kroll, J., Menasche, D.S., Noll, J., Paasivaara, M.: Survivability models for global software engineering. In: 9th IEEE International Conference on Global Software Engineering (ICGSE), pp. 100–109, August 2014
4. Beecham, S., O'Leary, P., Richardson, I., Baker, S., Noll, J.: Who are we ng global software engineering research for? In: Proceedings of the International Conference on Global Software Engineering (ICGSE 2013). Bari, Italy, August 2013
5. Bird, C., Nagappan, N., Gall, H., Murphy, B., Devanbu, P.: Putting it all together: using socio-technical networks to predict failures. In: 20th International Symposium on Software Reliability Engineering, ISSRE 2009, pp. 109–119 (2009)
6. Cataldo, M., Herbsleb, J.D., Carley, K.M.: Socio-technical congruence: A framework for assessing the impact of technical and work dependencies on software development productivity. In: Proceedings of the Second ACM-IEEE International Symposium on Empirical Software Engineering and Measurement, ESEM 2008, pp. 2–11. NY, USA (2008). http://doi.acm.org/10.1145/1414004.1414008
7. Damian, D., Marczak, S., Kwan, I.: Collaboration patterns and the impact of distance on awareness in requirements-centred social networks. In: Sutcliffe and Jalote [19], pp. 59–68
8. Espinosa, J.A., Carmel, E.: The effect of time separation on coordination costs in global software teams: a dyad model. In: Proceedings of the 37th Annual Hawaii International Conference on System Sciences (HICSS 2004). IEEE Computer Society, Big Island, Hawaii, USA, 5–8 Jan, 2004
9. Herbsleb, J.D., Mockus, A., Finholt, T.A., Grinter, R.E.: An empirical study of global software development: distance and speed. In: Proceedings of the 23rd International Conference on Software Engineering (ICSE 2001), pp. 81–90. Toronto, Ontario, Canada, 12–19 May, 2001
10. Herbsleb, J.D., Paulish, D.J., Bass, M.: Global software development at Siemens: Experience from nine projects. In: Proceedings of the 27th International Conference on Software Engineering (ICSE 2005), pp. 524–533. IEEE Computer Society Press, St. Louis, May 2005
11. Kwan, I., Schrter, A., Damian, D.: A weighted congruence measure. In: Socio-Technical Congruence Workshop, in Conjunction with International Conference Software Engineering. Vancouver, Canada (2009)
12. Lasser, S., Heiss, M.: Collaboration maturity and the offshoring cost barrier: the tradeoff between flexibility in team composition and cross-site communication effort in geographically distributed development projects. In: Proceedings of the International Professional Communication Conference (IPCC 2005), pp. 718–728, 10–13 July, 2005
13. Maiden, N., Lockerbie, J., Randall, D., Jones, S., Bush, D.: Using satisfaction arguments to enhance i* modelling of an air traffic management system. In: Sutcliffe and Jalote [19], pp. 49–52

14. Moe, N.B., Smite, D.: Understanding a lack of trust in global software teams: a multiple-case study. Softw. Process Improv. Pract. **13**(3), 217–231 (2008)
15. Nguyen, T., Wolf, T., Damian, D.: Global software development and delay: Does distance still matter? In: Proceedings of the 2008 IEEE International Conference on Global Software Engineering (ICGSE 2008), pp. 45–54. IEEE Computer Society, Bangalore, India, August 2008
16. Noll, J., Beecham, S., Richardson, I.: Global software development and collaboration: Barriers and solutions. ACM Inroads **1**(3), 66–78 (2010)
17. Portillo-Rodrguez, J., Vizcano, A., Piattini, M., Beecham, S.: Using agents to manage socio-technical congruence in a global software engineering project. Inf. Sci. **264**, 230–259 (2014)
18. Richardson, I., Casey, V., McCaffery, F., Burton, J., Beecham, S.: A process framework for global software engineering teams. Inf. Softw. Technol. **54**, 1175–1191 (2012)
19. Sutcliffe, A., Jalote, P. (eds.): 15th IEEE International Requirements Engineering Conference (RE 2007). IEEE Computer Society, New Delhi, India, 15–19 October, 2007

MAMD: Towards a Data Improvement Model Based on ISO 8000-6X and ISO/IEC 33000

Ana G. Carretero[(✉)], Ismael Caballero, and Mario Piattini

Alarcos Research Group, Institute of Software and System Technologies,
Escuela Superior de Informática, Paseo de la Universidad 4,
13071 Ciudad Real, Spain
{AnaIsabel.Gomez,Ismael.Caballero,
Mario.Piattini}@uclm.es

Abstract. Organizations are increasingly becoming aware that the better the data, the higher the benefits they can obtain from them. To maximize the benefits from data, it is highly recommended to institutionalize a set of good practices related to data management, data quality management and data governance. As a result of our research, we have developed MAMD (Alarcos' Model for Data Improvement). MAMD is a framework consisting of a process reference model addressing the best practices of data management, data quality management and data governance, and an assessment and improvement model of the level of institutionalization of these practices. This paper describes how we have developed MAMD from ISO 8000-6x and ISO/IEC 33000.

Keywords: Data quality · Data governance · Data quality management · Data management · Data improvement · Maturity model

1 Introduction

The potential of the organizations to develop their mission and to find new paths to innovate on an increasingly competitive market is mainly grounded on data. Due to this fact, organizations are becoming more and more conscious that the better the data, the higher the benefits they can obtain. As an example of benefits, a better economic performance can be cited. It stands to reason that enough resources in deploying solutions shall be invested. These solutions will be aimed to achieve proportional data quality levels according to both intended and future uses of data.

Hence, ensuring data quality is a task which must: (1) be planned well enough in advance; (2) consider clear objectives aligned with organizational strategy; (3) assign adequately qualified human, and sufficient materials and economic resources. Only then, commensurate results with organization potential can be guaranteed. This assurance of data quality levels must be achieved by implementing integrated data management, data quality management and data governance programs.

To facilitate software processes improvement to organizations, there are alternatives based on *de iure* and *de facto* standards like COBIT [1], CMMI [2], ISO/IEC 15504 [3], ISO/IEC 33000 [4] … unfortunately, they do not specifically address low levels of data quality concerns, and it is not easy to use them directly as regards working with data management, data quality management and data governance disciplines. However, in recent times, new process-oriented initiatives (DMM [5] or ISO 8000-60 [6]) emerged to cope with these disciplines. After a detailed study, we can conclude that DMM had two important problems: its application is not easy and it is focused primarily on financial domain. On the other hand, we posed that because of its general purpose, ISO 8000-6X is easier to apply and use, although it does not explicitly cover neither data government processes aspects and it nor does fully address data management processes.

To fill this gap, and as a main result of our research we have developed the Alarcos' Model for Data Improvement (MAMD stands for "*Modelo Alarcos de Mejora de Datos*" in Spanish). Our objective was to create a framework that allows organizations to develop continuous improvement projects based on PDCA cycle to progressive implantation of improvements to obtain a best performance of data. MAMD consists of two main components:

- A process reference model that extends ISO 8000-61 [7] with data governance processes and some data management processes.
- An assessment and improvement model based on ISO/IEC 33000 [4]. We decided to ground our proposal on ISO/IEC 33000 due to the lack of specific and standardized works in the area.

The main contribution of this paper is the presentation and description of the MAMD models. This paper is structured as follows: Sect. 2 presents related works, Sect. 3 presents MAMD framework, Sect. 4 has some conclusions obtained as result of this paper and introduce some future lines of work that we consider necessary to improve MAMD. Lastly, we include some acknowledge and references.

2 Related Works

This section is to show related works with the main content of our proposal. This implies:

1. To provide an overview of the assessment and improvement process models.
2. To compare the various existing process reference models to identify processes that will be part of the process reference model of MAMD.

A maturity model can be understood as a tool used to organize a set of elements ordered according to a given criterion [8]. In the domain of this work, the criterion is related to organizational maturity in respect of guarantee the success of business processes with regard to data quality management, data management and data governance.

The first researcher to apply the concept of maturity model in the field of computer science was probably Humphrey in 1987 [9]. He used it to explain organizations; how to have more capable processes in order to produce high quality software. Specifically, in data quality domain, English was the first one to apply the maturity concept to data management at the same time as he included the notion of "data quality" in [8]. Since then, there has been many works related to data management that try to address this issue. Following subsections will go deep into such data quality management maturity models.

2.1 Scope of the Existing Data Maturity Models

Regarding the scope of "*data management practices*" [10], it is easy to see how the evolution of the field has found data quality management and data governance. By the end of the twentieth century, organizations began to be aware of the need for data quality. It is difficult to provide a data quality definition because of multiple interpretations of the concept. In [11], professor Wang establishes a data quality definition as "fitness for use", and this definition has been widely used all over the last year as reference to the development of research works on the data quality management area. Nonetheless, soon, organizations realize that Data quality management needs an integrative support from high management. The concept of data governance was presented for the first time in the middle of the previous decade. Their objective is to align the data strategy to the organizational business strategy, what implies to invest the necessary efforts to carry out data management and data quality management [12, 13]. Figure 1 shows data management's evolution over time since 1950 to present.

The three mentioned disciplines are not on the focus of all the existing frameworks and currently only DMM [5] and MAMD - that is to be presented in this paper - address the three disciplines as it will be shown below. However, it is possible to find: (i) maturity models whose purpose is address only one of the three disciplines, as English [8], Caballero et al. [14, 15], Ryu et al. [16] or Baskarada [17] and (ii) frameworks that are not presented as a maturity model and include the three disciplines, like DAMA [13].

Along this work, "data maturity model" term is going to be used to refer to all maturity models that integrate data management, data quality management and data governance.

2.2 Frameworks Considered as Basis

Considering that the idea of maturity models was firstly applied to software processes, and up to now some software process maturity models have been developed, it makes sense that research work on data maturity models have used these models as a base.

A framework which is used as reference not only provides a structure to process reference model, but also other necessary components as an assessment methodology and an improvement model. CMMI [18] provides a process reference model that can be used with SCAMPI [19] or CBA-IBI [20], while ISO/IEC 15504 [21] provides an assessment model, including criteria that represents a maturity model and an assessment model that can be used with ISO 12207 [22].

In this sense, the process reference model, which has inspired most of the data maturity models is CMMI. The two representations of CMMI – staged and continuous – have been

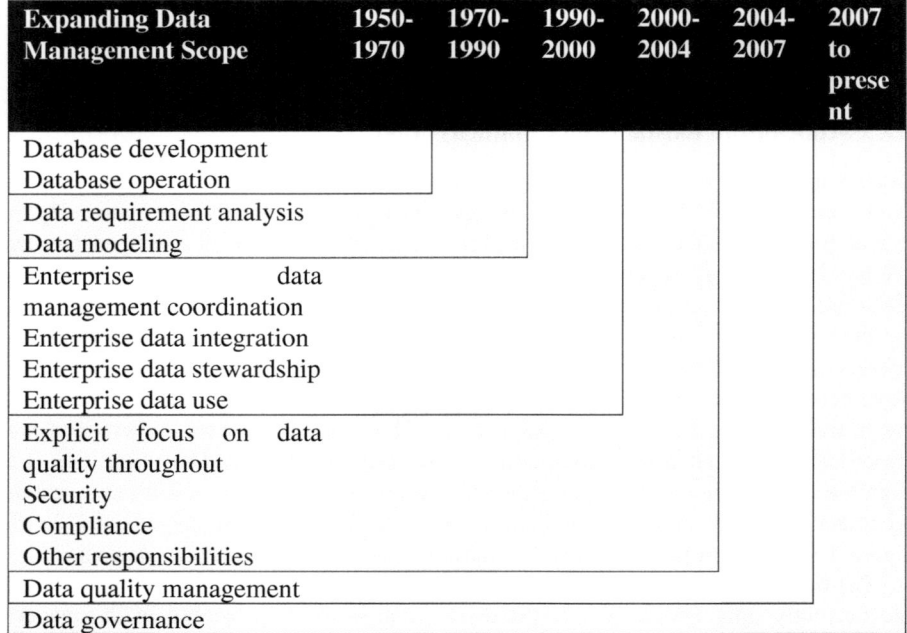

Fig. 1. Adapted from Aiken et al. [10] by using Trends.google.com

used in various proposals. To mention a few of them: IQM3 [15] is presented as a staged model, while IQMM [17] or recently DMM [5] are described as continuous models.

ISO 8000-6x project [23] includes a process reference model (ISO 8000-61) and a maturity model (ISO 8000-62) structured according to the established principles in ISO/IEC 33000.

Furthermore, it is noteworthy to mention the model proposed by Pierce et al. in [24] that is based on COBIT 4.1. Additionally, it is necessary to highlight the fact that many authors in the field of data quality use "data" and "information" as synonyms.

2.3 Existing Models Classification

To present the works in this area, they have been grouped against two criteria, reference framework and scope. In scope, there are three possible values: {"*data management*", "*data quality management*", "*data governance*"}, while in the reference framework the next values are been classified: CMMI, ISO/IEC 15504, COBIT and others. Table 1 gathers this classification.

Table 1. Data maturity models classification according to their scope.

Framework	Data management	Data quality management	Data governance
English [8]	X	X	
CALDEA [14]	X	X	
IQM3 [15]	X	X	
IQM [17]	X	X	
Aiken et al. [10]	X		
DMM [5]	X	X	X
IAIDQ [24]	X	X	X
ISO 8000-61 [7]	X	X	
DAMA [13]	X	X	X

Table 2 presents data maturity models classification according to the reference framework used.

Table 2. Data maturity models classification according to the reference framework used.

Framework	CMMI	ISO 15504	COBIT	Others
English [8]				X
CALDEA [14]	X			
IQM3 [15]	X			
IQMM [17]	X			
Aiken et al. [10]	X			
DMM [5]	X			
IAIDQ [24]			X	
ISO 8000-61 [7]		X		
DAMA [13]				X

3 MAMD, the Alarcos' Data Improvement Model

The MAMD framework is based on three aforementioned disciplines: data management [25], data quality management [11, 26] and data governance [27]. They are strongly dependant one from the others. This dependence is observed by [28] - where is revealed that the actual investigation in data quality involve the obvious need of adding certain governance, management, and technical aspects. The description of the three disciplines is showed below:

- Data governance is aimed to design and implement data management and data quality strategies, which allows the alignment of data strategies to business organizational strategies. Such strategies are implemented as organizational policies. This will give support to the business needs by providing the necessary resources to both areas and monitoring the use of the resources regarding the strategic objectives of the organization.

- From our perspective and for the sake of simplicity, we consider that data management implements and maintains a technological data infrastructure that must support business requirements. The requirements will be expressed through the data management policies. Likewise, the specific data quality requirements and their management shall be supported by the technological infrastructure.
- Data quality management implements and maintains a data quality organizational culture that shall produce, maintain, perform, and communicate data quality management good practices that must be applied by data management. The actions previously mentioned shall satisfy the data quality specific requirements that ensure the organization processes success.

In order to bring to reality not only the main outcome of the three disciplines, but also the dependency between them, the Process Reference model is introduced as a way to depict what organization could do rather than specifying what organization has to do.

3.1 Process Reference Model

According to the stated in clause 5.3.1 of ISO/IEC 33004 [29], a process reference model (PRM) is defined as a set of processes that can collectively provide support to the organizational processes. The process reference model of MAMD is composed by 18 processes grouped around the three disciplines: data management, data quality management and data governance. These processes have been identified by mapping ISO 8000-61, DMM, COBIT, and DAMA (see Table 3 for a mapping between ISO 8000-61, MAMD and DMM.)

The process reference model is shown below:

Data Management Processes (DM)

- **DM.1. Data requirement management.** This process aims at collecting and validate requirements referral to necessary data to manage the organization successfully.
- **DM.2. Technological infrastructure management.** The goal of this process is to specify and maintain the necessary technological infrastructure to support data meaning shared between applications.
- **DM.3. Historical data management.** The process addresses how to maintain and perform necessary policies to organizational historical data management.
- **DM.4. Data security management.** This process is aimed to define and enable mechanisms to make possible confidentiality, integrity, accessibility or availability, authenticity, non-repudiation, consistency, isolation, and data audit.
- **DM.5. Configuration management.** The process addresses how to define the processes by which an organization demand, determines, approves, and implements the reachable plans and evaluates the changes of data lifecycle.
- **DM.6. Master data management.** This process is aimed to identify the relevant concepts to organization business domain and the organizational data strategy alignment around these master data.

Table 3. DMM and ISO 8000-61 processes mapped to MAMD processes.

MAMD	DMM	ISO 8000-61
DM.1. Data Requirements Management	DO 4.1	I 1.1
DM.2. Technological Architecture Management	PA 5.1, PA 5.2, PA 5.3	DRS 2.1
DM.3. Historical Data Management	PA 5.5	
DM.4. Data Security Management	SP 6.4	DRS 2.4
DM.5. Configuration Management	SP 6.5	
DM.6. Master Data Management	DMS 1.1, DG 2.1	
DM.7. Data Design	DG 2.2, DG 2.3	
DM.8. Establishment of Data Sources and Data Targets	DO 4.3	DMS 2.2
DM.9. Data Integration	PA 5.4	I 1.8, DMS 2.2
DQM.1. Data Quality Measurement	SP 6.1, DQ 3.1, DQ 3.3	I 1.5, I 1.7, I 1.10
DQM.2. Data Quality Improvement	SP 6.1, DQ 3.1, DQ 3.3	I 1.11, I 1.12, I 1.14
DG.1. Establishment of Data Strategy	DMS 1.1, DQ 3.1, DG 2.1, DMS 1.2	I 1.2, I 1.4, I 1.5
DG.2. Management of the Data Lifecycle and Value of Data	DO 4.2	
DG.3. Definition of Standards, Policies and Procedures	DG 2.1, DMS 1.2, DQ 3.1, DQ 3.2, PA 5.2	I 1.3, I 1.9
DG.4. Human Resources Management	DMS 1.3	RP 3.2
DG.5. Financial Resources Management	DMS 1.5	
DG.6. Monitoring of Organizational Data Strategy	DG 2.1, DMS 1.1	I 1.7
DG.7. Management of Changes to Data Strategy	DMS 1.1	

- **DM.7. Data design.** The goal of this process is to develop a consistent data model, complete, comprehensive and extensible that covers the data requirements of all organizational units. In addition, the data model shall be aligned to the organizational data strategy.
- **DM.8. Data sources and data targets establishment.** The process addresses how to identify and characterize each data sources and destinations used in original business processes, as well as the agreements and interactions with providers and customers.
- **DM.9. Data integration.** The goal of this process is to ensure data integrity through flow control and relationships with transferred data to application systems or data bases.

Processes related to Data Quality Management (DQM)

- **DQM.1. Data quality measurement.** This process is aimed to establish necessary resources to satisfy requirement, and measure quality levels according to measurement criteria.
- **DQM.2. Data quality improvement.** The goal of this process is to implement a continuous improvement cycle based on PDCA model to data improvement in organizational repositories.

Processes related to Data Governance (DG)

- **DG.1. Data strategy establishment.** The process addresses how to identify and prioritize data management objectives, and work according to these prioritization to give support to the corporate strategic objectives.
- **DG.2. Data lifecycle management and data value.** The goal of this process is to identify the importance degree of data have to different business processes in corresponding stages.
- **DG.3. Standards, policies and procedures definition.** This process is aimed to establish those standards, policies, good practices and procedures to data management, data quality management and data governance to support as better as possible the data quality strategy.
- **DG.4. Human resources management.** The process address how to manage needs adequately to required specific formation to the human resources specifically destined to data management, data quality management and data governance.
- **DG.5. Financial resources management.** The goal of this process is to develop plans for financial resources provisioning and maintaining that can give support to organizational data strategy.
- **DG.6. Data organization strategies monitoring.** This process is aimed to develop and measure key indicators for monitoring the achievement of data management strategy and check that it is being actually aligned with the organizational data strategy.
- **DG.7. Change management in data strategy.** The goal of this process is to maintain coherently organizational data strategy according to the evolution of corporate strategic objectives.

3.2 Process Assessment Model

The purpose of a data quality management maturity assessment is to understand and assess how well the organizational processes address the requirements identified by the data quality management process reference model specified by ISO 8000-61.

ISO 8000-61 identifies needs that are covered by the data quality management process reference model. To evaluate data quality management maturity in the organizations is necessary to understand and to assess the processes efficacy to cover them.

Process Capability Levels and Process Attributes. As stated in ISO/IEC 33020 [30], process capability is defined on a six point ordinal scale that enables capability to be assessed from the bottom of the scale, incomplete, through the top end of the scale, innovating. The scale represents increasing capability of the implemented process – from failing to achieve the process purpose through continually improvements.

ISO/IEC 33020 defines process capability on a six point ordinal scale. The scale starts on level 0 labelled as "incomplete" and ends on level 5 labelled "innovating". Also, the scale represents capability of the implemented process.

To compute the process capability level is necessary to observe and assess the evidence of the achievement of the process attributes. For a detailed description of the full meaning of the process capability and the process attributes can be consulted in clause 5.2 of ISO/IEC 33020.

To calculate the process capability level is necessary to assess and observe the evidence of the achievement of the process attributes. The meaning of the process attributes and the process capability are described in ISO/IEC 33020. Table 4 summarises the processes attributes and capability levels that have to be achieved. Note that achieving the next level involves obtaining own level and above.

Rating Process Attributes and Process Capability. Rating a process attribute consists of a judgement of the extent to which a specific process attribute has been achieved for the assessed process. A process attribute (PA) is a measurable property within this process measurement framework of process capability. The capability levels and process attributes are described in ISO/IEC 33020 in clause 5.2 and the ordinal scale for rating capability levels are described in clause 5.3. In Table 4 the capability levels and process attributes, and in Table 5 the corresponding values and the ordinal scale are shown. Because of length paper restrictions, we have not include the way to develop how to compute the assessment indicator as ISO/IEC 33004 requires (Table 6).

Table 4. Capability levels and process attributes.

Process capability level	Process attributes
Incomplete process	n/a
Performed process	PA.1.1. Process performance
Managed process	PA.2.1. Performance management
	PA.2.2. Work product management
Established process	PA.3.1. Process definition
	PA.3.2. Process deployment
Predictable process	PA.4.1. Quantitative analysis
	PA.4.2. Quantitative control
Innovating process	PA.5.1. Process innovation
	PA.5.2. Process innovation implementation

Hence, when an organizational business process is to be assessed with regard to the data quality management, assessors shall investigate on an evidence-basis how much data quality management processes from the data quality management process reference model are achieved. As a result, it can be stated that one specific organizational process is capable of addressing the data quality management process with the level indicated by the ordinal.

Table 5. Ordinal scale for rating capability levels.

Ordinal	Meaning
N - Not achieved	There is little or no evidence of the defined process attribute in the assessed process.
P - Partially achieved	There is some evidence of an approach to, and some achievement of, the defined process attribute in the assessed process. Some aspects of achievement of the process attribute may be unpredictable.
L - Largely achieved	There is evidence of a systematic approach to, and significant achievement of, the defined process attribute in the assessed process. Some weaknesses related to this process attribute may exist in the assessed process.
F - Fully achieved	There is evidence of a complete and systematic approach to, and full achievement of, the defined process attribute in the assessed process. No significant weaknesses related to this process attribute exist in the assessed process.

3.3 Maturity Model

In the context of data quality management provided in this paper, a maturity level indicates how well an organizational unit's business process achieves the goals required for data quality management processes by using the resources provided by the organization.

The processes identified for each maturity level have been included by different criteria: priority of the processes for the business, relevance of the processes in other models, complexity, and necessary resources. The maturity levels that are proposed in MAMD, together with their meaning and the processes that are included are detailed below:

- **Maturity level 0 or Immature:** the organization cannot provide evidence about the effective implementation of good practices addressed by the process reference model. Therefore, there are no guaranties that their data is being used adequately.
- **Maturity level 1 or Basic:** the organization can evidence that it uses a set of good practices oriented to provide the minimum support necessary to the data management required to successfully support their business processes. Nevertheless, no special attention is given to data governance and data quality.
- **Maturity level 2 or Managed:** the organization can evidence that uses a set of good practices oriented to guarantee that the data used in business processes are aligned to organizational strategy. Consequently, there are guarantees that the organization has implemented the minimum necessary data governance processes to ensure the success in their business processes.
- **Maturity level 3 or Established:** the organization can evidence that it uses a set of good practices oriented to data quality management to guarantee that data used in their business processes have adequate quality levels.
- **Maturity level 4 or Predictable:** the organization can evidence that it uses a set of good practices oriented to monitoring that organizational data strategies are really effectives.

- **Maturity level 5 or Innovating:** the organization can evidence that it uses a set of good practices oriented to guarantee that organizational data strategies are evolving. An organization will be said to be at maturity level 5 when it monitors their data strategies and it executes the following processes of process reference model. This processes are oriented to update data strategies to improve known defects and also can be used to improve the global performance.

Table 6. Ordinal scale for rating capability levels.

AP.5.2																
AP.5.1																
AP.4.2																
AP.4.1																
AP.3.2																
AP.3.1																
AP.2.2																
AP.2.1																
AP.1.1																
DM.1	DM.2	DM.5	DM.8	DM.3	DM.4	DG.1	DG.2	DG.3	DM.9	DQM.1	DM.6	DM.7	DQM.2	DG.4	DG.6	DG.5	DG.7
ML1				ML2					ML3						ML4	ML5	

The maturity level is calculated based on the capability level of processes on the process reference model included in the evaluation. The capability level is calculated considering the degree of institutionalization of good practices and process attributes described in ISO/IEC 33020.

To calculate the capability level of this processes the different kind of evidences shall be inspected and it will be recollected to each business processes instances that have been chosen to make the evaluation. As result of the capability level a classification will be obtained. The classification for each one of the process attributes according to ISO/IEC 33020 is: "Not Achieved (N)", "Partially Achieved (P)", "Full Achieved (F)", and "Largely Achieved (L)".

To make the improvement, the objective of the organization will be to achieve the best and the most suitable level of organizational maturity. This implies to progressively implement and improve the requirements of the capability level for the processes in the process reference model of MAMD. The objective is to guarantee better quality levels to organizational processes.

4 Conclusions and Future Work

It is important to realize that the introduced components of MAMD and their relationship meet the requirements of ISO/IEC 33004 and ISO/IEC 33020 for a maturity model.

On the other hand, we have found that the implementation of MAMD can really bring benefits to the organizations, such benefits resulting from working with data that have adequate levels of quality. We are currently working in the application of MAMD to several study case to refine the model from lesson we are learning.

In the future, we want to quantitatively establish to what extent the improvement of the level of data management maturity, data governance and data quality management poses a clear advantage for organizations.

Acknowledgements. This work has been funded by VILMA project (Consejería de Educación, Ciencia y Cultura de la Junta de Comunidades de Castilla La Mancha, y Fondo Europeo de Desarrollo Regional FEDER, PEII-2014-048-P) and SEQUOIA project (Ministerio de Economía y Competitividad and Fondo Europeo de Desarrollo Regional FEDER, TIN2015-63502-C3-1-R).

References

1. ISACA: COBIT 5: Enabling Information, ed. ISACA (2013)
2. CMMI Project Team: Capability Maturity Model® Integration (CMMI SM), Version 1.1. CMMI for Systems Engineering, Software Engineering, Integrated Product and Process Development, and Supplier Sourcing (CMMI-SE/SW/IPPD/SS, V1. 1) (2002)
3. ISO/IEC-JTC1/SC7, ISO/IEC 15504-1:2004: Information Technology - Process Assessment - Part 1: Concepts and Vocabulary. International Organization for Standarization, Geneva (2004)
4. ISO: ISO/IEC 33000: Information technology: Process assessment. ISO (2015)
5. SEI: DMM: Data Management Maturity Model. SEI, Pittsburgh (2014)
6. ISO: ISO 8000-60: Data Quality Management: The Overview of Process Assessment. ISO (2015)
7. ISO: DIS/ISO 8000-61: Data quality: Information & data quality management process reference model. ISO (2015)
8. English, L.: Improving Data Warehouse and Business Information Quality: Methods for Reducing Costs and Increasing Profits. Wiley, New York (1999)
9. Humphrey, W.S.: Characterizing the Software Process: A Maturity Framework. Software Engineering Institute, Carnegie Mellon University, Pittsburgh (1987)
10. Aiken, P.H., et al.: Measuring data management practice maturity: a community's self-assessment. IEEE Comput. **40**(4), 42–50 (2007)
11. Wang, R.Y.: A product perspective on total data quality management. Commun. ACM **41**(2), 58–65 (1998)
12. Ladley, J.: Data Governance. How to Design, Deploy, and Sustain and Effective Data Governance Program. Morgan Kauffman, San Francisco (2012)
13. Mosley, M., et al. (eds.): The DAMA Guide to Data Management Body of Knowledge (DAMA-DMBOK Guide), 1st edn. Data Management International (2009)

14. Caballero, I., Gómez, Ó., Piattini, M.: Getting better information quality by assessing and improving information quality management. In: Ninth International Conference on Information Quality (ICIQ 2004). MIT, Cambridge (2004)
15. Caballero, I., et al.: IQM3: information quality maturity model. J. Univ. Comput. Sci. **14**, 1–29 (2008)
16. Ryu, K.-S., Park, J.-S., Park, J.-H.: A data quality management maturity model. ETRI J. **28**(2), 191–204 (2006)
17. Baskarada, S.: IQM-CMM: Information Quality Management Capability Maturity Model. Vieweg+Teubner Research (2009)
18. SEI: CMMI® for Development, Version 1.3 (CMMI-DEV, V1.3), in Improving processes for developing better products and services, Technical Report (2010)
19. SEI: CMMI® for SCAMPI Class A Appraisal Results 2011 End-Year Update. Software Engineering Institute, Carnegie Mellon University (2012)
20. Dunaway, D.K.: CMM SM - Based Appraisal for Internal Process Improvement, (CBA IPI) Lead Assessor™ Guide (CMU/SEI-96-HB-003). Software Engineering Institute, Pittsburgh (1996)
21. Pino, F., Piattini, M., Fernandez, C.M.: Modelo de Madurez de Ingeniería del Software de AENOR. AENORediciones, Madrid (2015)
22. ISO: ISO/IEC 12207-2008: Systems and software engineering — Software life cycle processes. International Standards Organization (2008)
23. Kim, S., Lee, C.: The process reference model for the data quality management process assessment. J. Soc. e-Bus. Stud. **18**(4), 1–14 (2013)
24. Pierce, E., et al.: The State of Information and Data Quality. 2012 Industry Survey & Report. Understanding how organizations manage the quality of their information and data assets. International Association for Information and Data Quality (IAIDQ) and University of Arkansas at Little Rock (UALR-IQ): Little Rock (AR), USA (2012)
25. Redman, T.C.: Data Driven: Profiting From Your Most Important Business Asset. Harvard Business School Press, Boston (2008)
26. Ballou, D.P., Tayi, G.K.: Managerial issues in data quality. Paper presented at the First International Conference on Information Quality (ICIQ 1996). MIT, Cambridge (1996)
27. Otto, B.: Organizing data governance: findings from the telecommunications industry and consequences for large service providers. Commun. Assoc. Inf. Syst. **29**(1), 45–66 (2011)
28. Sadiq, S., Indulska, M., Jayawardene, V.: Research and industry synergies in data quality management. In: International Conference on Information Quality, Adelaide, South Australia (2011)
29. ISO: ISO/IEC 33004: Information technology: Process assessment: Requirements for process reference, process assessment and maturity models. ISO (2015)
30. ISO: ISO/IEC 33020: Information technology: Process assessment: Process measurement framework for assessment of process capability. ISO (2015)

How to Integrate Risk Management in IT Settings Within Management Systems? Comparison and Integration Perspectives from ISO Standards

Béatrix Barafort[1(✉)], Antoni-Lluís Mesquida[2], and Antònia Mas[2]

[1] Luxembourg Institute of Science and Technology,
5 Avenue des Hauts-Fourneaux, 4362 Esch-sur-Alzette, Luxembourg
beatrix.barafort@list.lu
[2] Department of Mathematics and Computer Science,
University of the Balearic Islands, Cra. de Valldemossa,
Km 7.5, Palma de Mallorca, Spain
{antoni.mesquida,antonia.mas}@uib.es

Abstract. With the omnipresence of IT in any business, risk management is a critical and central activity. IT companies or IT department in companies may seek certification against one or several management system standard(s). Then risk management have to be tackled in the context of the domain targeted by each management system. This paper is investigating how risk management could be integrated from several ISO standards that are relevant for IT settings: quality management, project management, IT service management and information security management. Based on the reference standard ISO 31000 dedicated to risk management, a comparison is performed in order to identify risk management related activities in the ISO high level structure for management system standards, ISO 9001, ISO 21500, ISO/IEC 20000-1 and ISO/IEC 27001, and to elicit integration vectors. The paper concludes on future works aiming at proposing a process reference and assessment model for integrating risk management activities.

Keywords: Risk management · Risk management process · Integrated risk management · Management system · Integrated management system · IT settings · ISO standards

1 Introduction

Information Technology is more than ever present, for business matters within companies, between interconnected companies and/or private individuals, for cloud computing solutions, Internet of Things, connected and mobile devices and many more Internet usages. IT has then become omnipresent and essential for any business. Because of its indispensable nature, risk management has also become vital. In all domains, risk management activities must be under control. It can be for dedicated risk management purposes or from a broader perspective in management systems. In IT settings, many activities are strongly related to risk management: project management, information security and IT service management (ITSM) to quote the main domains.

Depending on their strategic goals, competitive advantage on the market, regulation and compliance constraints, IT companies or IT departments may need to be certified regarding management system standards such as the ISO/IEC 27001 [1] or the ISO/IEC 20000-1 [2]. They may also need to integrate these IT related standards with more general ones such as the ISO 9001 [3] for quality management system (QMS). This situation is more and more frequent and require integration and interoperability attentions for cost saving, complexity reduction, efficiency and effectiveness. This is particularly true for risk management which is central in IT organizations with integrated management systems and risk-based thinking.

The objective of this research is to investigate and compare risk management activities throughout various ISO (International Organization for Standardization) standards and to show that a centralized and integrated risk management approach can provide the basis to improve, coordinate and interoperate risk management activities in IT settings for various purposes such as project management, quality management, ITSM, information security management. The structured input for these works is the International reference in terms of Risk management: the ISO 31000 standard [4]. Hence, the research question studied is this paper is: *how to integrate risk management in IT settings within a management system context?* Moreover, in order to satisfy market constraints that many companies face today and to provide a broad and neutral perspective, the authors make the assumption that an integrated risk management approach for IT settings will benefit them by being based on ISO standards. International standards represent international consensus and provide an open access to structured technical domains as well as voluntary positioning towards certifications.

The paper is organized as follows: Sect. 2 describes related work; Sect. 3 is an overview of the studied standards; Sect. 4 proposes the comparison approach and the comparison itself; Sect. 5 discusses and analyses the findings in the conclusion and future works insights are proposed.

2 Related Work

Integrating management systems has been a topic of interest in research and industry for many years now [5, 6]. This has been particularly true for quality management, environmental management and health and safety domains [7]. It has been more and more necessary to integrate these systems for cost reductions, efficiency, effectiveness, and market positioning.

In the IT domain, with the first publication in 2005 of the ISO/IEC 20000-1 and ISO/IEC 27001, new management system standards appeared on the international scene, respectively for ITSM and Information Security. Some integration models and approaches have been tackled [8, 9] with a model proposition for integrating management systems [10], mainly driven by the ISO 9001 QMS implementation in a large number of companies.

In the meantime, maturity models, process assessment and improvement frameworks were very popular, such as CMMI [11] and ISO/IEC 15504 standards [12]. From a complementary perspective compared to a management system certification, performance management approaches dealing with process assessment and process improvement raised. Process Assessment Models (PAM), such as the PAM ISO/IEC 15504-8 [13], and the ISO/IEC 27001 Information Security one currently under development at ISO [14], provide new methodological approaches for measurement and continual improvement, contributing to certification preparation and monitoring of the management system. Recently, a research contribution proposed a maturity model for an integrated management systems assessment [15]; it enables the comparison of integrated systems implemented in different companies or contexts.

As management system standards (MSS) interest increased, ISO published in its Directives in 2012 (revised in 2014) an annex named "High-level structure (HLS), identical core text, common terms and core definitions" for MSS [16]. The goal was to standardize the core content of management systems and to impose the adoption of this structure to all management systems to the rhythm of their respective revision. The ISO/IEC 27001 standard is from now on aligned with the HLS since its second revision in 2013 [1]. The ISO 9001 has been upgraded in its last revision of 2015 [3]. The ISO/IEC 20000-1:2011 [2] standard is partially aligned and still needs to be fully aligned with the HLS.

With a management system integration mindset, some R&D works have defined different generic processes related to the core content requirements of the HLS in a Process Assessment Model, using a Transformation Process based on Goal-oriented requirements engineering techniques [17]. These works have been proposed to ISO and are incorporated within PRMs and PAMs under development for Information Security [14] and potentially for ISO/IEC 20000-1 and ISO 9001.

Among the integrative aspects of management systems, risk management is a particular topic of great importance and interest for organizations. A lot of research works exist, targeting risk management with applications in many domains. Thus Risk management plays an important part and is omnipresent in management systems. From the ISO standards perspective, the ISO 31000 standard on Risk management [4] is the main reference, with a holistic view on risk management. Furthermore in many domains there are dedicated risk management standards: i.e. for Information security, we can quote the ISO/IEC 27005 (Information security risk management) [18].

Last but not least, IT settings are commonly organized by projects, and have to face projects risks. From the ISO perspective, the ISO 21500 [19] standard provides guidance for project management: processes, continual improvement and risk management are important tackled concerns. This standard has been considered from a PRM and PAM point of view by the authors [20, 21] where a process-oriented organization can benefit from this high value structure for process assessment and process improvement purposes.

In the context of the problematic of integrated management systems, risk management is a critical cornerstone which has not been addressed specifically from the IT organizations point of view. Considering the gained experience by the authors from the various domains, this paper intends to explore risk management in IT settings from the angle of the following selected more relevant ISO standards: ISO 31000 as main theme, ISO Annex SL, ISO 9001, ISO 21500, ISO/IEC 20000-1, and ISO/IEC 27001. Other standards such as the ISO/IEC 12207 Software Engineering Lifecycle and ISO/IEC

15288 System Engineering Lifecycle are not considered as they are not directly targeting a PDCA neither a management system approach.

3 Overview of Targeted ISO Standards for Comparing Risk Management

Every year, ISO performs a survey [7] of certifications to MSSs. The 2014 results show again that ISO 9001 (which gives the requirements for quality management systems) is the leader of management system certification standards. This survey also indicates an increase of the certifications related to ISO/IEC 27001 (Requirements for information security management systems), and more recently ISO 22301 (Business continuity management systems). ISO/IEC 20000-1 (Requirements for IT Service Management Systems) does not appear in the survey and remains less present on the market, ITIL (IT Infrastructure Library) [22] still being the de facto standard. But ISO/IEC 20000-1 remains of interest for its alignment in intent and structure in our works, and a relative impact on the market [23].

Table 1 below summarizes the main characteristics of targeted ISO standards of the paper for comparing risk management.

Table 1. Main characteristics of ISO targeted standards.

Standard name	Main characteristics	Comment
ISO 31000:2009 Risk management – Principles and guidelines	Principles and generic guidelines on risk management	ISO 31000 is the appropriate standard candidate for driving the comparison of risk management from a generic perspective in various ISO standards
	Is not for the purpose of certification (does not provide requirements)	
	Can be used whether for IT or non-IT applications, in public, private, associations or group, for any type of risk (Not specific to any industry or sector)	
ISO Directives Part 1 Annex SL:2014 - High level structure for management system standards	Generic requirements for management systems with the goal to ensure consistency among various MSS and enable easier integration whatever the domain	The ISO Technical Management Board progressively enforces the use of the HLS to all MSSs, and then naturally targets risk management on a consistent way

(*Continued*)

Table 1. (*Continued*)

Standard name	Main characteristics	Comment
	(information security, service management, quality, etc.)	
	Reducing costs and providing the transversal approach via processes: fulfilled by integrated and interoperable management systems	
ISO 9001:2015 Quality management systems - Requirements	New version of ISO 9001 aligned with the changes that organizations have to face, focusing more on performance, combining the process approach with risk-based thinking and activating the Plan-Do-Check-Act cycle at all levels of the organization; also makes easier the integration of several management systems (alignment with HLS)	The flagship standard ISO 9001 providing requirements for quality management systems (QMS) has been revised and published in September 2015
ISO 21500:2012 Guidance on project management	Guidance for project management	It is admitted that the PMBOK Guide® had a great influence on the ISO 21500 standard development. As in PMBOK, risk management in one of the ten existing Subject groups with processes in planning, implementing and controlling phases of the project life cycle
	Can be used by any type of organization, for any type of project, irrespective of complexity, size or duration. Provides high-level description of concepts and processes that are considered to form good practice in project management	
	Identifies the recommended project management processes to be used during a project	

(*Continued*)

Table 1. (*Continued*)

Standard name	Main characteristics	Comment
ISO 20000-1: 2011 IT Service Management - Service management system requirements	Service management system (SMS) standard	As the HLS was released in 2012 by ISO, the current version of ISO/IEC 20000-1 is not fully aligned with the HLS but has many requirements related to risk management with a close mind-set
	Specifies requirements for the service provider to plan, establish, implement, operate, monitor, review, maintain and improve an SMS (requirements including the design, transition, delivery and improvement of services to fulfil agreed service requirements)	
ISO 27001:2013 Information security management	Information security management system (ISMS): systematic approach to managing sensitive company information so that it remains secure	The ISO/IEC 27001 is part of the ISO 27000 family of standards which is aiming at helping organizations keep information assets secure. ISO/IEC 27001 is the best-known standard in the family providing requirements for ISMS.
	Can be applied to small, medium and large businesses in any sector	
	Includes people, processes and IT systems by applying a risk management process and is aligned with the HLS	

4 Comparison of Risk Management in Targeted ISO Standards

In order to compare risk management approaches in the various selected ISO standards previously mentioned, the following systematic method has been followed:

- Step 1: Identification of risk-based activities in all standards (search on the keyword "Risk").
- Step 2: Mapping of the sections/requirements to some requirement in Clause 4 (Framework) or 5 (Process) of ISO 31000.
- Step 3: Description of relations or connection points among risk-based activities and the related requirements.

Table 2 summarizes the results of steps 1 and 2.

Table 2. Results from the comparison process.

	Sections/requirements of the Standard addressing "risks"	Sections mapped to some requirement in ISO 31000 clauses 4 or 5
Annex SL	1	1
ISO 9001	14	12
ISO 21500	17	17
ISO/IEC 20000-1	12	12
ISO/IEC 27001	9	7

The relations detected during step 3 are presented in the rest of this section according to the following classification:

- Context of risk management in all standards (Sect. 4.1)
- Leadership and commitment (Sect. 4.2)
- Plan-Do-Check-Act (PDCA) cycle (Sect. 4.3).

It should be noted that when no relation was found between a category and a standard, no reference to this standard is made in the section.

4.1 Context of Risk Management in All Standards

ISO 31000 recommends that organizations develop, implement and continuously improve a framework whose purpose is to integrate the process for managing risk into the organization's overall governance, strategy and planning, management, reporting processes, policies, values and culture.

Risk-based thinking is explicit in ISO 9001: *"an organization needs to plan and implement actions to address risks and opportunities. Addressing both risks and opportunities establishes a basis for increasing the effectiveness of the quality management system, achieving improved results and preventing negative effects"* (0.3.3).

ISO/IEC 27001 includes *"Requirements for the assessment and treatment of information security risks tailored to the needs of the organization"* (1). Moreover, *"The information security management system preserves the confidentiality, integrity and availability of information by applying a risk management process and gives confidence to interested parties that risks are adequately managed"* (0.1).

4.2 Leadership and Commitment

According to ISO 31000, the introduction of risk management and ensuring its ongoing effectiveness require strong and sustained commitment by management of the organization, as well as strategic and rigorous planning to achieve commitment at all levels.

ISO 9001 explicitly assigns some leadership responsibilities for risk management to Top management: *"Top management shall demonstrate leadership and commitment with respect to the quality management system by promoting the use of the process approach and risk-based thinking"* (5.1.1). *"Top management shall demonstrate leadership and commitment with respect to customer focus by ensuring that the risks and opportunities… are determined and addressed"* (5.1.2).

ISO/IEC 20000-1 also considers that *"Top management shall provide evidence of its commitment to planning, establishing, implementing, operating, monitoring, reviewing, maintaining, and improving the SMS and services by ensuring that risks to services are assessed and managed"* (4.1.1).

4.3 PDCA Cycle

4.3.1 Plan

According to ISO 31000, the risk management policy should clearly state the organization's objectives for, and commitment to, risk management.

ISO 9001 considers that *"Risk-based thinking is essential for achieving an effective quality management system"* (0.3.3) and recommends that *"The organization shall plan actions to address risks and opportunities…"* (6.1.2).

ISO 21500 considers risk management as part of the organizational strategy *"Opportunities selection includes consideration of various factors, such as how benefits can be realized and risks can be managed"* (3.4.1).

ISO/IEC 20000-1, when planning the SMS, proposes to take into consideration that *"the service management plan shall contain or include the approach to be taken for the management of risks and the criteria for accepting risks"* (4.5.2). Also, *"Planning for the new or changed services shall contain or include the identification, assessment and management of risks"* (5.2).

In the same way as in ISO 9001, when planning for the information security management system according to ISO/IEC 27001, we can find that *"The organization shall determine the risks and opportunities that need to be addressed"* (6.1.1). And that *"The information security objectives shall take into account risk assessment and risk treatment results"* (6.2).

According to ISO 31000, risk management should become part of those organizational processes and embedded in all the organization's practices and processes in a way that it is relevant, effective and efficient.

In order for a project following the ISO 21500 recommendations to be successful, *"The project scope within the constraints, while considering the project risks and resource needs to provide the project deliverables, should be defined and managed"* (4.1).

In ISO 9001, it can be read that *"The organization shall determine the processes needed for the quality management system and their application throughout the organization, and shall address the risks and opportunities"* (4.4.1).

The ISO/IEC 20000-1 Change management process (9.2) also consider the impact of risks in the organizational processes: *"Decision-making shall take into consideration the risks, the potential impacts to services…"*.

4.3.2 Do

In ISO 31000, when implementing risk management, an organization should implement the framework for managing risk and should ensure that the risk management process is applied through a risk management plan at all relevant levels and functions of the organization. The risk management process is shown in Fig. 1 and comprises the activities described in ISO 31000 clauses 5.2 to 5.6.

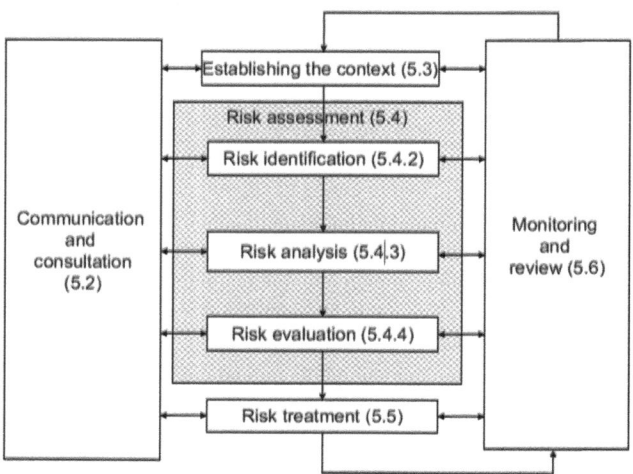

Fig. 1. ISO 31000 Risk management process

Communication and consultation (5.2) with external and internal stakeholders should take place during all stages of the risk management process.

ISO Annex SL defines a clause for understanding the needs and expectations of interested parties *"The organization shall determine the interested parties that are relevant to the XXX management system; and the relevant requirements of these interested parties"* (4.2). ISO 9001 contains an instantiation of this clause to the QMS (4.2). The same clause can be found in ISO/IEC 27001 for the ISMS (4.2).

ISO 21500 contains a specific process, Manage communications (4.3.40), which is focused on *"Resolving communication issues to minimize the risk that the project is negatively affected by...".*

By **establishing the context (5.3)**, the organization articulates its objectives, defines the external and internal parameters to be taken into account when managing risk, and sets the scope and risk criteria for the remaining process.

ISO Annex SL defines a clause for understanding the organization and its context *"The organization shall determine external and internal issues that are relevant to its purpose and that affect its ability to achieve the intended outcome(s) of its XXX management system"* (4.1). ISO 9001 and ISO/IEC 27001 contain instantiations of this clause for, respectively, a QMS and an ISMS.

ISO 21500 proposes to consider *"Factors outside the organizational boundary may have an impact on the project by imposing constraints or introducing risks affecting the project"* (3.5.2).

Risk assessment (5.4) is the overall process of risk identification, risk analysis and risk evaluation.

ISO/IEC 20000-1 states that *"The service provider shall assess and document the risks to availability and continuity of services. The agreed requirements shall take into consideration risks"* (6.3.1). In (6.6.1), this standard also suggests that *"Management with appropriate authority shall ensure that information security risk assessments are conducted at planned intervals"*.

Similarly, ISO/IEC 27001 considers that *"The organization shall perform information security risk assessments at planned intervals or when significant changes are proposed or occur..."* (8.2).

In **Risk identification (5.4.2)**, the organization should identify sources of risk, areas of impacts, events and their causes and their potential consequences.

ISO Annex SL defines a clause to *"...determine the risks and opportunities that need to be addressed"* (6.1). ISO 9001 contains an instantiation of this clause (6.1.1).

ISO 21500 contains a process named Identify risks whose purpose is *"To determine potential risk events and their characteristics that, if they occur, may have a positive or negative impact on the project objectives"* (4.3.28).

ISO/IEC 20000-1 considers that *"Requests for change shall be assessed to identify new or changed information security risks. Information security incidents shall be managed using the incident management procedures, with a priority appropriate to the information security risks"* (6.6.3).

ISO/IEC 27001 also contains a clause *"To identify the information security risks..."* (6.1.2).

Risk analysis (5.4.3) involves developing an understanding of the risk. Risk analysis provides an input to risk evaluation and to decisions on whether risks need to be treated, and on the most appropriate risk treatment strategies and methods.

ISO 21500 defines the Assess risks process (4.3.29) *"To measure and prioritize the risks for further action. This process includes estimating the probability of occurrence of each risk and the corresponding consequence for project objectives, if the risk does occur"*.

ISO/IEC 27001 explicitly considers *"analysing the information security risks"* (6.1.2).

Risk evaluation (5.4.4) purpose is to assist in making decisions, based on the outcomes of risk analysis, about which risks need treatment and the priority for treatment implementation.

ISO/IEC 27001 states that information security risks should be evaluated *"By comparing the results of risk analysis with the risk criteria and prioritizing the analysed risks for risk treatment"* (6.1.2).

Risk treatment (5.5) involves selecting one or more options for modifying risks, and implementing those options. Once implemented, treatments provide or modify the controls.

ISO Annex SL defines a clause to *"Plan actions to address these risks and opportunities"* (6.1). ISO 9001 contains an instantiation of this clause (6.1.2).

ISO 21500 Treat risks process (4.3.30) specifies that *"Risk treatment includes measures to avoid the risk, to mitigate the risk, to deflect the risk or to develop contingency plans to be used if the risk occurs"*.

ISO/IEC 27001 proposes that *"The organization shall define and apply an information security risk treatment process"* (6.1.3). Moreover, *"The organization shall retain documented information of the results of the information security risk treatment"* (8.3).

Both **monitoring and review (5.6)** should be a planned part of the risk management process and involve regular checking or surveillance. It can be periodic or ad hoc.

ISO 9001 claims that *"The organization shall analyse and evaluate appropriate data and information arising from monitoring and measurement. The results of analysis shall be used to evaluate the effectiveness of actions taken to address risks and opportunities"* (9.1.3). And adds *"When a nonconformity occurs, including any arising from complaints, the organization shall update risks and opportunities determined during planning, if necessary"* (10.2.1).

ISO 21500 defines a process named Control risks (4.3.31), whose goals are *"Tracking the identified risks, identifying and analysing new risks, monitoring trigger conditions for contingency plans and reviewing progress on risk treatments while evaluating their effectiveness"*.

4.3.3 Check

According to ISO 31000, in order to ensure that risk management is effective the organization should measure risk management performance against indicators; periodically measure progress against the risk management plan and review the effectiveness of the risk management framework, policy and plan. These activities are proposed to be done during Management reviews in ISO 9001, ISO/IEC 20000-1 and ISO/IEC 27001.

ISO 9001 states that *"The management review shall be planned and carried out taking into consideration the effectiveness of actions taken to address risks and opportunities"* (9.3.2). In ISO/IEC 20000-1 *"Top management shall review the SMS and the services at planned intervals to ensure their continued suitability and effectiveness. This review shall include risks"* (4.5.4.3). Similarly, in ISO/IEC 27001 *"The management review shall include consideration of results of risk assessment and status of risk treatment plan"* (9.3).

4.3.4 Act

According to ISO 31000, based on results of monitoring and reviews, decisions should be made on how the risk management framework, policy and plan can be improved.

Only ISO/IEC 20000-1 explicitly states that *"The service provider shall manage improvement activities including risk reduction"* (4.5.5.2). The rest of the analysed standards do not contain a sentence related to risk management improvement.

4.4 Summary

As listed in Table 3 below, the comparison shows that many similarities exist for risk management in the selected standards. The context of risk management is displayed via the policies, leadership and commitment, and the risk management itself is shown throughout the PDCA cycle with a dedicated process or set of processes for risk management in all standards.

Table 3. Comparison summary.

ISO 31000	Annex SL	ISO 9001	ISO 21500	ISO/IEC 20000-1	ISO/IEC 27001
4.2 Mandate and commitment		5.1.1, 5.1.2, 9.3.2		4.1.1	5.1
4.3.2 Establishing risk management policy		0.3.3, 6.1, A.5	3.4, 3.4.1, 4.3.3	4.5.2, 5.2, 6.6.1	5.2, 6.2.c
4.3.4 Integration into organizational processes		0.3, 0.3.1, 4.4, 4.4.1, 6.1	4.1, 4.3.6, 4.3.23-25-26	4.5.3, 6.6.2, 9.1, 9.2	4.4, 6.1
4.3.5 Resources			3.9		
4.3.6 Establishing internal communication and reporting mechanisms			3.6, 4.3.40		
4.3.7 Establishing external communication and reporting mechanisms			4.3.40		
4.5 Monitoring and review of the framework		6.1		4.5.4.3	6.1
4.6 Continual improvement of the framework				4.5.5.2	
5.2 Communication and consultation	4.2	4.2	4.3.40		4.2
5.3 Establishing the context	4.1	4.1, A.8	3.5.2, 3.11		4.1

(*Continued*)

Table 3. (*Continued*)

ISO 31000	Annex SL	ISO 9001	ISO 21500	ISO/IEC 20000-1	ISO/IEC 27001
5.4 Risk assessment				6.3.1, 6.6.1	6.1.2, 6.2, 8.2
5.4.2 Risk identification	6.1	6.1, 6.1.1	4.3.28	6.6.3	6.1.2.c
5.4.3 Risk analysis		9.1.3	4.3.29		6.1.2.d
5.4.4 Risk evaluation		9.1.3	4.3.29		6.1.2.e
5.5 Risk treatment	6.1	6.1, 6.1.2	4.3.30		6.1.3, 6.2, 8.3
5.6 Monitoring and review		9.1.3, 9.3.2, 10.2.1	4.3.31, 4.5.4.3		9.3.e

5 Conclusion and Perspectives

In this paper we present a comparison of how risk management is tackled in several ISO standards that can be deployed in IT settings with management systems. This comparison contributes to the exploration of how Risk Management can be integrated in such contexts. Several facets of management system(s) are integration vectors such as the understanding of the organisation and its context, risk-based thinking, leadership and commitment, process approach and PDCA structure.

It is important to quote that all ISO management systems standards from now on inherit from the HLS a clause specifying the *"Understanding of the organization and its context"*. This clause says: *"The organization shall determine external and internal issues that are relevant to its purpose and that affect its ability to achieve the intended outcome(s) of its XXX management system"*. This clause has in fact been inherited itself from the ISO 31000. The external context of the organization has to be considered, with for instance regulatory and legal aspects, relationships with external stakeholders, etc. The internal context may include governance, capabilities including processes, information systems, etc.

Then we can say that the risk management context is highly connected to the management system for ISO 9001, ISO/IEC 20000-1 and ISO/IEC 27001 and to the project environment in ISO 21500 with factors inside or outside the organizational boundary. These factors may have an impact by introducing risks to the project; then risks should be managed explicitly.

According to ISO 9001, one of the key purposes of a management system is to act as a preventive tool. The concept of preventive action is expressed through the use of risk-based thinking. Top management should provide leadership and commitment for introducing risk-based thinking at the needed levels in the organization. Each organization decides the degree of formalism for addressing risk management and is responsible for the application of risk-based thinking. This provides a great flexibility which has to be balanced with the fact to address several disciplines and risk areas (quality, project, IT services, and information security) with integrated management systems.

Process approach and PDCA structure used in ISO 9001, ISO/IEC 20000-1 and ISO/IEC 27001 facilitate the integration of the different specific activities for planning risk management, performing risk treatment plans, monitoring if risk management process is effective, and improving the applied risk management framework. ISO 21500 uses a similar structure at the level of a particular project by suggesting actions to identify risks, apply mitigation and contingency actions, monitor if risk treatment plan is effective, and improve the project risk management activities.

In management systems and in projects, the process approach can drive the transversal mechanisms in order to better perform risk management activities. The 2015 version of ISO 9001 supports the idea of a risk management process for federating activities (even if it is not prescriptive). From the project management perspective, the fact to establish a risk management process can enforce the influence of risk management in organizations. The intensity and the types of risks are important in the ISO 27001: even if an integrated approach of risk management related to the management system can be put in place, a dedicated instance may be implemented for the information security context which is very specific and critical. ISO 20000-1 may soon follow the same idea by fully aligning to the HLS. Again, each set of risks related to some dedicated scope (quality, project, IT service, information security) can be managed from a dedicated implementation derived from a unique generic risk management process.

Considering the above-mentioned management system integration vectors, we believe that organizational capabilities in companies with IT settings can be strengthened by an integrated risk management process or set of processes, based on ISO standards such as the compared ones in this paper. The selected standards were voluntarily limited because there are empirically considered as the most significant in IT settings. An integrated risk management process or set of processes can be described on a very structured way enabling process assessment against a capability measurement framework and facilitating process improvement. In this context the authors intend to develop a process reference model and a process assessment model (satisfying requirements of the ISO/IEC 33004 standard [24]) dedicated to risk management, for providing a centralized and integrated risk management approach with improvement, coordination and interoperability characteristics. This enables process assessment and improvement where management, definition and deployment, measurement and continual improvement are dealt with. Thus it will enable to integrate risk management in IT settings with a systemic management of quality, project, IT services and information security such as tackled by ISO standards related to these disciplines in the paper. Other ISO standards such as ISO/IEC 12207 & 15288 may be considered but the scope of the research question limited to a management system context and PDCA approach will remain the main driver. The doors for integrated risk management with management systems of other domains than IT may be opened.

Acknowledgments. This work has been partially supported by the Spanish Ministry of Science and Technology with ERDF funds under grants TIN2013-46928-C3-2-R.

References

1. ISO/IEC 27001: Information technology – Security techniques – Information security management systems – Requirements. International Organization for Standardization, Geneva (2013)
2. ISO/IEC 20000-1: Information Technology — Service management — Part 1: Service management system requirements. International Organization for Standardization, Geneva (2011)
3. ISO 9001: Quality management systems – Requirements. International Organization for Standardization, Geneva (2015)
4. ISO 31000: Risk management – Principles and guidelines. International Organization for Standardization, Geneva (2009)
5. Casadesús, M., Karapetrovic, S., Heras, I.: Synergies in standardized management systems: Some empirical evidence. TQM J. **23**(1), 73–86 (2011). Emerald Insight
6. Simon, A., Karapetrovic, S., Casadesús, M.: Difficulties and benefits of integrated management systems. Ind. Manage. Data Syst. **112**(5), 828–846 (2012). Emerald Insight
7. ISO Survey (2014). http://www.iso.org/iso/iso-survey
8. Mesquida, A.L., Mas, A.: Integrating IT service management requirements into the organizational management system. Comput. Stand. Interfaces **37**, 80–91 (2015). Elsevier
9. Mesquida, A.L., Mas, A., Amengual, E., Cabestrero, I.: Sistema de gestión integrado según las normas ISO 9001, ISO/IEC 20000 e ISO/IEC 27001. Rev. Esp. Innovación Calidad e Ing. del Softw. **6**(3), 25–34 (2010). ATI
10. Mesquida, A., Mas, A., San Feliu, T., Arcilla, M.: MIN-ITs: a framework for the integration of IT management standards in mature environments. Int. J. Software Eng. Knowl. Eng. **24**(06), 887–908 (2014). World Scientific
11. CMMI for Development, Acquisition & Services, version 1.3. Carnegie Mellon University, Software Engineering Institute (2010)
12. ISO/IEC 15504-2: Information Technology — Process assessment — Performing an assessment. International Organization for Standardization, Geneva (2003)
13. ISO/IEC TS 15504-8: Information Technology — Process assessment — An exemplar process assessment model for IT service management. International Organization for Standardization, Geneva (2012)
14. ISO/IEC 33072: TS Information Technology — Process Assessment — Process capability assessment model for information security management. International Organization for Standardization, Geneva (to be published)
15. Domingues, P., Sampaio, P., Arezes, P.M.: Integrated management systems assessment: a maturity model proposal. J. Cleaner Prod. (2016). doi:10.1016/j.jclepro.2016.02.103
16. ISO/IEC Directives, Part1. Annex SL. International Organization for Standardization, Geneva (2014)
17. Cortina, S., Mayer, N., Renault, A., Barafort, B.: Towards a process assessment model for management system standards. In: Mitasiunas, A., Rout, T., O'Connor, R.V., Dorling, A. (eds.) SPICE 2014. CCIS, vol. 477, pp. 36–47. Springer, Heidelberg (2014)
18. ISO/IEC 27005: Information technology– Security techniques – Information security risk management – Requirements. International Organization for Standardization, Geneva (2011)

19. ISO 21500: Guidance on project management. International Organization for Standardization, Geneva (2012)
20. Mesquida, A.-L., Mas, A., Lepmets, M., Renault, A.: Development of the project management SPICE (PMSPICE) framework. In: Mitasiunas, A., Rout, T., O'Connor, R.V., Dorling, A. (eds.) SPICE 2014. CCIS, vol. 477, pp. 60–71. Springer, Heidelberg (2014)
21. Mesquida, A.-L., Mas, A., Barafort, B.: The project management SPICE (PMSPICE) process reference model: towards a process assessment model. In: O'Connor, R.V., et al. (eds.) EuroSPI 2015. CCIS, vol. 543, pp. 193–205. Springer, Heidelberg (2015). doi:10.1007/978-3-319-24647-5_16
22. The Cabinet Office. ITIL Lifecycle Publication Suite. The Stationery Office Edition (2011)
23. Cots, S., Casadesús, M.: Exploring the service management standard ISO 20000. Total Qual. Manage. Bus. Excellence **26**(5-6), 515–533 (2015). Taylor Francis Online
24. ISO/IEC 33004: Information Technology - Process assessment - Requirements for process reference, process assessment and maturity models. International Organization for Standardization, Geneva (2015)

A Learning Tool for the ISO/IEC 29110 Standard: Understanding the Project Management of Basic Profile

Mary-Luz Sánchez-Gordón[1(✉)], Rory V. O'Connor[2,3], Ricardo Colomo-Palacios[4], and Sandra Sanchez-Gordon[5]

[1] Universidad Carlos III de Madrid, Madrid, Spain
mary_sanchezg@hotmail.com
[2] Lero, The Irish Software Research Centre, Limerick, Ireland
rory.oconnor@computing.dcu.ie
[3] Dublin City University, Dublin, Ireland
rory.oconnor@computing.dcu.ie
[4] Ostfold University College, Halden, Norway
ricardo.colomo-palacios@hiof.no
[5] Escuela Politecnica Nacional, Quito, Ecuador
sandra.sanchez@epn.edu.ec

Abstract. The *"best practices"* of international software standards are considered important in improving the software process. The ISO/IEC 29110 standard defines lifecycle profiles for Very Small Entities (VSEs) and VSEs have also been recognized important in the software industry. Since this standard is novel, practitioners need to be actively engaged in their own learning. Serious games offer the potential not only to entertain and educate, but can also operate as a strategy for promoting the standard itself. The findings of this explorative study make possible an initial judgment about its potential as a fun standard learning tool as well as to analyze its pertinence, engagement, strengths, and weaknesses as guidance for further evolution.

Keywords: VSE · ISO/IEC 29110 · ISO · Standards · Process improvement · Project management · Serious game · Learning tool

1 Introduction

According to Eurostat [1][1], in 2012, 99.8 % of enterprises in this software industry were medium-sized (< 250 employees). Small enterprises (< 50 employees) made up at least 98.8 % and micro (< 10 employees) were 93.9 %. In this sector, nearly 32.2 % of people were employed at micro enterprises. In this context, the term Very Small Entities (VSEs) has been defined as being "an enterprise, organization, department or project having up to 25 people" [2].

---

[1] The General Industrial Classification of Economic Activities within the European Communities (NACE Rev.2) that identifies computer software and related computer services as division 62: computer programming, consultancy and related activities and division 63: information service activities.

Although the acceptance level of any type or model of software quality or lifecycle standard in VSEs is very low and less priority [3], the level of awareness of standards and potential benefits are high. The relationship between the success of a software company and the software process it utilized has been investigated [4–6] showing the need for all organizations, not just VSEs to pay attention to software process practices, such as ISO standards [7]. However, most VSEs can neither afford the resources, in terms of number of employees, budget and time, nor do they see a net benefit in establishing software life cycle processes [8]. To rectify some of these constraints, a set of guides has been developed according to a set of VSE characteristics. Thus, ISO/IEC 29110 is an international standard which is aimed at meeting the specific needs of VSEs [9].

Despite the fact that ISO/IEC 29110 is a well-structured and detailed technical text on complex subject, easier than the ISO/IEC 12207, practitioners could find it difficult to understand and adopt it. In general, international software standards are considered important in improving the software process, but teaching international software standards remains a challenging issue [10]. Therefore, new learning tools to complement training among practitioners can be useful. The question is how such standards, particularly ISO/IEC 29110, can be learned with less time and efforts invested for both practitioners and VSEs.

A possible and feasible approach is using a serious game. Although, non-technological methods have still low usage in SE teaching [11], a non-digital game-based environment can be turned into a powerful tool for teaching [12]. Therefore, designed card games or board games as an activity (even instead of a computerized version) for software engineering and management training have great potential. Serious games offer the potential to not only entertains and educate [13], but can also operate as a strategy for promoting the standard itself. In fact, there is a growing interest in games for purposes beyond entertainment [10, 12] and a consensus that serious games have a significant potential as a tool for instruction [14]. Consequently, the goal of the study is to investigate the potential as a fun standard learning tool of a card game that is designed for raising awareness and understanding the project management process of ISO/IEC 29110.

The rest of the paper is structured as follows. Section 2 presents the background study of the study and outlines ISO/IEC 29110 and Games in Software Engineering (SE). Section 3 describes how the game was designed. Section 4 presents the results we obtained during the pilot study. Section 5 summarizes the conclusions of the paper and outlines challenges that may lead to future research.

2 Background

2.1 ISO/IEC 29110

The ISO/IEC 29110 is an international software engineering standard which defines lifecycle profiles for VSEs [2]. It is aimed at addressing the issues identified above and addresses the specific needs of VSEs [15–17] and to tackle the issues of low standards adoption by small companies [3, 18–20]. In fact, there is an increasing interest on the standard [21], although there is still much work to be completed. The approach [22, 23] used to develop ISO/IEC 29110 started with the pre-existing international standard ISO/IEC 12207 dedicated to software process lifecycles. The overall approach consisted of three steps: (1) Selecting ISO/IEC 12207 process subset applicable to VSEs of up to 25 employees; (2) Tailor the subset to fit VSE needs; and (3) Develop guidelines for VSEs.

The guides are based on subsets of appropriate standards elements. There are a profile Groups which are a collection of profiles which are related either by composition of processes (i.e. activities, tasks), or by capability level, or both. The "Generic" profile group has been defined [2] as applicable to a vast majority of VSEs that do not develop critical software and have typical situational factors. To date the Basic Profile [2] and Entry Profile [24] has been published, their purpose is to define a software development and project management guide for performing one project at a time. The Entry profile is defined for the case when more flexible and more light-weight software process is needed than the Basic profile scope, e.g. for the case when user-risk is very low, using period is very short, and process responsibility is appropriately divided between the acquirer and the developer. It is worth noting that Entry profile is contained in the Basic Profile.

At the core of this standard is a Management and Engineering Guide (ISO/IEC 29110-5) [2] focusing on *Project Management* and *Software Implementation*. The purpose of the Project Management process is to establish and carry out in a systematic way the tasks of a software implementation project, which complies with the project's objectives in terms of quality, time and cost. It is intended to be used by the VSE to establish processes to implement any development approach or methodology including, e.g., agile, evolutionary, incremental, test driven development, etc. based on the VSE organization or project needs.

In the nutshell, Project Management generates a *Project Plan* to direct the software project. During the execution of the project *Change Requests* may cause revisions to the *Project Plan*. The project is the subject of *Project Assessment and Control* during the lifetimes of the project until the *Software Implementation* is complete and *Project Closure* occurs.

Additionally, a series of Deployment Packages (DPs) and Implementation Guides, which are freely available from http://29110.org, have been developed to define guidelines and explain in detail more detail the processes defined in the ISO/IEC 29110 profiles in order to assist with the deployment of ISO/IEC 29110 and to provide guidance on the actual implementation of ISO/IEC 29110-5 in VSEs [25]. It is worth mentioning that a DP is not a process reference model, in other words, it is not prescriptive. The elements of a typical DP are: description of processes, activities, tasks, roles and products, template, checklist, example, reference and mapping to standards and models, and a list of tools.

2.2 Serious Games in Software Engineering

Accordingly to the overview about serious games carried out in [13], there are many different terms, that all point to what is here called serious games. However, one issue most definitions agree upon, more or less, is that serious games are concerned with the use of games and gaming technology for purposes other than mere entertainment or "fun". Such purposes include education, training, health, and so on.

Games have been used in software engineering and project management educational settings as a supplement to classroom-based teaching with some success [10]. However, there are only several ones which are related to software project management: SIMSE is an interactive, graphical, educational software engineering simulation game designed to teach students the process of software engineering, SIMSOFT is a kind of serious game which consists of two game boards, a printed board and a digital board, ProDec is a simulation-based serious game created with the intention to train and assess students in software project management, SESAM is a natural language based serious game which motivates players to gain software project management techniques, DELIVER is another type of serious game which consists of a printed board. It helps students to develop controlling projects performances. Problems and Programmers (PnP) is using a physical card game to teach students about the software engineering process. SimulES-W [26] is the digital version of SimulES, an educational board and card game. SimulES is an evolution of the ideas of the PnP game but differs because SimulES does not have any specific development process. In Software development Game [11], players must build origami boxes with one of the following four groups of letters, SO, FT, WA or RE. Every box represents a software module (a part of a software piece that can be exchangeable with others). One group of four modules forms one software piece (a complete word, SOFTWARE, made of four modules).

Furthermore, Semat (an acronym for Software Engineering Methods and Theory) have some games [27] - e.g., SemCards, MetricC, Semat board-crossing and Semat game - such as a strategy for promoting its theory and practice. Semat is an initiative for gathering together the core elements essential to the development of software projects [28]. In Semat game, players are encouraged to understand the concepts of the topic proposed by the game, such as the main features of a PMBOK process [27]. It is worth mentioning that using specialized decks of cards is not uncommon[2,3]. Games have also been designed to teach the practices, values and concepts behind XP and object-oriented programming, such as the popular XP War game.

Finally, no games were found in the state of the art for learning the ISO/IEC 29110. Although, there is a preliminary study [10] that investigates the need of a serious game to improve the ability of learners of ISO/IEC 12207 standard from an industrial perspective.

3 The Game – Go for It!

3.1 Design Process

Accordingly to Adams [29], there are three stages of the design process: concept, elaboration and tuning. In the concept stage, the following considerations were made: (i)

---

[2] See http://www.drdobbs.com/xp-war/184415908 for more details.
[3] See http://www.industriallogic.com/games for more details.

learning must be active and collaborative (ii) it does not need software and hardware resources, (iii) the approach to be fast, painless and cost-effective. Considering all of the above, this study adopted a familiar game concept: *Card Game*. The aim of the game has been to promote and provoke awareness, and ultimately, understanding of ISO/IEC 29110 standard among practitioners of SE.

During elaboration stage, the design work begins to move from the theoretical to the concrete. Some prototypes of the game were created and the rules were volatile. The topic of the game is ISO/IEC 29110 standard and how some of its elements - such as activities, tasks, work products, and roles - are related. The object of the game proposed is teaching the project management process and showing how to interact with its elements when a particular profile - Basic profile - is selected. The inputs of the activities are the required work products and the outputs of the activities are the generated work products when a team member performs a set of tasks. Furthermore, a process of iterative refinement was introduced. Early game models were created and sessions were played with friends and family of the first author. Based on what was learned from the experience, the game was refined. Once the authors felt that the design was completed and harmonious, the design was locked.

Then, design work entered the tuning stage, during which the authors made small adjustments to the rules of the game. At this point, the game was positively evaluated by an expert in the ISO/IEC 29110 standard and a play session was carried out with third year students (33) in a project management class at a university in Ecuador, to gain experience and fine tune the definition and satisfaction of the learning objectives.

3.2 Game Description

This section will only briefly describe the gameplay and the various components of the game. Go for it! was designed as a non-Technological educational game for contributing to teaching the ISO/IEC 29110 standard elements where players are encouraged to understand the project management process of Basic profile. It is designed for use in conjunction with PM education or reinforces PM teaching points. The game environment is one that forces them to follow good practices. They experience the consequence of lack of knowledge in a way that simulates the actual project experience, through the delays of a project - length of the game - and loss of credibility – loss of points. They are also challenged to do their best in order to win. The idea is to provide a participant engagement loop (i.e. the flow [30]), which help player to learn and participate more frequently and ultimately create planned participant behavior. As Kosa and Yilmaz stated in [12], the teacher do not actively participate. They act just like a game master to facilitate the game. Instead, students interact with each other and the game. After the play sessions, students draw their own conclusions about the experience based on time spent and points earned. The teacher actually just provides support mechanisms and follows an instructional scaffolding attitude. The game elements are presented in Fig. 1 and the key game concepts are described below.

A Learning Tool for the ISO/IEC 29110   275

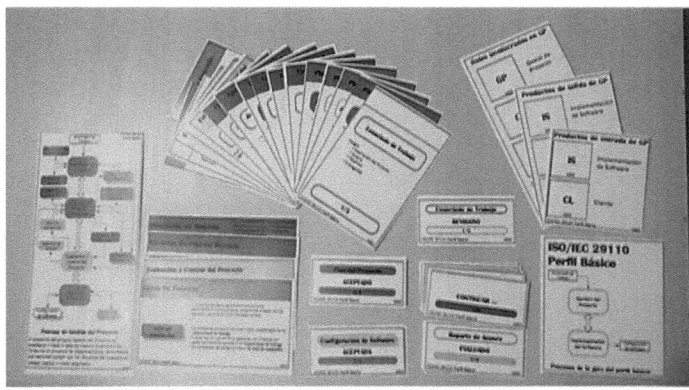

Fig. 1. Deck of cards (Color figure online)

Fig. 2. Project management processes - Basic profile adapted from [2]

Players, Go for it! is made for novices – 1 to 5 players new or relatively new to project management process. The players are the project team members.

Card Reference Guide is useful as a memory aid for the team. It includes the Fig. 2 which shows the Project Management processes, a brief description of its activities and task, roles involved and source/destination of input/output work products.

The Deck of Cards covers the four activities in the Project Management process: Project Planning, Project Plan Execution, Project Assessment and Control, and Project Closure. Each one of them corresponds to a group differenced with a color (blue, green, yellow or red) (see Fig. 1). The white color represents the input and the output of the Project Management processes - «*Statement of Work*» and «*Software Configuration*». Each one of them has two types of cards: Activity and State. A pair of cards is composed of one of each type.

Activity Card, an activity card is composed by four elements (see Fig. 3): On the top, the name of the activity "*Project Planning*". Below, the name of the resulting work products "*Project Plan*" the team generate when they do the activity, if it is an output the element is color and shadow. In the middle, it provides a checklist of tasks to be performed. On the bottom, the basic sequence of activities to follow.

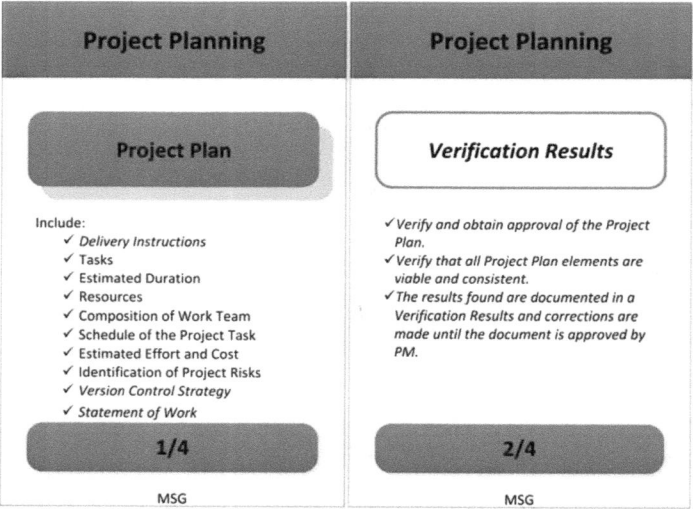

Fig. 3. Activity card

State Card, a state card is composed by three elements (see Fig. 4): On the top, the name of the work product associated "*Project Plan*". In the middle, the state achieved "*Verified*" by the product as result of the activity. On the bottom, the state sequence associated with the activity. When the word "*Continue* ..." appears in the state, the players should continue with the next activity card.

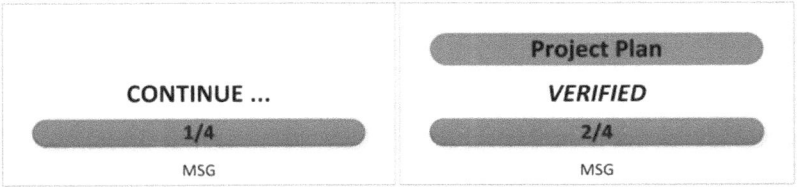

Fig. 4. State card

Gameplay has been defined as *"One or more causally linked series of challenges in a simulated environment"* [29]. Thus, a contest is organized as a single elimination (or knockout) tournament by teams. In this format, everyone on the team has to make an effort in order to advance to the next stage. The winner advances to the next round while the loser is eliminated from the competition.

First, two pairs of teams simultaneously compete in two semifinals. The two winners (one in each semifinal) compete in the final, and the winner of the final obtains the prize. The losers of the semifinals do not compete further. The prize is defined by the facilitator. In each round, a mission should be completed by the teams. In order to accomplish their mission, they must complete four sub-missions; each one of them is one activity. The sub-missions are: Project Planning (blue), Project Plan Execution (green), Project Assessment and Control (yellow), Project Closure (red). The *«Card Reference Guide»* could be used as a map to guide the future moves.

Each team designates a delegate (player) who will play the cards. Any player may deal first. The dealer shuffles the cards and then deals them out, one at a time face down, to each player in rotation, until all the cards have been dealt. Each player plays one card from their hand which is selected by consensus among the team members. The team should justify it clearly based on the standard and the facilitator decides if it is valid and well enough justified. Then, the player places it face up on the table to make a pile. Next, the state card associated should be played by who hold it.

The first sub-mission starts with the player who holds the *«Statement of Work»* activity card. Play continues with the blue suit until the highest card of it is reached. Next, the second and third mission must be carried out in the same way. The fourth mission starts with the player who holds the *«Software Configuration»* card. Finally, the red suit is played. The game is over when players run out of cards.

Winning. The winner of this game is the team that had more right moves in each round. As a result, they identify and recognize the largest number of best practices of the ISO/IEC 29110 standard.

4 Pilot Study

The research objective of this pilot study is to test the overall applicability of the game as learning tool. The game was applied to a 33-student group distributed in two sub-groups belonging of the course *"Software Quality"* from the *National Polytechnic School of Ecuador*. All the participants (25 men and 8 women) accepted voluntarily to take part in the study. Only four of them had previous Software Engineering experience in the industry. The game was practiced in two different sessions which had distinct facilitators and lasted 2 h each. Before the sessions, the facilitators encouraged participants to read the standard on their own pace. Also, the facilitators planned the game session and agreed what would be the prize for the winners. On the game day, the facilitator spend one hour in order to present the ISO/IEC 29110 standard and the card game using a power point presentation. The second hour, the game session started, teams were formed (3–5 individuals), the tables and chairs were placed properly, and the teams played a two-round tournament, the winner of which played the top player. Finally, the prize was allocated to the winner team. Each round lasted about 15 min. Also, it was observed that individuals overwhelmingly (94 %) agreed that would like to play again. Figure 5 depicts the interactions during the game session.

Fig. 5. Game session

After the game, it was applied a 20-item survey with the aim of gathering information from the players. It is important to note that this survey was validated by two experts for face validity and amendments were accordingly. The results are summarized as follows. Table 1 shows a snapshot of the background above mentioned. For most of the questions, a five point Likert scale was used (5 = strongly agree, 4 = agree, 3 = neutral, 2 = disagree, 1 = strongly disagree) in order to measure the level of agreement.

Table 1. Background to the two groups

Background	Groups	
	A	B
Gender (Female/Male)	4/11	4/14
SE experience (Industry)	1	3
SE experience (Academic)	15	18
Semester	7	7
Group size	15	18
Individuals per group	3–5	4–5
Game Length per round (minutes)	10–15	10–15
Would play again (YES/NO)	15/0	16/2

Table 2 presents the frequencies of each of the responses, along with their arithmetic means and standard deviation values.

Table 2. Frequencies, mean and standard deviation

	1	2	3	4	5	Mean	Standard deviation
Participant involvement			5	18	10	4.15	0.656954
Alternative to classroom	1		6	14	12	4.09	0.899954
Fun factor		2	3	20	8	4.03	0.758182
Engaging		2	5	18	8	3.97	0.797148
Design useful		2	6	17	8	3.94	0.814244
Kept me interested			9	17	7	3.94	0.693668
Knowledge acquisition		2	16	12	3	3.48	0.743506
Encourage to knowledge	2	2	13	11	5	3.45	1.017749

As a result, two groups arose from the data. The arithmetic means in the first group vary between 4.15 and 3.94. The question from the first group "Participant Involvement" has the highest average with a 4.15 arithmetic mean and 0.656954 standard deviation. From here, 85 % of students stated that they were involved during the game and pointed it was fun. In fact, 25 % of out of the total strongly agreed with the last statement. In addition, 79 % of participants report that the game is an alternative to a traditional classroom activity. Although one defeat was enough to eliminate a team from the tournament, the game engaged 79 % of the participants. And 73 % of the participants kept themselves interested during the game.

In this group, 76 % of the students also pointed that the game design is useful. They believe that the game has a meaningful design because the cards include color coding and numbered linked with the processes flow. Likewise, the card reference guide helped students to familiarize themselves with the standard.

The arithmetic means of the questions in the second group vary between 3.28 and 3.45. When the questions in this group are examined, it can be seen that 45 % of the students say that they improved their knowledge on the standard and 48 % of the respondents report that they are more encouraged to know more about the standard. And, nearly the same number of the participants remained neutral. Therefore, no indication for a significant difference on learning effectiveness could be shown.

In order to understand the lowest scores, the data were analyzed by participant and by answers. Bear in mind that two participants strongly disagree with the issues about encourage to knowledge and alternative to classroom - i.e. 100 % of these answers. Also, they disagree with the items about fun factor and design useful - i.e. 100 % of these answers. One of them also disagrees with the items about engaging and knowledge acquisition - i.e. 50 % of these answers. And the remaining (50 %) come from another participant (third). This last participant in conjunction with another one (fourth respondent) also disagree with the item of encourage to knowledge, his remaining answers has the average with a 3.57 arithmetic mean and 0.494871 standard deviation. In fact, the lowest scores in Alternative to Classroom Activity, Fun Factor, Engaging, Useful Design and Encourage to Knowledge appeared as outliers point when Pierces criterion were applied [31]. Below is a briefly description about the process and results (see Table 3).

Table 3. Pierces criterion

	Mean	Standard deviation	Pierce's criterion	
			R * SD	$|x_i - x_m|$
Alternative to classroom	4.09	0.899954	2.18	3.09
Fun factor	4.03	0.758182	1.63	2.03
Engaging	3.97	0.797148	1.71	1.97
Useful design	3.94	0.814244	1.75	1.94
Knowledge acquisition	3.48	0.743506	1.60	1.48
Encourage to knowledge	3.45	1.017749	2.18	2.45

First, obtain R from the table for one measured quantity assuming one/two doubtful observation and 33 measurements: R = 2.425/2.146. Secondly, calculate the maximum allowable deviation $|x_i - x_m|_{max}$ = R * SD where x_i is a measured data value and x_m is the mean of the data set. Third, obtain the actual deviations for the suspicious measurements $|x_i - x_m|$. Finally, eliminate the suspicious measurements if: $|x_i - x_m| > |x_i - x_m|_{max}$. Therefore, there are three respondents (9 %) disagree.

In the light of this, the two open questions about the game and the experience of these participants were analyzed in order to gain a more comprehensive view. The biggest issue rested with the game rules as exemplified by the next quotes from two of the participants "*A lack of easy understanding of the rules*" and "*I liked it [the game], but it requires a more detailed manual*". Furthermore, another participant stated "*It [the game] seems boring and little interactive*" and the last one of them pointed out "*In my opinion … there should [in the game] be a greater degree of complexity and not have many clues for playing …*", but conversely, most respondents commented that the game was interesting, fun, didactic and intuitive as exemplified by other respondent "*It's something fun and also teaches*", with another respondent confirming that "*It is a very interesting game and encouraging*". A further respondent highlights that "*It was cool to learn with a game*". With another respondent stating that "*you can learn about the standard in your own pace*". Consequently, the game was embraced by most of them as someone put it most succinctly, "*It's a good experience to understand the structure of the ISO/IEC 29110*".

In discussions after gameplay, the facilitators observed that participants were more comfortable with the ISO/IEC 29110 standard. The gameplay environment forced participants to gain awareness and understand what they had previously read about ISO/IEC 29110 standard in order to accomplish the mission. The main benefit appeared to be the ability to bring relative PM novices together to leverage each other's knowledge and begin a PM dialogue. Moreover, the facilitators supported the findings and recommended (i) create exclusive materials for them in order to lead the session game easily, and (ii) Translate the game to Spanish.

Finally, the respondents suggest improvements such as clarify the rules, create a demo or tutorial, translate it to Spanish, highlight color and numbering, and include figures.

5 Conclusions

This study was explorative in nature. Although, it could not statistically demonstrate a learning effect, subjective evaluations indicates the potential of such a game to support education. In addition, the study provided first insights on the game and its main strengths and weaknesses, which will systematically guide its further evolution. Based on results from this study, the game seems to be fun, immersive and certainly involve the participants, who engage in a game that reflect Project management demands in VSEs. Therefore, overall applicability of the game as a learning tool is achievable. However this study had reveled issues that need to be addressed through further studies. Thus, the authors are planning to repeat the experiment with certain modifications to the initial training of the facilitators to enable the acquisition of a more comprehensive understanding as well as adaptations to the experiment material and the game itself. Once the enhanced version of the game becomes available, the authors will repeat the experiment. In this sense, the results of the study presented in this paper will also be useful as a baseline for comparison.

Some work is still to be done about this topic: (i) improvement of the game by analyzing the suggestions made by the participants, (ii) improving the game by including other elements, like memory challenges, visual clues, time pressure, (iii) practicing the game with undergraduates students in others locations in order to reveal if the gameplay allow the transference of the concept across cultures, and (iv) future works should include new ways to game that involve more interaction among team members, hence extending the individual learning opportunities.

Acknowledgments. The authors would like to thank Andrés Larco, the course tutor, who played a major role in the use of the game. A special thanks also to all the students of the course "Software Quality" in 2015 of the National Polytechnic School of Ecuador, who participated in the evaluation of Go for It!.

References

1. Eurostat: annual enterprise statistics by size class for special aggregates of activities (NACE Rev. 2), http://ec.europa.eu/eurostat/web/structural-business-statistics/data/database
2. ISO: software engineering – lifecycle profiles for Very Small Entities (VSEs) part 5-1-1: management and engineering guide: generic profile group: basic profile, Geneva (2011)
3. Sanchez-Gordon, M.-L., O'Connor, R.V., Colomo-Palacios, R.: Evaluating VSEs viewpoint and sentiment towards the ISO/IEC 29110 standard: a two country grounded theory study. In: Rout, T., O'Connor, R.V., Dorling, A. (eds.) SPICE 2015. CCIS, vol. 526, pp. 114–127. Springer, Heidelberg (2015)

4. Clarke, P., O'Connor, R.V.: Business success in software SMEs: recommendations for future SPI studies. In: Winkler, D., O'Connor, R.V., Messnarz, R. (eds.) EuroSPI 2012. CCIS, vol. 301, pp. 1–12. Springer, Heidelberg (2012)
5. Clarke, P., O'Connor, R.V.: The influence of SPI on business success in software SMEs: an empirical study. J. Syst. Softw. **85**, 2356–2367 (2012)
6. O'Connor, R.V., Basri, S.: Understanding the role of knowledge management in software development: a case study in very small companies. Int. J. Syst. Serv.-Oriented Eng. **4**, 39–52 (2014)
7. O'Connor, R.V., Laporte, C.Y.: Software project management in very small entities with ISO/IEC 29110. In: Winkler, D., O'Connor, R.V., Messnarz, R. (eds.) EuroSPI 2012. CCIS, vol. 301, pp. 330–341. Springer, Heidelberg (2012)
8. Pino, F.J., García, F., Piattini, M.: Software process improvement in small and medium software enterprises: a systematic review. Softw. Qual. Control J. **16**, 237–261 (2008)
9. O'Connor, R.V., Laporte, C.Y.: Deploying lifecycle profiles for very small entities: an early stage industry view. In: O'Connor, R.V., Rout, T., McCaffery, F., Dorling, A. (eds.) SPICE 2011. CCIS, vol. 155, pp. 227–230. Springer, Heidelberg (2011)
10. Aydan, U., Yilmaz, M., O'Connor, R.V.: Towards a serious game to teach ISO/IEC 12207 software lifecycle process: an interactive learning approach. In: Rout, T., O'Connor, R.V., Dorling, A. (eds.) SPICE 2015. CCIS, vol. 526, pp. 217–229. Springer, Heidelberg (2015)
11. Zapata Jaramillo, C.M.: Teaching software development by means of a classroom game: the software development game. Dev. Bus. Simul. Exp. Learn. **36**, 156–164 (2014)
12. Kosa, M., Yilmaz, M.: Designing games for improving the software development process. In: O'Connor, R.V., et al. (eds.) EuroSPI 2015. CCIS, vol. 543, pp. 303–310. Springer, Heidelberg (2015). doi:10.1007/978-3-319-24647-5_25
13. Susi, T., Johannesson, M., Backlund, P.: Serious Games - An Overview. University of Skövde, Sweden (2015)
14. Bellotti, F., Kapralos, B., Lee, K., Moreno-Ger, P., Berta, R.: Assessment in and of serious games: an overview. Adv. Hum.-Comput. Interact. **2013**, 1–11 (2013)
15. O'Connor, R.V., Laporte, C.Y.: Deploying lifecycle profiles for very small entities: an early stage industry view. In: O'Connor, R.V., Rout, T., McCaffery, F., Dorling, A. (eds.) SPICE 2011. CCIS, vol. 155, pp. 227–230. Springer, Heidelberg (2011)
16. O'Connor, R., Laporte, C.Y.: Using ISO/IEC 29110 to harness process improvement in very small entities. In: O'Connor, R.V., Pries-Heje, J., Messnarz, R. (eds.) 18th European Software Process Improvement Conference on Workshop on SPI in SMEs, pp. 225–235. Springer, Heidelberg (2011)
17. O'Connor, R.V., Laporte, C.Y.: Towards the provision of assistance for very small entities in deploying software lifecycle standards. In: Proceedings of the 11th International Conference on Product Focused Software (PROFES 2010), pp. 4–7. ACM (2010)
18. Coleman, G., O'Connor, R.: Investigating software process in practice: a grounded theory perspective. J. Syst. Softw. **81**, 772–784 (2008)
19. O'Connor, R., Coleman, G.: Ignoring "Best Practice": why irish software SMEs are rejecting CMMI and ISO 9000. Australas. J. Inf. Syst. **16**, 7–30 (2009)
20. Sánchez-Gordón, M.-L., O'Connor, R.V.: Understanding the gap between software process practices and actual practice in very small companies. Softw. Qual. J. 1–22 (2015)
21. Moreno-Campos, E., Sanchez-Gordón, M.-L., Colomo-Palacios, R., de Amescua Seco, A.: Towards measuring the impact of the ISO/IEC 29110 standard: a systematic review. In: Barafort, B., O'Connor, R.V., Poth, A., Messnarz, R. (eds.) EuroSPI 2014. CCIS, vol. 425, pp. 1–12. Springer, Heidelberg (2014)

22. O'Connor, R.V., Laporte, C.Y.: An innovative approach to the development of an international software process lifecycle standard for very small entities. Int. J. Inf. Technol. Syst. Approach **7**, 1–22 (2014)
23. Laporte, C.Y., O'Connor, R., Fanmuy, G.: International systems and software engineering standards for very small entities. CrossTalk – J. Defense Softw. Eng. **26**, 28–33 (2013)
24. International Organization for Standardization (ISO): software engineering — lifecycle profiles for Very Small Entities (VSEs) — Part 5-1-1: management and engineering guide: generic profile group: entry profile, Geneva (2012)
25. Laporte, C.Y.: Contributions to software engineering and the development and deployment of international software engineering standards for very small entities (2009)
26. Monsalve, E.S., do Prado Leite, J.C.S., Werneck, V.M.B.: Transparently teaching in the context of game-based learning: the case of simulES-W. In: Proceedings of the 37th International Conference on Software Engineering, vol. 2, pp. 343–352. IEEE Press, Piscataway (2015)
27. Zapata-Jaramillo, C.M., Lopez, M.D.R., Sanchez, R.E.A., Pinzon, L.D.J.: SEMAT GAME: applying a project management practice. Dev. Bus. Simul. Exp. Learn. **42**, 133–143 (2015)
28. Jacobson, I., Ng, P.-W., McMahon, P.E., Spence, I., Lidman, S.: The Essence of Software Engineering: Applying the SEMAT Kernel. Addison-Wesley, Upper Saddle River (2013)
29. Adams, E.: Fundamentals of Game Design, 2nd edn. New Riders, Berkeley (2009)
30. Abuhamdeh, S., Csikszentmihalyi, M.: The importance of challenge for the enjoyment of intrinsically motivated. Goal-Directed Activities Pers. Soc. Psychol. Bull. **38**, 317–330 (2012)
31. Ross, S.M.: Peirce's criterion for the elimination of suspect experimental data. J. Eng. Technol. **20**, 38–41 (2003)

Empirical Research Case Studies of SPI

The Role of Process in Early Software Defect Prediction: Methods, Attributes and Metrics

Rana Ozakinci[1(✉)] and Ayca Tarhan[2]

[1] TÜBİTAK BİLGEM Software Technologies Research Institute (YTE),
06100 Ankara, Turkey
rana.ozakinci@tubitak.gov.tr
[2] Computer Engineering Department, Hacettepe University, Beytepe Yerleskesi,
06800 Ankara, Turkey
atarhan@hacettepe.edu.tr

Abstract. Software quality is the set of inherent characteristics that are built into a software product throughout software development process. An important indicator of software quality is the trend of software defects in the life-cycle. The models of software defect prediction and software reliability provide the opportunity for practitioners to observe the defectiveness distribution of their products in development and operation. However, reported studies are mostly focused on coding or testing stages. Though this is reasonable due to executable nature of the product, it prevents practitioners from taking the advantages (such as cost reduction) of identifying and predicting software defects earlier in the life-cycle. This paper, therefore, provides an overview of the trend of early software defect prediction studies as retrieved by a systematic mapping of the literature, and elaborates on the methods, attributes, and metrics of the studies that comprise software process data in the defect prediction.

Keywords: Early · Defect prediction · Software defect · Software reliability · Software quality · Prediction model · Process metrics · Systematic mapping

1 Introduction

Software systems have complex and continuously growing structure due to their nature. Ensuring software quality assurance throughout the development of software becomes an essential duty for both software managers and developers. Development of reliable software within limited time, budget and resources makes this duty more difficult. Predictive models are used early in the lifecycle to assess the software development risks from the beginning of the project [1].

Software reliability prediction is important for budget estimates, resource planning and time management if the prediction can be applied during early phases such as requirements analysis or design. During the past 30 years, numerous reliability and

---

The original version of this chapter was revised. An erratum to this chapter can be found at 10.1007/978-3-319-38980-6_34

defect prediction models have been developed and presented in the literature [2]. Generally, these studies are based on certain data processing methods and use various kinds of software metrics in order to build the prediction models based on the later phases of the software development life cycle (SDLC), i.e. testing or operational usage, thus causing a missed opportunity of controlling and ensuring the cost-effectiveness [3].

Early software reliability prediction is needed for the early identification of software quality, cost overrun, and optimal development strategy. A useful approach for early assessments is predicting the number of defects during the requirements, design, or coding phase, which may provide preventive actions such as additional reviews and more extensive testing, finally improving software process control and achieving high software quality [3].

In order to identify the characteristics and make use of the early phase data, information about the development process, its attributes and metrics gains importance. Since the defects are introduced into software during the process of product development, the attributes and metrics of the process in which the defects originate can be useful in the early prediction of the defects [4, 5]. In this paper, a review of the scientific literature on early software reliability and defect prediction is presented with respect to the features of methods, phases, and types of entities. In order to retrieve and categorize the studies that relate to our research, a systematic mapping study is conducted and the results are reported according to specified criteria. The focus of this paper is on identifying process attributes and metrics among the early defect prediction studies. To the best of our knowledge, there is no such study in the literature that evaluates the process characteristics in the early software defect prediction studies according to their prediction model information. Therefore, this paper contributes to the literature in various ways, such as identifying the early defect prediction studies and the role of process information with regard to different methods, attributes and metrics.

The remainder of the paper is organized as follows. Section 2 provides a summary of the literature-based studies on software reliability and defect prediction, and their findings. Section 3 explains the design of this research study. Section 4 provides results from an analysis of early defect prediction by highlighting the development phases, methods, attributes and process metrics mostly used in prediction studies. Section 5 closes the study by overall conclusions and the statement of future work.

2 Software Reliability and Defect Prediction

Many terms are used in the software engineering literature to describe a malfunction, notably fault, failure, and error [6]. Software reliability refers to the probability that software will not cause any failures for a specified time under specified conditions. Failure refers to the inability of a system or system component to perform a required function within specified limits. Fault is defined as a defect in the code that can be the cause of one or more failures [6]. IEEE Standard Classification for Software Anomalies [7] provides a uniform approach for these terms without regard to when they originate or which life cycle they are encountered. According to this standard; defect is an imperfection or deficiency in a work product where that work product does not meet its specifications, for example some omissions and imperfections found during early in the

SDLC [7]. Therefore, in order to address the anomalies in the early phases, "defect" term is used througout the study.

Software reliability prediction aims to predict the reliability of software, during software development life cycle phases, with the purpose of enabling development, test and management team to form an opinion about the reliability and quality of the software [8]. Since, the reliability of a software system depends upon the number of residual defects, early defect prediction gains importance. Defect prediction models allow software engineers to focus development activities on defect-prone code, consequently improving software quality and making better use of resources [9].

In general, these prediction models tend to use intermediate product attributes as dependent variables in order to determine the effects to the independent variable, i.e. number of defects. However, in order to take advantage of the early phase data to predict residual defects, process data becomes a major factor since it may represent the progress of the early phases more accurately [10].

2.1 Related Work

There are a number of literature analysis studies about software defect or reliability prediction. Catal and Diri [11] reviewed software fault prediction papers with a focus on types of metrics, methods and datasets. They did not describe all the prediction models in detail. They evaluated papers published before and after 2005 since PROMISE repository was created in 2005. The results show that the percentage of use of public databases and machine learning approaches increased significantly since 2005.

Catal [12] investigated 90 papers on software fault prediction published between 1990 and 2009. This review provided a guide for researchers to investigate the studies on software metrics, methods, datasets, and performance evaluation metrics, as well as the experimental results.

Hall et al. [9] published a systematic review about the performances of the fault prediction models that were similar in design to [11], which was more comprehensive in terms of the number of included studies and analyses. In the review, 208 papers published from January 2000 to December 2010, that focused on empirical studies on software fault prediction were included. The main objective was to assess context, independent variables and modeling techniques and their influences to the performance of fault prediction models. The main findings showed that models based on simple modeling techniques such as Naïve Bayes or Logistic Regression performed well. In addition, combinations of independent variables, and usage of feature selection techniques while performing the models resulted in better performance.

Recently, Jureczko and Madeyski [5] presented a review of research studies that investigated process metrics in software defect prediction. They focused on the most important results, recent advances and the summary regarding the use of these metrics in software defect prediction models. They reported that process metrics constitute a different source of information than the product metrics and employing process metrics in the defect prediction could lead to better results than working only with the product metrics.

Wahono [13] conducted a literature review that aims to identify and analyze the research trends, datasets, methods and frameworks used in software defect prediction research between the years 2000 and 2013. The results showed that 77.46 % of the research studies were related to classification methods, and 64.79 % of the research studies used public datasets.

Malhotra [14] performed a systematic literature review in order to analyze and assess the performance of the machine learning techniques for software fault prediction models and summarized the characteristics based on metrics reduction techniques, metrics, data sets and performance measures of the 64 primary studies published between 1991 and 2013. It was concluded that the machine learning techniques had acceptable fault prediction capability and could be used by software practitioners and researchers.

3 Research Design

Systematic mapping studies [15] compromise a broad review of primary studies in a specific topic that aims to identify the evidences available on the topic and said to complement systematic literature reviews [16]. The findings can help to direct focus of a future systematic review by allowing a comprehensive research of the primary studies. As a result, we conducted this mapping study with broader research questions for providing a wide overview about the early prediction of software reliability and defects, correspondingly.

3.1 Research Questions

The main goal of this systematic mapping study was to identify and classify early software defect prediction studies based on the main categorical attributes given in data extraction subsection. In order to focus these attributes properly, a set of research questions were defined (Table 1).

Table 1. Addressed research questions

Research questions		Motivation
RQ1	What is the trend of early prediction studies in the last 15 years?	Categorize the early prediction studies based on their features to see the overall trend.
RQ2	What types of methods are used in early software defect prediction?	Identify and categorize the methods used in early prediction studies in the literature.
RQ3	Which development phases are associated with early software defect prediction?	Investigate the phases that the prediction studies are conducted.
RQ4	Which software entities are subject to early software defect prediction?	Characterize the software entities that mostly used in models.
RQ5	What are the measurable process attributes associated with software process entity?	Categorize the measurable attributes which are used in studies that gather the process data.
RQ6	What are the software process metrics that are used to measure the process attributes?	Identify and categorize the software process metrics used in early prediction studies.

3.2 Search Strategy

PICOC (Population, Intervention, Comparison, Outcomes, and Context) suggested by [16] was developed in order to identify keywords and specify search strings:

Population: Early software defect prediction studies
Intervention: Early software defect prediction model
Comparison: The role of process in early software defect prediction models
Outcomes: The methods, attributes and metrics
Context: Academia (scientific literature)

In order to capture the phases of the data collected in studies, we constructed the search strategy as "early" and "earlier" words located in title. In spite of the fact that there are many terms used meaning the term "defect" (e.g. fault, error, and bug), only the "fault" keyword was included, since the other two words do not reflect the meaning of the faults that occur in the early phases. We also searched for the "reliability" keyword, which may return results that address early phases of the SDLC while building the prediction model. The main body of search strings and added keywords based on interventions were as follows:

Title: (("early" or "earlier") and
Title – abstract – keywords:
("software defect" or "software fault" or "software reliability") and
("prediction" or "estimation" or "analysis"))

We ran several searches for the studies reported between the years 2000 and 2015 in the following digital libraries of the scientific literature (in alphabetical order): ACM, ScienceDirect, Scopus, SpringerLink, Web of Science and Wiley. Table 2 shows the searches ran in the digital libraries, and the number of studies initially retrieved and selected.

Table 2. Number of studies initially retrieved and selected

Digital library	Initially retrieved	Initially selected
ACM	5	1
ScienceDirect	3	1
Scopus	64	20
SpringerLink	28	16
Web of science	25	9
Wiley	4	1
Total	129	48

Initially, 129 papers were retrieved from the searches. We then selected 48 papers that apply inclusion criteria C1, C2, C3 presented in Table 3. In order to ensure that study is conducted early in the SDLC, we eliminated 21 papers regarding to exclusion criteria C4. Then, through the rest of 27 papers, snowballing approach is applied by investigating the references of primary papers. Inclusion criteria defined in Table 3 were considered while applying the snowballing procedure.

3.3 Study Selection Criteria

To be included in this systematic mapping, a study must be reported in a paper published in English as journal paper, conference proceedings or book chapter. The criteria for studies to be included in the mapping study are based on the inclusion and exclusion criteria presented in Table 3. According to the criteria, 41 selected studies are included in the systematic mapping study.

Table 3. Inclusion and Exclusion Criteria

Inclusion criteria		Exclusion criteria
C1	Studies that focus on predicting reliability or classifying software as faulty or non-faulty and/or predicting defect numbers	Studies that detect or locate existing faults
C2	Studies that clearly state the prediction method	Studies that do not present any prediction method
C3	Studies that define context parameters, metrics used and datasets	Studies that focus on estimating cost or development effort
C4	Studies that use early SDLC information in order to make prediction, which includes requirement and design phases	Studies that focus on the phases of coding or later

3.4 Study Quality Assessment

The approach to identifying studies suitable for this mapping study is motivated by Kitchenham and Charter's [16] notion of a quality check. Quality assessment is specifically focused on determining the papers that report sufficient information to compare other studies in terms of answering defined RQs. To be able to do this, a basic set of information (prediction method, datasets, attributes, and metrics) must be reported in papers. Without this, it will be very difficult to accurately realize what is reported in the study. We have developed and applied a set of criteria in order to ensure that sufficient information is reported in defect prediction studies. Selected papers were examined in detail according to the criteria by the first author, and the examination was reviewed by the second author. The quality criteria are defined as follows.

- Is there a clear statement of that research is about defect or reliability prediction?
- Does the study clearly define which prediction methods or approaches were used?
- Does the study give used metrics and datasets to build the prediction model?
- Is it clearly identified which SDLC phase/phases were considered?

3.5 Data Extraction

Data extraction process is conducted according to some data attributes related to research questions that are shown in Table 4. The main classification scheme of the study was

Table 4. Data extraction process

Categorized information	Values	Explanation	Related RQ
Data collection type	- Quantitative - Qualitative - Hybrid	Represents whether data was gathered through numerical or computational way; such as formulas or statistical modeling, or a subjective way, based on questionnaires, expert opinions so on. Hybrid models use both methods together.	RQ1
Dataset type	- Public - Private - Both	Indicates whether data used in the study is accessed as public or private	RQ1
Method	- Machine learning - Statistical - Fuzzy logic - Bayesian network - Other	Expresses the approach used in the study regarding to prediction model built	RQ2
SDLC phase	- Requirement - Design - Code - Test	States the software development life-cycle stage that the metrics are collected and prediction model is built	RQ3
Software entity	- Product - Process - Resource	Describes the type of the entities used in the studies based on definitions of Fenton and Bieman's classifying software measures [17]	RQ4
Attributes associated with process entity	- Effort - Stability - Process maturity - Number of defects - Adequacy - Time	Explanation is given in research result section (RQ5)	RQ5

prepared based on key-wording described in [15]. First, all papers are identified and reviewed for specifying whether they will be included in the study or not, regarding to its compliance with the study selection criteria. Then, selected papers are analyzed deeply in order to map the attributes of each paper with determined categories. To gather all information about these attributes, full text of the study is read and recorded within a tabular form.

4 Research Results

In this section, we addressed our research questions and analyzed the finding in a systematic way for 41 studies.

RQ1 - What is the trend of early prediction studies in the last 15 years?
Number of studies about early prediction indicates a non-uniform distribution over the years. Although, there is an increase of the interest in software defect prediction research since 2005 [11, 13], number of studies that report early prediction has varied (Fig. 1). While seven studies focused on reliability prediction in early phases, 34 studies (83 % of total) applied defect prediction. In addition, data collection type is considered to be helpful for the approaches in gathering data in early studies. More than half of the studies (56 %) used quantitative methods to gather data. A great majority of the rest (39 %) used hybrid approaches that merge quantitative and qualitative methods. A small percentage of studies (5 %) applied qualitative techniques. Studies were also categorized with regard to their types of datasets. Private datasets (49 %) belong to industrial companies or individuals, which are not distributed as public datasets. Public datasets (34 %) frequently exist in PROMISE and NASA MDP (metrics data program) repositories which are open to access. A few studies both used public and private datasets (5 %) and others (12 %) did not state the type of the dataset.

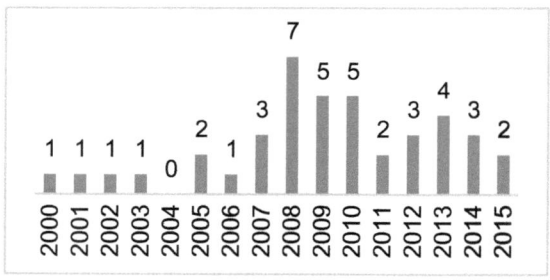

Fig. 1. Number of early studies per year

RQ2 - What types of methods are used in early software defect prediction?
Most frequently used method was machine learning (31 %), which is the main state-of-the-art approach in software defect prediction models. Machine learning methods included support vector machines, artificial neural networks, genetic algorithms, K-means clustering, decision trees and so on. Fuzzy logic methods (%21) were widely preferred thanks to its capability to measure abstract data which exists in early phases. Statistical methods (19 %) were next preferred and mostly covered regression based models. Bayesian belief network based models (17 %) were also used.

RQ3 - Which SDLC phases are most often associated with early prediction studies?
Twenty-five studies covered requirement phase-based data for the early prediction. Besides, 33 studies included design phase-based data in the prediction methods. While

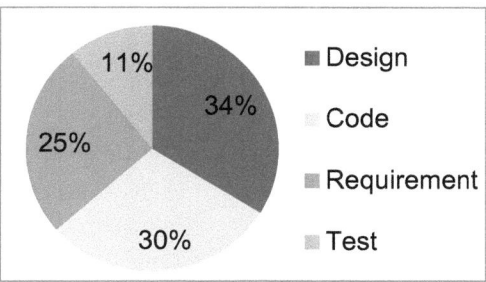

Fig. 2. Distribution of SDLC phases

18 studies focused on requirement, design and code phase-based data together, 10 studies included only design and code phase-based data for early prediction. Four studies used only requirement phase-based data, while nine studies used only design phase-based data. The percentages of the SDLC phases associated with early prediction studies can be seen in Fig. 2. Design phase-based data was mostly preferred while applying early prediction models. Since, studies that use requirement and design phase-based data have been mostly covered code phase-based data, its percentage was about 30 %. It can be seen that; early prediction studies chose requirement phase-based data (25 %) in order to provide earlier results. Test phase-based data (11 %) was rarely associated with the early prediction studies.

RQ4 - Which software entities are subject to software defect prediction studies?
The software entities subject to prediction studies were elicited from the software metrics used in the studies. Twenty-three studies used only product entity based data, and three studies used metrics based on product and process entities. Eleven studies used software metrics that are related to all entities. Two studies used both process and resource entities to gather software metrics. Only two studies used process entity based metrics. Overall, 18 studies (44 % of total) were used process entity related metrics to collect process data for early defect prediction.

Research questions RQ5 and RQ6 are answered below for only 18 studies that used process-based data as the indicator of the early defect prediction model and full references to these studies are given in the Appendix.

RQ5 - What are the measurable process attributes associated with software process entity?
In order to classify process attributes, a grouping approach has been applied to the studies that use process entity in their prediction method. The classification of the process attributes has been constructed from [18] and considered as follows.

- **Effort;** covers the measures related to the effort of a process activity as person-day.
- **Time;** represents the measures related to the time for applying a process activity.
- **Stability;** identifies the changefulness of a process artifact.
- **Process Maturity;** states the maturity of the organization about the process activities.

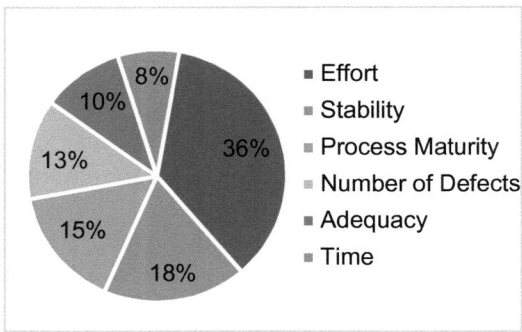

Fig. 3. The distribution of measurable attributes associated with software process entity

- **Number of Defects;** specifies the number of defects found during a process activity.
- **Adequacy;** represents the quality or completeness of a process artifact.

The distribution of the process attributes associated with each software process entity is shown in Fig. 3.

RQ6 - What are the software process metrics that are used to measure the process attributes?

We classified the studies that used process metrics with respect to their process attributes in Table 5. It is interesting to see that seven studies (out of 18) used metrics of stability, six studies used metrics of process maturity, and four studies used metrics of adequacy in their prediction studies.

Table 5. Mapping of process metrics used in the studies to process attributes

Process attribute	Related process metrics	Referencing studies
Effort	- Effort of the review activity of requirement analysis, design, coding or testing	S1, S5, S6, S7, S8, S9, S11, S12, S13, S14, S15, S16, S17, S18
Stability	- Requirement stability - Number of requirements' change request	S9, S10, S11, S15, S16, S17, S18
Process maturity	- Process maturity of the organization, i.e. CMMI level	S7, S9, S11, S12, S15, S16
Number of defects	- Number of defect data found from the review of requirement analysis, design, coding or testing	S1, S2, S3, S7, S13
Adequacy	- Quality of specification requirement document, design, code or test cases/scenarios	S10, S11, S12, S17
Time	- Requirement, design, code, test time - Rework time	S2, S4, S5

5 Conclusion

Software quality is the main evidence of compliance for software products that acquire proper and correct implementation of requirements. As a consequence, software quality assurance is essential in earlier phases of the software lifecycle and software prediction models help in early detection of defect proneness. Through it is not easy to collect process data from each kind of project, findings from software process assessments or process audits might be significant to gather the information that the early prediction models need.

According to this study, process-based software metrics play an important role on the early defect prediction. Although the analyzed early prediction studies based on process data report that the proposed early prediction methods will be useful for software management team and helpful for early quality assurance, there is a need for quantitative evidence about the benefits of using the process data in early defect prediction models.

In this paper, we have elaborated on the studies that use process based metrics for reliability or defect prediction in the early phases of the SDLC. To the best of our knowledge, this is the first systematic mapping study about the role of process in early software defect prediction. Our work makes contribution to the scope of defect prediction area by demonstrating the up-to-date picture of the literature and the distinctive features of the process information. We hope that this work will be exemplary for future analysis of the effects, benefits and contributions of process data within the context of early defect prediction. Our work has limitations due to its search string and selection criteria. To cope with this limitation, we applied snowballing through the primary studies to elicit the secondary ones, and also retrieved some studies from the references of the recently published systematic studies (as summarized in Sect. 2).

For future work, we plan to conduct case studies to investigate early lifecycle evidence based on the mostly used methods and process metrics in the models built (e.g., fuzzy based prediction models and review effort for requirements phase). We will then compare the results of the early prediction model on different datasets to analyze the success rates of the predictions. Apart from our plans, the most influential research characteristics on prediction accuracy and the set of evaluation criteria need to be investigated in the context of the early models.

A Appendix

See Table 6.

Table 6. Software defect prediction studies that covered process-based data

No	Study ref.	Data collection type	Dataset type	Method	SDLC phase	Entity
S1	[19]	Quantitative	Private	Bayesian network	Design, code, test	Product, process
S2	[20]	Quantitative	Private	Statistical	Requirement, design, code, test	Product, process, resource
S3	[21]	Hybrid	NA	Fuzzy	Requirement, design, code	Product, process, resource
S4	[22]	Quantitative	Private	Other	Requirement, design, code, test	Process
S5	[23]	Hybrid	Private	Statistical	Design, code, test	Process
S6	[24]	Hybrid	Both	Other	Requirement, design, code	Product, process, resource
S7	[25]	Hybrid	Private	Fuzzy	Requirement, design, code	Product, process
S8	[26]	Qualitative	Private	Fuzzy	Requirement, design, code, test	Process, resource
S9	[27]	Hybrid	Public	Fuzzy	Requirement, design, code, test	Product, process, resource
S10	[28]	Hybrid	Private	Other	Requirement, design, code, test	Product, process, resource
S11	[29]	Hybrid	Both	Machine learning	Requirement, design, code, test	Product, process, resource
S12	[30]	Hybrid	Private	Bayesian network	Requirement, design, code, test	Product, process, resource
S13	[31]	Quantitative	Private	Statistical	Requirement, design, code, test	Product, process
S14	[32]	Qualitative	Private	Bayesian network	Requirement, design, code	Process, resource
S15	[33]	Hybrid	NA	Fuzzy	Requirement, design, code	Product, process, resource
S16	[34]	Hybrid	Public	Fuzzy	Requirement, design, code	Product, process, resource
S17	[35]	Hybrid	Public	Bayesian network	Requirement, design, code	Product, process, resource
S18	[36]	Hybrid	Private	Fuzzy	Requirement	Product, process, resource

References

1. Smidts, C., Stoddard, R.W., Stutzke, M.: Software reliability models: an approach to early reliability prediction.In: Proceedings, of the Seventh International Symposium on Software Reliability Engineering, White Plains, NY, pp. 132–142 (1996)
2. Song, Q., Jia, Z., Shepperd, M., Ying, S., Liu, J.: A general software defect-proneness prediction framework. IEEE Trans. Softw. Eng. **37**(3), 356–370 (2011)
3. Pandey, A.K., Goyal, N.K.: Early Software Reliability Prediction. Springer, New Delhi (1987)
4. Aslan, D., Tarhan, A., Demirörs, V.O.: How process enactment data affects product defectiveness prediction – a case study. In: Lee, R. (ed.) SERA 2013. SCI, vol. 496, pp. 151–166. Springer, Heidelberg (2014)
5. Madeyski, L., Jureczko, M.: Which process metrics can significantly improve defect prediction models? An empirical study. Softw. Qual. J. **23**(3), 393–422 (2015)
6. IEEE Recommended Practice on Software Reliability, in IEEE STD 1633–2008, pp. 1–72, 27 June 2008
7. IEEE Standard Classification for Software Anomalies, in IEEE Std 1044–2009 (Revision of IEEE Std 1044-1993), pp.1–23, 7 January 2010
8. Cukic, B., Hayes, J.H.: The virtues of assessing software reliability early. IEEE Softw. **22**(3), 50–53 (2005)
9. Hall, T., Beecham, S., Bowes, D., Gray, D., Counsell, S.: A systematic literature review on fault prediction performance in software engineering. IEEE Trans. Softw. Eng. **38**(6), 1276–1304 (2012)
10. Radjenovic, D., et al.: Software fault prediction metrics: a systematic literature review. Inf. Softw. Technol. **55**(8), 1397–1418 (2013)
11. Catal, C., Diri, B.: A systematic review of software fault prediction studies. Expert Syst. Appl. **36**(4), 7346–7354 (2009)
12. Catal, C.: Software fault prediction: a literature review and current trends. Expert Syst. Appl. **38**(4), 4626–4636 (2011)
13. Wahono, R.S.: A systematic literature review of software defect prediction: research trends, datasets, methods and frameworks. J. Softw. Eng. **1**, 1–16 (2015)
14. Malhotra, R.: A systematic review of machine learning techniques for software fault prediction. Appl. Softw. Comput. J. **27**, 504–518 (2015)
15. Petersen, K., Feldt, R., Mujtaba, S., Mattsson, M.: Systematic mapping studies in software engineering. In: 12th International Conference on Evaluation and Assessment in Software Engineering, pp. 68–77
16. Kitchenham, B., Charters, S.: "Guidelines for Performing Systematic Literature Reviews in Software Engineering (Version 2.3)," Technical report EBSE-2007–01, Keele Univ., EBSE (2007)
17. Fenton, N.E., Bieman, J.: Software Metrics: A Rigorous and Practical Approach, 3rd edn. CRC Press, Boca Raton (2014)
18. Florac, W.A., Park, R.E., Carleton, A.: Practical software measurement: measuring for process management and improvement (1997)
19. Amasaki, S., Takagi, Y., Mizuno, O., Kikuno, T.: A Bayesian belief network for assessing the likelihood of fault content. In: 14th International Symposium on Software Reliability Engineering, ISSRE 2003, pp. 215–226 (2003)
20. Hong, Y., Baik, J., Ko, I.Y., Choi, H.J.: A value-added predictive defect type distribution model based on project characteristics. In: Proceedings of the 7th IEEE/ACIS International Conference on Computer and Information Science, 2008, pp. 469–474 (2008)

21. Kumar, K.S., Misra, R.B.: An enhanced model for early software reliability prediction using software engineering metrics. In: Second International Conference on Secure System Integration and Reliability Improvement, pp. 177–178 (2008)
22. Mohan, K.K., Verma, A.K., Srividya, A., Rao, G.V, Gedela, R.K.: Early quantitative software reliability prediction using petri-nets. In: IEEE Region 10 and the Third International Conference on Industrial and Information Systems, ICIIS 2008, pp. 1–6 (2008)
23. Yamada, S.: Early-stage software product quality prediction based on process measurement data. In: Misra, K.B. (ed.) Handbook of Performability Engineering, pp. 1227–1237. Springer, London (2008)
24. Fenton, N., Neil, M., Marsh, W., Hearty, P., Radliński, Ł., Krause, P.: On the effectiveness of early life cycle defect prediction with Bayesian Nets. Empirical Softw. Eng. **13**(5), 499–537 (2008)
25. Pandey, A., Goyal, N.: A fuzzy model for early software fault prediction using process maturity and software metrics. Int. J. Electron. Eng. **1**(2), 239–245 (2009)
26. Mohan, K.K., Verma, A.K., Srividya, A.: Early qualitative software reliability prediction and risk management in process centric development through a soft computing technique. Int. J. Reliab. Qual. Saf. Eng. **16**(6), 521–532 (2009)
27. Pandey, A.K., Goyal, N.K.: Fault prediction model by fuzzy profile development of reliability relevant software metrics. Int. J. Comput. Appl. Technol. **11**(6), 34–41 (2010)
28. Kläs, M., Nakao, H., Elberzhager, F., Münch, J.: Support planning and controlling of early quality assurance by combining expert judgment and defect data-a case study. Empir Softw. Eng. **15**(4), 423–454 (2010)
29. Sandhu, P.S., Lata, S., Grewal, D.K.: Neural network approach for software defect prediction based on quantitative and qualitative factors. Int. J. Comput. Theory Eng. **4**(2), 298–303 (2012)
30. Ba, J., Wu, S.: ProPRED: A probabilistic model for the prediction of residual defects. In: Proceedings of 2012 IEEE/ASME 8th IEEE/ASME International Conference on Mechatronic and Embedded Systems and Applications, pp. 247–251 (2012)
31. Dhiauddin, M., Suffian, M., Ibrahim, S.: A Systematic Approach to Predict System Testing Defects using Prior Phases Metrics for V-Model, 1, 1–17 (2013)
32. Kumar, C., Yadav, D.K.: Software defects estimation using metrics of early phases of software development life cycle. Int. J. Syst. Assurance Eng. Manag. **4**, 1–9 (2014)
33. Pandey, A.K., Goyal, N.K.: Early fault prediction using software metrics and process maturity. Early Softw. Reliab. Prediction **303**, 117–130 (2013)
34. Yadav, H.B., Yadav, D.K.: Early software reliability analysis using reliability relevant software metrics. Int. J. Syst. Assur. Eng. Manag. 1–12 (2014)
35. Kumar, C., Yadav, D.K.: Software defects estimation using metrics of early phases of software development life cycle. Int. J. Syst. Assur. Eng. Manag. **4**, 1–9 (2014)
36. Chatterjee, S., Maji, B.: A new fuzzy rule based algorithm for estimating software faults in early phase of development. Soft Computing, 1–13 (2015)

An Empirical Study on Software Testing Practices in Automotive

Giuseppe Lami[✉], Isabella Biscoglio, and Fabio Falcini

Consiglio Nazionale delle Ricerche - Istituto di Scienza e Tecnologie della Informazione, Via Moruzzi, 1, 56124 Pisa, Italy
{giuseppe.lami,isabella.biscoglio,
fabio.falcini}@isti.cnr.it

Abstract. This paper presents the results of an empirical study aimed at characterizing and analyzing recurrent software development weaknesses in automotive industry. In the automotive domain software development is mainly demanded to specialized software suppliers that are required by car makers to improve and measure the process quality of their projects by applying process models such as Automotive SPICE^{TM}. The authors, as Automotive SPICE assessors, have directly recorded and identified specific software process improvement opportunities on the basis of the evidences gathered from real software development projects during a significant number of assessments performed at several organizations world-wide. This paper, that focuses specifically on the software testing-related processes, is a step of a wider study that the authors are carrying out. Such a study aims at identifying, using data from real automotive software development projects, common software development weaknesses having negative impact according Automotive SPICE^{TM}, in order to derive a picture of the state of the practice of software development in automotive and to provide researchers and practitioners with a reference for improvement initiatives aimed at solving those weaknesses.

Keywords: Software process improvement · Automotive · Automotive SPICE® · Software testing

1 Introduction

Automotive is one of the application fields that witnessed, in the last years, the highest growing of technological innovation, in particular for software-intensive components. Car OEMs (Original Equipment Manufacturer) are nowadays turning their vehicles from mechanical devices into elaborated electronically controlled systems. Electronic systems, more and more complex and connected by CANs (Control Area Networks), control today over the 85 % of the automobile's functionalities. Consequently, software (with increased demand in terms of size and complexity) is a crucial car component since it is part of embedded systems called Electronic Control Units (ECU) that control electronically a large number of the vehicle functions (navigation and infotainment included). The number of ECUs, from economic to costly vehicle models, is remarkably increased during the last fifteen/twenty years.

Generally speaking, the software development is mainly demanded to ECU and software suppliers (car makers are lately involved more closely) that range from small-medium organizations to large and structured ones – it is important to notice that small and medium organizations are currently a significant percentage of the players in this challenging arena. In this context project management and software engineering, initially underestimated sides of the ECU development projects, have at present taken the attention of whole automotive industry that require projects to meet increasingly demanding timing and quality objectives - it is interesting to remark that budget efficiency is also important but mass production can partially mitigate this aspect in some circumstances. In particular, the market expectations (it is fact that the bulk of car issues currently come from electronics and software issues) and technology advances have produced a real need for improvement at managerial and technical levels in order to keep software developments on track, especially for SME small and medium-sized enterprises (SME).

Despite the Automotive SPICE^{TM} model for software process assessment and improvement is widely used in automotive (mainly as a mean for qualifying software suppliers by several car manufacturers), and consequently there is a potential availability of huge amount of data from assessments, in literature there is, at our understanding, scarceness of studies addressing common trends in such a technologically ever-increasing application domain. The reasons may be different, as the confidentiality of data from assessments and the difficulty of collecting data because the existence of many companies involved in the production of software-intensive automotive components and many assessors.

This study aims at providing a contribution in answering the following research questions:

RQ.1. What are the most frequently weak software testing practices in automotive?

RQ.2. Is the capability of a software testing-related practice influenced by the phase of software testing (software unit testing, software integration testing, and software functional testing) in which it is performed?

This study relies on full sets of data taken from a sample of 27 Automotive SPICE assessments performed by the authors. The average number of processes assessed in these assessments is 13, and for each assessment several projects may be used as sources of information for determining the Capability level of each process. For these reasons, the amount of information and process indicators available from the study sample is relevant.

The data sample includes information on several processes ranging from the technical ones (belonging to the Engineering category), as for instance Software Requirements Analysis, Software Design, Software Testing, System Integration and Test processes, to the managerial ones as for instance Problem Resolution Management, Change Management, Risk Management. In this paper we focus on those processes directly addressing software testing. According to the Automotive SPICE process reference model, there are three processes dealing with software testing: Software Construction, Software Integration Test, and Software Testing. Our aim is to complete in the future the study by taking into account all the software engineering-related processes available in the study's data sample.

Another significant characteristic that enforces the originality and the validity of this empirical study, is the fact that it uses real data from real software development projects collected in the last 5 years. In literature, empirical studies addressing the same topics very often rely on data taken from questionnaires and/or literature review instead of data and indicators from projects [9–11].

This paper is structured as follows: in Sect. 2 the Automotive SPICE model for software process assessment and improvement is presented and its principal components are described. In Sect. 3 the methodological approach set up and followed for conducting this empirical study is presented. Section 4 the data, related to the three processes in the scope of such a study, are presented with the support of tables and graphs for understandability and readability purposes. In Sect. 5 the available data are analyzed and, finally, in Sect. 6 conclusions are presented and the next steps of this research initiative are introduced.

2 Introduction to Automotive SPICE™

SPICE (Software Process Improvement and Capability Determination) is an acronym that identifies the ISO/IEC 33000 standard series (that recently substituted the former ISO/IEC 15504 standard) [3]. In early 2000s an initiative was launched by the Procurement Forum with the principal European Car Makers, their assessors and representative bodies to address the problems related to software assessments in automotive. In the framework of this initiative, a Special Interest Group (SIG) has been founded with the aim to design a special version of the SPICE model (called Automotive-SPICE) tailored on the needs and peculiarities of the automotive business area. The first results of the initiative was to create consensus on commonality of approach in order to avoid that suppliers face multiple assessments from multiple manufacturers using different models and criteria and consume resources that put additional pressure on delivery times. Furthermore, the focus on software capability determination by means of software process assessment has determined a common trend among the European Car Makers in using Automotive SPICE™ as a mean for determining a supplier's qualification mechanism.

Nowadays Automotive SPICE, as a *de-facto* process assessment and improvement standard, is used by car makers to push software process improvement among their ECU and software suppliers [4, 5]. Many of the car makers are using also this standard to assess supplier capabilities and are requiring the achievement of specific rating. Thus it provides both a scheme for evaluating the capability of software processes and a path for their improvement. In extreme synthesis the four basic pillars of Automotive SPICE are: Process Reference Model (PRM) [2], Process Assessment Model (PAM) [1], Measurement Framework and Assessment Scope. For the first three concepts we refer to the bibliography. The Assessment Scope is a subset of the processes contained in Automotive SPICE PRM, where each process is associated with a target process capability level. In particular, the Hersteller Initiative Software (HIS) Scope is a subset of the processes contained in Automotive SPICE, which will be assessed by each manufacturer at least at Capability Level 2. The HIS Scope of the Automotive SPICE is the reference scope used by automotive OEMs for the qualification of suppliers of software-intensive car components. In Table 1 the whole Automotive SPICE PRM is presented, the processes in bold are those belonging to the HIS assessment scope. The HIS scope requires to assess those processes up to capability level 2.

Table 1. HIS assessment scope

Process id.	Process name	Process id.	Process name
ACQ.3	Contract agreement	SUP.8	**Configuration management**
ACQ.4	**Supplier monitoring**	SUP.9	**Problem resolution management**
ACQ.11	Technical requirements	**SUP.10**	**Change request management**
ACQ.12	Legal and administrative requirements	PIM.3	Process improvement
ACQ.13	Project requirements	**ENG.1**	**Requirement elicitation**
ACQ.14	Request for proposals	**ENG.2**	**System requirements analysis**
ACQ.15	Supplier qualification	**ENG.3**	**System architectural design**
MAN.3	**Project management**	**ENG.4**	**Software requirements analysis**
MAN.5	Risk management	**ENG.5**	**Software design**
MAN.6	Measurement	**ENG.6**	**Software construction**
SPL.1	Supplier tendering	**ENG.7**	**Software integration test**
SPL.2	Product release	**ENG.8**	**Software testing**
SUP.1	**Quality Assurance**	**ENG.9**	**System integration test**
SUP.2	Verification	**ENG.10**	**System testing**
SUP.4	Joint review	REU.2	Reuse program management
SUP.7	Documentation		

From Table 1 it results that processes in Automotive SPICE® are conveniently grouped and large in number. The rational behind the HIS scope is to limit the impact on the practitioners by selecting the core of the engineering processes and only few additional fundamental processes.

3 The Methodological Approach

During the last five years the authors, in the capacity of qualified Automotive SPICE Principal Assessor (according to the IntACS international assessor certification scheme) [6], have performed more than twenty Automotive SPICE assessments of several organizations producing software-intensive systems for the automotive industry.

Typically these Automotive SPICE assessments have targeted the HIS scope (or variants of HIS scope) in several domains (e.g. body electronics, lighting, closures...) and they had one or more of the following purposes:

- Perform Gap Analysis for benchmarking
- Measure the progress after a SW Process Improvement effort
- Supplier process capability rating

as the typical software process improvement follows the pattern shown in Fig. 1.

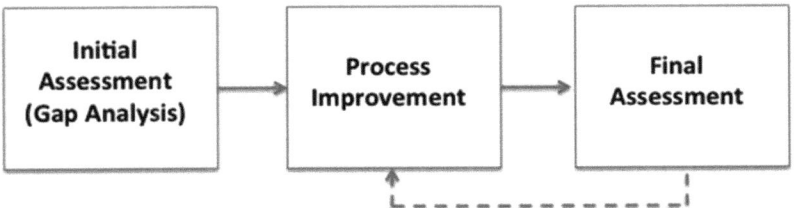

Fig. 1. Typical process Improvement path

Table 6 in Annex A summarizes in anonymous way the database that supports this study – although the sample is limited in number (27) and geographical distribution (Italy 22, China 2, Korea 2, Israel 1) it can be considered meaningful by all means due to the nature of the subject under analysis. Yet the following outcomes have not a statistical validity and are based on empirical observations. The column "Company Size" of Table 6 in Annex A has been left void for confidentiality reasons (the indication of company size could lead to the identification of the company itself).

It is key to remark that the organizations have been assessed:

- Before and after improvement (10 organizations) for a total of 21 assessments. With reference to Table 6, the value in the "Gap An. - Assessm." Column is 'YY'.
- After implementing a structured improvement initiative (7 organizations). With reference to Table 6, the value in the "Gap An. - Assessm." Column is 'NY'.

The available data target in total 42 projects (some of them having to comply with ISO 26262 requirements [8]). From a size point of views the organizations ranges from small (7), medium (11), large (9) ones.

This empirical study, that focuses on software testing-related practices only, represents only a step of a wider analysis aiming at getting a complete "in practice" view of the software process improvement internals in the automotive industry, in [14] a similar study, addressing a couple of Automotive SPICE management processes, has been reported.

During the assessments, evidences and data on the processes in scope are gathered by various means, including interviews, documents and work products analysis and these data are used to assess (using the expert judgment of the assessors as well) a set of indicators provided by the Automotive SPICE model itself. These indicators are the so-called Base Practices (process-specific) and the Generic Practices (applicable to all processes). Base Practices (BPs) are indicators of the performance of a specific process, i.e. they represent the set of practices necessary to fulfill the purpose of the process they refer to. Generic Practices (GPs) are indicators of the capability of a process. They are out of the scope of this study. In context of process improvement it is important to remark that the assessment activity is not limited to a mere rating of process indicators, but it includes also the provision of high-level improvement guidance for the projects under assessment. Assessments also enrich the assessors by exposing them to precious "behind-doors" experience of real projects.

The following step-wise approach has been adopted in this study:

S.1. The organizations assessed by the authors are classified in terms of product domain, organization size (omitted from annex A for confidentiality), location, and type of assessment.

S.2. The rating achieved by the Base Practices of the processes under investigation have been reported in tabular format.

S.3. The Base Practices having higher frequency of unsatisfactory ratings (i.e. achieving a rating N or P according the Automotive SPICE Measurement Framework) have been identified with the support of statistical techniques.

S.4. The rationales of Base Practices weaknesses have been investigated and analyzed in order to identify possible significant trends and commonalities in software testing in automotive.

Confidentiality issues has been considered and carefully addressed.

4 Study Results

As stated in Sect. 3, this paper addresses the software testing-related practices. Automotive SPICE PRM has been conceived to include three levels of software testing: unit, integration (against software architectural design), high-level (against software requirements). Such a multiplicity of software testing layers reflects the state of the practice in automotive embedded software development projects. For this reason the Automotive SPICE PAM doesn't group all the software testing-related practices into a unique process, indeed Software Construction process (ENG.6), Software integration Test process (ENG.7), and Software Testing process (ENG.8) include Base Practices addressing someway software testing. This section is structured in two sub-sections one aimed at describing what are the software testing-related Base Practices in the Automotive SPICE PAM and how they are mapped with respect to the processes, the other aims at presenting the results of the study.

4.1 Software Testing Practices in Automotive SPICE

Automotive SPICE PAM contains 17 Base Practices addressing software testing issues. These BPs are distributed among 3 different processes of the Automotive SPICE PRM:

Software Construction process (ENG.6), Software integration Test process (ENG.7), and Software Testing process (ENG.8). The ENG.6 process addresses unit testing, ENG.7 addresses software integration testing and ENG.8 addresses the higher level of software testing. In the following the 17 BPs addressing software testing are identified and grouped by process:

Software Construction process (ENG.6): ENG.6.BP1: Define a unit verification strategy; ENG.6.BP5: Develop unit verification criteria; ENG.6.BP6: Verify software units; ENG.6.BP7: Record the results of unit verification; ENG.6.BP10: Ensure consistency and bilateral traceability of software units to test specification for software units.

Software Integration Test process (ENG.7): ENG.7.BP2: Develop software integration test strategy; ENG.7.BP3: Develop test specification for software integration test; ENG.7.BP5: Verify the integrated software; ENG.7.BP6: Record the results of software integration testing; ENG.7.BP7: Ensure consistency and bilateral traceability of software architectural design and software detailed design to software integration test specification; ENG.7.BP8: Develop regression testing strategy and perform regression testing.

Software Testing process (ENG.8): ENG.8.BP1: Develop software test strategy; ENG.8.BP2: Develop test specification for software test; ENG.8.BP3: Verify integrated software; ENG.8.BP4: Record the results of software testing; ENG.8.BP5: Ensure consistency and bilateral traceability of software requirements to software test specification; ENG.8.BP6: Develop regression test strategy and perform regression testing.

4.2 Study Data Report

Table 2 reports, for each assessment, the ratings assigned to the seventeen Base Practices (BP) belonging to the Automotive SPICE PAM presented in Sect. 4.1. As stated in Sect. 2 the measurement scale is composed of 4 values (N, P, L, F). The first column the assessments belonging to the sample of this study are identified with the same OU Id. reported in Annex A. Figure 2 represents the same data in graphical format.

In order to facilitate the analysis of the data the rating value of each BP, originally expressed by a value in the four value scale N-P-L-F, is substituted by a numeric value. To do that, we start by describing the mechanism provided by Automotive SPICE to determine the rating of a BP. Such a mechanism associates a value in the four-value N-P-L-F scale to a percentage of achievement of the BP. In practice, the assessor shall gather evidences enough to establish at what extent a BP is performed, this extent is required to be expressed in percentage. Because the establishment of an exact percentage of the performance of a practice is very hard to be defined (this is not a measure, it is essentially a professional judgment), Automotive SPICE provides, in order to make assessment rating more repeatable and comparable, the mapping between percentages and rating values on the N-P-L-F scale shown in Table 3.

Table 2. Software testing-related base practices ratings

id.	ENG.6					ENG.7						ENG.8					
	Base practices					Base practices						Base practices					
	1	5	6	7	10	2	3	5	6	7	8	1	2	3	4	5	6
1	L	L	F	L	F	–	–	–	–	–	–	P	L	F	F	F	L
2	F	L	F	F	F	P	F	F	F	F	P	L	F	F	F	F	L
3	F	F	F	F	F	L	F	F	F	F	L	F	L	F	F	F	F
4	F	F	F	F	F	F	F	F	F	F	F	F	F	F	F	F	F
5	P	L	L	L	L	–	–	–	–	–	–	–	–	–	–	–	–
6	P	P	L	P	L	P	L	F	P	P	P	L	F	F	F	F	L
7	F	F	F	L	L	L	F	F	F	L	L	L	F	F	F	F	L
8	P	P	L	N	N	P	L	P	P	N	P	P	P	L	L	P	P
9	P	P	L	N	P	P	P	P	P	N	P	P	P	P	L	P	P
10	F	F	L	F	F	F	F	L	F	F	F	F	F	F	F	L	F
11	F	F	L	F	F	L	F	L	F	F	F	F	F	F	F	L	F
12	F	L	L	F	F	L	F	L	F	F	F	F	F	F	F	L	F
13	L	F	F	L	F	F	L	L	F	L	F	F	F	F	F	L	F
14	L	F	L	F	F	L	L	F	F	L	L	L	F	F	F	F	F
15	F	L	L	F	F	F	L	L	F	L	F	F	F	F	F	L	F
16	F	F	P	F	F	F	L	L	F	P	F	F	F	F	L	L	F
17	F	F	F	F	F	L	F	F	F	F	L	L	F	F	F	F	L
18	F	F	F	F	F	L	F	F	F	F	F	F	F	F	F	F	F
19	F	L	L	F	F	F	F	L	L	F	F	F	F	F	F	L	L
20	F	F	L	F	F	F	F	F	F	L	F	F	F	F	F	F	F
21	N	N	N	N	N	P	P	P	P	N	N	N	P	P	P	P	P
22	P	P	P	N	P	P	L	L	L	N	P	L	P	L	L	L	L
23	P	P	P	L	P	P	P	F	F	P	P	P	P	F	F	P	P
24	P	L	F	F	P	P	P	L	L	P	P	P	F	F	F	P	P
25	P	L	F	F	L	P	F	F	F	L	L	P	F	F	F	L	L
26	F	F	L	F	F	L	L	F	L	F	F	F	F	L	L	F	L
27	F	L	P	L	L	L	P	L	P	P	L	F	F	P	L	L	P

Then, if the percentage of performance of a certain BP is evaluated for instance as 70 %, the rating to be assigned to that BP is L, if the percentage of performance is evaluated as 25 % the rating is P, and so on.

In order to substitute values with numbers, we consider the middle value of each percentage range and we substitute it to the correspondent N-P-L-F value. According to this mechanism, the N rating will be substituted with the value 0,075 (7,5 %), P with 0,33 (33 %), L with 0,66 (66 %), and F with 0,925 (92,5 %).

Because of this it is possible to calculate the average value of the ratings of each BP in the sample of this study. The average values are represented in graphical format in Fig. 3.

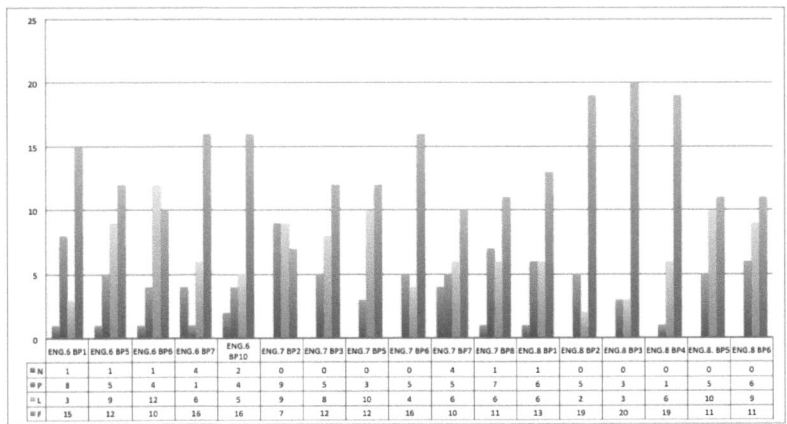

Fig. 2. Graphical representation of base practice ratings

Table 3. Ratings correspondence

Performance percentage range	0 %–15 %	16 %–50 %	51 %–85 %	86 %–100 %
Rating value	N	P	L	F

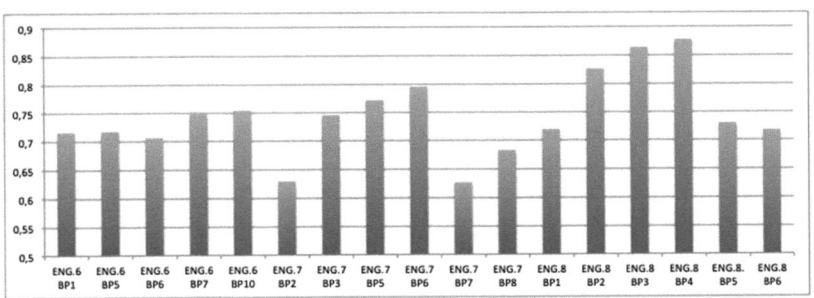

Fig. 3. Average ratings of base practices

5 Study Data Analysis

A characteristic of the set of processes related to software testing in the Automotive SPICE PRM is that they contains BPs with similarities. In particular, we can notice that the BPs of these processes can be grouped onto 6 clusters. Each cluster is composed of practices addressing the same topic, but in the context of a different process. In other words, some practices (e.g. defining testing strategy) are replicated in different process, but in each of them, a practice is defined taking into account the specific characteristics of the process it belongs to. The clusters that can be identified are:

C1 Definition of testing strategy it contains ENG.6.BP1, ENG.7.BP2, and ENG.8.BP.1
C2 Specification of Test Cases it contains ENG.6.BP5, ENG.7.BP3, and ENG.8.BP.2
C3 Execution of Test Cases it contains ENG.6.BP6, ENG.7.BP5, and ENG.8.BP.3
C4 Reporting of Test Cases results it contains ENG.6.BP7 for unit testing, ENG.7.BP6, and ENG.8.BP.3
C5 Bilateral traceability of Test Cases it contains ENG.6.BP10 for unit testing, ENG.7.BP7, and ENG.8.BP.5

According to the specific process, the test cases are requested to be traced with respect different items (test cases vs. software units in the case of ENG.6 process, test cases vs. software design elements in the case of ENG.7 process, and test cases vs. software requirements in the case of ENG.8 process.

C6 - Definition and application of a regression test strategy: it contains ENG.7.BP8 and ENG.8.BP.6. No regression strategy is required for the ENG.6 process.

Interesting outcomes can be derived by aggregating the BP belonging to the same cluster and by calculating the mean value of the ratings. The results are represented in graphical format in Fig. 4.

It can be noticed that the mean values of the rating of the C.1, C.5, and C6 are significantly lower than those of the other clusters. It indicates that the performance of the practices belonging to these clusters is weaker for the organizations in the study sample.

In order to make such an analysis more sophisticated, we are interested in understanding whether the ratings of the BPs belonging to the six clusters C.1 - C.6 are homogenous or not. To do that, we applied non-parametric tests, used for data measured by ordinal scale. The null hypothesis was that there are no differences among the 3 detected BPs (or 2 for Regression Testing), and then the median scores for the three variables are equal.

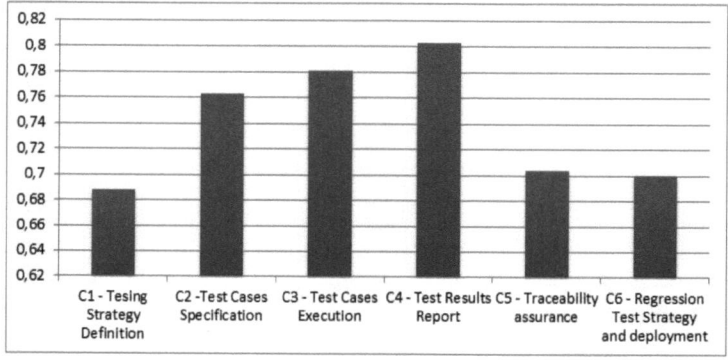

Fig. 4. Average ratings by base practices clusters

The alternative hypothesis was that at least one of the variables differs from at least one of the others and then there was a significant difference among the variables. Among the non parametric tests, the Friedman Test [7] has been used for the groups with three variables, and the Wilcoxon Test [7] for the group with two variables, that is Regression Testing. It was chosen a single significance level $\alpha = 0,01$ for the six groups, and then the null hypothesis has been rejected at this level. Data of the application of these Tests techniques are reported in Tables 4 and 5.

Table 4. Friedman test results

Test strategy definition		Test cases specification		Test cases execution		Test results record		Traceability	
BP	Mean rating	BP	Mean rating	BP	Mean rating	BP	Mean rating	BP	Mean rating
ENG.6 BP.1	2,14	ENG.6 BP.5	1,80	ENG.6 BP.6	1,68	ENG.6 BP.7	1,82	ENG.6 BP.7	1,82
ENG.7 BP.2	1,7	ENG.7 BP.3	1,94	ENG.7 BP.5	1,96	ENG.7 BP.6	1,96	ENG.7 BP.6	1,96
ENG.8 BP.1	2,16	ENG.8 BP.2	2,26	ENG.8 BP.3	2,36	ENG.8 BP.4	2,22	ENG.8 BP.4	2,22
Friedman test		Friedman test		Friedman test		Friedman test		Friedman test	
N	25	N	25	N	25	N	25	N	25
Chi-square	8,450	Chi-square	5,451	Chi-square	10,618	Chi-square	5,024	Chi-square	5,024
Df	2	Df	2	Df	2	Df	2	Df	2
Asymp. Sig.	0,015	Asymp. Sig.	0,066	Asymp. Sig.	0,005	Asymp. Sig.	0,081	Asymp. Sig.	0,081

According to the results reported in Tables 4 and 5, the only cluster containing BPs having ratings not homogeneous (i.e. with significant variability among them) is the Test Execution.

Table 5. Wilcoxon test results

		N	Mean rank	Sum of ranks
ENG.8.BP.6 – ENG.7.BP8	Native ranks	3	5,00	15,00
	Positive rank	6	5,00	30,00
	Ties	16		
	Total	25		

6 Conclusions

This paper presents an empirical study aimed at identifying and discussing possible recurrent weak and strong areas in the overall software testing process in automotive. The study has been carried out using data from Automotive SPICE assessment performed using real data from real software development project.

The results of the study, reported in detail, can be summarized as follows:

- The overall software testing process is addressed by three different processes in Automotive SPICE process reference model: Software Unit Testing, Software Integration and Test, and Software Testing processes. The Base Practices addressing software testing-related aspect are in total 17. It has been noticed that these Base Practices can be clustered by the testing activity they refer to. In total 6 clusters have been identified. Each cluster contains Base Practices that address the same kind of activity but deployed in one of the 3 processes.

- The first result of the study shows that the ratings of the Base Practices are not homogeneous. Some Base Practices are weaker than others. In particular, the average rating of the Base Practices ENG.7.BP.2 (Software Integration Test Strategy Definition), ENG.7.BP.7 (Bilateral traceability of software architectural design and software detailed design to software integration test specification) is the lowest. On the contrary, the Base Practices ENG.8.BP.4 (Record the results of software testing) and ENG.8.BP.4 (Verify integrated software) are those with highest ratings. This is in-line with the authors' experience. In fact, the software testing against the software requirements (addressed by the ENG.8 Software Testing process in Automotive SPICE) is often the most rigorous testing phase in automotive software development projects, while the software integration testing (i.e. the testing aimed at verifying the internal and external interfaces of software), that in Automotive SPICE is addressed by the ENG.7 Software Integration and Test process, is often poorly performed and documented.
- The second interesting result is the evidence about the average ratings achieved by the Base Practices clustered by testing-related activity. Data show that Testing Strategy Definition, Regression Test Strategy definition and deployment, and Traceability assurance are weaker that the other three clusters (i.e. Software Test Cases specification, Test Cases execution, and Test Results reporting). Again this is a confirmation of the authors' experience. In fact, while Testing is actually performed on the basis of documented test cases and the related results are reported, what is often not enough clearly defined and documented is the test strategy (inclusive of regression test strategy) to be followed; moreover the traceability often is not guaranteed to be complete. Statistic investigation on the available data of this study shown that the ratings of the Base Practices belonging to the six clusters are all homogeneous but those related to the Test Cases Execution Cluster, in that case there is a significant difference between the ratings of Test Cases Execution in Software Testing and in Unit Testing: the Test Cases Execution in the case of Unit Testing is significantly weaker than Test Case Execution in the case of Software Integration Test.

The study relies on a data taken from Automotive SPICE process assessments performed by the authors on a sample of 27 companies worldwide in the last five years. These data include evidences collected during the assessments related to procedures, work products, tools, software product characteristics, quality and management indicators. Although the average number of processes belonging to the scope of the assessments in the study sample is 13, this paper focuses on the three specific processes of Automotive SPICE addressing software Testing.

The principal originality of this study is the use of real data from real software development projects in automotive. In literature the empirical studies addressing similar topics are mainly based on literature reviews and surveys made by means of questionnaires.

The results of this study can represent a contribution in the identification of the most critical practices in automotive software development projects and can represent both a benchmark for automotive software players and a starting point for setting up process improvement initiatives.

The authors' aim is to continue this study by extending the analysis to the other processes available in the data sample and investigating possible correlations among BPs. The sample will be used also to find out possible characterizations of the weaknesses in terms of company size, the geographical location and the specific product domain.

ANNEX A

See Table 6.

Table 6. Study sample description

OU id.	Product domain	OU size	Project team size	Company size	Location	Gap an.- assessm.	Year scope
1	Body electronics	10	7		Italy	YY	2013 ENG.4, ENG.5, ENG.6, ENG.8, MAN.3, SUP.1, SUP.8, SUP.9, SUP.10 (CL2)
2	Infotainment & telematics	27	12		China	NY	2014 ENG.2, ENG.3, ENG.4, ENG.5, ENG.6, ENG.7, ENG.8, ENG.9, ENG.10, MAN.3, MAN.5, MAN.6, SUP.1, SUP.8, SUP.9, SUP.10 (CL2)
3	Electric vehicle control	1000	15		South Korea	YY	2014 ENG.2, ENG.3, ENG.4, ENG.5, ENG.6, ENG.7, ENG.8, ENG.,9, ENG.10, MAN.3, SUP.1, SUP.8, SUP.9, SUP.10 (CL2)
4	Electric vehicle control	18	15		South Korea	YY	2014 ENG.2, ENG.3, ENG.4, ENG.5, ENG.6, ENG.7, ENG.8, ENG.9, ENG.10, MAN.3, SUP.8, SUP.10 (CL2)
5	Electric steering	10	5		Italy	YN	2014 ACQ.4, ENG.1, ENG.2, ENG.3, ENG.4, ENG.5, ENG.6, MAN.3, MAN.5, SUP.1, SUP.4, SUP.8, SUP.9, SUP.10, SPL.2 (CL2)
6	Body electronics	5	5		Italy	NY	2013 ENG.1, ENG.2, ENG.3, ENG.4, ENG.5, ENG.6, ENG.7, ENG.8, ENG.,9, MAN.3, MAN.5, SUP.1, SUP.4, SUP.8, SPL.2 (CL2)
7	Body electronics	31	12		Italy	NY	2012 ACQ.4, ENG.1, ENG.2, ENG.3, ENG.4, ENG.5, ENG.6, ENG.7, ENG.8, ENG.9, ENG.10, MAN.3, MAN.5, SUP.1, SUP.8, SUP.9, SUP.10 (CL2)
8	Cooling fan	10	8		Italy	YN	2011 ENG.2, ENG.3, ENG.4, ENG.5, ENG.6, ENG.7, ENG.8, ENG.,9, ENG.10, MAN.3, SUP.1, SUP.8, SUP.9, SUP.10 (CL2)
9	Motor control	15	10		Italy	YN	2011 ENG.2, ENG.3, ENG.4, ENG.5, ENG.6, ENG.7, ENG.8, ENG.,9, ENG.10, MAN.3, SUP.1, SUP.8, SUP.9, SUP.10 (CL2)

(*Continued*)

Table 6. (*Continued*)

OU id.	Product domain	OU size	Project team size	Company size	Location	Gap an.-assessm.	Year scope
10	Cooling fan	10	9		Italy	YY	2013-2014 ENG.2, ENG.3, ENG.4, ENG.5, ENG.6, ENG.7, ENG.8, ENG.,9, ENG.10, MAN.3, SUP.1, SUP.8, SUP.9, SUP.10 (CL2)
11	Lighting control	10	6		Italy	YY	2013-2014 ENG.2, ENG.3, ENG.4, ENG.5, ENG.6, ENG.7, ENG.8, ENG.,9, ENG.10, MAN.3, SUP.1, SUP.8, SUP.9, SUP.10 (CL3)
12	Window lift	50+	10		China	YY	2014 ENG.2, ENG.3, ENG.4, ENG.5, ENG.6, ENG.7, ENG.8, ENG.,9, ENG.10, MAN.3, SUP.1, SUP.8, SUP.9, SUP.10 (CL2)
13	Driving assistance	100+	20+		Israel	NY	2013 ENG.2, ENG.3, ENG.4, ENG.5, ENG.6, ENG.7, ENG.8, ENG.,9, ENG.10, MAN.3, SUP.1, SUP.8, SUP.9, SUP.10 (CL2)
14	Closures	10	7		Italy	NY	2013 ENG.2, ENG.3, ENG.4, ENG.5, ENG.6, ENG.7, ENG.8, ENG.,9, ENG.10, MAN.3, MAN.5, MAN.6, SUP.1, SUP.8, SUP.9, SUP.10 (CL2)
15	Electric pumps	10	7		Italy	YY	2013 ENG.2, ENG.3, ENG.4, ENG.5, ENG.6, ENG.7, ENG.8, ENG.,9, ENG.10, MAN.3, SUP.1, SUP.8, SUP.9, SUP.10 (CL2)
16	Cooling fan	5	5		Italy	YY	2012 ENG.2, ENG.3, ENG.4, ENG.5, ENG.6, ENG.7, ENG.8, ENG.,9, ENG.10, MAN.3, MAN.5, MAN.6, SUP.1, SUP.8, SUP.9, SUP.10 (CL2)
17	Instrument cluster	6	7		Italy	NY	2011 ENG.2, ENG.3, ENG.4, ENG.5, ENG.6, ENG.7, ENG.8, ENG.,9, ENG.10, MAN.3, SUP.1, SUP.8, SUP.9, SUP.10 (CL2)
18	Body electronics	20	7		Italy	NY	2012 ENG.2, ENG.3, ENG.4, ENG.5, ENG.6,, ENG.7, ENG.8,, ENG.9, ENG.10, SUP.1, SUP.8, SUP.9, SUP.10, MAN.3 (CL3)
19	Window lift	5	4		Italy	YY	2012 ENG.4, ENG.5, ENG.6, ENG.7, ENG.8 (CL2)
20	Electric vehicle Control	20	8		Italy	YY	2010-2012 ENG.2, ENG.3, ENG.4, ENG.5, ENG.6, ENG.7, ENG.8, ENG.,9, ENG.10, MAN.3, SUP.1, SUP.8, SUP.9, SUP.10 (CL2)
21	Instrument Cluster	10	5		Italy	YN	2010 MAN.3, SUP.1, SUP.8, SUP.9, SUP.10, ENG.4, ENG.5, ENG.6, ENG.7, ENG.8 (CL1)
22	Electric vehicle Control	10	6		Italy	YN	2010 ENG.2, ENG.3, ENG.4, ENG.5, ENG.6, ENG.7, ENG.8, ENG.,9, ENG.10, MAN.3, SUP.1, SUP.8, SUP.9, SUP.10 (CL1)
23	Body electronics	50	8		Italy	YN	2015 ENG.1, ENG.4, ENG.5, ENG.6, ENG.7, ENG.8, MAN.3, MAN.5, MAN.6, SUP.1, SUP.4, SUP.8, SUP.9, SUP.10 (CL2)
24	Infotainment & Telematics	60	10		Italy	YN	2015 ENG.1, ENG.2, ENG.4, ENG.5, ENG.6, ENG.7, ENG.8, MAN.3, MAN.5, MAN.6, SUP.1, SUP.4, SUP.8, SUP.9, SUP.10, SPL.2 (CL2)
25	Body electronics	6	4		Italy	YN	2015 ENG.4, ENG.5, ENG.6, ENG.7, ENG.8, MAN.3, SUP.1, SUP.8, SUP.9, SUP.10 (CL2)

(*Continued*)

Table 6. (*Continued*)

OU id.	Product domain	OU size	Project team size	Company size	Location	Gap an. - assessm.	Year scope
26	HVAC	10	50		Italy	YN	2015 ENG.4, ENG.5, ENG.6, ENG.7, ENG.8, MAN.3, SUP.1, SUP.8, SUP.9, SUP.10 (CL2)
27	Vehicle Control	30	1000+		Italy	YY	2015 ENG.4, ENG.5, ENG.6, ENG.7, ENG.8, MAN.3, SUP.1, SUP.8, SUP.9, SUP.10 (CL2)

References

1. Automotive SPICE, Process Assessment Model (PAM) v2.5 (2010)
2. Automotive SPICE, Process Reference Model (PRM) v4.5 (2010)
3. ISO/IEC 33000 – Information Technology – Process Assessment, International Organization for Standardization (2013)
4. Hoermann, K., Mueller, M., Dittman, L., Zimmer, J.: Automotive SPICE in Practice: Surviving Implementation and Assessment. Rocky Noor, Santa Barbara (2008). ISBN 978-1933952291
5. Fabbrini, F., Fusani, M., Lami, G., Sivera, E.: A SPICE-based supplier qualification mechanism in automotive industry. Softw. Process Improv. Pract. J. **12**, 523–528 (2007). Wiley InterScience
6. www.intacs.info
7. Hollander, M., Wolfe, D.A., Chicken, E.: Nonparametric Statistical Methods. John Wiley & Sons, Hoboken (2014)
8. ISO 26262 - Road Vehicles - Functional Safety, International Organization for Standardization (2011)
9. Niazi, M., Wilson, D., Zowghi, D.: Critical success factors for software improvement implementation: an empirical study. Softw. Process Improv. Pract. **11**, 193–211 (2006). Wiley InterScience
10. Niazi, M., Ali Babar, M., Verner, J.M.: Software process improvement barriers: a cross-cultural comparison. Inf. Softw. Technol. **52**, 1204–1216 (2010). Elsevier
11. Hall, T., Rainer, A., Baddoo, N.: Implementing software process improvement: an empirical study. Softw. Process Improv. Pract. **7**, 3–15 (2002). Wiley InterScience
12. Kan, S.H.: Metrics and Models in Software Quality Engineering. Addison-Wesley Longman Publication, Boston (2002)
13. Benjamini, Y.: Opening the box of a boxplot. Am. Stat. **42**(4), 257–262 (1988)
14. Biscoglio, I., Falcini, F., Lami, G.: Investigation on common software process weaknesses in automotive. In: ACM/IEEE International Symposium on Empirical Software Engineering and Measurement (ESEM), Beijing (China) 22–23 October 2015, pp. 1–8. IEEE (2015)

Empirically Derived Recommendations for Personalised Text-Based Technical Support

Solomon Gizaw[1(✉)], Jim Buckley[2], and Sarah Beecham[1]

[1] Lero - The Irish Software Research Centre,
University of Limerick, Limerick, Ireland
Solomon.gizaw@ul.ie, Sarah.Beecham@lero.ie
[2] CSIS – Department of Computer Science and Information Systems,
Lero - The Irish Software Research Centre,
University of Limerick, Limerick, Ireland
Jim.Buckley@ul.ie

Abstract. Technical Support (TS) is a post sales service provided to users of Information Technology (IT) products. Effective customer support can increase an IT company's revenue, improve the quality of their software, build customer loyalty, and enhance their reputation. However, not all companies realise these benefits as many customers and users are choosing alternative forms of support such as open source non-proprietary support forums.

This paper posits that this movement to forums is because of a perceived improvement in service levels and thus presents a study of empirically-derived practices for Technical Support (TS) from these forums. In this analysis we identified types of users (personas) and grouped them according to levels of expertise and what they value. Additionally we identified characteristics of the communication handling process that influence desirable and undesirable outcomes. Focussing solely on text based support, we present ways that TS advisors can identify user types and, having identified the user type, how to tailor their response accordingly. Finally, we also indicate how ignoring user-types or through inappropriate handling of a question, the TS advisor/user interaction can fail.

Keywords: Information technology · Technical support · User characteristics · Online technical support forums · Individualisation · Human factors · Grounded theory

1 Introduction

There is some evidence to suggest that companies are failing in their efforts to provide effective TS, as users are ignoring what these companies offer in terms of user documentation, FAQs, chat, call centers, email and websites. They seek out alternative sources of help in the form of community forums where they appear to be better supported [1–3].

The literature indicates that, to achieve a much better user experience, TS should consider the individual characteristics of the user [4–8]. The current trend where user characteristics are poorly defined has proven to be unreliable, not repeatable, and inconsistent. A review of the literature suggests that a core problem is the neglect of user characterisation in TS, where, at best, a user's characteristics are captured in an ad hoc fashion [7, 9, 10]. This is somewhat surprising given that the user experience can be enhanced by channeling support to meet the user's individual needs [2, 3, 9]: Providing personalised response to each user is an effective user-satisfaction strategy [11]. The literature shows that personalised value-added services can meet users' requests at a deeper level than that of traditional TS services by providing accurate information and processing the information to satisfy user requirements [7]. Wang et al. [12] suggests that successful communication with users can even reduce software failure rates and produce better versions of the application [12].

In our research we aim to empirically derive and evaluate characteristics of users in order to determine prevalent user attributes, which can enhance the process of implementing personalised TS. Empirically derived personalised attributes could reinforce our current understanding of how to characterise users and, by taking a more inductive approach, may possibly provide novel perspectives and new work-practices that may in turn improve TS. Furthermore, we aim to validate the empirically identified characteristics in a survey with a group of TS advisors and TS users. Without such empirically grounded characterisation efforts to personalise TS practices may be misguided.

This paper presents empirically-derived recommendations for personalised text-based Technical Support (TS) as drawn from an analysis of TS online forums. We collected threads (messages) from each forum and using a grounded theory approach to identify successful and unsuccessful practices of TS services. The work we report here is based on data collected from one hundred and sixteen threads (3,064 messages) from eight online open source forums. We focused our findings on personalised TS practices that are shown satisfy user requirements. Our results aim to allow commercial organisations (and other interested parties) identify types of users and how successful tailored practices address their needs. Additionally we present lessons learned, and practices to avoid, that are likely to lead to unsuccessful outcomes where the user/TS advisor interaction breaks down before offering a solution to a given problem.

Consequently, we present ten empirically-derived recommendations for a personalised TS communication handling process. A higher level more encompassing description of Perso*nalisation* In Practice is described in Gizaw et al. [13]. In this paper, we describe the detailed successful and unsuccessful practices of personalised TS services that identify TS users according to groups of characteristics and suggest resultant work practices. To empirically-derive the recommendations we investigate the successful and unsuccessful threads in a forum with the following research question:

Research question one: What are the scenarios in TS that satisfy user requirements?
Research question two: How can the observed scenarios be used to more effectively construct TS systems for improved personalised TS services?
Research question three: What can we learn from the unsuccessful scenarios in TS?

This study is organised as follows: Sect. 2 describes the grounded theory method that underpins this study. Section 3 presents the results, where the user characteristics are categorised, and the associated work-practice recommendations. In Sect. 4 the limitations of the study are stated, and finally Sect. 5 concludes and summarizes this study.

2 Method

The purpose of this study is to inductively generate theory to gain a deeper understanding of the interaction of individuals in the context of TS forums. Adopting an inductive, qualitative approach, we generate theory to inform a framework for how user characteristics and the associated communication handling process affect the outcome of TS advisor/user interaction. Threads from TS forums are analyzed to understand communication patterns, and what people understand about a given issue when using text-based communication. In this way we elicit information on how people can be grouped together in a comprehensible and manageable way.

The research method is shown in Fig. 1. The methodology is iterative whereby we continue to investigate the phenomena until tending to saturation (i.e. where, after several analyses of the data, no new themes emerged [14]. Theoretical sensitivity was gained by literature reviews on Personalisation and Technical Support, which provided conceptual clarity of concepts that might be relevant to guide the research. It is the ability to see relevant data and to reflect upon the empirical data material with the help of theoretical terms [14]. To achieve this, the study uses existing related literature on personalisation to elicit information on how users can be modeled and grouped together [2, 3, 15]. The literature was also applied *ex post facto* to place the derived user characteristics with the context of the wider literature on human factors [14].

2.1 Grounded Theory Method

A qualitative grounded theory approach is adopted, as specified by Strauss and Corbin [14], to developing a theory (or framework) that specifically informs company-based TS systems and actors. The main distinguishing features of the Grounded Theory

	Theoretical Sensitivity	Data Collection And Analysis	Characteristics Refinement	Framework Refinement
Input/Data	Literature on: Personalisation Technical Support	Forum Threads	Categories: Characteristics of emergent concepts	Validated Categories
Method	Straussian Grounded Theory: Conceptualisation	Grounded Theory: Theoretical Sampling Constant Comparison	Cohen's Kappa Inter-rater reliability testing	Grounded Theory: Theoretical Sorting
Process	Conduct LR on: Personalisation Technical Support	Axial Coding / Data Collection / Open Coding	Refine / Agreement Level / Disagreement	Theory practice Integration Selective Coding Diagramming
Output	Goal Defined: TS Attributes of Personalisation	Categories: characteristics of emerged concepts Theoretical Saturation	Validated Code	Substantive Theory Framework
Rationale	Identify the gap Define RQs	Identify Concepts (Codes) Address RQs	Reduce Subjectivity Check Agreement	Validate Findings Refine Theory

Fig. 1. The research method

Method (GTM) include the continuous undertaking of theoretical sensitivity, data collection, coding and analysis, memo-ing, sorting and constant comparison, theoretical sampling, and theoretical saturation [14].

2.2 Data Collection and Sampling

TS forums are selected as a data source primarily because:

- Forums provide a naturally occurring data set that reflects the perspectives of real world users, and a higher possibility of uncovering good practice [2, 3, 15].
- Ralph and Parsons [16], in their conclusion suggest that many information sources such as user message posts to online forums have not been well-exploited for personalisation and those forums might be rich resources of data to mine towards characterisation of personalisation attributes.

In accordance with Strauss and Corbin's [14] Theoretical Sampling (Purpose Sampling) method, we started data collection with an initial sampling and the rest of the data collected iteratively, guided by the emerging theory. The dataset for the research was collected in three rounds until it tended towards theoretical saturation. Table 2 shows the total dataset collected in three iterations. The first dataset was selected by an initial sampling of TS forums based on a Google search using the search string: "IT Technical Support forums." Frequently used forums were selected (Table 1, forums 1-6). The sampling method was purposive, where the remaining two forums (7 and 8) were selected by looking for more diversified domains in terms of users' broader level of expertise. In the first six initial forums novice users were under represented. Therefore subsequent iterations focused on less technical domains, where novice users were better represented, in order to create a more balanced dataset.

Table 1. The eight TS forums used in the study

	Tech support [1]	Tech guy [2]	Computing [3]	Cybertech help [4]	Daniweb [5]	5star support [6]	PC help [7]	Technical assistance [8]
Number of threads	22	25	19	5	7	6	17	15
Number of messages	638	729	516	190	231	109	445	206

The eight technical support forums as shown in Table 2 are selected due to their support for many diversified IT domains in terms of level of expertise, bearing in mind more interaction patterns can be found and different user characteristics can be identified. In total 116 threads were collected within the three iterations; 3064 messages were found within these 116 threads.

Table 2. Dataset sampling

Dataset	Description	# Forums	# Threads	# Messages	# Messages per Thread
1	Exploratory sample	6/8	40	747	1-54 (range)
2	Focussed set	8/8	61	1217	1-87 (range)
3	Long interactive threads	8/8	15	1100	51-127 (range)
Total		8	**116**	**3064**	**1-127 (range)**

2.3 Data Analysis

According to the GTM of Strauss and Corbin [14] data interpretation involves three stages of coding: *open coding* to discover categories, *axial coding* to further develop and relate the categories and finally *selective coding* to integrate and refine the theory. The three coding techniques are not necessarily sequential analytic steps. For example, open and axial coding overlapped in this study and were iterative, as categories were developed and refined. In addition, axial and selective coding overlapped as categories were related and integrated into an explanatory theory.

In this research *open coding* began with the first thread and a message-by-message analysis. The purpose of open coding was to identify codes in the data and to begin to discover categories and their properties and dimensions [14]. Table 3 presents an example of open coding that began with a simple interpretation of each message that summarises the underlying concept (shown by the square bracketed text). For instance line 072 is coded as "**Problem of users not stating the question properly**". Consequently a memo about the concept is created as shown in line 073. We used the scientific software program called "Atlas.ti" version 6.2 to manage and analyse the textual data. The tool also helped to connect and visualize files as well as index the data.

Table 3. Open coding examples

Line	Text and [open code]
072	"Had you explained what your reason was we could have advised you sooner". [**Problem of users not stating the question properly**]
073	**Memo**: *The TS advisor reminded the user it would have been better to state the question and reason in the first place*
078	"I think this poster is not reading the answers" **Memo**: *Prior discussion shows the user has low level experience*
080	"It's hard to soar like an Eagle when you are flying with Turkeys" [**Novice User**] [**Insulting**]

After identifying categories through the open coding process, the next step is an intermediary coding process known as *axial coding* [14]. In axial coding, concepts are sorted, synthesised and reassembled. Each emerged concept is grouped into a new set of categories that represent the ideas. Strauss and Corbin [14] define a *property* as a general or specific characteristic of a category and a *dimension* as a location of a property along a continuum or range. For example, 'credibility', is one of the categories identified as something that is important to a user in this study. It has a dimension ranging from trust to mistrust. A property of 'credibility' is the differentiator *cause*, where credibility can be 'caused' by the product, the vendor, TS advisor, the instruction, the consequences of executing the instruction, or the software that diagnoses the problem.

Selective coding is the final coding process in GTM, and involves the selection of core categories of the data. *Selective coding* systematically relates the categories identified in axial coding, and integrates and refines them to derive theoretical concepts. This is achieved according to a coding framework that captures the phenomenon in terms of context, causal conditions, intervening conditions, action/interaction and consequences. The *context* captures the environment within which decisions and actions take place; the *causal and intervening conditions* reflect the why, when, how come, and where the phenomenon occurs; these culminate in a portrayal of *actions/interactions* of the people in response to what is happening in the situations (answers the questions 'by whom' and 'how'); and finally we consider the *consequences* of the action taken or inaction (answers what happen as a result of the actions/interactions).

After theoretical saturation, we conducted an inter-rater reliability test evaluation using Cohen's *kappa* [17]. Cohen's *kappa* inter-rater reliability test was performed using IMB SPSS version 20.0. A researcher coded 103 selected indicators to validate the first author's interpretation and findings. Initial results produced an inter-rater agreement of 0.673 k value, but subsequent discussions between the 'raters' led to the refinements of some category definitions. A further independent inter-rater test was performed which achieved a 75 % agreement which according to Landis and Koch is a "substantial agreement".

3 Results

3.1 Categories

Emergent concepts are categorised according to their properties and dimensions. These concepts are grouped into three main categories according to similar characteristics as outlined in Table 4:

- User characteristics: further decomposed to level of expertise and user values.
- Communication process: further decomposed to activity and emotions.
- Outcomes: further decomposed to successful and unsuccessful.

Table 4 shows the occurrence of each concept, category and the frequency counts of each attribute that occurred during the process of coding. Categories are explored in context with interactions that occurred in the 8 forums, and quotes from either a user or a TS advisor are given in italics and *"double quotes"* to act as exemplars of how concepts emerged.

Table 4. Ranked list of categories

Core Category	Category	Concept	Number of occurrence
1. User characteristics	1.1 Level of expertise	*Novice*	47
		Intermediate	11
		Experienced	16
	1.2 User Values	*Loyalty*	24
		Value for Money	27
		Credibility	26
		Security	10
2. Communication process	2.1 Activity	*Emphasis*	50
		Procedure	18
	2.2 Communication Issues	*Misinformation*	9
		Misunderstanding	22
		Confusion	12
	2.3 Technical issues	*Multi-Component*	22
	2.4 Emotions	*Frustration*	18
		Anger	12
3. Outcomes	3.1 Successful	*Satisfaction*	141
	3.2 Unsuccessful	*Insult*	5
		Frustration	10
		Anger	9

There were different outcomes for the TS forum threads, with some ending up as '*successful*' 72 threads, others as '*unsuccessful*' 17 threads as shown in Table 5. The remaining ones were those that were labeled as 'unknown' 27 threads. A successful outcome is a practice where the user's question is answered to their satisfaction e.g. "*Yep, seems to have fixed it. Thanks*" and where a good communication handling process occurred, e.g. "*Thanks for your help and response*". An unsuccessful outcome is a practice where the user's question is not answered to their satisfaction e.g. "*It's starting to get on my nerves*", "*I think I need to take it to a tech because this is way over my head*".

From analysis of the interaction data it was observed that most of the threads that ended up with a status of "unknown" finished after the right information had been posted. So indirectly, it could be assumed that participants just did not acknowledge it, or had maybe left the forum before the response was posted. It seems that users will not always come back to the thread after they have solved their problem to inform TS advisors. Hence we can assume that most of the threads of status "unknown" can be considered as successfully ending threads. Despite this assumption, we only use the threads with known outcomes to build our theory since the explicit outcome of the interaction is important to increase confidence.

Table 5. Observed success rate

Successful		Unsuccessful		Total	
Observed	%	Observed	%	Observed	%
72	80.9	17	19.1	89	100

3.2 Successful and Unsuccessful Practices of TS Forums

The empirically-derived personalised recommendations provide explanation of user characteristics found in TS forums and communication handling process. Considering the research questions, Personа*lisation* In Practice was identified as the central phenomenon [13]. The term Personа*lisation* In Practice emerged from the data analysis to describe the many successful practices of the personalised communication handling process. This Personа*lisation* In Practice framework must be viewed in the context of content predilection and communication patterns that satisfy user requirements in a more targeted manner. But it should also encompass some of the unsuccessful practices that do not satisfy user requirements, and how these unsuccessful stories can be turned around to be successful.

Based on the successful and unsuccessful outcomes we now present ten recommendations with examples extracted from the empirical data, indicating how the empirically-derived practices might help improve the quality of TS through focusing on the communication flow observed within TS forums. These practices, while providing only a small set of examples, can provide important insights into how user profiling and communication handling in TS forums can impact on success.

P1: Establish and handle user's *level of expertise*.

P1.1 Establish user level of expertise: TS advisors can establish a user's *level of expertise* by noticing their explicitly-stated user *level of expertise* or analysing the implicit performance of users' diagnosis processes. As a result, users' *level of expertise* can be described in three ranges:

- *Experienced*: - A user who is skillful or knowledgeable as shown through extensive contact, participation or observation. Experience is exposed either implicitly, for example, through the painstaking steps the user has taken in order to diagnose the problem (E.g. *"Here is what I did so far to troubleshoot problem"*) or explicitly through mentioning or categorising themselves as experienced, knowledgeable, expert (E.g. *"I work as (technical) support professional"*).
- *Intermediate*: - A user who is not familiar with a given domain but displays skills in using different software applications. An intermediate participant is exposed implicitly through the practical steps they have taken in order to diagnose the problem while explicitly pointing out their lack of experience on a specific domain.
- *Novice*: - A user who is new or inexperienced in a certain task or situation. Typically a novice user explicitly mentions or categorises themselves as a novice (E.g. *"IT HAS BEEN YEARS SINCE I HAVE TAKEN A COMPUTER CLASS AND I AM LEARNING"*).

Establishing a user's level *of expertise* seems to be an important aspect of the TS-forum service. For example, out of the total of 89 *'successful'* and *'unsuccessful'* threads users either explicitly or implicitly describe their *level of expertise* in 74 threads. Among these threads the *'successful'* rate is 81 % and *'unsuccessful'* rate is 19 %. In episodes where the TS advisor did not capture user *level of expertise* the thread frequently ended in confusion, misinformation and misunderstanding: This happened 53 % of the time.

P1.2 Handle user *level of expertise*: The empirical data suggest that being able to gauge the level of the user's expertise greatly influences the personalised communication handling process that will prompt a successful outcome. For example, of the 47 threads where the user declared themselves as novices, the TS advisor tended to provide *procedural instructions (a fixed step-by-step sequence of activities)* (74.5 % of the time - 35 threads). Of these 35 threads that were answered procedurally, 31 had *'successful'* outcomes with, on average, 5 messages per thread. This is a high success rate, over a short message span, suggesting that *procedural instructions* suit *novice* users. In contrast, the 12 novice queries that were not answered procedurally had a success rate of 33.3 % and took, on average, 10 messages to reach a conclusion. This, allied with the comments of some of the novice users when not provided with procedural instruction, re-enforces the impression that procedural instruction may suit novice users: *"WHAT THE < Abusive Word > IS GOING ON?*[1]*", "You seem to think that everyone thinks as you, well, < NAME > we don't GO AND PLAY WITH YOUR TOY!!!!!"*

On the other hand, when it becomes clear that the user has a high level of expertise different handling patterns are observed. The TS advisor enquires as to the diagnostics performed by the user and provides a greater proportion of *declarative answers (stating only facts)*, and providing *procedural* answers only 50 % of the time (in contrast to the 74.5 % associated with *novice* users). Of the 16 threads where the user declared themselves as experienced, 8 were handled *declaratively* and they had a 62.5 % success rate, and only 31 % of the threads were above 10 messages long whereas 8 were handled procedurally and they only had a 50 % success rate. However, not considering the *level of expertise* of the user has a big influence on the flow of the communication handling process and the consequences of the results.

P2: Provide different options with regard to the affordability of the service to the user

In TS forums, users often mention the *affordability* of the product. The *affordability* of the service which users' request are: **Free**: *"I want a free one"*; **Cheap**: *"I'll find one cheap enough"*; and surprisingly **Costly**: *"I'm looking for PAID PRODUCT – not free"*. Here they are typically looking for additional services like a warranty. In the case of users first ask about the *affordability* of the service the success rate is 99.3 % out of 27 occurrences of *affordability*. The empirical data shows that TS advisors sometimes provide different options regardless the user asks about the affordability: **Free**: *"You*

---

[1] The use of capitalisation is taken directly from the forums, in this context suggests anger, as a textural form of shouting.

can try many commercial cleaners with no cost and there are totally free available too." and **Costly**: "*There are good and paid alternatives out there*". In this case where user has got different options regarding affordability of the service ended in '*successful*' in 77.8 % of the threads. This shows the importance of different options with regards of the *affordability* of the service to the user.

P3: Manage third-party products
Usually TS advisors support only specific products and might not have detailed knowledge of other software which works together with the product. TS advisors may not be an expert in *third-party* software and drivers that are involved in the problem. The empirical data shows that TS advisors provide support for *third-party* software e.g. "*What happens if you try using < Name > or < Name > rather than the < Name > software? Personal experience suggests that you're better off using something other than the < Name > software, even with < Name>*"; "*<Name > wouldn't be a factor since neither < Name > or < Name > can use it.*" And "*You may want to try the < Name > manufactures diagnostic program. Check the manufactures web page for their diagnostic tools.*"

Not managing *third-party* software has a big impact for the successful communication handling process and problem solving. For example out of 22 occurrences where *third-party software* is involved in the problem, TS advisors recommend a solution over half results in '*successful*'. TS advisor sometimes asked for help with *third-party* software (software they are not directly familiar with) this will lead to variable outcomes. Although over half were '*successful*', TS advisor needs to be careful in a system where they are not familiar with the *third-party* software.

P4: Generate visually appealing material
According to the findings of this study, effective personalised TS requires spending sufficient time giving information and suggestions to users and increasing the clarity of information by generating visually appealing materials. TS advisors were found to use the practices *augmenting step-by-step instructions* and *signifying the main point of the instruction* to make the material more visually appealing:

P4.1 Augmenting Step-by-step procedural instruction: The empirical study shows that TS advisors often provide augmented by a bullet pointed or numbered *step-by-step* sequence of instruction that must be followed in the same order to correctly perform the task in order to solve the problem. TS advisors use *step-by-step* instruction for the following purposes: to explain the actions to take in solving the problem: "*Please follow these instructions*", "*follow these steps*"; to clarify each state-what else happened: "*Please post all of your hardware, giving as much detail as possible*". The successful and unsuccessful rates of augmenting step-by-step instruction are described in *P1.2 Handle user level of expertise practice*. The success rate for procedure provided to the user is 72.2 % out of 55 occurrences in threads. When providing instruction for the question asked, the TS advisor might, for example, explains the GUI of each step. The empirical study shows that TS advisor often includes a screenshot of each step of the instruction pointing out where the users take the next action.

P4.2 Signify the main point of the instruction: *Emphasis* is used to signify the main point of discussion. *Emphasis*, in this context, is defined as a stress laid on particular words, by means of position, repetition, or other indication; intensity or force of expression. Instructions that the user should follow were emphasised by bolding a word or phrase: *"Please read and follow all these instructions very carefully"* and changing the color: *"<--Very important Ensure you have...."* Or *"**Note: It is important..."* TS advisor also emphasis the text to remind a user to be careful as a cautionary reminder by: Upper case: *"I would advise you not to use ANYTHING"*. We found that 44.4 % of the emphases were 'to-do' instructions, 30 % were as a warning 'not-to-do' instructions 25 % were a reminder 'not-to-forget' instructions.

The evidence suggests that emphasising important parts of the instructions helps the user to follow the instruction accordingly. Among 88 occurrences where *emphasis* is used by TS advisor in their instruction threads ended *'successful'* in 78.4 %. Additionally the successful rate where *emphasis* was not used in the instruction is 50 %. This suggests that TS advisors need to use emphasis 'to-do' instructions, 'not-to-do' warning and 'not-to-forget' reminders using colors and upper cases in order to signify the main point of instruction.

P5: Prompt user to provide individual context
TS advisor should prompt the user to provide information regarding the steps they have tried and action taken to try to solve their problem; the tools used to diagnose the problem, and detailed information regarding what happened at each stage of the problem. In this study, a detailed clarification process preceded a successful outcome the majority of times. Unsuccessful outcomes were more frequently associated with queries where clarification was not sought. Out of all 89 threads, 53 had clarifications and 46 of these were *'successful'*. 36 threads did not have clarifications and only 26 threads were *'successful'*.

P6: Avoid premature response with respect to the problem context
This data suggests that TS advisors should be aware of trying to obtain full context before committing to a diagnosis or solution. In fact, in situations where a premature response was given by the TS advisor in general, the success rate was only 2 out of 12.

That is, the empirical data suggests that by-passing clarification doesn't prove very successful; the subsequent responses being premature and leading to misinformation. This is well illustrated by the frustrated comments of users to show that going to diagnosis stage without understanding the context of the question through clarification as the threads proceed: *"Just trying different fixes willy-nilly in hopes of resolving the problem is a waste of time and energy and more likely to make things worse than better"*. In some cases when the communication is unsuccessful, moderators may be involved in solving an argument between the user and TS advisor and helping resolve the actual problem leading to a successful conclusion.

P7: Establish privacy and security requirements of the user
The empirical data shows that users' *security* and *privacy* requirements are important factors in personalised communication in this context. This happened in ten threads out of 29. Usually users' show their concern about *security* by stating how much the

problem or the software used to diagnose the issue is free from risk or danger e.g. *"I was worried in case it could be some kind of virus that key logs the password"*. In response, TS advisors establish users' security concern and take different kinds of measures to protect users from risk or danger (e.g. *"That suggests to me that < NAME > might have a dodgy < NAME > setup."* and request the user to make sure whether the user has already taken the necessary measures to avoid the risks as a caution (e.g. *"Have you changed all your passwords for your online accounts to something more secure Strong Passwords"*). According to the empirical data in the forum shows that 80 % of the ten threads where security and privacy risks raised ended up *'unsuccessful'* whereas 20 % ended up *'successful'*. The conclusion I draw from this is that these issues are not well supported and that there is an information gap here that needs to be addressed (in terms of TS support forums).

P8: Establish users expected perceived value of the service.
The empirical data shows that user' expectations and perceived quality are determined by their loyalty to a specific product/brand. Usually users provide what they prefer: *"More my thing, I like the strength of < NAME > Software."* or what they do not: *"I swore I would not ever purchase another < NAME > product"*. Expressions of loyalty were found in 24 threads.

Additionally, it seems important to users that TS advisors do not affiliate themselves with specific vendors and provide balanced suggestions to the user. Suggestions judged to be unbiased ended up successful in 75 % of the 24 threads where the user shows their loyalty to a specific product. The empirical data shows that 25 % ended up as *'unsuccessful'*. However, indications are that among this 25 %, only 16.7 % were unsuccessful due to TS criticizing a product (and the user losing trust in the TS as a result). TS advisors who promote or denigrate a product may change the discourse of the communication process from a positive to a negative interaction. For instance a user responded to a promotion with, *"<Abusive Word > guys you are good marketers!"* indicating that blatant promoting of a given product can result in a loss of trust.

P9: Monitoring the communication flow
P9.1 TS advisors need to avoid misinforming users: *Misinformation* can create communication difficulties and loss of user confidence and can delay the solution. In TS forums, users can be misinformed in the following ways: leaving out important steps from the process: *"I assume you meant to put the/s after the}."*; not providing necessary information: *"I tried to follow your advice on the < NAME > Software, but it kept saying..."* and assuming the user is familiar with the topic and using technical words that novice users cannot understand: *"Just what is SF???"*. *Misinforming* users may lead to unsuccessful terminations of threads which in turn results in disappointing users. Out of 9 occurrences of *misinformation,* 22.3 % had an *'unsuccessful'* outcome, whereas 77.7 % occurrences ended as *'successful'* of which 55.5 % occurrences were corrected by the TS advisor themselves and 22.2 % occurrences needed the involvement of moderators. In order to avoid misinforming users TS advisors need to (a) make sure not to leave important steps out of the process, (b) provide all necessary information and (c) not assume the user is familiar with the subject matter and terminology.

P9.2 TS advisor need to avoid misunderstanding user requirements: *Misunderstanding* in this context is when one person in an interaction has the wrong perception of the other person's idea. In a forum, users *misunderstand* the TS advisor due to (a) the TS advisor implying one thing and meaning another; (b) the TS advisor using technical words, and (c) the TS advisor assuming the user knows what they are referring to. These misunderstanding can be reversed by the TS advisor acknowledging the problem, for example, "*I think you misinterpreted my post, but I'll try to help you out with that*" and "*I should have been more specific*" are the best practices of TS advisor. Sometimes moderators may involve when the misunderstanding continues "*You are being advised correctly*"; "*The above suggestion is best and user-friendly, provided you follow all instructions word-for-word*". The importance of understanding the user's intention and requirement is most apparent when the user does not explain the problem properly. Out of 22 occurrences of users *misunderstanding*, 72.7 % end up '*successful*' but among those, 22.7 % needed moderators' involvement. 27.3 % of users *misunderstanding* communication issues lead to the '*unsuccessful*' ending. Thus it is important to understand user requirements before TS provide any information, and to present that information clearly and concisely.

P9.3 Do not confuse users with multiple solutions: *Confusion*, in this context, is the uncertainty of accepting the advice or suggestion provided or the hesitation of performing instructions to solve the problem. In a forum, *confusion* can occur when more than one TS advisor is involved "*As it's counterproductive to have more than one person working on the same issue, I've passed on the information to < NAME>*" or when users are provided with different options for the solution "*Given two options what will be the right one to follow?*", "*Which method is best; I'm a little confused*". In a forum, out of 12 occurrences of user *confusion*, 58.3 % of *confusion* occurred because of multiple responses from one TS advisor and 41.7 % of *confusion* occurred because of the involvement of multiple TS advisors. Among the 12 occurrences of user *confusion* 8.3 % of *confusion* ended with *frustration* and 33.3 % of the *confusion* ended with *anger*.

P10: Manage Emotions
TS advisors should be trained to understand the emotional state of the user by examining the written submissions provided by the user. Our data suggests that it is better for a TS advisor to address the emotions before providing further instructions to solve the problem.

P10.1 TS advisors need to calm down an annoyed user: *Anger* is one of the emotions triggered by communication issues. There are different circumstances observed in TS forums that trigger users' *anger*, for example, (a) incorrect instructions offered to the user, as shown in the user reply: "*Please reread your "instructions" before you say that they weren't followed*" and (b) promoting products, where the user wrote: "*<Abusive Word > tricked me*". TS advisor can calm down the annoyed user by directly asking them to "*please tone down your language*" or can offer practical guidance as to a more desirable communication and problem solving process e.g., "*If you want help, be nice, or go elsewhere. If you continue with this attitude, then I will* *ban you*". Out of the 12 occurrences of user *anger*, 33.3 % occurred because of TS advisor *misunderstanding* the user's question, 41.6 % of *anger* occurred because the clarification process took too long and 25 % occurred because users were angry with vendors before they posted their query in the forum. This study shows that failing to calm down an annoyed user led to 21 *'unsuccessful'* outcomes, among these bad outcomes, 42.8 % included evidence of user *Anger*.

P10.2 Respond quickly and give high priority attention to frustrated user: *Frustration* is defined as unfulfilled expectations or dissatisfaction of users. Among the 18 occurrences of users' *frustration* in the communication handling process 38.9 % occurred because of the clarification process taking longer (e.g. explanations took many interactions over several days, or detailed instructions took time to process) and 61.1 % occurred because users were frustrated by the product performance before they came to the forum. When frustration occurs the user may lose confidence in the TS advisor, and may leave the thread prematurely and consequently to an *'unsuccessful'* ending. However, by giving the user high priority and empathizing, the user may rebuild confidence in the service. These TS responses seemed to work: "*I understand you're frustrated*" and "*The task will be time consuming and frustrating but doable*" are good examples of the practice. For instance, among the 28 occurrences of user *frustration* during communication 64.3 % ended up *'successful'*. However, not giving high priority attention to frustrated users often resulted in *'unsuccessful'* threads, for example 35.7 % of 28 occurrences of user *frustration* ended up *'unsuccessful'*. Among the 35.7 % occurrences of user *frustration*, 70 % of users left the TS service (as when searching for the user in subsequent threads they could not be found, or tell the TS advisor that they are going to look for alternative forms of help).

P10.3 Remove inappropriate users: the empirical data shows that some users insult TS advisors which can be de-motivating and upsetting, and may lead to the TS advisor also becoming offensive. Among the 5 occurrences of insulting user behaviour, we found that 40 % were annoyed because the TS advisor did not established and handle a user's *level of expertise*, 40 % of TS advisors *misunderstood* the users and 20 % occurred because users were *frustrated* by the clarification process. On the other hand, TS advisors insulted the users in 68.5 % of cases because the user *misunderstood* them. The empirical data in the forum shows that when TS advisors *insult* users, *moderators intervene* in the communication. For instance among the 19 occurrences of TS advisor *insul*ting behavior, 31.5 % times *moderators* intervened. *Moderators* calm down the situation by warning the TS advisors and users not to insult each other and by warning inappropriate behavior is not acceptable in the TS forum.

4 Discussion

Returning to our research questions, we now summarize our results as follows:

RQ1: What are the scenarios in TS forums that satisfy user requirements?

The users can be identified according to groups of characteristics such as level of expertise. These characteristics can be determined by either directly asking, by users telling (explicit), or by implicit means (e.g. through the painstaking steps the user has taken in order to diagnose the problem). Once grouped in terms of personas, the communication can be adjusted accordingly e.g. procedural instructions (a fixed step-by-step sequence of activities) for novices, a mix of step-by-step guidance and declarative for intermediate, and mainly declarative answers (stating only facts) for expert users. Observing how users are handled in scenarios provide good guidelines to better understand the user-TS advisor communication process.

RQ2: How can the observed scenarios be used to more effectively construct TS systems for improved personalised TS services?

Our empirical study indicates that users can be characterized not only according to a level of expertise, but also according to how they value system security, credibility of the service, and whether the system represents value for money to them personally. These emerging user characteristics can be considered during company-based TS system development to enhance the service in a more targeted, personalised manner. The successful communication handling process, based on these emerging user characteristics, provides a degree of manageable individuality with economies of scale. Groups of people can be aggregated into persona clusters to customise systems or content for their intended users.

There are some cross cutting practices such as a moderator's involvement that are beneficial in many scenarios. Moderators become involved when recommendations have not been followed by the user, or when the TS advisor is unsure of how best to help the user. Moderators are shown to be important in resolving any disagreements, or in adding clarity where needed. The involvement of moderators can turn an unsuccessful interaction between the user and TS advisor into a successful interaction. It could be implemented in the context of company based TS for example when TS advisors are in doubt of the communication handling process: they can use a moderator or indeed pass a query onto an expert to other area of knowledge. This is fairly transparent to the user in a text based scenario, where the interaction is asynchronous, and short delays between interactions are expected.

One scenario of note is when the user is abusive. This is perhaps also an example of where dealing with users in an open source forum varies from a company based scenario. In open source forums, we found that some abusive users were banned from participating. The context of the forums is different to a company-based service agreements and therefore it needs to be discussed in the company, where rather than banning a customer, the company may choose to escalate the thread to a manager. A company needs to have a policy about how to deal with abusive users; creating such policies is outside of the scope of this study.

RQ3: What can we learn from the unsuccessful scenarios in TS?

The study also observed reasons why unsuccessful practices occur and what can be learnt from these practices in future TS advisor/user interactions in a company-based context. Practices such as not establishing a user level of expertise, not establishing privacy and security user requirements, managing third-party software, and avoiding premature response has a big impact on the outcome of the communication handling process and problem solving. Such practices can lead to miscommunication and can confuse users, which may cause uncertainty about the information provided; create communication difficulties and loss of confidence of the user and delay of the solution thereby leading to the failure of the communication.

We concur with other researchers [2, 3, 15, 16] that using on-line forums provides a rich source of data, and in our case given the high success rate of the interactions (see Table 5), suggests that many of our empirically grounded concepts work, at least in an Open Source context. The challenge now is to consider how valid these concepts are in a commercial company-based scenario.

5 Limitations

This research is limited by the choice of forum datasets, which in turn were in some ways limited by our access to them. The characteristics of online users may differ from the user that will interact directly with a development organization. While, data collected from our 8 selected forums (comprising 116 conversation threads from 116 different users) allowed us to identify characteristics across a range of different user types, and may share the characteristics of the wider population of TS users; we do not suggest that these findings can be totally generalised outside of the context of 8 Open Source forums.

Specifically, some the practices identified as leading to success in an Open Source forum (such as multiple TS advisors engaging with the user at run time) may not be feasible in a company based TS scenario. Future work could include a validation of our findings through a comparison of company-based datasets to produce more externally valid results.

Data derived from the TS forums contained different types of expression such as texts, symbols, and gestures and abbreviated words. This research only concentrated on analysing text since the core purpose of this research is text-based communication in TS. The other expressions (such as emails, telephone calls, gestures and symbols in the text) have not been collected or analysed in this empirical study. These complementary expressions could be included in the future studies to find more concrete and rich set of personalised characteristics.

Since the success of a given interaction is determined by a clear sign-off from the user, there were many threads that were indeterminate (we class as outcome 'unknown'). While we were careful not to use these data in our analysis, it may contain patterns of communication that run counter to our findings.

6 Conclusion

In conclusion, based on the empirical study of 8 open source forums we addressed our research questions, which were to investigate successful and unsuccessful practices of TS forums to improve technical support systems to satisfy user requirements in a more targeted and personalised manner. We have shown ten recommendations: Establish and handle user's level of expertise, provide different options with regard to the affordability of the service to the user, manage third-party products, generate visually appealing material, prompt users to provide individual context, avoid premature response with respect to the problem context, establish privacy and security requirements of the user, establish users expected perceived value of the service, and monitor the communication flow. The recommendations are interconnected in several situations that enable to better understand the user-TS advisor communication handling process. The recommendations also include reasons why unsuccessful practices occur and what can be learnt from these practices in future user-TS advisor interactions in a company-based context. The idea is that by applying the recommendations of the successful threads, the user will have a better experience, and the number of unsuccessful outcomes will be reduced.

Future work includes a triangulation of data sources to include interviews with the TS experts giving advice, as well as the users asking for advice to gain further confidence in our interpretations.

We are currently validating the practices with a representative group of TS advisors and TS users, through a survey to ask them which practices TS persona practices they currently use (to highlight any gaps), and which of the proposed practices they think would help them in their various roles (to add confidence to our framework of practices).

Acknowlegments. This work was supported, in part, by Science Foundation Ireland grant 10/CE/I1855 to Lero - the Irish Software Engineering Research Centre (www.lero.ie). This research is also supported by the Science Foundation Ireland (Grant 07/CE/I1142) as part of the Centre for Next Generation Localisation (CNGL) at the University of Limerick.

References

1. Stefani, A., Xenos, M.: E-commerce system quality assessment using a model based on ISO 9126 and belief networks. Softw. Qual. J. **16**(1), 107–129 (2008)
2. Oxton, G.: The power and value of on-line communities. In: 2010: Consortium for Service Innovation, Keynote address in Centre for Next Generation Localisation Public Showcase, Localisation Research Centre CSIS Department, University of Limerick, 27 April 2010
3. Steichen, B., Wade, V.: Adaptive retrieval and composition of socio-semantic content for personalised customer care. In: International Workshop on Adaptation in Social and Semantic Web (2010)
4. Negash, S., Ryan, T., Igbaria, M.: Quality and effectiveness in web-based customer support systems. Inf. Manage. **40**(8), 757–768 (2003)
5. Gao, N., Zhao, S., Jiang, W.: Researched customer requirements representation and mapping on ontology. In: 2011 International Conference on Management and Service Science (2011)
6. Lee, Z., Kim, Y., Lee, S.-G.: The influences of media choice on help desk performance perception. In: Proceedings of the 34th Annual Hawaii International Conference on System Sciences. IEEE (2001)
7. Na, C., et al.: A value-added service model of mining right information. In: 2010 International Conference on E-Business and E-Government (ICEE). IEEE (2010)
8. Tam, K.Y., Ho, S.Y.: Web personalization: is it effective? IT Prof. **5**(5), 53–57 (2003)

9. Wu, D., et al.: A framework for classifying personalization scheme used on e-commerce websites. In: Proceedings of the 36th Annual Hawaii International Conference on System Sciences. IEEE (2003)
10. Viviani, M., Bennani, N., Egyed-Zsigmond, E.: A survey on user modeling in multi-application environments. In: Proceedings of the 2010 Third International Conference on Advances in Human-Oriented and Personalized Mechanisms, Technologies and Services, pp. 111–116. IEEE Computer Society (2010)
11. Kim, W., Song, Y.U., Hong, J.S.: Web enabled expert systems using hyperlink-based inference. Expert Syst. Appl. **28**(1), 79–91 (2005)
12. Wang, G.A., et al.: ExpertRank: a topic-aware expert finding algorithm for online knowledge communities. Decis. Support Syst. **54**(3), 1442–1451 (2013)
13. Gizaw, S., Buckley, J., Beecham, S.: Characterising users through an analysis of on-line technical support forums. In: Abrahamsson, P., et al. (eds.) PROFES 2015. LNCS, vol. 9459, pp. 528–545. Springer, Heidelberg (2015). doi:10.1007/978-3-319-26844-6_39
14. Strauss, A., Corbin, J.M.: Basics of Qualitative Research Techniques and Procedures for Developing Grounded Theory, 2nd edn. Sage Publications, London (1998)
15. Vesanen, J.: What is personalisation? a conceptual framework. Eur. J. Mark. **41**(5–6), 409–418 (2007)
16. Ralph, P., Parsons, J.: A framework for automatic online personalization. In: Proceedings of the 39th Annual Hawaii International Conference on System Sciences (HICSS 2006). IEEE (2006)
17. Cohen, J.: Weighted kappa: nominal scale agreement provision for scaled disagreement or partial credit. Psychol. Bull. **70**(4), 213 (1968)

SPI Sustainment Model Validation: Two Exploratory Case Studies

Nazrina Khurshid[1,2(✉)] and Paul L. Bannerman[1,2]

[1] School of Computer Science and Engineering, UNSW, Sydney, Australia
{nkm,pbannerman}@cse.unsw.edu.au
[2] Data61, CSIRO, Australian Technology Park, Sydney, Australia

Abstract. Research has shown that adopting and implementing Software Process Improvement (SPI) reference frameworks can produce benefits in software product quality and delivery. However, limited attention has been given to sustaining SPI over time and the influence of the organizational context on SPI activities. The authors have previously proposed a theoretical SPI Sustainment Model derived from the literature to address this gap. This paper extends that work by empirically validating the model using longitudinal case studies of companies that have adopted CMMI. The validation supports the underlying theory of the model that SPI program benefits can be reinforced and sustained by nurturing influential factors, identified in the model, in the organizational context in which the SPI activities take place. The paper concludes that viewing SPI more broadly as an organizational investment rather than just an incremental product or process improvement tool may support sustained benefits.

Keywords: Software process improvement · Sustainment · SPI · CMMI · Case studies

1 Introduction

Existing Software Process Improvement (SPI) literature suggests that the implementation of SPI initiatives can assist software-developing organizations to create strategic advantages to remain competitive [1, 2]. While most organizations are motivated to adopt and implement SPI, challenges arise as they face difficulties when adapting the selected SPI reference model to their organizational context [3, 4]. In addition, SPI can add complexity as contextual realities change and organizations face multiple challenges during and after implementation. As a result, improvement efforts can fail, resulting in resistance towards, or abandonment of, adopted SPI practices [5].

Further, some SPI implementation research focusing on success factors suggests that the challenges organizations experience in sustaining SPI may have less to do with the adoption of a specific reference model and/or toolset than with how SPI was introduced and integrated into the organization [6]. Even though a wide range of SPI frameworks and process models to support SPI implementation is available, some software-developing organizations are not able to sufficiently address their needs and the critical challenges they face [6]. To help overcome this problem, we have proposed [7] and provide here an initial validation of an *SPI Sustainment Model*. In this context, SPI sustainment is defined as the enablement of SPI activities, effort and outcomes to continuously improve and/or maintain improvements in software development processes.

The study aims to validate the theoretical model developed in [7], focusing on the research question: *What influences software-developing organizations to sustain SPI?* The key contribution of the paper is an *SPI Sustainment Model* that looks outside the box of existing process reference models to organizational contextual factors (internal and external) that may positively reinforce and sustain SPI activities.

In the next section, the proposed model is briefly reintroduced. Then, the study environment, research design, and data analysis for the validation are described in Sects. 3, 4 and 5 before the case study results are presented in Sect. 6. Finally, Sect. 7 discusses contributions and implications of the model before conclusions are drawn.

2 Prior Research– SPI Sustainment Model

The proposed *SPI Sustainment Model* was developed from the literature on process improvement as described in [7]. The model comprises nine factors from the organizational context of SPI initiatives clustered into three categories that the literature suggests are influential in sustaining SPI activities (see Fig. 1). Model development was motivated by the observation that the organizational context in which SPI frameworks and reference models are applied is under-researched in the literature, in favor of a narrower focus on SPI framework adoption and implementation. Taking account of the broader context enables best practices around SPI frameworks to be augmented at the organizational level to positively influence SPI outcomes over time. While other research has also sought to look beyond existing reference models (such as [8, 9] and other related work reported in [7]), our approach is characterized by its focus on supporting SPI sustainment.

The model postulates that having the right skills (individuals and team operational capabilities), organizational support (capacity for change), and the leverage of external stakeholders and industry experts can positively influence SPI sustainment in software-developing organizations. However, realizing these benefits requires close alignment and integration of SPI activities with the organizational infrastructures that can add survival value to SPI, both as an organizational initiative and a software engineering function. *Operational capabilities* includes applying relevant principles, behaviors and practices in adopting and implementing process improvements (Implementation); engaging appropriate skills to enact SPI initiatives (Competencies); and incentive and reinforcement mechanisms to encourage and promote improvement of the organization's software processes (Reward System). The organization's *Capacity for change* particularly includes the strategic intent, goals, governance and policies that motivate and frame SPI initiatives (Strategy & Policy); the engagement, support and commitment of senior executives to signal the relevance and importance of SPI to the organization (Leadership & Commitment); provisioning suitable training programs and tools to equip individuals and teams for SPI activities (Education & Training); and allocating, empowering and managing appropriate resources to achieve the SPI goals (Resourcing). Finally, *External stakeholder* influences include conformance with

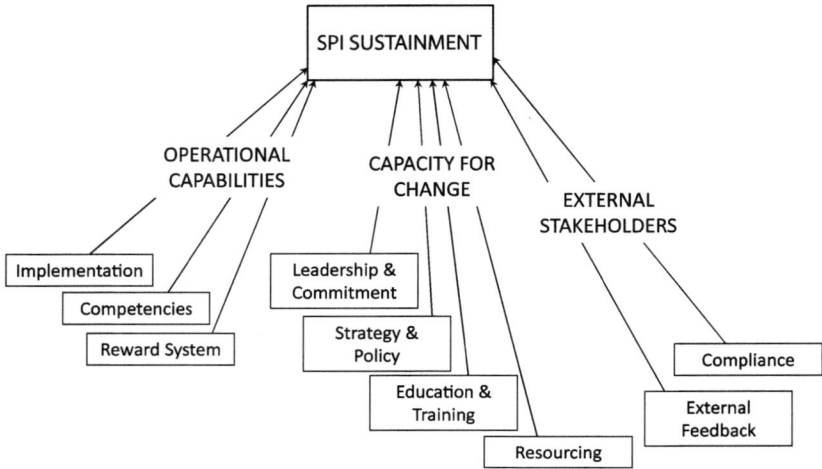

Fig. 1. SPI Sustainment Model (adapted from [7])

customer and industry-based process quality assurance expectations, reference models and standards (Compliance); and process/product quality feedback from customers and SPI assessors, as well as advocacy from industry experts and stories about competitors' SPI activities (External Feedback).

3 Study Environment

In 2004, the Malaysia government introduced a funding subsidy program to enable local software companies to adopt and implement CMMI between Levels 2 and 5. The SPI initiative was introduced to assist companies to increase their process capabilities through the adoption of a recognized SPI reference model. Thirty eight (38) companies participated in the SPI initiative to achieve CMMI Levels from 2 to 5. Six companies were used in the model validation, two of which are reported here in detail (see further in Sect. 4).

3.1 Study Timeline

The study timeline is shown in Table 1. Key milestones (mostly around transition to a new maturity level) in this timeline framed the periods during which comparative data were collected from the program (referred to as Measurement Periods in the table). Data on contextual factors were collected before, during, and after the SPI adoption and implementation. This was supported by CMMI SCAMPI C [10] measurement performed by a government appointed SPI consultant. Additional supporting data were also gathered, including an SPI initiative post implementation survey commissioned by the government, CMMI audit reports, and newspaper clippings. Through multiple contacts with case participants during the study timeline, the study followed the SPI journey from the start of adoption to post assessment (to sustainability or otherwise).

Table 1. Study timeline

Timeline	Measurement Period (MP)	SPI events
2004	MP 0	SPI initiative introduced by government (CMMI Level 2-5 adoption and implementation)
2005	MP 0	CMMI Level 2 Gap analysis & measurement
2005-06	MP 0	CMMI SCAMPI A appraisals [10]
2007	MP 1	Post implementation interview & CMMI Level 2 measurement
2008	MP 2	Governments' SPI initiative post implementation survey
2009	MP 2	SPI goal questionnaire & self-assessment process measures (CMMI Level 2)
2010	MP 2	Focus group discussions
2011	MP 2	CMMI Level 2 process measurement
2014	MP 3	Post implementation interview & CMMI Level 2 measurement

3.2 Roles and Requirements

As each company adopted and started implementing an SPI program, they chose the representation of the process model, maturity level goal, roles, training program and appraisal strategies they would use throughout the implementation. Table 2 summarizes the key roles and responsibilities of study participants to illustrate the scope of SPI activities included in the evaluation of SPI sustainment.

4 Research Design: Case Study Analysis

As this research is exploratory in nature, and time is a fundamental dimension in sustaining any activity, the *SPI Sustainment Model* lends itself to validation via a longitudinal case study design. We use the case study method as an empirical tool based on real-life software-developing companies practicing SPI [11]. In this study, we investigate what influences companies to sustain SPI using grounded theory coding methods. We then assess these findings against the influences proposed in the *SPI Sustainment Model*. Figure 2 depicts the overall design of the study as a continuation of the previous model development study (highlighted in Fig. 2 and described in [7]).

4.1 Case Study Selection

The fundamental task of validation of the proposed *SPI Sustainment Model* requires evaluation of sustainment measures and process improvement outcomes against the organizations' improvement goals over time. The basic proposition is that the process improvement outcomes should vary proportionately with the level of SPI sustainment influence in the SPI program's organizational context (that is, high sustainment influence should be associated with achievement of sustainment goals).

Table 2. Study participant roles and responsibilities

SPI companies	• Attend CMMI briefing overview • Determine CMMI maturity level goal and overall SPI goal • Set up engineering process group with defined roles and responsibilities • Participate in various CMMI process training • Prepare initial gap analysis report and interact with executive leadership to ensure support • Tailor training materials and provide CMMI process training to rest of team/company • Attend Assessment Team Member (ATM) training and participate in SCAMPI A appraisals • Track all SPI projects and CMMI process areas for reporting • Participate in local SPI network community program (SPIN) • Provide input during the post implementation review activities (survey/questionnaires/interviews) • Participate in SCAMPI C post implementation appraisals
SPI consultant	• Provide SPI overview briefings, CMMI process area training and coaching to SPI companies • Conduct gap analysis and CMMI process measurement (SCAMPI C) • Lead CMMI SCAMPI A appraisal activities
Government agency	• Promote SPI awareness through industry briefings and seminar • Provide funding assistance for SPI • Conduct a post implementation survey one year after SPI adoption and implementation • Provide contact information to SPI companies participating in the subsidy program • Set up Software Process Improvement Network (SPIN) • Track SPI initiative impact using industry wide impact survey, questionnaires, post interview sessions, focus group discussions

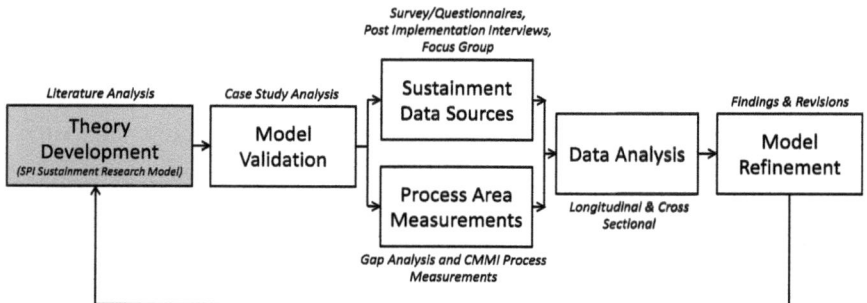

Fig. 2. SPI sustainment model research design

The Malaysian SPI program was chosen due to the first author's involvement and knowledge of the initiative and its participants. A convenience sample [12] of participating companies was selected from the program for evaluation based on availability of data spanning multiple measurement periods (as explained in Subsect. 3.1) and contrasting SPI outcomes. This was done using a selection criteria questionnaire to determine SPI goals and motivation, SPI outcomes and impact, future implementation plans, and resourcing availability. On this basis, 6 case study companies were selected. Due to space limitations, two contrasting cases are presented in detail in this paper (comprising improvement sustained and not sustained outcomes) to illustrate the analysis process. The results for all 6 cases are summarized in Table 4.

4.2 Data Collection

The data for this study was obtained from a government agency database tracking the SPI initiative between 2006 and 2014. All data were anonymized and stored electronically in a basic editor tool, sorted by case study, for analysis.

Sustainment Data Sources: Data were sourced from feedback forums such as questionnaires and focus group discussions during measurement period (MPs) and after participation in SPI initiatives (see Table 1) as well as a program post-implementation survey commissioned by the government agency, conducted after the SPI funding initiative ended to better understand the impact of the SPI program on participating organizations and capture lessons learned. In addition, semi-structured post implementation interviews with case study participants from the Engineering Process Group (EPG) and senior management knowledgeable about SPI also provided relevant data. Interview questions were mostly open-ended to attract free comment and were audio taped with the permission of company representatives. Confidentiality was maintained by using pseudonyms for companies and informants in transcripts and reports. Interview questions were informed by the researchers' knowledge of the program and observations during its operation. Researchers sought to elicit responses relating to the companies' experience, understanding and perceptions of SPI, its implementation, outcomes and organizational changes to support SPI.

Process Area Measurements: The government agency implementing the SPI program and participating consultants provided rich sources of relevant process measurements data. CMMI process area measurements and gap analysis reports were obtained from the government appointed SPI consultant to support validation of the sustainment influences found in the case analyses. To provide commonality in the process assessment results, CMMI Level 2 process areas were used to track the process capabilities across the study period.

4.3 Case Studies

4.3.1 ORG 1– Goal to Improve

The first company is a provider of digital library systems involving design, development, installation and implementation of information and knowledge management systems. It was incorporated in 1994 and employs over 50 systems engineers and consultants. The company adopted and implemented CMMI v1.1 Level 2 for the companies' flagship application project. With realization of benefits after the first year of implementation, the company renewed its SPI goal to improve processes by implementing CMMI v1.3 Level 3 and participating in other SPI programs, including completion of local Software Testing certifications and training C-Level managers as Lean Six Sigma Project Champions. These activities reflected the company's commitment to sustain SPI via the goal to continue improving its processes.

4.3.2 ORG 2 – Goal to Maintain

Established in 1999 and with less than 50 employees, ORG 2 develops custom web based applications with data visualization using Google Earth Enterprise, Maps and Search Application to deliver universal searches across heterogeneous enterprise environments. The company provides Drupal-related services including installation, configuration, design, and module development. With limited SPI experience and knowledge, ORG 1 formally adopted CMMI v1.1 Level 2 when the SPI initiative was introduced and achieved the maturity rating the following year. The company then chose to maintain and fully institutionalize the improvements already made rather than pursue higher CMMI maturity levels at that time.

5 Data Analysis

Data analysis was performed at the level of individual variables (influencing factors) within the *SPI Sustainment Model* (Fig. 1). Analyses were conducted both *within case* (to identify the presence of variables that informants believed influenced SPI outcomes) and *cross-case* (to verify that identified variables behaved consistently in all cases). Data analysis comprised three main activities: developing empirical indicators to guide factor identification and measurement; coding case study data to identify and measure the presence of influencing factors in the case data for variables in the *SPI Sustainment Model* and any other factors that emerged from the data; and evaluation of findings against SPI goals using CMMI Level 2 process area assessment data. The first two activities are described below while the last one is the subject of Sect. 6.

5.1 Development of Empirical Indicators

To operationalize the *SPI Sustainment Model*, a set of empirical indicators was developed for each sustainment variable in the model to guide identification of the factor in the data. A rating guide was also developed to aid in measuring the relative strength of the influence evidenced in the data. Each variable was defined relative to its role as an influencing factor in the organizational context of an SPI program (some variables were also found in the literature as success factors *within SPI programs* but these were defined differently). The empirical indicators were developed specifically to help identify and measure factors in the organizational context (not within SPI programs themselves). The developed empirical indicators are summarized in Table 3.

The strength of sustainment factors identified in the data was measured using a simple ratio variable scale of 0 to 5 with Low valued as 1; Medium as 3 and High as 5 within each measurement period. To ensure rating consistency, a rating guide was

Table 3. Empirical indicators of model variables

Variables	Sample empirical indicators
Implementation	• Demonstrable SPI initiative improvement outcomes • Established SPI implementation and review mechanisms • SPI is applied to all relevant areas and activities and is widely understood
Competencies	• Individuals/teams demonstrate capabilities in SPI initiatives • Key SPI roles and responsibilities clearly identified • Availability of skilled SPI champions within the organization • Access to external specialist skills as needed
Reward system	• Role definitions incorporate statements on desirable SPI initiative-related behavior • Appropriate SPI performance indicators and reward schemes are articulated
Leadership and commitment	• Organization demonstrates commitment towards SPI activities through leadership, resourcing (managerial & financial) and organizational culture • Leadership involvement in and support of SPI activities
Strategy and policy	• SPI objectives developed and linked to the organization's mission, vision and strategic goals • Active management and support of SPI is expressly legitimated and practiced • Software development methodology is defined in reference to SPI process model/framework • SPI practice procedures, tools and/or templates exist and are used
Education & training	• SPI training is part of organization's education & training curriculum (including induction) • Participation of SPI education & training programs by all relevant business units
Resourcing	• Key roles clearly identified • Availability of resources (people, technology, financials) to prepare, implement and conduct SPI • Adequate SPI resources are allocated
Compliance	• Comparisons/benchmarking with external influencers such as organizations (suppliers, competitors), established process models and/or recognized process standards
External feedback	• Availability of SPI experts to infuse knowledge in process analysis, training and assessments • Understanding of what customers value, now and into the future, influences organizational direction, strategy and action in pursuit of software quality

prepared for each variable. Statements of what a low, medium or high influence might look like were developed for each variable. For example, a case describing low availability of resources with SPI skills or experience to perform SPI activities would attract a Low rating for the *Competencies* sustainment variable.

5.2 Coding and Measurement

Grounded theory coding methods were used to identify sustainment influences in the case study data [13]. The sustainment data sources were manually scanned by the first author for evidence of potential influences on the sustainment of SPI program improvements and outcomes in each measurement period. Relevant text fragments were loaded into the editing tool for referencing, coding and memoing during the iterative analysis process. Open coding was used to mark evidence of sustainment influences; axial coding was used to cluster influences into related variables; and selective coding was used to group variables into related theme-based categories (of which 3 emerged) [13]. Identification of influences was aided by the empirical indicators summarized in Table 3. Variables (and categories) that mapped to those identified in the *SPI Sustainment Model* adopted the names used in the model. Any other variables not represented in the model were also identified and recorded (but not measured in this study).

Finally, each variable identified from the model in each measurement period of the study in which it was identified was then measured with the aid of the rating guide (that is, it was given a strength rating of low, medium or high). Indicators, coding and ratings were discussed and agreed with another researcher (the second author).

6 Results

The empirical results are summarized below in two figures for each case study. The first is a radar chart showing the values of each sustainment variable identified in the case data in each measurement period (MP) examined. In both case studies, three MPs were analyzed (MP 1, MP 2 and MP 3). Each measurement period reflects a milestone in the organization's SPI journey (such as progression to a new maturity level).

The second figure (a bar chart) records assessment results from the program consultants for the CMMI Level 2 process areas in which improvements or maintenance was undertaken (for a description of the process area codes, refer to a CMMI specification, accessible online). In this chart, MP 0 reflects the baseline process area capabilities before any improvements were made. The other process area measurements were made at the end of each measurement period, enabling evaluation of process improvement outcomes against the SPI goals for each measurement period.

6.1 ORG 1 - an 'Improver'

Analysis using SPI Sustainment Model (Fig. 3): Based on ORG 1 case study data, the sustainment factor evaluation results are shown in Fig. 3. The chart shows values for each variable in the model found as an influencing factor in each measurement period (MP 1 to MP 3). Overall, the chart shows a gradual increase in the strength of influencing factors from the start of the SPI program, from medium to medium-high. Throughout the study period, we particularly noted strong development in the organization's *Leadership & Commitment* to SPI; high individual and team *Competencies* in enacting SPI; and maintenance of medium-high SPI practice *Implementation*

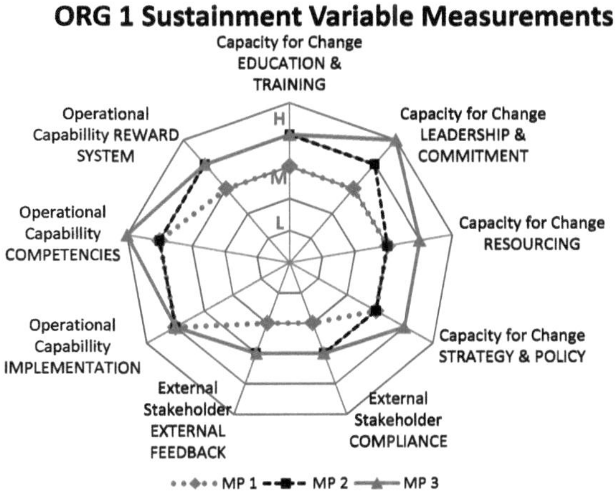

ORG 1 Sustainment Variable Measurements

Fig. 3. ORG 1 sustainment measures

capabilities. Applying the underlying theory of the model, this suggests that ORG 1 has improved its ability to sustain SPI gains and activities across the study period.

Analysis of CMMI Process Areas (Fig. 4): ORG 1 had two distinct sustainment goals during the study evaluation period: (1) to maintain its improved processes after the implementation of CMMI Level 2 and; (2) to improve its processes by implementing CMMI maturity Level 3. Achievement of these goals is illustrated in the process area measurements for MP 0 to MP 3 in Fig. 4, showing an overall increase in process capabilities from Maturity Level 2 to Level 3. This supports the theoretical proposition that maintenance and improvement of software development processes are enabled by medium to high SPI organizational sustainment capabilities.

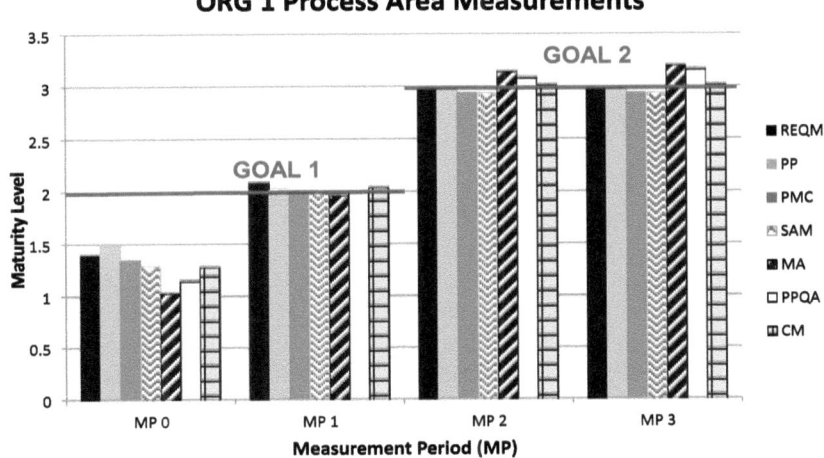

Fig. 4. ORG 1 CMMI process measures

6.2 ORG 2 - a 'Reverter'

Analysis using *SPI Sustainment Model* (Fig. 5): ORG 2 case study data also provided evidence of the influence of all 9 variables in the *SPI Sustainment Model* on that organization's SPI outcomes. In contrast to ORG 1, ORG 2 showed a progressive decline in its SPI sustainment capabilities for all variables across the three measurement periods (MP 1 to MP 3). After the initial adoption of SPI (in MP 1), all sustainment variable values were Medium (except for *Education & Training*, which was High due to the development of strong internal SPI education and training programs). However, due mainly to a high turnover of participants upon completion of various *Education & Training* programs and shallow *Leadership and Commitment* towards the SPI initiatives, these capabilities waned over MP 2 and MP 3. Accordingly, ORG 2's SPI sustainment capability substantially diminished to a Low level across the study period.

ORG 2 Sustainment Variable Measurements

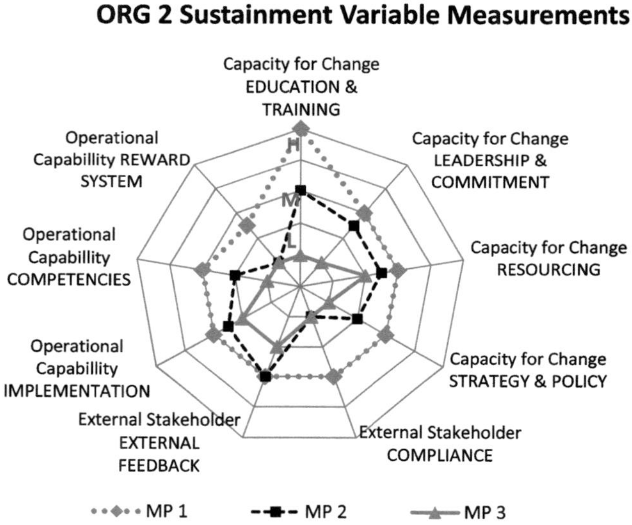

Fig. 5. ORG 2 sustainment measures

Analysis of CMMI Process Areas (Fig. 6): Unlike ORG 1, ORG 2 made a conscious decision to only maintain its improved processes after the initial implementation of CMMI Level 2 (Goal to maintain). The company made no formal plans to improve its processes by pursuing higher maturity ratings. It was more interested in institutionalizing the initial changes introduced under the SPI initiative. Process measures across the study period showed a steady decline in ORG 2's software processes during MP 2 and MP 3, failing to meet its goal of sustaining the SPI improvements made. This result supports the proposed theory that maintenance of software development processes is unlikely with diminished (Low) SPI sustainment capabilities.

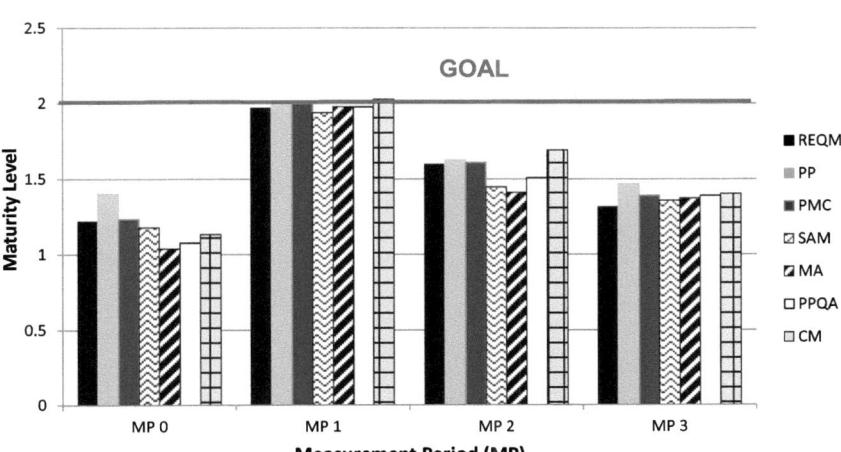

Fig. 6. ORG 2 CMMI process measures

6.3 Summary of Results

The evaluation results from all six validation case studies showed a consistent pattern of behavior to ORG 1 and ORG 2. These are summarized in Table 4. This supports the underlying theory of the model, detailed in [7], that improvements in the identified organization level contextual variables positively influence sustainment of software-developing organizations' SPI program level improvements and efforts over time. Furthermore, the empirical analyses identified two potential additional influence factors to those shown in the *SPI Sustainment Model* (which was derived from the literature), also shown in Table 4: External Leadership (influential role models from outside of the organization) and; Political influences (internal power politics). Further investigation is required to determine whether these variables should also be integrated into the *SPI Sustainment Model*.

Finally, while no claims are made here relating to causality, we note that: there are theoretical explanations for the influence of each variable on the sustainment of SPI, drawn from the literature when the model was formulated (in [7]); in each case study, evidence of the existence of the sustainment influences preceded in time or coincided with measurement of the CMMI process area change effects; the relationships for all variables were consistent in each of the 6 cases studies, and; no plausible alternative explanations for the effects have as yet been found. However, some limitations of the study are noted in the next section.

Table 4. Summary of results from six validation cases studies

ORG	SPI Goal(s)	Sustainment model findings	Process area findings	Sustainment variables found	Potential additional variables
1	Improve / maintain Level 2, 3	Improved from med to med-high	Achieved and sustained	All (9)	External leadership
2	Achieve / maintain Level 2	Decreased from medium to low	Process capabilities declined	All (9)	Political influences
3	Improve (CMMI Level 2, 3, 4, 5)	Improved from medium to high	Achieved and sustained	All (9)	Political influences
4	Achieve / maintain Level 2	Minimal change (M/L – M – M/L)	Slight decline in MP 3	All (9)	
5	Achieve / maintain Level 2	Decreased from medium to low	Process capabilities declined	All (9)	
6	Achieve / Maintain Level 2	Minimal change (M/L – M – M/H)	Slight decline in MP 2	All except reward system in MP 2	

7 Discussion and Conclusion

This paper extends work presented in [7] by empirically validating a proposed *SPI Sustainment Model* developed from the process improvement research literature. The model argues that SPI program gains can be reinforced and sustained by nurturing certain influential factors in the organizational context in which the SPI activities take place. Six case studies of SPI implementations (two of which were evaluated in detail) provide support for the model.

This work is exploratory and requires further validation and development within the SPI community. For example, any effects of the government sponsorship in the case study data need to be isolated. Also, as found in these cases, further work is needed in refining the set of influential factors in the model. Organization size and maturity levels may also present threats to validity. Inclusion of additional larger organizations and higher maturity levels may alter the variables set. Furthermore, while great effort was taken in ensuring the discriminate validity of model variables (in relation to factors that are influential both within some SPI programs such as CMMI and outside in the organizational context of the program) further work is needed to make differentiations more visible (this is beyond the scope and space limitations of this paper). Finally, further work is also needed on developing and measuring SPI Sustainment as the dependent variable.

The model provides a timely reminder for SPI researchers and practitioners that an organization can have a powerful influence (both positive and negative) on the activities that are undertaken within its domain. Success is critically dependent on aligning project level activities with organizational level capabilities (and vice versa) to gain sustained benefits. The *SPI Sustainment Model* also offers opportunities to extend SPI best practice with organizational strategies to integrate both levels in SPI initiatives and ongoing functional programs (such as those administered by a Software Engineering Process Group or SEPG).

In conclusion, to achieve sustained impact in practice, researchers and practitioners need to fundamentally recognize SPI as an organizational investment rather than just an incremental product or process improvement tool. The *SPI Sustainment Model* offers a broader way of looking at factors that influence SPI initiatives and practices as well as the potential to reap sustained benefits in software product delivery and quality over time.

Acknowledgements. This research was partly supported by NICTA, funded by the Australian Government through the Department of Communications and the Australian Research Council through the ICT Centre of Excellence Program.

References

1. Gupta, J.N., Sharma, S.K., Hsu, J.: An overview of knowledge management. In: Jennex, M. (ed.) Knowledge Management: Concepts, Methodologies, Tools, and Applications. Information Science Reference, Hershey, PA (2008)
2. Turban, E., Aronson, J.E., Liang, T.-P.: Knowledge management. In: Decision Support Systems and Intelligent Systems, Prentice Hall, Upper Saddle River, NJ (2005)
3. Potter, N., Sakry, M.: Developing a plan. In: Making Process Improvement Work, pp. 1–19. Addison-Wesley, Reading, MA (2006)
4. Morgan, P.: Process improvement: Is it a lottery? methods & tools, practical knowledge for the software developer. Tester Proj. Manag. **15**(1), 3–12 (2007)
5. Calvo-Manzano, J.A., Cuevas, G., Gómez, G., Mejia, J., Muñoz, M., Feliu, T.S.: Methodology for process improvement through basic components and focusing on the resistance to change. J. Softw. Evol. Process. **24**(5), 511–523 (2012)
6. Conradi, H., Fuggetta, A.: Improving software process improvement. IEEE Softw. **19**(4), 92–99 (2002)
7. Khurshid, N., Bannerman, P.L.: Modeling SPI sustainment in software-developing organizations: a research framework. In: Mitasiunas, A., Rout, T., O'Connor, R.V., Dorling, A. (eds.) SPICE 2014. CCIS, vol. 477, pp. 214–225. Springer, Heidelberg (2014)
8. Ogasawara, H., Takumi, K., Minoru, A.: Proposal and practice of software process improvement framework – toshiba's software process improvement history since 2000. J. Softw. Evol. Process. **26**(5), 521–529 (2014)

9. Clarke, P., O'Connor, R.V., Leavy, B., Yilmaz, M.: Exploring the relationship between software process adaptive capability and organisational performance. IEEE Trans. Softw. Eng. **41**(12), 1169–1183 (2015)
10. Standard CMMI Appraisal Method for Process Improvement (SCAMPI), Version 1.1: Method Definition Document (2001)
11. Yin, R.K.: Case Study Research: Design and Methods, 5th edn. Sage Publications, Thousand Oaks, CA (2014)
12. Bryman, A.: Social Research Methods, 4th edn. Oxford University Press, New York, NY (2012)
13. Corbin, J., Strauss, A.: Grounded Theory Research: Procedures, Canons, and Evaluative Criteria. Qual. Sociol. **13**(1), 3–21 (1990)

Knowledge and Human Communications Issues in SPI

An Investigation of Software Development Process Terminology

Paul Clarke[1,2](✉), Antoni-Lluís Mesquida[4], Damjan Ekert[5], J.J. Ekstrom[6], Tatjana Gornostaja[7], Milos Jovanovic[4], Jørn Johansen[8], Antonia Mas[4], Richard Messnarz[5], Blanca Nájera Villar[9], Alexander O'Connor[1,3], Rory V. O'Connor[1,2], Michael Reiner[10], Gabriele Sauberer[9], Klaus-Dirk Schmitz[11], and Murat Yilmaz[12]

[1] Dublin City University, Dublin, Ireland
paul.m.clarke@dcu.ie, {alexander.oconnor,rory.oconnor}@dcu.ie
[2] Lero, The Irish Software Research Centre, Limerick, Ireland
[3] ADAPT, The Global Centre of Excellence for Digital Content Technology, Dublin, Ireland
[4] Universitat de les Illes Balears, Palma, Mallorca, Spain
{antoni.mesquida,milos.jovanovic,antonia.mas}@uib.es
[5] ISCN, The International Software Consulting Network, Graz, Austria
{dekert,rmess}@iscn.com
[6] Brigham Young University, Provo, UT, USA
jekstrom@byu.edu
[7] Tilde Company, Riga, Latvia
tatjana.gornostaja@tilde.com
[8] Whitebox Aps, Hørsholm, Denmark
jj@whitebox.dk
[9] TermNet, The International Network for Terminology, Vienna, Austria
{bnajera,gsauberer}@termnet.org
[10] European Certification and Qualification Association (ECQA), Krems, Austria
michael.reiner@fh-krems.ac.at
[11] Technical University of Cologne, Cologne, Germany
klaus.schmitz@th-koeln.de
[12] Çankaya University, Ankara, Turkey
myilmaz@cankaya.edu.tr

Abstract. The practice of software development has evolved considerably in recent decades, with new programming technologies, the affordability of hardware, pervasive internet access and mobile computing all contributing to the emergence of new software development processes. The newer process initiatives, which include those which are sometimes referred to as agile or lean methods, have brought with them new terms, which sometimes reflect the introduction of novel concepts. Other times, new terms correspond to long established concepts that have been repackaged. The net position is that we have a proliferation of language and term usage in the software development process domain, a problem which has implications for assessors and assessment frameworks, and for the broader community. In this paper, we explore this problem, finding that it is worthy of further research. Plus, we identify a technique suited to addressing this concern: the establishment of a canonical software process ontological model.

Keywords: Software engineering · Software development process · Software development roles · Specialised communication · Terminology · Ontology

1 Introduction

Software development is a complex activity [1] that is highly sensitive to human interaction and team work [2]. We should therefore pay very careful attention to human communication mechanisms, including language and terminology. The concern of the authors of this paper is that we are perhaps not paying sufficient attention to the area of language and terminology in software development, and in particular our focus is on a potentially large, latent terminology problem concerning software development activities and roles. That a terminology problem may exist in our field ought not to come as any major surprise – our domain has witnessed rapid expansion over the past thirty years, an expansion that has been fueled by innovation. Such innovation is very welcome and a foundation for many of the advancements witnessed, and with it comes diversity and innovation in use of language. It is for this reason that we have *iterations* that are sometimes called *sprints*, *team leaders* that might be considered to be *ScrumMasters*, *use cases* that some might confuse with *user stories*, and *reviews* that some refer to as *retrospectives*. This type of drift in terminology is not always accompanied by expansion of the underlying concepts and therefore, it could be claimed that some new terminology is neither required nor desirable.

The importance of systematic terminology work is of concern to many fields of endeavour with the result that methods have been developed to help address issues related to language diversity. One technique that can be employed to address issues of terminology diversity is the grounding of a set of terms in a conceptual framework called an ontology. An ontology sets out by first identifying the concepts of importance to an area of interest, an important step as this can help to interrelate terminology which has emerged in a field. Thus, the ontological focus is first on the concepts or meanings of interest in a field and thereafter in the terms associated with these meanings.

In this paper we briefly examine the scale of the terminological problem in software development processes (Sect. 2) and introduce the methods of systematic terminology concept-orientation (Sect. 3). Section 4 presents a discussion on the implications of our initial research findings, with Sect. 5 containing the conclusion.

2 Software Development Language and Terminology

A key question to ask in the early stages of any research effort is: *Does the envisaged problem appear worthy of research?* Correspondingly, our primary work to date has focused on just this question. Although our research remains at a nebulous stage, our present findings indicate that there is problem regarding software process terminology and that this problem extends into the identification of various software development roles. In this position paper, we seek only to very broadly scope the problem such that readers can gain an initial appreciation for the impact and nature of terminology drift in the software development space. In undertaking our research, we have looked to the early days of software development, seeking to identify the origin of some of the central concepts and terminology in our field. This search, which is far from complete, has rendered the view presented in Fig. 1.

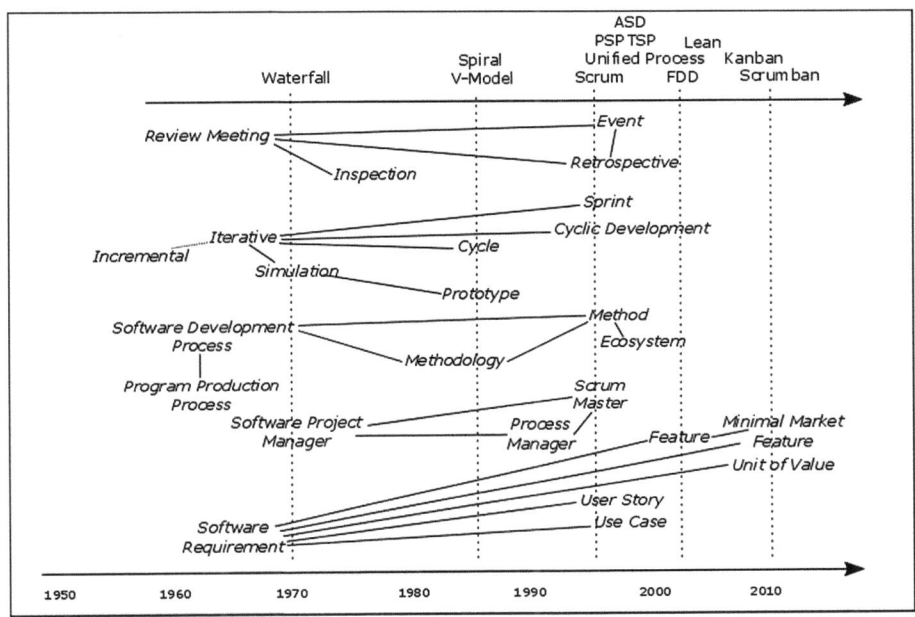

Fig. 1. Software terminology landscape – a process and role viewpoint

The *software development process* – or *software process* as it is sometimes shortened - exists as a documented concept since at least the early 1960 s [3]. More recently, the agile software development community has opted for the term *method* to identify the software process or aspects of the software process, though it has been observed by one of the agile founding fathers that the terms *method* and *methodology* should be replaced by the term *agile software development ecosystems* [4]. Perhaps the inclination to describe the *process* as a *method* or *methodology* in the agile domain emanates from the concept that the agile structure adopted should be of a *barely sufficient* nature [4], containing only as much process as is beneficial, and therefore the use of the term *method* or *methodology* sets the agile approach apart from more comprehensive process elaborations – if this was the intention, then it could have probably been satisfied just as well (and with less recourse to terminological debate) through use of an alternative label, perhaps: *agile software process*. Whatever the case, and whatever your *process* or *method* or *methodology* or *ecosystem* persuasion, that such debate and deviation exists concerning the labelling of the domain itself is indicative of intrinsic terminology issues in our field – if we cannot agree on the name for the domain, it does not bode well for our ability to consistently apply terminology in identifying concerns within the domain – including the roles involved in producing software.

When it is considered that the term *method* has a long-established and very specific meaning in programming [5], it could be suggested that it was unhelpful to overload the term *method* when labelling an agile software development process. Concerning the adoption of the term *agile method*, it may be the case that this terminological divergence from the more traditional *process* term was considered important by early agile innovators as a mechanism to distinguish the agile development philosophy from its precursors. Central to this innovation is the degree of agility enabled by agile methods, a point that is well made by Barry Boehm and Richard Turner [6]. Though, on the subject of language, it is worth highlighting that the juxtaposition of the terms *Agility* and *Discipline* in the title of Boehm and Turner's work is unfortunate as it carries with it the implicit suggestion that agile software development is something that is not disciplined or which may not require discipline (which of course is not the case, and which one suspects was not intended by the authors). And this is not an issue that is evident only in Boehm and Turner's work – one of the primary advocates for agile software development, Jim Highsmith, has employed an equally unsatisfactory juxtaposition when outlining the difference between the two camps as balancing *Flexibility* and *Structure* [4]. Of course, flexibility is not achieved through the removal of structure, rather it is achieved through the adoption of structures that support flexibility – and one suspects that this is a further instance of unintended language implications from the perspective of the original author. So, all around we appear to have some lack of clarity with respect to term usage and even a weak concept-to-language coupling, and this is something which the authors consider to be leading to misunderstanding in our profession in general, the full cost of which could be greater than many might expect.

Two concepts that appear to be central to many software development process models are *iterations* and *increments*. Iterative software development, which is a core feature of agile software development, is a not an invention of the agile movement [7], and along with incremental development, it has been noted as beneficial for software development since at least the 1960 s [8, 9]. Indeed, some in our field may be surprised to learn that the waterfall model [10] also caters for iterative development – a fact which the authors suspect may be largely over looked in some quarters. The basic point here is that the *iteration* and *increment* concepts are long established in the software development domain. Yet, these concepts are not necessarily immediately or intuitively obvious across all life cycle models – at least not from a language and terminology perspective. Perhaps the most obvious example is to be found in the term *sprint*. A *Sprint* is "*an iterative cycle of development work*" [11] and as such, is essentially the same concept as an *iteration* (in Royce's Waterfall) *or cycle* (in Boehm's Spiral [12]). One could therefore legitimately claim that a *sprint* could have been described using existing terms - perhaps as a *short iteration* - and it is not difficult to see how such language use would have benefited those hordes of software developers already familiar with the term *iteration*. Even today, one suspects that the exact relationship between a sprint and a traditional iteration is not entirely clear to all in our field. Those outside our field could not be blamed for seeing no relationship whatsoever from looking at the terminology employed.

Beyond the inconsistent use of terminology across various software development processes, in recent times we have the added confusion that there would appear to be an increasing tendency to create new titles for individual actors (or software development roles). In [13] we are told that *"the ScrumMaster fills the position normally occupied by the project manager"* with the ScrumMaster responsible for managing the Scrum process but not for the definition and management of the work itself. However, it has been observed in some case studies that pure self-organisation can be difficult to achieve in practice, with the theoretical disjoint between work management and process management being difficult to realise in some Scrum environments where teams may need a team member pushing the workload towards completion [13, 14] or where the ScrumMaster may tend to naturally assume this authority [15] (though it should be noted that [13] puts this issue down to a failure to implement Scrum correctly). It is therefore the case, that at least in some cases, the ScrumMaster may – even if incorrectly so – operate as a traditional project manager.

Advocates of Scrum have legitimised this role naming with the assertion that the ScrumMaster needs to be distinguished from the traditional Software Project Manager role (which has existed at least since the 1960 s [16]), that their authority should essentially be indirect, with their knowledge and policing of Scrum practices being the limit of their power [13]. This being the case, the role of traditional process manager (for which the following definition has been suggested: "to provide information to specialise and instantiate the process model, and to activate and monitor the execution of this instantiated model" [17] would appear to overlap greatly with that of a ScrumMaster, thus questioning the need to introduce another new role title. Even in rugby, from which Scrum claims to draw its inspiration in metaphor, there is no such role as a ScrumMaster (there is a Scrum Half, who has varying degrees of authority in terms of calling different pre-planned plays at different times). So the software process terminology issue is broad, it is not just concerned with the adoption of different terms for similar (or equivalent) concepts across different software process models, it also extends to the terminology adopted for different roles within software development teams.

Further examples of issues related to terminology may be found in the treatment of software requirements, which may sometimes be referred to as *requirements*, other times as *use cases*, other times again as *user stories* and *features* (and one expects many other labels besides). With the passing of time, what was once the single homogenous *software requirements* activity has come to be tackled using a variety of different techniques. The term *software requirements* is in use at least as early as 1965 [18] and was quite possibly common parlance for some time prior to that point. *Use Cases* can be adopted when gathering requirements and have been reported to have "fulfilled the role of software requirements well" [19]. Within agile software development there would appear to be a number of terms used for the purpose of identifying software requirements, many of which appear to be related to the *use case* concept. In Adaptive Software Development [20], the term *feature* is preferred with a number of features constituting the *scope* (and a number of features may be required in order to deliver a single piece of *functionality*). Feature Driven Development (FDD) [21] adopts a similar convention, where *features* are small client-valued functions that can be delivered in two weeks and where sets of features may be utilised to deliver higher level complex *functions*. Consequently, on the evidence accumulated in our cursory investigation, a significant research effort might be required just to harmonise the current software requirements concepts and terminology. The broader process terminology issue is certainly current and if anything, our findings suggest that we may have a large and perhaps mostly latent terminology problem – and to answer the question we set forth at the start of this research: *Does the envisaged problem appear worthy of research?* Our conclusion, based on early efforts, suggests that it is a problem worthy of further research.

3 Terminology and Ontology

In order to reduce a terminological problem, the common approach is to retrieve and store already existing terms, approve definitions and, if necessary, coin new terms. It is what the terminology science call systematic terminology work. In this case, we propose applying this to software development process terminology. To address this task, there is no need to start from scratch. As we have illustrated in Sect. 2, many terms are already in use and, in some cases, may be confusing users. The first step would be an assessment of the field of knowledge by identifying and evaluating the preexisting related resources. For example, the ISO terminology about software process, to be found in the official ISO Online Browsing Platform [22] or the International Software Testing and Qualifications Board Glossary [23], just to mention two examples (there are a great many sources of software process terminology in existence – too many to list in this paper). The reliability of such resources is a key factor while retrieving information.

The role of the experts is essential in this process. The terminologist can only draft the methodology for a successful terminology project. But the software process engineers are the experts that have the knowledge to select the best term candidates, draft definitions and validate relevant information. A study of the field of knowledge will allow the collection of the concepts and terms of this specific field and, thus, to develop a conceptual structure of the domain in the form of an ontology. This ontology is essential to study the relations between concepts in order to reduce some of the problems presented in Sect. 2.

An ontology is the collection of concepts and terms in a certain language in a specific subject field, but also the formal, explicit (conceptual) models of object ranges in a computational representation [24]. According to the ISO, a model of product knowledge is achieved by a formal and consensual representation of the concepts of a product domain in terms of identified characterization classes, class relations and identified properties [25]. An ontology also gives an indication about the degree of necessity of a prescriptive approach as it will show if there is proliferation of terms for one concept, why this happens and which term candidate is the most adequate in each case. The ontological approach will also set the path for the concept orientation of the terminology database. It should be highlighted that there is no single approach to ontology development that is universally applied, and that tooling can be utilised in order to support the development task [26].

This ontology approach to the software process conceptual structure would also help to delimit and clarify roles and tasks in the working environment. This can help not just to harmonise existing resources but also to standardise curricula and skills for professions related to knowledge-driven software development. The software process community will directly benefit from a terminology database and ontology to guide them through the terminology related to tasks, roles, competences and skills.

All this work would result in a much-needed, industry standard terminological database with an ontology component for knowledge-driven holistic application development. The existence of such a terminological database (or TermBase) would facilitate lower friction, higher quality development in multi-party projects, and assist in tacit knowledge maintenance as teams evolve, and ultimately can be a canonical collection of the state-of-art terminology for the software development process that could be used as lookup reference tool not only for experts and peers, but also for new-comers in the community as well as laymen.

The effectiveness of ontologies in addressing terminology concerns has been demonstrated to be effective in many fields [27] and given the type of findings identified in Sect. 2, there are good reasons to consider its use in the software development process space. In the following section, we present some discussion on the implications of adopting ontology structures for the software process and software development roles.

4 Discussion

In Sect. 2, we demonstrated that there is diversity in the use of language and terminology in the software development process domain. This diversity has accumulated over the decades, with various waves of process innovation often introducing new terminology. For example, we highlighted the new terminology introduced in the Scrum process [28], with *ScrumMasters* and *Sprints* seeming to overlap heavily with the pre-existing concepts of *Project/Process managers* and *Iterations*. It should not be inferred from the examples that we highlight in this work that they originate from process models or approaches that might be considered especially problematic from a terminology perspective. Rather, the examples employed are often from some of the most important and impactful process innovations (for example, Scrum, the Waterfall model and the Spiral model). Through looking to some of the most impactful process models, we can also start to get some indication of the depth and nature of the diversity of language, and in this case, our finding is that a software professional familiar with Scrum may have difficulty relating some Scrum terminology to the Waterfall model (and vice versa). Indeed, when it is further considered that a wide variety of situational or environmental factors inform process selection [29], that processes may be tailored for individual project needs [30], and that the software process itself may be continually evolving [31, 32], the problem of term usage is perhaps amplified – since a hybrid software development process may further confuse language and terminology usage. Our general impression is that there is a wide variety of different terminology adopted to represent similar or overlapping concepts, and perhaps a lack of clarity with respect to the salient concepts of concern across different software development efforts.

If we accept that diversity exists in software development process terminology – and few, we suspect, would argue to the contrary – the debate shifts to examining the scale of the diversity and its potential impact. Our initial research in this space suggests that there may be a large degree of diversity in software development process terminology and we plan further, more expansive, investigations to fully evaluate the problem size. However, our initial standpoint is that the diversity of terminology is a sizeable problem at present, with implications for many software development projects. For large software development undertakings requiring multiple suppliers, the absence of a common and cohesive understanding of scope, roles and processes may prove to be a challenging and costly issue. All we have to do is consider the case where one of the suppliers is working with a process that deals with *User Stories*, *Sprints* and *ScrumMasters*. Meanwhile, a second supplier deals in the different terminological currency of *Requirements*, *Iterations* and *Project Managers*. Given the reported tendency to tailor and adapt software development processes [30, 32] and the potential importance of such actions in supporting business performance [31, 33], the ability to precisely relate terms between different methods may be particularly beneficial for software development process evolution – and efforts in this respect would be eased through the establishment of a canonical software development process ontology.

And this is not merely a problem of terminology, it is deeper than just that – it is likely to be a problem whereby we have not as a community managed to render the core concepts of our field in a universally digestible form (a form which must permit the interaction of concepts from different process models and lifecycles in the first instance, while the labels and terms adopted in individual process approaches would ideally be related to concepts from different approaches). Added into this mix is the further suspicion of the authors that there may even an issue concerning appropriate levels of completeness of individual understandings of the various software development process models that have been proposed. Anecdotal evidence from the experience of the authors suggest that there may insufficiencies in understanding for the models that do exist – with one example being the Waterfall model which it seems may have become associated with single-pass, sequential software development in some quarters, even though Royce's original contribution in fact dedicates specific attention to the need to utilize multiple iterations in software development (those seeking clarification on this point should refer to [10]).

This problem of terminology diversity is not just manifested in large multiple-supplier software projects, it may be a problem for the field in general. Each time a company hires a new software developer, there is inevitably going to be some distance between the newcomer's personal dictionary of terms and the established practice in the new company. Partly this is a problem of education both within the educational sector and also personal professional development, but is also a problem that is not assisted by the unfortunate reality that we do not presently have a single canonical software development process ontology (incorporating roles) – and therefore, associations between individual software development process models are difficult to achieve. And this is not a problem that has gone entirely unnoticed in our field, for example [34] has proposed an initial ontology for the purpose of ISO/IEC Sub Committee 7 (SC7), a welcome contribution in the eyes' of the authors. Our proposal however is greater than just SC7 language and terminology concerns, we seek to address the broader software engineering community, large swathes of which have (at best) only loose interaction with software engineering standards. Furthermore, we have established a cross disciplinary team of expertise that we feel is essential to achieving the goal of our research to reduce the problem of unintended or harmful terminological diversity in our field. This team includes software development process expertise, terminological and ontological specialisms, proficiency in knowledge management, and computational linguistics skills. With this team, we seek to develop a canonical ontology for software development processes which incorporates all major software development process lifecycles and associated terminology, with the systematic community-led establishment of a commonly accepted set of concepts and definitions for our field (based upon the many sources of software process terminology that are presently in existence) and the enablement of access to this knowledge store (either directly with queries or through published APIs) through readily available channels (such as internet/cloud-based services).

For the software process assessment community, especially those who are regularly engaged in process assessments, there can be a challenge when formulating discussions with individuals and organizations in order to establish precisely the extent to which a process is enacted, or to understand the boundary to individual roles within companies. Therefore, the challenge of process assessment could potentially be eased – if only slightly – through the introduction of mechanisms that might improve the consistency of use of terminology related to software processes and roles such as is proposed by the authors. A cautionary note should be registered concerning our proposed undertaking though: it is neither small nor simplex. It is for this reason that we have assembled a cross-disciplinary team and it is also the foundation of our determination to pursue a community-led approach to the work program. This could include, for example, engagement with relatively large numbers of software development experts so as to systematically agree concepts, terms and definition. Naturally, within individual software development approaches where clarity exists in relation to software process terms, we would not seek to redefine individual terms – but rather clearly identify their relationship to other process models. Finally, work of the proposed nature requires many participants and many years, and therefore substantial funding, the pursuit of which is ongoing.

5 Conclusion

In this paper, we have provided a brief snapshot of some of the terminology issues that exist in contemporary software development. This snapshot suggests that there is a large, complex and potentially very costly problem concerning the present application of terminology to both processes and roles involved in software development. This perceived problem does not have a quick or simple solution but rather a solution will require the sustained engagement of multiple disciplines, including terminology expertise, software development specialists, knowledge management know-how, and computational linguistics. It should also be emphasised that it would be a folly to attempt to eliminate the problem, but that the challenge is to reduce the problem to more manageable proportions.

Our proposal is to systematically develop a canonical software development process and roles ontology. In this proposed community-led work program, the contributions of earlier working groups and process initiatives should not be overlooked, but rather carefully incorporated so as to maximize the benefit of earlier important work in this space. The resultant canonical ontology should be capable of seamlessly integrating emerging and future software development lifecycles, and it should comfortably accommodate the primary process models in active use, including more recent innovations in agile and lean software development – with this accommodation taking care to fully appreciate the conceptual differences between approaches rather than attempting to force dissimilar concepts together. The proposed ontology can be used in educational settings, in professional training programs, it may be integrated into existing software tooling solutions, and also adopted by industrial software developers. To draw analogy with an established programming practice, it would in a sense represent a *refactoring* of the terminology and language usage in our domain. A refactoring which, we suggest, is overdue and essential to future smooth and professional operation of our field, including but not limited to those involved in process assessment.

References

1. Clarke, P., O'Connor, R. V., Leavy, B.: A complexity theory viewpoint on the software development process and situational context. In: Proceedings of the 2016 International Conference on Software and System Process (ICSSP 2016). IEEE, San Francisco (2016)
2. Yilmaz, M., O'Connor, R.V., Clarke, P.: A systematic approach to the comparison of roles in the software development processes. In: Mas, A., Mesquida, A., Rout, T., O'Connor, R.V., Dorling, A. (eds.) SPICE 2012. CCIS, vol. 290, pp. 198–209. Springer, Heidelberg (2012)
3. Singleton, J.W.: Software design and implementation. System Development Corporation, Santa Monica (1963)
4. Highsmith, J.: What is agile software development? Crosstalk – the journal of defense. Softw. Eng. **15**(10), 4–9 (2002)
5. Cox, B.J.: Object-Oriented Programming -an Evolutionary 'Approach, 1st edn. Addison-Wesley Inc., Reading (1986)
6. Boehm, B., Turner, R.: Balancing Agility and Discipline - A Guide for the Perplexed. Pearson Education Limited, Boston (2003)
7. Lindvall, M., et al.: Empirical findings in agile methods. In: Wells, D., Williams, L. (eds.) XP 2002. LNCS, vol. 2418, pp. 197–207. Springer, Heidelberg (2002)
8. Larman, C., Basili, V.R.: Iterative and incremental development: a brief history. IEEE Comput. **36**(6), 47–56 (2003)
9. Basili, V.R., Turner, A.J.: Iterative enhancement: a practical technique for software development. IEEE Trans. Softw. Eng. **SE-1**(4), 390–396 (1975)
10. Royce, W.: Managing the development of large software systems: concepts and techniques. In: Western Electric Show and Convention Technical Papers, IEEE Computer Society, Los Alamitos (1970)
11. Schwaber, K.: SCRUM development process. In: Business Object Design and Implementation Workshop at the 10th Annual Conference on Object-Oriented Programming Systems, Languages and Applications (OOPSLA 1995). Springer-Verlag, Berlin (1995)
12. Boehm, B.: A spiral model of software development and enhancement. IEEE Comput. **21**(5), 61–72 (1988)
13. Schwaber, K.: Agile Project Management with Scrum. WP Publishers & Distributors Pvt Ltd., Bangalore (2004)

14. Cristal, M., Wildt, D., Prikladnicki, R.: Usage of SCRUM practices within a global company. In: IEEE International Conference on Global Software Engineering, pp. 222–226. IEEE (2008)
15. Moe, N.B., Dingsoyr, T., Dyba, T.: Overcoming barriers to self-management in software teams. IEEE Softw. **26**(6), 20–26 (2009)
16. Jones, M.M., McLean, E.: Management problems in large-scale software development projects. Ind. Manage. Rev. **11**, 1–15 (1970)
17. Conradi, R., Fernström, C., Fuggetta, A., Snowdon, R.: Towards a reference framework for process concepts. In: Derniame, J.-C. (ed.) EWSPT 1992. LNCS, vol. 635, pp. 1–17. Springer, Heidelberg (1992)
18. Bauer, W.F., Campbell, E.K.: Advanced naval tactical command and control study (informatics report TR-65-58-2). 1st edn. Prepared for Advanced Warfare Systems Division, Naval Analysis Group, Office of Naval Research by Informatic Inc. (1965)
19. Kulak, D., Guiney, E.: Use Cases: Requirements in Context, 1st edn. Addison-Wesley, Boston (2004)
20. Highsmith, J.: Adaptive Software Development: A Collaborative Approach to Managing Complex Systems. Dorset House Publishing, New York (2000)
21. Palmer, S.R., Felsing, J.: A Practical Guide to Feature-Driven Development. Prentice Hall, Upper Saddle River (2002)
22. ISO, Online Browsing Platform. https://www.iso.org/obp/ui/#home
23. ISTQB, Standard Glossary of Software Testing Terms. http://www.istqb.org/downloads/glossary.html
24. Budin, G.: Methodology for dynamic ontology creation from terminologies to ontologies – tools of knowledge organization. In: Proceedings of International Terminology Summer School 2009, TermNet, Cologne, Germany (2009)
25. ISO: ISO 13584-32:2010 - industrial automation systems and integration - OntoML: Product ontology markup language. 1st edn. ISO, Geneva, Switzerland (2010)
26. Aardi, G., Falbo, R.D.A., Pereira Filho, J.G.: Using objects and patterns to implement domain ontologies. J. Braz. Comput. Soc. **8**(1), 43–56 (2002)
27. Wache, H., Vögele, T., Visser, U., Stuckenschmidt, H., Schuster, G., Neumann, H., Hübner, S.: Ontology-based integration of information - a survey of existing approaches. In: Proceedings of IJCAI-01 Workshop: Ontologies and Information Sharing, Seattle, WA, pp. 108–117 (2001)
28. Schwaber, K., Beedle, M.: Agile software development with SCRUM. Prentice Hall, Upper Saddle River (2002)
29. Clarke, P., O'Connor, R.V.: The situational factors that affect the software development process: towards a comprehensive reference framework. J. Inf. Softw. Technol. **54**(5), 433–447 (2012)
30. Coleman, G., O'Connor, R.: Investigating software process in practice: a grounded theory perspective. J. Syst. Softw. **81**(5), 772–784 (2008)
31. Clarke, P., O'Connor, R., Leavy, B., Yilmaz, M.: Exploring the relationship between software process adaptive capability and organisational performance. IEEE Trans. Softw. Eng. **41**(12), 1169–1183 (2015)
32. Clarke, P., O'Connor, R.V.: An empirical examination of the extent of software process improvement in software SMEs. J. Softw. Evol. Process **25**(9), 981–998 (2013)
33. Clarke, P., O'Connor, R.V.: The influence of SPI on business success in software SMEs: an empirical study. J. Syst. Softw. **85**(10), 2356–2367 (2012)
34. Henderson-Sellers, B., McBride, T., Low, G., Gonzalez-Perez, C.: Ontologies for international standards for software engineering. In: Ng, W., Storey, V.C., Trujillo, J.C. (eds.) ER 2013. LNCS, vol. 8217, pp. 479–486. Springer, Heidelberg (2013)

Representing Software Process in Description Logics: An Ontology Approach for Software Process Reasoning and Verification

Edward Kabaale[2(✉)], Lian Wen[1,2], Zhe Wang[1,2], and Terry Rout[1]

[1] Institute for Integrated and Intelligent Systems, Griffith University,
170 Kessels Rd, Nathan, QLD 4111, Australia
`{l.wen,z.wang,t.rout}@griffith.edu.au`
[2] School of Information and Communication Technology, Griffith University,
170 Kessels Rd, Nathan, QLD 4111, Australia
`e.kabaale@griffith.edu.au`

Abstract. Software process is critical for producing high quality software. However, software processes are usually described in natural language which makes it difficult to verify if they have been fully or how well implemented in complex software projects. It's also hard for practitioners to implement processes from different standards and make sure they work harmonically, consistently and completely. Composition Tree (CT) notation, a Behavior Engineering approach has been successfully used to formalize software process in previous work. However, there are no reasoning tools for CT to automatically check and verify the modeled software processes. In this study we explore the synergy of software process modeling and Description Logics (DLs). Given the rich expressiveness of DLs and their efficient and automated reasoning support, DLs can be used to reason and verify software processes more effectively. We propose an algorithm for transforming CT software process model into a DL so that DL reasoning engines can be used to perform automated software process analysis. Case studies and simple examples are also given to justify the feasibility of this proposed approach.

Keywords: Software process · Composition tree · Description logics · Automatic reasoning · Process verification · Behavior engineering · Software engineering

1 Introduction

Software processes represented in international standards such as ISO/IEC 12207, ISO/IEC/29110 [5, 6] among others are explicitly described in formal documents using natural language. Compliance to the processes described in these prescriptive process models is considered as best practices to ensure successful completion of software development projects. They guide, support and advise software developers by prescribing activities, tasks and steps to be followed in quality and repeatable software production. However, these process models are commonly specified using natural language and/or graphical representations, both lacking the computational semantics needed to enable their automated verification and reasoning. They consist of verbose description that seeks to accurately and completely describe the processes and activities to be followed in software development. Such comprehensive natural language based descriptions present a number of challenges for implementing organizations.

It's difficult to compare the similarity and difference between two similar processes described in different standards. For example comparing a process from ISO/IEC 12207 and its counterpart in ISO/IEC 15228. This comparison is always necessary for process understanding, correctness verification and classification. It's also crucial when designing new standards and choosing appropriate process models for efficient process definition and improvement.

Similar to the above challenge is when two processes are to be merged and integrated. There are current efforts in aligning process models in the system and software engineering community. While these two fields are working closely, their process models use different terminologies, process sets, process structures and levels of description [23]. When process models are used in isolation on the same project, they tend to be less effective and redundant which results into inconsistencies among the implemented processes. On the other hand, merged and aligned processes enable common vocabulary, single process structure, jointly planned level of prescription and effective communication across the project [23].

Thirdly, although processes described in natural language provide a recipe in overall software development guidance, they are seldom implemented and followed exactly. As software developers often need to collect data by questionnaires to validate their organizational processes against the process models. This leads to problems of ambiguity, subjectivity, inconsistency and inaccuracy in process implementation and validation [13].

Even though the Composition Tree (CT) approach has proven to be useful in formalizing, modeling and comparing software processes [2], it has some limitations. Firstly, CT models can grow big and this presents a problem to software engineers to analyze and verify such models due to human memory lapse and state explosion [22]. Secondly, its language for logic tests in the tools for Behavior Engineering is limited subsequently no reasoners currently can be used to automatically verify and reason the consistency and completeness of software process models produced. On the other hand Description Logics (DLs), a family of knowledge representation languages with well understood semantics provide means by which models can be understood by machines and therefore reasoners can be used to automatically verify and reason the consistency and completeness of the software process. Highly optimized and efficient DL reasoners such as PELLET [26], FACT ++ [27] and HERMIT [24, 25] are readily available off shelf for this purpose.

Therefore in this paper we propose an algorithm to translate CT models to a DL. We also present an example of the translation algorithm, and a case study to demonstrate the DL services in software process verification and reasoning. The rest of the paper is organized as follows; Sect. 2 introduces background information about software process modeling, Composition Trees and Description Logics while our approach forms Sect. 3. Sections 4 and 5 look at related work and conclusion respectively.

2 Background

2.1 Software Process Modeling

Software Process Modeling (SPM) refers to the activities in creating abstract representations of the methodology, design or definition of the software process [1]. SPM incorporates a representation approach and comprehensive analysis capabilities (a range of tests in the areas of consistency, completeness, and correctness). The goals of SPM are to abstract and organize software process information into well-defined models, analyze the inter-relationships among model elements and attributes, and predict the outcome of software process [1]. Process models can be analyzed, validated and simulated [1]. And if represented by a formal language with clear semantics like DL then they can also be reasoned on for inconsistencies.

Process models are of great importance in software engineering as summarized below by [3]; (i) Process models ease understanding and communication between different stakeholders in software development, (ii) Process models help in process management support and control; requiring a project specific software process and monitoring, management and coordination, (iii) They provide automated orientations for process performance and reasoning, (iv) They provide automated support; requiring automated process parts, cooperative work support, a compilation of metrics and process integrity assurance, (v) Process model enhance process improvement.

The resulting software process models from SPM can be *descriptive* or *prescriptive* [14]. *Prescriptive* process modeling defines how software development processes should be performed, including methodologies, rules, guidelines, and behavior patterns that would lead to the desired process performance. *Prescriptive* process models are used as guidelines or frameworks to organize and structure how software development activities should be performed, and in what order [1]. Thus, *prescriptive* process models can also be referred to as reference process models – see, for example ISO/IEC 12207 [5], ISO/IEC 29110 [6] among others. These models determine a set of essential, but unordered activities, which have to be completed to obtain a software product. They do not prescribe a specific life cycle. Each organization that uses the standard must instantiate the prescribed process as a specific process.

ISO/IEC 24774: 2007 *Software and Systems Engineering–life cycle management— Guideline for process description* [4] is one important example of prescriptive Process Reference Models that defines a general format for any process reference model without specifying a specific life cycle. Any organization that uses the standard must instantiate their own specific process based on the guidelines provided by the standard. This general purpose standard outlines the elements used to describe a process as; title, purpose statement, outcomes, activities and tasks [2].

- The **purpose** describes the goal of performing the process it is expressed as a high level goal for performing the process, preferably stated in a single sentence. The implementation of the process should provide measurable, tangible benefits to the stakeholders through the expected outcomes.
- The **outcomes** express the observable results expected from the successful performance of the process. Outcomes are expressed in terms of a positive, observable

objective or benefit. The list of outcomes associated with a process shall be prefaced by the text, 'As a result of successful implementation of this process:' the outcomes should be no longer than two lines of text, about twenty words. The number of outcomes for a process should fall within the range 3 to 7. Outcomes should express a single result. The use of the word 'and' or 'and/or' to conjoin clauses should be avoided. Outcomes should be written so that it should not require the implementation of a process at any capability level higher than 1 to achieve all of the outcomes, considered as a group.

- The **activities** are a list of actions that may be used to achieve the outcomes. Each activity may be further elaborated as a grouping of related lower level actions.
- The **tasks** are specific actions that may be performed to achieve an activity. Multiple related tasks are often grouped within an activity.

Despite the fact that software processes represented in international standards are well-structured and contain detailed technical description on a complex subject, their implementation is still a challenge. Their natural language representation lacks formal semantics for automated analysis, consistency checking and reasoning. It makes it difficult to rigorous analyze and compare information from the many different versions of the same standard. It may also be complicated to tailor processes to specific software development projects [2]. This situation calls for a formal modelling formalism that can produce precise, unambiguous and consistent models. In CT and DL formalisms we can find a solution to the above shortcomings of processes modeled in natural language.

2.2 Composition Trees

Behavior Engineering (BE) is a general high level graphical modeling notation [16]. BE approaches have proven successful in elimination of ambiguity and incompleteness in requirements and process models with great success [2, 17]. Just like UML diagrams are used in various phases of software design, BE approaches are used in modeling and verifying various software artefacts such as functional requirements, software architecture and traceability [17, 18], and process models [2].

The main modeling techniques of BE are Behavior Trees (BTs) and Composition Trees (CTs). Well as BTs are used in modeling dynamic system aspects [17], CTs similar to UML class diagrams, model static system aspects in terms of entities, relationships, attributes and component states [2]. CT just like BT is constructed through a careful step wise approach and later integrated into one complete tree like graphical model. The created models are more intuitive, less ambiguous and easier to read and verify than the original natural language processes [2]. The application of BE approaches and CT in particular to process modeling and verification has highlighted the importance of using a simple yet intuitive modeling notation than the more complicated UML with teens of diagrams to contend with. Being simple and easy aids communication and understanding among the different SE stakeholders with different domain backgrounds. We believe the simple created CT models can easily be reasoned on using DL reasoners for consistence further enhancing the effectiveness of this approach in process modeling.

2.3 Using Composition Trees to Model Software Processes

ISO/IEC 24774:2007, prescribes the standard elements to define a process as the title, purpose, outcomes, activities and tasks. The purpose and outcomes are more suitable static elements of a process that can easily be modelled by CT. These process elements have been successfully used to model software processes in previous works [2, 7]. More information about how to model software process using CT can be found in these studies. In this case study, we translate the Human Resource Management Process from ISO/IEC TS 33053, a draft Process Reference Model for Quality Management [28], to CT.

Process Name: *Human Resource Management*
Purpose: *The purpose of Human Resource Management is to provide the organization with necessary competent human resources and to improve their competencies, in alignment with business needs.*
Outcomes: As a result of successful implementation of this process;

1. *The competencies required by the organization to produce products and services are identified*
2. *Identified competency gaps are filled through training or recruitment*
3. *Understanding of role and activities in achieving organizational objectives in product and service provision is demonstrated by each individual*

CT Modeling
The first step as indicated already is to identify the components from the process;

HRM: *Human Resource Management*
HR: *Human Resource*
BN: *Business needs*
Gap: *Competency gaps*
TR: *Training and Recruitment*
TR: *Roles and activity*
PS: *Products and services*

The CT model above shows a more intuitive and less ambiguous process as compared to the natural language process. It's easy to establish the relationships between the different components of the process. It also makes it possible to follow the consistency of the process and makes the process available for automation.

The benefit of modelling a software process in a CT is that the graph gives an overall view of the process and it's less ambiguous and intuitive. Formal verification such as comparing two processes can be performed by using automated tools [4]. However, reasoning of processes modeled in CT is not possible because they are no mature reasoning tools for CT models currently. This has propelled us to look at knowledge representation where DLs can be used to model and reason processes efficiently there by enabling automated process analysis.

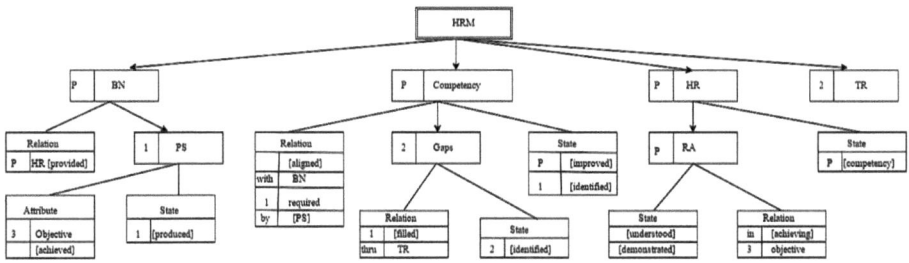

Fig. 1. The CT for Human Resource Management Process

2.4 Description Logics

Description Logics (DLs) [9] are a family of logics specifically designed to represent and reason on structured knowledge. DLs are a collection of logics that are less expressive than for example first order logic but highly structured with improved computational complexity [11]. DLs are class based representation formalisms that represent aspects of the domain of interest in terms of concepts, roles and individuals. Knowledge modeling in DL is done using Boolean constructors to build complex concepts from simple ones. Depending on the modeling needs of the domain of interest more expressive variants of DL can be obtained by adding more constructors. One of the most expressive DLs is *SROIQ* that underpins the OWL 2 a W3C standard for the Semantic Web. Some DL constructors and their syntax are shown in the table below (Table 1).

Table 1. Syntax and examples of some DL constructors.

Construct	Syntax	Example
Atomic concept	A	*Teacher*
Atomic role	P	*hasChild*
Atomic negation	$\neg A$	$\neg$*Teacher*
Conjunction	$C \sqcap D$	*Human* $\sqcap$ *Male*
Existential restriction	$\exists R.C$	$\exists$*hasChild.Male*
Value restriction	$\forall R.C$	$\forall$*hasChild.Male*
Top concept	$\top$	
Bottom concept	$\bot$	
Disjunction	$C \sqcup D$	*Father* $\sqcup$ *Mother*

A precise specification of the meaning of DL axioms is given by their model theoretical mapping via an interpretation function to the domain of interest. In the standard set-theoretic semantics of concept descriptions, concepts are interpreted as subsets of a domain of interest, and roles as binary relations over this domain. An interpretation I consists of a non-empty set Δ^I (domain of I) and a function $\cdot^I$ (the interpretation function of I) which maps each atomic concept A to a subset A^I of Δ^I, and each atomic role R to a subset R^I of $\Delta^I \times \Delta^I$ and each individual name a to an element $a^I \in \Delta^I$ [11]. A DL knowledge base is mainly composed of two main components. The Terminological knowledge represented in the TBox (schemata) and the Assertional knowledge forming the ABox (data instances).

The *TBox* is also referred to as the ontology in DL. It defines the intensional knowledge by which a concrete world can be described. This knowledge is represented by axioms in the form of logical sentences. The TBox axioms include (i) Concept inclusions in the form of $C \sqsubseteq D$, where C and D are arbitrary concepts. *For example, Mother $\sqsubseteq$ Parent*, (ii) Concept equivalence in the form of $C \equiv D$; meaning that C and D have the same instances and model. For example, *Mother $\equiv$ Parent $\sqcap$ Female*. Generally a TBox is a finite set of axioms of the above forms. A model of a TBox is an interpretation that satisfies all its axioms.

The *ABox* represents assertional knowledge that complies with the intensional knowledge in the TBox. There are two main types of assertions for DL systems, i.e. a concept assertion that asserts an individual belongs to a given concept in the form of $C(a)$, *for instance Mother(Mary) means that Mary belongs to the concept of mothers;* and a role assertion that asserts two individuals are related via a given role in the form of $R(a, b)$. For example, we can express that Mary has a child called Peter as *hasChild(Mary, Peter)*. An ABox is a finite set of concept and role assertions. The interpretation function in the ABox is extended to individual names, as each individual is mapped to an element of the domain by the interpretation function.

The DL knowledge base *KB* is a pair of a TBox T and an ABox A, i.e. $KB = (T, A)$. An interpretation I satisfies a DL knowledge base iff it satisfies both the TBox and the ABox. A DL knowledge base *KB* entails a DL statement ϕ, written as $KB \vDash \phi$, iff every interpretation that satisfies *KB* also satisfies ϕ.

DL systems have been used to model different domains of interest such as conceptual modeling [8], natural science [20], databases [19] and above all ontological modeling. DLs underpin the logical foundation of Web Ontology Language (OWL) which is now a W3C standard for the Semantic Web [20]. Generally DL can be used to model anything that can be modelled by a directed graph [10].

Starting with the design of a TBox is a popular approach in developing DL complex ontologies, however, there is little discussion on practical ways of dealing with real world challenges that must be overcome to build, refine and maintain TBox models [12]. Nevertheless it provides the basic structure of the ontology to be developed and it is here where the conceptualization of the domain under study is enumerated. In [12] a methodology is provided for modeling DL knowledge bases based on TBox approach. The ABox complements the TBox by relating individuals to concepts and to other individuals via roles [11]. While it is possible to split the TBox from ABox in modeling DL knowledge bases for various reasons and benefits; see for example [12]. In this paper we adopt a methodology in [12] that allows the knowledge base structure to be constructed first as a TBox and later complimented with ABox at run time. This approach enables TBox maximum reasoning capabilities. We are more interested in the benefits that happen in the knowledge base in the middle of TBox and ABox as shown below [12] (Fig. 2).

3 Translating CT Diagrams to DL TBoxes

In this section we describe how a CT model can be translated to a DL TBox. In addition, using DL ABox we can enumerate the instances and properties of the components. The goal of such translation is that the resulting knowledge base (both the TBox translated from the CT model and the additional ABox) can be used for verification and automated reasoning. For instance, using the resulting knowledge base we can verify organizational processes through instance checking. The application will be discussed in detail in Sect. 4, whereas in what follows we will focus on the TBox translation.

3.1 CT to DL Translation

Our translation process is based on the following Composition Tree Axioms in Table 2, which aims to maximally preserve the structure of the tree. Our translation is different from the approach in [8, 10] but shares the same spirit. In particular, we formalize the CT model into a DL TBox (ontology) as follows:

Table 2. CT to DL translation.

CT Statement	DL Axiom
A component C has a subcomponent C_i	$C \sqsubseteq \exists hasSubComponent.C_i$
A component C has an attribute a_i with value type T_i	$C \sqsubseteq \exists a_i.T_i$
A component C has relation R with another component C'	$C \sqsubseteq \exists R.C'$
A component C has a state S	$C \sqsubseteq \exists hasState.S$
Two components C_1 and C_2 are disjoint	$C_1 \sqsubseteq \neg C_2$
A component C is constituted from all its properties (incl. subcomponents, attributes, relations to other components, and states)	$C \equiv$ $\exists hasSubComponent.C_1 \sqcap \cdots$ $\sqcap \exists hasSubComponent.C_n \sqcap \exists a_1.T_1 \sqcap \cdots \sqcap \exists a_m.T_m$ $\sqcap \exists R_1.C'_1 \sqcap \cdots \sqcap \exists R_l.C'_l$ $\sqcap \exists hasState.S_1 \sqcap \cdots \sqcap \exists hasState.S_k$

a. *Each component is represented by an atomic concept.*
b. *Each component is associated with its subcomponent through a universal role hasSubComponent.*
c. *Each state is represented by an atomic concept and each component is associated with its states through a universal role hasState.*
d. *Each attribute is represented by a role and each value type is represented by an atomic concept.*
e. *Each relation is represented by a role.*

Note that the final axiom provides a definition of the component. This assumes the CT model provide complete information about each component. Such axioms are useful for process verification as we will discuss in the following section.

3.2 Reasoning Services

DL systems provide users with various reasoning services that deduce implicit knowledge from the explicitly represented knowledge [11]. The basic reasoning service in DL systems is to test for satisfiability of a concept or a TBox. That is to test whether the conceptualization specified in the TBox has a contradiction or not. In an unsatisfiable TBox any consequence can flow logically but this will be without meaning. Testing for satisfiability is often a first step in checking whether a TBox models anything meaningful. Let C be a concept description and T a TBox. The concept C is satisfiable w.r.t. T *iff* there is a model of T in which C can be interpreted as nonempty, i.e. there exists an interpretation I such that $C^I \neq \emptyset$. A TBox is satisfiable iff it has a model. Satisfiability checking can capture CT coherence and consistency checking in our approach as follows.

CT Coherence: A *CT* is *coherent*, if it can represent all the intended information about its components from natural languages without violating any of the constraints in the CT diagram. This may help to check its composition and completeness. Exploiting the formalization in *DL*, CT coherence can be checked by checking satisfiability of the corresponding concepts in the *DL* TBox representing the CT diagram.

CT Consistency: A CT diagram is *consistent*, if it does not violate any of the constraints in the diagram. This is important as different CT can be integrated to form one integrated CT, and CT consistency check guarantees whether such integration violates any of the constraints in the initial CT diagrams; as otherwise the integration of the different CTs may make it very difficult to detect inconsistencies. By exploiting the formalization in *DL*, the consistency of an Integrated Composition Tree (ICT) diagram can be checked by checking the satisfiability of the corresponding *DL* TBox [10].

CT Consistency with Instances: Another DL reasoning service that is of importance in our case is checking the consistency of a TBox related to an ABox. As mentioned at the beginning of Sect. 3, the ABox comes from logged processes, i.e. instances of a process. Just like for consistency of a TBox, we can also test for (i) contradictions in the ABox and (ii) At run time, we can check whether the ABox is consistent with the conceptualization in the TBox.

Instance Checking: An individual a is an instance of a concept C w.r.t a knowledge base *KB*, iff $KB \models C(a)$. Instance checking denotes the task of testing whether a given individual is an instance of a given concept, i.e., whether $KB \models C(a)$ holds. Instance checking is the central reasoning service for information and instance retrieval from knowledge bases. Instance checking can also be used to verify whether an individual can be classified into some defined DL concepts in the knowledge base. In our case study to be presented in the next section, we demonstrate that instance checking can be used to verify whether the implemented organizational processes in the ABox confirm (instances of) to the standard processes specified out in the TBox.

ABox realization: Realization of an individual, in turn denotes the retrieval of all named concepts from the knowledge base that a given individual is an instance of. This reasoning service is also central in automated verification of organizational process models. Again, using ABox instances as a practice model for an organization we can verify the processes against the standard processes in the TBox by checking all the possible components an instance belongs to. In the section below we illustrate how DL TBox translation and how to use ABox reasoning for software process consistency, completeness and conformance checking.

4 A Case Study

In this section, we translate the CT model for Human Resource Management Process from Fig. 1 to a DL for consistency checking and other reasoning. To ensure faithful translation to a DL, we use the method in Table 2 in the previous section.

Table 3. ABox fragment for Process P

$Process(P)$	$hasSubComponent(P, Need)$
$hasSubComponent(P, JP)$	$hasSubComponent(P, Peter)$
$HR(Peter)$	$Competency(JP)$
$hasSubComponent(Need, System)$	$isProvidedBy(Need, Peter)$
$hasObjective(System, Objective)$	$hasState(System, State)$

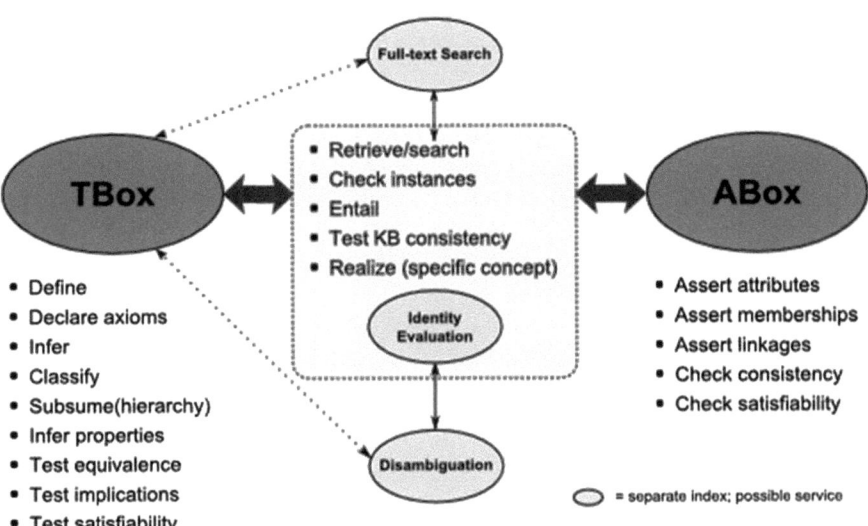

Fig. 2. Showing the benefits of TBox and ABox working together in the Knowledge

4.1 DL TBox Translation

Following the approach we introduced in the previous section, the above CT is translated to the following TBox axioms.

$$HRM \equiv \exists hasSubComponent.BN \sqcap \exists hasSubComponent.Competency \sqcap \exists hasSubComponent.HR \sqcap \exists hasSubComponent.TR \quad (1)$$

$$BN \equiv \exists hasSubComponent.PS \sqcap \exists isProvidedBy.HR^- \quad (2)$$

$$PS \equiv \exists hasState.Produced \sqcap \exists hasObjective.Achieved^- \quad (3)$$

$$Competency \equiv \exists hasSubComponent.Gaps \sqcap \exists isAlignedTo.BN \sqcap \exists isRequiredBy.PS \sqcap \exists hasState.(Improved \sqcap Identified) \quad (4)$$

$$Gaps \equiv \exists hasState.Identified \sqcap \exists isFilledThru.TR \quad (5)$$

$$HR \equiv \exists hasSubComponent.RA \sqcap \exists hasState.Competency \quad (6)$$

$$RA \equiv \exists hasState.(Understood \sqcap Demonstrated) \sqcap \exists isUsedInAchieving.Objectives \quad (7)$$

4.2 Process Verification

Organizational Process *P* is recorded for an organization that has a business need of developing an accounting software system in Java platform following the human resource process as defined in the draft Process reference model for quality management [28] as modeled above. It has a human resource (individual) *Peter* who has competency in C programming. The organizational objective is to develop an accounting software system in Java platform. This means that, there is a competency gap in the organization that can be filled through training or recruitment. This shows that *Peter* needs training in Java in order to meet the organizational object of developing the software system. This will help to align the human resource competency with the business needs.

This information can be modeled as an ABox and instance checking reasoning service can be used to check if Process *P* is HRM process described previous. Table 3 below represents the ABox fragment.

The ABox says *P* is a process and it has three subcomponents a *Need*, the individual human resource *Peter*, and the competency of Java programming, denoted *JP*. The *Need* has a subcomponent that is the *System* to be developed, and the *Need* must be provided by *Peter*, the only human resource available. The implementation of the *Sysem* has an *Objective* and a *State*.

From the above example, we can use a DL reasoner, e.g., HERMIT, to check if $HRM(P)$ is entailed by the knowledge base consists of both the TBox (1)-(7) and the ABox in Table 3 to check for the completeness of the process. The DL reasoner can easily detect that $HRM(P)$ is not entailed by the knowledge base because it's missing an important component, that is, *Peter* is not trained in Java to enable him have competency in using Java to produce the software system needed. Hence, by adding the training for

Java programming, denoted *JP_Training*, as an instance of the concept *TR*, i.e., *TR(JP_Training)*, and as a subcomponent of the process *P*, i.e., *hasSubComponent(P, JP_Training)*, it will help to complete the process. The training should enable Peter to produce the system, i.e., *Produced(State)*, and achieve the objective of the system, i.e., *Achieved(Objective)*. After all these steps, the process *P* is complete, and the new knowledge base by adding the above facts will entail *HRM(P)*.

The above case study shows how organizations can check and reason their processes in terms of consistency and conformance with standard process reference models modeled as the TBox. Our application scenario appears to be simple, but it exemplifies the main issues of our approach in order for the reader to comprehend the steps followed in the approach. It forms a simple and intuitive theoretical basis for automated process analysis in our approach.

Compared our approach with the natural language description of software process analysis and verification, it is easy to see how simple and scalable our approach can be when dealing with the same tasks. The benefit of modelling and verifying a software process by this approach is that, it gives an overall view of the process both in graphical and formal notation and yet less ambiguous, precise and intuitive. Formal verification and reasoning can be performed using readily available automated tools off shelf [2, 26, 27].

5 Related Work

There is a common agreement that software engineering in general and software process in particular can benefit from DL (Ontology) based approaches to modeling and reasoning. However, many approaches focus on software process modeling and knowledge sharing, instead of what ontology reasoning support to use for software process consistency and verification. Recent research efforts concentrate on generic solutions for introducing different levels of abstraction and formalisation for software process [13, 15].

The approach described in [15, 30] represents the Software Process Engineering Metamodel (SPEM) in DL to give it precise semantics. This enables the application of process analysis techniques to the models created using SPEM. While the approach uses DL just like in our approach, no DL based reasoning was used. Similar to our work, is the work presented in [21], where conceptual graph theory is used to represent and compare organisational processes and the practice models in various combination. While this work has the same sprit like ours in formalising and validating software process, no reasoning services are employed to detect inconsistencies in software process. Similarly the work presented in [29] is in the same vain like ours, where ontology reasoning is used to detect inconsistencies and incompleteness in requirements specification. Specifically the use of TBox as a requirement Meta model against which requirements instances of a particular project can be checked for consistency and completeness. The checks are complimented with consistence and completeness rules written in Semantic Web Rule Language (SWRL). However, in this work it's assumed that the requirements ontology and its instances will be provided by the same project hence its main concern is more on consistence and completeness checking than validation and verification.

The need for the use of ontology reasoning in software engineering and in particular software process has been recognised by many other researchers. However, in most cases the purpose has been to establish a common vocabulary and formalizing the software process concepts [13, 15, 30]. To our knowledge, none of the reviewed studies provides for the use of ontology reasoning in software process analysis and verification like our approach does.

6 Conclusion and Outlook

This paper presents a formal approach for software process verification and reasoning. A software process presented in natural language is firstly translated into a composition tree, and then to a description logic TBox with formal semantics. The DL presentation enables automated verification and reasoning tools to be used for process analysis. Using description logics, we modeled the Human resource process in the quality management process as a TBox against which organizational implemented processes in form of ABox at run time can be verified for consistency, completeness and compliance.

We plan to refine the modeling and apply our approach also to a wide spectrum of processes. For engineering processes. It can also be extended to other application domains and more complex scenarios. Besides this, our work can be extended in many ways. On the practical side we are working on developing an operational ontology for a given standard process against which organizational processes can be verified and reasoned for consistency and conformance. On the theoretical side, we are looking into the trade-off between expressiveness and performance as well as the limits of modeling and reasoning a software process in CT and DL, especially in comparison to other modeling and reasoning approaches for software process.

References

1. Feiler, P.H., Humphrey, W.S.: Software process development and enactment: Concepts and definitions. In: 2rd International Conference on Software Process, pp. 28–40 (1993)
2. Wen, L., Tuffley, D., Rout, T.: Using composition trees to model and compare software process. In: O'Connor, R.V., Rout, T., McCaffery, F., Dorling, A. (eds.) SPICE 2011. CCIS, vol. 155, pp. 1–15. Springer, Heidelberg (2011)
3. Curtis, B., Kellner, M., Over, J.: Process modeling. Commun. ACM **35**, 75–90 (1992)
4. ISO/IEC TR 24774. Software and systems engineering – Life cycle management – Guidelines for process description (2007)
5. ISO/IEC IEEE 12207 CD1 - revision of 12207:2008 Systems and software engineering Software life cycle processes (2014)
6. ISO/IEC TR 29110-5-1-2, Software engineering – Lifecycle profiles for Very Small Entities (VSEs): Management and engineering guide: Generic profile group: Basic profile (2011)

7. Wen, L., Rout, T.: Using composition trees to validate an entry profile of software engineering lifecycle profiles for very small entities (VSEs). In: Mas, A., Mesquida, A., Rout, T., O'Connor, R.V., Dorling, A. (eds.) SPICE 2012. CCIS, vol. 290, pp. 38–50. Springer, Heidelberg (2012)
8. Calvanese, D.: Description Logics for Conceptual Modeling. EPCL Basic Training Camp Dresden, Germany (2012)
9. Baader, F., Calvanese, D., McGuinness, D., Nardi, D., Patel-Schneider, P.F. (eds.): The Description Logic Handbook: Theory, Implementation and Applications. Cambridge University Press, Cambridge (2003)
10. Berardi, D., Calvanese, D., Giacomo, G.D.: Reasoning on UML class diagrams. Artif. Intell. **168**, 70–118 (2005)
11. Krotzsch, M., Simancik, F., Horrocks, I.: A Description Logic Primer. University of Oxford, Oxford (2013)
12. Bergman, M.: The Fundamental importance of keeping an ABox and TBox Split, AI3 Adaptive Information (2009). http://www.mkbergman.com
13. Thaddeus, S., Kasmir Raja, K.: Ontology for software Engineering Process Automation (2006). http://www.researchgate.net/publication/278241783
14. Acuna, S.T., Jusristo, N., Moreno, A.M.: A Software Process Model Handbook for Incorporating People's Capabilities XXVIII, 324 p. 90 (2005)
15. Rodriguez, D., Garcia, E., Sanchez, S., Nuzzi, C.R.: Defining software process model constraints with rules using OWL and SWRL. International Journal of Software Engineering and Knowledge Engineering, World Scientific Publishing Company (2010)
16. Behavior Engineering Web Site. http://www.behaviorengineering.org/
17. Dromey, R.G.: System Composition: Constructive Support for the Analysis and Design of Large Systems, SETE, Systems Engineering Conference, Brisbane, Australia (2005)
18. Wen, L., Dromey, R.G.: From Requirements Change to Design Change: A Formal Path. In: Proceedings of the 2nd IEEE International Conference on SEFM (2004)
19. Borgida, A., Lenzerini, M., Rosati, R.: Description logics for databases. In: [5], pp. 462–484. Cambridge University Press (2003)
20. Horrocks, I., Kutz, O., Sattler, U.: The even more irresistible *SROIQ*. In: Doherty, P., Mylopoulos, J., Welty, C. (eds.) Proceedings of the 10th International Conference on the Principles of Knowledge Representation and Reasoning KR, pp. 57–67. AAAI Press (2006)
21. Moor, A., Delugach, H.: Software process validation: comparing process and practice models. In: Eleventh International Workshop on Exploring Modeling Methods in Systems Analysis and Design (EMMSAD 2006. Conjunction with 18th Conference on Advanced Information Systems Engineering, Luxembourg (2006)
22. Yatapanage, N., Winter, K., Zafar, S.: Slicing behavior tree models for verification. In: Calude, C.S., Sassone, V. (eds.) TCS 2010. IFIP AICT, vol. 323, pp. 125–139. Springer, Heidelberg (2010)
23. Roedler, G.: An Overview of ISO/IEC/IEEE 15288, System Life Cycle Processes. Asian Pacific Council on Systems Engineering (APCOSE) Conference (2010)
24. Motik, B., Shearer, R., Horrocks, I.: A hypertableau calculus for SHIQ. In: Calvanese, D., Franconi, E., Haarslev, V., Lembo, D., Motik, B., Tessaris, S., Turhan, A.-Y. (eds.) Proceedings of the 2007 Description Logic Workshop (DL 2007) (2007)
25. Motik, B., Shearer, R., Horrocks, I.: Optimized reasoning in description logics using hypertableaux. In: Pfenning, F. (ed.) CADE 2007. LNCS (LNAI), vol. 4603, pp. 67–83. Springer, Heidelberg (2007)
26. Sirin, E., Parsia, B.: Pellet system description. In: Parsia, B., Sattler, U., Toman, D. (eds.), Description Logics. CEUR Workshop Proceedings, vol. 189. CEUR-WS.org (2006)

27. Tsarkov, D., Horrocks, I.: FaCT ++ description logic reasoner: System description. In: Proceedings of the 3rd International Joint Conference on Automated Reasoning (IJCAR 2006), 2006. FaCT ++ download page http://owl.man.ac.uk/factplusplus/
28. ISO/IEC 33053 PDTS1 Information Technology — Process Assessment — Process reference model for quality management (2016)
29. Siegemund, K., Thomas, E., Zhao, Y., Pan, J., Assmann, U.: Towards ontology-driven requirements engineering. In: The 10th International Semantic Web Conference (ISWC2011)
30. Wang, S., Jin, L., Jin, C.: Represent software process engneering metamodel in description logic. In: Proceedings of World Academy of Science, Engineering and Technology. 11 ISSN 1307-6884 (2006)

A Behavior Tree-Based Model for Supporting the Analysis of Knowledge Transferred in Software R&D Teams

Alvaro Fernández Del Carpio[✉]

Universidad La Salle, Arequipa, Peru
alfernandez@ulasalle.edu.pe

Abstract. Software R&D teams require proper forms of representing knowledge at carrying out software engineering processes and researches. In this context, transfer of knowledge becomes a dynamic process because team members participating in the process acquire, communicate and integrate knowledge from different sources. In this paper, a behavior tree-based model is presented for representing knowledge generated from research and development activities. Through structured nodes representing pieces of knowledge, it is possible to identify key points of new challenges, concerns, issues, gaps, etc., and shed lights on new insights and knowledge of importance to team members, contributing to improve and provide solutions to the domain analyzed.

Keywords: R&D teams · Knowledge transfer · Knowledge representation · Software process

1 Introduction

Knowledge transfer becomes a strategic area of knowledge management for practitioners, researchers [1], and organizations [2, 3]. In software R&D teams, an effective sharing of ideas, know-hows and feedback related to processes influence the characteristics of the software product [4]. Knowledge transfer is a dynamic process which includes knowledge acquisition, communication, application, acceptance and integration [5]. This process requires taking into account appropriate forms of representing knowledge to tap into the knowledge received, considering that several studies have demonstrated that knowledge transfer can benefit productivity [6].

An effective transference among individuals is critical for teams [3, 7] working on development and research, being important that members have the right knowledge at the right time [8]. Considering that different communication means have different effects on knowledge management [9], a common language for exchanging knowledge encourages a better understanding and absorption of knowledge [7], facilitating rapid reflections and frequent introspections, for example, when exploring aspects at developing and designing software products [4].

Work groups carrying out research and development (R&D) imply knowledge-intensive activities and specialized knowledge [10], performing an important role in the creation of knowledge because they provide a sharing environment for interaction and the promotion of knowledge that can be represented using different forms, such as ontologies, frames, etc. But, how expressive is a representation of the knowledge for supporting analysis? Hence, it is important to consider suitable symbolic representations and clear associations [11]. The knowledge representation maps the knowledge required into data structures in order to solve problems [12]. According to characteristics mentioned by [13], a knowledge representation should be flexible enough in order to present different focus, given the possibility of reasoning, usage of context, work with incomplete information, consistent and easy to use it.

This paper proposes a model incorporating the features above-mentioned for representing knowledge transferred from processes carried out by R&D teams. A structure based on behavior trees allows the reasoning, generation and integration of knowledge in order to promote the analysis of their structural elements, shedding lights on new challenges, initiatives, issues, gaps, proposals and solutions when team members perform researches and development related to software engineering area.

The rest of the paper is organized as follows. Section 2 presents the background. Section 3 discusses the proposal of the knowledge representation model. Section 4 describes the case study. Section 5 presents the threats to validity. Finally, discussion and conclusions are given in Sect. 6.

2 Background

R&D teams become the kernel of organizations oriented to develop software [14]. Software R&D activities are related to improving the quality of products, researching knowledge from various sources, exchanging information related to tasks, activities, processes, models, etc. Research and development teams gather and share all kind of knowledge in order to propose solutions to problems [15]. Interaction and cooperation between R&D team members conduct to integrate knowledge, identifying the interactions of information into a knowledge base [16].

According to [17], activities in transferring knowledge in R&D teams are proposed under a three-stage model: (1) sharing information, (2) selection and integration of the different knowledge, and (3) getting new knowledge through cooperation and communication. R&D processes imply that knowledge presents a dynamic behavior when building the knowledge basis according to goals. As a whole, representing knowledge is addressed to hierarchy of data, rule-based representations and logic-based representations [18]. Fuzzy logic and fuzzy set theory are useful for aggregating and representing knowledge, paying special attention about how aggregated knowledge is represented in order to allow an active process of the knowledge [19]. A graph-based representation expresses knowledge on a logical basis and in a structured way, showing how the knowledge is built, and allowing the control over the formation process [19], facilitating an easy understanding by users.

Ontologies are a common form of representing knowledge, defining the semantic meaning and represent data in a relational hierarchy [19]. They can be used for supporting different activities [20]: the Knowledge Representation Requirements Model (KRRM) provides levels of conceptual interoperability that may be reached if the requirements are met [21]; modeling the knowledge in intelligent learning systems [12, 22]; reusing knowledge in engineering change through an ontology-based method [23]; service configuration knowledge [24]; capturing the software engineering knowledge for a multi-site software development and helping to clear up ambiguities in terms used in SE context [25]; understanding of the domain knowledge and project matters [26]; software architecture [27]: software testing [28];and representing the knowledge of claims [29].

Likewise, a RDF-based representation method is used to model the knowledge when developing innovative design [30]. Graphs-based knowledge representation enables knowledge-based reasoning, allowing handling uncertainty through fuzzy technology [31], such as fuzzy Petri nets [32, 33] and building nodes of knowledge for displaying types of human knowledge and detecting new knowledge with grouping terms into complex expressions [34]. A tree-like graphical form structures the representation of system behavior through functional requirements expressed in terms of natural language and translated into a formal representation [35]. The graphical notation supports composition, events, control-flow, and threads. State realization, selection, event, guard, input, output and, assertion were considered as types of behavior for expressing the requirements specifications [36].

The above-mentioned approaches provide different forms of representing knowledge over certain software engineering areas; however such representations do not provide team members with forms of expressing insight about research and development viewed as objects of knowledge connected between them according to features of states, conditions, compositions, etc. with the capability of offering analysis of relevant items.

3 Specification of the Model

This section describes the model for representing knowledge in research and development activities in order to understand and communicate clearly different analysis aspects of a knowledge area among team members. By performing a research process in software engineering, it involves performing research strategies that delineate the orientation and purpose of the research.

Appropriate representations of knowledge can contribute to an effective development of complex analysis. This model focuses on integrating the knowledge from several sources, facilitating the analysis and the foundations of new insights and knowledge orderly and consistently, and taking as reference the phases in transferring knowledge in a team: generation, growth, and maturity [2]. The proposed model for representing knowledge in research and development activities is based on a hierarchical structure called behavior trees [35, 36].

The model is composed of two parts: the Analysis Tree Modeling Process (ATMP) and the Analysis Tree Modeling Language (ATML). Each part is described as follows:

3.1 Analysis Tree Modelling Process (ATMP)

The ATMP comprises a set of activities for getting a formal representation from knowledge sources. A formal representation is expressed through tree-like structures called

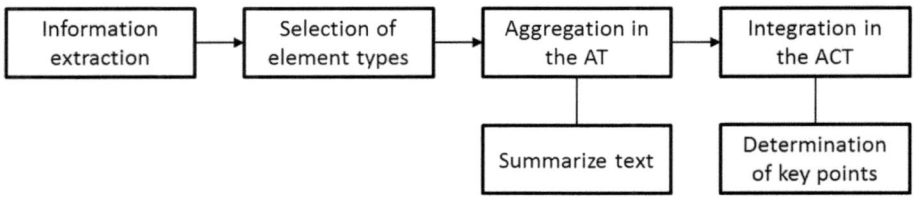

Fig. 1. The Analysis Tree Modelling Process (ATMP)

Analysis Tree (AT) and Analysis Composition Tree (ACT). They both provide a holistic view of the knowledge for analysis, highlighting key points for new concerns. The process begins with the searching and selection of sources for collecting data, and then integration of existing and new knowledge is performed (Fig. 1):

The activities of the process are described below:

(a) Information extraction: firstly, information is selected from the sources by a team member, and secondly, segmentation techniques are applied on the extracted information in accordance to grammatical rules for gathering entities, actions, objects, and relationships.
(b) Selection of element types: a piece of information is associated with a tree node's element type.
(c) Aggregation in the AT: a piece of information is included into a node's element in correspondence to its type. When creating a new node, all information elements must be completed before inserting the node into the AT.
(d) Summarize text: in long sentences, a summarization technique can be executed to make transformations into a smaller information chunk without losing the semantic meaning.
(e) Integration in the ACT: Analysis Trees are integrated to form the Composition Tree, which contains relevant information from sources. This activity is carried out conforming to team member's point of view. The integration process requires the accomplishment of some of the following premises:
   a. Existence of a logical sequence between a root node and a child node belonging both to different trees.
   b. A root node is the answer to a child node, provided that both nodes belong to different trees.
(f) Determination of key points: once the ACT has been created, concerns can be extracted in order to identify main concepts, questionings, gaps, issues, solutions, new challenges, etc. related to the knowledge domain.

3.2 Analysis Tree Modelling Language (ATML)

ATML defines the graphical notation to represent structured tree nodes specifying key points of the knowledge and the connectors to link nodes. This structure represents objects of a specific domain and shows states, changes, consequence of changes, causes, responses, and interactions as product of its evolution and interrelationship. The AT establishes a formal representation of researching and developing the knowledge domain expressed often in natural language. Transferring sentences from sources to tree-like notations is performed following the team member's criteria, interests and points of views.

The ATML definition, based on [36], describes the visual notation of the tree elements, where nodes are depicted as structured rectangles and connections are lines with different kinds of terminals depending on the type of semantic relationship. The ATML describes both the Analysis Tree and the Analysis Composition Tree.

The Analysis Tree contains nodes representing pieces of knowledge, constituting the basic units called Analysis Component (AC) within the knowledge area. The Composition Tree integrates the different Analysis Trees, providing a holistic view of the whole knowledge of analysis. The specification of a tree node is as follows (Fig. 2):

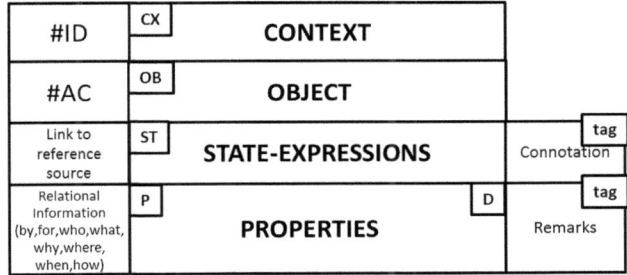

Fig. 2. Analysis Component (AC)

The node elements are described as follows:
- #ID: the team member's identification responsible for elaborating the AC
- #AC: the AC's identification
- Context: specifies the object domain
- Object: specifies a piece of knowledge within the specified context
- State-expressions: specifies the situation of an object through different kinds of expressions:

- *look-state*: indicates the perspective, focusing, representation or scope of the object.
- (comparative-state): indicates comparatives or relationships to other elements or components
- {parts-state}: specifies the structure, organization or composition of the object
- ? if-state? : represents conditions of the object that can determine a sequence flow to other AC.
- ??when-state?? : a sequence flow is passed if the when-state expression has been performed.
- [state]: indicates the realization of the state by the object
- [[occurrence-state]]: specifies the realization of events or happenings produced by the object.

Further details such as diagrams, formulas, images, and graphics can be linked to get a better understanding.
- Properties: specifies actions or aspects related to state-expressions.
- Link to reference source: specify the link to the data source.
- Relational Information: specify a questioning term about the state-expression.
- Connotation: expresses a particular opinion given by the source author regarding either the state-expression or properties of the object. In case that there was no information related to the author's connotation, a tag is labeled with (-). On the contrary, the tag is labeled with (+).
- Remarks: expresses the team member's opinion regarding state-expression or properties of the object. In case that there was no information related to the team member's opinion, a tag is labeled with (-). On the contrary, the tag is labeled with (+). The remark cell is colored in red to highlight critical points.

Tree nodes can be linked by three kinds of connectors:

(a) ⟶ Sequence connector: sets the sequence flow between two ACs.
(b) ---- Similarity connector: links two similar ACs having each one different reference sources.
(c) •—• Contrast connector: links two contrary ACs having each one different reference sources.

The connection between nodes can be done using different ways in order to provide a greater semantic meaning:

(a) Component – Component.
(b) Connotation – Component.
(c) Remark – Component.
(d) Property – Component.

When an element between two nodes is equal or similar, it is not specified in the target component. Figure 3 depicts the elaboration of an AT with connections between nodes from a section of a standard for quality management in the field of innovation, knowledge and technology transfer (InnoSPICE), based on the ISO/IEC 15504. This example describes the analysis of some base practices belonging to the Human Resource Management process as part of the Organizational Process category.

Figure 4 depicts the elaboration of an AT from a part of a research document related to requirements process. Note that key points (cell in dark grey) are assigned to some nodes as result of analyzing expressions and properties of objects.

Integration among several ATs (differentiated by greyscale) is depicted in Fig. 5, using the three kinds of connectors. Each root node corresponds to a specific source, and key points (cells colored in dark grey) are highlighted to be easily identified by the team members.

A Behavior Tree-Based Model

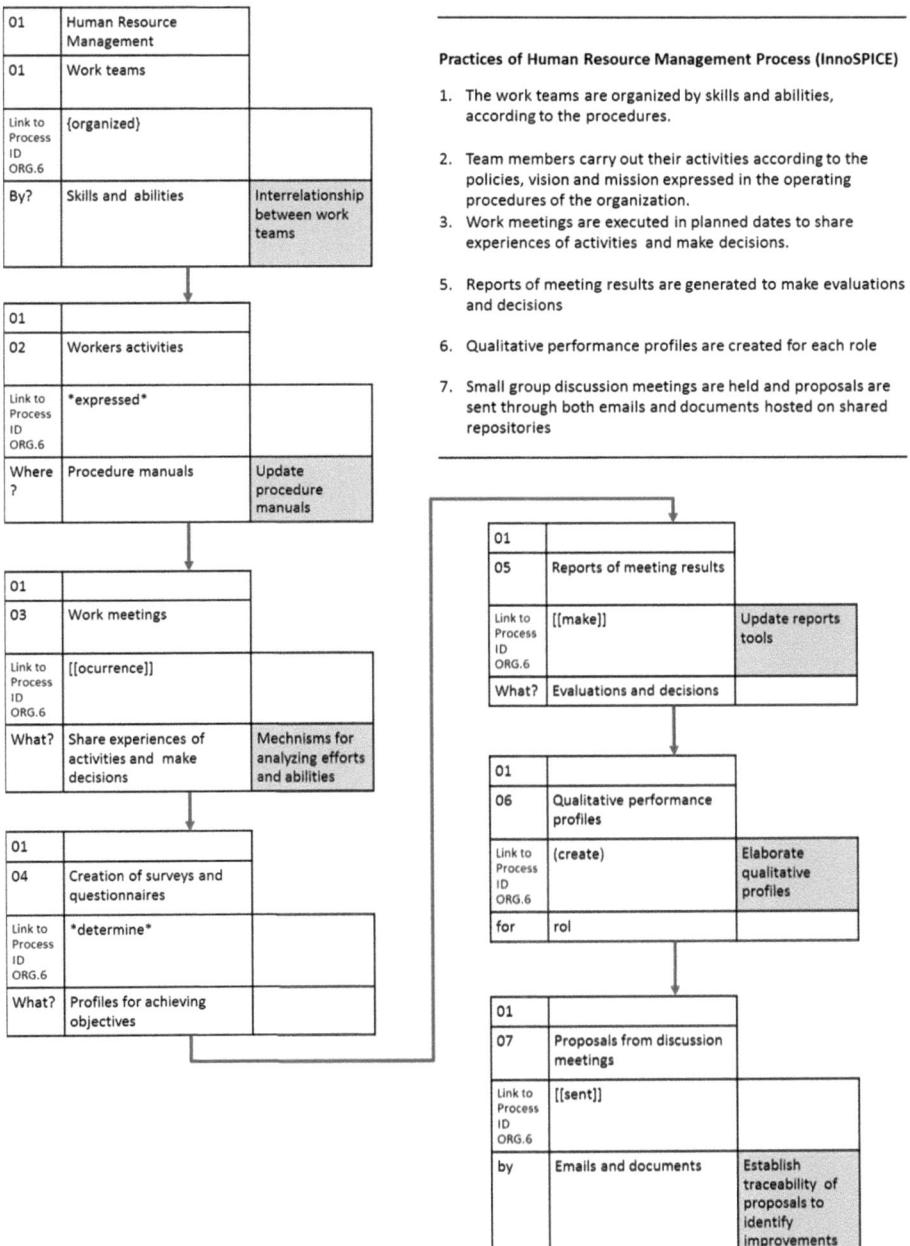

Fig. 3. An AT with connections between ACs from practices of the Human Resource Management Process (InnoSPICE)

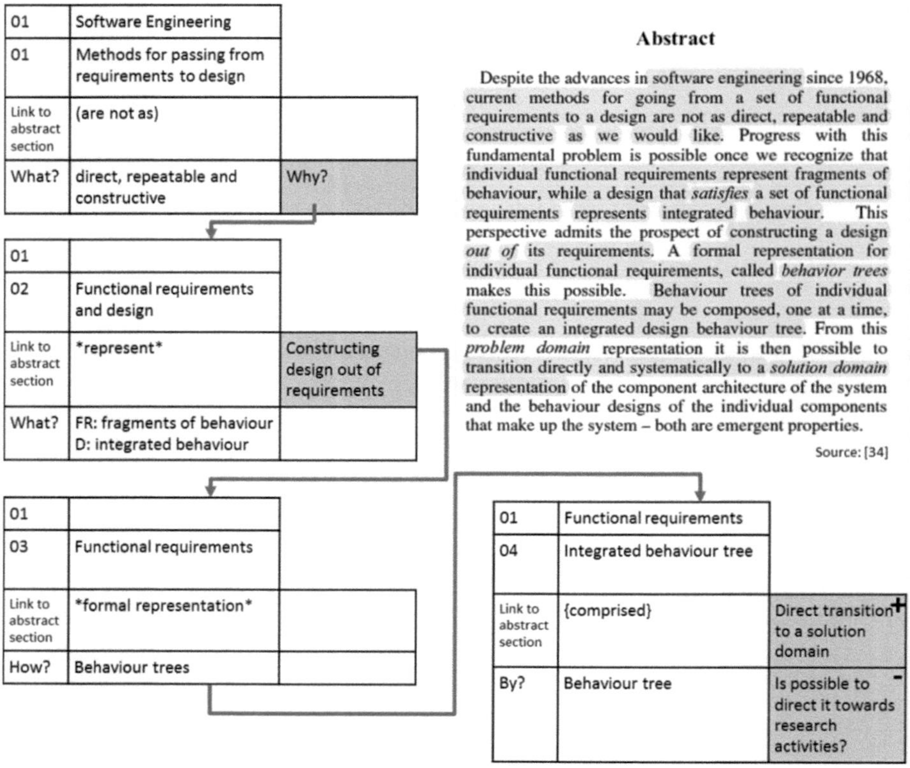

01	Software Engineering	
01	Methods for passing from requirements to design	
Link to abstract section	(are not as)	
What?	direct, repeatable and constructive	Why?

01		
02	Functional requirements and design	
Link to abstract section	*represent*	Constructing design out of requirements
What?	FR: fragments of behaviour D: integrated behaviour	

01		
03	Functional requirements	
Link to abstract section	*formal representation*	
How?	Behaviour trees	

Abstract

Despite the advances in software engineering since 1968, current methods for going from a set of functional requirements to a design are not as direct, repeatable and constructive as we would like. Progress with this fundamental problem is possible once we recognize that individual functional requirements represent fragments of behaviour, while a design that *satisfies* a set of functional requirements represents integrated behaviour. This perspective admits the prospect of constructing a design *out of* its requirements. A formal representation for individual functional requirements, called *behavior trees* makes this possible. Behaviour trees of individual functional requirements may be composed, one at a time, to create an integrated design behaviour tree. From this *problem domain* representation it is then possible to transition directly and systematically to a *solution domain* representation of the component architecture of the system and the behaviour designs of the individual components that make up the system – both are emergent properties.

Source: [34]

01	Functional requirements	
04	Integrated behaviour tree	
Link to abstract section	{comprised}	Direct transition to a solution domain
By?	Behaviour tree	Is possible to direct it towards research activities?

Fig. 4. An AT with connections between ACs from a section of a document about requirements process

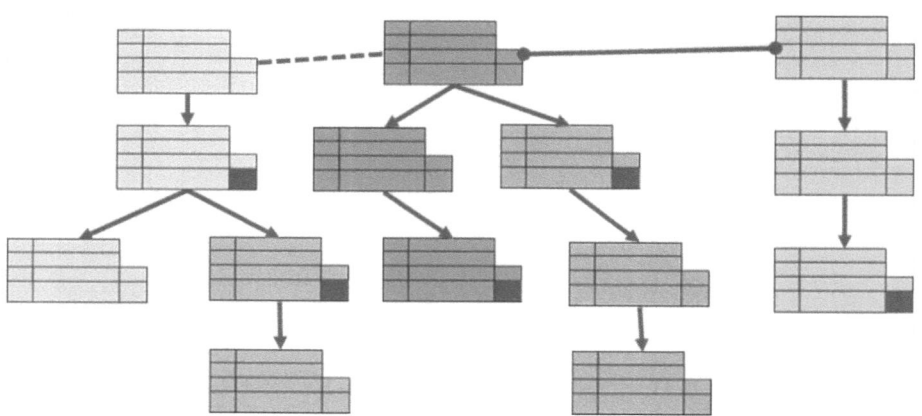

Fig. 5. Various ACTs corresponding to different source documents

4 Case Study

In this section a case study organization is introduced, and collection and analysis of data are reported.

Study Design. This case study aims at establishing a model for representing knowledge from R&D teams in structures called Analysis Trees which depicts properly key points of a knowledge area and allows identifying concerns about researches and developments.

This study was conducted in R&D groups belonging to the academy with connections to business sector : Procasoft Group formed by engineers and researchers from the System Engineering Programme of the Universidad Católica de Santa María (UCSM), the Software Engineering Programme of the Universidad La Salle (ULS), and the Latin-American Institute of Innovation, Research and Technological Studies (ILIIET); CIET Group formed by engineers and researchers belonging to Electronics and Telecommunications Programme of the Universidad Católica de San Pablo (UCSP), and IPRODAM group formed also by engineers and researchers working in Image Processing and Data Mining (UCSP-ULS). All team members have used the model for acquisition (establishing the research and development basis), communication, generation and integration of knowledge.

As for analysis units for validation, activities related to modelling and applying the notation for building analysis trees were defined to be analyzed. As sources considered for gathering evidence were work documents, emails, and instant messaging. The techniques applied for collecting data were questionnaires and interviews.

The following activities were considered for executing the validation strategy:

A. Selection of participants: A total of 24 R&D team members participated in the process.
B. Specification of the knowledge domain: team members carried out researches and development in areas related to software engineering, computer science, electronics and system engineering. The knowledge areas were selected to initiate the exploration of information and were determined by group managers.
C. Managing the process: the building process of analysis trees was analyzed considering the participants' background and interactions among them.

Data Collection and Analysis. The research was performed based on questionnaires and interviews where 24 interviewees were selected from R&D teams performing researches and developments about knowledge domains specified in point (B) of the previous subsection. A questionnaire was handed out to evaluate unit of analysis regarding modelling and use of the notation for building analysis trees. Team members rated the items on a 5-point Likert-type scale where 1 = - Strongly Disagree, 2 = Disagree, 3 = Uncertain, 4 = Agree, 5 = Strongly Agree.

A. Analysis of activities related to model process. Table 1 shows that on the whole team members are satisfied with the operation of the model. Some difficulties at identifying elements types in the selected text were expressed by the respondents (48.8 %), node elements can be identified from the interpretation and summarization of text (45.8 %), an acceptable number of respondents are agreed that connectors provide an appropriate semantic meaning (37.5 %), performing integration of analysis trees (41.7 %), and obtaining key points for the analysis from the composition tree (45.8 %).

Table 1. Rating the model process

Items	1	2	3	4	5
(a)		8.3 %	**45.8 %**	29.2 %	16.7 %
(b)		8.3 %	33.3 %	**45.8 %**	12.5 %
(c)			25.0 %	37.5 %	37.5 %
(d)			29.2 %	**41.7 %**	29.2 %
(e)			20.8 %	33.3 %	**45.8 %**

The scale items are: (a) "Identifying elements types from text selected by the team member is performed without difficulty"; (b) "The interpretation and summarization from the source document maintain the correlation with the node elements, especially with the context, object, state-expression, and properties"; (c) "The different connection points between nodes provide flexibility and semantic meaning"; (d) "The integration of Analysis Trees is carried out following the accomplishment of the premises"; (e) "Useful information is obtained from the Composition Tree about the analysis, such as gaps, contradictions, similarities, issues, trends, and new challenges in order to shed light on new concerns and insights".

B. Analysis of activities related to model notation. Table 2 shows that an acceptable number of respondents are completely agreed with the connectors notation (41.7 %), they consider that the node notation provides a proper representation of the knowledge pieces of the source document (45.8 %), state-expressions notation provides a clear description of object situations (33.3 %), it is easy to analyze through the composition tree (58.3 %), the analysis tree shows key points of the source document (45.8 %), and the model notation is suitable for transferring knowledge among team members (54.2 %).

Table 2. Rating the model notation

Items	1	2	3	4	5
(a)			25.0 %	33.3 %	**41.7 %**
(b)		4.2 %	25.0 %	**45.8 %**	25.0 %
(c)		25.0 %	**33.3 %**	20.8 %	20.8 %
(d)			16.7 %	25.0 %	**58.3 %**
(e)			20.8 %	33.3 %	**45.8 %**
(f)			16.7 %	29.2 %	**54.2 %**

The scale items are: (a) "The connectors notation are suitable for its purpose"; (b) "The node notation structures properly the knowledge units in the analysis; (c) "Notations for state-expressions describe clearly the different situations of the object"; (d) "The proposed structure facilitates the analysis of a source document"; (e) "The analysis tree clearly represents important aspects of the source document", (f) "The representation of a source document using hierarchical structures facilitates the transfer of knowledge among R&D team members".

5 Threats to Validity

As a possible threat to this work is the inaccuracy in elaborating properly the analysis tree with respect to data source due to perception capability of some team member. The node notation regarding elements was not easily identified by some participants, especially regarding state-expressions. At the beginning of the evaluation process, the model notation was not really understood but in the course of applying the model they felt more acquainted with the model language. Also, some of them had difficulty in summarizing text and identifying some node elements. That is due to selecting and identifying key terms from documents was not an easy task for some participants. It depends on capacity of reading and comprehension before specifying the tree nodes.

To mitigate this threats and as future works, some mechanisms for assisting in identifying more easily node elements will be incorporated, as well as an assistant to guide the extraction of node elements types from summarized text. Finally, the model will be extended towards other R&D teams to be evaluated, working in different contexts of software engineering in order to incorporate improvements in the notation and mechanisms of the model.

6 Discussion and Conclusions

Knowledge transfer is a dynamic process in teams working on research and development. Therefore, a suitable knowledge representation will benefit to teams at identifying easily concerns, issues, gaps, new challenges, etc. as key points within the information analyzed. This paper presents a model for representing knowledge in a hierarchical structure based on the behavior tree approach. This model provides a formal representation depicting how the knowledge is acquired and transformed from sources like text documents into structured nodes, which are considered as pieces of knowledge for analysis.

Results of applying the model in R&D teams have shown that using a tree-like structure, including different types of connectors to provide sequence, opposition and correlation between different sources, belonging to the same knowledge domain, allows having a holistic view of a determined domain. Analysis and sharing appreciations would allow getting better understanding at elaborating processes or exploring knowledge from information sources. Most of participants agreed that this kind of representation facilities perform a more precise analysis by using a hierarchical representation and attaching questionings on topics to the object being analyzed, and also establish traceability towards information sources. This proposal helps to team members to get a better communication between them and take insight on aspects considered of importance by the work team.

As important factors to be considered by applying the model are the team member's criteria, interest and experience in extracting and interpreting information from documented sources and integrating them into the model structure.

Acknowledgements. The ILIIET (Latin-American Institute of Innovation, Research and Technological Studies) and the researches groups Procasoft, CIET and IPRODAM have collaborated with the development of this research.

References

1. Hongli, L., Yao, F., Zhigao, C.: Effects of social network on knowledge transfer within R&D team. In: 2009 International Conference on Information Management, Innovation Management and Industrial Engineering, vol. 3, pp. 158–162. IEEE (2009)
2. Chen, T., Fu, H.: The subject knowledge representation and utilizations in E-learning. In: 2010 2nd International Symposium on Information Engineering and Electronic Commerce (IEEC), pp. 1–4. IEEE (2010)
3. Xiao-hong, W., Bao-sheng, Z., Wen-jing, W.: Research on stability of knowledge transfer in virtual technology innovation team. In: 2010 International Conference on Management Science and Engineering (ICMSE), pp. 969–975. IEEE (2010)
4. Ghobadi, S.: What drives knowledge sharing in software development teams: a literature review and classification framework. Inf. Manag. **52**(1), 82–97 (2015)
5. Mingfei, L., Jie, Z.: Study on the mechanisms of team learning upon knowledge transfer: a research based on social constructivism learning theory. In: 2010 International Conference on Information Management, Innovation Management and Industrial Engineering (ICIII), vol. 1, pp. 196–200. IEEE (2010)
6. Baum, J.A.C., Calabrese, T., Silverman, B.S.: Don't go it alone: alliance network composition and startups' performance in Canadian biotechnology. Strateg. Manag. J. **21**, 267–294 (2000)
7. Xiao-na, B., Gang, Q., Guo-liang, Z.: An empirical study of the relationship between team social capital and knowledge transfer: mediating role of transactive memory system. In: 2013 International Conference on Management Science and Engineering (ICMSE), pp. 1370–1378. IEEE (2013)
8. Dwivedi, A.N.: Knowledge Management for Healthcare: Using Information and Communication Technologies for Decision Making, p. 315. Idea Group Inc., Hershey (2005)
9. Yang, W., Chang-Xiong, S., Zou, L., Li-Yan, M., Ying, J.: Constructing the application models of knowledge management and innovation based on communication means in research team. In: 2008 4th International Conference on Wireless Communications, Networking and Mobile Computing, WiCOM 2008, pp. 1–4. IEEE (2008)
10. Huang, C.C.: Knowledge sharing and group cohesiveness on performance: an empirical study of technology R&D teams in Taiwan. Technovation **29**(11), 786–797 (2009)
11. Lee, I., Portier, B.: An empirical study of knowledge representation and learning within conceptual spaces for intelligent agents. In: Innull, pp. 463–468. IEEE (2007)
12. Wang, H.: Research on the model of knowledge representation ontology based on framework in intelligent learning system. In: International Conference on Electrical and Control Engineering (ICECE), pp. 6757–6760. IEEE (2011)

13. Grigorova, D., Nikolov, N.: Knowledge representation in systems with natural language interface. In: Proceedings of the 2007 International Conference on Computer Systems and Technologies, p. 68. ACM (2007)
14. Yi, Y., Song, H., Bin, H., Xiao-ming, L.: Research on network of relationship in the large software research and development team based on complex network theory. In: 2010 Third International Conference on Information and Computing (ICIC), vol. 2, pp. 285–288. IEEE (2010)
15. Wang, L., Chen, J.: Empirical study on the influence factors of R&D team creativity in China. In: 4th IEEE International Conference on Management of Innovation and Technology, ICMIT 2008, pp. 260–265. IEEE (2008)
16. Huang, C. C., Jiang, P. C.: Examining transactive memory system in R&D teams. In: International Conference on Industrial Engineering and Engineering Management (IEEM) 2010, pp. 885–890. IEEE (2010)
17. Zhao, S., Wu, S.: The analysis on the impact of knowledge transfer process between Corporate R & D staff to technological innovation. Technol. Manag. **11**, 330–332 (2009)
18. Mohamed, R., Watada, J.: Evidence theory based knowledge representation. In: Proceedings of the 13th International Conference on Information Integration and Web-based Applications and Services, pp. 74–81. ACM (2011)
19. Portmanna, E., Kaltenriedera, P., Pedryczb, W.: Knowledge representation through graphs. Procedia Comput. Sci. **62**, 245–248 (2015)
20. Abdalla, G., Damasceno, C. D. N., Guessi, M., Oquendo, F., Nakagawa, E. Y.: A systematic literature review on knowledge representation approaches for systems-of-systems. In: IX Brazilian Symposium on Components, Architectures and Reuse Software (SBCARS), pp. 70–79. IEEE (2015)
21. Turnitsa, C., Tolk, A.: Knowledge representation and the dimensions of a multi-model relationship. In: Proceedings of the 40th Conference on Winter Simulation, pp. 1148–1156. Winter Simulation Conference (2008)
22. Yu, S., Zhiping, L.: Ontology-based domain knowledge representation. In: 4th International Conference on Computer Science&Education, pp. 174–177 (2009)
23. Wang, Z., Wan, Y.: Research on engineering change knowledge representation and retrieval technology based on ontology. In: 19th International Conference on Automation and Computing (ICAC), pp. 1–5. IEEE (2013)
24. Shen, J., Wu, B.: Service configuration knowledge representation, acquisition and reasoning. In: 11th International Conference on Service Systems and Service Management (ICSSSM), pp. 1–5. IEEE (2014)
25. Wongthongtham, P., Kasisopha, N., Chang, E., Dillon, T.:A software engineering ontology as software engineering knowledge representation. In: Third International Conference on Convergence and Hybrid Information Technology, ICCIT 2008. vol. 2, pp. 668–675. IEEE (2008)
26. Jianping, W.: A novel software engineering knowledge representation method for multi-site software development. In: 3rd International Conference on Software Engineering and Service Science (ICSESS), pp. 523–526. IEEE (2012)
27. Babu, L., Seetha Ramaiah, M., Prabhakar, T. V., Rambabu, D.:. Archvoc–towards an antology for software architecture. In: 2nd Workshop on SHAring and Reusing Architectural Knowledge Architecture, Rationale, and Design Intent (SHARK-ADI 2007), p. 5, Washington, DC, USA. IEEE Computer Society (2007)
28. Barbosa, E. F., Nakagawa, E. Y., Maldonado, J. C.: Towards the establishment of an ontology of software testing. In: 18th International Conference on Software Engineering and Knowledge Engineering (SEKE 2006), pp. 522–525, San Francisco, CA (2006)

29. Wen-zhou, Y., Jun-jie, D.: A study of knowledge representation of construction claims based on ontology. In: International Conference on Management Science and Engineering (ICMSE), pp. 2132–2136. IEEE (2013)
30. Zhen, L., Jiang, Z., Su, H., Liang, J.: RDF-based innovative design knowledge represent. In: First International Conference on Semantics, Knowledge and Grid, 2005. SKG 2005, p. 77. IEEE (2005)
31. Shetty, R. T., Riccio, P. M., Quinqueton, J.: Hybrid model for knowledge representation. In: 2006 International Conference on Hybrid Information Technology, ICHIT 2006. vol. 1, pp. 355–361. IEEE (2006)
32. Ribarić, S., Zadrija, V.: An object-oriented implementation of a knowledge representation scheme based on Fuzzy Petri nets. In: Seventh International Conference on Fuzzy Systems and Knowledge Discovery (FSKD), vol. 2, pp. 987–993. IEEE (2010)
33. Suraj, Z.: Knowledge representation and reasoning based on generalised fuzzy Petri nets. In: 12th International Conference on Intelligent Systems Design and Applications (ISDA), pp. 101–106. IEEE (2012)
34. Jakupovic, A., Pavlic, M., Mestrovic, A., Jovanovic, V.: Comparison of the nodes of knowledge method with other graphical methods for knowledge representation. In: 36th International Convention on Information & Communication Technology Electronics & Microelectronics (MIPRO), pp. 1004–1008. IEEE (2013)
35. Dromey, R. G.: From requirements to design: formalizing the key steps. In: First International Conference on Software Engineering and Formal Methods, Proceedings, pp. 2–11. IEEE (2003)
36. Wendland, M. F., Schieferdecker, I., Vouffo-Feudjio, A.: Requirements-driven testing with behavior trees. In: Fourth International Conference on Software Testing, Verification and Validation Workshops (ICSTW), pp. 501–510. IEEE (2011)

The Need for Obtaining Real Sponsor Satisfaction that Leads to Steady Generation of SPI Effects

Takeshige Miyoshi[✉]

Miyoshi Art of Software Process Inc., Saitama, Japan
miyoshi.gunta@mirror.ocn.ne.jp

Abstract. The SPICE frameworks and conformant models have considerably evolved in the past two decades. However, producing SPI effects to such levels as sponsors expect is not necessarily easy, because it is closely related to the "process context" of each organization. One of the key strategies for getting over this hurdle is to assiduously consider the "process context" in each of the SPI steps, and to determine the sponsor's satisfaction level with performance of assessment/appraisal. In most cases, the SPI sponsor, who has authority over the SPI effort, has issues in his/her business activities. By addressing these issues in the assessment/appraisal, the sponsor can recognize that the SPI activities are really connected to actual business. As an extension of the previous paper [1] that described the importance of producing 'quality' assessment outputs, this paper describes critical success factors for obtaining real satisfaction levels, that lead to steady generation of SPI effects.

Keywords: ISO/IEC 330xx family · CMMI® · SCAMPI^{SM} · Organization's process context · Sponsor Satisfaction Level (SSL)

1 Introduction

Since the "Software Process" came into the limelight in the 1980's, many efforts have been made by "Software Process" communities. The SPICE frameworks (ISO/IEC 15504 series [2–11] and ISO/IEC 330xx family [12–17]), their conformant process models (including CMM(I) [18], and appraisal methods [19]) have greatly evolved in the past two decades, and various benefits of using them have been reported. Accordingly, users of those frameworks and models have spread across many fields. However, still the effects of using them are not necessarily easily obtained to such levels as sponsors expect, in various cases. This is because producing SPI (Software Process Improvement) effects depends on how to interpret abstract model practices and how to practically implement them at their actual tasks, based on accurate understanding of their organization's "process context." Therefore, careful recognition of the definition of "Continual process improvement" is required today: It is defined as *"an on-going cycle of process improvement programs to strengthen and improve the processes supporting business"* in ISO/IEC 33001 [12]. Accordingly, the SPI activities must support the organization's business.

The importance of "Understanding the organization's 'process context' in SPI activities" was emphasized in the previous paper [1]. This is, however, not always so easy, because of the complexity of the organization's structure, management's pressure to produce business effects quickly, among many other issues. Therefore, in every step of an SPI program, the sponsor's positive support and participation is critical. In order to realize this, it is meaningful to perform assessment/appraisal during the early steps of the SPI cycle and to obtain a feeling of sponsors' real satisfaction with assessment outputs. In order to prove this, the author's experience-based qualitative data[1] were organized and analyzed from the viewpoint of "Sponsor Satisfaction Level (SSL) with assessment/appraisal outputs." Then Critical Success Factors (CSF) for increasing SSLs have been identified and examined.

In this paper, the background and data of SSL with performance of assessment/appraisal are explained in Sect. 2. Analysis of SSL data is shown in Sect. 3. Then CSFs for increasing SSL are described in Sect. 4. Those CSFs are examined from an SPI practitioner's viewpoint in Sect. 5, and finally, Sect. 6 concludes the paper.

2 Data of Sponsor Satisfaction Level (SSL) with Performance of Assessment/Appraisal

2.1 Background of This Paper

For the past two decades, personal notes have been taken at every opportunity of leading or participating in assessment/appraisal. From the early days, insufficient consideration of "process context" was sometimes observed in assessed organizations, resulting in modest support and participation by the sponsor, because he/she couldn't explicitly recognize that the SPI activities were really connected to their actual business performance. Actually, as described in ISO/IEC 33014 [13], the Sponsor has the following responsibilities;

> "The Sponsor has the overall responsibility for aligning the improvement program according to the actual **business goals**. The responsibility for initiating and supporting the improvement activities in the organization is located here. The sponsor – typically a person from top management - is the person (or group) that endorses the improvement programs or projects and demands the results. This type of role is found among top managers with responsibility for business, product and process development. Only at that level of the organization is there enough power and influence to make the necessary impact."

On the other hand, "process context" is emphasized as one of the cornerstones of achieving reliability and repeatability of assessment ratings [20];

> "An understanding of the **context** within which a process operates within an OU [Organizational Unit] is critical to accurately assessing whether a practice that has been implemented fulfills its purpose. The implementation of a practice that fully meets its purpose in a small, noncritical development environment may be totally inadequate in a large, critical environment. Therefore, the context within which a process is deployed fundamentally influences judgments of practice adequacy."

---

[1] See Sect. 2.2 for these data. Since the author's SPI experience is primarily focused on CMM(I)-based appraisals, these data are described in a CMM(I)-based setting.

This quotation implies that carefully organized data of the organization's "process context" should be considered when developing the organization's process manuals and guidelines in the early steps of an SPI program. Therefore, from the early steps of SPI programs, the sponsor should play an important role in clearly organizing such attribute data of the organization. Subsequently, the sponsor's positive support and participation in the SPI program can have a great impact on the effect of every step of the SPI activities. Among them, obtaining a feeling of real satisfaction with assessment/appraisal outputs could be the most important factor. Furthermore, the various elements of "process context," e.g., the organization's size & demographics, application domain, product attributes, will be gradually recognized by the sponsor to be quite meaningful in business-driven SPI, as the level of process capability and/or organizational maturity are increased.

2.2 Sources of Collected Assessment/Appraisal Data

For this study, a total of seventy personal notes taken from the late 1990's to the present are reviewed with special attention to the SSL. The personal notes include impressions of CMM(I)-based assessments/appraisals as well as 'self-evaluation data' of participants' performance during the Onsite period. The 'self-evaluation data' means one's evaluation results of SSL with assessment/appraisal findings, concerning nine Process Areas (PAs) of CMMI as well as corresponding Key Process Areas (KPAs) of SW-CMM. Mapping of KPAs to PAs is shown in Table 1[2].

2.3 Selected Attributes to Determine Sponsor Satisfaction Level (SSL)

Having been involved in Japan's national R&D project of evaluating the quality of software development tools [21], the importance of "simple or concise" evaluation factors due to cognitive and practical reasons came to mind. Therefore a total of ten attributes, divided into two factors, are selected as shown in Table 2.

The first factor is 'ATMs (Appraisal Team Members) Competency Level' (Factor (a)), especially, capability of interpreting the process model's practices considering the organization's "process context," so that those practices will effectively work in the organization's software development environment. This competency requires sufficient knowledge of the process model as well as enough experience of real-world software development projects.

---

[2] Since the basic policy of "Process Improvement" underlies both SW-CMM-based assessment (CBA-IPI) and CMMI-based appraisal (SCAMPI^{SM} Class A, 'Internal Process Improvement' mode), it is reasonable to use the evaluation data of both SW-CMM and CMMI together.

Table 1. Mapping of SW-CMM KPA to CMMI PA

Category	KPA in SW-CMM	PA in CMMI
Project Management	Software Project Planning	Project Planning (PP)
	Software Project Tracking and Oversight	Project Monitoring and Control (PMC)
Support	Measurement-1 in each KPA	Measurement and Analysis (MA)
Engineering	Software Product Engineering	Requirements Development (RD), Technical Solution (TS), Product Integration (PI)
Process Management	Organization Process Focus	Organizational Process Focus (OPF)
	Organization Process Definition	Organizational Process Definition (OPD)
	Training Program	Organizational Training (OT)

Table 2. SSL evaluation factors and attributes

Evaluation Factor	Evaluation Attribute			Evaluation Indicator & Level Scale
(a) ATMs Competency Level	Comprehensive ATMs Competency (This attribute includes capability of interpreting the process model's practices considering the "process context.")			From a comprehensive view, ATMs demonstrate, in every session of the Onsite period, a performance level of High ("3"), Middle ("2") or Low ("1").
(b) PA Findings Satisfaction Level by the sponsor	Project Management	PP	PMC	Sponsor's level of satisfaction with the Findings statements of each PA, classified to High ("3"), Middle ("2") or Low ("1") [a].
	Support	MA		
	Engineering	RD	TS	
		PI		
	Process Management	OPF	OPD	
		OT		

[a] Although the rating values of the nine attributes is sensitively and intuitively determined to be "3," "2," or "1," during the Final Findings Presentation session, they can be supplemented or modified in the Executive session that allows discussion with the sponsor. In this kind of sensitive & intuitive-based style, the evaluation results are more reasonable and useful in real-world SPI situations, because the actual voice of the sponsor can be directly considered. Although this style sounds 'subjective,' it is an attempt to get over the hurdle to realize steady generation of SPI effects.

The second factor is 'PA Findings Satisfaction Level by the sponsor' (Factor (b)). This means how deeply the sponsor is satisfied with the Findings statements of PAs. From a practical viewpoint, nine PAs from four process categories were selected: PP[3] and PMC[4] from 'Project Management' category, MA[5] from 'Support' category, RD[6], TS[7] and PI[8] from 'Engineering' category, as well as OPF[9], OPD[10] and OT[11] from 'Process Management' category.

The evaluation data of Factor (a) can be gained, in every session of the Onsite period as well as at the Executive session, which is usually conducted after the Final Findings Presentation, and which offers the opportunity for free discussion between the sponsor and ATMs (See Table 2). On the other hand, the data of Factor (b) can be collected at the Final Findings Presentation session, where all PA Findings are presented to the sponsor by the appraisal team leader. While reading the PA Findings, the team leader can see the reaction on the sponsor's face, from which his/her satisfaction level of the evaluation attributes can be determined. In addition, free conversation with the sponsor at an informal gathering after the assessment/appraisal is also an important source of assessing his/her satisfaction level (See Table 2).

2.4 Data Evaluation Results Representation Technique

As collected data gradually increases, the need for an easy way to represent the results of evaluation became evident. In order to see the similarity or difference with evaluation data of previously conducted assessments/appraisals, the evaluation results should be expressed as simply as possible to be understood at a glance. This, coupled with previous experience [21, 22], led to the development of a unique pie chart model shown in Fig. 1.

In the pie chart, ten attributes and the SSL are expressed by eleven segments. Each of the evaluated levels of the nine PAs and the ATMs Competency is represented by its radius. The radius is scaled in three levels corresponding to the three grade rating levels.

---

[3] PP: Project Planning.
[4] PMC: Project Monitoring & Control.
[5] MA: Measurement and Analysis.
[6] RD: Requirements Development.
[7] TS: Technical Solution.
[8] PI: Product Integration.
[9] OPF: Organizational Process Focus.
[10] OPD: Organizational Process Definition.
[11] OT: Organizational Training.

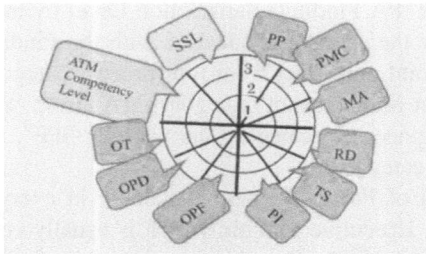

Fig. 1. SSL pie chart

3 Analysis of Sponsor Satisfaction Level (SSL) Data with Performance of Assessment/Appraisal

3.1 Steps of Data Analysis

The attribute data explained in the previous section were reviewed and analyzed during the past years, according to the following two recursive steps:

(1) When an assessment/appraisal was completed, a personal note was reviewed and organized. Then relevant data of ten attributes were extracted into a "SSL Attribute Table" (See Table 3). Then SSL was determined according to simple rating rules as follows:

> **<SSL rating rules>**
> High (3): more than 60% out of 10 attributes are rated "3"
> Middle (2): more than 60% out of 10 attributes are rated "3" or "2"
> Low (1): Any situation not covered by above

(2) Next, in order to understand, at a glance, the tendency of each data item of the organization, the Attribute Table data were transcribed into a SSL pie chart. Examples are shown in Fig. 2.

Table 3. An example of SSL data

SSL	Scale	ATMs Competency Level	PA Findings Satisfaction Level								
			Project Mgt/ Support			Engineering			Process Management		
			PP	PMC	MA	RD	TS	PI	OPF	OPD	OT
	3:High			O							
O	2:Middle	O	O				O	O	O		O
	1:Low				O	O				O	

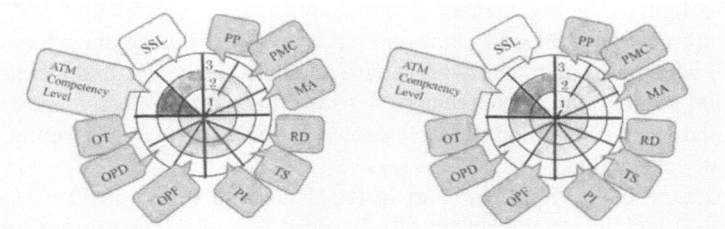

Fig. 2. Examples of SSL pie chart data

The number of extracted data from a total of seventy assessments/appraisals to each cell of the Attribute Table is shown in Table 4. Although 60 % of the total 70 cases are rated with Satisfaction Level 2 (Middle), approximately 27 % and 13 % are rated to be Satisfaction Level 3 (High) and 1 (Low) respectively. Looking globally, by considering the background context of each case, they can be broadly classified into three patterns, corresponding to the three grade rating levels. This analysis showed the tendency that higher ATMs competency level and meaningful PA Findings make SSL "High (3)." Lower ATMs competency level and less accurate PA Findings lead to lower SSLs (i.e., Middle ("2") or Low ("1")[12]. The characteristic tendencies of each pattern are described in the following subsections.

Table 4. Number of extracted data to each cell of SSL Attribute Table

S S L	Scale	ATMs Competency Level	PA Findings Satisfaction Level								
			Project Mgt/Support			Engineering			Process Management		
			PP	PMC	MA	RD	TS	PI	OPF	OPD	OT
19	3:High	19	20	19	19	18	18	21	15	15	20
42	2:Middle	44	35	35	31	40	40	40	40	40	40
9	1:Low	7	15	16	20	12	12	9	15	15	10

3.2 Three Patterns of Sponsor Satisfaction Level (SSL) Data

3.2.1 Pattern 1: Satisfaction Level-3

In the first pattern (Satisfaction level-3), the ATMs' capability of mapping the organization's activities to process model practices is high. Actually the organization's work environment and activities are clearly mapped to the process model's practices of relevant PAs. This shows their high capability of interpreting the process model's

---

[12] One of the notable points here is that the high SSL comes, not necessarily from just achieving the target maturity level, but rather from correctly understanding clarified PA Findings statements (Strengths & Weaknesses), in which the organization's real-world status is reflected. ("Whether a target capability/maturity level is achieved or not" is out of scope of this study.)

practices in light of the organization's "Process Context." The Strength and Weakness Findings are clearly expressed using unique terms (i.e., the organization's own terminology) which is used in their work environment and activities. In the Final Findings Presentation session and the Executive session, the sponsor clearly understands the meaning and intent of the Findings statements. He/she offers a vivid greeting indicating a feeling of satisfaction.

An example of the SSL pie chart in this Pattern is shown in Fig. 3, and a few examples of Findings statements are as follows: < Part of statements are simplified or edited, for preserving confidentiality, in these Subsects. from 3.2.1 to 3.2.3. >

<Project Planning (PP)>: *Having a reliable basis on historical data and process performance baselines, the quality and process performance objectives are clearly defined in the Project Planning document.*

<Requirements Development (RD), Technical Solution (TS)>: *The organization continues "process improvement" effort by addressing new improvements for upper development phases such as introduction of uniquely developed in-house tools. As a result, the total effort of reworking in lower phases is decreased, and this led to improved software quality and a decrease of development costs.*

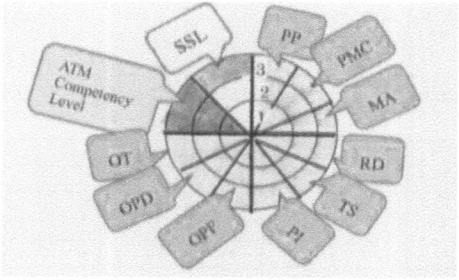

Fig. 3. An example of SSL pie chart in Pattern 1

3.2.2 Pattern 2: Satisfaction Level-2

In the second pattern (Satisfaction level-2), although the organization's issues are moderately mapped to the process model's PAs, and relevant PA Findings appear to be useful. However, they are expressed in somewhat abstract and superficial language. The meaning and intent of the Findings statements are not fully understood by the sponsor. In the Final Findings Presentation session and the Executive session, the sponsor offers a greeting indicating an intention of continuing their SPI activities.

An example of the SSL pie chart in this Pattern is shown in Fig. 4, and examples of Findings statements are as follows:

<Technical Solution (TS)>: *In the basic design phase, the decision experience is not shared among software projects, by documenting the rationale, when doing important decision-making on critical themes.*

<Organizational Process Focus (OPF)>: Since the procedures of collecting exemplary documents or useful data have not yet penetrated across the organization, useful process assets are not yet accumulated on the organization's process library.

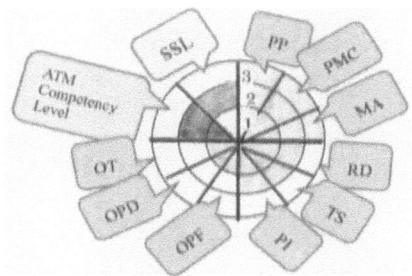

Fig. 4. An example of SSL pie chart in Pattern 2

3.2.3 Pattern 3: Satisfaction Level-1

In the third pattern (Satisfaction level-1), neither meaningful Strengths nor Weaknesses are observed. Sponsor's needs seem not to be understood by the organization's people. In addition, critical factors of "process context" are not clearly organized. The description of statements seems superficial, or they are 'pro-forma' and 'boiler-plate' statements using the model's wording. The sponsor greeting indicates their SPI activities are not clearly connected to their business.

An example of the SSL pie chart in this Pattern is shown in Fig. 5, and a few examples of Findings statements are as follows:

<Project Planning (PP)>: Estimates of project planning parameters are establish and maintained. And, a project plan is established as the basis for managing the project.

<Measurement and Analysis (MA)>: Measurement data are collected in every project according to the standard procedure. However, the MA activities are not effectively performed because the concept of MA process is not yet correctly recognized.

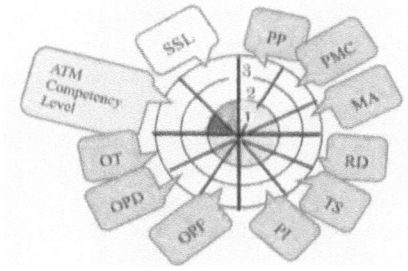

Fig. 5. An example of SSL pie chart in Pattern 3

4 Critical Success Factors (CSFs) for Increasing Sponsor Satisfaction Levels (SSLs)

In order to increase the effect of assessment/appraisal, one has been playing the role of lead assessor/appraiser, keeping a policy of having a pragmatic viewpoint in interpreting process models' practices and in observing the organization's processes. In addition, a convinced policy of discovering as many benefits as possible during assessment/appraisal, regardless of how large or small their SPI effects, was empirically proven to be valuable. Based on these policies and in light of the analysis results of SSL data described in the previous section, three CSFs have been identified for increasing the SSLs, as listed in Table 5.

Table 5. CSFs for Increasing SSLs[a]

CSF-1	Understanding the Organization's "Process Context" and Sponsor's Needs
CSF-2	Pragmatically Interpreting Model Practices and Mapping Them Flexibly to the Organization's Work
CSF-3	Developing High Comprehensibility Findings in Assessment/Appraisal

[a] These CSFs come from [23] and the author's actual experience in real-world assessments/ appraisals.

4.1 CSF-1: Understanding the Organization's "Process Context" and Sponsor's Needs

In order to promote 'continual process improvement' activities for supporting business, the organization's "process context" and sponsors' SPI needs should be clarified. In many cases, factors of "process context" differ, based on the nature of the organization's business. The "process context" includes application domain, size, criticality, complexity, and quality characteristics of its products or services. In addition, the organization should notice in the earliest step that the clarified factors of the "process context" could be very useful for establishing 'stable' processes, when moving forward to higher process capability levels or organizational maturity levels.

In general, sponsors' needs in software organizations include 'Quality,' 'Cost,' 'Delivery,' and 'Performance.' Typical examples are 'increasing quality of products,' 'decreasing cost of development,' 'keeping on schedule' and 'increasing productivity.' Therefore, when an assessment/appraisal is conducted, the sponsor's needs and aims of the SPI program should be clarified. Then the appraisal team should develop the Final Findings and other appraisal output documents which meet the sponsor's needs as closely as possible.

4.2 CSF-2: Pragmatically Interpreting Model Practices and Mapping Them Flexibly to the Organization's Work

Usually, in the early steps of an SPI program, the organization's process manuals and guidelines are developed. In this stage, it is critical to carefully organize data of the aforementioned factors of the organization's "process context". In real-world SPI situations, however, it is not always so easy to consider them, clearly and accurately. In addition to management's pressure, the reasons for this will broadly range from a simple reason, such as a lack of the "SPI frame of mind" among senior management to a complicated situation, caused by the organizational structure and problems at the human level. Therefore, the personal attributes/skills described in a previous paper [1], especially, "Communicative competence with composure and perseverance" and "Capability to organize complicated issues in real-world situations, and to clearly explain them to the point" are very helpful for those who promote the SPI program.

On the other hand, in the process frameworks and models such as SPICE and CMM (I), every process and practice has its own specific intent. Accordingly, the process model's abstract practices need to be interpreted in light of the "process context" and business objectives. Consequently, those practices effectively work for the real-world project situations of the organization. Empirically, the aforementioned personal attributes/skills could be helpful to do this interpretation, as well as for mapping the model practices to the real-world tasks conducted in the organization.

4.3 CSF-3: Developing High Comprehensibility Findings in Assessment/Appraisal

In order to obtain a feeling of sponsors' real satisfaction with assessment/appraisal outputs, the high capability of interpreting the process model's practices considering the organization's "process context" is necessary. As we see in Pattern 1 in 3.2.1, this capability is useful for developing and presenting high comprehensibility Findings that work under the organization's context. Besides, this makes it possible to clearly map the organization's work environment and activities to the process model's practices of relevant PAs. In this situation, the sponsor can clearly understand the meaning and intent of the Findings statements, because they are expressed using unique terminology which is used in their work environment and activities. Again, in order to do this, it would be helpful to keep in mind the importance of the "Capability to organize complicated issues in real-world situations, and to clearly explain them to the point" which was discussed and emphasized in a previous paper [1].

5 Examination of Critical Success Factors (CSFs)

From the perspective of business-driven SPI, "reducing variation in process performance" should be the primary topic for improving QCD (Quality/Cost/Delivery). In order to reduce variation as the organization improves in its process capability or organizational maturity, "understanding process context" and "obtaining sponsor participation" are key factors of successful SPI. (See CSF-1)

The steps or phases of organizational SPI programs are defined in SPICE's current Technical Report, *ISO/IEC TR 33014* [13], as well as in the SEI's IDEAL^{SM} approach [24] in a CMM(I) context. At one of the improvement phases, an assessment/appraisal is conducted, which is a meaningful and sensitive event in the SPI cycle. By conducting assessment/appraisal, gaps between the organization's current activities and model's goals/practices are identified. Then the current status of the organization is clarified from the viewpoint of each process. In this paper, nine PAs are selected for determining SSL, which include basic functions for software organizations to improve their processes. (See Table 1) Fundamental practices required in project management are included in PP and PMC in 'Project Management' category. MA in 'Support' category has basic but very meaningful practices for understanding by "number" the effects of SPI activities. RD, TS and PI in 'Engineering' category have comprehensive practices for software development. OPF, OPD and OT in 'Process Management' category also include meaningful practices for promoting organization level SPI program.

At an early step of the SPI program, an organization's unique factors of "process context" should be clarified. (See CSF-1) Then, in light of the unique "process context" factors, the organization's unique process manuals and guidelines should be developed that will effectively work in the organization's environment. (See CSF-2) For example, if an organization wants to improve QCD, with "Delivery" as the highest priority, (most probably,) "Project Management" practices can be primarily focused in the first stage (i.e., "Managed" level in both of SPICE and CMMI). Starting this "Managed" level, the "Measurement and Analysis (MA)" process plays a very meaningful role. Measurement is not so much about collection of numbers but rather about understanding what information is useful to take necessary improvement actions. In the MA activities in every maturity level, establishing 'operational' definitions in key metrics for QCD, considering the unique "process context" factors could be extremely useful. At the assessment/appraisal in this stage, using the organization's terminology (instead of the model's wording) is very important in order to attract the interest of the sponsor and participants.

After implementation of the "project management" practices, the organization can focus on establishment or improvement of their software engineering practices. At this stage (i.e., "Established" level in SPICE, and "Defined" level in CMMI), the organization can enrich their software engineering tasks and keep balance with management practices. In addition, projects' data and experience are shared at the organization level, by making good use of the "Process Assets," which have accumulated experience data within the organization. Using such development environments, the defects injected during upper and middle phases decrease, while defects removed in reviews will increase; then it is possible to reduce the variability of actual results around the QCD targets.

When the management and engineering practices are effectively and practically functioning in the organization's context, it is possible to move toward "high maturity" process activities (i.e., "Predictable" and "Innovating" levels in SPICE, and "Quantitatively Managed" and "Optimizing" levels in CMMI), by using accumulated data, which are quantitatively connected to the organization's business objectives of QCD. Concerning the comprehensibility of appraisal Findings, especially at this stage, the Strength and Weakness Findings are clearly expressed using unique terminology which is used in their work environment and activities. The sponsor clearly understands the meaning and intent of the Findings statements. (See CSF-3)

As was mentioned at the beginning of this section, "reducing variation in process performance" should be the primary topic for improving QCD and 'stable' process is so fundamental that its importance cannot be over-emphasized. Although, in several cases, it takes considerable time and effort to make process variation 'stable,' this kind of effort is critical and worthwhile toward establishing reliable Process Performance Baselines[13]. These can be used as bases of critical business decisions on QCD. However, in real-world situations, due to management's pressure to produce SPI effects and to achieve target maturity levels quickly, in some cases, people are apt to select an easy way to reach 'stable' processes. The fundamentals of SPC (Statistical Process Control) thinking such as "to isolate and eliminate elements that are making the process unstable" should be firmly kept in mind. Without this understanding, using complicated theories and methods is just a play on numbers. For example, improper use of statistical methods, such as nonlinear transformations of the data lead to confusion in reality. The following quotation indicates a quite persuasive example [25]. The argument by H.C. Tippett can be truly applied, even today, to the real-world software organizations which are trying to produce business effects through implementing "high maturity" practices.

> *"When using data in a business setting one should take care to present the data in a form that is easy to interpret. This will generally mean that one should avoid nonlinear transformations of the data such as logarithms, square roots, trigonometric functions, and probabilistic transformations... (A fascinating paraphrase of an argument by H.C. Tippett bears on this point [26].)*
> *Since nonlinear transformations are rarely used in business, their use in the analysis of business data is to be discouraged. Robust yet simple methods, such as the control chart, will be much better than less robust, more complex, analyses which depend upon transformations of the data."*

The most crucial point is that the high-maturity practices should be implemented using the accumulated meaningful data from 'stable' processes. From these real-world SPI viewpoints, the three CSFs are vital for "Obtaining Real Sponsor Satisfaction that Leads to Steady Generation of SPI Effects" as expressed in the title of this paper.

6 Conclusions

This paper emphasizes the importance of business-driven SPI activities. It requires assiduous consideration of "process context" of the organization, and positive support by a sponsor. In order to realize this, it is critical to obtain high level satisfaction by a sponsor with assessment/appraisal outputs. In order to prove this, accumulated personal notes of CMM(I)-based assessments/appraisals are reviewed and analyzed, with special attention to the SSL. In order to discuss the SSL at an assessment/appraisal, nine processes corresponding to the four process categories of CMMI-DEV model are used.

---

[13] In order to establish reliable Process Performance Baselines, data from 'stable' processes are required. Such data can sometimes be obtained by appropriate 'Subgrouping' or 'Stratification.' In addition, it is also critical to consider the interaction of processes and sub-processes.

Then, based on the analysis results, the CSFs are explained and examined. In the CSF examination, an example of a typical condensed scenario of elevation of an organization's process maturity level is explained, and a moderate caution about incorrect use of model interpretation in high maturity practices is presented. In this way, honest practitioners of SPI activities should contribute to the promising further development of the process frameworks and models, using their steady efforts and experience in real-world SPI fields. Of course, using process frameworks and models requires a steady, but sometimes difficult effort. However, such process frameworks and models should be used to help people, especially engineers and managers, in real-world software development situations. Eventually, this kind of 'Field-oriented' thinking could most realistically lead to steady generation of SPI effects.

References

1. Miyoshi, T.: Emphasis on personal attributes/skills to produce 'quality' assessment outputs that lead to steady generation of spi effects. In: Rout, T., O'Connor, R.V., Dorling, A. (eds.) SPICE 2015. CCIS, vol. 526, pp. 87–99. Springer, Heidelberg (2015)
2. ISO/IEC 15504-1:2004, Information technology- Process assessment - Part 1: Concepts and vocabulary
3. ISO/IEC 15504-2:2003, Information technology - Process assessment - Part 2: Performing an assessment
4. ISO/IEC 15504-3:2004, Information technology - Process assessment - Part 3: Guidance on performing an assessment
5. ISO/IEC 15504-4:2004, Information technology - Process assessment - Part 4: Guidance on use for process improvement and process capability determination
6. ISO/IEC 15504-5:2012, Information technology - Process assessment - Part 5: An exemplar Process Assessment Model
7. ISO/IEC 15504-6:2013, Information technology - Process assessment - Part 6: An exemplar system life cycle process assessment model
8. ISO/IEC TR 15504-7:2008, Information technology - Process assessment - Part 7: Assessment of organizational maturity
9. ISO/IEC TS 15504-8:2012, Information technology - Process assessment - Part 8: An exemplar process assessment model for IT service management
10. ISO/IEC TS 15504-9:2011, Information technology - Process assessment - Part 9: Target process profiles
11. ISO/IEC TS 15504-10:2011, Information technology - Process assessment - Part 10: Safety extension
12. ISO/IEC-33001:2015, Information technology - Process assessment - Concepts and terminology
13. ISO/IEC TR 33014:2013, Information technology — Process assessment — Guide for process improvement
14. ISO/IEC-33002:2015, Information technology - Process assessment - Requirements for performing process assessment
15. ISO/IEC-33003:2015, Information technology - Process assessment - Requirements for process measurement frameworks

16. ISO/IEC-33004:2015, Information technology - Process assessment - Requirements for process reference, process assessment and maturity models
17. ISO/IEC-33020:2015, Information technology - Process assessment - Process measurement framework for assessment of process capability
18. CMMI Product Team, CMMI for Development, Version 1.3, Technical report CMU/SEI-2010-TR-033, Software Engineering Institute (2010)
19. SCAMPI Upgrade Team, Standard CMMI® Appraisal Method for Process Improvement (SCAMPI[SM]) A, Version 1.3: Method Definition Document, HANDBOOK CMU/SEI-2011-HB-001 (2011)
20. Emam, K.E., Drouin, J.N., Melo, W.: SPICE – The Theory and Practice of Software Process Improvement and Capability Determination. IEEE Computer Society Press (1998)
21. Miyoshi, T., Azuma, M.: An empirical study of evaluating software development environment quality. IEEE TSE **19**(5), 425–435 (1993)
22. Miyoshi, T.: Early Experience with Software Process Assessment Using SPICE Framework at Software Research Associates, Inc., SOFTWARE PROCESS – Improvement and Practice, vol. 2(3), pp. 211–235. John Wiley & Sons Ltd. (1996)
23. Paulk, M.C., et al.: The Capability Maturity Model – Guidelines for Improving the Software Process. Addison Wesley, Reading (1997)
24. Bush, M., Dunaway, D.: CMMI Assessments–Motivating Positive Change. Addison Wesley, Reading (2005)
25. Wheeler, D.J., Chambers, D.S.: Understanding Statistical Process Control. SPC Press, New York (1992)
26. Tippett, L.H.C.: The Methods of Statistics, 4th edn., pp. 344–345. Williams & Norgate Ltd. (1952)

Short Papers

Investigating the Suitability of Using Agile for Medical Embedded Software Development

Surafel Demissie^(✉), Frank Keenan, and Fergal McCaffery

Regulated Software Research Centre and Lero, Department of Computing and Mathematics,
Dundalk Institute of Technology, Dundalk, Co. Louth, Ireland
{surafel.demissie,frank.keenan,fergal.mccaffery}@dkit.ie

Abstract. Agile has been the subject of safety and critical domain in recent years. Emerging medical devices are highly relying on embedded software that runs on the specific platform in real time. The development of embedded software is different from ordinary software development due to the hardware-software dependency. Previous literature reviews discussed the challenges of bringing Agile practices to embedded software developments in general. This paper outlines the challenges and addresses the future work from medical embedded software development perspective.

Keywords: Medical device software · Agile software development · Embedded software · Challenges

1 Introduction

The medical device market is breaking through the world economy and showing substantial impact. Industry experts anticipate this market to register robust growth over the next years with figures expected to expand from 133.6bn USD in 2014 to 173.3bn USD in 2019 [1]. A key characteristic of many medical devices is that of embedded software systems. Essentially, such systems are computerized systems that are unique as they are designed to perform specific task on specific platform. The complexity and growth rate of embedded software has been increasing over the past decades. From insulin pumps, pacemakers, cardiac monitors, to anesthesia machines, software is playing a major role in the functionalities of these devices. For example, implanted cardiac pacemakers and defibrillators have approximately 80,000 to 100,000 lines of software code [2]. However, the development of embedded software adds different challenges to the software engineer due to their complexity.

The development of Medical embedded software development brings challenges from embedded software development which is related to technological factors including platform, hardware-software dependency and real-time nature. Also, progress typically requires input from multiple diverse stakeholder groups including, for example, software developers, hardware engineers, and possibly mechanical engineers in addition to the expected medical domain experts. Such diversity requires much interaction and multi domain communication.

To attempt to control risk and overcome the challenges presented for such development, teams typically follow a plan-driven approach, such as the V-model, and need to provide an evidence to show their software development process to get pre-market and post-market approval [3]. As such, they are obliged to conform to regulations outlined by Medical Device Directive (MDD) in Europe or Food and Drug Administration (FDA) in the US. However, there have been calls for a better software development framework to address the trustworthiness of critical embedded software development. Indeed, most these regulations are high-level and don't dictate about low-level implementation [4]. These regulatory environments are complicated and changing. This is due to the amendments that these regulations went through periodically [5].

One approach that may offer assistance is the agile software development [6] which has been a hot issue in recent embedded software development projects. Generally, agile methods recommend a high degree of expert customer involvement, ability to incorporate changing requirements and short development cycles producing working software. Numerous agile methods are available including eXtreme Programming (XP) [7], Scrum and Feature Driven Development (FDD) [8].

The purpose of this paper is to identify these challenges and discuss the future work on how medical device makers need to improve their software development process to address the challenges. The next section summarizes Medical device software development process. This is followed by medical embedded software issues. Finally we will address how we can benefit from Agile to address the challenges of medical embedded software development.

2 Medical Device Software Development

Safety critical systems are systems whose failure or abnormal functionality will result on a loss or damage to human life or the environment. Medical devices are a subset of such systems. Modern medical devices are getting too complex and most of their functionalities are relying on software. In fact software itself is considered as medical device [MDD 2007/47/EC].

Given their criticality, documented evidence through highly-regulated process is required. Depending on their geographical location, medical device companies need to provide evidence that they went through the desired process to get the approval by the regulatory body. For example, in the European Union medical devices must have the CE mark [29]. This process includes satisfying standards such as medical device quality management standard (EN ISO 13485:2003) [30], medical device risk management standard (EN ISO 14971:2009) [31] and the medical device product level standard (IEC 60601-1 [32]).

The challenges that software development companies in the medical device domain face when they want to market a device can be categorized in two ways:

2.1 Software Development Life-Cycle Choice

The traditional plan-driven software development approaches such as waterfall [9] or V-model approaches emphasize a structured progression between defined phases.

Each phase consists on a definite set of activities and deliverables that must be accomplished before the following phase can begin [10]. Conformance to such a process makes the regulatory process structured and organized and enables traceability. Despite having a structural balance and their disciplined nature, these models are reported to be risky and their implementation invites failure because if requirements change during development phase the amount of rework is costly. The other main concern of these models is that the actual development comes late in the process and this makes the results invisible for a long time. This delay can be disconcerting to management and customers [10].

2.2 Large and Complex Regulatory Process

The need to adherence to a large number of regulatory requirements specified in various international standards is also one of the challenges that medical device companies need to deal with [3]. These regulations are complex and need a unified framework that can serve as a reference by medical device companies. Recently a framework named MDevSPICE® has been proposed by our research center that integrates requirements from various international medical device standards and guidance documents with the generic software development best practices while providing a possibility to assess processes [11]. This framework also includes system level processes that have an impact on software requirements. Using this framework a medical device software developer can produce software that will be safe and easily integrated with other sub-systems of the overall medical device. The purpose of our project is to add flexibility to MDevSPICE® framework through incorporating tailored agile practices to suit embedded medical software development.

3 Medical Embedded Software

The development of embedded software is different from commercial or application software as it has to interact to the hardware in real-time [12]. While commercial software development focus on algorithm and data processing, embedded software development aims at managing and controlling system or hardware. Even though there would be data and algorithm in embedded software, it would be only to control and manage the hardware in a better way.

Embedded software development has grown complex and attract the attention of researchers. The challenges of embedded software development has been addressed frequently [12, 13]. The addressed challenges are related to issues such as functionality, real-time behavior, system complexity, optimization, interdependency, verification and tools.

Developing embedded software requires the simultaneous work of hardware and software which is known as co-design. Multi domain experts aim at optimizing both applications and hardware for some combination of performance, power, and cost. Thus effective communication between these diverse roles is a factor for the success of an embedded software development team.

Emerging medical embedded software development, as a subset of embedded software, shares these challenges. These devices are getting complex functionalities and most of these functionalities are relying on the correct functionality of the embedded software. For example, [14] reports that in medical device industry system complexity is exceeding software maturity and the industry is not taking full advantage of well-known techniques for engineering software for critical systems. The same report suggests the need to apply system engineering approach to deal with complexity. Thus the industry is calling for a better software development practice.

4 Agile Software Development as a Means to Face the Challenges

Medical device software developer has to deal with challenges at high level concerning certification and regulation [15] and technical challenges associated with embedded software at a lower level.

4.1 Related Work

To understand the challenges associated with the applicability of agile for medical embedded software development, we have performed a mini-literature review. There exist very little research on the applicability of agile for safety critical regulated environments and most of previous works are industrial reports and case studies [16]. Barriers such as lack of documentation, traceability issues, lack of up-front planning and management of multiple releases have also been reported by medical device companies on the implementation of agile [17]. Despite progress, there are limited reports on the adaption of agile practices for medical embedded software development. One recent technical document released by the Association for the Advancement of Medical Instrumentation (AAMI:TIR 45:2012) comments on the applicability of Agile practices for the development medical devices [4]. According to this technical document, both agile and regulatory perspectives value high-quality software and we've to align both goals. The nature of embedded software development brings its own challenges. To overcome the embedded challenge previous reports on agile adaption fall into three categories.

1. Creation of a new agile method: for example [18] report the development of a new agile method using XP and Scrum as well as organizational patterns as agile patterns.
2. Modifying the agile principles to suit embedded behavior: the authors of [19] modified the agile principles and created their own set principle.
3. Tailoring different agile processes by selecting and combining practices from different methods.

The majority of previous work fits in the third category. Most of these reports employ the implementation of Scrum and XP [20–23]. The reports also suggest that there is no reason why agile methods could not–at least to some extent-be used for embedded domain. The reports also suggest that there is a clear gap due to lack of empirical research.

Numerous challenges are reported. Quite a few are related to the highly regulated and complex process [16, 24–26] which still needs rigorous research. Regarding multi domain communication, modification to Scrum practices, including the Product Owner (PO) role and scrum master role, brought benefits but required significant effort [27].

5 Supporting Multiple Stakeholder Input

The proposal here is to expand the MDevSPICE® framework by increasing its flexibility through incorporating tailored agile practices to suit embedded medical software development. One question that needs to be addressed is which combination of practices can support multi-domain stakeholder communication. At a general level each Agile Method claims to support the principles of the Agile Manifesto. Two principles appear to offer guidance for interaction between different parties. One claims that "the most efficient and effective method of conveying information to and within a development team is face-to-face conversation". Another emphasizes that for success knowledgeable and important stakeholders must work directly with developers "daily throughout the project". Specific Agile Methods then recommend practices that can help to realize these principles.

Our overall approach will incorporate practices drawn from XP and Scrum, the two most popular Agile Methods. However, as Scrum is essentially a project management approach and offers little guidance on main lifecycle phases we consider here the practices of XP that can be used to support the main life cycle phases. The most recent version of XP describes 24 individual practices of which 13 are listed as primary practices. Those that offer support for multi domain communication and offer potential for Embedded Medical Device Software Development [28].

- *Pair Programming:* All code is written with two programmers at one machine. For each pair two interchanging roles are recommended. One is in control of the keyboard and is thinking about the best way to solve the problem. The other thinks strategically questioning the whole approach, looking for test cases and performing code inspections.
- *Sit Together:* Teams should sit together and work in an open space to support open, collaborative and effective communication between members
- *Whole Team:* Teams should consist of the relevant expertise, a set of a diverse roles are necessary to effectively complete a given project
- *Real Customer Involvement:* Those who are directly affected have the most representative perspective of the problem and should be involved with the team *throughout* development
- *Informative Workspace:* This practice encourages the use of the wall to post informative artifacts such as user stories and wall charts depicting progress including potential problems that require attention keeping everyone informed
- *User stories:* Requirements should *initially* be described using user stories to provoke a discussion between the customer and developers. Each user story is required to include an Acceptance Test written by a domain expert

- *Weekly cycles:* Lengthy development cycles can increase the complexity of problems encountered during deployment so weekly cycles are encouraged to mitigate this
- *Quarterly Cycles:* For larger projects where it is not suitable to deliver weekly, work should be divided into quarterly cycles which helps check on "alignment with larger goals" and taking account of the "big picture" as progress is made

6 Conclusion and Future Work

As part of our in-progress project, we have discussed the current activities that we're performing for the challenges of medical embedded software development. To deal with the challenge associated with multiple stakeholder input we have proposed a tailored approach incorporating practices drawn from XP. But for the overall challenges we will incorporate practices from both XP and Scrum. In the future we're planning to expand the MDevSPICE® framework by adding flexibility through tailoring. The future work also includes performing a survey with medical device companies to further analyze additional challenges and apply the proposed tailored approach.

Acknowledgments. This research is supported by the SFI through Lero - the Irish Software Research Centre (http://www.lero.ie) grant 10/CE/I1855 & 13/RC/20194.

References

1. Espicom: United States Medical Devices Report. http://www.espicom.com/usa-medical-device-market.html
2. Jiang, Z., Mangharam, R.: High-confidence medical device software development. Found. Trends® Electron. Des. Autom. **9**, 309–391 (2015)
3. Munzner, R.F.: Entering the U.S. Medical Device Marlket, pp. 3548–3550 (2003)
4. AAMI: AAMI TIR45: Guidance on the use of AGILE practices in the development of medical device software (2012)
5. McHugh, M., McCaffery, F., Casey, V.: Changes to the international regulatory environment. J. Med. Devices **6**, 021004 (2012)
6. Greer, D., Hamon, Y.: Agile software Development. Softw. Pract. Exp. **41**, 943–944 (2011)
7. Beck, K.: Embracing change with extreme programming. Computer **32**, 70–77 (1999). (Long. Beach. Calif)
8. Palmer, S.R., Felsing, M.: A Practical Guide to Feature-Driven Development. Prentice Hall, Upper Saddle River (2001)
9. Royce, D.W.W.: Managing the development of large software systems. In: IEEE WESCON, pp. 1–9 (1970)
10. Munassar, N.M.A., Govardhan, A.: A comparison between five models of software engineering. Int. J. Comput. Sci. **7**, 94–101 (2010)
11. Mccaffery, F., Lepmets, M., Clarke, P.: Medical device software as a subsystem of an overall medical device. In: Proceedings of First International Conference Fundamentals and Advances in Software Systems Integration (2015)
12. Woodward, M.V., Mosterman, P.J.: Challenges for embedded software development. In: 2007 50th Midwest Symposium on Circuits and Systems, pp. 630–633 (2007)

13. Ebert, C., Jones, C.: Embedded software: facts, figures, and future. Computer **42**, 42–52 (2009). (Long. Beach. Calif)
14. Fu, K.: Trustworthy medical device software. In: Institute of Medicine Workshop on Public Health Effectiveness of the FDA 510, vol. 510, pp. 1–20 (2011)
15. Hrgarek, N.: Certification and regulatory challenges in medical device software development. In: Proceedings of 2012 4th International Workshop on Software Engineering in Health Care, SEHC 2012, pp. 40–43 (2012)
16. Fitzgerald, B., Stol, K.J., O'Sullivan, R., O'Brien, D.: Scaling agile methods to regulated environments: an industry case study. In: Proceedings of International Conference on Software Engineering, pp. 863–872 (2013)
17. McHugh, M., McCaffery, F., Casey, V.: Barriers to adopting agile practices when developing medical device software. In: Mas, A., Mesquida, A., Rout, T., O'Connor, R.V., Dorling, A. (eds.) SPICE 2012. CCIS, vol. 290, pp. 141–147. Springer, Heidelberg (2012)
18. Cordeiro, L., Barreto, R., Barcelos, R., Oliveira, M., Lucena, V., Maciel, P.: TXM: an agile HW/SWDevelopment methodology for building medical devices. ACM SIGSOFT Softw. Eng. Notes. **32**, 4 (2007)
19. Kaisti, M., Mujunen, T., Mäkilä, T., Rantala, V., Lehtonen, T.: Agile principles in the embedded system development. In: Cantone, G., Marchesi, M. (eds.) XP 2014. LNBIP, vol. 179, pp. 16–31. Springer, Heidelberg (2014)
20. Kaisti, M., Rantala, V., Mujunen, T., Hyrynsalmi, S., Könnölä, K., Mäkilä, T., Lehtonen, T.: Agile methods for embedded systems development - a literature review and a mapping study. EURASIP J. Embed. Syst. **2013**, 15 (2013)
21. Xie, M., Shen, M., Rong, G., Shao, D.: Empirical studies of embedded software development using agile methods: a systematic review. J. Inf. Syst. **2**, 21–26 (2012)
22. Srinivasan, J., Dobrin, R., Lundqvist, K.: "State of the Art" in using agile methods for embedded systems development. In: 2009 33rd Annual IEEE International Computer Software and Application Conference, vol. 2, pp. 522–527 (2009)
23. Albuquerque, C.O., Antonino, P.O., Nakagawa, E.Y.: An investigation into agile methods in embedded systems development. In: Murgante, B., Gervasi, O., Misra, S., Nedjah, N., Rocha, A.M.A., Taniar, D., Apduhan, B.O. (eds.) ICCSA 2012, Part III. LNCS, vol. 7335, pp. 576–591. Springer, Heidelberg (2012)
24. Jonsson, H., Larsson, S., Punnekkat, S.: Agile practices in regulated railway software development. In: Proceedings of - 23rd IEEE International Symposium on Software Reliability Engineering Workshops, ISSREW 2012, pp. 355–360 (2012)
25. Rasmussen, R., Hughes, T., Jenks, J.R., Skach, J.: Adopting agile in an FDA regulated environment. In: Proceedings of the Agile 2009 Conference (Agile 2009), pp. 151–155 (2009)
26. Zema, M., Rosati, S., Gioia, V., Knaflitz, M., Balestra, G.: Developing medical device software in compliance with regulations, pp. 1331–1334 (2015)
27. Goncalves, G.S., Luiz, G., Lima, B., Maria, R.E., Tadeu, R., Valeria, M., Ferreira, M.A., Chaves, A., Olimpio, A., Gomes, A., Otero, L., Eduardo, L., Vasconcelos, G. De, Yukio, L., Sato, C., Nunweiler, H., Silva, A., Marques, J.C., Pierre, A.L.: An interdisciplinary academic project for spatial critical embedded system agile development. In: DASC (2015)
28. Beck, K., Andres, C.: Extreme Programming Explained. Addison-Wesley, Reading (2005)
29. British Standards Online (America). http://www.bsiamerica.com/en-us/Sectors-and-Services/Industry-sectors/Healthcare-and-medical-devices/CE-marking-for-medicaldevices/
30. EN ISO 13485:2003 Medical Device: Quality Management Systems. Requirements for the Regulatory Process, 24 July 2003

31. EN ISO 14971:2009 Medical Devices. Application of Risk management to medical devices, 31 July 2009
32. EN 60601-1 Medical Electrical Equipment. General requirements for basic safety and essential performance. Collateral standard. Usability, 31 May 2010

Agile – Is it Suitable for Medical Device Software Development?

Fergal McCaffery^(✉), Kitija Trektere, and Ozden Ozcan-Top

Regulated Software Research Centre, Dundalk Institute of Technology,
Dublin Road, Dundalk, Co.Louth, Ireland
{fergal.mccaffery,kitija.trektere}@dkit.ie,
ozdentop@gmail.com

Abstract. Medical device software is typically developed through adopting a prescribed plan driven software development lifecycle approach based upon variations of the waterfall or V-Model. Organisations wishing to satisfy regulations have to define software development processes and also that these processes have been implemented throughout the complete development lifecycle. Agile development techniques report to offer solutions within other industries that would solve challenges encountered within the medical device industry. However, there are some concerns with using agile for medical device software development in relation to satisfying the regulatory bodies. In this short paper, we highlight the issues in traditional medical device software development. Secondly, we discuss the challenges and highlight agile practices that have been successfully adopted in the medical device software industry.

Keywords: Medical device · Agile software development · Plan driven · V–model

1 Introduction and Background to the Medical Device Software

The proportion of software used in the medical device (MD) industry has grown significantly with the amount of software increasing within traditional MDs. Also due to a change in regulations a MD can consist entirely of software or have software as a component of the overall MD system [1]. In the US, the Food and Drug Administration (FDA) oversees regulation. To assist manufacturers to satisfy regulations the FDA provides guidance documents for MD manufacturers and software developers [2]. The challenge that MD software development companies face when wanting to market a device is that they need to adhere to a large number of regulatory requirements specified in various international standards. Due to the demands to satisfy the documentation required by the regulatory requirements, MD software development has typically adopted a plan driven development lifecycle. In this study, we outline the issues with implementing a plan driven lifecycle and by conducting a literature review discuss both the challenges and success stories from adopting an agile software development approach.

1.1 Research Approach

This research forms part of a larger research project to develop an agile framework for mobile medical software application development. This research project will involve initially performing an extensive literature review of 3 areas of interest: mobile application development, medical device software development processes and agile software development practices. In Sect. 2, the benefits and barriers from implementing a Waterfall or V-Model lifecycle are described. In Sect. 3, agile development is introduced with a focus on its usage in highly regulated environments based upon information obtained from performing a literature review. The conclusions from this research along with future plans are detailed in Sect. 4.

2 Traditional MD Software Development

Medical software development is typically performed in a plan-driven manner, usually through adopting either Waterfall or V-Model lifecycles. When using a Waterfall approach [3] it is crucial to set stable requirements that are well known and are not subject to change. It follows a predefined sequence. Royce also stated that following a sequential cascading lifecycle is "risky and invites failure".

The Waterfall Model is easy to understand and is suitable whenever staff are inexperienced as it provides clearly defined steps and deliverables [4]. With this approach requirements are defined at the start of the development and help maintain stability. Where quality is the primary factor, the Waterfall Model is well suited as each stage can be completed before moving on to the next stage. However, if cost and time are more important other lifecycles should be considered the waterfall model can consume considerable effort.

The V-Model is a variation of the waterfall model that specifically includes different types of testing at the various stages of the lifecycle [5]. With the V-model testing is planned in parallel with a corresponding development phase. Therefore, the V-model is particularly well suited to MD software development as verification is required at each phase of the lifecycle to indicate that the requirements of each phase have been fulfilled, this verification is important in terms of the objective evidence that is required to satisfy the regulatory bodies. Additionally, traceability is an integral part of a regulatory compliant MD software development process [6] and the performance of verification in parallel with each corresponding phase of development, makes the V-Model very suitable for achieving regulatory requirements [7–9]. Consequently, the V-model can be particularly beneficial to follow in the development of safety critical software (Ge et al. 2010).

2.1 Barriers When Implementing Waterfall/V-Model Software Development

When adopting a strictly traditional waterfall/V-Model software development lifecycle there is no specific focus upon iterations, therefore making it more difficult to deliver frequent releases and to amend incorrect decisions in a timely manner. Consequently, no working software is produced until late in the development cycle, therefore increasing the risk of delivering an invalid product. Such lifecycles do not include a prototyping practice that would actively engage users in the development process and help to detect errors as well through increased communication [10]. The traditional lifecycle involves spending a considerable amount of time producing and verifying documentation. However, a lot of time and effort is spent producing documentation and therefore less time is left for the development and testing phases of the lifecycle. Such lifecycles do not embrace change easily; therefore, any changes introduced once the project has started can create financial overruns.

3 Agile Software Development

Agile software development has been used successfully in many different domains to improve the efficiency of software development. This created interest from the medical device community in relation to the suitability of agile for the development of regulatory compliant software. A working group was formed by the Association for the Advancement for Medical Instrumentation (AAMI) and they produced AAMI:TIR 45:2012 [11] which is an internationally accepted technical report outlining that "agile practices can be successfully adopted to develop regulatory compliant software" [12]. Agile software development literature reports "the promise of improved software quality and reduced delivery times" [13]. There are several reported benefits for adopting agile development practices including: delivering working software frequently; getting fast feedback and adjusting and embracing change accordingly; and minimized bureaucracy [14].

3.1 Use of Agile in Highly Regulated Environments

In this section, we provide findings within regulated domains that have benefited from using agile methods/techniques and/or discovered challenges during the implementation of the agile methods and techniques.

Agile adoption challenges in the medical domain. Gathering evidence that defined processes have been adhered to is an essential part of MD development. This evidence consists of different types of documents which need to be kept up-to-date and traceable. It is therefore not suitable to generate such documents and key artefacts at the end of the project, agile principles therefore need to cater for the generation of such documentation within each iteration along with other essential work [9]. Given the increased number of iterations in agile development appropriate tool support is important for the generation of evidence documentation. Different tool solutions were proposed such as having a wiki that is continuously updated, automated online documentation created from source or freely available in a book which is created from the source tree [15].

As the approval of medical product by regulatory bodies is mandatory, adoption of agile practices will only be permitted by senior management if proof exists of being able to provide the same level of traceability, verification, risk mitigation and validation as when using the V-model [16]. One significant experience reported the un-approval of executed test cases due to a lack of detail in test steps during an FDA audit [9], even though the intent of the device was satisfied and the software functioned as intended.

Besides regulatory requirements, there are issues that make it difficult to adapt and implement agile approaches in MD development. One of them is the hardware components of MDs (mostly including embedded software). Rottier and Rodrigues describe the need for extensive manual testing for verification as those systems may have interfaces with external hardware [16]. In addition, hardware development has its own independent life cycle that has to be integrated with software development on specific milestones. Achieving balance between upfront design and just in time design especially for the systems that rely heavily on hardware decisions like MDs is difficult. Rodriguez mentions that the lack of revisiting the architectural design regularly during development and not evolving will lead to the need for major code refactoring in the future [16]. Paulk states that "agile methods may be inappropriate for life-critical and essential moneys projects to the degree they oversimplify design and lack documentation" [17] however he also outlines that XP and Scrum methods have been used successfully within other domains.

Some other challenges include "adoption of an agile methodology in specific projects while the rest of the organization is still implementing a waterfall approach combined with an iterative software development approach, managing changes in requirements [16] and restructuring of the organization (especially the QA teams) [18]. Additionally, few studies specifically emphasised the impact of agile adoption upon the company and the team culture [12].

Successful Stories of Agile Adoption. In one of his key principles E. Deming states *"Eliminate the need for massive inspection by building quality into the product in the first place"* [19]. Manjunath et al. describe how they used continuous integration, coding guidelines and code reviews to obtain built-in quality in the first instance [20]. From this perspective, agile software development doesn't conflict with MD regulations, as it facilitates achievement of safety and built-in quality.

While an agile philosophy is thought to be in conflict with regulatory requirements, the use of agile software development for MDs goes back to the 2000 s [21]. Fitzgerald et al. [22] present an adopted Scrum approach for regulated environments called *R-Scrum*. This study details an adapted Scrum approach (*R-Scrum*) for achieving compliance to regulatory requirements and documents the results of the application of R-Scrum in a MD development project. In 2005, Sutherland evaluated Scrum using a medical company [21]. Since then Scrum has been adopted in various MD development projects [18, 22–24]. It is significant that more than half of the projects referenced in this study adopted Scrum to some extent. What makes Scrum so popular is its clear roadmap and easy to understand and implement structure. However, Scrum is only one part of the solution. The heart of the agile manifesto is "working software over comprehensive documentation". The practices to achieve working software in regular intervals throughout a project require adaptation of highly technical practices such as Test Driven Development (TDD), automated testing and continuous integration. Rottier and Rodrigues explain how applying extensive amounts of manual testing degraded their velocity in one MD project and how the significant amount of work required for test automation was worth the effort. Initially, they used basic Scrum and then integrated TDD and test automation during the project. They mentioned that *"Scrum started showing its strengths finally"* as they improved in TDD and automated verification. Therefore, to achieve full success, teams should incorporate technical practices [16]. For example, Pair Programming and TDD worked well for Medtronic providing them early feedback and improved quality [23]. A survey of 20 Irish MD software development organisations in 2012 revealed that 50 % of organisations were using the V-Model, 25 % of them were following an agile approach and the "remaining 25 % used other development lifecycles such as the Waterfall, and Iterative & Incremental approaches" [25]. The case studies [9, 16, 23, 26] highlighted that following an agile approach "can resolve problems associated with plan driven software development" [25].

4 Conclusion

In this paper, we discussed the benefits and challenges that are likely to be observed when implementing waterfall/V-Model in MD software development lifecycles. As these models have been widely adopted in MD software development, we sought evidence on the use of agile software development in the MD domain to encourage practitioners to evaluate the benefits of performing agile software development. This work supported findings from previous research that was conducted in relation to using agile for regulatory environments in 2013 [22], observing that there is still very little evidence on explaining experiences on the use of agile methods/practices in the medical domain.

Acknowledgments. This research is supported by the SFI through Lero - the Irish Software Research Centre (http://www.lero.ie) grant 10/CE/I1855 & 13/RC/20194.

References

1. FDA: Chapter I - Food and drug administration, department of health and human services subchapter H - Medical devices, Part 820 - Quality system regulation, USA
2. FDA, Guidance Document - Medical Devices and Radiation-Emitting Products. Center for Devices and Radiological Health (2015)
3. Royce, W.W.: Managing the development of large software systems. In: Proceedings of IEEE WESCON, vol. 26, pp. 1–9, August 1970
4. ExecutiveBrief, Which Life Cycle Is Best for Your Project? (2008). https://www.projectsmart.co.uk/which-life-cycle-is-best-for-your-project.php
5. Rook, P.: Controlling software projects. Softw. Eng. J. **1**(1), 7–16 (1986)
6. Casey, V., Mccaffery, F.: Med-Trace: Traceability Assessment Method for Medical Device Software Development, vol. 1, pp. 1–5 (2011)
7. Mc Hugh, M., Cawley, O., McCaffery, F., Richardson, I., Wang, X.: An agile V-model for medical device software development to overcome the challenges with plan-driven software development lifecycles. In: Proceedings of 2013 5th International Workshop on Software Engineering in Health Care, SEHC 2013, pp. 12–19 (2013)

8. McCaffery, F., McFall, D., Donnelly, P., Wilkie, F.G., Sterritt, R.: A software process improvement lifecycle framework for the medical device industry. In: Proceedings of IEEE International Conference and Workshops on the Engineering of Computer-Based Systems (ECBS 2005), p. 8 (2005)
9. Rasmussen, R., Hughes, T., Jenks, J.R., Skach, J.: Adopting agile in an FDA regulated environment. In: Proceedings of Agile Conference, pp. 151–155 (2009)
10. Schrage, M.: Never go to a client meeting without a prototype. Softw. IEEE **21**(2), 42–45 (2004). [software prototyping]
11. AAMI, AAMI TIR 45:2012 - Guidance on the use of Agile practices in the development of medical device software (2012)
12. McHugh, M., McCaffery, F., Fitzgerald, B., Stol, K.-J., Casey, V., Coady, G.: Balancing agility and discipline in a medical device software organisation. In: Woronowicz, T., Rout, T., O'Connor, R.V., Dorling, A. (eds.) SPICE 2013. CCIS, vol. 349, pp. 199–210. Springer, Heidelberg (2013)
13. Cawley, O., Wang, X., Richardson, I.: Lean/agile software development methodologies in regulated environments – state of the art. In: Abrahamsson, P., Oza, N. (eds.) LESS 2010. LNBIP, vol. 65, pp. 31–36. Springer, Heidelberg (2010)
14. Principles behind the Agile Manifesto. http://www.agilemanifesto.org/principles.html
15. Gary, K., Enquobahrie, A., Ibanez, L., Cheng, P., Yaniv, Z., Cleary, K., Kokoori, S., Muffih, B., Heidenreich, J.: Agile methods for open source safety-critical software. Softw. Pract. Exp. **41**(9), 945–962 (2011)
16. Rottier, P.A., Rodrigues, V.: Agile development in a medical device company. In: Proceedings of Agile Conference, pp. 218–223 (2008)
17. Paulk, M.C.: On Empirical Research into Scrum Adoption. Prentice Hall, Upper Saddle River (2011)
18. Sumrell, M.: From waterfall to agile - how does a QA team transition? In: Proceedings of Agile Conference, pp. 291–295 (2007)
19. Deming, W.D.: https://en.wikipedia.org/wiki/W._Edwards_Deming. Accessed 06 Jan 2016
20. Manjunath, K.N., Jagadeesh, J., Yogeesh, M.: Achieving quality product in a long term software product development in healthcare application using Lean and Agile principles: Software engineering and software development. In: Proceedings - 2013 IEEE International Multi Conference on Automation, Computing, Control, Communication and Compressed Sensing, iMac4s 2013, pp. 26–33 (2013)
21. Sutherland, J.: Future of scrum: Parallel pipelining of sprints in complex projects. In: Proceedings of Agile Confernce, pp. 90–99 (2005)
22. Fitzgerald, B., Stol, K.J., O'Sullivan, R., O'Brien, D.: Scaling agile methods to regulated environments: an industry case study. In: International Conference on Software Engineering Proceedings, pp. 863–872 (2013)
23. Spence, J.W.: There has to be a better way! In: Agile Development Conference Proceedings, pp. 272–278 (2005)
24. Upender, B.: Staying agile in government software projects. In: Proceedings of Agile Development Conference (ADC 2005), pp. 153–159 (2005)
25. McHugh, M., McCaffery, F., Casey, V.: Barriers to adopting agile practices when developing medical device software. In: Mas, A., Mesquida, A., Rout, T., O'Connor, R.V., Dorling, A. (eds.) SPICE 2012. CCIS, vol. 290, pp. 141–147. Springer, Heidelberg (2012)
26. Heeager, L.T., Nielsen, P.A.: Agile software development and its compatibility with a document-driven approach? a case study. In: Australasian Conference on Information Systems Proceedings, pp. 205–214 (2009)

Using Enterprise SPICE in Very Small Entities

Linda Ibrahim[1(✉)], Ernest Wallmüller[2], and Wolfgang Daschner[2]

[1] Enterprise SPICE, Washington, DC, USA
rlibrahim@aol.com
[2] Qualität & Informatik, Geroldswil, Switzerland

Abstract. The purpose of this paper is to show how the Enterprise SPICE model [1, 2] can be used to help very small entities (VSEs). The Enterprise SPICE model is a comprehensive integrated model intended for use in any domain, or in an enterprise of any size, including VSEs. The preponderance and importance of VSEs is described as well as challenges and issues they face. Examples of common VSE situations are provided and some case studies are presented where Enterprise SPICE can be helpful for VSEs.

Keywords: Enterprise SPICE · ISO/IEC 33071 · Very small entities · Process improvement

1 Introduction

The purpose of this paper is to show how the Enterprise SPICE model ([1] ISO/IEC FDIS 33071) [2] can be used to help very small entities (VSEs) defined as "enterprises, organizations, departments or projects having up to 25 people" [3]. The Enterprise SPICE model was developed to support enterprises of any size, in any domain. It is a comprehensive integrated model, but it is intended to be used selectively, depending on the needs of the enterprise. In this paper we illustrate how Enterprise SPICE might help VSEs be successful.

2 Predominance of VSEs

One may consider 2 types of VSEs: independent and embedded. Independent VSEs are the predominant form of enterprises globally. A widely quoted study [4] indicates that 92.2 % of independent European enterprises have up to 9 employees (called Micro-enterprises), and another 6.5 % have from 10 to 49 employees. Micro enterprises account for 70 % to 90 % of enterprises in OECD (Organisation for Economic Co-operation and Development) countries and about 57 % in USA [5, 6]. Babson [7] reports that 98 % of businesses in the US have fewer than 20 employees. Furthermore, many if not most medium and large enterprises have departments or projects with 25 or fewer staff members, rendering them what might be called "embedded" VSEs. Such VSEs may follow process standards and improvement paths as used by their parent companies. Also, VSEs who are contractors or subcontractors may need to comply with process standards that are mandated by their acquirers. But "stand-alone" or independent VSEs may not typically consider the use of process standards. Some situations where process standards can help VSEs are provided in Sect. 5 below.

3 Importance of VSEs

VSEs can be considered a main driver for innovation and employment as well as social and local integration. VSEs also develop and/or maintain systems and/or software that is used in larger systems, therefore, recognition of VSEs as suppliers of high quality systems and/or software is often required. In general, VSEs provide valuable services across the spectrum of products and services people need every day. It is important to recognize VSE contributions, promote VSE entrepreneurship, and reward their innovation and risk-taking efforts. The best possible environment for small business and entrepreneurship needs therefore to be created.

In urging for this, we:

- Acknowledge the dynamic capacities of VSEs in answering to new market needs and in providing jobs
- Stress the importance of VSEs in fostering social and regional development, while behaving as examples of initiative and commitment
- Recognise entrepreneurship as a valuable and productive life skill, at all levels of responsibility
- Applaud successful enterprises, which deserve to be fairly rewarded
- Consider that some failure is concomitant with responsible initiative and risk-taking and must be mainly envisaged as a learning opportunity
- Recognise the values of knowledge, commitment and flexibility in the new economy
- Seek to encourage the use of best practices and standards in VSEs, in a way that readily provides value to these critical entities

4 VSE Issues and Challenges

What are the challenges facing small businesses? A study by Babson College [7] surveyed about 1300 participants in their Goldman Sachs 10,000 Small Businesses program and found:

Challenge #1: Finding and keeping customers (31 %)
Challenge #2: Financing the business (21 %)
Challenge #3: Developing and updating a business strategy (16 %)
Challenge #4: Hiring and keeping good employees at reasonable wages (15 %)

Sanchez-Gordon et al. [8] found that major issues in IT-specific VSEs regarding the use of models or standards relate to low levels of customer or market requirements, lack of resources, difficult procedures, and the need for more guidance and assistance. That publication focuses on the use of ISO/IEC 29110 [6] in IT-specific VSEs, as 29110 is designed to support VSEs in the IT sector. However our target community is broader, to include all VSEs in all domains as applicable to their needs. VSEs are the most sensitive of all to changes in the business environment. They are the first to suffer if weighed down with excessive bureaucracy. And they are the first to flourish from initiatives to cut red tape and reward success.

5 Can Standards Help VSEs?

As risk and process management increasingly become a subject of concern, and as process approaches are maturing and earning the confidence of companies, the use of ISO/IEC international standards is spreading in organizations of all sizes.

Small companies can use processes as the foundation of their quality assurance process and quality management system and to help them become established initially and then to help with everything their business entails.
Consider the following situations and questions for example:

- Why should a very small entity care about processes and practices?
- How could they help a VSE that is just starting up?
- How could they help a sub-contractor focusing on security services?
- Why would processes benefit an independent electrician?
- How could processes and practices help a VSE open a barber shop, a catering business, a lawn service, a training consultancy?
- What should one do to grow an idea for a brand new product/service?
- Can processes and practices help a small voluntary board be more effective?

There are many useful best practices that can be helpful in situations such as these. They can be found in Enterprise SPICE [1, 2]. Since Enterprise SPICE is domain-independent, it provides guidance for any small (or large) enterprise; it is not specific to software or IT enterprises.

The idea is to select subsets of processes, and of practices within those processes, that might be most relevant to VSEs that provide any product or service. Look at those practices to see if using them might help the enterprise. It is not necessary to seek levels or certification to help business performance. But it just makes sense to look at recognized best practice to see if that might provide value. For a VSE new in the field of project management for example, why not check best practice in this area? For VSEs that seek certification, that is possible as well, since Enterprise SPICE is conformant with ISO/IEC 33004 [9] requirements.

Small enterprises are likely to have different needs, depending on their objectives. A few general alternatives are described below. Each may have a different profile of most useful processes and practices. References are given to Enterprise SPICE processes that might be most useful for each example. The list of Enterprise SPICE processes is provided in the Appendix to this paper.

1. Start-up – identify what the enterprise is about, what are our goals, what is our strategy (use Enterprise Governance)
2. Determine products/services to be offered – study the market, identify customers and their needs (use Needs, Tendering, Business Relationship Management, Research and Innovation)

3. Develop the products/services – plan product/service development, hire and train staff, execute the plan (use Human Resource Management, Project Management, Quality Assurance, Configuration Management and selected life cycle processes)
4. Deliver the products/services (use Deployment and Disposal, Operation and Support)

Once the important processes and practices are identified, various process improvement approaches can be used to help the VSE. General guidelines can be found in [10]. Some VSE-specific case studies and examples are provided below.

5.1 Case Study – Embedded VSE

This case study pertains to the use of Enterprise SPICE in an embedded VSE, a small part of the very large US Department of Transportation. An Enterprise SPICE assessment was performed on a selected Investment Review Board (a board that makes and oversees investment decisions). The process scope of the assessment was the Investment Management process of Enterprise SPICE, up to capability level 2. This was the process most relevant to the needs of this VSE. The results indicated strengths in their process and also areas of future improvement opportunities [11].

This case illustrates the use of Enterprise SPICE in an embedded VSE, focusing on the use of a single process, the Investment Management process, to support improved performance. It indicates the value of using the Enterprise SPICE model selectively, in areas most needed by the VSE.

5.2 Case Study – Independent VSE

This case illustrates the use of Enterprise SPICE for strategy development and implementation in a small voluntary independent advisory board [12]. The board is the Enterprise SPICE Advisory Board, responsible for governance of the Enterprise SPICE project. To help in achieving the Enterprise SPICE vision, the Board developed a strategy with four goals and several initiatives associated with each. Enterprise SPICE processes were used as follows.

- For the Deployment goal, the Deployment and Disposal, Training, and Tendering processes were used.
- For the Model Evolution goal, the Change and Configuration Management, Needs, and Research and Innovation processes were used.
- For the Governance/Management goal, the Enterprise Governance, Business Relationship Management, and Supplier Agreement Management processes were used.
- For the Operation and Support goal, the Operation and Support, Knowledge Management, Training, and Process Improvement processes were used.

As the strategy continues to be implemented, the Board has been using the practices in these processes to carry out the initiatives in the strategy.

5.3 Case Study – A Business Management Approach

A case study was done by Dallas and Wynn [13] on business process management (BPM) for small business. In that context a Process Governance Framework provides a high-level layer of BPM definition and a frame of reference to guide activities and ensure consistency of approach. [14]. A Process Governance Framework was developed that addressed the following:

- Decision-making—Key categories of process decisions were identified and responsibilities for each category were assigned to organizational roles.
- Process Roles and Responsibilities—Guidelines were developed to assist in determining who should be appointed as the Process Owner of each process.
- Responsibilities were also outlined for process approval, feedback and analysis support.
- Process Standards—Standards were detailed for process referencing, storage, modeling notation and tools.
- Measurement and Compliance—A set of performance measures and compliance activities were identified. Due to the relative infancy of The Business, these were focused on near-term BPM activities.

The following Enterprise SPICE processes can be used to implement the Framework:

- Enterprise Governance for Govern (1.) and Plan (2.).
- Business Relationship Management for Manage Client Relationship (3.).
- Life Cycle Processes for Deliver Core Services (4.).
- Support Processes for Support (5. till 9. plus selected Governance/Management processes like Investment Management and Human Resource Management)

An example of a Process Governance Framework for small business is illustrated below:

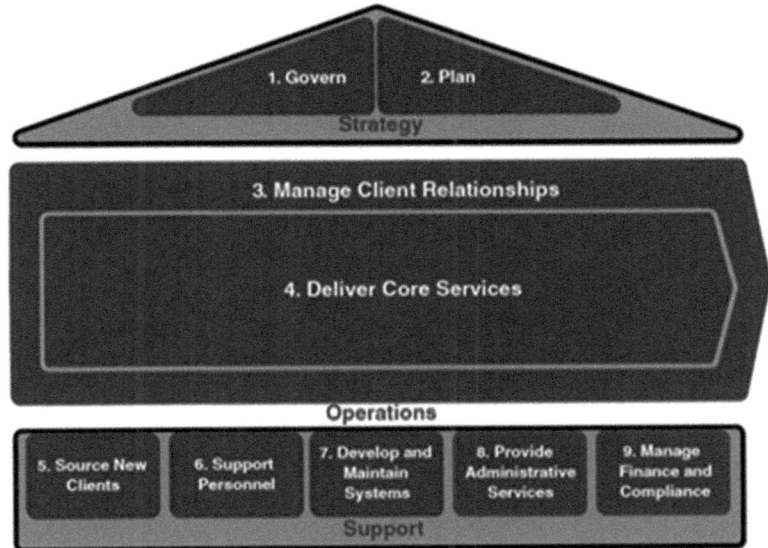

6 Benefits of Using Enterprise SPICE

When an organization has implemented processes by using Enterprise SPICE as a best practice model, the following benefits can be realized:

- a simple, easy to use model for business process improvement
- a best practice model for small organizations that would like to do the first steps in process management
- a best practice model that can easily be extended for process model development
- a process reference model that can be used for business process assessments
- a source for best and good practices if someone is looking for practices in a given process

The benefits are based on the proximity to the customer for any self-employed, freelancer or small business is - in contrast to the wholesale and consumer goods companies - always in direct contact with its customers.

7 Conclusions

We believe that VSEs are critical enterprises and that processes and practices of Enterprise SPICE can help them be successful. We have provided some examples to help illustrate that the Enterprise SPICE model, when used selectively, can provide value to VSEs.

Appendix: Enterprise SPICE Process Dimension

Governance / Management Category	Special Applications
Enterprise Governance Investment Management Human Resource Management Enterprise Architecture Business Relationship Management Supplier Agreement Management Tendering Project Management Risk Management	Safety and Security
Life Cycle Category	
Needs Requirements Design Design Implementation Integration Evaluation Deployment and Disposal Operation and Support	
Support Category	
Alternatives Analysis Measurement and Analysis Quality Assurance and Management Change and Configuration Management Information Management Knowledge Management Training Research and Innovation Work Environment Process Definition Process Improvement	

References

1. ISO/IEC FDIS 33071 Information Technology- Process assessment – An integrated process capability assessment model for Enterprise Processes 2016
2. Enterprise SPICE Project Team: Enterprise SPICE An Integrated Model for Enterprise-wide Assessment and Improvement, Technical report – Issue 1. SPICE User Group (2010)

3. Laporte, C.Y., Alexandre, S., O'Connor, R.V.: A software engineering lifecycle standard for very small enterprises. In: O'Connor, R., Baddoo, N., Smolander, K., Messnarz, R. (eds.) Proceedings of EuroSPI, pp. 129–141. Springer, Heidelberg (2008)
4. Moll, R.: Being prepared – A bird's eye view of SMEs and risk management, ISO Focus+, February 2013
5. O'Connor, R.V., Laporte, C.Y.: An innovative approach to the development of an international software process lifecycle standard for very small entities. Int. J. Inf. Technol. Syst. Approach **7**, 1–22 (2014)
6. Laporte, C.Y., O'Connor, R., Fanmuy, G.: International systems and software engineering standards for very small entities. CrossTalk – J. Defense Softw. Eng. **26**, 28–33 (2013)
7. Babson: Stimulating Small Business Growth, A Report on the Goldman Sachs 10,000 Small Businesses Program, Babson College, MA, USA, February 2014
8. Sanchez-Gordon, M.-L., O'Connor, R.V., Colomo-Palacios, R.: Evaluating VSEs viewpoint and sentiment towards the ISO/IEC 29110 standard: a two country grounded theory study. In: Rout, T., O'Connor, R.V., Dorling, A. (eds.) SPICE 2015. CCIS, vol. 526, pp. 114–127. Springer, Heidelberg (2015)
9. ISO/IEC 33004: Information technology — Process assessment — Requirements for process reference, process assessment and maturity models (2014)
10. Daschner, W., Ibrahim, L., Henschelchen, W., Wallmueller E.: Guide to Applying the Enterprise SPICE Model (2013)
11. Carnaroli, H.G., Ibrahim, L.: Assessing Investment Management Processes in the US Department of Transportation using Enterprise SPICE, SPICE 2010
12. Ibrahim, L.: Developing the enterprise SPICE strategy using enterprise SPICE. In: Woronowicz, T., Rout, T., O'Connor, R.V., Dorling, A. (eds.) SPICE 2013. CCIS, vol. 349, pp. 252–255. Springer, Heidelberg (2013)
13. Dallas, I., Wynn, T.: Information Systems for Small and Medium-sized Enterprises. In: Devos, J. et al. (eds.) Progress in IS Springer, Berlin (2014)
14. Kirchmer, M.: Small and medium enterprises also benefit from MPE. In: Kirchmer, M. (ed.) High Performance Through Process Excellence, pp. 147–157. Springer, Berlin (2011)

Smart Requirements: How Smart Can They Get?

Danilo Assmann(✉)

Vector Informatik GmbH, Ingersheimer Str. 24, 70499 Stuttgart, Germany
`danilo.assmann@vector.com`

Abstract. In current practice requirements engineering is a text based process. The available theory and tools do not address the internal elements–the semantic structure–of requirements. We present an approach to extract a first domain model, which can also serve as basis for the system architecture, directly from the requirements. Besides the model, the approach provides also new and insightful metrics, which focus on product characteristics instead of process characteristics. The model and metrics can be used to fulfill the SPiCE (and AutomotiveSPICE 3) requirements, concerning consistency and completeness of requirement specifications.

Keywords: Requirements · SPiCE (ISO15504/ISO330xx) · AutomotiveSPICE 3 · Consistency · Model

1 What Is Wrong with Current Requirements Engineering?

One of the basic beliefs of software engineering still is that requirements are useful. They have an important influence on the final product. Actually they define and shape the product and capture the customer expectation in a reliable form [1, 2].

Coming back to the question in the header: nothing is wrong. But we can do more. We can improve our understanding of the requirements engineering process, and we can improve the usefulness of the requirements related work products. We need to make them worthwhile so developers can see and feel the advantage to create and maintain them.

Despite their importance, the way we treat requirements is not very advanced. Basically we can distinguish two existing engineering directions:

- usage of patterns (simplified grammar) [3–6]
- improved writing (clear terms and data dictionaries) [7, 8]

Even applying these techniques still leave requirements quite dumb text. This reflects also the current tooling: we can count and prioritize requirements. We can give them attributes, we can link text blocks. But actually not much has changed from using good old Word. We have sentences, paragraphs, and a lack of logic; with slightly improved usability.

Sure, there is also the area of formal specification (e.g., Z, VDM, B). Which is fascinating, amazingly complex, and still has little practical influence. [11–13].

Nevertheless, we can learn something from the usage of formal specification, and also from the successful application of function points:

© Springer International Publishing Switzerland 2016

- requirements describe the behavior (functionality) of the system
- everything we need to build the system, and understand the domain, is already in the requirements

In my own words: the *requirements* already *contain* a (in-complete) *model of the* application domain and the *system* (software).[1]

So how can we improve requirements engineering based on this knowledge? How can requirements become smart? And what does smart mean anyhow? Simple benefits of being smart should be:

- a complete and working data dictionary or object hierarchy
- completeness (per requirements, but also for the specification)
- consistency (for the specification and with other work products)
- freedom of conflict (for the specification)
- compliance to AutomotiveSPICE 3 and ISO 26262

That's what we want to achieve, when we make our requirements smart. Our approach to smartness relies on three techniques, which combine proven approaches with new ideas:

- usage of (domain specific) patterns
- domain-specific language (terms)
- explicit extraction of the semantic model

2 Our Concept

2.1 Why Do You Amplify "Domain Specific"?

For conferences and generic tool provider it is very nice to talk on an abstract level. But in practice most of the time life is much easier: you can be concrete. You have a given context. And when you build your model, based on this context you can make a lot of assumptions, which will simplify your life.

So in practice you will have only certain patterns of requirements. You will also have certain objects, messages, mechanisms, architectures. From what we learned so far, you can cluster your domain context in:

- software at runtime
- states (in case of finite state machines)
- messages, events
- data and data access
- runtime environment (other objects including hardware and other software)
- build environment (including configuration of the software)
- process (logical flow; technical process of the domain)

---

[1] Why incomplete? Many things we expect from the system are just basic needs, which are not specified anymore. It is basic knowledge of the domain. Refer to the Kano model for deeper insight on this topic [9, 10].

The objects in the last three groups will be specific to the topic (domain); and some of the others also. So it is not possible to provide a standard dictionary. Based on our experience the built up of such a dictionary does not take long.

The relations (defined by the verbs) follow the context. For generic contexts (data access, software, messages) we propose to use a generic standard set, with a minimal set of actions. They all should be clear and redundancy free defined.

E.g., "check" and "validate" have some overlap. So use only one of them, or use a third more clear/precise term.

2.2 What About Our Patterns?

Now we provide a short insight into our approach. Based on the needs from complying with the safety standard we provided a set of basic patterns (top-down). These patterns where applied in several AUTOSAR components. Basically we can distinguish three areas of patterns:

- services (functionality used via API, callback, callout)
  - e.g., <Subject> shall provide a service to <functionality>
- states (description of a finite state machine)
  - e.g., <Subject> shall provide a mode to <state>
- use cases (all pre-build and post-build configuration)
  - e.g., <Subject> shall be used in <scenario>

The next step was to take a sample (around 10 %) of used specifications and analyze the real-world requirements and refine the patterns. We did this in two steps:

(1) extracting refined patterns from the examples. E.g., Object - <pattern indicator> - relation - [definition] - attribute - object[2]
(2) After having the sample and the application distribution of patterns, we could derive meta-patterns (grammar): e.g., Object - [[object - condition] - relation - [definition] - [attribute] - object]

By additionally applying a simple writing guide, the readability of requirements improves. The structure helps to make clear what should happen through this requirement. It simplifies the process of writing, because you know what to place where.

Requirements for a safety process complying with ISO 26262 demand semi-formal notations (ASIL C and D). Our patterns fulfill this requirement. So we do not use formal specification, but a reduced set of words and grammar of natural language.

2.3 Does Semantics Mean Smart?

Now we become real "smart" by going to the next level. The refined patterns allow us to recognize (and check) the relevant elements of a requirement. This allows us to access the inner structure of a requirement and create a kind of a model.

---

[2] <pattern indicator> is the predefined text segment from our basic patterns above.

The model gives us possibility to transform the text into a graph. A graph shows the inherent structure of a requirement and also of a requirement specification. It is a sketch of the natural architecture. This changes also the perspective: instead of looking at requirements, the defined objects are the main elements of the model. The requirements provide only different views of object relation.

The object based view has the advantage that all relations to an object can be seen in one place, even if they are scattered through the whole document (or several documents). This simplifies the review for consistency and completeness (also in case of state machines). That is requirements "engineering". Not just read and check. So how does this work?

Fig. 1. Simple example for requirement with markup.

Basically we do two things: remove the basic pattern elements (and other phrases) *and* tag the words following the grammar of the sentence (Fig. 1).

As you can see in the examples the tagging is quite easy (Figs. 1 and 2). You do it sentence by sentence and the number of objects and relations is limited by the natural length.

Some direct benefits while doing it manually:

- deep check on patterns: how many requirements conform to which pattern? Justify with clear reasons all deviations from pattern.
- build and maintain a data dictionary: build up the data dictionary including an object model (hierarchy)
- relation check: keep your writing clear and tidy; also for the verbs. Do the same words (verbs) have same meaning, and have different words always different meaning. It is possible to create a white-list, which covers the common terms (Fig. 2).

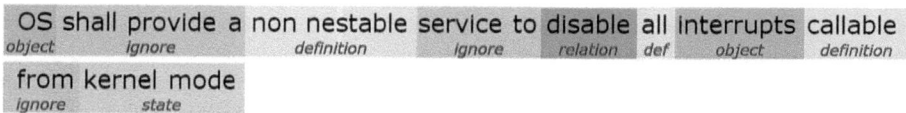

Fig. 2. Medium complexity requirement example.

2.4 Tooling

So up to now it is quite boring manual work, with high maintenance effort if you have to do it again for a new version of a specification.

The idea was to support this process with a very simple tooling. Which are around 100 lines of Java code.

It works completely text based (just text replace) and has currently no support for natural language processing. It performs a cleanup of unnecessary text, replaces matches with tags and counts and removes unused elements. As final output the tool provides tagged text. We use simple hash-tags with type identifier. During the learning process different output is possible, such as the not used words.

Besides the output, which can easily be translated in GraphViz syntax, it provides some metrics. We use it as a transformation tool (input to output) with a given threshold, so it reports after each run, if the transformation is "passed" or "failed" (Fig. 3).

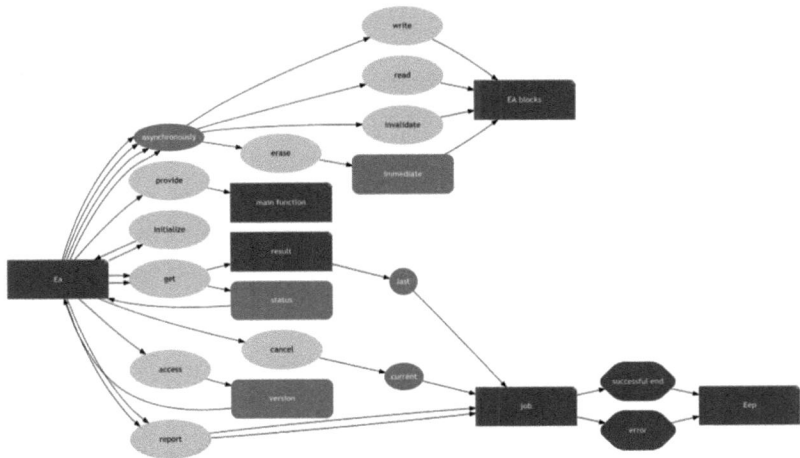

Fig. 3. Simple example of a generated requirement model.

2.5 Graph and Metrics

One advantage of the content based transformation of requirements into a model is that we can draw charts. And we can get these charts without any additional effort. They are kind of a side-effect. The chart gives you immediate feedback on the complexity and structure of your specification, and this in one page (Fig. 3). Basic metrics are visualized: #objects (#objects per requirement), #states, #levels (depth of requirements), #conditions, #relation (and the linkage [the edges]), #areas of cohesion. Based on these factors every requirement specification can be characterized. They define an individual "flavor". They have a characteristic on first sight.

3 Conclusion and Outlook

As mentioned throughout the paper, we haven't done but our first steps. So we still need more experience.

- Still learning: first we need to understand deviations in the process, then we will really understand the product.

- Improve tooling, if necessary: in commercial tooling NLP support needs to be provided. This will be still fast enough, but will give more precise results and much easier handling. E.g., the automation can be much higher during learning phase.
- Support for data dictionaries/object models: currently we rely only on word lists. From process modeling we have a lot of experience how to build hierarchical models. This can also be applied here.
- Diffs on versions: re-read for new versions of specifications will be fast (no effort) and allow checks on the model. So we can evaluate if there are relevant/risky changes.
- Integration with agile (e.g., SBE or BDS) practices: the notion would be to generate the headers of the data tables directly out of the requirements (objects/attributes/environment/states/…). And with changes you can easily see if relevant elements were added or removed.

References

1. ISO 33060
2. ISO 12207 (2008)
3. Hagge, L., Houdek, F., Lappe, K., Paech, B.: Using patterns for sharing requirements engineering process rationales. In: Dutoit, A.H., McCall, R., Mistrík, I., Paech, B., et al. (eds.) Rationale Management in Software Engineering, vol. 1. Springer, Heidelberg (2006)
4. Konrad, S., Cheng, B.H.C.: Requirements patterns for embedded systems. In: Proceedings of the 10th Anniversary IEEE Joint International Conference on Requirements Engineering, pp. 127–136 (2002)
5. van Lamsweerde, A.: Requirements engineering in the year 00: a research perspective. In: Proceedings of the 22nd international conference on Software engineering, pp. 5–19, New York (2000)
6. Coplien, J.O.: Software design patterns: common questions and answers. In: Rising L. (ed.) The Patterns Handbook: Techniques, Strategies, and Applications, pp. 311–320 (1998)
7. Houdek, F.: Messung in der Erstellung und Prüfung von Lastenheften, Metrikon (2014)
8. Houdek, F.: Anforderungen verbessern mit DESIRe, REConf (2008)
9. Noriaki, K., Seraku, N., Takahashi, F., Tsuji, S.: Attractive quality and must-be quality. J. Japanese Soc. Quality Control (in Japanese) **14**(2), 39–48 (1984). ISSN: 0386-8230
10. Cadotte, E.R., Normand, T.: Dissatisfiers and satisfiers: suggestions from consumer complaints and compliments. J. Consum. Satisfaction, Dissatisfaction Complaining Behavior **1**, 74–79 (1988). ISBN: 0-922279-01-2, ISSN: 0899-8620
11. Behm, P., Benoit, P., Faivre, A., Meynadier, J.-M.: Météor: a successful application of B in a large project. In: Wing, J.M., Woodcock, J. (eds.) FM 1999. LNCS, vol. 1708, pp. 369–387. Springer, Heidelberg (1999)
12. Bernot, G., Gaudel, M.C., Marre, B.: Software testing based on formal specifications: a theory and a tool. Softw. Eng. J. **6**(6), 387–405 (1991)
13. Clarke, E.M., Wing, J.M., et al.: Formal methods: state of the art and future directions. ACM Comput. Surv. **28**(4), 626–643 (1996)

Current Challenges and Proposed Software Improvement Process for VSEs in Developing Countries

Tatsuya Nonoyama[1,2], Lian Wen[1,2], and Terry Rout[1(✉)]

[1] Institute for Integrated and Intelligent Systems, Griffith University, Brisbane, Australia
{l.wen,t.rout}@griffith.edu.au
[2] School of Information and Communication Technology, Griffith University,
170 Kessels Rd, Brisbane QLD 4111, Australia

Abstract. Many software development organizations are classified as Very Small Entities (VSEs) with limited number of staff to implement full size of software development lifecycles standards (SDLC) such as ISO/IEC 12207 in their software projects. To make VSEs easier to implement lifecycles, ISO/IEC 29110 is a Standard specifically for VSEs; one of the parts defines a cut-down set of processes specifically tailored for VSEs. There are two frequently used processes (Software Development Process and Project Management Process) however; some VSEs seek for more support in SDLC selection. This paper investigates the differences of VSEs from different economic regions and argues that VSEs in developing countries usually can afford more staff due to much lower salary rates in those countries. Therefore they are capable of implementing more labor consuming processes compared to their counterparts in the developed countries. The paper then proposes an additional process (Process Improvement Process) as an extension for the current ISO/IEC 29110. Furthermore, through the aspects of economic feasibility and development sustainability, the paper justifies that the proposed process is valuable for VSEs in developing countries.

Keywords: Software process improvement · Very small entity · Software process

1 Introduction

ISO/IEC 29110 is an essential guidance for VSEs to develop their software on time and budget [1–3]. ISO/IEC 29110 consists of Project Management Process and Software Implementation Process to help VSEs to reach their expected performance. In the early days, ISO standards are lengthy and difficult to fully implemented by small organizations.

According to Laporte and Alexandre [4] a large number of IT organizations are categorized as very small entities (VSEs), where the total staff number is less than 10. On the other hand, Small and Medium Enterprises (SME) may face different stages of financial situations compared to VSEs. To satisfy these VSEs, tailor-made light weight SDLC standard ISO/IEC 29110 was introduced. Roldan [5] suggested that the current ISO/IEC 29110 is highly used in developed and some developing countries. However, this is not the case for the rest of developing countries [6, 7]. This indicates that, the single generic standard 29110 is not adequate for some developing countries such as Indonesia and Philippines.

Majority of VSEs are still facing financial difficulties and lack of resources. The findings suggest that the financial difficulties caused other challenges such as defined policies and training [8]. In this paper, we propose an extension for the ISO/IEC 29110, so the extended version could ease the challenges in developing countries.

The paper is structured as following: the second section introduces the background information which includes the current standards for VSE and the different characteristics of VSEs in different regions. In section three, we propose a Process Improvement Process (PI) as an optional extension for ISO/IEC 29110. The following discussion section we argue the feasibility and practical value of the proposed process. Finally a conclusion and some future work with limitations.

2 Background

2.1 Current Challenges of VSEs

Financial difficulties are major concerns for most VSEs, it creates other challenges such as lack of resources and employee training [8–10]. For VSEs in developing countries, accessing reliable resource can be more expensive than human resources. Sanchez-Gordon et al. [11] stated that financial constrains makes it challenging to adapt ISO standards compared to developed countries. Although, light weight 29110 is feasible for some regions, majority of developing countries still view ISO/IEC 29110 as a challenge.

In relation to retaining reliable resources, VSEs in developing countries, shows higher concerns for collecting and allocating relevant resources to implement 29110 or other standards. Many VSEs from developing countries, feel less confident to implement and manage the processes in 29110 [6, 10]. Although, ISO/ICE 29110 is currently active in some parts of developing countries, it is still worth customizing ISO/IEC 29110 to satisfy other VSEs in developing countries.

2.2 Current Standards for VSE Subsection

The current ISO/IEC 29110 standards address the generic profile group of VSE. The standard consists of relevant information to improve and sustain the overall capability level of VSEs. The current ISO/IEC 29110 for those VSEs that do not develop critical or complex software [12]. Furthermore, Suryamimgrum [7] stated that more guidance and explanations are needed for those VSEs to select compatible and affordable processes.

ISO/IEC 29110 consists of two processes and the outcomes of these two processes (PM process) [13] and (SI process) can be found in different set of standards such as standard ISO/IEC 12207 (ISO/IEC 29110-5-1-2). In Sect. 2.2.1, it includes two software processes and activities are listed.

2.2.1 Software Processes for ISO/IEC 29110

Project Management Process (PM process)

"The purpose of the Project Management process is to establish and carry out in a systematic way the tasks of the software implementation project, which allows complying with the project's objectives in the expected quality, time and costs" as quoted in (ISO/IEC TR 29110-5-1-2). PM process is an essential part of reaching project objectives. This is particularly the case for VSEs in developing countries, where policies are not well defined. Establishment of project planning and clear software activity lists are extremely important.

Software Implementation Process (SI process)

"The purpose of the Software Implementation process is the systematic performance of the analysis, software component identification, construction, integration and tests, and product delivery activities for new or modified software products according to the specified requirements" as quoted in (ISO/IEC TR 29110-5-1-2).

For VSEs in developing countries SI process becomes critical to ensure all the software components are necessary and feasible to avoid reconstructions. For most VSEs, project or software reworks can leads to project failure (Table 1).

Table 1. Include process activities for SI and PM.

SI process activities	PM process activities
SI.1 Software Implementation Initiation	*PM.1 Project Planning*
SI.2 Software Requirements Analysis	*PM.2 Project Plan Execution*
SI.3 Software Component Identification	*PM.3 Project Assessment and Control*
SI.4 Software Construction	*PM.4 Project Closure*
SI.5 Software Integration and Tests	(Wen & Rout, 2012 :
SI.6 Product Delivery	ISO/IEC TR 29110-5-1-2)
(Wen & Rout, 2012: ISO/IEC TR 29110-5-1-2)	

2.3 Software Process Improvement (SPI) Subsection

In regardless of sizes and circumstances, software process improvement (SPI) is an essential part of software development for VSEs. To conduct software development, there are two approaches to develop software. Plan-driven approach with evaluate software quality based on the capability level and agile development methods with SCRUM.

Agile methods are based on iterative and incremental development using short development cycles [14]. In agile methods, it is a top priority to meet the expectations of customer(s) in early and continuous stages of software delivery [15]. Although agile software development methods became commonly used by some VSEs, both approach methods could result positive outcomes depending on the nature of VSEs.

On the other hand, the traditional software development world, still advocates the traditional plan-driven approach, which focus on the quality of the software artifacts and the predictability of their processes [14]. In the case of developing countries, we highly recommend VSEs to follow the traditional plan-driven approach to enhance software quality. Software improvement process should address the challenge of financial difficulties by providing step by step guidelines for software quality to avoid software reconstructions [16, 17]. Appropriate usage of knowledge management and experience management can increase the productivity of plan-driven approach.

2.4 Characteristic Trends of VSEs in Developing Countries

In order to propose realistic and useful software process, it is essential to understand the characteristic trends of VSEs in developing countries to support the implementation of ISO/IEC 29110. To design the purpose and objectives needs to be reachable and simple enough for inexperienced developers could understand. These characteristic of VSE are relatively common in developing countries such as Indonesia and Philippines [5–7]. Despite the fact that these characteristic trends do not directly impacts on the software improvement process. However, ISO/IEC standards and other guidelines may consider the trends of developing countries when updating ISO/IEC 29110 and other standards.

3 Proposed Extension for ISO/IEC 29110

3.1 The New Software Process Improvement Process

Purpose of the proposed process is to provide the knowledge of software quality and guide VSEs to determine which area needs software quality improvement. The proposed process also helps VSEs to understand a plan-driven approach for software development [18]. A plan-driven approach is highly recommended for VSEs that needs a further enhancement on overall business capabilities.

3.1.1 Outcomes of Proposed Process

The definition of outcome is observable results expected from the successful performance of the process. Outcomes are expressed in terms of a positive, observable objective or benefit. The list of outcomes associated with a process shall be prefaced by the text, 'As a result of successful implementation of this process'. Outcomes should be no longer than two lines of text, about twenty words. Outcomes should express a single result [19].

The outcome of proposed process is based on the existed model of software process improvement from ISO12207. In this proposed process, the objectives are modified to meet the nature of VSEs in developing countries. In other words, these objectives are reconstructed to be more realistic for VSEs [5]. As the results of implementing the proposed process is to improve the overall capability level by producing better software. VSEs are essential to understand that well-disciplined and well-targeted approach expand their software quality [16].

It is important for VSEs to attempt all the listed objectives and process outcomes to check software quality. The description of each outcome is generic and almost identical as regular software process improvement. To ensure these outcomes are achieved, the extensive use of knowledge management and experience management are necessary to customize it to their organization. Table 2: can be used for initial guidance for VSEs.

Table 2. Objectives and process outcomes

Objectives of proposed process	Process outcomes
To understand the current state of software engineering and the overall capability level (company's current capability level)	(a) Record historical information for process improvement.
	(b) Exam current status
To focus on archiving technical results. Step aside from relationship bonding or achieving unrealistic expectations from clients.	(c) Setup improvement goal
	(d) Create improvement plan
	(e) Execute improvement plan
	(f) Monitor the progress
To learn and combine traditional process and new concepts to encourage the skilled, motivated, and creative people.	(g) Adjust the plan

3.2 Feasibility Level of Proposed Software Process Improvement

In order to determine the degrees of feasibility, VSE should meet the characteristic trends and the condition of labor costs. VSEs are necessary to make a decision on whether the time and investments are worth it to implement proposed process. Laporte et al., [3] reported that, the rate of labor cost differs in various regions which impacts on the amount of investments and time constraints. The labor cost differences can be a major concern for some VSEs with higher rate of labor costs.

For example: European or developed countries concerns about the labor cost, even they had adequate knowledge and experiences to implement a standard such as ISO/IEC 29110, it is challenging to focus on expending or improving their software quality within the budget. On the other hand, VSEs in developing countries are more likely to have lower labor costs compared to other regions such as Europe and Western countries [5, 7]. In comparison between two countries, this proposed process may be more feasible for developing countries where labor cost is low.

3.3 Technical Importance

In this section, we discuss the importance of knowledge and experience management for VSEs to stay competitive in their business. The purpose of knowledge management is intended to gather, link, and reuse knowledge to improve the productivity of software process [20]. Knowledge and experience management helps VSEs to determine which resources and skills are needed to improve software quality. According to Habra et al. [16] mentioned that existing knowledge management and experience management practices are rarely seen in the context of VSEs. It is extremely important for VSEs to customize the processes if necessary. Having a better knowledge increases the confidence to make better decisions which leads to less software reworks. Knowledge management can support making better decisions in finance, process implementation and software quality.

A better knowledge in software processes help VSEs to generate positive experiences. According to Suryaningrum [7] VSEs in developing countries are generally inexperienced in implementing new software processes and guidelines to assist their capability level. Ribaud et al. [20] stated that the purpose of experience management is to provide a way to relate and integrate project experiences and knowledge to increase business revenue. Furthermore, VSEs in developing countries also need to consider their policies and regulations [6, 7]. In other words, developing clear and strict guidelines are needed in developing countries.

4 Discussions

Identifying challenges and characteristic trends of developing countries provides better guidance for VSEs in countries such as Indonesia and Philippines. The proposed process was built based on the characteristic trends and challenges of developing countries. The purpose of this proposed process is to support VSEs to improve their capability level and business opportunities. Our intention is not to focus on resolving all the challenges of VSEs but, to ease their challenges and improve their software quality by introducing a proposed process. Furthermore, the current 29110 is not compatible in some developing countries [7]. We also aim to help VSEs in developing countries to improve their knowledge and experience management.

At this stage, we propose this software process improvement (proposed process) with the support to expand their knowledge and experience. Ribaud et al. [20] claimed that, for VSEs from developing countries, it is crucial to recognize the concepts of knowledge management and experience management. The purposes of these two concepts is to assists on making better decisions in software quality and generate ideas to expand business opportunities for VSEs.

We discovered that three major challenges that causes VSEs in developing countries which made it difficult to implement software processes and ISO/IEC standards such 29110. We discovered that (1) financial difficulties, (2) lack of resources or human resources and (3) less structured policies and regulations. Developing countries such as Indonesia and Philippines have less structured policies and regulations which made it difficult to implement structured standard.

5 Conclusion and Future Research Studies

The current state of VSEs in developing countries not only face challenges but, also need to consider knowledge management and experience management for making better decisions in regards to implementing software process improvement (proposed process) [21, 22]. The findings suggested that VSEs in developed countries are not feasible to implement the proposed process under two reasons. (1) high rate of labor cost makes it challenging to afford additional process, (2) the characteristic mismatch. One of the major differences between developed and developing countries was the management prospective and style. VSE in developing countries show greater interests in relationship bonding between workers and clients.

For those VSEs in developing countries, we proposed software process improvement (proposed process) particularly for VSEs in developing countries such as Indonesia and Philippines. We made a recommendation for VSEs to recognize the concepts of knowledge management and experience management for further supporting tools to help sustain the proposed process. We do not intend to see immediate changes in management prospective in developing countries. Instead, the proposed process is to help understand the different prospective in management styles to improve the business opportunities.

In this paper, a number of limitations were identified. First limitation: lack of research studies conducted in VSEs in general and mostly targeted towards SME which made it challenging to find relevant information of VSEs. Second limitation: Due to limited amount of research studies in VSEs, we are unable to provide a detailed guidance for proposed process. Third limitation: the proposed process is intended for VSEs with a certain characteristic trends of Asian region. The proposed process may not be compatible for VSEs from developing countries (European and Western countries). These limitations suggest that more research studies are necessary to propose better software process improvement for VSEs in developing countries.

References

1. Laporte, C.Y., O'Connor, R., Fanmuy, G.: International systems and software engineering standards for very small entities. CrossTalk J. Defense Softw. Eng. **26**, 28–33 (2013)
2. O'Connor, R.V., Laporte, C.Y.: An innovative approach to the development of an international software process lifecycle standard for very small entities. Int. J. Inf. Technol. Syst. Approach **7**, 1–22 (2014)
3. Laporte, C.Y., O'Connor, R.V., Paucar, L.H.G.: The implementation of ISO/IEC 29110 software engineering standards and guides in very small entities. In: Maciaszek, L.A., Filipe, J., Venkatesh, R., et al. (eds.) ENASE 2015. CCIS, vol. 599, pp. 162–179. Springer, Heidelberg (2016). doi:10.1007/978-3-319-30243-0_9
4. Laporte, C.Y., Alexandre, S., O'Connor, R.V.: A software engineering lifecycle standard for very small enterprises. In: O'Connor, R.V., Baddoo, N., Smolander, K., Messnarz, R. (eds.) EuroSPI 2008. CCIS, vol. 16, pp. 129–141. Springer, Heidelberg (2008)
5. Roldan, M.D.: Sustaining "Lilliputs" in the global knowledge-based economy: prospects for micro, small, and mediumscale enterprises in the developing world. Eur. J. Sustain. Dev. **4**(2), 269–274 (2015)
6. Devos, J., Landeghem, H.V., Deshoolmeester, D.: Rethinking IT governance for SMEs. J. Ind. Manag. Data **112**(2), 206–223 (2011)
7. Suryaningrum, D.H.: Knowledge management and performance of small and medium entities in Indonesia. Int. J. Innov. Manag. Technol. **3**(1), 35–41 (2012)
8. Yan, H., Li, Y.: Research on the relationship of government subsidies and enterprise performance. In: 3rd International Conference on Management, Education, Information and Control, p.1806 (2015)
9. Clarke, P., O'Connor, R.V.: Business success in software SMEs: recommendations for future SPI studies. In: Winkler, D., O'Connor, R.V., Messnarz, R. (eds.) EuroSPI 2012. CCIS, vol. 301, pp. 1–12. Springer, Heidelberg (2012)
10. Bergeron, F., Croteau, A.M., Uwizeyemungu, S., Raymond, L.: IT governance framework applied to SMEs. Int. J. IT/Bus. Alignment Gov. **6**(1), 33–49 (2015)
11. Sanchez-Gordon, M.-L., O'Connor, R.V., Colomo-Palacios, R.: Evaluating VSEs viewpoint and sentiment towards the ISO/IEC 29110 standard: a two country grounded theory study. In: Rout, T., O'Connor, R.V., Dorling, A. (eds.) SPICE 2015. CCIS, vol. 526, pp. 114–127. Springer, Heidelberg (2015)

12. Mesquida, A., Mas, A.: A project management improvement program according to ISO/IEC 29110 and PMBOK®. J. Softw. Evol. Process **26**, 846–854 (2014)
13. O'Connor, R.V., Laporte, C.Y.: Software project management in very small entities with ISO/IEC 29110. In: Winkler, D., O'Connor, R.V., Messnarz, R. (eds.) EuroSPI 2012. CCIS, vol. 301, pp. 330–341. Springer, Heidelberg (2012)
14. Ogasawara, H., Kusanagi, T., Aizawa, M.: Proposal and practice of software process improvement framework – Toshiba's software process improvement history since 2000. J. Softw. Evol. Process **26**, 521–529 (2014)
15. Sánchez-Gordón, M.L., O'Connor, R.V.: Understanding the gap between software process practices and actual practice in very small companies. Softw. Qual. J. 1–22 (2015)
16. Habra, N., Laporte, C.Y., Alenxandre, S., Desharnais, J.: Initiating software process improvement in very small enterprises experience with a light assessment tool. J. Inf. Softw. Technol. **50**, 763–771 (2007)
17. Hommes, M., Khan, A., Gerber, C., Kinpis, H., Hamm, K.: Out of the shadow and into the banks: financing very small and informal enterprises. J. Enterp. Dev. Microfinance **25**(3), 212–225 (2014)
18. O'Connor, R.V., Laporte, C.Y.: Using ISO/IEC 29110 to harness process improvement in very small entities. In: O'Connor, R.V., Pries-Heje, J., Messnarz, R. (eds.) EuroSPI 2011. CCIS, vol. 172, pp. 225–235. Springer, Heidelberg (2011)
19. Wen, L., Rout, T.: Using composition trees to validate an entry profile of software engineering lifecycle profiles for very small entities (VSEs). In: Mas, A., Mesquida, A., Rout, T., O'Connor, R.V., Dorling, A. (eds.) SPICE 2012. CCIS, vol. 290, pp. 38–50. Springer, Heidelberg (2012)
20. Ribaud, V., Saliou, P., O'Connor, R.V., Laporte, C.Y.: Software engineering support activities for very small entities. In: Riel, A., O'Connor, R., Tichkiewitch, S., Messnarz, R. (eds.) EuroSPI 2010. CCIS, vol. 99, pp. 165–176. Springer, Heidelberg (2010)
21. Clarke, P., O'Connor, R.V.: The situational factors that affect the software development process: towards a comprehensive reference framework. J. Inf. Softw. Technol. **54**, 433–447 (2012)
22. Galván-Cruz, S., Mora, M., Connor, R., Acosta-Escalante, F., Alvarez, F.: On project management process in agile systems development methodologies and the ISO/IEC 29110 standard (entry profile). In: International Conference on Informatics and Computing (CNCIIC-ANIEI), Mexico (2014)

Erratum to: Software Process Improvement and Capability Determination

Paul M. Clarke[1(✉)], Rory V. O'Connor[2], Terry Rout[3], and Alec Dorling[4]

[1] Lero Irish Software Research Centre, Dublin City University, Dublin, Ireland
paul.m.clarke@dcu.ie
[2] Dublin City University, Dublin, Ireland
[3] Software Quality Institue, Griffith University, Brisbane, QLD, Australia
[4] Impronova AB, Drabergsvagen, Lindome, Sweden

Erratum to:
Chapter 1 in: P.M. Clarke et al. (Eds.)
Software Process Improvement and Capability Determination
DOI: 10.1007/978-3-319-38980-6_1

In the original version the quality of Figure 1, Tables 2 and 3 was low. This has been corrected. They appear now in better quality.

Erratum to:
Chapter 21 in: P.M. Clarke et al. (Eds.)
Software Process Improvement and Capability Determination
DOI: 10.1007/978-3-319-38980-6_21

(1) In the original version the affiliation of Ayça Tarhan is not presented correctly. The correct affiliation is Ayça Tarhan, Computer Engineering Department, Hacettepe University, Beytepe Yerleskesi, 06800, Ankara, Turkey, e-mail: atarhan@hacettepe.edu.tr.
(2) In the original version the e-mail address of Rana Ozakinci is not presented correctly. The correct e-mail address is rana.ozakinci@tubitak.gov.tr.

The updated original online version for the original chapters can be found at
10.1007/978-3-319-38980-6_1
10.1007/978-3-319-38980-6_21

© Springer International Publishing Switzerland 2016
P.M. Clarke et al. (Eds.): SPICE 2016, CCIS 609, p. E1, 2016.
DOI: 10.1007/978-3-319-38980-6_34

Author Index

Adalı, Onat Ege 135
Annanperä, Elina 150
Assmann, Danilo 431

Bannerman, Paul L. 334
Barafort, Béatrix 254
Beecham, Sarah 227, 316
Behari, Suren 195
Biscoglio, Isabella 301
Buckley, Jim 316
Bujok, Andrzej Beniamin 17

Caballero, Ismael 241
Cairns, Paul 109
Calderón, Alejandro 59
Calvo-Manzano, Jose A. 123
Carretero, Ana G. 241
Cater-Steel, Aileen 195
Clarke, Paul 71, 351
Colomo-Palacios, Ricardo 98, 270
Corona, Brisia 123

Daschner, Wolfgang 423
Demirörs, Onur 135, 169, 210
Demissie, Surafel 409

Earle, Clara Benac 3
Ekert, Damjan 351
Ekstrom, J.J. 351

Falcini, Fabio 301
Fernández Del Carpio, Alvaro 377
Flood, Derek 43

Gallina, Barbara 3
Gizaw, Solomon 316
Gökalp, Ebru 169, 210
Gómez-Martínez, Elena 3
Gornostaja, Tatjana 351

Ibrahim, Linda 423

Johansen, Jørn 98, 351
Jovanovic, Milos 351

Kabaale, Edward 362
Keenan, Frank 409
Khurshid, Nazrina 334

Lami, Giuseppe 301
Liukkunen, Kari 150

MacMahon, Silvana Togneri 17
Mas, Antònia 254, 351
McCaffery, Fergal 17, 43, 409, 417
Mejia, Jezreel 123
Mesquida, Antoni-Lluís 254, 351
Messnarz, Richard 351
Miramontes, Juan 123
Miranda, Eduardo 181
Miyoshi, Takeshige 391
Mulcahy, Bernard 17
Muñoz, Mirna 123

Noll, John 227
Nonoyama, Tatsuya 437

O'Connor, Alexander 351
O'Connor, Rory V. 71, 98, 270, 351
Oivo, Markku 150
Orta, Elena 84
Ozakinci, Rana 287
Özcan-Top, Özden 135, 417

Paige, Richard 109
Piattini, Mario 241

Reiner, Michael 351
Rickard, William J. 17
Rout, Terry 195, 362, 437
Ruiz, Mercedes 59, 84
Rust, Peter 43

Salah, Dina 109
San Feliu, Tomas 123
Sánchez-Gordón, Mary-Luz 270
Sanchez-Gordon, Sandra 270
Sauberer, Gabriele 351
Schmitz, Klaus-Dirk 351
Shrestha, Anup 195
Söylemez, Mehmet 31

Tarhan, Ayca 31, 287
Toleman, Mark 195

Trektere, Kitija 417
Tripathi, Nirnaya 150

Villar, Blanca Nájera 351

Wallmüller, Ernest 423
Wang, Zhe 362
Wen, Lian 362, 437
Whelan, Dick 17

Yilmaz, Mert 71
Yilmaz, Murat 71, 351

MIX
Papier aus verantwortungsvollen Quellen
Paper from responsible sources
FSC® C105338

If you have any concerns about our products,
you can contact us on
ProductSafety@springernature.com

In case Publisher is established outside the EU,
the EU authorized representative is:
**Springer Nature Customer Service Center GmbH
Europaplatz 3, 69115 Heidelberg, Germany**

Printed by Libri Plureos GmbH
in Hamburg, Germany